GUIDE TO SPECIAL ISSUES AND INDEXES OF PERIODICALS
3RD EDITION

Miriam Uhlan, Editor

Special Libraries Association
New York

Copyright © 1985 by Special Libraries Association
235 Park Avenue South, New York, NY 10003

Printed in the United States of America

Library of Congress Cataloging in Publication Data
Main entry under title:

Guide to special issues and indexes of periodicals.

Includes index.
1. Business--Periodicals--Bibliography. 2. Business--Periodicals--Indexes--Bibliography. 3. Industry--Periodicals--Bibliography. 4. Industry--Periodicals--Indexes--Bibliography. 5. Commerce--Periodicals--Bibliography. 6. Commerce--Periodicals--Indexes--Bibliography. I. Uhlan, Miriam.
Z7164.C81G85 1985   [HF5351]   016.051   85-2351
ISBN 0-87111-263-9

Contents

Introduction v

Classified List of Periodicals 1

List of Canadian Periodicals 9

Guide to Special Issues of Periodicals 11

Subject Index to Special Issues 135

Introduction

The editors of the second edition of *Guide to Special Issues and Indexes of Periodicals* wrote, in their introduction:

> Consumer, trade and technical periodicals furnish a vast amount of specialized data vital to the business and professional communities. At a time when information needs are more demanding than ever, this second edition...is designed to facilitate the rapid location of such essential materials.

Almost a decade has passed since the publication of the second edition, and the highly publicized "information explosion" has made it even more vital to locate up-to-date information quickly and efficiently.

The format of the third edition is similar to the second edition. The *Guide* details, in alphabetical sequence, 1362 U.S. and Canadian periodicals which publish *Special Issues* (directories, buyers' guides, convention issues, statistical outlooks or reviews, and other features or supplementary issues appearing on a continual, annual or other basis). It also indicates whether periodicals provide an *Editorial Index* (annual, semiannual or other) and an *Advertiser Index* (a page locator of the advertisers appearing in the issue). Each entry lists the subscription address and subscription price of each periodical and the price of each *Special*. All prices are in U.S. dollars. When two prices are given for Canadian periodicals, the first price is in U.S. dollars and the second price is in Canadian dollars. Unless otherwise indicated, special issues are published in the regular issue and are included in the subscription price. The directory will indicate if the special issue is a separate release (not bound into the regular issue).

There are several features new to this edition:

1. The name of the periodical publisher is given.
2. Each entry also indicates whether the price of a *Special* is included as part of the annual subscription or must be ordered and paid for separately.
3. When known, the first year the *Special* appeared is listed.
4. If the periodical is indexed or abstracted in a computerized database, the name of the database is given.
5. If the periodical has an *Editorial Index,* it is classified as subject, author or title.
6. Expanded annotations on each *Special Issue* are provided when its title is not sufficiently descriptive.

As in the second edition, a *Classified List of Periodicals* precedes the main text, and a comprehensive *Subject Index to Special Issues* follows the main text. New to this edition is also a separate *List of Canadian Periodicals*.

The information for this edition of the *Guide* was gathered by questionnaires and extensive telephone calls to magazine editors; personal examination of selected periodicals; examination of editorial schedules; and reference to the second edition of the *Guide* and other resources detailing contents of periodicals. The editor wishes to express particular thanks to the following persons who provided valuable advice and information: Doris Katz (coeditor of the second edition); Mary McNierney Grant and the staff of the Center for Business Research, C.W. Post College; Lorna Daniells; and Sylvia Mechanic and the staff of the Brooklyn Business Library. The editor also wishes to thank Richard Reed for his valuable assistance in preparing this edition; Naomi Drucker, Alice Berridge, and Nicholas Massa; Sophie Zimmerman and Terry Cohen for their clerical help; and Michael J. Esposito, Special Libraries Association.

Although every effort has been made to provide up-to-date information, the world of periodicals publishing is constantly changing, on short notice. Each week brings news of publishers buying magazines from each other; corporate moves to new locations; new magazine formats; and of course ever-rising subscription rates. (It is suggested that subscription prices be verified with publishers -- hence the inclusion of publishers' names in this edition.) Omissions or errors are unintentional; and it is hoped that changes and corrections will be brought to the attention of the Editor. This *Guide* does not attempt to be all-inclusive, but it represents major sources of industry and consumer information, for convenient reference.

Miriam Uhlan

Classified List of Periodicals

A

Abstracts/Indexes
Index Medicus; 0668
International Aerospace Abstracts; 0704
Meteorological and Geoastrophysical Abstracts 0868
NFAIS Newsletter; 0920
Resources in Education (RIE); 1120

Accounting
Accounting Review; 0016
The CPA Journal; 0232
CA Magazine; 0234
International Tax Journal; 0708
Journal of Accountancy; 0724
Journal of Accounting, Auditing and Finance; 0725
Journal of Real Estate Taxation; 0757
Journal of Taxation; 0762
Management Accounting; 0823
Practical Accountant; 1059
Price Waterhouse Review; 1064
Review of Taxation of Individuals; 1128
Tax Executive; 1245
Tax Law Review; 1246
Tax Lawyer; 1247
Taxation For Accountants; 1248
Taxes; 1249

Advertising/Promotion/Public Relations
Ad Day/U.S.A.; 0017
Ad East; 0018
The Adcrafter; 0019
Advertising Age; 0024
Advertising World; 0025
Adweek; 0026
Agri Marketing; 0033
American Demographics; 0058
Art Direction; 0120
Business Marketing; 0224
Communications Arts; 0347
Fund Raising Management; 0572
Incentive Marketing Incorporating Incentive Travel; 0665
Journal of Advertising Research; 0726
Magazine Age; 0820
Marketing; 0831
Marketing and Media Decisions; 0832
Marketing Communications; 0833
Media Industry Newsletter; 0847
Medical Marketing & Media; 0853
New England Advertising Week; 0943
Premium/Incentive Business; 1061
Public Relations Journal; 1080
Public Relations Review; 1081
Specialty Advertising Business; 1216

Agriculture
AgMarketer; 0031
Agri Finance; 0032
Agribusiness World-Wide; 0034
Agricultural Economics Research; 0035
Agricultural Engineering Magazine; 0036
Agri-Equipment Today; 0037
American Bee Journal; 0053
American Fruit Grower/Western Fruit Grower; 0063
Big Farmer Entrepreneur; 0177
Canada Poultryman; 0240
The Canadian Fruitgrower; 0261
Cash Crop Farming; 0296
Citrus & Vegetable Magazine; 0328
Dairy Record; 0403
Farm Equipment Quarterly; 0502
Farm & Power Equipment; 0503
Farm Store Merchandising; 0504
Farm Supplier; 0505
Farmline; 0506
Feed & Farm Supply Dealer; 0511
Feed Industry; 0512
Feedlot Management; 0513
Feedstuffs; 0514
Grain Age; 0596
Grain Journal; 0597
Grain Storage & Handling; 0598
Hog Farm Management; 0637
Implement and Tractor; 0661
Northwest Farm Equipment Journal; 0954
The Packer; 0986
Poultry Digest; 1052
Poultry & Egg Marketing; 1053
Poultry Tribune; 1055
Solutions; 1206
Sugar y Azucar; 1233
Turkey World; 1293

Amusements/Vending
American Automatic Merchandiser; 0049
Canadian Vending; 0287
Play Meter; 1040
Vending Times; 1303

Antiques
The Antique Trader Weekly; 0103
Antiques Dealer; 0104
The Magazine Antiques; 0821
Spinning Wheel: The Magazine of Antiques & Early Crafts; 1219

Apparel/Accessories/Furs
Bobbin; 0186
Body Fashions/Intimate Apparel; 0187
Earnshaw's Infants, Girls and Boys Wear Review; 0443
Fashion Accessories Magazine; 0507
Fur Age Weekly; 0573
Hoisery & Underwear; 0638
Intimate Fashion News; 0710
Knitting Times/Apparel World; 0783
Men's Wear of Canada; 0860
SportStyle; 1227
Teens & Boys Magazine; 1251

Appliances/Consumer Electronics
Appliance; 0105
Appliance Manufacturer; 0106
Consumer Electronics; 0374
Mart Magazine; 0836

Architecture
Architectural Record; 0113
Architecture; 0114
Canadian Architect; 0242
Progressive Architecture; 1075

Art
American Artist; 0048
Art in America; 0121
Art Material Trade News; 0122
Arts & Activities; 0124
Museum News; 0917

Audio-Visual Communications
A/V Canada Business Communications; 0014
Audio Visual Directions; 0131
Audio-Visual Communications; 0132
Broadcast Technology; 0199
Communications News; 0348
PhotoVideo; 1015
Video Systems; 1308
Videodisk/Videotex; 1309

Automotive
Advanced Vehicle News; 0023
Auto Laundry News; 0133
Auto Merchandising News; 0134
Auto Trim News; 0135
Automotive Age; 0138
Automotive Body Repair News; 0139
Automotive Engineering; 0140
Automotive Industries; 0141
Automotive Marketing; 0142
Automotive News; 0143
Automotive Rebuilder; 0144
Automotive Volume Distribution; 0145
The Battery Man; 0162
Body Shop Business; 0188
Brake & Front End; 0195
Canadian Automotive Trade; 0243
Car and Driver; 0292
Family Motor Coaching; 0500
Home & Auto; 0639
Import Car; 0662
Jobber News; 0720
Jobber Topics; 0721
Motor; 0911
Motor/Age; 0912
Motor in Canada; 0913
Road & Track; 1134
Specialty & Custom Dealer; 1217
Super Service Station; 1234
Taxicab Management; 1250
Tire Review; 1266
Ward's Auto World; 1319
Warehouse Distributor News; 1320

Aviation/Aerospace
AIAA Journal; 0004
The AOPA Pilot; 0007
Aerospace; 0028
Air Line Pilot; 0041
Air Transport World; 0042
Airline Executive; 0043
Airport Services Management Magazine; 0044
Astronautics & Aeronautics; 0128
Aviation Equipment & Maintenance; 0146
Aviation, Space and Environmental Medicine; 0147
Aviation Week & Space Technology; 0148
Business and Commercial Aviation; 0216
Canadian Aircraft Operator; 0241
Canadian Aviation; 0244
Commuter Air; 0350
Flying; 0545
ICAO Bulletin; 0657
International Aerospace Abstracts; 0704
Journal of Aircraft; 0727
Journal of Energy; 0740
Journal of Guidance, Control and Dynamics; 0743
Journal of Spacecraft & Rockets; 0760
Professional Pilot; 1072
Rotor & Wing International; 1139
Vertiflite; 1305
Wings; 1341

B

Banking/Finance
ABA Banking Journal; 0003
Bank Administration; 0154
Bank Marketing Magazine; 0155
Bank Systems & Equipment; 0156
The Banker; 0157
The Bankers Magazine; 0158
Bankers Monthly: National Magazine of Banking & Investments; 0159
Banking Law Journal; 0160
Business Review—Federal Reserve Bank of Philadelphia; 0225
Canadian Banker & ICB REview; 0245
Credit; 0389
Credit & Financial Management; 0390
Credit Union Executive; 0391, 0392
Credit Union Magazine; 0393
Credit World; 0394
Economic Review—Federal Reserve Bank of Atlanta; 0448
Economic Review—Federal Reserve Bank of Kansas City; 0449
Federal Home Loan Bank Board Journal; 0508
Federal Reserve Bulletin; 0509
Financial Executive; 0525
The Financial Post; 0526
Financial Times of Canada; 0527
Financial World; 0528
Institutional Investor; 0690
The Journal; 0722
Journal of Commercial Bank Lending; 0734
Journal of Finance; 0741
Journal of Financial and Quantitative Analysis; 0742
Mergers & Acquisitions; 0862
Mortgage Banking; 0909
Mountain States Banker; 0915
New England Economic Review; 0945
Pacific Banker & Business; 0980
Quarterly Journal—Comptroller of the Currency 1093
Quarterly Review; 1094
Review—Federal Reserve Bank of St. Louis; 1130
Savings Bank Journal; 1154
Savings Institutions; 1155
The Southern Banker; 1210
United States Banker; 1298

Beauty Culture
American Hairdresser/Salon Owner; 0066
Beauty Fashion; 0163

Beverages
BIN Merchandiser; 0150
Beer Wholesaler; 0165
Beverage Canada; 0171
Beverage Industry; 0172
Beverage Retailer Weekly; 0173
Beverage World; 0174
Beverages/Bebidas; 0175
Brewers Digest; 0196
Canadian Beverage Review; 0246
Impact; 0660
Liquor Store Magazine; 0806
Modern Brewery Age; 0890
Wines & Vines; 1340

Bibliographies
The International Executive; 0705
Monthly Catalog of United States Government Publications; 0907

Bicycles/Motorcycles
Cycle; 0398
Cycle World; 0399
Motorcycle Product News; 0914

Boats/Boating
Boat and Motor Dealer Magazine; 0183
Boating; 0184
Boating Industry; 0185
Canadian Boating; 0247
Pacific Yachting; 0983
Rudder; 1143
Yacht Racing/Cruising; 1361
Yachting; 1362

Building/Construction
Alaska Construction & Oil; 0046
Automation in Housing/Systems Building News; 0137
Builder; 0204
Building Design & Construction; 0205
Building Guide Magazine; 0206
Building Supply and Home Centers; 0209
Buildings: The Facilities Construction and Management Magazine; 0210
Concrete; 0360
Concrete Construction; 0361
Construction; 0363
Construction Contracting; 0364
Construction Digest; 0365
Construction Equipment; 0366
Construction Equipment Distribution; 0367
Construction Review; 0368
The Construction Specifier; 0369
Constructioneer; 0370
Constructor; 0371
Daily Commercial News and Construction Record; 0401
Dixie Contractor; 0431
Engineering & Contract Record; 0483
Farm Building News; 0501
Fence Industry; 0515
Florida Builder; 0541
Genie-Construction; 0583
Heavy Construction News; 0632
Journal of Commerce (Canada); 0733
Journal of the American Concrete Institute; 0765
Journal of the Prestressed Concrete Institute; 0776
Manufactured Housing Business; 0827
Mid-West Contractor; 0876
Mobile/Manufactured Home Merchandiser; 0887
Multi-Housing News; 0916
National Development; 0927
Pacific Builder & Engineer; 0981
Parking; 0994
Professional Builder; 1069
Qualified Remodeler; 1091
RSI - Roofing, Siding, Insulation; 1102
U.S. Glass, Metal & Glazing; 1295
Walls & Ceilings; 1318
Window Energy Systems; 1339
Worldwide Projects; 1358

Building Maintenance
Building Operating Management; 0207
Building Services Contractor; 0208
Cleaning Management; 0331
Maintenance Supplies; 0822
Sanitary Maintenance; 1152

Business/Industry
Alaska Business & Industry; 0045
Barron's—National Business and Financial Weekly; 0161
Business America; 0215
Business and Society Review; 0217
Business History Review; 0221
Business Horizons; 0222
Business Week; 0226
Canadian Business; 0249
Columbia Journal of World Business; 0341
Corporate Report Minnesota; 0384
Dun's Business Month; 0440
Economic World; 0450
Executive; 0494
The Executive Combination; 0495
Financial World; 0528
Forbes; 0558
Fortune Magazine; 0565
Harvard Business Review; 0616
Horizons; 0641
Inc. Magazine; 0664
Income Opportunities; 0666
Industry Week; 0685
Journal of Small Business Management; 0759
Metropolitan Toronto Business Journal; 0871
Modern Africa; 0888
Modern Asia; 0889
Nation's Business; 0939
New Jersey Business; 0948
Seattle Business; 1169
Survey of Current Business; 1238
Survey of Wall St. Research; 1239
Women in Business; 1344
Working Woman; 1348

C

Ceramics/Glass
American Ceramic Society Bulletin; 0054
American Glass Review; 0065
Canadian Clay & Ceramics Quarterly; 0251
Ceramic Industry; 0304
Ceramic Scope; 0305
The Glass Industry; 0590
National Glass Budget; 0930
Tile & Decorative Surfaces; 1262
U.S. Glass, Metal & Glazing; 1295

Chemicals/Chemical Process Industries
AIChE Journal; 0005
Aerosol Age; 0027
Analytical Chemistry; 0101
Canadian Chemical Processing; 0250
Chemical Engineering; 0312
Chemical & Engineering News; 0313
Chemical Engineering Progress; 0314
Chemical Equipment; 0315
Chemical Marketing Reporter/Chemical Business; 0316
Chemical Processing; 0317
Chemical Purchasing; 0318
Chemical Week; 0319
Energy Progress; 0480
Industrial Chemical News; 0670
Journal of the American Oil Chemists Society; 0769
Pest Control Technology; 1002
Plant/Operations Progress; 1029
Soap/Cosmetics/Chemical Specialties; 1198

Commerce/Trade
American Import/Export Management; 0069
German American Trade News; 0585
International Trade Forum; 0709
Italian American Business; 0716

Communications/Telecommunications
APCO Bulletin; 0009
Business Communications Review; 0218
Journal of Communication; 0735
Sound & Communications; 1209
Telephone Engineer & Management; 1252
Telephony; 1253

Computers/Data Processing
Annals of the History of Computing; 0102
Byte; 0228
CIPS Review/La Revue ACI; 0231
Canadian Datasystems; 0255
Collegiate Microcomputer; 0340
Computer; 0352
Computer Decisions; 0353
Computer Design; 0354
Computer Pictures; 0356

ComputerData; 0357
Computers and People; 0358
Computerworld; 0359
Creative Computing; 0387
Data Communications; 0405
Data Management; 0406
Datamation; 0408
Desktop Computing; 0420
IBM Systems Journal; 0656
ICP Software Business Review; 0658
Infosystems; 0687
Journal of Systems Management; 0761
Journal of the Association for Computing Machinery; 0774
Microcomputing; 0872
Mini-Micro Systems; 0883
Small Systems World; 1191
Softalk; 1202

Confectionery
Candy Industry; 0289
Candy Marketer Quarterly; 0290
United States Tobacco and Candy Journal; 1299

Consumer Interests
Changing Times; 0310
Consumer Reports; 0375
Consumers' Research Magazine; 0376
FDA Consumer; 0498

D

Dairying/Dairy Products
Dairy Field; 0402
Modern Dairy; 0893

Dentistry
Dental Laboratory Review; 0415

Design Engineering
Design Engineering; 0417
Design News; 0418
Hydraulics & Pneumatics; 0654
Industrial Design; 0671
Machine Design; 0819
Materials Engineering; 0840
Power Transmission Design; 1058

Drugs/Cosmetics/Health and Beauty Aids
American Druggist; 0059
Drug & Cosmetic Industry; 0437
Drug Store News; 0438
Drug Topics; 0439
Product Marketing and Cosmetic & Fragrance Retailing; 1067

E

Earth Science
Geophysics; 0584

Economics
American Economic Review; 0061
Business Economics; 0219
Econometrica; 0446
Economic Report; 0447
Economic Review—Federal Reserve Bank of Atlanta; 0448
Economic Review—Federal Reserve Bank of Kansas City; 0449
History of Political Economy; 0635
Journal of Economic Literature; 0737
New England Economic Indicators; 0944
New England Economic Review; 0945
Review of Economics and Statistics; 1126

Education
American Quarterly; 0088
American School Board Journal; 0091
American School & University; 0092
Catechist; 0300
Change: The Magazine of Higher Learning; 0309
Collegiate Microcomputer; 0340
Community and Junior College Journal; 0349
Curriculum Product Review; 0397
The Education Digest; 0452
Educational Dealer; 0453
Educational Digest; 0454
Engineering Education; 0485
Health Education; 0622
The Horn Book Magazine; 0642
Instructor; 0691
Journal of Home Economics; 0745
Journal of Learning Disabilities; 0748
Journal of Physical Education, Recreation and Dance; 0754
Journalism Education; 0778
PMLA; 0977
PHI Delta Kappan; 1009
Plays, the Drama Magazine for Young People; 1042
Research Quarterly for Exercise and Sport; 1118
Resources in Education (RIE); 1120
School Business Affairs; 1157
School Product News; 1159
School Shop; 1160
Sociology of Education; 1201
Today's Catholic Teacher; 1268
Training and Development Journal; 1281
Voc Ed; 1312
The Volta Review; 1314

Electronics/Electrical Engineering
CEE/Contractors' Electrical Equipment; 0229
Canadian Electronics Engineering; 0257
Circuits Manufacturing; 0327
Dealerscope; 0409
Defense Electronics; 0412
Digital Design; 0426
EDN; 0441
Electrical Apparatus; 0458
Electrical Business; 0459
Electrical Construction and Maintenance; 0460
Electrical Consultant; 0461
Electrical Contractor; 0462
The Electrical Distributor; 0463
Electrical Equipment News; 0464
Electrical Wholesaling; 0465
Electrical World; 0466
Electricity Canada; 0467
Electri-Onics; 0468
Electronic Business; 0469
Electronic Component News; 0470
Electronic Design; 0471
Electronics; 0472
Electronics & Communications; 0473
Electro-Optics; 0474
Evaluation Engineering; 0493
Fiber Optics and Communications Newsletter; 0516
Fiberoptics Report; 0518
Laser Focus with Fiberoptic Technology; 0792
Laser Report; 0793
Microwave Journal; 0873
Microwave Systems News; 0874
Microwaves & RF; 0875
Signal; 1183
Solid State Technology; 1205
Transmission & Distribution; 1283

Engineering
AIPE Journal; 0006
Agricultural Engineering Magazine; 0036
The B.C. Professional Engineer; 0149
Canadian Consulting Engineer; 0253
Civil Engineering; 0330
Consulting Engineer; 0373
Cost Engineering; 0385
Engineering Digest; 0484
Engineering News-Record; 0487
Graduating Engineer; 0595
Lubrication Engineering; 0813
Mechanical Engineering; 0846
National Utility Contractor; 0938
New Equipment Digest; 0947
Specifying Engineer; 1218

Entertainment Industry
American Cinematographer; 0055
Amusement Business; 0099
Boxoffice; 0194
Tourist Attractions & Parks; 1272
Variety; 1302

Environmental Protection/Pollution Control
American Industrial Hygiene Association Journal; 0070
The Conservationist; 0362
Ecology; 0445
Environmental Progress; 0491
Environmental Science & Technology; 0492
Journal of the Air Pollution Control Association; 0764
Journal Water Pollution Control Federation; 0777
Land and Water; 0788
Pollution Engineering; 1045
Pollution Equipment News; 1046
Professional Sanitation Management; 1074
Sierra; 1182
Water & Pollution Control; 1325

F

Fashion
Vogue Magazine; 1313

Fire Protection
Fire Command; 0530
Fire Engineering; 0531
Fire Journal; 0532

Firearms
Handloader Magazine; 0609
Rifle; 1131

Fish/Fisheries
Aquaculture Magazine; 0108
The Fishermen's News; 0533
Fishery Bulletin; 0534
Fishing Gazette; 0535
Marine Fisheries Review; 0830
National Fisherman; 0928
Western Fisheries; 1333

Floors/Floor Coverings
Carpet & Rug Industry; 0294
Floor Covering News; 0538
Floor Covering Weekly; 0539
Flooring; 0540

Food/Food Industries
Bakery Production and Marketing; 0152
Baking Industry; 0153
Cereal Foods World; 0306
FDA Consumer; 0498
Focus on the Baking Industry; 0547
Food Engineering; 0549
Food Engineering International; 0550
Food in Canada; 0551
Food Processing; 0552
Food Production/Management; 0553
Frozen Food Age; 0569
The Macaroni Journal; 0817
The Manufacturing Confectioner; 0828
Meat Industry; 0843
Milling & Baking News; 0881
Modern Grocer; 0894
Processed Prepared Foods; 1066
Quick Frozen Foods; 1095

Snack Food; 1194
World Coffee & Tea; 1350

Footwear/Leather Goods
American Shoemaking; 0094
Canadian Footware Journal; 0259
Footwear News; 0557
The Leather Manufacturer; 0797
Leather & Shoes; 0798
Luggage & Leathergoods News; 0814
Shoe Service; 1178

Foundations/Philanthropy
Foundation News; 0566
Grants Magazine; 0599
Philanthropy Monthly; 1010

Funeral Services
Southern Funeral Director; 1211

Furniture
Casual Living; 0297
Flotation Sleep Industry; 0544
Furniture Design and Manufacturing; 0574
Furniture Manufacturing Management; 0575
Furniture Production; 0576
Furniture World; 0577
Juvenile Merchandising; 0780
Plywood & Panel World; 1044
Professional Furniture Merchant; 1070
Small World; 1192
Upholstering Today; 1300
Upholstery Manufacturing Management; 1301
Wood & Wood Products; 1345

G

Gardening/Horticulture/Landscaping
American Nurseryman; 0083
The American Rose Magazine; 0090
American Vegetable Grower; 0097
Canadian Florist, Greenhouse & Nursery; 0258
Florists' Review; 0543
Garden Supply Retailer; 0579
Golf Course Management; 0591
Grounds Maintenance; 0606
Horticulture, The Magazine of American Gardening; 0644
Landscape Architecture Magazine; 0789
The Landscape Contractor; 0790
Lawn Care Industry; 0796
Seed World; 1173
Seedsmen's Digest; 1174
Weeds Trees & Turf; 1328

Genealogy
The American Genealogist; 0064
The Genealogical Helper; 0582

General Interest
Analog Science Fiction/Science Fact; 0100
Commentary; 0342
En Route; 0479
Family Circle; 0499
50 Plus; 0520
Future Survey; 0578
Harper's; 0615
House Beautiful; 0652
Life; 0803
Los Angeles Magazine; 0812
The Mother Earth News; 0910
National Geographic; 0929
New York Magazine; 0949
Playboy; 1041
Popular Mechanics; 1049
Time; 1265
U.S. News & World Report; 1297
Woman's Day; 1343

Gerontology
Aging; 0030
Journal of the American Geriatrics Society; 0767

Government/Politics/Social Issues
Commonweal; 0346
The Crisis; 0395
Foreign Affairs; 0559
Foreign Service Journal; 0560
The Nation; 0924
Public Opinion Quarterly; 1078
State Government News; 1229
The Washington Monthly; 1321
World Press Review; 1355

Grocery Trade
Canadian Grocer; 0262
Convenience Store News; 0381
C-Store Business; 0396
Deli News; 0414
Grocers' Spotlight; 0603
Grocery Distribution Magazine; 0604
L'Epicier; 0799
Progressive Grocer; 1076
Supermarket Business; 1235
Supermarket News; 1236

H

Hardware/Housewares
Brushware; 0203
Doors and Hardware; 0433
Entree; 0490
Hardware Age; 0611
Hardware Merchandiser; 0612
Hardware Merchandising; 0613
Hardware Retailing; 0614
Housewares; 0653

Health Care/Hospitals
AARTimes; 0002
AORN Journal; 0008
American Journal of Nursing; 0074
The American Journal of Occupational Therapy; 0075
American Journal of Optometry and Physiological Optics; 0076
American Journal of Physiology; 0078
Archives of General Psychiatry; 0115
Archives of Ophthalmology; 0116
Aviation, Space and Environmental Medicine; 0147
Bulletin of the Medical Library Association; 0212
Children Today; 0320
Continuing Education for the Family Physician; 0377
Dental Products Report; 0416
Dialysis & Transplantation; 0421
Dimensions In Health Service; 0427
Emergency Medical Services; 0475
Federation of American Hospitals Review; 0510
Health; 0618
Health Care; 0619
Health Care Financing Review; 0620
Health Care Systems; 0621
Health Industry Today; 0624
Healthcare Financial Management; 0626
Hearing Instruments; 0627
The Hearing Journal; 0628
Hospital Forum; 0645
Hospital Practice; 0647
Hospital Progress; 0648
Hospital Topics; 0649
Hospitals; 0650
The Journal of Nursing Administration; 0752
Journal of Occupational Medicine; 0753
Journal of the American Geriatrics Society; 0767
The Journal of the American Medical Association; 0768
MLO/Medical Laboratory Observer; 0816
Medical Economics; 0848
Medical Electronics & Equipment News; 0849
Medical Group Management; 0850
Medical Group News; 0851
Medical Instrumentation; 0852
Medical Meetings; 0854
Medical Post; 0855
Medical Products Sales; 0856
Modern Healthcare; 0895
The Nurse Practitioner: The American Journal of Primary Health Care; 0956
Nursing Homes; 0957
Nursing Outlook; 0958
Nutritional Support Services; 0959
Patient Care; 0997
The Physician and Sportsmedicine; 1016
RNM Images; 1098
Respiratory Care; 1121
RN Magazine; 1133
Trustee; 1290
U.S. Medicine; 1296
The Volta Review; 1314

Heating/Plumbing/Refrigeration
ASHRAE Journal; 0011
Air Conditioning, Heating, & Refrigeration News; 0038
Contractor Magazine; 0379
Electric Comfort Conditioning News; 0455
Fueloil/Oil Heat and Solar Systems; 0571
Heating/Piping/Air Conditioning; 0630
Heating, Plumbing, Air Conditioning; 0631
Industrial Heating; 0678
RSC - Refrigeration Service and Contracting; 1101
Reeves Journal, Plumbing-Heating-Cooling; 1113
Service Reporter Distributor; 1176
Snips; 1195
Solar Age; 1203
Solar Engineering & Contracting; 1204
Supply House Times; 1237
The Wholesaler; 1337

Hobbies/Novelties/Toys
Craft & Needleworking Age; 0386
Creative Crafts & Miniatures; 0388
Flying Models Magazine; 0546
Hobby Merchandiser; 0636
Jewelry Making, Gems and Minerals; 0719
Lapidary Journal; 0791
Playthings; 1043
Railroad Model Craftsman; 1104
Rock & Gem; 1136
Sew Business; 1177
Souvenirs and Novelties; 1213
Toy & Hobby World; 1273
Toys & Games; 1274
Toys, Hobbies & Crafts; 1275

Home Furnishings
Bedding Magazine; 0164
China Glass & Tableware; 0321
The Designer; 0419
Furniture World; 0577
Gifts & Decorative Accessories; 0587
Gifts & Tablewares; 0588
Giftware Business; 0589
Home Goods Retailing; 0640
Interior Textiles; 0701

Hotels/Motels/Restaurants
Canadian Hotel & Restaurant; 0263
Club Management; 0335
The Cornell Hotel & Restaurant Administration Quarterly; 0383
Food Service & Hospitality; 0554
Foodservice Equipment Specialist; 0555
Foodservice Product News; 0556
Hotel & Motel Management; 0651
Independent Restaurants; 0667

Institutional Distribution; 0689
Lodging; 0808
Lodging & Food-Service East; 0809
Lodging Hospitality; 0810
NRA News; 0923
Nation's Restaurant News; 0941
Resort Management; 1119
Restaurant Business; 1122
Restaurant Hospitality; 1123
Restaurants & Institutions; 1124

Housing/Urban Planning
Journal of Housing; 0746
Journal of The American Planning Association; 0770

I

Industrial Management/Products
Canadian Industrial Equipment News; 0264
Industrial Engineering; 0674
Industrial Equipment News; 0675
Industrial Product Ideas; 0683
Quality; 1092

Instruments/Control Systems
Canadian Controls & Instruments; 0254
Control Engineering; 0380
I & C S; 0693
Intech; 0698

Insurance
Best's Review: Life/Health Edition; 0167
Best's Review: Property/Casualty Edition; 0168
Business Insurance; 0223
CPCU Journal; 0233
Canadian Insurance; 0265
Canadian Underwriter; 0286
CLU Journal; 0334
Employee Benefit Plan Review; 0476
Health Insurance Underwriter; 0625
Insurance Advocate; 0694
Insurance Field; 0695
Insurance Journal; 0696
Insurance Sales Magazine; 0697
International Insurance Monitor; 0706
Journal of Insurance; 0747
Life Association News; 0804
Life & Health National Underwriter; 0805
National Underwriter Property and Casualty; 0937
Risk Management; 1132
Rough Notes; 1140

Interior Design/Decoration
Architectural Record; 0113
Better Homes and Gardens; 0169
Canadian Interiors; 0266
Contract; 0378
Decorating Retailer; 0410
Decorative Products World; 0411
The Designer; 0419
House Beautiful; 0652
Interior Design; 0700
Interiors; 0702
Kitchen & Bath Business; 0782
Tile & Decorative Surfaces; 1262
Wallcoverings; 1317

Investments
Benefits Canada; 0166
The Bond Buyer; 0189
Commodities, The Magazine of Futures Trading 0345
Financial Analysts Journal; 0524
Investment Dealers' Digest; 0712
Money; 0906
Pension World; 0998
Pensions & Investment Age; 0999
Trusts & Estates; 1291

Venture; 1304
Wall Street Journal; 1316

J

Jewelry
American Jewelry Manufacturer; 0073
Canadian Jeweller; 0267
Jeweler/Gem Business; 0717
Jewelers' Circular-Keystone; 0718
Modern Jeweler; 0896
Precious Gem Investor; 1060
Watch & Clock Review; 1323

Journalism/Writing
Catholic Journalist; 0301
Editor & Publisher; 0451
Journalism Education; 0778
Journalism Quarterly; 0779
The Quill; 1096
The Writer; 1359
Writer's Digest; 1360

L

Labor/Industrial Relations
Employment and Earnings; 0478
Industrial and Labor Relations Review; 0669

Laboratory Techniques
American Laboratory; 0079
Biomedical Products; 0180
Canadian Clinical Laboratory; 0252
International Laboratory; 0707
Lab Animal; 0784
Laboratory Equipment; 0785
Laboratory Management; 0786
Laboratory Product News; 0787

Laundry/Dry Cleaning
American Coin-Op; 0057
Coinamatic Age; 0338
Textile Rental; 1258

Law Enforcement
Harvard Law Review; 0617
Law and Order; 0794
Law Enforcement Communications; 0795

Legal
American Bar Association Journal; 0052
Arbitration Journal; 0109
Banking Law Journal; 0160
Computer/Law Journal; 0355
Copyright Management; 0382
Invention Management; 0711

Library/Information Science
American Libraries; 0080
Bulletin of the Medical Library Association; 0212
Catholic Library World; 0302
Choice; 0322
Journal of Education for Librarianship; 0738
Journal of the American Society for Information Science; 0771
Library Journal; 0800
Library Quarterly; 0801
Library Trends; 0802
RQ; 1100
School Library Journal; 1158
Special Libraries; 1215
Wilson Library Bulletin; 1338

Lumber/Forest Industries
Canadian Forest Industries; 0260
Fingertip Facts & Figures; 0529
Forest Farmer; 0561
Forest Industries; 0562
Forest Products Journal; 0563
Logging & Sawmilling Journal; 0811
The Lumber Co-Operator; 0815

Timber Harvesting; 1263
Timber Processing Industry; 1264
World Wood; 1357

M

Management
Advanced Management Journal; 0022
Association Management; 0127
Compensation Review; 0351
Consultants News; 0372
Executive Recruiter News; 0497
Interfaces; 0699
Managerial Planning; 0826
Personnel Administrator; 1000
Personnel Journal; 1001
SAM Advanced Management Journal; 1151

Maritime
Canadian Shipping and Marine Engineering; 0280
Sea Ports & The Shipping World; 1166
Waterways Journal; 1327
The Work Boat; 1347
World Dredging & Marine Construction; 1352

Marketing/Merchandising
Agency Sales Magazine; 0029
American Automatic Merchandiser; 0049
Catalog Show Room Merchandiser; 0298
Catalog Showroom Business; 0299
The College Store Journal; 0339
Greetings Magazine; 0602
Hospital Gift Shop Management; 0646
Journal of Marketing; 0749
Journal of Marketing Research; 0750
Marketing and Media Decisions; 0832
Marketing Communications; 0833
Marketing News; 0834
Merchandising; 0861
Opportunity Magazine; 0973
Sales and Marketing Management in Canada; 1149
Sales & Marketing Management; 1150
Selling Direct; 1175
Visual Merchandising & Store Design; 1311

Materials Handling/Distribution
Handling & Shipping Management; 0608
Industrial Distribution; 0673
Material Handling Engineering; 0839
Materials Management & Distribution; 0841
Modern Materials Handling; 0898
Traffic Management; 1277

Meat Industry
Meat Plant; 0844
Meat Processing; 0845

Meetings/Conventions
Medical Meetings; 0854
Meeting & Conventions; 0857
Meeting News; 0858
Meetings & Incentive Travel; 0859
Successful Meetings; 1232
World Convention Dates; 1351

Metals/Metalworking/Machinery
Abrasive Engineering Society Magazine; 0015
American Machinist; 0081
American Metal Market; 0082
Assembly Engineering; 0126
Automatic Machining; 0136
Canadian Machinery & Metalworking; 0268
Canadian Welder & Fabricator; 0288
Carbide & Tool Journal; 0293
Die Casting Engineer; 0423
Foundry Management & Technology; 0567
Heating/Combustion Equipment News; 0629
Industrial Finishing; 0677
Industrial Machinery News; 0680
Iron Age; 0713

Iron & Steel Engineer; 0714
Iron & Steelmaker; 0715
Journal of Electronic Materials; 0739
Journal of Metals; 0751
Machine and Tool Blue Book; 0818
Manufacturing Engineering; 0829
Metal Center News; 0863
Metal Finishing; 0864
Metal Progress; 0865
Metal Stamping; 0866
Metalworking Digest; 0867
Modern Casting; 0892
Modern Machine Shop; 0897
NC Shop Owner; 0919
Plating and Surface Finishing; 1039
Products Finishing; 1068
Robotics Today; 1135
33 Metal Producing; 1261
Tooling & Production; 1270
Wire Journal International; 1342

Meteorology
Bulletin of the American Meteorological Society; 0211
Journal of Climate and Applied Meteorology; 0731
Journal of the Atmospheric Sciences; 0775
Meteorological and Geoastrophysical Abstracts; 0868
Monthly Weather Review; 0908

Military
Air Force Magazine; 0039
Air Force Times; 0040
Army; 0118
Army Times; 0119
Defense Management Journal; 0413
The Military Engineer; 0878
Military Market Magazine; 0879
National Defense; 0926

Mines/Mining Industry
Asbestos; 0125
Brick and Clay Record; 0197
CIM Bulletin; 0230
Canadian Mining Journal; 0269
Coal Age; 0336
Coal Mining & Processing; 0337
Engineering & Mining Journal; 0486
Industrial Minerals; 0682
Mines Magazine; 0882
Mining Congress Journal; 0884
Mining Engineering; 0885
Mining/Processing Equipment; 0886
The Northern Miner; 0953
Pit & Quarry; 1024
Rock Products; 1137
Skillings' Mining Review; 1188
Western Miner; 1335
World Coal; 1349
World Mining; 1353

Mobile Homes/Recreational Vehicles
RVBusiness; 1103

Motion Pictures
Back Stage; 0151
Film Comment; 0521
The Film Journal; 0522
Film Quarterly; 0523
SMPTE Journal; 1148

Music/Sound Recording
Audio; 0130
Billboard; 0178
Cash Box; 0295
Music Trades Magazines; 0918
RPM Weekly; 1099
Rolling Stone; 1138
Sound Canada; 1208
Stereo Review; 1230

N

Nutrition
Health Foods Business; 0623
Journal of the American Dietetic Association; 0766
Nutritional Support Services; 0959
Prevention Magazine; 1063
Weight Watchers Magazine; 1329

O

Oceanography
Journal of Physical Oceanography; 0755
Sea Frontiers; 1165
Sea Technology; 1167

Office Management/Methods/Supplies
Adminstrative Digest; 0021
Business Forms & Systems; 0220
Canadian Office; 0270
Canadian Office Products & Stationery; 0271
Canadian Secretary; 0279
Form Magazine; 0564
Geyer's Dealer Topics; 0586
Information Management; 0686
Management World; 0825
Marking Industry; 0835
Modern Office Procedures; 0899
NOMDA Spokesman; 0921
NOPA Special Report; 0922
The Office; 0961
Office Administration and Automation; 0962
Office Equipment & Methods; 0963
Office Products Dealer; 0964
The Secretary; 1170

Outdoor Living/Parks
Camping Magazine; 0239
National Parks; 0933
Park Maintenance; 0993
Recreation Canada; 1112
Scope Camping News; 1164

P

Packaging
Boxboard Containers; 0193
Canadian Packaging; 0272
Food & Drug Packaging; 0548
Package Engineering; 0984
Paper, Film & Foil Converter; 0988
Paperboard Packaging; 0992

Paints/Coatings
American Paint & Coatings Journal; 0085
American Painting Contractor; 0086
Journal of Coatings Technology; 0732
Modern Paint & Coatings; 0900
Painting & Wallcovering Contractor; 0987
Western Paint & Decorating; 1336

Paper/Pulp
PPI-Pulp & Paper International; 0978
Paper, Paperboard and Wood Pulp Monthly Statistical Summary; 0989
Paper Sales; 0990
Paper Trade Journal; 0991
PIMA Magazine; 1019
Pulp & Paper; 1086
Pulp & Paper Canada; 1087
Pulp & Paper Journal; 1088
Southern Pulp & Paper; 1212
TAPPI Journal; 1243

Performing Arts
American Squaredance; 0096
Dance Magazine; 0404
The Diapason; 0422
Frets; 0568
Guitar Player; 0607
The Instrumentalist; 0692
Keyboard; 0781
Plays, the Drama Magazine for Young People; 1042
Square Dancing; 1228
Symphony Magazine; 1242
Theatre Crafts; 1260

Personnel
Employee Services Management; 0477

Petroleum/Gas/Oil/Energy
Alaska Construction & Oil; 0046
Butane-Propane News; 0227
Canadian Petroleum; 0273
Drilling Contractor; 0434
Drilling, The Wellsite Publication; 0435
Drillsite; 0436
Energy User News; 0482
Fuel Oil News; 0570
Gas Digest; 0580
Gas Industries; 0581
Geophysics; 0584
Hydrocarbon Processing; 0655
National Petroleum News; 0934
Ocean Industry; 0960
Offshore; 0965
The Oil Daily; 0966
Oil & Gas Journal; 0967
Oil & Gas (OGD's) Digest; 0968
Oil, Gas & Petrochem Equipment; 0969
Oil Patch; 0970
Oilweek; 0971
Petroleum Engineer International; 1006
Petroleum Equipment; 1007
Pipe Line Industry; 1020
Pipeline; 1021
Pipeline & Gas Journal; 1022
Pipeline & Underground Utilities Construction; 1023
World Oil; 1354

Pets/Supplies
Cats Magazine; 0303
Dogs in Canada; 0432
Pet Age; 1003
The Pet Dealer; 1004
Petfood Industry; 1005
Pets/Supplies/Marketing; 1008

Photography
PSA Journal; 0979
Photo Marketing; 1011
Photogrammetric Engineering and Remote Sensing; 1012
Photographic Trade News; 1013
Photomethods; 1014
PhotoVideo; 1015
Popular Photography; 1050
The Professional Photographer; 1071

Physics
Journal of Applied Physics; 0728
Journal of the Acoustical Society of America; 0763
Physics in Canada; 1017
Sound and Vibration; 1207

Plant Engineering
Engineer's Digest; 0489
Industrial Maintenance & Plant Operation; 0681
Materials Performance; 0842
Plant Engineering; 1027
Plant Management & Engineering; 1028
Plant Services; 1030

Plastics and Rubber
Adhesives Age; 0020
Canadian Plastics; 0274
Modern Plastics; 0901
Plastics Business; 1031
Plastics Compounding; 1032

Plastics Design Forum; 1033
Plastics Design & Processing; 1034
Plastics Engineering; 1035
Plastics Machinery & Equipment; 1036
Plastics Technology; 1037
Plastics World; 1038
Rubber & Plastics News; 1141
Rubber World; 1142

Poultry/Livestock
Broiler Industry; 0202
National Hog Farmer; 0931
The Poultry Times; 1054

Power/Power Plants
Diesel & Gas Turbine Worldwide; 0424
Diesel Progress North American; 0425
Electric Light & Power; 0456
Electric Power Monthly; 0457
Energy Systems Product News; 0481
Nuclear News; 0955
Power Engineering; 1056
Power Magazine; 1057
Power Transmission Design; 1058
Public Power; 1079
Public Utilities Fortnightly; 1083
Rural Electrification; 1147
Turbomachinery International; 1292

Printing/Reprographics
American Ink Maker; 0072
American Printer; 0087
Artes Graficas USA (Spanish); 0123
Canadian Printer and Publisher; 0276
Graphic Arts Monthly; 0600
Graphic Arts Product News; 0601
Package Printing; 0985
Plan and Print; 1025
Printing Impressions; 1065
Review of the Graphic Arts; 1129
Typeworld; 1294

Public Administration/Works
APWA Reporter; 0010
American City & County; 0056
Civic Public Works; 0329
Government Product News; 0594
National Civic Review; 0925
National Development; 0927
National Utility Contractor; 0938
Nation's Cities Weekly; 0940
Planning; 1026
Public Administration Review; 1077
Public Works Magazine; 1084
Worldwide Projects; 1358

Publishing/Book Trade
The Booklist; 0190
Christian Bookseller & Librarian; 0323
The Horn Book Magazine; 0642
The New York Times Book Review; 0950
Presstime; 1062
Publishers Weekly; 1085
Quill & Quire; 1097
Top of the News; 1271

Purchasing
Midwest Purchasing; 0877
Modern Purchasing; 0902
Purchasing Magazine; 1089
Purchasing World; 1090

R

Radio/Television/Cable
Back Stage; 0151
Broadcast Engineering; 0198
Broadcaster; 0200
Broadcasting; 0201
Cable Communications Magazine (CCM); 0235
Cable Tech; 0236
Cablevision; 0237
E•ITV; 0442
Inside Radio; 0688
Journal of Broadcasting; 0729
Millimeter Magazine; 0880
Television Digest; 1254
Videography; 1310

Railroads
Modern Railroads; 0903
Railway Track & Structures; 1105
Trains; 1282

Real Estate
American Industrial Properties Report; 0071
The Appraisal Journal; 0107
Canadian Building; 0248
Industrial Development/Site Selection Handbook; 0672
Journal of Property Management; 0756
National Mall Monitor; 0932
National Real Estate Investor; 0935
New England Real Estate Journal; 0946
The Real Estate Appraiser and Analyst; 1106
Real Estate Forum; 1107
Real Estate News; 1108
Real Estate Review; 1109
Realty; 1110
Realty and Building; 1111
Skylines; 1190

Regional
Florida Builder; 0541
Florida Trend; 0542

Religion
America; 0047
The Christian Century; 0324
Christian Herald; 0325
Christianity Today; 0326
The Clergy Journal; 0332

Rental Services
Canadian Rental Service; 0277
Rental Equipment Register; 1115
Rental Product News; 1116

Retail Trade
Chain Store Age Executive with Shopping Center Age; 0307
Chain Store Age—General Merchandise Edition; 0308
The Discount Merchandiser; 0428
Discount Store News; 0429
Farm Store Merchandising; 0504
Journal of Retailing; 0758
Mass Market Retailers; 0837
Monday Report on Retailers; 0905
Non-Foods Merchandising; 0951
Retail Control; 1125
Shopping Center World; 1180
Shopping Centre Canada; 1181
Stores; 1231

Roads/Traffic Management
Better Roads; 0170
Highway & Heavy Construction; 0634
ITE Journal; 0659
Public Roads; 1082
Rural and Urban Roads; 1146
Traffic Management; 1277
Traffic Safety; 1278

S

Safety/Security
Industrial Hygiene News; 0679
Industrial Safety & Hygiene News; 0684
Locksmith Ledger; 0807
National Safety News; 0936
Professional Safety; 1073
Security Management; 1171
Security World; 1172

Science/Research/Development
ASTM Standardization News; 0013
American Journal of Physics; 0077
American Scientist; 0093
Archives of Otolaryngology; 0117
Biomedical Communications; 0179
Bioscience; 0181
Bulletin of the New York Academy of Medicine; 0213
Canadian Research; 0278
Industrial Hygiene News; 0679
Journal of Chromatographic Science; 0730
Medical Instrumentation; 0852
Natural History; 0942
Operations Research; 0972
The Physician and Sportsmedicine; 1016
Physics Today; 1018
Popular Science; 1051
Research & Development; 1117
The Review of Scientific Instruments; 1127
Science; 1161
Science News; 1162
Scientific American; 1163
Smithsonian Magazine; 1193

Social Sciences
American Sociological Review; 0095
Archaeology; 0110
Journal of Consumer Research; 0736
Journal of Health & Social Behavior; 0744
Social Psychology Quarterly; 1199
Sociology of Education; 1201

Social Services
Social Security Bulletin; 1200

Specialized Markets
American Baby; 0050
Black Enterprise; 0182
Ebony; 0444

Sports/Sporting Industry
American Firearms Industry; 0062
American Hockey & Arena; 0067
American Hunter; 0068
American Rifleman; 0089
Archery Retailer; 0111
Archery World; 0112
Bicycle Dealers Showcase; 0176
Bowlers Journal; 0191
The Bowling Proprietor; 0192
Camping Canada; 0238
Canadian Pool & Spa Marketing; 0275
Canoe; 0291
Executive Golfer; 0496
Field & Stream; 0519
Fishing Tackle Trade News; 0536
Golf Course Management; 0591
Golf Digest; 0592
Golf Magazine; 0593
Horse & Rider; 0643
Outdoor Canada; 0974
Outdoor Life; 0975
Pool Industry Canada; 1047
Pool & Spa News; 1048
Runner's World; 1144
Running & Fitness; 1145
Shooting Industry; 1179
Ski; 1184
Ski Area Management; 1185
Ski Business; 1186
Skiing; 1187
Skin Diver; 1189
Snowmobile Canada; 1196
Snowmobile Sports; 1197
Spa and Sauna Trade Journal; 1214
The Sporting Goods Dealer; 1220
The Sporting News; 1221
Sports Afield; 1222
Sports Illustrated; 1223
Sports Merchandiser; 1224

Sports Retailer; 1225
Sports Trade Canada; 1226
SportStyle; 1227
Swimming Pool Age & Spa Merchandiser; 1240
Swimming World—Junior Swimmer; 1241
Tack 'N Togs Merchandising; 1244
Tennis; 1255
Track & Field News; 1276
The Water Skier; 1326
Western Canada Outdoors; 1332
Western Horseman; 1334
Woodall's Campground Management; 1346
World Tennis; 1356

Statistics
Data User News; 0407
Journal of the American Statistical Association; 0772
Metropolitan Life Statistical Bulletin; 0870
Paper, Paperboard and Wood Pulp Monthly Statistical Summary; 0989

T

Textile Industry
American Dyestuff Reporter; 0060
America's Textiles; 0098
Canadian Textile Journal; 0281
Fiber Producer; 0517
Impressions; 0663
Industrial Fabric Products Review; 0676
Nonwovens Industry; 0952
Textile Chemist and Colorist; 1256
Textile Industries; 1257
Textile World; 1259

Tobacco
Tobacco International; 1267
United States Tobacco and Candy Journal; 1299

Transportation/Shipping
Canadian Transportation & Distribution Management; 0282
Commercial News; 0344
Distribution; 0430
Handling & Shipping Management; 0608
Harbour & Shipping; 0610
Mass Transit; 0838
Metropolitan (A.K.A. Metro); 0869
Passenger Transport; 0996
School Bus Fleet; 1156
Sea Trade; 1168
Today's Transport International; 1269
Traffic World; 1279
Truck & Off-Highway Industries; 1289
WWS/World Ports; 1315

Travel/Tourism
ASTA Travel News; 0012
Canadian Travel Courier; 0283
Canadian Travel News; 0284
Canadian Travel Press; 0285
Interline Reporter; 0703
Meetings & Incentive Travel; 0859
Pacific Travel News; 0982
Saskatchawan Motorist; 1153
Travel Agent; 1285
Travel & Leisure; 1286
Travel Printout; 1287
Travel Weekly; 1288

Trucks/Trucking
Atlantic Truck Transport Review; 0129
Bus & Truck Transport; 0214
Canadian Driver/Owner; 0256
Commercial Carrier Journal; 0343
Fleet Owner; 0537
Heavy Duty Trucking; 0633
Modern Bulk Transporter; 0891
Owner Operator; 0976
Refrigerated Transporter; 1114
Today's Transport International; 1269
Trailer/Body Builders; 1280
Transport Topics; 1284

V

Veterinary Science
DVM; 0400
Journal of the American Veterinary Medical Association; 0773
Modern Veterinary Practice; 0904
Veterinary Economics; 1306
Veterinary Medicine/Small Animal Clinician; 1307

W

Water Supply/Wastes Disposal
Ground Water Age; 0605
Journal American Water Works Association; 0723
Journal Water Pollution Control Federation; 0777
Management of World Wastes; 0824
Waste Age; 1322
Water Conditioning and Purification; 1324

Welding
Welding Design & Fabrication; 1330
Welding Journal; 1331

List of Canadian Periodicals

A/V Canada Business Communications; 0014
Adminstrative Digest; 0021
Atlantic Truck Transport Review; 0129
The B.C. Professional Engineer; 0149
Benefits Canada; 0166
Beverage Canada; 0171
Broadcast Technology; 0199
Broadcaster; 0200
Building Guide Magazine; 0206
Bus & Truck Transport; 0214
CIM Bulletin; 0230
CIPS Review/La Revue ACI; 0231
CA Magazine; 0234
Cable Communications Magazine (CCM); 0235
Camping Canada; 0238
Canada Poultryman; 0240
Canadian Aircraft Operator; 0241
Canadian Architect; 0242
Canadian Automotive Trade; 0243
Canadian Aviation; 0244
Canadian Banker & ICB REview; 0245
Canadian Beverage Review; 0246
Canadian Boating; 0247
Canadian Building; 0248
Canadian Business; 0249
Canadian Chemical Processing; 0250
Canadian Clay & Ceramics Quarterly; 0251
Canadian Clinical Laboratory; 0252
Canadian Consulting Engineer; 0253
Canadian Controls & Instruments; 0254
Canadian Datasystems; 0255
Canadian Driver/Owner; 0256
Canadian Electronics Engineering; 0257
Canadian Florist, Greenhouse & Nursery; 0258
Canadian Footware Journal; 0259
Canadian Forest Industries; 0260
The Canadian Fruitgrower; 0261
Canadian Grocer; 0262
Canadian Hotel & Restaurant; 0263
Canadian Industrial Equipment News; 0264
Canadian Insurance; 0265
Canadian Interiors; 0266
Canadian Jeweller; 0267
Canadian Machinery & Metalworking; 0268
Canadian Mining Journal; 0269
Canadian Office; 0270
Canadian Office Products & Stationery; 0271
Canadian Packaging; 0272
Canadian Petroleum; 0273
Canadian Plastics; 0274
Canadian Pool & Spa Marketing; 0275
Canadian Printer and Publisher; 0276
Canadian Rental Service; 0277
Canadian Research; 0278
Canadian Secretary; 0279
Canadian Shipping and Marine Engineering; 0280
Canadian Textile Journal; 0281
Canadian Transportation & Distribution Management; 0282
Canadian Travel Courier; 0283
Canadian Travel News; 0284
Canadian Travel Press; 0285

Canadian Underwriter; 0286
Canadian Vending; 0287
Canadian Welder & Fabricator; 0288
Cash Crop Farming; 0296
Civic Public Works; 0329
ComputerData; 0357
Daily Commercial News and Construction Record 0401
Design Engineering; 0417
Dimensions In Health Service; 0427
Dogs in Canada; 0432
Drillsite; 0436
Educational Digest; 0454
Electrical Business; 0459
Electrical Equipment News; 0464
Electricity Canada; 0467
Electronics & Communications; 0473
En Route; 0479
Engineering & Contract Record; 0483
Engineering Digest; 0484
Engineering Times; 0488
Executive; 0494
Farm Equipment Quarterly; 0502
Feed & Farm Supply Dealer; 0511
The Financial Post; 0526
Financial Times of Canada; 0527
Floor Covering News; 0538
Focus on the Baking Industry; 0547
Food in Canada; 0551
Food Service & Hospitality; 0554
Gifts & Tablewares; 0588
Harbour & Shipping; 0610
Hardware Merchandising; 0613
Health Care; 0619
Heating, Plumbing, Air Conditioning; 0631
Heavy Construction News; 0632
Home Goods Retailing; 0640
ICAO Bulletin; 0657
Industrial Product Ideas; 0683
Jobber News; 0720
Journal of Commerce (Canada); 0733
Laboratory Product News; 0787
L'Epicier; 0799
Logging & Sawmilling Journal; 0811
Luggage & Leathergoods News; 0814
Marketing; 0831
Materials Management & Distribution; 0841
Medical Post; 0855
Meetings & Incentive Travel; 0859
Men's Wear of Canada; 0860
Metropolitan Toronto Business Journal; 0871
Modern Dairy; 0893
Modern Purchasing; 0902
Monday Report on Retailers; 0905
Motor in Canada; 0913
The Northern Miner; 0953
Office Equipment & Methods; 0963
Oilweek; 0971
Outdoor Canada; 0974
Pacific Yachting; 0983
PhotoVideo; 1015
Physics in Canada; 1017
Plant Management & Engineering; 1028

Plastics Business; 1031
Pool Industry Canada; 1047
Pulp & Paper Canada; 1087
Pulp & Paper Journal; 1088
Quill & Quire; 1097
RPM Weekly; 1099
Recreation Canada; 1112
Sales and Marketing Management in Canada; 1149
Saskatchawan Motorist; 1153
Scope Camping News; 1164
Sea Ports & The Shipping World; 1166
Shopping Centre Canada; 1181
Snowmobile Canada; 1196
Snowmobile Sports; 1197
Sound Canada; 1208
Sports Trade Canada; 1226
Toys & Games; 1274
Water & Pollution Control; 1325
Western Canada Outdoors; 1332
Western Fisheries; 1333
Western Miner; 1335
Wings; 1341

Guide to Special Issues of Periodicals

0001. AAPG BULLETIN.
1444 South Boulder, Tulsa, OK 74101.
Annual Subscription: $70. **Frequency:** Monthly.
Publisher: American Association of Petroleum Geologists.
Editorial Index: Annual. Subject/Title/Author. December.
Indexed or Abstracted Online: GeoRef.
Special Issues:
Membership Directory. Started 1917. Published as a separate issue. $6. November.

0002. AARTIMES.
P.O. Box 35886, Dallas, TX 75235.
Annual Subscription: $25. **Frequency:** Monthly.
Publisher: Daedalus Enterprises.
Advertiser Index: Every issue.
Special Issues:
Convention Issue: American Association of Respiratory Therapy. Started 1977. $3. September.
Government Health Care Regulations. Started 1982. $3. November.

0003. ABA BANKING JOURNAL.
P.O. Box 530, Bristol, CT 06010.
Annual Subscription: $15 (members)/20 (others).
Frequency: Monthly.
Publisher: Simmons-Boardman Publishing Co.
Advertiser Index: Every issue.
Editorial Index: Annual. Subject/Title/Author. February or March.
Indexed or Abstracted Online: NEXIS; Management Contents.
Special Issues:
Bankers' Washington Guide. $1.75. January.
Community Banking. $1.75. March.
Banking Buyers Guide—product listing for 1000+ suppliers. $1.75. May.
Banking Organization. $1.75. July.
ABA Convention Issue. $1.75. October.
IRA Update. $1.75. November.

0004. AIAA JOURNAL.
1633 Broadway, New York, NY 10019.
Annual Subscription: $185. **Frequency:** Monthly.
Publisher: American Institute of Astronautics and Aeronautics.
Editorial Index: Annual. Subject/Author. December.
Indexed or Abstracted Online: Recon (limited access—NASA contractors only).
Special Issues:
AIAA Membership Roster. Published as a separate issue. $50. Not included in the subscription price. Biennially. January.

0005. AICHE JOURNAL.
345 East 47th St., New York, NY 10017.
Annual Subscription: $85. **Frequency:** Monthly.
Publisher: American Institute of Astronautics and Aeronautics.
Editorial Index: Annual. Subject/Title/Author.

0006. AIPE JOURNAL.
3975 Erie Ave., Cincinnati, OH 45208.
Annual Subscription: $34. **Frequency:** 6/yr.
Publisher: American Institute of Plant Engineers.
Editorial Index: Annual. Subject.
Special Issues:
AIPE Conference Issue. Started 1981. $5.75. September.

0007. THE AOPA PILOT.
421 Aviation Way, Frederick, MD 21701.
Annual Subscription: $16. **Frequency:** Monthly.
Publisher: Aircraft Owners and Pilots Association.
Special Issues:
Annual Aircraft Directory—performance, specifications and cost data on 9 categories: single-engine fixed gear; single-engine retractable gear; multi-engine turboprop; turbo jet; STOL; agricultural; rotary wing; sailplanes. $2. March.
Annual Avionics Directory. $2. June.

0008. AORN JOURNAL.
10170 East Mississippi Ave., Denver, CO 80231.
Annual Subscription: $32. **Frequency:** Monthly.
Publisher: Association of Operating Room Nurses.
Advertiser Index: Every issue.
Editorial Index: Semi-Annual. Subject/Author. June/December.
Indexed Online: Medlars.
Special Issues:
AORN Convention Proceedings. 2/yr. February/April.

0009. APCO BULLETIN.
105 1/2 Canal St., P.O. Box 669, New Smyrna Beach, FL 32070.
Annual Subscription: $18. **Frequency:** 11/yr.
Publisher: Associated Public Safety Communications Officers, Inc.
Editorial Index: Annual. Subject. December.
Special Issues:
APCO Conference Issues (preconference, conference, postconference). $2. 3/yr. July/August/September.

0010. APWA REPORTER.
1313 East 60 St., Chicago, IL 60637.
Frequency: Monthly.
Publisher: American Public Works Association.
Editorial Index: Annual. Subject. January.
Special Issues:
Convention Issue. Started 1981. September.

0011. ASHRAE JOURNAL.
1791 Tullie Circle, NE, Atlanta, GA 30329.
Annual Subscription: $15.
Publisher: American Society of Heating and Refrigeration.
Advertiser Index: Every issue.
Editorial Index: Annual. Subject/Title/Author. December.

0012. ASTA TRAVEL NEWS.
488 Madison Ave., New York, NY 10022.
Annual Subscription: $10. **Frequency:** Monthly.
Publisher: American Society of Travel Agents.
Special Issues:
ASTA Convention Issue. $1. September/October.

0013. ASTM STANDARDIZATION NEWS.
1916 Race St., Philadelphia, PA 19103.
Annual Subscription: $12. **Frequency:** Monthly.
Publisher: American Society for Testing Materials.
Advertiser Index: Every issue.
Editorial Index: Annual. Subject/Title/Author. December.
Special Issues:
Analytical Chemistry. Started 1982. February.

0014. A/V CANADA BUSINESS COMMUNICATIONS.
777 Bay St., Toronto, Ontario, Can. M5W 1A7.
Annual Subscription: $24/13. **Frequency:** 9/yr.
Publisher: Maclean Hunter Ltd.
Advertiser Index: Every issue.

Special Issues:
Technology Forecast/COMMTEX Show. $4. January.
Source Book—directory of A/V companies in Canada, with international manufacturers. Started 1979. $12. May.

0015. ABRASIVE ENGINEERING SOCIETY MAGAZINE.
1700 Painters Run Rd., Pittsburgh, PA 15243.
Annual Subscription: $30. **Frequency:** 6/yr.
Publisher: Abrasive Engineering Society.
Advertiser Index: Every issue.
Special Issues:
Annual Conference, Abrasive Engineering Society. $6. March/April.

0016. ACCOUNTING REVIEW.
5717 Bessie Drive, Sarasota, FL 33583.
Annual Subscription: $25. **Frequency:** Quarterly.
Publisher: American Accounting Association.
Editorial Index: Annual. Author. October; Cumulative index 1926-78 available separately; $25 (members)/50 (nonmembers).
Indexed or Abstracted Online: Management Contents; ABI/Inform.
Special Issues:
American Accounting Association Committee's Survey of Doctoral Programs in Accounting in the U.S. January.

0017. AD DAY/U.S.A.
919 Third Ave., New York, NY 10022.
Annual Subscription: $75. **Frequency:** Weekly.
Publisher: Executive Communications, Inc.
Indexed or Abstracted Online: AMI.
Special Issues:
Handbook of Independent Advertising & Marketing Services—"hard-to-find" sources. Published as a separate issue. $50. Not included in the subscription price. Biennially (even years). January.
New Business Report—accounts being solicited by agencies. Published as a separate issue. $4.50. Not included in the subscription price. Monthly.

0018. AD EAST.
907 Park Square Bldg., Boston, MA 02116.
Annual Subscription: $20. **Frequency:** Monthly.
Publisher: Ad East Enterprises Inc.
Indexed or Abstracted Online: AMI.
Special Issues:
World of New England. $1.50. September.
Agency-Advertiser Special Issue. $1.50. November.

0019. THE ADCRAFTER.
2630 Book Tower, Detroit, MI 48226.
Annual Subscription: $20. **Frequency:** Weekly.
Publisher: Adcraft Club of Detroit, Inc.
Advertiser Index: May.
Special Issues:
Adcrafter Roster—directory of Adcraft club members and other trade organizations. $10. May.

0020. ADHESIVES AGE.
6285 Barfield Rd., Atlanta, GA 30328.
Annual Subscription: $21. **Frequency:** Monthly.
Publisher: Communication Channels, Inc.
Advertiser Index: Every issue.
Editorial Index: Annual. Subject/Title/Author. December.
Special Issues:
Adhesives Age Directory: U.S. and Canadian manufacturers, suppliers, arranged alphabetically, geographically, and by type; industry consultants, sales offices. $29.50. Not included in the subscription price. May.

0021. ADMINSTRATIVE DIGEST.
1450 Don Mills Rd., Don Mills, Ontario, Can. M3B 2X7.
Annual Subscription: $43/30. **Frequency:** 10/yr.
Publisher: Southam Communications Ltd.
Advertiser Index: Every issue.
Special Issues:
Telecommunications. January.
Records Management/Small Business Machinery. March/November.
Reprographics. April.
Computers. May.
Word Processing. June.
Business Directory. July/August.
Office Environment. September.

0022. ADVANCED MANAGEMENT JOURNAL.
Trudeau Rd., Saranac Lake, NY 12983.
Annual Subscription: $19. **Frequency:** Quarterly.
Publisher: Society for Advancement of Management.
Editorial Index: Annual. Title/Author. Fall.

0023. ADVANCED VEHICLE NEWS.
P.O. Box 5200, Westport, CT 06881.
Annual Subscription: $15. **Frequency:** Quarterly.
Publisher: Porter Corporation.
Advertiser Index: Every issue.
Special Issues:
Directory Issue—suppliers of electric vehicles and nonpetroleum vehicles. Started 1973. $5. February.

0024. ADVERTISING AGE.
740 North Rush St., Chicago, IL 60611.
Annual Subscription: $50. **Frequency:** Weekly.
Publisher: Crain Communications, Inc.
Advertiser Index: Every issue.
Indexed or Abstracted Online: AMI.
Special Issues:
Corporate Image Advertising. $1.25. January.
Direct Marketing. $1.25. January.
Job Hunting. $1.25. January.
Tobacco Marketing. $1.25. January.
Wine Marketing. $1.25. January.
Hispanic Marketing. $1.25. February.
Sports Marketing. $1.25. February.
Test Marketing. $1.25. February.
Toiletries & Beauty Aids Marketing. $1.25. February.
Beer Marketing. $1.25. March.
Chicago. $1.25. March.
Co-op Advertising. $1.25. March.
Extra Issue: U.S. Agency Income. $1.25. March.
TV Syndication. $1.25. March.
Home Computers. $1.25. April.
Marketing to Affluents. $1.25. April.
Travel & Tourism. $1.25. April.
Business Press. $1.25. May.
Grocery Marketing. $1.25. May.
Premiums & Promotions. $1.25. May.
Research Business Review. $1.25. May.
Suburban Media. $1.25. May.
Automotive Marketing. $1.25. June.
Business/Professional Advertising. $1.25. June.
Consumer Electronics. $1.25. June.
100 Top Media Companies. $1.25. June.
Fitness Marketing. $1.25. July.
International—Latin America, Canada. $1.25. July, October, December.
Radio. $1.25. July.
Retail Marketing. $1.25. July.
Liquor Marketing. $1.25. August.
Maturity Market. $1.25. August.
Outdoor Advertising. $1.25. August.
Sales Promotion. $1.25. August.
Youth Marketing. $1.25. August.
Dallas-Fort Worth. $1.25. September.
Extra Issue: 100 Leading Advertisers. $1.25. September.
Fashion Marketing. $1.25. September.
Healthcare Marketing. $1.25. September.
Newspapers. $1.25. September.
Grocery Marketing. $1.25. October.
Magazines. $1.25. October.
Market/Advertising Research. $1.25. October.
Marketing to Women. $1.25. October.
Cable TV. $1.25. November.
Fast Food Marketing. $1.25. November.
Florida. $1.25. November.

Media Outlook. $1.25.   November.
Entertainment Marketing. $1.25.   December.
100 Top Markets. $1.25.   December.

0025. ADVERTISING WORLD.
150 Fifth Ave., Ste. 610, New York, NY 10011.
Annual Subscription: $30.   **Frequency:** 6/yr.
Publisher: Directories International.
Advertiser Index: Every issue.
Editorial Index: Annual. Subject. February.
Indexed or Abstracted Online: Management Contents.
Special Issues:
   International Advertising Agency Billings Review.   Started 1978. $6.   June/July.

0026. ADWEEK (published in five regional editions: East, Southeast, Midwest, Southwest and West).
820 Second Ave., New York, NY 10017.
Annual Subscription: $45.   **Frequency:** Weekly.
Publisher: ASM Communications, Inc.
Indexed or Abstracted Online: AMI.
Special Issues:
   BADvertising Awards.   Started 1983. $1.50.   January.
   Art Directors Index.   Published as a separate issue. $3.   February.
   Creativity Report. $1.50.   February.
   Regional Market Reports. $1.50.   February/May/August/November.
   Agency Report.   Started 1984. $1.50.   March.
   Magazine Report.   Published as a separate issue. $3.   March.
   Best & Worst Clients. $1.50.   April.
   Newspaper Report.   Published as a separate issue. $3.   April.
   Women and Advertising.   Started 1983. $1.50.   May.
   Directories of Advertising.   Published as a separate issue. $3.   June.
   Salary Report. $1.50.   June.
   Markets & Marketing. $1.50.   July.
   Retailing Special Report.   Started 1983. $1.50.   August.
   Television Industry Special Report (Broadcast, Cable, Video, Satellite).   Started 1984.   Published as a separate issue. $3.   August.
   Fall Preview/Calendar of Events.   Started 1983. $1.50.   September.
   Advertising & the Entertainment Business (Movies, Sports, Music, the Arts).   Started 1984. $1.50.   October.
   Radio in American Life.   Published as a separate issue. $3.   November.
   Special Report on Design.   Started 1984. $1.50.   November.
   Frontiers of Knowledge—learning from universities.   Started 1984. $1.50.   December.

0027. AEROSOL AGE.
200 Commerce Rd., Cedar Grove, NJ 07009.
Annual Subscription: $14.   **Frequency:** Monthly.
Publisher: Industry Publications Inc.
Advertiser Index: Annually.
Special Issues:
   Cosmetic, Toiletry and Fragrance Association Annual Meeting Issue. $2.   February.
   Chemical Specialties Manufacturers Association Meeting Issues. $2.   2/yr.   May, December.
   Annual International Buyers Guide. $2.   October.

0028. AEROSPACE.
1725 De Sales St. NW, Washington, DC 20036.
Annual Subscription: Free.   **Frequency:** Quarterly.
Publisher: Aerospace Industries Association of America, Inc.
Special Issues:
   Review and Forecast.   Winter.

0029. AGENCY SALES MAGAZINE.
P.O. Box 3467, Laguna Hills, CA 92653.
Annual Subscription: $20.   **Frequency:** Monthly.
Publisher: Manufacturers' Agents National Association (MANA).
Editorial Index: Annual. Subject/Title. January.
Special Issues:
   MANA Membership Directory—lists manufacturers agents/agencies, lines carried, territory covered, year established, number of salesmen.

0030. AGING.
Superintendent of Documents, GPO, Washington, DC 20402.
Annual Subscription: $13.   **Frequency:** 6/yr.
Publisher: U.S. Department of Health And Human Services.
Indexed Online: Magazine Index.
Special Issues:
   Older Americans Month Issue. $4.75.   May/June.

0031. AGMARKETER.
P.O. Box 1467, Yakima, WA 98907.
Annual Subscription: $8.   **Frequency:** Monthly.
Publisher: Columbia Publishing.
Special Issues:
   Chemical & Fertilizer.   Started 1975. $1.   January.
   Potatoes.   Started 1975. $1.   February.
   Beans.   Started 1975. $1.   March.
   Irrigation.   Started 1975. $1.   April.
   Asparagus.   Started 1975. $1.   May.
   Pre-Harvest.   Started 1975. $1.   June.
   Packing & Shipping.   Started 1975. $1.   October.
   Irrigation.   Started 1975. $1.   November.

0032. AGRI FINANCE.
5520 West Touhy Ave., Ste. G, Skokie, IL 60077.
Annual Subscription: $22.95.   **Frequency:** 10 times/yr.
Publisher: Century Communications, Inc.
Editorial Index: Annual. Title. December.
Special Issues:
   List of Top 100 Ag Banks.   November.
   Farm Manager Listing (survey).   December.

0033. AGRI MARKETING.
5520-G Touhy Ave., Skokie, IL 60077.
Annual Subscription: $28.   **Frequency:** Monthly.
Publisher: Century Communications.
Advertiser Index: Every issue.
Editorial Index: Annual. Subject. December.
Special Issues:
   Focus Report: Agri-marketing in Canada. $3.   February.
   Focus Report: Marketing Research. $3.   March.
   NAMA Conference Issue. $3.   April.
   Focus Report: Farm Broadcasting. $3.   June.
   Farm Show Guide. $3.   July.
   Focus Report: Direct Marketing. $3.   September.
   Top 150 Farm Print Advertisers/Focus Report: Premiums & Incentives in AgBusiness. $3.   October.
   Ag's Biggest Advertising Agencies. $3.   November.
   Special Annual: Marketing Services Guide.   December.
   Year-End Outlook. $3.   December.

0034. AGRIBUSINESS WORLD-WIDE.
P.O. Box 5017, Westport, CT 06881.
Annual Subscription: $50.   **Frequency:** 6/yr.
Publisher: Intercontinental Publications.
Advertiser Index: Every issue.
Special Issues:
   Dairy Supplement. $10.   March/April.
   Asia Agribusiness Show. $10.   May/June.
   Consultants and Agritech. $10.   July/August.
   Annual Outlook. $10.   September/October.

0035. AGRICULTURAL ECONOMICS RESEARCH.
Superintendent of Documents, GPO, Washington, DC 20402.
Annual Subscription: $8.50.   **Frequency:** Quarterly.
Publisher: Economic Research Service.
Editorial Index: Cumulative. Author. Available separately from Economic Research Service.

0036. AGRICULTURAL ENGINEERING MAGAZINE.
2950 Niles Rd., St. Joseph, MI 49085.

Annual Subscription: $18. **Frequency:** Monthly.
Publisher: American Society of Agricultural Engineers.
Advertiser Index: Every issue.
Editorial Index: Annual. Subject. February.
Indexed Online: Agricola.
Special Issues:
   Up Front in Agricultural Machinery—agricultural equipment manufacturing industry. Started 1973. $2.50. 4/yr. July, October, January, April.

0037. AGRI-EQUIPMENT TODAY.
P.O. Box 1467, Yakima, WA 98907.
Annual Subscription: $6. **Frequency:** Monthly.
Publisher: Columbia Publishing.
Advertiser Index: Every issue.
Special Issues:
   Farm Show Issue. Started 1977. $1. January.
   Buyer's Guide. Started 1977. $1. July.

0038. AIR CONDITIONING, HEATING, & REFRIGERATION NEWS.
P.O. Box 2600, Troy, MI 48007.
Annual Subscription: $41. **Frequency:** Weekly.
Publisher: Business News Publishing Co.
Advertiser Index: Every issue.
Editorial Index: Annual. Subject. January.
Special Issues:
   Directory—lists 1,600 manufacturers of a/c, heating, and commercial refrigeration, including some solar. No domestic refrigeration, no plumbing. Plus product listing and the ARW wholesalers nationwide. Trade names. Started 1932. Published as a separate issue. $15. January.
   Statistical Panorama. Started 1966. Published as a separate issue. $15. April.
   Schedule of Special Impact Reports. Published as a separate issue. October.

0039. AIR FORCE MAGAZINE.
1750 Pennsylvania Ave., NW, Washington, DC 20006.
Annual Subscription: $15. **Frequency:** Monthly.
Publisher: Air Force Association.
Advertiser Index: Every issue.
Special Issues:
   Almanac Issue—command-by-command survey of U.S. Air Force. May.
   Electronics Issue. July.
   Anniversary Issue. September.
   AFA Convention Issues. October/November.
   Military Balance—country-by-country survey of world's military might. December.

0040. AIR FORCE TIMES.
475 School St. SW, Washington, DC 20024.
Annual Subscription: $32.50. **Frequency:** Weekly.
Publisher: Army Times Publ. Co.
Special Issues:
   Retirement—all aspects of retirement from military service. 3/yr. February/July/November.
   Education—educational opportunities for military personnel and their dependents. 2/yr. April/November.
   Travel. 2/yr. May/September.
   Auto. October.

0041. AIR LINE PILOT.
1625 Massachusetts Ave., NW, Washington, DC 20036.
Annual Subscription: $15. **Frequency:** Monthly.
Publisher: Air Line Pilots Association International.
Editorial Index: Annual. Subject/Title/Author. December.

0042. AIR TRANSPORT WORLD.
Penton Plaza, 1111 Chester Ave., Cleveland, OH 44114.
Annual Subscription: $30. **Frequency:** Monthly.
Publisher: Penton/IPC.
Advertiser Index: Every issue.
Special Issues:
   Industry Forecast. $2.50. January.
   Air Cargo Statistics. $2.50. February.
   Airframe & Engine. $2.50. March.
   Annual Market Development Issue—yearend update. Started 1964. $2.50. May.
   Maintenance & Engineering. $2.50. July.
   International Air Transport Association—member airline report. $2.50. October or November.
   New product preview. $2.50. December.

0043. AIRLINE EXECUTIVE.
6255 Barfield Rd., Atlanta, GA 30328.
Annual Subscription: $23. **Frequency:** Monthly.
Publisher: Communications Channels, Inc.
Special Issues:
   Airline Product Buying Survey. $2.50. January.
   Airline Industry Yearbook. $2.50. May.
   International Air Transport Association Meeting. $2.50. October.

0044. AIRPORT SERVICES MANAGEMENT MAGAZINE.
731 Hennepin Ave., Minneapolis, MN 55403.
Annual Subscription: $24. **Frequency:** Monthly.
Publisher: Lakewood Publications.
Advertiser Index: Every issue.
Editorial Index: Semi-Annual. Subject/Author. June.
Special Issues:
   Planning Aids Showcase for FBO resale items (FBO—Fixed-base operations, ie., airport businesses offering flight training, aircraft sales, etc.). Started 1970. March.
   Annual Blue Book Directory of FBO Suppliers (aircraft/aviation parts, accessories, equipment). Started 1961. April.
   Planning Aids Showcase for Airport Equipment. Started 1970. May.
   Annual Red Book Directory of Airport Suppliers (airport/airline ground support equipment, services). Started 1961. October.

0045. ALASKA BUSINESS & INDUSTRY.
1519 Ship Ave., Anchorage, AK 99501.
Annual Subscription: $25. **Frequency:** Monthly.
Publisher: Alaska Business Magazine, Inc.
Special Issues:
   Construction. Started 1969. $2.50. April.
   Native Corporations. $2.50. September.
   Computer Edition. Started 1982. $2.50. October.

0046. ALASKA CONSTRUCTION & OIL.
109 West Mercer, Seattle, WA 98119.
Annual Subscription: $18. **Frequency:** Monthly.
Publisher: Vernon Publications.
Advertiser Index: Every issue.
Editorial Index: Annual. Subject/Title. December.
Special Issues:
   Forecast & Review. $2. January.
   Transportation. $10. February.
   Research & Technology. $2. March.
   Top Contractors / Top Projects. $2. April.
   Timber Report. $2. May.
   Private Construction. $2. June.
   Equipment Directory. $10. July.
   Construction Around State. $2. August.
   Mining. $2. October.
   Highway & Heavy Construction. $2. November.
   Electrical Power Generation. $2. December.

0047. AMERICA.
106 West 56 St., New York, NY 10019.
Annual Subscription: $21. **Frequency:** Weekly.
Publisher: America Press.
Editorial Index: Semi-Annual. Subject/Title/Author. January/July.
Indexed or Abstracted Online: Magazine Index.
Special Issues:
   Vocations. Started 1981. $.75. February.
   Lenten Reading. Started 1970. $.75. March.
   Theological Education. Started 1975. $.75. March.
   Spring Book Roundup. Started 1970. $.75. May.
   Fall Book Review. Started 1970. $.75. September.

Religious Education.   Started 1976. $.75.   September or October.
Fall Term.   Started 1970. $.75.   October.
Christmas Books. $.75.   November.
Books on the Bible.   Started 1960. $.75.   December.

0048. AMERICAN ARTIST.
1515 Broadway, New York, NY 10036.
Annual Subscription: $18.   **Frequency:** Monthly.
Publisher: Billboard Publications Inc.
Advertiser Index: Every issue.
Editorial Index: Annual. Subject/Title/Author. December.
Special Issues:
Art School Directory.   Started 1964. $2.   March.
New Art Books. $2.   April.
Annual Trade Supplement. $2.   May.
Annual Business Issue for Artists. $2.   June.
Annual Art Instruction Supplement.   Started 1978. $2.   September.
Annual Gift Issue. $2.   December.

0049. AMERICAN AUTOMATIC MERCHANDISER.
7500 Old Oak Blvd., Middleburg Heights, OH 41307.
Annual Subscription: $15.   **Frequency:** Monthly.
Publisher: Harcourt Brace Javanovich.
Advertiser Index: Every issue.
Editorial Index: Annual. Subject/Title. July.
Special Issues:
New Products Review.   Started 1975. $2.   January.
Hot Beverages.   Started 1959. $2.   February.
Industry Census Edition.   Started 1979. $2.   April.
Blue Book Directory.   Started 1969. $15.   July.
Office Coffee Service Edition.   Started 1970. $2.   August.
Candy/Snacks/Confections.   Started 1959. $2.   September.
NAMA Showbook (industry convention).   Started 1958. $2.   October.
Convention Report.   Started 1959. $2.   November.
Tobacco Products.   Started 1959. $2.   December.

0050. AMERICAN BABY.
575 Lexington Ave., New York, NY 10022.
Annual Subscription: $9.97.   **Frequency:** Monthly.
Publisher: American Baby Inc.
Indexed or Abstracted Online: Magazine Index.
Special Issues:
Nutrition—for mothers and infants.   February.
Nursery Furniture.   March/October.
Maternity.   April.
Toddler Fashions.   3/yr.   May/August/November.
Fathers.   June.
Early Learning.   August.
Toys & Sleepwear.   December.

0051. AMERICAN BANKER.
One State St. Plaza, New York, NY 10004.
Annual Subscription: $225.   **Frequency:** Daily.
Publisher: Same.
Editorial Index: Monthly. Subject.
Indexed or Abstracted Online: Information Bank; NEXIS.
Special Issues:
Austria/Switzerland.   Started Pre-1970. $2.50.   January.
Holiday Clubs. $2.50.   January.
100 Largest Savings Banks.   Started Pre-1970. $2.50.   January.
Professional Education Review. $2.50.   January.
Trust Management Annual. $2.50.   January.
Asset/Liability Review. $2.50.   February.
Bank Security Annual. $2.50.   February.
International Banking Annual. $2.50.   February.
Telecommunications Review. $2.50.   February.
Top 300 Savings and Loans.   Started Pre-1970. $2.50.   February/August.
European Financial Marketing Review.   Started Pre-1970. $2.50.   March.
Savings Banks Operations Annual. $2.50.   March.
Top Bank Holding Companies.   Started Pre-1970. $2.50.   March.
Top Earners.   Started Pre-1970. $2.50.   March.
Top 300 Commercial Banks.   Started Pre-1970. $2.50.   March/August.
Trust Operations Review. $2.50.   March.
American Banker 5000.   Started Pre-1970. $2.50.   April.
Brazil.   Started Pre-1970. $2.50.   April.
Electronic Funds Transfer Review. $2.50.   April.
Installment Credit Annual. $2.50.   April.
Benelux.   Started Pre-1970. $2.50.   May.
Executive Compensation. $2.50.   May.
Marketing to the Affluent.   Started 1981. $2.50.   May.
Mortgage Banking Review. $2.50.   May/October.
Real Estate Finance Annual. $2.50.   May.
Savings Banks Review.   Started 1981. $2.50.   May.
Technology Annual. $2.50.   May.
Top 100 Trust Banks.   Started Pre-1970. $2.50.   May.
Venezuela.   Started Pre-1970. $2.50.   May.
Bank Performance Annual. $2.50.   June.
Edge Act Banking Annual. $2.50.   June.
Finance Company Review. $2.50.   June.
France.   Started Pre-1970. $2.50.   June.
Germany.   Started Pre-1970. $2.50.   June.
Japan.   Started Pre-1970. $2.50.   June/December.
Pacific Rim.   Started Pre-1970. $2.50.   June.
Top Commercial Bank Lenders.   Started Pre-1970. $2.50.   June.
United Kingdom.   Started Pre-1970. $2.50.   June.
Italy.   Started Pre-1970. $2.50.   July.
Singapore & Hong Kong.   Started Pre-1970. $2.50.   July.
World's Top 500 Banks by Assets.   Started Pre-1970. $2.50.   July.
World's Top 500 Banks by Deposits.   Started Pre-1970. $2.50.   July.
Argentina.   Started Pre-1970. $2.50.   August.
World Savings Banks Review. $2.50.   August.
Canada.   Started Pre-1970. $2.50.   September.
IMF/World Bank Annual. $2.50.   September.
International Data Networks. $2.50.   September.
Personnel & Management. $2.50.   September.
Scandinavia.   Started Pre-1970. $2.50.   September.
Transaction Card Annual. $2.50.   September.
ABA Annual Convention. $2.50.   October.
Bank Marketing. $2.50.   October.
Cash Management Annual. $2.50.   October.
Commercial Lending. $2.50.   October.
Mortgage Banking Secondary Market. $2.50.   October.
Agribusiness Review. $2.50.   November.
Australia.   Started Pre-1970. $2.50.   November.
Commercial Finance. $2.50.   November.
Correspondent Banking Annual. $2.50.   November.
Insurance. $2.50.   November.
Oil-Producing Nations. $2.50.   November.
Real Estate Management. $2.50.   November.
Top Savings and Loans Holding Companies.   Started Pre-1970. $2.50.   November.
Turkey.   Started Pre-1970. $2.50.   November.
Annual Statistical Guide.   Started Pre-1970. $2.50.   December.
Chile.   Started Pre-1970. $2.50.   December.
Credit Union Annual. $2.50.   December.
EEC.   Started Pre-1970. $2.50.   December.
Eastern Bloc.   Started Pre-1970. $2.50.   December.
Non-Bank/Bank Linkages. $2.50.   December.
Operations & Automation Preview. $2.50.   December.
Self-Service Banking. $2.50.   December.
Year-End Forecast Guide.   Started Pre-1970. $2.50.   December.

0052. AMERICAN BAR ASSOCIATION JOURNAL.
1155 East 60th St., Chicago, IL 60637.
Annual Subscription: $20.   **Frequency:** Monthly.
Publisher: American Bar Association.
Advertiser Index: Every issue.

Editorial Index: Annual. Subject/Author. December.
Indexed Online: LEXIS.
Special Issues:
Lawyers' Directolog. Started 1982. Published as a separate issue. Not included in the subscription price. April.
American Bar Association Annual Report. Started 1978. December.

0053. AMERICAN BEE JOURNAL.
51 South 2nd St., Hamilton, IL 62341.
Annual Subscription: $10.50. **Frequency:** Monthly.
Publisher: Dadant & Sons, Inc.
Advertiser Index: Every issue.
Editorial Index: Annual. Subject/Title/Author. December.

0054. AMERICAN CERAMIC SOCIETY BULLETIN.
65 Ceramic Dr., Columbus, OH 43214.
Annual Subscription: $12.50. **Frequency:** Monthly.
Publisher: American Ceramic Society, Inc.
Advertiser Index: Every issue.
Editorial Index: Annual. Subject/Author. December.
Special Issues:
Company Directory—1500 ceramic organizations; product guide. $5. January.
Annual meeting official program. $3. March.
Refractories Issue. $3. July.
Membership Roster—including National Institute of Ceramic Engineers. $3. October.
Index Issue—complete subject/author index. $5. December.

0055. AMERICAN CINEMATOGRAPHER.
P.O. Box 2230, Hollywood, CA 90028.
Annual Subscription: $20. **Frequency:** Monthly.
Publisher: A.S.C. Holding Co.
Editorial Index: Annual. Title/Author. December.

0056. AMERICAN CITY & COUNTY.
6255 Barfield Rd., Atlanta, GA 30328.
Annual Subscription: $36. **Frequency:** Monthly.
Publisher: Communications Channels, Inc.
Advertiser Index: In Municipal Index.
Indexed Online: Trade & Industry Index.
Special Issues:
Industry Outlook. $3.50. January.
APWA (American Public Works Association) Public Works Leader Awards. $3.50. May.
Municipal Index—buyers guide to vendors of materials, equipment and services for municipal use. Includes listing of municipal officials in major U.S. cities. Published as a separate issue. $20. May.
American Water Works Association Conference/National Solid Wastes Management Association Exposition. $3.50. June.
Salary Survey—Top Public Administrators. $3.50. July.
American Public Works Association Convention/American Public Transit Association Convention/Water Pollution Control Federation Conference. $3.50. September.
National Recreation and Park Association Congress. $3.50. October.
Survey of City and County Administrators. $3.50. November.

0057. AMERICAN COIN-OP.
500 North Dearborn, Chicago, IL 60610.
Annual Subscription: $20. **Frequency:** Monthly.
Publisher: American Trade Magazines.
Advertiser Index: Every issue.
Special Issues:
Industry Outlook. $4. January.
Buyers Guide. $4. March.
Coin Laundry Association Convention. $4. Biennially. June (odd years).

0058. AMERICAN DEMOGRAPHICS.
P.O. Box 68, Ithaca, NY 14850.
Annual Subscription: $42. **Frequency:** Monthly.
Publisher: American Demographics, Inc.
Editorial Index: Annual. Subject/Author. December.
Indexed Online: AMI.
Special Issues:
Close-Up—demographic profile of different state each month. Started 1982. $5. Monthly.
Special Research Section—useful statistics from the U.S. Census Bureau. Started 1981. $5. December.

0059. AMERICAN DRUGGIST.
555 West 57th St., New York, NY 10019.
Annual Subscription: $24. **Frequency:** Monthly.
Publisher: Hearst Corp.
Advertiser Index: Every issue.
Indexed or Abstracted Online: Trade & Industry Index.
Special Issues:
Prescription Survey. $2. May.
Home Health Care Study. $2. Biennially. June (even years).
American Druggist Blue Book—price and product reference guide. Published as a separate issue. $16. Not included in the subscription price. July.
Open Call Study — OTC products. $2. September.
Generic Products. $2. October.

0060. AMERICAN DYESTUFF REPORTER.
50 West 23 St., New York, NY 10010.
Annual Subscription: $17. **Frequency:** Monthly.
Publisher: SAF International.
Advertiser Index: Every issue.
Editorial Index: Annual. Subject/Title/Author. January or February.
Special Issues:
Flame Retardants. January.
Carpets Technology. June.
American Textile Machinery Association Convention. August, every four years.
International Textile Machinery Association Convention. August, every four years.
Conference Preview: National Technical Conference of the American Association of Textile Chemists. September or October.
Wet Processing "How to" Reports. Started 1969. September.
Process Control Buyers Guide. November.
New Product Review. December.

0061. AMERICAN ECONOMIC REVIEW.
1313 21st Ave. South, Ste. 809, Nashville, TN 37212.
Annual Subscription: $100. **Frequency:** 5/yr.
Publisher: American Economic Association.
Editorial Index: Annual. Title/Author. December.
Indexed or Abstracted Online: Predicasts; Trade & Industry Index; Magazine Index; Management Contents; ABI/Inform.
Special Issues:
American Economic Association Conference Papers and Proceedings. May.

0062. AMERICAN FIREARMS INDUSTRY.
2801 E. Oakland Park Blvd., Ft. Lauderdale, FL 33306.
Annual Subscription: $20. **Frequency:** Monthly.
Publisher: American Association of Federally Licensed Firearms Dealers.
Advertiser Index: Every issue.
Special Issues:
Shooting Hunting Outdoor Trade (SHOT) Show Issue. Started 1975. Published as a separate issue. December.

0063. AMERICAN FRUIT GROWER/WESTERN FRUIT GROWER.
37841 Euclid Ave., Willoughby, OH 44094.
Annual Subscription: $10. **Frequency:** Monthly.
Publisher: Meister Publishing Co.
Special Issues:
Winter Conventions & Shows/Peaches. $2. January.
Pest Control & Frost Control. $2. February.
Herbicide Roundup & Fertilization. $2. March.

Irrigation. $2.   April.
Vineyards & Small Fruits. $2.   May.
Direct Marketing. $2.   June.
Buyers Guide & Directory. $2.   July.
Nuts. $2.   August.
Apple Merchandising. $2.   September.
Orchard & Vineyard Machinery. $2.   October.
Pruning/Washington & Michigan Horticultural Shows. $2.   November.
Fruit Outlook/Money Management. $2.   December.

0064. THE AMERICAN GENEALOGIST.
1232 39th St., Des Moines, IA 50311.
Annual Subscription: $12.   **Frequency:** Quarterly.
Publisher: George E. McCracken.
Editorial Index: Annual. Subject. October.

0065. AMERICAN GLASS REVIEW.
P.O. Box 2147, Clifton, NJ 07015.
Annual Subscription: $20.   **Frequency:** Monthly.
Publisher: Ebel-Doctorow Publications.
Advertiser Index: Every issue.
Special Issues:
Glass Factory Directory—U.S. manufacturers and suppliers. Published as a separate issue.   February.

0066. AMERICAN HAIRDRESSER/SALON OWNER.
100 Park Ave., Ste. 1000, New York, NY 10017.
Annual Subscription: $20.   **Frequency:** Monthly.
Publisher: Service Publications Inc.
Advertiser Index: Every issue.
Special Issues:
Beauty and Barber Supply Institute Convention Issues. Published as a separate issue. $2.   August.
Green Book: Confidential Buying Guide—lists manufacturers, products, key personnel, trade marks, brand names, beauty salon chains.   Published as a separate issue. $40.   Not included in the subscription price.   December.

0067. AMERICAN HOCKEY & ARENA.
2997 Broadmoor Valley Rd., Colorado Springs, CO 80906.
Annual Subscription: $12.   **Frequency:** 7/yr.
Publisher: Amateur Hockey Association of the United States.
Advertiser Index: Every issue.
Special Issues:
Annual Summer Camp Guide.   February.
USA Hockey Team Yearbook—special edition for the 1984 Olympic year.   One time special issue.   August (1983).
Buyer's Guide.   Summer.

0068. AMERICAN HUNTER.
1600 Rhode Island Ave. NW, Washington, DC 20036.
Annual Subscription: $15.   **Frequency:** Monthly.
Publisher: National Rifle Association.
Special Issues:
Hunter's Directory—U.S. and Canada hunting areas, fees, etc., state-by-state and province-by-province; also lists outfitters, guides, taxidermists.   Published as a separate issue. $5.50.   Not included in the subscription price.   September.

0069. AMERICAN IMPORT/EXPORT MANAGEMENT.
401 N. Broad St., Philadelphia, PA 19108.
Annual Subscription: $25.   **Frequency:** Monthly.
Publisher: North American Publishing Co.
Advertiser Index: Every issue.
Special Issues:
Annual Showcase of Services.   Started 1978. $3.   January.
Directory of Customs and Marine Attorneys. $3.   January.
Marking of Imports. $3.   February.
U.S. Foreign Trade Zones. $3.   March.
Directory of Marine Insurance Companies. $3.   April.
Catalog of Customs Forms. $3.   May.
Directory of Container Manufacturers and Lessors.   Started 1966. $3.   June.
Directory of Steamship Lines and Airlines. $3.   July.
Directory of Custom House Brokers. $3.   August.
Air Cargo Agents and Air Freight Forwarders. $3.   September.
Major U.S. Banks Doing Business Overseas. $3.   October.
Foreign Freight Forwarders. $3.   November.
Ports of the Far East. $3.   December.

0070. AMERICAN INDUSTRIAL HYGIENE ASSOCIATION JOURNAL.
475 Wolf Ledges Pkwy., Akron, OH 44311.
Annual Subscription: $60.   **Frequency:** Monthly.
Publisher: American Industrial Hygiene Association.
Editorial Index: Annual. Subject/Author. December.

0071. AMERICAN INDUSTRIAL PROPERTIES REPORT.
P.O. Box 2060, Red Bank, NJ 07701.
Annual Subscription: $20.   **Frequency:** 10/yr.
Publisher: Indprop Publishing Co.
Advertiser Index: Every issue.
Special Issues:
Economic Forecast.   Started 1980. $5.   January.
Worldwide Guide for Foreign Investment.   Started 1970. $5.   February.
Site Seekers Guide.   Started 1968.   Published as a separate issue. $10.   March/April.
Finance Directory.   Started 1982. $5.   July/August.
Office/Industrial Park Guide.   Started 1975. $5.   September.
Site Seekers Guide for Reverse Investment.   Started 1968. Published as a separate issue. $10.   November.

0072. AMERICAN INK MAKER.
101 West 31st St., New York, NY 10001.
Annual Subscription: $16.   **Frequency:** Monthly.
Publisher: MacNair Dorland Co.
Advertiser Index: Every issue.
Editorial Index: Annual. Title. January.
Special Issues:
National Association of Printing Ink Manufacturers Convention.   Started 1923. $3.   February.
Organic and Inorganic Pigments.   Started 1982. $3.   June.
Buyer's Guide.   Started 1962. $3.   October.

0073. AMERICAN JEWELRY MANUFACTURER.
Chilton Way, Radnor, PA 19089.
Annual Subscription: $14.   **Frequency:** Monthly.
Publisher: Chilton Co.
Advertiser Index: Every issue.
Editorial Index: Annual. Subject. January.
Special Issues:
Expo/New York Issue.   Started 1968.   February.
Expo/Providence Issue.   Started 1973.   Biennial.   March.
Expo/West Issue.   Started 1976.   March or April.
Electroplating Issue.   Started 1976.   May.
Casting Issue.   Started 1973.   August.

0074. AMERICAN JOURNAL OF NURSING.
555 West 57 St., New York, NY 10019.
Annual Subscription: $24.   **Frequency:** Monthly.
Publisher: American Journal of Nursing Co.
Advertiser Index: Every issue.
Editorial Index: Annual. Subject/Author. February.
Indexed Online: Medlars; Medline.
Special Issues:
Books of the Year.   Started 1969.   January.
Official Directory—nursing organizations.   Started 1905.   April.

0075. THE AMERICAN JOURNAL OF OCCUPATIONAL THERAPY.
1383 Piccard Dr., Rockville, MD 20850.
Annual Subscription: $45.   **Frequency:** Monthly.
Publisher: The American Occupational Therapy Association, Inc.
Editorial Index: Annual. Subject/Author. December.
Indexed or Abstracted Online: Medline.

Special Issues:
Buyers Guide. February.

0076. AMERICAN JOURNAL OF OPTOMETRY AND PHYSIOLOGICAL OPTICS.
428 East Preston St., P.O. Box 1496, Baltimore, MD 21203.
Annual Subscription: $45. **Frequency:** Monthly.
Publisher: American Academy of Optometry.
Editorial Index: Annual. Subject/Author. December.
Indexed Online: ISI, Index Medicus.

0077. AMERICAN JOURNAL OF PHYSICS.
Graduate Physics Bldg., SUNY, Stony Brook, NY 11794.
Annual Subscription: $82. **Frequency:** Monthly.
Publisher: American Institute of Physics.
Advertiser Index: Every issue.
Editorial Index: Annual. Subject/Title/Author. December.
Special Issues:
Directory of Physics and Astronomy Staff Members—colleges, universities, federally funded R&D centers, government laboratories and not-for-profit laboratories in U.S., Canada, Mexico and Central America. Published as a separate issue. $60. Not included in the subscription price. Fall.
Graduate Programs in Physics, Astronomy and Related Fields (U.S. and Canada). Published as a separate issue. $15. Not included in the subscription price. Fall.
10-year Cumulative Index. Started 1933. Published as a separate issue. Every 10 yrs. 1972 (last).

0078. AMERICAN JOURNAL OF PHYSIOLOGY.
9650 Rockville Pike, Bethesda, MD 20814.
Annual Subscription: $315. **Frequency:** Monthly.
Publisher: American Physiology Society.
Editorial Index: Semi-Annual. Subject/Author. June/December.

0079. AMERICAN LABORATORY.
808 Kings Highway, Fairfield, CT 06430.
Annual Subscription: $54. **Frequency:** Monthly.
Publisher: International Scientific Communications, Inc.
Advertiser Index: Every issue.
Editorial Index: Annual. Subject/Author. December.
Special Issues:
Laboratory Buyers Guide. Started 1977. Published as a separate issue. $4.50. January.
Thermal Analysis. $4.50. January.
Laboratory Automation. $4.50. February/September.
Spectroscopy. $4.50. March/November.
Microscopy. $4.50. April.
Chromatography. $4.50. May/August.
Chemical Analysis. $4.50. June.
Environmental Analysis. $4.50. July/December.
Separation Techniques. $4.50. October.

0080. AMERICAN LIBRARIES.
50 East Huron St., Chicago, IL 60611.
Annual Subscription: $30. **Frequency:** 11/yr.
Publisher: American Library Association.
Advertiser Index: Irregular.
Editorial Index: Annual. Subject/Author. December (none in 1982).
Indexed or Abstracted Online: Magazine Index.
Special Issues:
Professional Literature for Librarians. Started 1983. $3. April or May.
Reference Books. Started 1984. $3. April.
ALA Conference Issue. $3. June.
Midwinter Conference (Show) Issue. $3. December or January.

0081. AMERICAN MACHINIST.
1221 Ave. of the Americas, New York, NY 10020.
Annual Subscription: $35. **Frequency:** Monthly.
Publisher: McGraw-Hill Publishing.
Advertiser Index: Every issue.
Editorial Index: Annual. Subject/Author. April.
Indexed or Abstracted Online: Compendex; CA Search; Metadex.
Special Issues:
Economic & Technical Outlook for Metalworking. $4. January.
Machine-Tool Standings of the Leading Nations. $4. February.
Robotics. $4. April.
Computer-Integrated Manufacturing. $4. July.
International Machine Tool Show/Buyers Guide. $4. September.
Inventory of Metalworking Equipment. $4. November.
AM Manufacturing Achievement Award. $4. December.

0082. AMERICAN METAL MARKET.
73 East 21 St., New York, NY 10003.
Annual Subscription: $285. **Frequency:** Daily.
Publisher: Fairchild Publications.
Indexed or Abstracted Online: Trade & Industry Index.
Special Issues:
Contract Shops. $1.50. January.
Electrical Discharge Machines. $1.50. January.
Ferrous Scrap. $1.50. January.
Silver. $1.50. January.
Strategic Metals. $1.50. January.
Copper Club. $1.50. February.
Nickel. $1.50. February.
Steel Service Center Institute. $1.50. February.
Tungsten. $1.50. February.
Aerospace Metals & Machines/Westec Show (Society of Manufacturing Engineers). $1.50. March.
Batteries. $1.50. March.
Computers in Manufacturing. $1.50. March.
Copper & Brass Service Centers. $1.50. March.
Nonferrous Scrap. $1.50. March.
Stainless Steels. $1.50. March.
Exchange Trading. $1.50. April.
Lead & Zinc. $1.50. April.
Machine Tool Distributors. $1.50. April.
Metal Purchasing. $1.50. April.
Pipe & Tube. $1.50. April.
Vacuum Metallurgy. $1.50. April.
Ferroalloys. $1.50. May.
Foundry. $1.50. May.
Modern Manufacturing/Society of Manufacturing Engineers Show. $1.50. May.
Steel Capital Equipment & Financing. $1.50. May.
Steel Service Center. $1.50. May.
European Machine Tools. $1.50. June.
Japanese Machine Tools. $1.50. June.
Powder Metallurgy. $1.50. June.
Precious Metals. $1.50. June.
Robotics. $1.50. June.
Titanium. $1.50. June.
Metal Trading. $1.50. July.
Molybdenum. $1.50. July.
Tin. $1.50. July.
U.S. Machine Tools. $1.50. July.
Aluminum Recycling. $1.50. August.
Cobalt. $1.50. August.
International Machine Tool Show. $1.50. August.
Specialty Steels. $1.50. August.
Copper. $1.50. September.
Die Casting. $1.50. September.
Platinum. $1.50. September.
Tantalum & Columbium. $1.50. September.
International Steel. $1.50. October.
Japanese Machine Tool Fair. $1.50. October.
London Metal Exchange. $1.50. October.
Steelmaking Today. $1.50. October.
Aluminum. $1.50. November.
Gold. $1.50. November.
Nickel Stainless. $1.50. November.
Superalloys. $1.50. November.
Chromium. $1.50. December.
Galvanizing. $1.50. December.
Manganese. $1.50. December.

Market Mills. $1.50. December.

0083. AMERICAN NURSERYMAN.
310 South Michigan Ave., Chicago, IL 60604.
Annual Subscription: $17. **Frequency:** 24/yr.
Publisher: American Nurseryman Publishing Co.
Advertiser Index: Every issue.
Editorial Index: Annual. Title/Author. December 15.
Special Issues:
Container Production/Interior Landscaping. $2. January.
Christmas Preview. $2. February.
Exterior Landscaping. $2. March.
Flower & Garden. $2. May.
Foreign Technology. $2. August.
Association of American Nurserymen (AAN) Convention Report. $2. September.
Nursery Management. $2. October.
Energy Conservation. $2. November.
Winter Trade Show. $2. December.

0084. AMERICAN OPINION.
395 Concord Ave., Belmont, CA 02178.
Annual Subscription: $20. **Frequency:** 11/yr.
Publisher: American Opinion.
Special Issues:
Scoreboard Almanac—articles reviewing political conditions in U.S. and world. Started 1958. $3. July/August.

0085. AMERICAN PAINT & COATINGS JOURNAL.
2911 Washington Ave., St. Louis, MO 63103.
Annual Subscription: $25. **Frequency:** Weekly.
Publisher: American Paint Journal Co.
Advertiser Index: Every issue.
Editorial Index: Annual. Subject. March.
Indexed Online: Trade & Industry Index.
Special Issues:
Convention Daily—National Paint and Coatings Association/Federation of Societies for Coatings Technology. Started 1916. Published as a separate issue. Convention days (5). November.

0086. AMERICAN PAINTING CONTRACTOR.
2911 Washington Ave., St. Louis, MO 63103.
Annual Subscription: $24. **Frequency:** Monthly.
Publisher: American Paint Journal Co.
Advertiser Index: Every issue.
Editorial Index: Annual. Subject/Title. February.
Special Issues:
Industrial Maintenance Painting. March, June, September, December.

0087. AMERICAN PRINTER.
300 West Adams St., Chicago, IL 60606.
Annual Subscription: $25. **Frequency:** Monthly.
Publisher: Maclean Hunter Publishing Corp.
Editorial Index: Annual. Subject/Author. December.
Indexed Online: Trade & Industry Index.
Special Issues:
Annual Gravure Update. March.
Gutenberg Festival Show Issue. May.
Newspaper Industry Report. June.
Mid-Year Industry Report. July.
Forecast. December.

0088. AMERICAN QUARTERLY.
303 College Hall, University of Pennsylvania, Philadelphia, PA 19104.
Annual Subscription: $25. **Frequency:** 5/yr.
Publisher: American Studies Association.
Editorial Index: Annual. Author. Winter.
Special Issues:
Bibliography Issue—includes articles; American studies research-in-progress list; directory of officers and committee members of the American Studies Association. $5. December.
Survey of American Studies Programs in the U.S. (included in Bibliography issue). $5. Biennially (even years). December.

0089. AMERICAN RIFLEMAN.
1600 Rhode Island Ave., NW, Washington, DC 20036.
Annual Subscription: $15. **Frequency:** Monthly.
Publisher: National Rifle Association.
Editorial Index: Annual. Subject/Author. December.
Indexed Online: Magazine Index.

0090. THE AMERICAN ROSE MAGAZINE.
P.O. Box 30,000, Shreveport, LA 71130.
Annual Subscription: $18.00 (full membership); $12.50 (magazine). **Frequency:** Monthly.
Publisher: American Rose Society.
Advertiser Index: Every issue.
Editorial Index: Biennial. Subject/Title/Author. December, even years.

0091. AMERICAN SCHOOL BOARD JOURNAL.
1055 Thomas Jefferson St., NW, Washington, DC 20007.
Annual Subscription: $32. **Frequency:** Monthly.
Publisher: National School Board Association.
Advertiser Index: Every issue.
Editorial Index: Annual. Subject/Author. Published separately in March (free).
Special Issues:
National School Boards Association Convention Preview. $4. April.

0092. AMERICAN SCHOOL & UNIVERSITY.
401 North Broad Street, Philadelphia, PA 19108.
Annual Subscription: $25. **Frequency:** Monthly.
Publisher: North American Publishing Co.
Advertiser Index: Every issue.
Indexed Online: Magazine Index.
Special Issues:
Maintenance & Operations Cost Report. $3. March.
Educational Construction Cost Report. $3. April.
Annual Buyers Guide for Educators. $3. May.

0093. AMERICAN SCIENTIST.
345 Whitney Ave., New Haven, CT 06511.
Annual Subscription: $24. **Frequency:** 6/yr.
Publisher: Sigma Xi, The Scientific Research Society.
Editorial Index: Annual. Author. November/December.

0094. AMERICAN SHOEMAKING.
P.O. Box 198, Cambridge, MA 02140.
Annual Subscription: $18. **Frequency:** Weekly.
Publisher: Shoe Trades Publishing Co.
Advertiser Index: Every issue.
Special Issues:
Canadian Shoe Fair Preview. August.
National Shoe Fair. August.
Semaine de Cuir Show Issues. September/October.
New Products Preview. December.

0095. AMERICAN SOCIOLOGICAL REVIEW.
1722 N Street, NW, Washington, DC 20036.
Annual Subscription: $27. **Frequency:** Bimonthly.
Publisher: American Sociological Association.
Editorial Index: Annual. Author. December.

0096. AMERICAN SQUAREDANCE.
P.O. Box 488, Huron, OH 44839.
Annual Subscription: $9. **Frequency:** Monthly.
Publisher: Stan & Cathie Burdick.
Editorial Index: Annual. Title. December.
Special Issues:
Vacation—square dance vacations. Started 1969. $1. April.
Distaff—focus on women. Started 1969. $1. July.

0097. AMERICAN VEGETABLE GROWER.
37841 Euclid Ave., Willoughby, OH 44094.
Annual Subscription: $10. **Frequency:** Monthly.
Publisher: Meister Publishing.
Advertiser Index: Annual (July).
Special Issues:
Buyers Directory. $1. July.
Flower Power (w/photos). $1. November.

Vegetable Varieties (w/photos). $1. December.

0098. AMERICA'S TEXTILES.
106 East Stone Ave., P.O. Box 88, Greenville, SC 29602.
Annual Subscription: $43. **Frequency:** Monthly.
Publisher: Billian Publishing Co.
Advertiser Index: Every issue.
Special Issues:
Outlook. $3.50. January.
Financial Issue. $3.50. June.
Membership Guide: American Textile Machinery Association. $3.50. August.

0099. AMUSEMENT BUSINESS.
Box 24970, Nashville, TN 37202.
Annual Subscription: $40. **Frequency:** Weekly.
Publisher: Billboard Publications Inc.
Special Issues:
Western Fairs. $2. January.
Funparks Directory—U.S. and Canada. Published as a separate issue. $30. Not included in the subscription price. February.
Managing the Leisure Facility. $2. February/May/August/December.
Buyers Guide for the Mass Entertainment Industry. Published as a separate issue. $15. Not included in the subscription price. March.
Spring Special—fairs and exhibition dates. $2. April.
Trade Show & Convention Guide. Published as a separate issue. $65. Not included in the subscription price. June.
International Association of Auditorium Managers convention. $2. July.
Carnival & Circus Booking Guide—U.S. and Canada. Published as a separate issue. $5. Not included in the subscription price. September.
Amusement Rides and Games Buyers Guide—U.S. and Canada. Published as a separate issue. $7.50. Not included in the subscription price. October.
AudArena Stadium Guide—U.S., Canada, foreign. Published as a separate issue. $40. Not included in the subscription price. October.
Country Music Talent Buyers. $2. October.
International Association of Amusement Parks and Attractions Convention. $2. November.
Cavalcade of Acts & Attractions—U.S., Canada, foreign. Published as a separate issue. $30. Not included in the subscription price. December.
Directory of North American Fairs and Festivals. Published as a separate issue. $35. Not included in the subscription price. December.

0100. ANALOG SCIENCE FICTION/SCIENCE FACT.
P.O. Box 1936, Marion, OH 44306.
Annual Subscription: $19.50. **Frequency:** 13/yr.
Publisher: Davis Publications, Inc.
Editorial Index: Annual. Author. January.
Special Issues:
Analog Anthology—selections from 1930-present (first published as "Astounding Stories of Science Fiction"). Started 1981. Published as a separate issue. $2.95. Not included in the subscription price. 2/yr. Varies.

0101. ANALYTICAL CHEMISTRY.
1155-16th St. NW, Washington, DC 20036.
Annual Subscription: $18 (ACS members)/24 (nonmembers). **Frequency:** Monthly.
Publisher: American Chemical Society.
Advertiser Index: Every issue.
Editorial Index: Annual. Subject/Author. December.
Abstracted Online: CA Search.
Special Issues:
ACS Conference Preview. $6. February.
Review Issue—application reviews on oil, coal, food, air pollution, pesticides, water quality. Major developments in biochemical analysis, clinical chemistry, coatings, ferrous metallurgy, etc. Started 1949. Published as a separate issue. $7.25. April.
ACS Laboratory Guide—instruments, equipment and materials. Geographical guide to laboratory supply houses, research instruments and equipment, chemicals and materials guide, research services, new books, trade names index, company directory of firms selling research products. Started 1966. Published as a separate issue. $7.25. August.

0102. ANNALS OF THE HISTORY OF COMPUTING.
1899 Preston White Dr., Reston, VA 22091.
Annual Subscription: $50 (institutional rate). **Frequency:** Quarterly.
Publisher: American Federation of Information Processing Societies, Inc.
Editorial Index: Annual. Subject/Title/Author. January.
Special Issues:
Office Automation Conference: Proceedings. Published as a separate issue. $28. Not included in the subscription price. January.
National Computer Conference: Proceedings. Published as a separate issue. $80. Not included in the subscription price. June.

0103. THE ANTIQUE TRADER WEEKLY.
Box 1050, Dubuque, IA 52001.
Annual Subscription: $22. **Frequency:** Weekly.
Publisher: Babka Publishing Co.
Advertiser Index: Every issue.
Editorial Index: Irregular. Subject. Varies.
Special Issues:
Price Guide to Antiques. Published as a separate issue. $10.50. Not included in the subscription price. 6/yr. January/March/May/July/September/November.
"Annual of Articles"—Complete reprints of articles in Weekly, bound in hard cover, indexed by subject. Note: "Annual" is published irregularly; usually every nine months. Cumulative indexes available on request. Published as a separate issue. $10.95. Not included in the subscription price. Irregular. Irregular.

0104. ANTIQUES DEALER.
1115 Clifton Ave., Clifton, NJ 07013.
Annual Subscription: $15. **Frequency:** Monthly.
Publisher: Ebel-Doctorow Publications.
Advertiser Index: Every issue.
Special Issues:
Annual Directory of Wholesale Sources (listed alphabetically, geographically and by merchandise categories). Started 1950. $7.50. Annual. September.

0105. APPLIANCE.
1000 Jorie Blvd., CS5030, Oak Brook, IL 60521.
Annual Subscription: $30. **Frequency:** Monthly.
Publisher: Dana Chase Publications, Inc.
Advertiser Index: Every issue.
Special Issues:
Appliance Industry Purchasing Directory. Started 1974. $12. January.
Annual Profiles of Appliance Industry Suppliers. Started 1978. $3. March.
Portrait of the U.S. Appliance Industry/Home Laundry Appliances. Started 1978. $3. September.
Calendar of Events. Started 1977. $3. October.
New Products/Annual Consumer Electronics Report. Started 1969. $3. December.

0106. APPLIANCE MANUFACTURER.
P.O. Box 5772, Denver, CO 80217.
Annual Subscription: $35. **Frequency:** Monthly.
Publisher: Cahners Publishing Co.
Advertiser Index: Every issue.
Indexed Online: Trade & Industry Index.
Special Issues:
Annual Profile Issue—who's who; market shares. $10. January.
Money-Saving Ideas. $4. March.
Directory. $10. June.
Symposium and Trade Show. $4. September.

0107. THE APPRAISAL JOURNAL.
430 North Michigan Ave., Chicago, IL 60611.
Annual Subscription: $25. **Frequency:** Quarterly.
Publisher: American Institute of Real Estate Appraisers.
Editorial Index: Annual. Subject/Title/Author. October (cumulative index approx. every 10 yrs).
Abstracted Online: Management Contents.
Special Issues:
Membership Directory. January/July.

0108. AQUACULTURE MAGAZINE.
P.O. Box 2329, Asheville, NC 28802.
Annual Subscription: $15. **Frequency:** 6/yr.
Publisher: Achill River Corp.
Advertiser Index: Every issue.
Editorial Index: Annual. Subject/Title. November.
Special Issues:
Buyer's Guide. Started 1977. Published as a separate issue. $7. December.

0109. ARBITRATION JOURNAL.
140 West 51st St., New York, NY 10020.
Annual Subscription: $30. **Frequency:** Quarterly.
Publisher: American Arbitration Association.
Editorial Index: Annual. Subject/Title/Author. December.
Indexed or Abstracted Online: Trade & Industry Index; Legal Resource Index; ABI/Inform; Management Contents.

0110. ARCHAEOLOGY.
P.O. Box 928, Farmingdale, NY 11735.
Annual Subscription: $18. **Frequency:** 6/yr.
Publisher: Archaeologial Institute of America.
Editorial Index: Every 10 yr. Subject/Title/Author.
Special Issues:
Archaeology Around the World (Travel Guide). $3.50. March/April.
Archaeology in the USA (Travel Guide). $3.50. May/June.

0111. ARCHERY RETAILER.
715 Florida Ave. South, Suite 306, Minneapolis, MN 55426.
Annual Subscription: Free (qualified persons). **Frequency:** 6/yr.
Publisher: Winter Sports Publishing Inc.
Special Issues:
Annual Archery Directory—manufacturers. Published as a separate issue. $3. October.
SHOT Show (Shooting, Hunting, Outdoor Trade). $3. December.

0112. ARCHERY WORLD.
715 Florida Ave. South, Suite 306, Minneapolis, MN 55426.
Annual Subscription: $9. **Frequency:** 6/yr.
Publisher: Winter Sports Publishing Inc.
Advertiser Index: Every issue.
Special Issues:
Annual Bowhunting Guide. Published as a separate issue. $2.95. June.

0113. ARCHITECTURAL RECORD.
1221 Ave. of the Americas, New York, NY 10020.
Annual Subscription: $33. **Frequency:** Monthly.
Publisher: McGraw-Hill Inc.
Advertiser Index: Every issue.
Editorial Index: Annual. Subject/Title/Author. December.
Indexed Online: Magazine Index.
Special Issues:
Dodge/Sweet Construction Outlook. $6. February/May/August/November.
Record Houses—best designed houses. Started 1952. Published as a separate issue. $6. April.
Record Interiors—best interiors. Started 1980. Published as a separate issue. $6. September.
Product Reports—new building products. $6. December.

0114. ARCHITECTURE.
1735 New York Ave., NW, Washington, DC 20006.
Annual Subscription: $24. **Frequency:** Monthly.
Publisher: American Institute of Architects.
Advertiser Index: Every issue.
Editorial Index: Annual. Subject/Title/Author. December.
Special Issues:
Annual Review of New American Architecture. Started 1978. May.
Annual Review of Recent World Architecture. Started 1982. August.

0115. ARCHIVES OF GENERAL PSYCHIATRY.
535 North Dearborn St., Chicago, IL 60610.
Annual Subscription: $30. **Frequency:** Monthly.
Publisher: American Medical Association.
Advertiser Index: Every issue.
Editorial Index: Annual. Subject/Author. December.
Indexed Online: Medline.

0116. ARCHIVES OF OPHTHALMOLOGY.
535 North Dearborn St., Chicago, IL 60610.
Annual Subscription: $30. **Frequency:** Monthly.
Publisher: American Medical Association.
Editorial Index: Annual. Subject/Author. December.
Indexed Online: Medline.

0117. ARCHIVES OF OTOLARYNGOLOGY.
535 North Dearborn St., Chicago, IL 60610.
Annual Subscription: $30. **Frequency:** Monthly.
Publisher: Archives of Otolaryngology.
Editorial Index: Annual. Subject/Title/Author. October.
Special Issues:
American Academy of Facial and Plastic Reconstructive Surgery: Annual Meeting Papers. $3. 2/yr. March and July.
American Society for Head and Neck Surgery: Annual Meeting Papers. $3. November.

0118. ARMY.
2425 Wilson Blvd., Arlington, VA 22201.
Annual Subscription: $16. **Frequency:** Monthly.
Publisher: Association of the U.S. Army.
Advertiser Index: Every issue.
Editorial Index: Annual. Title/Author. February.
Special Issues:
ARMY Green Book—annual report by top military people on the current status of the Army. Started 1964. $1.50. October.

0119. ARMY TIMES.
475 School St., SW, Washington, DC 20024.
Annual Subscription: $32.50. **Frequency:** Weekly.
Publisher: Army Times Publishing Co.
Special Issues:
Retirement Supplement—articles for military retirees. Started 1970. $1.50. 3/yr. February/July/November.
Education Supplement—educational opportunities for military & dependents. Started 1969. $1.50. April/November.
Travel Supplement—vacations, resorts. Started 1975. $1.50. May/September.
Auto Supplement—new cars, fix-it articles. Started 1977. $1.50. October.
Christmas Shopping guide—gift ideas. $1.50. October.
Holiday Food & Party Issue—ideas, recipes. Started 1975. $1.50. November.

0120. ART DIRECTION.
10 East 39th St., 6th Floor, New York, NY 10016.
Annual Subscription: $20. **Frequency:** Monthly.
Publisher: Advertising Trade Publications Inc.
Advertiser Index: Every issue.
Special Issues:
Ad Typography. Started 1975. $2.50. May.
Ad Directions Trade Show. Started 1978. $2.50. August.
Ad Photography. Started 1979. $2.50. September.
Television Advertising. Started 1976. $2.50. November.

0121. ART IN AMERICA.
850 Third Ave., New York, NY 10022.
Annual Subscription: $34.95. **Frequency:** 11/yr.
Publisher: Whitney Communications Corp.
Advertiser Index: Every issue.
Editorial Index: Annual. Subject/Title/Author. August.
Indexed Online: Magazine Index.
Special Issues:
Guide to Galleries, Museums & Artists—by state and city. Index to artists with cross-refernces to their gallery affiliations. Catalog listings, arranged by artists' names. Started 1983. $5.95. August.

0122. ART MATERIAL TRADE NEWS.
6255 Barfield Rd., Atlanta, GA 30328.
Annual Subscription: $23. **Frequency:** Monthly.
Publisher: Syndicate Magazines.
Advertiser Index: Every issue.
Special Issues:
International Art Material Directory/Buyer's Guide. Published as a separate issue. $15. Not included in the subscription price. May.

0123. ARTES GRAFICAS USA (SPANISH).
399 Conklin St., Ste. 306, Farmingdale, NY 11735.
Annual Subscription: $25. **Frequency:** Bimonthly.
Publisher: Graphic Arts Trade Journals International Inc.
Advertiser Index: Every issue.
Special Issues:
Export Graficas USA (Spanish). Started 1968. Published as a separate issue. $15. Not included in the subscription price. March.
Export Graficas USA (Spanish)—buyers guide (company product listings); directory; trade name section; company profiles of their manufacturing or export program. Started 1968. Published as a separate issue. $15. Not included in the subscription price. March.
Export Graphics USA (English). Started 1980. Published as a separate issue. $15. Not included in the subscription price. September.

0124. ARTS & ACTIVITIES.
P.O. Box 85103, San Diego, CA 92138.
Annual Subscription: $15. **Frequency:** 10/yr.
Publisher: Publishers' Development Corporation.
Advertiser Index: Every issue.
Editorial Index: Semi-Annual. Subject/Author. January/June.
Special Issues:
Fibers & Threads. January.
Annual Buyer's Guide. February.
Summer Art Experiences Directory. March.
Ceramics/Crafts. May.
Guide to Summer Ordering. June.
Back to School. September.

0125. ASBESTOS.
131 North York Rd., P.O. Box 471, Willow Grove, PA 19090.
Annual Subscription: $18. **Frequency:** Monthly.
Publisher: D & B Enterprises Inc.
Advertiser Index: Annually in December issue.
Editorial Index: Annual. Subject. December.
Special Issues:
International Asbestos Mining Review. Started 1940. $5. January.
International Asbestos Company/Product Review. Started 1940. $5. March.
International Asbestos Occupational Safety & Health Review. Started 1972. $5. May/June.
Greetings From Asbestos Industry Leaders. Started 1936. $5. December.

0126. ASSEMBLY ENGINEERING.
Hitchcock Building, Wheaton, IL 60187.
Annual Subscription: $55. **Frequency:** Monthly.
Publisher: Hitchcock Publishing Co.
Advertiser Index: Every issue.
Editorial Index: Annual. Title. January.
Special Issues:
Productivity Improvement/Cost Reduction. Started 1974. $4.50. January.
High-Technology Special Issue. Started 1983. $4.50. May.
Assembly Technology Expo. Started 1975. $4.50. September.
Master Catalog—includes manufacturers directory and engineering reference handbook. Started 1961. Published as a separate issue. $25. September.

0127. ASSOCIATION MANAGEMENT.
1575 Eye Street, NW, Washington, DC 20005.
Annual Subscription: $24 (free to ASAE members).
Frequency: Monthly.
Publisher: American Society of Association Executives.
Advertiser Index: Every issue.
Editorial Index: Annual. Subject/Title/Author. January.
Special Issues:
Insurance. January.
Convention Hall Directory. February.
ASAE Spring Convention. March.
Who's Who in Association Management—1) Membership Directory; 2) Yellow Pages—suppliers of services to associations; 3) special speakers and speakers bureau directory. Started 1983. Published as a separate issue. $10 (members)/$45 (nonmembers). March.
International Issue/Small Meetings Report. April.
ASAE Pre- and Post-Convention Reports. 3/yr. May/June/October.
Financial Management. May.
Publishing/Group Travel. July.
ASAE Annual Meeting & Report. August/October.
Profiles of Key Award Winners. September.
Staff Management/Fund Raising. October.
Management Conference Issue. November.
Leadership—for executive boards. December.

0128. ASTRONAUTICS & AERONAUTICS.
1633 Broadway, New York, NY 10019.
Annual Subscription: $51. **Frequency:** 11/yr.
Publisher: American Institute of Astronautics & Aeronautics.
Advertiser Index: Every issue.
Editorial Index: Annual. Subject/Author. December.
Indexed or Abstracted Online: Recon (limited access—NASA contractors only).

0129. ATLANTIC TRUCK TRANSPORT REVIEW.
567 Coverdale Rd., Ste. 7A, Riverview, New Brunswick, Can. E1B 3K7.
Annual Subscription: $7.50. **Frequency:** Quarterly.
Publisher: Atlantic Providence Trucking Association.
Special Issues:
Directory of Trucking Services. $7.50. Spring.
APTA Truck Roadeo. $3. Summer.
APTA Annual Convention Program. $3. Fall.
APTA Convention Review/Year's Highlights. $3. Winter.

0130. AUDIO.
1255 Portland Pl., P.O. Box 5318, Boulder, CO 80321.
Annual Subscription: $13.94. **Frequency:** Monthly.
Publisher: CBS Publications.
Advertiser Index: Every issue.
Editorial Index: Subject/Title/Author. December.
Indexed Online: Magazine Index.
Special Issues:
Car Stereo Directory. $1.75. May.
Product Review Directory—specifications and prices on over 1000 stereo components. $2.25. October.

0131. AUDIO VISUAL DIRECTIONS.
25550 Hawthorne Blvd., Torrance, CA 90505.
Annual Subscription: $18. **Frequency:** Monthly.
Publisher: Montage Publishing, Inc.
Advertiser Index: Every issue.
Special Issues:
National Audio-Visual Association Show. January.
A/V Producer Directory. August.

Audio Buyers Guide.   December.

0132. AUDIO-VISUAL COMMUNICATIONS.
475 Park Ave. South, New York, NY 10016.
Annual Subscription: $13.50.   **Frequency:** Monthly.
Publisher: United Business Publications, Inc.
Advertiser Index: Every issue.
Editorial Index: Annual. Subject. January.
Indexed Online: Trade & Industry Index.
Special Issues:
  Corporate Communications Centers Guide.   Started 1975. $1.50.   February.
  Videotape Production Facilities Directory.   Started 1970. $1.50.   April.
  Motion Picture Laboratory Services Directory.   Started 1971. $1.50.   June.
  Who's Who in AV Presentation Directory.   Started 1969. $1.50.   June.
  AV Equipment Buyer's Guide/Slide Lab Services Directory.   Started 1964/1970. $4.75.   October.

0133. AUTO LAUNDRY NEWS.
370 Lexington Ave., New York, NY 10017.
Annual Subscription: $12.   **Frequency:** Monthly.
Publisher: Columbia Communications.
Advertiser Index: Every issue.
Special Issues:
  Buyers Guide. $10.   January.

0134. AUTO MERCHANDISING NEWS.
234 Greenfield St., Fairfield, CT 06430.
Annual Subscription: $24.   **Frequency:** Monthly.
Publisher: Mortimer Communications, Inc.
Advertiser Index: Every issue.
Special Issues:
  Directory of Aftermarket Suppliers (1982 only).   Published as a separate issue. $5.   Not included in the subscription price.   July.
  Show Issue/Automotive Parts and Accessories Association.   Started 1971.   August.

0135. AUTO TRIM NEWS.
1623 Grand Ave., Baldwin, NY 11510.
Annual Subscription: $9.   **Frequency:** Monthly.
Publisher: National Association of Auto Trim Shops.
Special Issues:
  Directory of Product Sources.   Published as a separate issue. $5 (members)/10 (nonmembers).   Not included in the subscription price.   December.

0136. AUTOMATIC MACHINING.
228 North Winton Rd., Rochester, NY 14610.
Annual Subscription: $15.   **Frequency:** Monthly.
Publisher: Same.
Advertiser Index: Every issue.
Special Issues:
  Machine Tool Show Issue. $3.   August.

0137. AUTOMATION IN HOUSING/SYSTEMS BUILDING NEWS.
P.O. Box 120, Carpinteria, CA 93013.
Annual Subscription: $30 (domestic); $70 (foreign).
  Frequency: Monthly.
Publisher: CMN Associates, Inc.
Advertiser Index: Every issue.
Editorial Index: Annual. Subject/Title. December.
Special Issues:
  Annual Buyers Guide/Industry Statistics.   Started 1975. $10.   January.
  Top 100 Home Producers.   Started 1965. $5.   August.

0138. AUTOMOTIVE AGE.
2950-A7 Airway Ave., Costa Mesa, CA 92626.
Annual Subscription: $20.   **Frequency:** Monthly.
Publisher: Freed-Crown-Lee Publishing.
Advertiser Index: Every issue.
Special Issues:
  December Buyers Guide—for new car dealerships; includes Western regional supplement.   Started 1970.   Published as a separate issue. $5.   December.

0139. AUTOMOTIVE BODY REPAIR NEWS.
65 East South Water St., Chicago, IL 60601.
Annual Subscription: Free to qualified persons.   **Frequency:** Monthly.
Publisher: Stanley Publishing Co.
Advertiser Index: Buyers Guide.
Special Issues:
  Body Shop Buyers Guide and Fact Book.   Published as a separate issue.   March.

0140. AUTOMOTIVE ENGINEERING.
400 Commonwealth Dr., Warrendale, PA 15096.
Annual Subscription: $30.   **Frequency:** Monthly.
Publisher: Society of Automotive Engineers.
Advertiser Index: Every issue.
Special Issues:
  Technical Highlights of European Vehicles. $4.   January.
  Society of Automotive Engineers Congress Issue. $4.   February.
  Materials Issue. $4.   March.
  S.A.E. Roster Issue/Directory and Catalog File.   Published as a separate issue. $50.   Not included in the subscription price.   April.
  Passenger Car Issue. $4.   June.
  Automotive Electronics Issue. $4.   August.
  Off-Highway Issue. $4.   September.
  Technical Highlights of U.S. Vehicles. $4.   October.
  Truck and Bus Issue. $4.   November.

0141. AUTOMOTIVE INDUSTRIES.
Chilton Way, Radnor, PA 19089.
Annual Subscription: $30.   **Frequency:** Monthly.
Publisher: Chilton Co.
Advertiser Index: Every issue.
Special Issues:
  Specifications & Statistics Issue—passenger cars, trucks, engines.   Started 1918. $10.   April.
  Suppliers Issue—financial analysis of automotive OEM suppliers.   Started 1975. $10.   June.
  New Cars.   October.
  Auto Industry Report.   December.

0142. AUTOMOTIVE MARKETING.
Chilton Way, Radnor, PA 19089.
Annual Subscription: $30.   **Frequency:** Monthly.
Publisher: Chilton Co.
Advertiser Index: Every issue.
Indexed Online: Trade & Industry Index.
Special Issues:
  Buyers Guide.   July.
  Automotive Parts and Accessories Association Show.   August.
  Supplier and Retailer Profiles.   December.

0143. AUTOMOTIVE NEWS.
965 East Jefferson Ave., Detroit, MI 48207.
Annual Subscription: $40.   **Frequency:** Weekly.
Publisher: Crain Communications, Inc.
Indexed or Abstracted Online: AMI; Trade & Industry Index.
Special Issues:
  National Automobile Dealers Association Show. $1.   February.
  Society of Automotive Engineers Show. $1.   February.
  Import World. $1.   March.
  Market Data Book. $1.   April.
  Custom Market. $1.   June.
  Service Profits. $1.   July.
  Showroom Profits. $1.   August.
  World Expo Show. $1.   August.
  Marketing Forecast. $1.   September.
  Japan. $1.   October.
  Leisure Motor Vehicles (recreational vehicles). $1.   November.
  Forecast. $1.   December.

0144. AUTOMOTIVE REBUILDER.
   11 South Forge St., Akron, OH 44304.
   Annual Subscription: $20. **Frequency:** Monthly.
   Publisher: Babcox Automotive Publications.
   Advertiser Index: Every issue.
   Special Issues:
   Annual Purchasing Directory.   January.
   Annual Core Supplier Directory.   July.
   Heavy Duty Parts Supplier Directory.   November.
   Import Parts Supplier Directory.   December.

0145. AUTOMOTIVE VOLUME DISTRIBUTION.
   7300 North Cicero Ave., Lincolnwood, IL 60646.
   Annual Subscription: $20. **Frequency:** 10/yr.
   Publisher: Irving-Cloud Publishing Co.
   Advertiser Index: Every issue.
   Special Issues:
   Pacific Automotive Show. $2.50.   January.
   Automotive Service Industries Convention/Big "I" Show. $2.50.   February.
   Automotive Warehouse Distributors Association Conference. $2.50.   October.

0146. AVIATION EQUIPMENT & MAINTENANCE.
   7300 Cicero Ave., Lincolnwood, IL 60646.
   Annual Subscription: $10. **Frequency:** 6/yr.
   Publisher: Irving-Cloud Publishing Co.
   Advertiser Index: Every issue.
   Special Issues:
   Airfield & Aircraft Maintenance Equipment Review. $2.50.   September/October.

0147. AVIATION, SPACE AND ENVIRONMENTAL MEDICINE.
   Washington National Airport, Washington, DC 20001.
   Annual Subscription: $55. **Frequency:** Monthly.
   Publisher: Aerospace Medical Association.
   Editorial Index: Annual. December.
   Special Issues:
   Pre-Prints: Aerospace Medical Association Conference.   Published as a separate issue. $10/15.   May.
   Directory.   December.

0148. AVIATION WEEK & SPACE TECHNOLOGY.
   P.O. Box 503, Hightstown, NJ 08520.
   Annual Subscription: $45. **Frequency:** Weekly.
   Publisher: McGraw-Hill.
   Advertiser Index: Every issue.
   Editorial Index: Annual. Subject. December.
   Abstracted Online: Information Bank; Magazine Index; Trade & Industry Index.
   Special Issues:
   Helicopter Air Show Issue (HAI).   February.
   Forecast & Inventory.   March.
   Aerospace Materials (Special Section).   April.
   Paris Air Show Issue.   Biennially odd years.   May.
   Electronic Warfare: Part I & II (Special Section).   August.
   Farnborough Air Show—Biennial.   September.
   Business Flying & NBAA Show Issue.   October.
   International Air Transport.   November.
   International Marketing Directory.   December.
   Special Section: Computers in Aerospace.   December.

0149. THE B.C. PROFESSIONAL ENGINEER.
   2210 West 12 Ave., Vancouver, British Columbia, Can. V6K 2N.
   Annual Subscription: $10. **Frequency:** Monthly.
   Publisher: Association of Professional Engineers of British Columbia.
   Special Issues:
   Directory Issue.   August.

0150. BIN MERCHANDISER.
   703 Market St., San Francisco, CA 94103.
   Annual Subscription: $29. **Frequency:** Monthly.
   Publisher: Industry Publications, Inc.
   Special Issues:
   BIN California Gold Book—reference file for distilled spirits licenses in California. Includes summaries of current federal and state laws governing industry; biographical data on senators and assemblymen in California legislature; industry directory for California.   Started 1961.   Published as a separate issue. $4.26.   June.

0151. BACK STAGE.
   330 West 42 St., New York, NY 10036.
   Annual Subscription: $32. **Frequency:** Weekly.
   Publisher: Back Stage Publications, Inc.
   Advertiser Index: Film/Tape Directory.
   Indexed Online: Trade & Industry Index.
   Special Issues:
   Business Screen News—industrial, training & sponsored films. $.75.   Monthly.
   Film/Tape Directors Salute. $.75.   January.
   Pennsylvania Salute. $.75.   January.
   Western Studios & Facilities. $.75.   January.
   Film & Tape Directory—nationwide listings of TV commercial and industrial film producers, TV station suppliers.   Published as a separate issue. $20.   Not included in the subscription price.   March.
   IBCA Awards—Broadcast Commercials. $.75.   March.
   NAB (National Association of Broadcasters) Convention. $.75.   April.
   Art Directors Special. $.75.   May.
   Chicago-Midwest Special/U.S. Industrial Film Festival. $.75.   May.
   Video/Tape Production Salute/Los Angeles Video Show. $.75.   May.
   CLIO Awards Special—coverage of awards for TV commercial excellence. $.75.   June.
   New York Film & Tape Production Week.   Started 1981. $.75.   June.
   Southern States. $.75.   June.
   National Audio-Visual Association Meeting/(AV America). $.75.   July.
   AMI—American Multi-Image. $.75.   August.
   Animation, Opticals & Special Effects. $.75.   August.
   Texas and Western States. $.75.   August.
   New England Production Highlights. $.75.   September.
   Salute to Minnesota. $.75.   September.
   SMPTE (Society of Motion Picture and Television Engineers) Convention. $.75.   October.
   Video Expo. $.75.   October.
   Film Production Houses. $.75.   November.
   International Film & TV Festival of New York. $.75.   November.
   Anniversary Issue.   Started 1961. $.75.   December.
   Editors and Post-Production. $.75.   December.

0152. BAKERY PRODUCTION AND MARKETING.
   5725 East River Rd., Chicago, IL 60631.
   Annual Subscription: $45. **Frequency:** Monthly.
   Publisher: Gorman Publishing Co.
   Advertiser Index: Every issue.
   Special Issues:
   Bakery In-Store—special issues with features for supermarket in-store bakers.   Published as a separate issue. $10.   2/yr.   March/September.
   Biscuit & Bakers Manufacturers Association Conference/ American Society of Bakery Engineers Meeting. $6.   April.
   Retail Bakers of America Show Guide.   Published as a separate issue.   April.
   RBA and Supermarket Bakery Conference Reports. $6.   June.
   Red Book—annual directory of major bakeries and distributors of equipment and ingredients.   Published as a separate issue. $95.   June.
   Food Marketing Institute Meeting/Exhibition. $6.   July.
   American Bakers Association Meeting. $6.   August.
   Southern Bakers Production Conference. $6.   November.
   Buyers Guide—annual directory of suppliers of equipment, ingredients, services. $21.   December.

0153. BAKING INDUSTRY.
301 East Erie St., Chicago, IL 60611.
Annual Subscription: $24. **Frequency:** Monthly.
Publisher: Putman Publishing Co.
Advertiser Index: Every issue.
Special Issues:
  Packaging Guide and Directory. $2. February.
  Processing Systems Guide and Directory. $2. May.
  Ingredients Guide and Directory. $2. August.
  Baking Show-in-Print. $2. September.
  Material Handling. $2. November.
  Snack Processing. $2. December.

0154. BANK ADMINISTRATION.
2550 Golf Rd., Rolling Meadows, IL 60008.
Annual Subscription: $30. **Frequency:** Monthly.
Publisher: Bank Administration Institute.
Advertiser Index: Every issue.
Editorial Index: Annual. Subject/Author. December.
Indexed or Abstracted Online: Management Contents; ABI/Inform.
Special Issues:
  Bank Security Directory (suppliers, products & services). Started 1982. $3. March.
  Check Processing Equipment Directory/Top 50 Profit Performing Banks. Started 1983. $3. April.
  Cash Dispensing Equipment and Automated Tellers Directory. $3. May.
  Bank Administration Institute Officers. $3. July.
  Automated Teller Machine (ATM) Directory/Coin and Currency Processing Directory. Started 1983. Published as a separate issue. $3. August.
  Bank Administration Institute Convention. $3. September.

0155. BANK MARKETING MAGAZINE.
309 West Washington St., Chicago, IL 60606.
Annual Subscription: $36/48 (nonmembers). **Frequency:** Monthly.
Publisher: Bank Marketing Association.
Advertiser Index: Every issue.
Editorial Index: Annual. Subject. December.
Special Issues:
  Directory of Financial Marketing Services. January.
  Premiums and Incentives. August.
  Annual Convention Issue. October.

0156. BANK SYSTEMS & EQUIPMENT.
1515 Broadway, New York, NY 10036.
Annual Subscription: $20. **Frequency:** Monthly.
Publisher: Gralla Publications.
Advertiser Index: Every issue.
Editorial Index: Annual. Subject. February.
Abstracted Online: ABI/Inform.
Special Issues:
  Directory and Buyers Guide. January.
  EFT (electronic funds transfer) Network Directory. March.
  Annual Software Review. August.
  ABA Annual Convention. October.

0157. THE BANKER.
Minster House, Arthur St., London, , England EC 4R 9AX.
Annual Subscription: $100. **Frequency:** Monthly.
Publisher: Financial Times Business Publishing Ltd.
Editorial Index: Annual. Subject/Author. April.
Indexed Online: Trade & Industry Index.
Special Issues:
  Foreign Banks in New York. Started 1965. February.
  Top 500 World Commercial Banks Listing. Started 1960. Published as a separate issue. June.
  Foreign Banks in London. Started 1960. November.
  Top 100 Arab Bank Listing. Started 1979. December.

0158. THE BANKERS MAGAZINE.
210 South St., Boston, MA 02111.
Annual Subscription: $60. **Frequency:** 6/yr.
Publisher: Warren, Gorham & Lamont Inc.
Editorial Index: Biennial (even years). Subject/Author. January/February.
Indexed or Abstracted Online: ABI/Inform; Management Contents.

0159. BANKERS MONTHLY: NATIONAL MAGAZINE OF BANKING & INVESTMENTS.
601 Skokie Blvd., Northbrook, IL 60062.
Annual Subscription: $18. **Frequency:** Monthly.
Publisher: Bankers Monthly, Inc.
Indexed or Abstracted Online: ABI/Inform; Management Contents.
Special Issues:
  100th Anniversary Special Issue. $1.50. One time only. January (1984).
  Finance Industry Survey—roster of leading companies; key financial statistics for each. $1.50. May.

0160. BANKING LAW JOURNAL.
210 South St., Boston, MA 02111.
Annual Subscription: $68. **Frequency:** 8/yr.
Publisher: Warren, Gorham & Lamont.
Editorial Index: Annual. Subject/Title. November/December. Provides subject guide to judicial decisions and articles; title index to articles; title and index of books reviewed; and table of cases, by case name.
Indexed or Abstracted Online: ABI/Inform; Management Contents; Legal Resource Index.

0161. BARRON'S—NATIONAL BUSINESS AND FINANCIAL WEEKLY.
200 Burnett Rd., Chicopee, MA 02101.
Annual Subscription: $63. **Frequency:** Weekly.
Publisher: Dow-Jones & Co.
Editorial Index: Annual. Subject. Annual index to Barron's now appears in annual index to Wall Street Journal.
Indexed or Abstracted Online: Information Bank; Trade & Industry Index; Magazine Index; Management Contents; ABI/Inform; Dow-Jones News Retrieval.
Special Issues:
  Year-End Round-Up, Investment Scene. $1.50. January.
  Mutual Fund Investments—portfolio report, by company, on the funds listed in the performance record. $1.50. Usually February/May/August/November.

0162. THE BATTERY MAN.
100 Larchwood Dr., Largo, FL 33540.
Annual Subscription: $9. **Frequency:** Monthly.
Publisher: Independent Battery Manufacturers Association, Inc.
Advertiser Index: Every issue.
Editorial Index: Annual. Subject. January.
Special Issues:
  International SLIG Buyers Guide—listing of 2000 automotive battery manufacturers and related suppliers in the free world. Started 1969. Published as a separate issue. $7. Biennially (odd-numbered years). June, biennially.

0163. BEAUTY FASHION.
48 East 43rd St., New York, NY 10017.
Annual Subscription: $15. **Frequency:** 11/yr.
Publisher: Beauty Fashion, Inc.
Special Issues:
  Sun Products. $5. January.
  Men's Cosmetics Directory—men's products and their manufacturers. $10. April.
  Treatments Directory—products by size and price. $10. June.
  Fragrance Directory—women's fragrances, forms available, and manufacturers. $10. July.
  Cosmetics Directory—products by type and manufacturer. $10. October/November.

0164. BEDDING MAGAZINE.
1235 Jefferson, Davis Hwy., Arlington, VA 22202.
Annual Subscription: $30. **Frequency:** Monthly.

Publisher: National Association of Bedding Manufacturers.
Advertiser Index: Every issue.
Special Issues:
Yearbook and Suppliers Guide—National Association of Bedding Manufacturers. Started 1973. $3. December.

0165. BEER WHOLESALER.
75 S.E. 4th Ave., Delray Beach, FL 33444.
Annual Subscription: $12. **Frequency:** 6/yr.
Publisher: Dogan Publications.
Advertiser Index: Every issue.
Special Issues:
Imported Beers. Started 1969. $5. July/August.

0166. BENEFITS CANADA.
777 Bay St., Toronto, Ontario, Can. M5W 1A7.
Annual Subscription: $48/26. **Frequency:** 6/yr.
Special Issues:
Directory of Employee Benefit Consultants. Started 1978. $8/5. March/April.
Real Estate Vehicles for Pension Funds. Started 1982. $8/5. May/June.
Directory of Group Insurance. Started 1977. $8/5. July/August.
Top 20 Pension Funds. Started 1980. $8/5. September/October.
Directory of Pension Fund Investment Services. Started 1978. $8/5. November/December.

0167. BEST'S REVIEW: LIFE/HEALTH EDITION.
Ambest Rd., Oldwick, NJ 08858.
Annual Subscription: $14. **Frequency:** Monthly.
Publisher: A.M. Best Company.
Advertiser Index: Every issue.
Indexed or Abstracted Online: ABI/Inform; Insurance Abstracts; Trade & Industry Index; Management Contents.
Special Issues:
Insurance Stock Trends. $1.50/3.00 (minimum order). February.
Best's Insurance Convention Guide. Published as a separate issue. $3. Not included in the subscription price. 3/yr. March/July/November.
Life Insurance Company Changes. $1.50/3.00 (minimum order). March.
Insurance Accounting & Systems Association. Started 1975. $1.50/3.00 (minimum order). May.
Insurance Technology. $1.50/3.00 (minimum order). May/November.
Individual and Group Annuities/Universal Life Insurance. $1.50/3.00 (minimum order). June.
Leading Life Insurance Companies. $1.50/3.00 (minimum order). July.
Lapse Ratios on Individual Businesses/500 Leading Life Companies in Total Premium Income. $1.50/3.00 (minimum order). August.
Average Policy Size. $1.50/3.00 (minimum order). September.
Asset Allocation and Yield. $1.50/3.00 (minimum order). October.
Participating & Non-Participating Whole Life Policy Comparison. $1.50/3.00 (minimum order). October.
Accident and Health Premiums. $1.50/3.00 (minimum order). November.
Dividend Comparisons. $1.50/3.00 (minimum order). December.

0168. BEST'S REVIEW: PROPERTY/CASUALTY EDITION.
Ambest Rd., Oldwick, NJ 08858.
Annual Subscription: $14. **Frequency:** Monthly.
Publisher: A.M. Best Company.
Advertiser Index: Every issue.
Indexed or Abstracted Online: ABI/Inform; Insurance Abstracts; Trade & Industry Index; Management Contents.
Special Issues:
Review and Preview. $1.50/3.00 (minimum order). January.
Insurance Stock Trends. $1.50/3.00 (minimum order). February.
Corporate Changes. $1.50/3.00 (minimum order). March.
Insurance Accounting & Systems Association Meeting. Started 1975. $1.50/3.00 (minimum order). May.
Technology Emphasis. $1.50/3.00 (minimum order). May/November.
Excess & Surplus. Started 1982. $1.50/3.00 (minimum order). June/September/December/March.
200 Leading Property/Casualty Companies & Groups. $1.50/3.00 (minimum order). June.
Insurance Premium Distribution. $1.50/3.00 (minimum order). July.
Auto Insurance Premiums. $1.50/3.00 (minimum order). August.
Property Insurance Marketing. $1.50/3.00 (minimum order). September.
General Liability/Medical Malpractice Insurance Marketing. $1.50/3.00 (minimum order). October.
Inland Marine and Bond Marketing. $1.50/3.00 (minimum order). November.

0169. BETTER HOMES AND GARDENS.
Locust at 17th, Des Moines, IA 50336.
Annual Subscription: $12.97. **Frequency:** Monthly.
Publisher: Meredith Corporation.
Indexed Online: Magazine Index.
Special Issues:
Better Homes and Gardens Brides' Book. Started 1980. Published as a separate issue. $2.50. Not included in the subscription price. January/August.
Better Homes and Gardens Building Ideas—for readers who want to have a house custom-built. Started 1937. Published as a separate issue. $2.50. Not included in the subscription price. January/April/July/October.
Better Homes and Gardens Country Home—country lifestyle, building renovation, furnishings, antiques, collectibles, crafts, cooking, gardens. Started 1979. Published as a separate issue. $2.50. Not included in the subscription price. 6/yr. January/March/May/July/September/November.
Better Homes and Gardens Garden Ideas & Outdoor Living. Started 1940. Published as a separate issue. $2.50. Not included in the subscription price. January (Spring)/March (Summer).
Better Homes and Gardens 100's of Needlework and Craft Ideas. Started 1977. Published as a separate issue. $2.25. Not included in the subscription price. January/June.
Better Homes and Gardens Baking Ideas. Started 1977. Published as a separate issue. $2.50. Not included in the subscription price. February/November.
Better Homes and Gardens Decorating Ideas. Started 1941. Published as a separate issue. $2.50. Not included in the subscription price. February/May/August/November.
Better Homes and Gardens Kitchen & Bath Ideas—new and remodeled. Started 1973. Published as a separate issue. $2.50. Not included in the subscription price. February/May/September/December.
Better Homes and Gardens Remodeling Ideas. Started 1958. Published as a separate issue. $2.50. Not included in the subscription price. February/May/September/December.
Better Homes and Gardens Country Crafts—quilts, rugs, samplers, etc. Started 1980. Published as a separate issue. $2.25. Not included in the subscription price. March.
Better Homes and Gardens Window & Wall Ideas. Started 1975. Published as a separate issue. $2.50. Not included in the subscription price. April.
Better Homes and Gardens Holiday Crafts—decorations and trims for home; children's wear; sweaters to knit and crochet; toys; quilting; lace; etc. Started 1974. Published as a separate issue. $2.50. Not included in the subscription price. August.

Better Homes and Gardens Christmas Ideas.   Started 1952. Published as a separate issue. $2.50.   Not included in the subscription price.   September.
Better Homes and Gardens Do-It Yourself Home Improvement and Repair.   Started 1968.   Published as a separate issue. $2.50.   Not included in the subscription price.   September.
Better Homes and Gardens Country Cooking.   Published as a separate issue. $2.50.   Not included in the subscription price.   September.
Better Homes and Gardens Holiday Cooking & Entertaining Ideas.   Started 1969.   Published as a separate issue. $2.50.   Not included in the subscription price.   October.
Better Homes and Gardens All-Time Favorite Recipes.   Started 1977.   Published as a separate issue. $3.95.   Not included in the subscription price.   November.
Better Homes and Gardens Low-Calorie Recipes.   Started 1978.   Published as a separate issue. $2.50.   Not included in the subscription price.   December.

0170. BETTER ROADS.
P.O. Box 558, Park Ridge, IL 60068.
Annual Subscription: $15.
Publisher: Same.
Advertiser Index: Every issue.
Special Issues:
Annual Legislative and Funding Issue—by states.   January.
Roadside Maintenance.   February.
Herbicide Application, Geotextiles.   March.
Recycling Equipment.   April.
Semi-annual Bridge Issue.   May, November.
Winter Maintenance Buyers Guide.   June.
Traffic Control & Safety.   July.
Roadside Maintenance.   August.
American Public Works Association Congress Issue.   September.
Pavement Management/Computerized Traffic Control.   October.
Geotextiles.   November.
Equipment Materials Users Specifications.   December.

0171. BEVERAGE CANADA.
5200 Dixie Rd., Ste. 204, Mississauga, Ontario, Can.
Annual Subscription: $10.   **Frequency:** 10/yr.
Publisher: Arthurs Publications Ltd.
Editorial Index: Annual. Subject. October.
Special Issues:
Market Leaders—outstanding performers in spirits industry.   Started 1982. $2.   April.
Imports Issue—import agents' profile.   Started 1982. $2.   June.
New Products Issues.   Started 1981. $2.   August.

0172. BEVERAGE INDUSTRY.
120 West 2nd St., Duluth, MN 55802.
Annual Subscription: $35.   **Frequency:** 26/yr.
Publisher: Harcourt, Brace Jovanovich Inc.
Advertiser Index: Every issue.
Indexed or Abstracted Online: AMI; Trade & Industry Index.
Special Issues:
Beverage Industry Annual Manual—round-up of year's industry developments, plus industry statistics. Covers beverage plants for alcoholic and non-alcoholic products. Buyers guide; brand name directory.   Started 1967. Published as a separate issue. $35.   Not included in the subscription price.   September.

0173. BEVERAGE RETAILER WEEKLY.
250 W. 57 St., New York, NY 10107.
Annual Subscription: $20.   **Frequency:** Weekly.
Publisher: Beverage Retailer Weekly.
Special Issues:
Report to the Industry. $.75.   January/June.
BRW Wines, Cordials, Liqueurs Trade Exposition. $.75.   March.
National Liquor Stores Association Convention. $.75.   April.
New York-New Jersey Beverage Guide Annual. $.75.   April.
Wine and Spirit Wholesaler of America Convention. $.75.   May.
Beer Issue. $.75.   July.
Special Women's Issue. $.75.   August.
Bourbon. $.75.   September.
National Beer Wholesaler Convention/New Jersey Liquor Stores Convention. $.75.   October.
New Jersey Licensed Beverage Association Convention. $.75.   October.
New York State Beer Wholesalers Convention. $.75.   October.
Holiday Gift Packaging and Merchandising. $.75.   November.
Holiday Promotions. $.75.   November/December.
National Licensed Beverage Association Convention. $.75.   November/December.

0174. BEVERAGE WORLD.
150 Great Neck Rd., Great Neck, NY 11021.
Annual Subscription: $30.   **Frequency:** Monthly.
Publisher: Keller International Publishing Corp.
Advertiser Index: Every issue.
Editorial Index: Subject/Title. December.
Indexed Online: Trade & Industry Index.
Special Issues:
Beverage Business Forecast/Convention Review: National Soft Drink Association. $3.50.   January.
Quality Control. $3.50.   February.
Top 10 Soft Drink Brands.   Started 1981. $3.50.   March.
Top 10 Beer Brands.   Started 1982. $3.50.   April.
Vending. $3.50.   May.
Packaging. $3.50.   June.
Top 100 Beverage Companies. $3.50.   July.
Beverage Market Index/International Roundup.   Started 1977. $3.50.   August.
Buyers Guide—includes Soft Drink Franchise Company Directory. $3.50.   September.
Truck Trends. $3.50.   October.
100 Year History of the Beverage Marketplace and Future Probe.   Started 1982 only.   Published as a separate issue. $20 softcover; $25 hardcover.   1 time only.   October.
Beverage Brand Directory: "Living" Directory and Plant Specification Guide (includes telephone update service).   Started 1983. $3.50.   November.
Hall of Fame.   Started 1982. $3.50.   December.
Periscope—newsletter on soft drink, beer, wine and fruit juice segments. $3.50.   12/yr.   Monthly.

0175. BEVERAGES/BEBIDAS.
All Americas Publishers Service Inc., P.O. Box 807, Winnetka, IL 60093.
Annual Subscription: $15.   **Frequency:** 7/yr.
Publisher: Charles Hahn.
Special Issues:
Buyers Guide (English edition and Spanish edition). $2.   July.

0176. BICYCLE DEALERS SHOWCASE.
P.O. Box 19531, Irvine, CA 92713.
Annual Subscription: Free to qualified persons.   **Frequency:** Monthly.
Publisher: Hester Communications Inc.
Special Issues:
Dealer Survey.   February.
Buyers Guide—bicycle and moped manufacturers and distributors; trade name index; service directory.   Published as a separate issue. $15.   November.

0177. BIG FARMER ENTREPRENEUR.
131 Lincoln Hwy., Frankfort, IL 60423.
Annual Subscription: Controlled Circulation.   **Frequency:** Monthly.
Publisher: Ralph Bralle.
Advertiser Index: Every issue.

Special Issues:
Machinery Management & Equipment.   January.
Irrigation Management & Equipment.   March.
Livestock Management.   April.
Harvest Preview.   June.

0178. BILLBOARD.
P.O. Box 1413, Riverton, NJ 08077.
Annual Subscription: $135.   **Frequency:** Weekly.
Publisher: Billboard Publications, Inc.
Advertiser Index: Every issue.
Indexed or Abstracted Online: AMI; Trade & Industry Index.
Special Issues:
Beatles 20th Anniversary. $3.   One time only.   February 1984.
Country Music Source Book.   Published as a separate issue. $15.   Not included in the subscription price.   March.
Retail Guide to Computer Software. $3.   March.
International Directory of Recording Studios.   Published as a separate issue. $20.   Not included in the subscription price.   September.
International Buyers Guide.   Published as a separate issue. $35.   Not included in the subscription price.   December.

0179. BIOMEDICAL COMMUNICATIONS.
470 Park Ave. South, New York, NY 10016.
Annual Subscription: $10.   **Frequency:** 6/yr.
Publisher: United Business Publications.
Advertiser Index: Every issue.
Editorial Index: Bimonthly. Subject/Title/Author. Every issue.
Special Issues:
Medical Media Directory.   Started 1975. $5.   March.
Equipment Specification and Purchasing Guide.   Started 1975. $5.   November.

0180. BIOMEDICAL PRODUCTS.
P.O. Box 1952, Dover, NJ 07801.
Annual Subscription: Free to qualified persons.   **Frequency:** Monthly.
Publisher: Gordon Publications, Inc.
Advertiser Index: Every issue.
Special Issues:
Fundamental Lab Equipment and Labware Buyers Guide. $1.   January.
American Society for Microbiology Show. $1.   February.
Laboratory Filters Buyers Guide. $1.   March ('83)/April ('84).
Federation of American Societies for Experimental Biology Show. $1.   April ('83)/March ('84).
American Association of Immunologists Show. $1.   Biennially.   May 84.
American Society of Biological Chemists Show. $1.   May.
Laboratory Chemicals Buyers Guide. $1.   May.
Liquid Scintillation and Gamma Counting Buyers Guide/Tissue Culture Association Show. $1.   June.
Electrophoresis and Isoelectric Focusing Buyers Guide. $1.   July.
Bioresearch Computerization. $1.   Biennially.   August.
Budget Planning Aids. $1.   August.
Microscopic, Optic and Photographic Buyers Guide. $1.   August ('83)/February ('84).
Laboratory Animal Directory Issue/AALAS Show. $1.   September ('83)/October ('84).
Chromatography Equipment Buyers Guide. $1.   Annual.   October ('83)/September ('84).
American Society for Cell Biology Show/Cell Biology Buyers Guide. $1.   November.
Biotechnology Instrumentation and Antibodies and Antisera Buyers Guides. $1.   December.

0181. BIOSCIENCE.
1401 Arlington Blvd., Arlington, VA 22209.
Annual Subscription: $43.   **Frequency:** Monthly.
Publisher: American Institute of Biological Sciences.
Advertiser Index: Every issue.
Editorial Index: Annual. Subject/Title/Author. December.
Indexed Online: Magazine Index.

0182. BLACK ENTERPRISE.
P.O. Box 5600, Bergenfield, NJ 07621.
Annual Subscription: $15.   **Frequency:** Monthly.
Publisher: Earl G. Graves Publishing Co.
Indexed Online: Magazine Index; Trade & Industry Index.
Special Issues:
Careers and Opportunities.   Started 1977. $1.75.   February.
Black Enterprise 100.   Started 1973. $3.   June.
Money Management.   Started 1973. $1.75.   October.

0183. BOAT AND MOTOR DEALER MAGAZINE.
340 Linden Ave., Wilmette, IL 60091.
Annual Subscription: $20.   **Frequency:** Monthly.
Publisher: Van Zevern Publications Inc.
Advertiser Index: Every issue.
Special Issues:
Trade Boat Show Issue. $3.   September.
Market Manual—year-end sales statistics; manufacturers and distributors.   Published as a separate issue. $10.   December.

0184. BOATING.
One Park Ave., New York, NY 10016.
Annual Subscription: $18.   **Frequency:** Monthly.
Publisher: Ziff-Davis Publishing Co.
Advertiser Index: Every issue.
Editorial Index: Subject. December.
Indexed Online: Magazine Index.
Special Issues:
Boat Show Issue/Buyers Guide to New Powerboats. $2.50.   January.
America's Cup Race Issue. $2.   Every 4 yrs.   September.

0185. BOATING INDUSTRY.
850 Third Ave., New York, NY 10022.
Annual Subscription: $14.97.   **Frequency:** Monthly.
Publisher: Same.
Advertiser Index: Every issue.
Editorial Index: Annual. Subject. December.
Indexed Online: Trade & Industry Index.
Special Issues:
Marine Buyers' Guide—suppliers of pleasure boats.   Started 1961. $7.95.   December.

0186. BOBBIN.
1110 Shop Rd., P.O. Box 1986, Columbia, SC 29202.
Annual Subscription: $18.   **Frequency:** Monthly.
Publisher: Bobbin Publications, Inc.
Advertiser Index: Every issue.
Editorial Index: Semi-Annual. Subject/Title/Author. July (six months)/December (cumulative).
Special Issues:
Bobbin Show Issue. $2.   September.
Management Review. $2.   December.

0187. BODY FASHIONS/INTIMATE APPAREL.
7500 Old Oak Blvd., Middleburg Heights, OH 44130.
Annual Subscription: $16.   **Frequency:** Monthly.
Publisher: Harcourt Brace Jovanovich.
Indexed Online: Trade & Industry Index.
Special Issues:
Market Maker for Fall/Holiday and Spring/Summer markets- for buyers and merchandise managers.   Published as a separate issue.   January/May/October/November.
Directory—U.S. and Canadian manufacturers, product classification, trade name listing.   Started 1913.   Published as a separate issue. $10.   September.

0188. BODY SHOP BUSINESS.
11 South Forge St., Akron, OH 44304.
Annual Subscription: $20.   **Frequency:** Monthly.
Publisher: Babcox Automotive Publications.
Advertiser Index: Every issue.
Editorial Index: Annual. Subject/Title. December.
Special Issues:
Who's Who Directory.   April.

Certification and Training Update. December.

0189. THE BOND BUYER.
One State St. Plaza, New York, NY 10004.
Annual Subscription: $495 (weekly)/$1095 (daily).
Frequency: W and daily.
Publisher: The Bond Buyer, Inc.
Special Issues:
Index to Bonds Proposed and Issued. $5.50. January/April/July/October.
American Bankers Association Investments Conference. $5.50. February.
Dealer Bank Association Investments Conference. $5.50. March.
Mutual Finance Officers Association Conference. $5.50. April.
Pollution Control Federation Conference. $5.50. April.
Directory of Municipal Bond Dealers of the U.S. Published as a separate issue. $60 each/85 combined. Not included in the subscription price. May/October.
Municipal Bond Analysts Association Conference. $5.50. May.
American Public Power Association Conference. $5.50. June.
National Association of Counties. $5.50. June.
Public Securities Association Conference. $5.50. October.
National Association of State Treasurers Conference. $5.50. November.
National League of Cities Conference. $5.50. November.
Council of State Housing Agencies Conference. $5.50. December.

0190. THE BOOKLIST.
50 East Huron St., Chicago, IL 60611.
Annual Subscription: $40. **Frequency:** 23/yr.
Publisher: American Library Association.
Editorial Index: Semi-Annual. Subject/Title/Author. February/August.
Special Issues:
Reviewer's Choice. $2.25. January.
Notable Books—50 outstanding books/Notable Children's Books—selected by ALA Children's Services Division/Basic Books for Young Adults—selected by ALA Young Adult Services Division/Newberry and Caldecott Award Winners. $2.25. March.
Publisher's Spring Announcements. $2.25. March.
Hi-Low Reading. $2.25. April.
Vo-Tech. $2.25. April.
Notable Films, Filmstrips, Recordings. $2.25. May.
Outstanding Reference Books. $2.25. May.
ALA Conference. $2.25. June.
Reference Books Bulletin. $2.25. September.
Best Young Adult Books. $2.25. October.
Publisher's Fall Announcements. $2.25. October.
Audiovisual Showcase. $2.25. November.
Popular Reading. $2.25. December.

0191. BOWLERS JOURNAL.
875 North Michigan Ave., Ste. 1801, Chicago, IL 60611.
Annual Subscription: $15. **Frequency:** Monthly.
Publisher: National Bowlers Journal, Inc.
Advertiser Index: Every issue.
Special Issues:
Annual—special recap of prior year. Started 1978. $3. January.
American Bowling Congress Tournament Issue. Started 1920. $2. February.
Women's International Bowling Congress Issue. Started 1945. $2. March.
Billiard/Bowling Institute Convention Issue. Started 1962. $2. April.
Bowling Proprietors Convention Edition. Started 1933. $2. May.
All-American Team Issue. Started 1938. $2. August.
International Issue. Started 1981. $2. September.

0192. THE BOWLING PROPRIETOR.
615 Six Flags Dr., Arlington, TX 76011.
Annual Subscription: $5. **Frequency:** 11/yr.
Publisher: Bowling Proprietors' Association of America, Inc.
Advertiser Index: Every issue.
Editorial Index: Annual. Subject/Title. January.
Special Issues:
Bowling Proprietors' Association of America Convention and Annual Report. June.

0193. BOXBOARD CONTAINERS.
300 West Adams St., Chicago, IL 60606.
Annual Subscription: $15. **Frequency:** Monthly.
Publisher: Maclean Hunter Publishing Corp.
Advertiser Index: Every issue.
Special Issues:
Boxmakers' Buying Guide. $2. January.

0194. BOXOFFICE.
1020 South Wasbash Ave., Chicago, IL 60605.
Annual Subscription: $25. **Frequency:** Monthly.
Publisher: RLD Communications.
Advertiser Index: Every issue.
Indexed or Abstracted Online: AMI.
Special Issues:
Trade Show Issues. Started Pre-1960. 3/yr. February/May/November.
Barometer Issue—review of prior year's films. Started Pre-1960. April.
Buyer's Directory. Started Pre-1960. August.

0195. BRAKE & FRONT END.
11 South Forge St., Akron, OH 44304.
Annual Subscription: $23. **Frequency:** Monthly.
Publisher: Babcox Publications, Inc.
Advertiser Index: Every issue.
Editorial Index: Annual. Subject. December.
Special Issues:
Buyers' Guide—Brake Parts. $3. August.
Buyers' Guide—Chassis and Suspension Parts. $3. September.
Buyers' Guide—Tools and Equipment. $3. October.

0196. BREWERS DIGEST.
4049 West Peterson Ave., Chicago, IL 60646.
Annual Subscription: $14. **Frequency:** Monthly.
Publisher: Siebel Publishing Co.
Advertiser Index: Every issue.
Editorial Index: Annual. Subject/Title/Author. December.
Indexed or Abstracted Online
Special Issues:
Annual Buyers Guide & Brewery Directory. Started 1926. Published as a separate issue. $8. January.
Point of Purchase—USA Sales Figures. $8. February.
Brewing Chemistry Abstracts/Import Sales. $8. March.
Micro-Brewing/Home Brewing. $8. May.
Plant Equipment/Maintenance & Sanitation. $8. June.
Recycling. $8. July.
Waste Water Treatment. $8. August.
Transportation. $8. September.
Keg Handling/Refrigeration. $8. November.

0197. BRICK AND CLAY RECORD.
1350 East Touhy Ave., P.O. Box 5080, Des Plaines, IL 60018.
Annual Subscription: $15. **Frequency:** Monthly.
Publisher: Cahners Publishing Co.
Indexed Online: Trade & Industry Index.
Special Issues:
Refractories. Started Pre-1976. $3. January.
American Ceramic Society Convention. Started Pre-1976. $3. April.
Annual Industry Forecast. Started Pre-1976. $3. June.
Autoclaymation. Started Pre-1976. $3. September.
Brick Institute of America Convention/Annual Structural Clay Marketing Awards. Started Pre-1976. $3. October.
International Market Outlook. Started Pre-1976. $3. December.

0198. BROADCAST ENGINEERING.
P.O. Box 12901, Overland Park, KS 66212.
Annual Subscription: $25. **Frequency:** Monthly.
Publisher: Intertech Publishing Corp.
Advertiser Index: Every issue.
Special Issues:
  Cable Engineering Demographic Section. Started 1982. $3. 4/yr. February/April/August/November.
  National Association of Broadcasters Convention Preview. Started 1959. $3. March.
  Buyers' Guide Special. Started 1959. $15. September.
  Annual Engineering & Management Salary Survey. Started 1980. $3. October.
  Chinese Language Edition. Started 1981. Published as a separate issue. November.
  Spec Book—radio and TV broadcasting equipment. Started 1982. Published as a separate issue. $15. November.

0199. BROADCAST TECHNOLOGY.
P.O. Box 420, Bolton, Ontario, Can. L0P 1A0.
Annual Subscription: $12. **Frequency:** 6/yr.
Publisher: Diversified Publications Ltd.
Advertiser Index: Every issue.
Special Issues:
  Buyer's Guide. Started 1976. $2. July/August.

0200. BROADCASTER.
7 Labatt Ave., Toronto, Ontario, Can. M5A 3P2.
Annual Subscription: $15. **Frequency:** Monthly.
Publisher: Norther Miner Press.
Advertiser Index: Every issue.
Special Issues:
  Spring and Fall Directories—listing all Canadian radio & television stations, cable companies, video & audio production houses, etc. $7.50. Semianually. May/November.

0201. BROADCASTING.
1735 DeSales St., NW, Washington, DC 20036.
Annual Subscription: $60. **Frequency:** Weekly.
Publisher: Broadcasting Publications, Inc.
Advertiser Index: Every issue.
Editorial Index: Annual. Subject/Title. Irregular.
Indexed or Abstracted Online: Trade & Industry Index; AMI.
Special Issues:
  Annual Special on Baseball. $2. February.
  National Association of Broadcasters Convention. $2. April.
  Broadcast Billings of Top 100 Advertising Agencies. $2. May.
  Awards Issue. $2. July.
  Annual Special on Football. $2. August.
  Broadcasting/Cablecasting Yearbook—radio, TV, cable systems which service U.S. & Canada, including networks, multiple system operators, pay cable services; charges to subscribers; program suppliers; equipment manufacturers; FCC rules; ad agencies for radio & TV; associations; brokers & consultants; engineering consultatns; satellite TV services. Published as a separate issue. $75. Not included in the subscription price. Spring.

0202. BROILER INDUSTRY.
Mt. Morris, IL 61054.
Annual Subscription: $15. **Frequency:** Monthly.
Special Issues:
  Southeastern International Poultry Trade Show. $1.50. January.
  Marketing. $1.50. April/October.
  Broiler Production. $1.50. June.
  Export/Import Opportunities. $1.50. August.
  Top Broiler Companies. $1.50. December.

0203. BRUSHWARE.
5 Willowbrook Ct., Potomac, MD 20854.
Annual Subscription: $15.50. **Frequency:** 6/yr.
Publisher: Centaur Co.
Advertiser Index: Every issue.
Special Issues:
  Buyers Guide and Manufacturers Directory—equipment manufacturers and finished products in the broom, brush and mop industry. $15.50. May/June.

0204. BUILDER.
P.O. Box 1434, Riverton, NJ 08077.
Annual Subscription: $20. **Frequency:** Monthly.
Publisher: Hanley-Wood, Inc.
Advertiser Index: Every issue.
Indexed or Abstracted Online: Architectuaral Index; CIS.
Special Issues:
  Home Buyers Survey. $5. January.
  New Products. $3. February.
  National Association of Home Builders Convention. $3. March.
  Preview—sketches of new, unbuilt projects. Started 1982. $3. March/April.
  Best of the West—gold nugget design award winners. $3. July.
  Builder's Choice—design award winners. Started 1981. $3. October.

0205. BUILDING DESIGN & CONSTRUCTION.
1350 East Touhy Ave., P.O. Box 5080, Des Plaines, IL 60018.
Annual Subscription: $35. **Frequency:** Monthly.
Publisher: Cahners Publishing Co.
Advertiser Index: Irregular.
Indexed Online: Trade & Industry Index.
Special Issues:
  300 Design/Construction Giants. Started 1979. $4. July.
  Annual of Emerging Technology. Started 1982. $4. November.
  300 Owner-Giants. Started 1979. $4. December.

0206. BUILDING GUIDE MAGAZINE.
34 St. Patrick St., Toronto, Ontario, Can. M5T 1V2.
Annual Subscription: $20.50. **Frequency:** 5/yr.
Publisher: Alan Heisey.
Advertiser Index: Every issue.
Special Issues:
  Construction Reference File. February, April, June, October.

0207. BUILDING OPERATING MANAGEMENT.
2100 West Florist Ave., P.O. Box 694, Milwaukee, WI 53201.
Annual Subscription: $20. **Frequency:** Monthly.
Publisher: Trade Press Publishing Co.
Advertiser Index: Every issue.
Editorial Index: Annual. Subject/Title. December.
Special Issues:
  The Building Envelope. $2. January.
  Public Areas. $2. February.
  Energy Management. $2. March.
  Building Maintenance. $2. April.
  Lighting. $2. May.
  Building Owners and Managers Association Convention/Office Design. $2. June.
  Contract Services. $2. July.
  Safety/Security. $2. August.
  Remodeling. $2. September.
  Energy Loss Control. $2. October.
  Building Interiors. $2. November.
  Mechanical/Electrical Systems. $2. December.

0208. BUILDING SERVICES CONTRACTOR.
101 West 31 St., New York, NY 10001.
Annual Subscription: $12. **Frequency:** Bimonthly.
Publisher: MacNair-Dorland Co.
Advertiser Index: Every issue.
Editorial Index: Annual. Title. December.
Special Issues:
  BSCA Convention Issue—Building Services Contractors Ass'n. $3. April.
  Advances in Cleaning Technology. $3. June.
  Grounds Maintenance—including parking lots. $3. August.

Buyers Guide—products, services, equipment. $3. December.

0209. BUILDING SUPPLY AND HOME CENTERS.
5 South Wabash Ave., Chicago, IL 60603.
Annual Subscription: $35. **Frequency:** Monthly.
Publisher: Cahners Publishing Co.
Advertiser Index: Every issue.
Indexed Online: Trade & Industry Index.
Special Issues:
Do-It-Yourself Home Center Catalog.   Started 1977.   February.
New Products.   February.
Awards Issue: Retailer of the Year.   Started 1976.   June.
Drummer Awards.   July.
Buyers Guide.   November.

0210. BUILDINGS: THE FACILITIES CONSTRUCTION AND MANAGEMENT MAGAZINE.
427 Sixth Ave. SE, P.O. Box 1888, Cedar Rapids, IA 52906.
Annual Subscription: $25.   **Frequency:** Monthly.
Publisher: Stamats Communications, Inc.
Advertiser Index: Every issue.
Editorial Index: Annual. Subject. December.
Special Issues:
Forecast. $2.50.   January.
Interiors. $2.50.   March.
Life Safety/Security. $2.50.   May.
Modernization. $2.50.   June.
Open Office. $2.50.   August.
Buildings Census—Listing of top readers. $2.50. September.
Energy. $2.50.   November.

0211. BULLETIN OF THE AMERICAN METEOROLOGICAL SOCIETY.
45 Beacon St., Boston, MA 02108.
Annual Subscription: $60.   **Frequency:** Monthly.
Publisher: American Meteorological Society.
Advertiser Index: Every issue.
Editorial Index: Annual. Subject/Author. December.
Abstracted Online: MGA.
Special Issues:
Annual Index.   Started 1920. $15.   December.

0212. BULLETIN OF THE MEDICAL LIBRARY ASSOCIATION.
919 North Michigan Ave., Ste. 3208, Chicago, IL 60611.
Annual Subscription: $45.   **Frequency:** Quarterly.
Publisher: Medical Library Association.
Advertiser Index: Every issue.
Editorial Index: Annual. Subject/Title/Author. October.
Indexed or Abstracted Online: Medline; LISA.
Special Issues:
Association Record: Annual Meeting Proceedings.   January.
Association Record: Roster of Officers & Committees. October.

0213. BULLETIN OF THE NEW YORK ACADEMY OF MEDICINE.
2 East 103rd St., New York, NY 10029.
Annual Subscription: $18.   **Frequency:** 10/yr.
Publisher: The New York Academy of Medicine.
Editorial Index: Annual. Title/Author. December.

0214. BUS & TRUCK TRANSPORT.
Box 9100, Postal Station A, Toronto, Ontario, Can. M5W 1Y5.
Annual Subscription: $20.   **Frequency:** Monthly.
Publisher: Maclean Hunter Ltd.
Advertiser Index: Every issue.
Special Issues:
Canadian Special Truck Equipment Manual.   Started 1974. Published as a separate issue. $11.   Not included in the subscription price.   January.

0215. BUSINESS AMERICA.
Superintendent of Documents, U.S. Government of Printing Office, Washington, DC 20402.
Annual Subscription: $55.   **Frequency:** 26/year.
Publisher: International Trade Administration.
Editorial Index: Annual. Subject/Title. January.
Indexed or Abstracted Online: Trade & Industry Index; Magazine Index; Predicasts.
Special Issues:
World Trade Outlook. $3.25.   February/August.
World Trade Week. $3.25.   May.
Trade Fairs Around the World. $3.25.   November.
World Commercial Holiday Calendar. $3.25.   December.

0216. BUSINESS AND COMMERCIAL AVIATION.
One Park Ave., New York, NY 10016.
Annual Subscription: $30.   **Frequency:** Monthly.
Publisher: Ziff-Davis Publishing Co.
Advertiser Index: Every issue.
Special Issues:
Planning and Purchasing Handbook.   Started 1958. $6. April.
Salary Survey.   Started 1974. $3.50.   September.
Fortune 1000 Corporate Aircraft Survey.   Started 1973. $3.50.   December.

0217. BUSINESS AND SOCIETY REVIEW.
210 South St., Boston, MA 02111.
Annual Subscription: $56.   **Frequency:** Quarterly.
Publisher: Warren, Gorham & Lamont.
Indexed or Abstracted Online: ABI/Inform; Trade & Industry Index; Management Contents; Legal Resource Index.
Special Issues:
Black Corporate Directors Directory.   Fall.

0218. BUSINESS COMMUNICATIONS REVIEW.
950 York Rd., Hinsdale, IL 60521.
Annual Subscription: $78.   **Frequency:** 6/yr.
Publisher: BCR Enterprises Inc.
Editorial Index: Annual. Subject/Title. November.

0219. BUSINESS ECONOMICS.
28349 Chagrin Blvd., Cleveland, OH 44122.
Annual Subscription: $20.   **Frequency:** Quarterly.
Publisher: National Association of Business Economists.
Special Issues:
Membership Directory. $8.   March.

0220. BUSINESS FORMS & SYSTEMS.
401 North Broad St., Philadelphia, PA 19108.
Annual Subscription: $43.   **Frequency:** Monthly.
Publisher: North American Publishing Co.
Advertiser Index: Every issue.
Special Issues:
Business Forms Man of the Year.   January or February.
National Business Forms Association (NBFA) Award Winners. January.
Business Forms Trends and Projections—from U.S. Industrial Outlook SIC 2761.   March.
International Business Forms Industries Convention.   April.
National Business Forms Association Convention.   October.
Directory of Forms Manufacturers and Supplies.   Started 1982. $25.   December.

0221. BUSINESS HISTORY REVIEW.
D-126 Gallatin Hall, Soldiers Field, Boston, MA 02163.
Annual Subscription: $25.   **Frequency:** Quarterly.
Publisher: Harvard University, Graduate School of Business Administration.
Editorial Index: Annual. Subject/Title/Author. Winter; 5-year Cumulative Indexes in 1966, 1971, 1976, 1981.
Indexed Online: Trade & Industry Index; Management Contents.

0222. BUSINESS HORIZONS.
School of Business, Bloomington, IN 47405.
Annual Subscription: $15.   **Frequency:** 6/yr.
Publisher: Graduate School of Business.
Editorial Index: Annual & Bimonthly. Subject/Author. Cumulative to date in each issue; full volume index in November/December.

Indexed or Abstracted Online: ABI/Inform; Magazine Index; Trade & Industry Index; Management Contents.

0223. BUSINESS INSURANCE.
740 Rush St., Chicago, IL 60611.
Annual Subscription: $40. **Frequency:** Weekly.
Publisher: Crain Communications Inc.
Editorial Index: Annual. Subject/Title/Author. March/June/September/December.
Indexed Online: Trade & Industry Index.
Special Issues:
Market Preview/Info for Buyers. $1. January.
Risk Management Services. $1. February.
Employee Benefits. $1. March, June, September, December.
Agent/Broker Profiles—includes 20 largest brokers. $1. June.
Excess/Surplus Lines—financial report. $1. July.
Marine/Aviation Insurance. $1. September.
International Risk Management/Insurance. $1. November.

0224. BUSINESS MARKETING.
740 North Rush, Chicago, IL 60611.
Annual Subscription: $20. **Frequency:** Monthly.
Publisher: Crain Communications.
Advertiser Index: Every issue.
Indexed or Abstracted Online: PTS/Prompt; AMI; Management Contents; Trade & Industry Index; NEXIS.
Special Issues:
Advertising Readership Studies by Business Publications. Started 1947. $3. January/April/July/October.
Annual Survey of Advertising Budgets/Best Ad of the Year. $3. January.
Advertising Volume Statistics for Business Publications. Started 1933. $3. February/May/August/November.
Special Issues in Business Publications. Started 1950. $3. March/June/September/November.
Best Trade Show Exhibit of the Year. $3. April.
Annual Report on Buying Trends at Trade Shows. $3. May.
100 Largest Business Advertisers; Update. Started 1981. $3. May and October.
Business/Industrial Ad Agency Roster. Started 1981. $3. September.
Forecast for Advertising Page Volume and Revenues. $3. December.

0225. BUSINESS REVIEW—FEDERAL RESERVE BANK OF PHILADELPHIA.
100 North 6th St., Philadelphia, PA 19106.
Annual Subscription: Free. **Frequency:** 6/yr.
Publisher: Federal Reserve Bank of Philadelphia.
Editorial Index: Annual. Title/Author. November/December.
Indexed Online: Predicasts.

0226. BUSINESS WEEK.
1221 Ave. of the Americas, New York, NY 10020.
Annual Subscription: $39.95. **Frequency:** Weekly.
Publisher: McGraw-Hill, Inc.
Special Issues:
Industry Outlooks — includes basic manufacturing, natural resources, high technology, food & services. $2. January.
World Economic Outlook: The Industrial Nations. $2. February/August.
Corporate Scoreboard—lists companies in key industries; March issue includes 4th quarter and yearly totals. $2. March/May/August/November.
Liquor Sales by Brands. $2. March.
Bank Scoreboard—top 200 banks ranked by assets. Started 1973. $2. April.
Executive Compensation Survey—top 25 highest paid executives; also listing by industry identifying top executives in over 36 industries. $2. May.
Inflation Scoreboard—reported & inflation adjusted earnings for over 500 largest U.S. industrial companies by industry. Started 1981. $2. May.
R&D Scoreboard—includes companies in 31 industries; also top 15 companies by total dollars; percent of roles; and dollars spent per employee. $2. June.
International Corporate Scoreboard—sales & earnings by country for over 900 public, private and state owned companies in 57 countries; also Top 20 non U.S. companies. Started 1973. $2. July.
World Economic Outlook: Third World Countries. $2. November.
Corporate Balance Sheet Scoreboard—covers almost 900 largest U.S. nonfinancial & industrial companies ranked by assets in 36 key industries. $2. Irregularly. Approximately every 18 months.
Investment Outlook—year end double issue; includes articles; economic forecasts; and forecasts for earnings per share for almost 900 companies. $2. Last December or first January.

0227. BUTANE-PROPANE NEWS.
P.O. Box 419, Arcadia, CA 91006.
Annual Subscription: $10. **Frequency:** Monthly.
Publisher: Same.
Advertiser Index: Every issue.
Editorial Index: Annual. Subject/Title. December.

0228. BYTE.
70 Main St., Peterborough, NH 03458.
Annual Subscription: $21. **Frequency:** Monthly.
Publisher: McGraw-Hill, Inc.
Advertiser Index: Every issue.
Editorial Index: Annual. Subject.
Abstracted Online: NEXIS.
Special Issues:
Benchmarks. February.
Simulation. March.
Real World Interfacing. April.
Professional Computing. May.
Education. June.
Graphics. September.
Mass Storage. October.
New Chips. November.
Communications. December.

0229. CEE/CONTRACTORS' ELECTRICAL EQUIPMENT.
707 Westchester Ave., White Plains, NY
Annual Subscription: Free. **Frequency:** 13/yr.
Publisher: Sutton Publishing Co.
Advertiser Index: Every issue.
Special Issues:
Instrumentation and Controls. January.
Switchgear and Distribution Equipment. February.
Electrical Systems in Industry. March.
Lighting: Commercial and Industrial. April.
Electrical Comfort Conditioning. May.
The Electrical Consultant: Impact/Interface. June.
Energy Management Systems and Devices. July.
Electrical Construction Tools. August.
Emergency/Security Systems. September.
PRI—Product Reference Issue (Directory). Published as a separate issue. $20. Not included in the subscription price. September.
NECA Show Issue and Show Book. October.
Modern Office Wiring. November.
Power Sources and Controls. December.

0230. CIM BULLETIN.
1130 Sherbrooke St. W., Ste. 400, Montreal, Quebec, Can. H3A 2MB.
Annual Subscription: $50/65. **Frequency:** Monthly.
Publisher: Canadian Institute of Mining & Technology.
Advertiser Index: Every issue.
Special Issues:
Underground Mining Conference. January.
Mine Safety. February.
Annual General Meeting. March.
Mineral Exploration. April.
Conference of Metallurgists. June.

Directory. Published as a separate issue. $75. Not included in the subscription price. June.
Open Pit Mining. July.
Manpower Training and Computer Technology. November.
Equipment and Maintenance Special. December.

0231. CIPS REVIEW/LA REVUE ACI.
243 College St., Toronto, Ontario, Can. M5T 2Y1.
Annual Subscription: $25. **Frequency:** 6/yr.
Publisher: Canadian Information Processing Society.
Advertiser Index: Every issue.
Special Issues:
Annual Canadian Computer Census—lists all hardware installations by corporations, by province and city. Published as a separate issue. $25. March.
CIPS Conference Preview. March/April.
Canadian Computer Show Preview. September/October.

0232. THE CPA JOURNAL.
600 Third Ave., New York, NY 10016.
Annual Subscription: $20. **Frequency:** Monthly.
Publisher: New York State Society of CPA's.
Advertiser Index: Every issue.
Editorial Index: Annual. Title/Author. December.

0233. CPCU JOURNAL.
Kahler Hall, Providence Rd., Malvern, PA 19355.
Annual Subscription: $12. **Frequency:** Quarterly.
Publisher: Society of Chartered Property and Casualty Underwriters.
Editorial Index: Annual. Subject/Title/Author. March.
Abstracted Online: ABI/Inform; Insurance Abstracts.

0234. CA MAGAZINE.
150 Bloor St., West, Toronto, Ontario, Can. M5S 2Y2.
Annual Subscription: $20. **Frequency:** Monthly.
Publisher: Canadian Institute of Chartered Accountants.
Advertiser Index: August.
Editorial Index: Subject/Author. December.
Indexed or Abstracted Online: ABI/Inform.
Special Issues:
Machines & Management—EDP, office equipment & systems, state-of-the-art technology for accountants. Started 1978. $3.50/2.50. August.

0235. CABLE COMMUNICATIONS MAGAZINE (CCM).
4 Smetana Dr., Kitchener, Ontario, Can. N2B 3B8.
Annual Subscription: $24. **Frequency:** Monthly.
Publisher: Same.
Advertiser Index: Every issue.
Editorial Index: Annual. Subject. November.
Special Issues:
Annual Buyer's Guide. Started 1958. March.
Canadian Cable Television Association Convention Issue. Started 1958. May.
Convention Report Issue. Started 1958. July.
Who's Who Handbook & Trade Directory. Started 1958. November.
Review/Forecast Issue. Started 1958. December.

0236. CABLE TECH.
P.O. Box 27277, Denver, CO 80227.
Annual Subscription: $10. **Frequency:** 6/yr.
Publisher: National Cable Television Institute.
Special Issues:
National Cable Television Association Convention Issue. May.
Western CATV Convention Issue. November.

0237. CABLEVISION.
2500 Curtis St., Denver, CO 80205.
Annual Subscription: $64. **Frequency:** Weekly.
Publisher: Titsch Communications.
Advertiser Index: Every issue.
Indexed or Abstracted Online: AMI.
Special Issues:
Construction Forecast. Started 1976. $3. January.
Contractors Callbook—directory of contractors for installation and other services to industry. Started 1983. $3. March.
National Cable Television Association Convention. $3. June.

0238. CAMPING CANADA.
3414 Park Ave., Ste. 221, Montreal, Quebec, Can. H2X 2H5.
Annual Subscription: $9. **Frequency:** 6/yr.
Publisher: CRV Publications Ltd.
Advertiser Index: Every issue.
Special Issues:
Motorcycle Buyer's Guide. Started 1975. Published as a separate issue. $2.50. Not included in the subscription price. March.
Camping and RV Guide to Canada. Started 1971. $3.50. April.

0239. CAMPING MAGAZINE.
Bradford Woods, Martinsville, IN 46151.
Annual Subscription: $15. **Frequency:** 7/yr.
Publisher: American Camping Association.
Advertiser Index: Every issue.
Editorial Index: Annual. Subject/Title/Author. May.
Indexed Online: Magazine Index.
Special Issues:
Parents Guide to Accredited Camps. Published as a separate issue. $5.95 (non-subscriber); $4.00 (subscriber). Not included in the subscription price. January.

0240. CANADA POULTRYMAN.
605 Royal Ave., New Westminster, British Columbia, Can. V3M 1J4.
Annual Subscription: $12.
Publisher: Same.
Advertiser Index: Every issue.
Special Issues:
Canada's Who's Who of the Poultry Industry. Started 1965. June.

0241. CANADIAN AIRCRAFT OPERATOR.
Streetsville Postal Station, P.O. Box 669, Mississauga, Ontario, Can. L5M 2C2.
Annual Subscription: $15/13. **Frequency:** 24/yr.
Publisher: Canadian Aircraft Operator Publishing Ltd.
Special Issues:
Commercial Aviation Review. November.

0242. CANADIAN ARCHITECT.
1450 Don Mills Rd., Don Mills, Ontario, Can. M3B 2X7.
Annual Subscription: $15. **Frequency:** Monthly.
Publisher: Southam Communications Ltd.
Advertiser Index: Every issue.
Special Issues:
Yardsticks for Costing. Published as a separate issue. $85. Not included in the subscription price. July.
Yearbook. $2. December.

0243. CANADIAN AUTOMOTIVE TRADE.
777 Bay St., Toronto, Ontario, Can. M5W 1A7.
Annual Subscription: $50/23. **Frequency:** 6/yr.
Publisher: Maclean Hunter Ltd.
Advertiser Index: Every issue.
Special Issues:
Tool & Equipment Buyers' Guide. Started 1975. $6. January.
New Car Showcase. $6. September.
Aftermarket Forecast. $6. December.
Automotive Service Data Book—total specifications for all cars available in Canada for five years previous to issue date. Started 1960. Published as a separate issue. $25. Not included in the subscription price. December.

0244. CANADIAN AVIATION.
Box 9100, Station A, Toronto, Ontario, Can. M5W 1V5.
Annual Subscription: $30/19. **Frequency:** Monthly.
Publisher: Maclean Hunter Ltd.
Advertiser Index: Every issue.

Special Issues:
  Aircraft Buyers Guide.   Started 1968. $1.75.   February.
  Aviation Directory of Canada.   Started 1949. $5.   April.
  Avionics Buyers Guide.   Started 1970. $1.75.   July.
  Corporate/Business Aviation in Canada. $1.75.   October.
  Update on Commercial Aviation. $1.75.   November.

0245. CANADIAN BANKER & ICB REVIEW.
T-D Centre, P.O. Box 282, Toronto, Ontario, Can. M5K 1K2.
Annual Subscription: $18. **Frequency:** Every 2 mos.
Publisher: The Canadian Bankers' Association.
Advertiser Index: Every issue.
Editorial Index: Annual. Subject/Title/Author. June.
Special Issues:
  Agricultural Credit Issue.   Started 1978. $3.   August.

0246. CANADIAN BEVERAGE REVIEW.
106 Lakeshore Rd. E., Ste. 209, Port Credit, Ontario, Can. L5G 1E3.
Annual Subscription: $25. **Frequency:** 6/yr.
Publisher: Naef Publishing Ltd.
Advertiser Index: Every issue.
Special Issues:
  Buyers Guide Directory—Canadian, U.S. and overseas manufacturers and suppliers. $5.   January.
  Mineral Water Issue—company directory. $2.   March.
  Brewery Issue—statistics. $2.   May.
  Canadian Soft Drink Association Convention/Soft Drinks. $2.   July.
  Distillery Issue—statistics. $2.   October.
  Winery Issue. $2.   November.

0247. CANADIAN BOATING.
5200 Dixie Rd., #204, Mississauga, Ontario, Can. L4W 1E4.
Annual Subscription: $10. **Frequency:** 8/yr.
Publisher: Arthurs Publications Ltd.
Special Issues:
  Buyers Guide.   October.

0248. CANADIAN BUILDING.
777 Bay St., Toronto, Ontario, Can. M5W 1A7.
Annual Subscription: $50/23. **Frequency:** 10/yr.
Publisher: Maclean Hunter Ltd.
Advertiser Index: Every issue.
Special Issues:
  Industry Spending Plans.   Started 1968. $7.   June.
  Real Estate Development Annual—membership listings (10,000 names), financial reports.   Started 1965. Published as a separate issue. $40.   Not included in the subscription price.   September.

0249. CANADIAN BUSINESS.
70 The Esplanade, Toronto, Ontario, Can. M5E 1R2.
Annual Subscription: $30/18.
Publisher: C B Media Ltd.
Advertiser Index: Every issue.
Indexed or Abstracted Online: ABI/Inform; Magazine Index.
Special Issues:
  Personal Finance.   January.
  International Business.   February.
  Information Technology.   March, June, September, November.
  Banking & Finance.   April.
  Small Business Source Book.   May.
  Top 500 Canadian Companies/Annual Reports.   July.
  Executive Guide.   August.
  Small Business Finance.   October.
  Industrial Locations Guide.   December.

0250. CANADIAN CHEMICAL PROCESSING.
1450 Don Mills Rd., Don Mills, Ontario, Can. M3B 2X7.
Annual Subscription: $33. **Frequency:** Every 6 weeks.
Publisher: Southam Communications Ltd.
Advertiser Index: Every issue.
Special Issues:
  Equipment Buyers Guide.   July.
  Chemical Buyers Guide.   December.

0251. CANADIAN CLAY & CERAMICS QUARTERLY.
2175 Sheppard Ave. E., Suite 110, Willowdale, Ontario, , Can. M2J 1W8.
Annual Subscription: $12; $10. **Frequency:** Quarterly.
Publisher: Harold L. Taylor Enterprises.
Advertiser Index: Every issue.
Special Issues:
  Roster Issue.   March.
  Directory and Buyers Guide.   June.
  Convention Issue.   December.

0252. CANADIAN CLINICAL LABORATORY.
777 Bay St., Toronto, Ontario, Can. M5W 1A7.
Annual Subscription: $11. **Frequency:** Quarterly.
Publisher: Maclean Hunter Ltd.
Advertiser Index: Every issue.
Special Issues:
  Laboratory Reference Guide.   Started 1980.   February.

0253. CANADIAN CONSULTING ENGINEER.
1450 Don Mills Rd., Don Mills, Ontario, Can. M3B 2X7.
Annual Subscription: $36.00/26.50. **Frequency:** Monthly.
Publisher: Southam Communications Ltd.
Advertiser Index: Every issue.
Editorial Index: Annual. Subject/Title/Author. December.
Special Issues:
  Annual Awards Issue.   Started 1966. $2.   October.
  CAD Systems & Software Survey. $2.   December.

0254. CANADIAN CONTROLS & INSTRUMENTS.
777 Bay St., Toronto, Ontario, Can. M5W 1A7.
Annual Subscription: $47/21. **Frequency:** 6/yr.
Publisher: Maclean Hunter Ltd.
Advertiser Index: Every issue.
Special Issues:
  Valve Selection Guide, with Canadian Suppliers. $8.   April.
  Controls & Instruments Buyers Guide.   Started 1960. $18.   August.

0255. CANADIAN DATASYSTEMS.
777 Bay St., Toronto, Ontario, Can. M5W 1A7.
Annual Subscription: $60/26. **Frequency:** Monthly.
Publisher: Maclean Hunter Ltd.
Advertiser Index: Every issue.
Editorial Index: Annual. Subject/Title. January.
Special Issues:
  Directory Issue—DP equipment, suppliers, service organizations (hardware and software). $20.   January.
  Show Preview: Canadian Computer Show. $5.   October.

0256. CANADIAN DRIVER/OWNER.
P.O. Box 9100, Postal Station A, Toronto, Ontario, Can. M5W I4S.
Annual Subscription: $15. **Frequency:** Bimonthly.
Publisher: Maclean Hunter Ltd.
Advertiser Index: Every issue.
Special Issues:
  Anaheim International Truck Show. $3.50 (U.S.)/1.50 (Can.).   May/June.

0257. CANADIAN ELECTRONICS ENGINEERING.
777 Bay St., Toronto, Ontario, Can. M5W 1A7.
Annual Subscription: $25/22. **Frequency:** Monthly.
Publisher: Maclean Hunter Ltd.
Advertiser Index: Every issue.
Editorial Index: Annual. Subject. December.
Special Issues:
  Canada and the World of Electronics.   Started 1980. Published as a separate issue. $25.   Not included in the subscription price.   January.
  CEE Electronics Directory and Buyers Guide.   Started 1955. $10.   July.

0258. CANADIAN FLORIST, GREENHOUSE & NURSERY.
1090 Aerowood Dr., Unit 1, Mississauga, Ontario, Can. L5L 1J9.
Annual Subscription: $12 (Can.); $18 (U.S.). **Frequency:**

Monthly.
Publisher: Heywood Publications Ltd.
Advertiser Index: Every issue.
Special Issues:
  Annual Buyers' Guide.   Started 1980. $15.   September.
  Canadian Greenhouse Conference Issue.   Started 1980. $1.50.   October.

0259. CANADIAN FOOTWARE JOURNAL.
1450 Don Mills Rd., Don Mills, Ontario, Can. M3B 2X7.
Annual Subscription: $24/18.   **Frequency:** 9/yr.
Publisher: Southern Business Publications.
Advertiser Index: Every issue.
Special Issues:
  Directory of Shoe Manufacturers. $2.   February/March.
  Shoemaking Directory. $2.   November.

0260. CANADIAN FOREST INDUSTRIES.
1450 Don Mills Rd., Don Mills, Ontario, Can. M3B 2X7.
Annual Subscription: $39.50/30.00.   **Frequency:** Monthly.
Publisher: Southam Communications Ltd.
Advertiser Index: Every issue.
Editorial Index: Annual. Subject/Title. December or January.
Special Issues:
  Annual Buyers Guide.   July.
  Forest Industries Equipment Exhibition Preview.   August.
  Capital Expenditures & Budgets.   September.
  Mill Automation.   November.
  Year-End Literature Review.   December.

0261. THE CANADIAN FRUITGROWER.
222 Argyle Ave., Delhi, Ontario, Can. N4B 2W9.
Annual Subscription: $4.   **Frequency:** 9/yr.
Special Issues:
  Mechanization. $.75.   February.
  Chemicals. $.75.   November.

0262. CANADIAN GROCER.
777 Bay St., Maclean Hunter Building, Toronto, Ontario, Can. M5W 1A7.
Annual Subscription: $26.   **Frequency:** Monthly.
Publisher: Maclean Hunter Ltd.
Advertiser Index: Every issue.
Special Issues:
  Food Broker Directory & Market Facts—lists Canadian food brokers, brand directory, and Canadian retail food statistics by cities and provinces. $15.   February.
  Survey of Chains & Groups—directory of all major Canadian retail food chains and voluntary groups with key personnel, stores served, etc. $12.   August.

0263. CANADIAN HOTEL & RESTAURANT.
777 Bay St., Toronto, Ontario, Can. M5W 1A7.
Annual Subscription: $27/24.   **Frequency:** Monthly.
Publisher: Maclean Hunter Ltd.
Advertiser Index: Every issue.
Special Issues:
  Fall Market Report. $6.   October.
  Directory—industry suppliers, products and services; associations. $10.   November.

0264. CANADIAN INDUSTRIAL EQUIPMENT NEWS.
1450 Don Mills Rd., Don Mills, Ontario, Can. M3B 2X7.
Annual Subscription: $30/56.   **Frequency:** Monthly.
Publisher: Southam Communications Ltd.
Advertiser Index: Every issue.
Special Issues:
  Industrial Literature Review.   Started 1973. $3.50.   Semi-annually.   March/October.

0265. CANADIAN INSURANCE.
100 Simcoe St., Toronto, Ontario, Can. M5H 3G2.
Annual Subscription: $12.   **Frequency:** 13/yr.
Publisher: Stone & Cox Ltd.
Advertiser Index: Every issue.
Special Issues:
  Computers and Automation.   Started 1977.   January.
  Marine Insurance.   Started 1975.   February.
  Surety.   Started 1978.   March.
  Adjusting & Claims Management.   Started 1976.   May.
  Statistical Issue.   Started 1930.   May.
  Reinsurance.   Started 1975.   July.
  Office Management.   Started 1978.   September.
  I.B.A.O. Convention.   Started 1920.   November.

0266. CANADIAN INTERIORS.
777 Bay St., Toronto, Ontario, Can. M5W 1A7.
Annual Subscription: $50/24.   **Frequency:** 8/yr.
Publisher: Maclean Hunter Ltd.
Advertiser Index: Every issue.
Editorial Index: Subject. November/December.
Special Issues:
  CI Product Finder. $5.   January/February, April, July/August, October.
  NEOCON Preview (contract furniture show). $5.   May/June.
  CI Sources Directory—suppliers in contract design industry. $12.   July/August.

0267. CANADIAN JEWELLER.
Box 9100, Station A, Toronto, Ontario, Can. M5W 1V5.
Annual Subscription: $50/23.   **Frequency:** Monthly.
Publisher: Maclean Hunter Ltd.
Advertiser Index: Every issue.
Special Issues:
  Jewelry Shows Issue (6 Canadian Shows). $5.   June.
  Annual Directory. $15.   December.

0268. CANADIAN MACHINERY & METALWORKING.
777 Bay St., Toronto, Ontario, Can. M5W 1A7.
Annual Subscription: $24/22.   **Frequency:** Monthly.
Publisher: MacLean Hunter Ltd.
Advertiser Index: Every issue.
Editorial Index: Annual. Subject. December.
Special Issues:
  Industrial Surface Finishing.   Started 1981. $10.   February/May/August/November.
  Annual Computer Numerical Control Census.   Started 1963. $10.   March.
  Hi-Tech Engineering & Manufacturing.   Started 1983. $10.   March/June/September/November.
  Annual National Productivity Awards Issue.   Started 1982. $10.   June.
  Annual Metalworking Directory & Buying Guide.   Started 1925. $15.   December.

0269. CANADIAN MINING JOURNAL.
1450 Don Mills Rd., Don Mills, Ontario, Can. M3B 2X7.
Annual Subscription: $65.00/31.75.   **Frequency:** Monthly.
Publisher: Southam Business Publications Ltd.
Advertiser Index: Every issue.
Editorial Index: Annual. Subject/Title/Author. December.
Special Issues:
  Reference Manual & Buyers Guide.   Published as a separate issue. $65/40.   Not included in the subscription price.   October.

0270. CANADIAN OFFICE.
P.O. Box 190, Harbour Centre, Ontario, Can. L5G 4L7.
Annual Subscription: $20.   **Frequency:** Monthly.
Publisher: Whitsed Publishing Ltd.
Special Issues:
  Redbook Buyers Guide to Office Equipment & Supplies. $2.50.   June/July.
  Communications Update & Forecast. $2.50.   December.

0271. CANADIAN OFFICE PRODUCTS & STATIONERY.
1450 Don Mills Rd., Don Mills, Ontario, Can. M3B 2X7.
Annual Subscription: $26.50/20.50.   **Frequency:** 6/yr.
Publisher: Southam Communications Ltd.
Advertiser Index: Every issue.
Special Issues:
  Forecast.   January/February.
  New Products.   September/October.
  Dealers Guide/Literature Review.   November/December.

0272. CANADIAN PACKAGING.
777 Bay St., Toronto, Ontario, Can. M5W 1A7.
Annual Subscription: $35/23. **Frequency:** 11/yr.
Publisher: MacLean Hunter Ltd.
Advertiser Index: Every issue.
Editorial Index: Title/Author. December.
Special Issues:
 Package Machinery Specifications & Directory. $15. January.
 Package Printing. February.
 Bottling. March.
 Flexible Packaging. April.
 Industrial Packaging. May.
 Pilfer-proof Packaging. June.
 Buyers' Guide and Directory. $15. July/August.
 PACK-EX Pre-Show Issue. September.
 Labeling/Coding & Marking. October.
 Converting & Boxmaking/Adhesives. November.
 Protective & Transit Packaging/Palletizing. December.

0273. CANADIAN PETROLEUM.
1201 5th St. SW, Ste. 200, Calgary, Alberta, Can. T2R 1L1.
Annual Subscription: $26.50/36.00. **Frequency:** 10/yr.
Publisher: Southam Communications Ltd.
Special Issues:
 Petrochemicals/Well Completions Statistical Report. January/February.
 Pipelines. March.
 Offshore Forecasts — Nova Scotia. April.
 Heavy Oil/Oil Sands. May.
 Petrochemical Processing Exhibition Showguide. Published as a separate issue. May.
 Audit of Industry Performance/Capital Spending. June.
 Annual Petrochemical Census. Started 1959. July.
 Canadian Offshore Resources Exposition/East Coast exploration. July.
 Drilling Activity/rig fleets. August.
 Annual Refining Census, Capital Spending and Manpower Reports/Energy Pricing Report. September.
 Canadian Oil Register. Published as a separate issue. $85. Not included in the subscription price. Annual. October.
 Computers, Instruments and Controls—annual review. Started 1982. October.
 Natural Gas Report/Geophysical Review. October.
 Finance and Government Regulations. November/December.

0274. CANADIAN PLASTICS.
1450 Don Mills Rd., Don Mills, Ontario, Can. M3B 2X7.
Annual Subscription: $36.00/26.50. **Frequency:** 9/yr.
Publisher: Southam Communications Limited.
Advertiser Index: Every issue.
Special Issues:
 Canadian Plastics Industry Outlook. January/February.
 Plastics Additives. April.
 Canadian Exports of Plastics Products, Resins, Machinery, Molds. June.
 Canadian Plastics Anniversary Issue. Started 1943. July/August.
 Plastics Industry in Quebec. September.
 Canadian Plastics Directory and Buyers Guide—processors, processes, products; materials and machinery suppliers; mold, tool & die makers; trade names; associations, consultants and government. Started 1960. Published as a separate issue. $25. December.

0275. CANADIAN POOL & SPA MARKETING.
Station Q, P.O. Box 282, Toronto, Ontario, Can. M4T 2M1.
Annual Subscription: $10. **Frequency:** 6/yr.
Publisher: Hubbard Marketing & Publishing Ltd.
Advertiser Index: Every issue.
Special Issues:
 Statistical Issue Special. Started 1979. $2. February.
 Hot Water Trade Directory. Started 1982. Published as a separate issue. $3. April.
 Special Technical Reprint Issue. Started 1981. Published as a separate issue. $3. June.
 Buyer's Digest and Trade Directory. Started 1979. $2. December.

0276. CANADIAN PRINTER AND PUBLISHER.
777 Bay St., Toronto, Ontario, Can. M5W 1A7.
Annual Subscription: $42/25. **Frequency:** Monthly.
Publisher: Maclean Hunter Ltd.
Special Issues:
 Buyers Guide & Directory. $15. March.
 Specifications: Film Processors. $6. September.
 Specifications: Typesetting Equipment/Printing Product Guide. $6. November.

0277. CANADIAN RENTAL SERVICE.
P.O. Box 247, Station A, Weston, Ontario, Can. M9N 3M7.
Annual Subscription: $18/9. **Frequency:** 6/yr.
Publisher: J. Peter Watkins Ltd.
Special Issues:
 Directory of Rental Goods Services. $2. April.
 Rental Mart Pre-Show Issue. $2. December.

0278. CANADIAN RESEARCH.
777 Bay St., Toronto, Ontario, Can. M5W 1A7.
Annual Subscription: $64/24. **Frequency:** 8/yr.
Publisher: Maclean Hunter Ltd.
Advertiser Index: Every issue.
Special Issues:
 Canadian Laboratory Reference Guide. Started 1980. February.

0279. CANADIAN SECRETARY.
777 Bay St., Toronto, Ontario, Can. M5W 1A7.
Annual Subscription: $8/7. **Frequency:** Quarterly.
Publisher: Maclean Hunter Ltd.
Special Issues:
 Typewriters. September.
 Communications/Information Delivery. November.

0280. CANADIAN SHIPPING AND MARINE ENGINEERING.
5200 Dixie Rd., Ste. 204, Mississauga, Ontario, Can. L4W 1E4.
Annual Subscription: $40/25. **Frequency:** Monthly.
Publisher: Arthurs Publications Ltd.
Advertiser Index: Every issue.
Abstracted Online
Special Issues:
 Offshore Buyer's Directory. Started 1982. $20. June.
 Marine Buyer's Directory. Started 1956. $20. December.

0281. CANADIAN TEXTILE JOURNAL.
4920 de Maisonneuve Blvd. W., Ste. 307, Montreal, Quebec, Can. H3Z 1N1.
Annual Subscription: $35 (U.S.). **Frequency:** Monthly.
Publisher: Canadian Textile Journals, Inc.
Advertiser Index: Every issue.
Special Issues:
 Manual of the Textile Industry of Canada. Published as a separate issue. $30. May.

0282. CANADIAN TRANSPORTATION & DISTRIBUTION MANAGEMENT.
1450 Don Mills Rd., Don Mills, Ontario, Can. M3B 2X7.
Annual Subscription: $26.50. **Frequency:** Monthly.
Publisher: Southam Communications Ltd.
Advertiser Index: Every issue.
Special Issues:
 Canadian Ports and Seaway Directory. Started 1934. Published as a separate issue. $28.95. Not included in the subscription price. March.
 Canadian Industrial Traffic League Convention Issue. $2. April.
 Transportation Guide—directory. Published as a separate issue. $28.95. July.
 Traffic Managers Salary Survey. Started 1980. $10. September.
 Canadian Highway Carriers Guide—directory. Published as a separate issue. $28.95. Not included in the subscription price. November.
 Presidents' Issue. Started 1977. $2. November.

0283. CANADIAN TRAVEL COURIER.
777 Bay St., Toronto, Ontario, Can. M5W 1A7.
Annual Subscription: $36/22. **Frequency:** 26/yr.
Publisher: Maclean Hunter Ltd.
Special Issues:
Britain. March.
Newfoundland/Europe. March.
Pacific. March.
Greece. April.
Tour Canada. April.
Appointment Diary/Industry Directory. $10. November.
Mexico. November.

0284. CANADIAN TRAVEL NEWS.
1450 Don Mills Rd., Don Mills, Ontario, Can. M3B 2X7.
Annual Subscription: $39.50/30.00. **Frequency:** Biweekly.
Publisher: Southam Communications Ltd.
Special Issues:
Travel Agents Pull-Out Sales Guide: Europe. Started 1980. $2.50. February.
Travel Agents Pull-Out Sales Guide: Canada. Started 1980. $2.50. March.
Travel Agents Pull-Out Sales Guide: Cruise Guide. Started 1980. $2.50. March/August.
Travel Agents Pull-Out Sales Guide: Eastern Europe. Started 1983. $2.50. March.
Travel Agents Pull-Out Sales Guide: Business Travel Guide. Started 1980. $2.50. April.
Travel Agents Pull-Out Sales Guide: Caribbean/Bahamas. Started 1980. $2.50. April/October.
Convention & Trade Show Preview—Alliance of Canadian Travel Associations. Started 1978. $2.50. May/June.
Travel Agents Pull-Out Sales Guide: Pacific Area Directory. Started 1978. $2.50. July.

0285. CANADIAN TRAVEL PRESS.
100 Adelaide St. West, Ste. 1300, Toronto, Ontario, Can. M5H 1S3.
Annual Subscription: $25/20. **Frequency:** 26/yr.
Publisher: Baxter Publishing Company.
Special Issues:
Cruise Issues. $3. March/September.
American Society of Travel Agents Convention Issue/Marketing & Media. $3. October.
Industry Forecast. $3. December.

0286. CANADIAN UNDERWRITER.
109 Vanderhoof Ave., Ste. 101, Toronto, Ontario, Can. M4G 2J2.
Annual Subscription: $12/10. **Frequency:** Monthly.
Publisher: Wadham Publications Ltd.
Special Issues:
Statistical Issue. $6. March.
Industry Education. $2. August.
Commercial Insurance. $2. September.

0287. CANADIAN VENDING.
833 Second Ave., E., Owen Sound, Ontario, Can. N4K 2H2.
Annual Subscription: $18.
Publisher: Sound Publishing Ltd.
Special Issues:
New Equipment. February.
C.A.M.A. Convention. April.
Food Service. June.
Coffee & Beverage. August.
Buyers' Guide & Directory. October.
Snack Foods. December.

0288. CANADIAN WELDER & FABRICATOR.
1077 St. James St., Winnipeg, Manitoba, Can. R3C 3B1.
Annual Subscription: $30/18. **Frequency:** Monthly.
Publisher: Sanford Evans Publishing Ltd.
Special Issues:
Canadian Welding Society Issue—lists members, chapters, meeting subjects for coming year. $2.50. June.
Directory & Buyers Guide. $2.50. September.

0289. CANDY INDUSTRY.
1 East First St., Duluth, MN 55802.
Annual Subscription: $18. **Frequency:** Monthly.
Publisher: Magazines for Industry.
Advertiser Index: Every issue.
Editorial Index: Annual. Subject/Author. December.
Indexed or Abstracted Online: Trade & Industry Index.
Special Issues:
Annual European Report. $2. January.
Biscuit Bakers Technical Conference. $2. March.
National Confectioners Association Convention. $2. May.
Retail Confectioners International. $2. June.
Ingredient & Flavor Issue. $2. July.
Packaging Issue. $2. August.
Chocolate Issue. $2. September.
National Candy Bar Survey. $2. October.
Candy Industry Buying Guide. Published as a separate issue. $25. Not included in the subscription price. December.

0290. CANDY MARKETER QUARTERLY.
1 East First Street, Duluth, MN 55802.
Annual Subscription: $18. **Frequency:** Quarterly.
Publisher: Magazines for Industry.
Advertiser Index: Every issue.
Special Issues:
Buyers Directory. January/April/July/October.
National Candy Wholesalers Association Conventions. January/July.
National Candy Buyers Brands Survey. April.
Year-end Review. October.

0291. CANOE.
P.O. Box 10748, Des Moines, IA 50349.
Annual Subscription: $15. **Frequency:** 6/yr.
Publisher: New England Publications.
Special Issues:
Guide to Canoeing & Kayaking. Started 1983. Published as a separate issue. $2.95. Not included in the subscription price. April.

0292. CAR AND DRIVER.
P.O. Box 2770, Boulder, CO 80302.
Annual Subscription: $12.98. **Frequency:** Monthly.
Publisher: Ziff-Davis Publishing Co.
Special Issues:
C/D Buyers Guide. Started 1950. Published as a separate issue. $4.95. Not included in the subscription price. February.

0293. CARBIDE & TOOL JOURNAL.
P.O. Box 437, Bridgeville, PA 15017.
Annual Subscription: $30. **Frequency:** 6/yr.
Publisher: Society of Carbide & Tool Engineers.
Advertiser Index: Every issue.
Special Issues:
Grinding Tools. Started 1979. $6. January/February.
Abrasives-Super Abrasives. Started 1979. $6. March/April.
Powder Metal Technology. Started 1979. $6. March/April.
Cutting Tools. Started 1979. $6. May/June.
NC Machinery. Started 1979. $6. September/October.
Non-Traditional Machinery. Started 1979. $6. September/October.
Forming Tools. Started 1979. $6. November/December.

0294. CARPET & RUG INDUSTRY.
26 Lake St., Ramsey, NJ 07446.
Annual Subscription: $18. **Frequency:** Monthly.
Publisher: Rodman Publications, Inc.
Advertiser Index: Every issue.
Editorial Index: Annual. Subject/Title/Author. December.
Special Issues:
Top 25 Carpet Mills. $5. June.
Machinery & Equipment Buyers Guide. $3. September.
Dye and Chemical Buyer's Guide. $3. November.

0295. CASH BOX.
1775 Broadway, New York, NY 10019.
Annual Subscription: $125. **Frequency:** Weekly.
Publisher: Same.
Advertiser Index
Special Issues:
International Directory—music record labels; distributors; pressing plants; publishing companies; managers; export/import, etc. Published as a separate issue. $20. July.
Year-End Issue—poll results of top records from charts. $3. December.

0296. CASH CROP FARMING.
222 Argyle Ave., Delhi, Ontario, Can. N4B 2Y2.
Annual Subscription: $4. **Frequency:** 11/yr.
Publisher: Cash Crop Publications Ltd.
Special Issues:
Corn Issues. $.75. February/September.
Grain Drying Equipment. $.75. July.
Soybean Issue. $.75. November.

0297. CASUAL LIVING.
370 Lexington Ave., New York, NY 10017.
Annual Subscription: $15. **Frequency:** 11/yr.
Publisher: Columbia Communications.
Advertiser Index: Every issue.
Special Issues:
Accessory Directory & Buyers Guide. February.
Spas and Hot Tubs. March.
Suppliers Issue. June/July.
Directory & Buyers Guide. $10. October.
Industry Calendar—market dates for new year. December.

0298. CATALOG SHOW ROOM MERCHANDISER.
1020 West Jericho Tpk., Smithtown, NY 11787.
Annual Subscription: $25. **Frequency:** Monthly.
Publisher: CSM Marketing, Inc.
Advertiser Index: December.
Special Issues:
National Housewares Manufacturers Association Show/Winter Consumer Electronics Show/China & Glass Exposition. $3. January.
National Sporting Goods Show/Jewelers of America Show/American Toy Fair/N.Y. Gift Show/National Leather & Luggage Goods Show/CSM Awards Issue. $3. February.
Photo Marketing Association Show. $3. March.
Flyer Merchandising/National Association of Tobacco Distributors Convention. $3. April.
Annual Catalog Buying Shows Issue. $3. May.
Accessories Merchandising/Summer Consumer Electronics Show. $3. June.
NHMA Show/Jewelers of America Show/American Fishing Tackle Show. $3. July.
Spring/Summer Catalog Selection Issue/National Hardware Show/Automotive Parts & Accessories Association Show. $3. August.
CSM Industry Census. $3. September.
Christmas Merchandising/National Office Products Association Show. $3. October.
CSM Milestone Issue. Started 1980. $3. November.
CSM Suppliers Directory. Started 1972. $3. December.

0299. CATALOG SHOWROOM BUSINESS.
1515 Broadway, New York, NY 10036.
Annual Subscription: $20. **Frequency:** Monthly.
Publisher: Gralla Publications.
Advertiser Index: Every issue.
Special Issues:
Consumer Electronics Show. $2. January/June.
Jewelers of America Trade Show. $2. February/July.
Photo Marketing Association Trade Show/National Housewares Manufacturing Association Exposition. $2. April.
Annual Consumer Audit—statistics on income, age, frequency of visits, catalog use, dollars spent per visit, etc. Started 1975. $2. May.
Annual Rep Guide—national and regional. $2. August.
Annual Market Audit—statistics on sales by product category, profit margins, turns, ad expenditures, catalog & flyer usage, etc. Lists top 40 catalog showroom firms. Started 1975. $2. September.
Supplier Directory—2000 showroom suppliers. Started 1974. $2. December.
Who's Who Among Catalog Publishers. $2. December.

0300. CATECHIST.
3451 East River Rd., Dayton, OH 45439.
Annual Subscription: $14.95. **Frequency:** 8/yr.
Publisher: Peter Li, Inc.
Special Issues:
School-Opening. September.

0301. CATHOLIC JOURNALIST.
119 North Park Ave., Rockville Centre, NY 11570.
Annual Subscription: $10. **Frequency:** Monthly.
Publisher: Catholic Press Association.
Special Issues:
Catholic Press Directory. Started 1923. Published as a separate issue. $10. Not included in the subscription price. February.
Awards Issue. $1. May.

0302. CATHOLIC LIBRARY WORLD.
461 W. Lancaster Ave., Haverford, PA 19041.
Annual Subscription: $30. **Frequency:** Monthly.
Publisher: Catholic Library Association.
Editorial Index: Annual. Subject/Author. May.
Special Issues:
Membership Directory. Started 1929. $20. January.
Convention Issue. Started 1929. $3. Annual. March.

0303. CATS MAGAZINE.
445 Merrimac Dr., P.O. Box 37, Port Orange, FL 32019.
Annual Subscription: $15.50. **Frequency:** Monthly.
Publisher: Cats Magazine, Inc.
Editorial Index: Annual. Title/Author. January.
Special Issues:
Directory Annual—lists 1200/1500 U.S. and Canada cat breeders by state (province) and breed; also all major national cat organizations and registries. Started 1953. $2. April.
Cat Show Awards Issues—U.S. and Canada award-winning cats of the past show season. Started 1947. $2. September and October.

0304. CERAMIC INDUSTRY.
1350 Touhy Ave., Des Plaines, IL 60018.
Annual Subscription: $15. **Frequency:** Weekly.
Publisher: Cahners Publishing Co.
Advertiser Index: Every issue.
Special Issues:
Raw Materials Handbook. $2.50. January.
Container Glass. $2.50. March.
American Ceramic Society Convention. $2.50. April.
Batching Techniques. $2.50. May.
Annual Review & Forecast. $2.50. June.
Ceramic Industry Giants. Started 1983. $2.50. August or December.
Autoramics. $2.50. September or November.
Ceramic Data Book. Published as a separate issue. $7.50. October.
International Issue. $2.50. December.

0305. CERAMIC SCOPE.
5208 West Pico Blvd., Los Angeles, CA 90019.
Annual Subscription: $9. **Frequency:** Monthly.
Publisher: Same.
Advertiser Index: Every issue.
Special Issues:
Ceramic Hobby Industry Buyers Guide. Started 1973. Published as a separate issue. $4. January.

0306. CEREAL FOODS WORLD.
3340 Pilot Knob Rd., St. Paul, MN 55121.
Annual Subscription: $45. **Frequency:** Monthly.
Publisher: American Association of Cereal Chemists.
Advertiser Index: Every issue.
Editorial Index: Annual. Subject/Author. December.
Special Issues:
  AACC PostConvention Issue: Show in Print/Buyers Guide/ Membership Directory. $6. January.
  Readership Study. $6. May.
  AACC Preconvention Issue. $6. September.

0307. CHAIN STORE AGE EXECUTIVE WITH SHOPPING CENTER AGE.
425 Park Ave., New York, NY 10022.
Annual Subscription: $20 (free to qualified persons).
Frequency: Monthly.
Publisher: Lebhar-Friedman, Inc.
Advertiser Index: Every issue.
Special Issues:
  Construction & Operations Forecast. January.
  SPECS (Store Planning Equipment Construction Services) Convention. March.
  New Construction Materials. April.
  FMI (Food Marketing Institute), ICSC (International Council of Shopping Centers), NMRI (National Mass Retailing Institute) previews. May.
  Annual Census of Chain Retail Stores—with industry profiles. July.
  Retailing's $100 Million Club—ranking of chains with $100 million or more annual volume. August.
  Annual Big Builders Survey—statistics on chains with largest capital expenditures. November.
  New Store of the Year Design Competition Winners. Started 1982. December.

0308. CHAIN STORE AGE—GENERAL MERCHANDISE EDITION.
425 Park Ave., New York, NY
Annual Subscription: $15. **Frequency:** Monthly.
Publisher: Lebhar-Friedman, Inc.
Indexed Online: Predicasts; Trade & Industry Index.
Special Issues:
  Annual "Yardsticks" Report: Top 100 Chains. $2. June.
  Top 20 Merchandising Departments Study. $2. July.
  Annual Consumer Intentions Study. $2. August.
  Great Retail Institutions—company profile. $2. December.

0309. CHANGE: THE MAGAZINE OF HIGHER LEARNING.
4000 Albermarle St., NW, Washington, DC 20016.
Annual Subscription: $20 (individual)/30 (institution).
Frequency: 8/yr.
Publisher: Heldref Publications.
Editorial Index: Author. January/February.

0310. CHANGING TIMES.
Editors Park, MD 20782.
Annual Subscription: $15. **Frequency:** Monthly.
Publisher: Kiplinger Washington Editors.
Editorial Index: Annual. Subject. December.
Indexed Online: Magazine Index.
Special Issues:
  Job Outlook for College Graduates—list of companies seeking graduates, with occupational breakdown. $1.75. February.
  Top Performing Mutual Funds. $1.75. October.
  Car Chart: Domestic—facts and figures on new models. $1.75. November.
  Car Chart: Imported—facts and figures on new models. $1.75. December.

0311. THE CHEESE REPORTER.
6401 Odana Rd., Madison, WI 53719.
Annual Subscription: $12. **Frequency:** Weekly.
Publisher: Cheese Reporter Publishing Co., Inc.
Special Issues:
  Special Seminar Issue. Started 1965. $1. May.
  Special Convention Issue. Started 1963. $1. October.

0312. CHEMICAL ENGINEERING.
P.O. Box 430, Hightstown, NJ 08520.
Annual Subscription: $22.50. **Frequency:** 26/yr.
Publisher: McGraw-Hill, Inc.
Advertiser Index: Every issue.
Editorial Index: Annual. Subject/Author. December.
Indexed or Abstracted Online: CIN.
Special Issues:
  Chemical Process Industry Forecast. $4.50. January.
  Petro-Expo Show. $4.50. Biennially. March (odd yrs).
  CE Construction Alert—major chemical process industries projects in planning stages, under construction, or newly completed. $4.50. 3/yr. April/May/July.
  Chemical Engineering Equipment Buyers Guide. Started 1974. $4.50. July.
  CE Personal Achievement Awards. $4.50. Biennially. November (even yrs).
  Petro-Chem Show. $4.50. Biennially. November (even yrs).
  Kirkpatrick CE Achievement Awards. $4.50. Biennially. December (even yrs).

0313. CHEMICAL & ENGINEERING NEWS.
1155 16th St., NW, Washington, DC 20036.
Annual Subscription: $34. **Frequency:** Weekly.
Publisher: American Chemical Society.
Advertiser Index: Every issue.
Editorial Index: Annual. Subject/Title. February.
Indexed Online: CA Search; Predicasts; CIN; Trade & Industry Index.
Special Issues:
  Chemical R&D budget outlook (industry). Started 1968. $2. January.
  Congressional outlook. Started Early 1970's. $2. January.
  Chemical R&D budget outlook (government). Started Early 1970's. $2. February.
  Quarterly Financial Report (Chemical Industry). Started 1975. $2. February/May/August/November.
  Instrumentation. Started 1970's. $2. March.
  Plant Capacity Use Survey (Chemical Industry). Started 1977. $2. 2/yr. May/October.
  Top 50 Chemical Companies, Products. Started 1969. $2. May.
  Facts & Figures (Chemical Industry). Started 1950's. $2. June.
  Professional Salary Survey (Chemists, Engineers). Started 1960's. $2. July.
  R&D Facts & Figures (Industry, Government, Universities). Started 1979. $2. July.
  Employment Outlook (Industry, Universities). Started 1960's. $2. October.
  Capital Spending Outlook (Industry). Started 1968. $2. December.
  World Chemical Industry Outlook. Started 1960's. $2. December.

0314. CHEMICAL ENGINEERING PROGRESS.
345 East 47 St., New York, NY 10017.
Annual Subscription: $35. **Frequency:** Monthly.
Publisher: American Institute of Chemical Engineers.
Advertiser Index: Every issue.
Editorial Index: Annual. Subject/Author. December.
Indexed or Abstracted Online: ISI; Compendex; CA Search.
Special Issues:
  New Engineering Data. Started 1963. $4. January.
  Petro/Expo, Biennial. Started 1961. $4. February/March.
  Chemical Plant Exposition. Started 1978. $4. May.
  Heat Transfer Conference. Started 1952. $4. July.
  AIChE Winter Conference. $4. September.
  Institute, Division & Intersociety Awards. $4. October.
  75th Anniversary/Diamond Jubilee. Started 1983. $4. One time only. October '83.
  Chem Show. $4. Biennially. November.

0315. CHEMICAL EQUIPMENT.
13 Emery Ave., Randolph, NJ 07869.
Annual Subscription: Free to qualified persons. **Frequency:** Monthly.
Publisher: Gordon Publications.
Advertiser Index: Every issue.
Special Issues:
  Buyer's Guide Issue/Budget Planning Aids. January.
  Valve Issue. February.
  Pump Issue. March.
  Bulk Material Handling. April.
  Energy Awards Issue; energy conservation controls and equipment. May.
  Heat Exchangers; Mid-Year Budget Planning Aids. June.
  Piping/Tubing/Fittings. July.
  Pollution Control. August.
  Instrumentation and Controls. September.
  Mixing/Blending/Drying. October.
  Chem Show Issue. November.
  Filtration/Separation. December.

0316. CHEMICAL MARKETING REPORTER/CHEMICAL BUSINESS.
100 Church St., New York, NY 10007.
Annual Subscription: $55. **Frequency:** Weekly.
Publisher: Schnell Publishing Company.
Advertiser Index: Every issue.
Indexed Online: CIN; Trade & Industry Index.
Special Issues:
  Chemicals Outlook. Started 1973. January.
  Detergents. Started 1982. January.
  Petrochemicals. Started 1975. March.
  Specialties. Started 1974. May.
  Beauty Chemicals. Started 1973. June.
  Oil, Paint & Drug Chemical Buyers Directory. Published as a separate issue. August.
  Chemicals Shipping. Started 1973. October.
  Coatings. Started 1974. November.
  Chemical Business (feature magazine—part 2 of CMR). Started 1979. 12/yr. Monthly.

0317. CHEMICAL PROCESSING.
301 East Erie St., Chicago, IL 60611.
Annual Subscription: $24. **Frequency:** 14/yr.
Publisher: Putman Publishing Co.
Special Issues:
  Filtration and Separation. January.
  Fluid Flow. February.
  Corrosion Control. March or April.
  Material Handling, Packaging and Transportation/Energy Conservation. April or May.
  Compressors, Blowers and Fans. May.
  Valves and Piping. June.
  Mixing/Size Reduction. July.
  Heat Transfer. August.
  Instrumentation/Process Controls/Pollution/Environmental Advances. September or October.
  Drying and Evaporation/Chem Show. November.
  Pumping. December.

0318. CHEMICAL PURCHASING.
2135 Summer St., P.O. Box 3837, Stamford, CT 06905.
Annual Subscription: $18. **Frequency:** Monthly.
Publisher: Myers Publishing Co.
Advertiser Index: Every issue.
Special Issues:
  Chemical Industry Outlook. Started 1965. $2. July.
  Chemical Buyer Salary Survey. Started 1976. $2. September.
  Chemicals Directory—chemical & raw materials sources of supply. Started 1965. Published as a separate issue. October.
  Chemical Briefs Commodity Studies. Started 1965. $2. 26/yr. Monthly (except July).

0319. CHEMICAL WEEK.
P.O. Box 430, Hightstown, NJ 08520.
Annual Subscription: $35. **Frequency:** Weekly.
Publisher: McGraw-Hill Publications.
Advertiser Index: Every issue.
Editorial Index: Semi-Annual. Subject/Author. September (prev. Jan-June)/March (prev. July-Dec); each volume $15, bound separately, on request. Not included with subscription.
Indexed or Abstracted Online: NEXIS; CIN.
Special Issues:
  Forecast: Domestic & International. $5. January.
  Chemical Week 300: Corporate Profiles. $5. April.
  Compensation Survey. $5. May.
  Maintenance Survey. $5. July.
  Top Foreign CPI (chemical processing industries) Firms. $5. August.
  Chemical Week Buyers Guide (includes Packaging). Published as a separate issue. $50. October.
  Directory of Worldwide Engineering and Construction. Published as a separate issue. $5. December.

0320. CHILDREN TODAY.
Superintendent of Documents, GPO, Washington, DC 20402.
Annual Subscription: $14. **Frequency:** 6/yr.
Publisher: U.S. Department of Health & Human Services.
Editorial Index: Annual. Subject/Author. November/December.
Indexed Online: Medline; ERIC; Magazine Index.

0321. CHINA GLASS & TABLEWARE.
P.O. Box 2147, Clifton, NJ 07015.
Annual Subscription: $15. **Frequency:** Monthly.
Publisher: Ebel-Doctorow Publications.
Advertiser Index: Every issue.
Special Issues:
  Redbook Directory—includes current manufacturers and importers of China glass, silver ware in the US, plus Backstamps and services. Started 1893. Published as a separate issue. $7.50. September.

0322. CHOICE.
100 Riverview Ctr., Middletown, CT 06457.
Annual Subscription: $85. **Frequency:** 11/yr.
Publisher: Association of College & Research Libraries, A.L.A.
Advertiser Index: Every issue.
Editorial Index: Title/Author.
Special Issues:
  Spring Announcements. $8. March.
  Outstanding Academic Books/Nonprint Materials. $8. May.
  American Library Association Conference. $8. June.
  Fall Announcements. $8. September.

0323. CHRISTIAN BOOKSELLER & LIBRARIAN.
396 East St. Charles Rd., Wheaton, IL 60187.
Annual Subscription: $18. **Frequency:** Monthly.
Publisher: Christian Life Missions.
Advertiser Index: Every issue.
Special Issues:
  Spring & Summer Religion Books. $2. March.
  CBA Convention Preview. $2. June/July.
  Fall & Winter Religion Books. $2. August.
  Jewish & Catholic Book Markets. $2. October.

0324. THE CHRISTIAN CENTURY.
5615 West Cermak Rd., Cicero, IL 60650.
Annual Subscription: $21. **Frequency:** Weekly.
Publisher: The Christian Century Foundation.
Editorial Index: Semi-Annual. Subject/Title/Author. June/December.
Indexed Online: Magazine Index.
Special Issues:
  Theological Education Issue. February.
  Arts Issue. March.
  Book Issues. $.75. Spring/Fall.

0325. CHRISTIAN HERALD.
40 Overlook Dr., Chappaqua, NY 10514.
Annual Subscription: $13.97. **Frequency:** 11/yr.
Publisher: Christian Herald Association.
Indexed Online: Magazine Index.
Special Issues:
   Vacation Bible Schools. $1.75.   February.
   Books Issue.   Started 1978. $1.75.   March.
   Easter Missions Travel. $1.75.   April.
   Music. $1.75.   May.
   Christian Booksellers Association Conference. $1.75.
      July/August.
   Youth Programs. $1.75.   September.
   College Directory. $1.75.   October.
   Christmas—books and music. $1.75.   December.

0326. CHRISTIANITY TODAY.
465 Gundersen Dr., Carol Stream, IL 60187.
Annual Subscription: $21.   **Frequency:** 18/yr.
Publisher: Christianity Today Inc.
Editorial Index: Annual. Subject/Title/Author. February.
Indexed or Abstracted Online: Magazine Index.
Special Issues:
   Books. $1.50.   February/September.
   Seminary or Pastoral Education. $1.50.   February.
   Easter. $1.50.   March or April.
   Bible/Theology. $1.50.   October.
   Youth. $1.50.   October.
   College/Higher Education. $1.50.   November.
   Christmas. $1.50.   December.

0327. CIRCUITS MANUFACTURING.
1050 Commonwealth Ave., Boston, MA 02215.
Annual Subscription: $35.   **Frequency:** Monthly.
Publisher: Morgan-Grampion Publishing Co.
Advertiser Index: Every issue.
Editorial Index: Annual. Subject/Title. December.
Special Issues:
   Special Report: Surface Mounting. $4.   January/March.
   NEPCOM West (electronics production show)/New
      Technologies for Printed Circuit Boards. $4.   February.
   Production Ideas Notebook. $4.   April.
   Special Report: Military Electronics. $4.   May.
   Special Report: Building Advanced Printed Circuit Boards.
      $4.   July.
   ISHM Show (International Society for Hybrid Microcircuits)/
      Special Report: Computer-Aided Manufacturing. $4.
      September.
   Buyers Guide. $4.   November.

0328. CITRUS & VEGETABLE MAGAZINE.
P.O. Box 2349, Tampa, FL 33601.
Annual Subscription: $10.   **Frequency:** Monthly.
Publisher: Kyle Publishing Co.
Advertiser Index: Every issue.
Special Issues:
   Buyers Guide for Florida Irrigation Society. $.50.   March.
   Equipment Directory. $.50.   July.
   Irrigation. $.50.   September.
   Agricultural Chemical Directory. $.50.   October.

0329. CIVIC PUBLIC WORKS.
777 Bay St., Toronto, Ontario, Can. M5W 1A7.
Annual Subscription: $47/21.   **Frequency:** Monthly.
Publisher: MacLean Hunter Ltd.
Advertiser Index: Every issue.
Editorial Index: Annual. Subject/Title. July.
Special Issues:
   Road and Streets. $6/4.   January.
   Water. $6/4.   March.
   Parks & Recreation. $6/4.   April.
   Environment. $6/4.   May.
   Wastes. $6/4.   June.
   Public Works Reference Manual and Buyers Guide. $15.
      July.
   Snow & Ice. $6/4.   September.
   Water & Sewage. $6/4.   October.
   Solid Waste. $6/4.   November.
   Convention Calendar. $6/4.   December.

0330. CIVIL ENGINEERING.
345 East 47th St., New York, NY 10017.
Annual Subscription: $36 (free with membership).
   Frequency: Monthly.
Publisher: American Society of Civil Engineers.
Advertiser Index: Every issue.
Editorial Index: Annual. Subject/Author. January.
Abstracted Online: Compendex.
Special Issues:
   Materials of Construction. $5.   March or May.
   Water Resources. $5.   April.
   Environment Engineering Annual. $5.   May or September.
   Outstanding Civil Engineering Project Achievement Award.
      $5.   June.
   Structures/Buildings. $5.   July.
   Transportation Engineering. $5.   November.
   Energy Engineering. $5.   December.

0331. CLEANING MANAGEMENT.
17911-C Sky Park Blvd., Irvine, CA 92714.
Annual Subscription: $12.   **Frequency:** Monthly.
Publisher: Harris Communications.
Advertiser Index: Every issue.
Editorial Index: Annual. Subject. January.
Special Issues:
   Buyer's Guide.   Started 1978. $2.   January.
   Training Issue.   Started 1978. $2.   August.

0332. THE CLERGY JOURNAL.
P.O. Box 1625, Austin, TX 78767.
Annual Subscription: $18.   **Frequency:** 10/yr.
Publisher: Church Management, Inc.
Advertiser Index: Every issue.
Special Issues:
   Annual Planning Issue—52 sermons, hymns for each week,
      calls to worship, dedications.   Started 1950. $7.90.
      May/June.

0333. CLIMATOLOGICAL DATA.
Federal Bldg., Asheville, NC 28801.
Annual Subscription: $19.50 per state.   **Frequency:**
   Monthly.
Publisher: National Climatic Center.
Special Issues:
   Monthly heating degree days and snow data, July-June (per
      state). $1.50.   July.
   Climatological Data Annual—per state—monthly and annual
      average temperatures, total precipitation, temperature
      extremes, freeze data, soil temperatures, evaporation,
      recap of monthly total cooling degree days.   Published as
      a separate issue.   Varies.

0334. CLU JOURNAL.
270 Bryn Mawr Ave., Bryn Mawr, PA 19010.
Annual Subscription: $10.   **Frequency:** Quarterly.
Publisher: American Society of CLU (Chartered Life
   Underwriters).
Editorial Index: Annual. Subject/Author. October.

0335. CLUB MANAGEMENT.
408 Olive St., St. Louis, MO 63102.
Annual Subscription: $6.   **Frequency:** Monthly.
Publisher: Commerce Publishing Co.
Special Issues:
   Club Managers Association of America Convention.
      February.

0336. COAL AGE.
1221 Ave. of the Americas, New York, NY 10020.
Annual Subscription: $18.   **Frequency:** Monthly.
Publisher: McGraw-Hill Publications.
Editorial Index: Annual. Subject/Title/Author. December.
Special Issues:
   Review and Outlook Issue. $3.50.   February.
   American Mining Congress—pre- and post-conventions.
      $3.50.   April, June.
   Mining Guide-Buying Directory. $3.50.   July.

Model Mining Issue (company profile). $3.50. October.
American Mining Congress Equipment Show (next show 1984). $3.50. Every 4 yrs. December 1984.

0337. COAL MINING & PROCESSING.
300 West Adams St., Chicago, IL 60606.
Annual Subscription: $35. **Frequency:** Monthly.
Special Issues:
Forecast. $3.50. January.
American Mining Congress Convention. $3.50. April.
Surface Mining. $3.50. June.
Preparation. $3.50. September.
Underground Mining. $3.50. December.

0338. COINAMATIC AGE.
5 Beekman St., New York, NY 10038.
Annual Subscription: $15. **Frequency:** 6/yr.
Publisher: Coinamatic Trade Publications.
Special Issues:
Energy. Started 1984. January/February.
Vending. March/April.
Equipment Specifications/Multi-Housing Laundry Association Convention. May/June.
Diversification. July/August.
Dry cleaning/National Automatic Laundry and Cleaning Council Convention. September/October.

0339. THE COLLEGE STORE JOURNAL.
528 East Lorain St., Oberlin, OH 44074.
Annual Subscription: $20. **Frequency:** 6/yr.
Publisher: National Association of College Stores.
Advertiser Index: Every issue.
Editorial Index: Annual. Title.
Special Issues:
Special Section—Emblematic Merchandise. $4. April/May.
Special Section—Soft Goods. $4. June/July.
Special Section—Textbooks. $4. August/September.
Special Section—NACS (National Association fo College Stores) Buyer's Guide. $4. December/January.

0340. COLLEGIATE MICROCOMPUTER.
Rose-Hulman Institute of Technology, Terre Haute, IN 47803.
Annual Subscription: $28. **Frequency:** Quarterly.
Publisher: Way With Words.
Editorial Index: Annual. Author. November.

0341. COLUMBIA JOURNAL OF WORLD BUSINESS.
815 Uris Hall, Columbia University, New York, NY 10027.
Annual Subscription: $20(Individual); $40 (Corporate).
Frequency: Quarterly.
Publisher: Trustees of Columbia University.
Editorial Index: Annual. Subject/Author. Winter.

0342. COMMENTARY.
165 East 56th St., New York, NY 10022.
Annual Subscription: $30. **Frequency:** Monthly.
Publisher: American Jewish Committee.
Editorial Index: Semi-Annual. Author. February/September.

0343. COMMERCIAL CARRIER JOURNAL.
P.O. Box 2045, Radnor, PA 19089.
Annual Subscription: $30. **Frequency:** Monthly.
Publisher: Chilton Company.
Advertiser Index: Every issue.
Editorial Index: Annual. Subject. December.
Special Issues:
Fleet Reference Annual. $6. April.
Top 100 Common Carriers—trends in the trucking industry. $6. June.
Fleet Buyers Guide and Specifications—lists new vehicles: makes, models, components. $6. October.

0344. COMMERCIAL NEWS.
3181 Fernwood, Lynwood, CA 90262.
Annual Subscription: $5. **Frequency:** Weekly.
Publisher: C. A. Page Publishing.

Special Issues:
Wheels of Progress (Trucking) (contained in the last issue of the month, entitled Cargo, Air Routing Guide). Started 1950. Published as a separate issue. January.
California Manufacturers Association, Transportation & Distribution Committee Convention (contained in the last issue of the month, entitled Cargo, Air Routing Guide). Started 1973. Published as a separate issue. March.
World Trade Week/National Transportation. Started 1925. May.
Traffic Managers Conference (contained in the last issue of the month, entitled Cargo, Air Routing Guide). Started 1972. Published as a separate issue. November.

0345. COMMODITIES, THE MAGAZINE OF FUTURES TRADING.
219 Parkade, Cedar Falls, IA 50613.
Annual Subscription: $34. **Frequency:** Monthly.
Publisher: Commodities Magazine Inc.
Advertiser Index: Every issue.
Editorial Index: Annual. Subject/Title. May.
Special Issues:
Reference Guide to Futures Markets—directory of futures trading firms, services, and materials. Includes annual Index of Articles and trading facts and figures. Started 1976. Published as a separate issue. $6. May.

0346. COMMONWEAL.
232 Madison Ave., New York, NY 10016.
Annual Subscription: $24. **Frequency:** 26/yr.
Publisher: Commonweal Publishing Co.
Editorial Index: Subject/Title. December.
Indexed Online: Magazine Index.
Special Issues:
Contemporary Theology. $1.25. January.
Religious Books. $1.25. February.
Spring Books. $1.25. May.
Fall Books. $1.25. November.
Christmas Books. $1.25. December.

0347. COMMUNICATIONS ARTS.
410 Sherman Avenue, P.O. Box 10300, Palo Alto, CA 94303.
Annual Subscription: $36. **Frequency:** 6/yr.
Publisher: Coyne & Blanchard, Inc.
Editorial Index: Annual. Subject. January/February.
Special Issues:
Arts Annual—reproduction of award of excellence winners in the photography and illustration competition. Started 1976. $12. July/August.
Annual reproduction of award of excellence winners in the design and advertising competition. Started 1960. $18. November/December.

0348. COMMUNICATIONS NEWS.
124 South First St., Geneva, IL 60134.
Annual Subscription: $21. **Frequency:** Monthly.
Publisher: Harcourt Brace Jovanovich Publications.
Advertiser Index: Every issue.
Indexed Online: Trade & Industry Index.
Special Issues:
Forecast. $2.50. January.
Satellites & Earth Stations. $2.50. March.
Broadcast, CATV and CCTV Equipment Review. $2.50. April.
Data Communications. $2.50. May/December.
International Communications Association Conference. $2.50. May.
Antennas and Towers. $2.50. June.
PBX (Private Branch Exchange). $2.50. July.
Two-way Radio. $2.50. August.
Twentieth Anniversary Issue (1984). $2.50. One time. September.
Microwave. $2.50. October.
Test Equipment/Telecommunications Association Conference. $2.50. November.

0349. COMMUNITY AND JUNIOR COLLEGE JOURNAL.
80 South Early St., Alexandria, VA 22304.
Annual Subscription: $12. **Frequency:** 8/yr.
Publisher: American Association of Community & Junior Colleges.
Editorial Index: Annual. Title/Author. May.
Indexed Online: ERIC.

0350. COMMUTER AIR.
6255 Barfield Rd., Atlanta, GA 30328.
Annual Subscription: $23. **Frequency:** Monthly.
Publisher: Communication Channels.
Advertiser Index: Every issue.
Special Issues:
 Yearbook Edition. Started 1979. May.

0351. COMPENSATION REVIEW.
P.O. Box 319, Saranac Lake, NY 12983.
Annual Subscription: $28.25. **Frequency:** Quarterly.
Publisher: AMACOM Periodicals Division, American Management Association.
Editorial Index: Annual. Subject/Author. Fourth Quarter.

0352. COMPUTER.
10662 Los Vaqueros Circle, Los Alamitos, CA 90720.
Annual Subscription: With membership in IEEE Computer Society. **Frequency:** Monthly.
Publisher: Institute of Electrical and Electronic Engineers Computer Society.
Editorial Index: Annual. Subject/Title/Author. December.

0353. COMPUTER DECISIONS.
50 Essex St., Rochelle Park, NJ 07662.
Annual Subscription: $28 (Free to qualified persons).
Frequency: Monthly.
Publisher: Hayden Publishing.
Advertiser Index: Every issue.
Editorial Index: Annual. Subject/Author. January.
Special Issues:
 Top 100 in DP. Started 1982. June or July.

0354. COMPUTER DESIGN.
119 Russell St., Littleton, MA 01460.
Annual Subscription: $50. **Frequency:** Monthly.
Publisher: Pennwell Publishing Co.
Advertiser Index: Every issue.
Editorial Index: Annual. Subject. Sent on request only.
Special Issues:
 Memory Systems Design. Started 1981. $5. January.
 Innovations in Systems Architecture. $5. February.
 Designing With Advanced System ICs. $5. March.
 Peripheral Integration/High Technology Approaches. $5. April.
 Future Directions in Systems Design. $5. May.
 Microsystems Design Techniques. $5. June.
 Graphics System Design Technology. $5. July.
 Super Systems/Designing for High Performance. $5. August.
 Data Communications Systems Design. $5. September.
 Intelligence in Systems Components. $5. October.
 Designing for Automation and Control. $5. November.
 Designers' Hall of Fame. $5. December.

0355. COMPUTER/LAW JOURNAL.
P.O. Box 54308 T.A., Los Angeles, CA 90054.
Annual Subscription: $66. **Frequency:** Quarterly.
Publisher: Center for Computer/Law.
Editorial Index: Annual. Subject/Title/Author. Winter.
Indexed or Abstracted Online: Legal Resource Index; Management Contents.
Special Issues:
 Current Developments in Computer Law. Started 1979. $18. Irregular.

0356. COMPUTER PICTURES.
330 West 42 St., New York, NY 10036.
Annual Subscription: $15. **Frequency:** 6/yr.
Publisher: Back Stage Publications, Inc.
Advertiser Index: Every issue.
Special Issues:
 Directory of Production Companies for Animation and Special Effects. $3. January/February.
 Product Manufacturers Directory of Computer Pictures—hardware and software for computer graphics. $3. November/December.

0357. COMPUTERDATA.
501 Oakdale Rd., Downsview, Ontario, Can. M3N 1W7.
Annual Subscription: $20. **Frequency:** Monthly.
Publisher: Page Communications.
Indexed or Abstracted Online: ABI/Inform.
Special Issues:
 Canadian Data Processing Directory-Vol. I: Hardware. Published as a separate issue. $25 (for Vol. 1 and 2). Not included in the subscription price. May.
 Canadian Data Processing Directory-Vol. II: Software. Published as a separate issue. $25 (for Vol. 1 and 2). Not included in the subscription price. August.

0358. COMPUTERS AND PEOPLE.
815 Washington St., Newtonville, MA 02160.
Annual Subscription: $34.50. **Frequency:** 6/yr.
Publisher: Berkeley Enterprises, Inc.
Editorial Index: Annual. Author. March/April.
Special Issues:
 Computer Directory and Buyers Guide—includes over 3300 organizations in computers and data processing. Started 1951. Published as a separate issue. $27.90. March/September.

0359. COMPUTERWORLD.
375 Cochituate Rd., Framingham, MA 01701.
Annual Subscription: $44. **Frequency:** Weekly.
Publisher: C. W. Communications Inc.
Advertiser Index: Every issue.
Indexed or Abstracted Online: ABI/Inform; Predicasts; Trade & Industry Index.
Special Issues:
 Computerworld OA (Office Automation). Started 1983. Published as a separate issue. $5/12 for the year. Bimonthly. February/April/June/August/October/December.
 Computerworld on Communications. Started 1983. Published as a separate issue. $1.50. May/September.
 Annual Hardware Roundup: Mainframes; Minicomputers; Microcomputers—each survey is in a different August issue. Started 1981. $1.50. August.
 Computer Systems Buyers Guide: Mainframes, Superminis, Minis, Small Business Systems, Micros. Started 1983. Published as a separate issue. $1.50. August.
 Terminals & Peripherals Buyers Guide. Started 1983. Published as a separate issue. $1.50. October.
 Software Buyers Guide. Started 1983. Published as a separate issue. $1.50. November.

0360. CONCRETE.
205 West Wacker Dr., Chicago, IL 60606.
Annual Subscription: $12.
Publisher: Pit & Quarry Publications, Inc.
Advertiser Index: Every issue.
Editorial Index: Annual. Subject. December.
Special Issues:
 Review & Outlook. $1.50. January.
 Precast/Prestressed. $1.50. April.
 Ready-Mixed. $1.50. June.
 Concrete Masonry (Block). $1.50. August.
 Buyers Guide. $1.50. September.
 Concrete Pipe. $1.50. October.

0361. CONCRETE CONSTRUCTION.
426 S. Westgate, Addison, IL 60101.
Annual Subscription: $12. **Frequency:** Monthly.
Publisher: Concrete Construction Publications.
Advertiser Index: Every issue.
Editorial Index: Annual. Subject. December.

Special Issues:
Concrete Sourcebook. Started 1983. Published as a separate issue. $19.50. Not included in the subscription price. February.
Annual Reference and Buyer's Guide. Started 1975. $2. December.

0362. THE CONSERVATIONIST.
50 Wolf Rd., Room 504, Albany, NY 12233.
Annual Subscription: $5. **Frequency:** 6/yr.
Publisher: NYS Department of Environmental Conservation.
Editorial Index: Biannual. Subject/Title/Author. December.
Indexed Online: Magazine Index.

0363. CONSTRUCTION.
7297-R Lee Highway, Falls Church, VA 22042.
Annual Subscription: $38. **Frequency:** 26/yr.
Publisher: Construction Publishing Co.
Special Issues:
Forecast. January.
Directory and Buyers Guide. $2. March.
New Truck & Trailer Preview. November.

0364. CONSTRUCTION CONTRACTING.
P.O. Box 3030, Redondo Beach, CA 90277.
Annual Subscription: $17. **Frequency:** Bimonthly.
Publisher: Nolan Sands Publishing Co.
Advertiser Index: Every issue.
Editorial Index: Annual. Subject. December.
Special Issues:
Equipment Specs. $3. January.

0365. CONSTRUCTION DIGEST.
101 E. 14th St., P.O. Box 603, Indianapolis, IN 46206.
Annual Subscription: $24. **Frequency:** 24/yr.
Publisher: Construction Digest, Inc.
Advertiser Index: Every issue.
Editorial Index: Annual. Subject/Title. Annually.
Special Issues:
Buyers Guide & Directory—Eastern Region: Indiana, Ohio and Kentucky. Western Region: Illinois and Eastern Missouri. Started 1970. Published as a separate issue. $18 (East or West)/30 (for both). March.
Truck Issue. Started 1970. November.

0366. CONSTRUCTION EQUIPMENT.
1350 East Touhy, Box 5080, Des Plaines, IL 60018.
Annual Subscription: $35. **Frequency:** Monthly.
Publisher: Cahners Publishing Co.
Advertiser Index: Every issue.
Indexed Online: Trade & Industry Index.
Special Issues:
Rebuilding America-Highways. Started 1983. $4. January/July.
Rebuilding America-Bridges. Started 1983. $4. February/August.
Industry Equipment-Owning Giants—top 270 industry equipment-owning giants. Started 1982. $4. March.
Rebuilding America-Mass Transportation. Started 1983. $4. March/September.
Rebuilding America-Urban Redevelopment. Started 1983. $4. April/October.
Buyers Guide. Started 1965. Published as a separate issue. $20. May.
Rebuilding America-Water Resources. Started 1983. $4. May/November.
Rebuilding America-Energy Systems. Started 1983. $4. June/December.
Construction Contractor Equipment-Owning Rights—top 314. Started 1974. $4. September.

0367. CONSTRUCTION EQUIPMENT DISTRIBUTION.
615 W. 22nd St., Oak Brook, IL 60521.
Annual Subscription: $15. **Frequency:** 10/yr.
Publisher: Associated Equipment Distributors.
Advertiser Index: Every issue.
Editorial Index: Annual. Title. January/February.
Special Issues:
Convention Issue—Associated Equipment Distributors. January/February.
Membership Directory. Started 1948. May.

0368. CONSTRUCTION REVIEW.
Superintendent of Documents, GPO, Washington, DC 20402.
Annual Subscription: $17. **Frequency:** 6/yr.
Publisher: Department of Commmerce.
Editorial Index: Title. Cumulative 4-year title index in each issue.
Indexed or Abstracted Online: Trade & Industry Index; Predicasts.
Special Issues:
Historical Data Issue—on construction, construction materials, interest rates, etc., for years 1947-82. $4.75. One time only. July/August '83.
Construction Outlook—statistics and outlook on construction employment; private residential construction; mobile homes; hotels and other nonresidential; office buildings; industrial; electric and gas utilities; farm, hospital and institutional; mining structures; public construction; schools; highways and streets; sewer and water supply systems; military facilities; federal construction. $4.75. November/December.

0369. THE CONSTRUCTION SPECIFIER.
601 Madison St., Alexandria, VA 22314.
Annual Subscription: $40. **Frequency:** Monthly.
Publisher: Construction Specifications Institute.
Advertiser Index: Every issue.
Editorial Index: Annual. Subject/Title/Author. December.
Special Issues:
Annual Specifiers' Guide to Products. Started 1980. Published as a separate issue. $3. February.
Annual Specifiers' Compendium of Handbooks and Manuals. Started 1982. Published as a separate issue. $3. August.
Legal Feature. Started 1980. $3. November.

0370. CONSTRUCTIONEER.
One Bond St., Chatham, NJ 07928.
Annual Subscription: $25. **Frequency:** Biweekly.
Publisher: Reports Corp.
Advertiser Index: Every issue.
Special Issues:
Construction Forecast. Started 1957. $1. January.
Directory. Started 1957. $10. March.
Utility Contracting. Started 1965. $1. April.
Public Works. Started 1965. $1. July.
Winter Operations. Started 1965. $1. September.
Trucks, Trailers/Heavy Haul & Rigging. Started 1965. $1. November.

0371. CONSTRUCTOR.
1957 E Street, NW, Washington, DC 20006.
Annual Subscription: $10. **Frequency:** Monthly.
Publisher: Associated General Contractors of America.
Special Issues:
Membership Directory and Buyer's Guide. $35. July.

0372. CONSULTANTS NEWS.
Templeton Rd., Fitzwilliam, NH 03447.
Annual Subscription: $66. **Frequency:** Monthly.
Publisher: Kennedy & Kennedy, Inc.

0373. CONSULTING ENGINEER.
1301 South Grove Ave., Barrington, IL 60010.
Annual Subscription: $35. **Frequency:** Monthly.
Publisher: Technical Publishing Co.
Advertiser Index: Every issue.
Editorial Index: Semi-Annual. Subject. December/June.
Special Issues:
Specification Update—700+ Literature offerings from manufacturers. $4. February/May/August/November.

0374. CONSUMER ELECTRONICS.
135 West 50th St., New York, NY 10022.
Annual Subscription: $50. **Frequency:** Monthly.
Publisher: CES Publishing.
Special Issues:
  Annual Buyer's Guide.   January.
  Annual Statistical Forecast.   March.
  Comdex Computer Issue.   Started 1983.   Published as a separate issue.   March.
  Media Specials (consumer electronics show daily).   June/January.

0375. CONSUMER REPORTS.
P.O. Box 1949, Marion, OH 43305.
Annual Subscription: $12. **Frequency:** Monthly.
Publisher: Consumer Union of U.S., Inc.
Editorial Index: Monthly. Subject. Every issue.
Special Issues:
  Auto Issue. $1.50.   April.
  "Best Buy" Gifts. $1.50.   November.
  Consumer Buying Guide. $3.50.   December.

0376. CONSUMERS' RESEARCH MAGAZINE.
401 C Street NE, Ste. 301, Washington, DC 20002.
Annual Subscription: $15. **Frequency:** Monthly.
Publisher: Consumers' Research Inc.
Editorial Index: Monthly. Subject. Monthly (cumulative to date).
Indexed Online: Magazine Index.

0377. CONTINUING EDUCATION FOR THE FAMILY PHYSICIAN.
53 Park Pl., New York, NY 10007.
Annual Subscription: $40/60. **Frequency:** Monthly.
Publisher: Le Jacq Publishing, Inc.
Editorial Index: Annual. Subject/Author. December.

0378. CONTRACT.
1515 Broadway, New York, NY 10036.
Annual Subscription: $18. **Frequency:** Monthly.
Publisher: Gralla Publications.
Advertiser Index: Every issue.
Editorial Index: Annual. Subject. January.
Special Issues:
  Directory/Buyers Guide—for interior designers and architects; lists sources of supply for furniture and furnishings, with emphasis on commercial and institutional design and space planning.   Started 1970. $8.   January.
  NEOCON-Annual Exposition of Contract Furniture and Furnishings. $8.   May.
  Open Plan Specifiers Guide.   Started 1973. $8.   July.
  Whos Who in Contract Design.   Started 1976. $8.   August.
  Institute of Business Designers Awards. $8.   November.

0379. CONTRACTOR MAGAZINE.
1301 South Grove Ave., Barrington, IL 60010.
Annual Subscription: $36. **Frequency:** 24/yr.
Publisher: Technical Publishing Co.
Indexed Online: Trade & Industry Index.
Special Issues:
  ASHRAE (American Society of Heating, Refrigerating and Air Conditioning Engineers) Show/Home Builders Show (National Association of Home Builders). $3.   January.
  MCAA (Mechanical Contractors Association of America) Show. $3.   February.
  ACCA (Air Conditioning Contractors of America) Show/American Subcontractors Association Convention. $3.   March.
  ASSE (American Society of Sanitary Engineering) Convention. $3.   May.
  ASA (American Supply Association) Annual Meeting/PHCC (National Association of Plumbing, Heating, Cooling Contractors) Exposition/SMACNA (Sheet Metal and Air Conditioning Contractor National Association) Convention/Hydronics Institute (boiler manufacturers). $3.   June.

0380. CONTROL ENGINEERING.
875 Third Ave., New York, NY 10022.
Annual Subscription: $45. **Frequency:** Monthly.
Publisher: Technical Publishing Co.
Advertiser Index: Every issue.
Editorial Index: Annual. Subject. December.
Indexed Online: Trade & Industry Index.
Special Issues:
  Control Products Specifier—product catalog.   Started 1983.   Published as a separate issue. $15.   September.

0381. CONVENIENCE STORE NEWS.
254 West 31st St., New York, NY 10001.
Annual Subscription: $18. **Frequency:** 16/yr.
Publisher: BMT Publications.
Special Issues:
  National Association of Convenience Stores Convention.   October.
  C-Store Chain Directory. $10.   December.
  Industry Report.   Published as a separate issue. $30.   Not included in the subscription price.   Fall.
  Quarterly Gallup Marketing Trends Report.   Varies.

0382. COPYRIGHT MANAGEMENT.
85 Irving St., P.O. Box 436, Arlington, MA 02174.
Annual Subscription: $96. **Frequency:** Monthly.
Publisher: Richard A. Onanian.
Editorial Index: Annual. Title. December.

0383. THE CORNELL HOTEL & RESTAURANT ADMINISTRATION QUARTERLY.
327 Statler Hall, Ithaca, NY 14853.
Annual Subscription: $25. **Frequency:** Quarterly.
Publisher: Cornell University Hotel School.
Editorial Index: Annual. Title. February.
Special Issues:
  Educators' Forum.   Started 1982. $7.50.   August.
  Bibliography of Hotel and Restaurant Administration.   Started 1940.   Published as a separate issue. $20.   Not included in the subscription price.   Fall.

0384. CORPORATE REPORT MINNESOTA.
7831 East Bush Lake Rd., Minneapolis, MN 55435.
Annual Subscription: $18. **Frequency:** Monthly.
Publisher: Doin Communication.
Special Issues:
  Guide to Leasing. $2.   April.
  Meetings and Conventions. $2.   September.
  Corporate Report Fact Book. $2.   October.
  Private 100 (major companies). $2.   December.

0385. COST ENGINEERING.
308 Monongahela Bldg., Morgantown, WV 26505.
Annual Subscription: $18. **Frequency:** Monthly.
Publisher: American Association of Cost Engineers.
Advertiser Index: Every issue.
Editorial Index: Annual. Title/Author. February.
Special Issues:
  Transactions of the American Association of Cost Engineers.   Started 1967.   Published as a separate issue. $27.50 (members); $33.50 (non-members).   Not included in the subscription price.   July.
  American Association of Cost Engineers—highlights of annual meeting.   October.

0386. CRAFT & NEEDLEWORKING AGE.
490 Rte. 9, Rd. 3, Box 420, Englishtown, NJ 07726.
Annual Subscription: $15. **Frequency:** Monthly.
Publisher: Hobby Publications Inc.
Advertiser Index: Every issue.
Special Issues:
  Hobby Industry Association Trade Show/Fall and Christmas Merchandising—buyers guide. $1.   January.
  Hobby Publications Annual Directory—includes doll house miniatures.   Published as a separate issue. $15.   June.

0387. CREATIVE COMPUTING.
P.O. Box 5214, Boulder, CO 80321.
Annual Subscription: $24.97. **Frequency:** Monthly.
Publisher: Ahl Computing, Inc.
Advertiser Index: Every issue.
Indexed Online: Magazine Index; Trade & Industry Index.
Special Issues:
Software Buyers Guide. Started 1982. Published as a separate issue. $3.95. Not included in the subscription price. May.
Buyers Guide to Personal Computers and Peripherals—hardware buyers guide. Started 1982. Published as a separate issue. $3.95. Not included in the subscription price. September.
Computer Games Reviews. $2.95. September.
Educational Software Reviews. $2.95. October.

0388. CREATIVE CRAFTS & MINIATURES.
P.O. Box 700, Newton, NJ 07860.
Annual Subscription: $7. **Frequency:** 6/yr.
Publisher: Carstens Publication Inc.
Advertiser Index: Every issue.
Editorial Index: Biennial. Subject/Title/Author. February/(even years).
Special Issues:
Buyers Guide. Monthly.

0389. CREDIT.
1101 14th St., Washington, DC 20005.
Annual Subscription: $16. **Frequency:** 6/yr.
Publisher: American Financial Services Association.
Special Issues:
Convention Issue: National Consumer Finance Association. Started 1982. $2. July/August.

0390. CREDIT & FINANCIAL MANAGEMENT.
475 Park Ave. South, New York, NY 10016.
Annual Subscription: $18. **Frequency:** 11/yr.
Publisher: National Association of Credit Management.
Advertiser Index: Every issue.
Editorial Index: Annual. Subject/Title/Author. December.
Indexed or Abstracted Online: Predicasts; Management Contents; Trade & Industry Index; ABI/Inform.
Special Issues:
Credit Manual of Commercial Laws—feature articles; state and federal regulations and laws; specimen contracts and credit instruments; statistics; etc. Published as a separate issue. $38.50. Not included in the subscription price. January.
National Association of Credit Management Annual Report. $2. February.
National Association of Credit Management Convention Report. $2. July/August.

0391. CREDIT UNION EXECUTIVE.
P.O. Box 4311, Madison, WI 53701.
Annual Subscription: $16. **Frequency:** Quarterly.
Publisher: Credit Union National Assn.
Advertiser Index: Every issue.
Editorial Index: Annual. Subject/Author. Spring.

0392. CREDIT UNION EXECUTIVE.
P.O. Box 431, Madison, WI 53701.
Annual Subscription: $16. **Frequency:** Quarterly.
Publisher: Credit Union National Association.
Advertiser Index: Every issue.
Editorial Index: Annual. Subject/Author. Spring.

0393. CREDIT UNION MAGAZINE.
P.O. Box 431, Madison, WI 53701.
Annual Subscription: $15. **Frequency:** Monthly.
Publisher: Credit Union National Association.
Advertiser Index: Every issue.
Editorial Index: Annual. Subject. December.
Special Issues:
Annual Gallup Poll of Public Attitudes Toward the Public Schools. Started 1969. $2.50. September.

0394. CREDIT WORLD.
243 North Lindbergh Blvd., P.O. Box 27357, St. Louis, MO 63141.
Annual Subscription: $18. **Frequency:** 6/yr.
Publisher: International Consumer Credit Association.
Editorial Index: Cumulative, August (1980-83). Subject/Title/Author. September/October.
Indexed or Abstracted Online: ABI/Inform; Management Contents.
Special Issues:
International Consumer Credit Association Conference Report. Started 1980. $3. June/July.
Who's Who of Consumer Credit Management. Published as a separate issue. $15. Not included in the subscription price. September.
Consumer Credit Buyers Guide—products and services for consumer credit executives. Started 1980. $3. December/January.

0395. THE CRISIS.
186 Remsen St., Brooklyn, NY 11201.
Annual Subscription: $6. **Frequency:** Monthly.
Publisher: National Association for the Advancement of Colored People.
Editorial Index: Annual. Author. December.
Indexed or Abstracted Online: ERIC.
Special Issues:
NAACP Annual Convention Resolutions. $2. December.

0396. C-STORE BUSINESS.
1351 Washington Blvd., Stamford, CT 06902.
Annual Subscription: $21. **Frequency:** 10/yr.
Publisher: Maclean Hunter Media, Inc.
Advertiser Index: Every issue.
Special Issues:
Annual Report of the Convenience Store Industry. Started 1971. $3. October.
Equipment Guide. $3. November/December.

0397. CURRICULUM PRODUCT REVIEW.
19 Davis St., Belmont, CA 94002.
Annual Subscription: Free (controlled circulation).
Frequency: 9/yr.
Publisher: Pitman Learning, Inc.
Advertiser Index: Every issue.
Special Issues:
Early Childhood/Careers. $2. January.
Science/The Arts. $2. February.
Social Studies/Bilingual Ed, Foreign Language. $2. March.
Computer Learning. $2. April.
Professional Development. $2. August.
Testing and Guidance/Life Skills. $2. September.
Social Studies/Values Education. $2. October.
Reading. $2. November.
Learning Technology/Audiovisual and Computer Software Award Winners. $2. December.

0398. CYCLE.
P.O. Box 2776, Boulder, CO 80302.
Annual Subscription: $13.98. **Frequency:** Monthly.
Publisher: Ziff-Davis Publishing Co. Inc.
Advertiser Index: Every issue.
Editorial Index: Annual. Subject/Title. January.
Indexed Online: Magazine Index.
Special Issues:
Cycle Buyers Guide—includes 10 best motorcycle buys of the year. Started 1968. Published as a separate issue. $2.95. Not included in the subscription price. April.
Street and Touring guide. Started 1980. Published as a separate issue. $2.95. Not included in the subscription price. May.

0399. CYCLE WORLD.
P.O. Box 5338, Boulder, CO 80321.
Annual Subscription: $13.94. **Frequency:** Monthly.
Publisher: CBS Publications.

Advertiser Index: Every issue.
Indexed Online: Magazine Index.
Special Issues:
Cycle World Road Test Annual & Buyers Guide (Motorcycles). Started 1963. Published as a separate issue. $2.95. January or February.

0400. DVM.
1 East First St., Duluth, MN 55802.
Annual Subscription: $20. **Frequency:** Monthly.
Publisher: Harcourt Brace Jovanovich Inc.
Special Issues:
Eastern States Veterinary Conference. $2. January.
Intermountain Veterinary Association Convention/American Association of Bovine Practitioners Convention Report. $2. February.
American Animal Hospital Association Convention. $2. March.
American Veterinary Medical Association Convention. $2. July.

0401. DAILY COMMERCIAL NEWS AND CONSTRUCTION RECORD.
34 St. Patrick St., Toronto, Ontario, Can. M5T 1V2.
Annual Subscription: $230. **Frequency:** Daily.
Publisher: Southam Communications Ltd.
Special Issues:
Progress Reports (Monday Supplement): Economic Review. January/April/July/October.
Progress Reports (Monday Supplements): Steel. June.
Progress Reports (Monday Supplements): Municipal Construction. August.
Progress Reports (Monday Supplements): Concrete. September.
Progress Reports (Monday Supplements): Trucking, Rigging, Hauling. November.
Progress Reports (Monday Supplements): Ontario Construction Handbook. December.

0402. DAIRY FIELD.
111 East Wacker Dr., Chicago, IL 60601.
Annual Subscription: $34. **Frequency:** Monthly.
Publisher: Harcourt, Brace, Jovanovich.
Advertiser Index: Every issue.
Editorial Index: Annual. Subject. December.
Special Issues:
Frozen Products/Consumer Survey: Ice Cream. $3. January.
Milk Products. $3. April.
Ingredients and Flavors. $3. May.
Fluid Milk/Consumer Survey: Fluid Dairy Products. $3. June.
Packaging/Aseptic Packaging. $3. July.
Cultured Products. $3. August.
Expo-in-Print: New Products. $3. September.
Cheese/Consumer Survey: Cheese Products. $3. October.
Dairy Regulators—Washington "Who's Who". $3. November.
Buying Guide/Industry Trends. $3. December.

0403. DAIRY RECORD.
5725 East River Rd., Chicago, IL 60631.
Annual Subscription: $40. **Frequency:** Monthly.
Publisher: Gorman Publ. Company.
Advertiser Index: Every issue.
Special Issues:
Buyer's Guide. Published as a separate issue. $17. June.
Dairy Expo Show Report. $6. Every 2 years. November.
Processor of the Year. Started 1980. $6. November or December.

0404. DANCE MAGAZINE.
P.O. Box 960, Farmingdale, NY 11737.
Annual Subscription: $22. **Frequency:** Monthly.
Publisher: Danad Publishing.
Special Issues:
College Guide—list of college dance programs. Published as a separate issue. $10.95. Not included in the subscription price. January.
Calendar of Summer Dance Events. $3. May.
Awards Issue. $2.50. September.
Directory of Dance Services—international listing of dancers, choreographers, retailers of dance-related merchandise, etc. Started 1970. Published as a separate issue. $20. Not included in the subscription price. October.
Nutcracker Issue—lists international performances of "The Nutcracker" for holiday season. $2.50. December.

0405. DATA COMMUNICATIONS.
1221 Ave. of the Americas, New York, NY 10020.
Annual Subscription: $24. **Frequency:** Monthly.
Publisher: McGraw-Hill, Inc.
Advertiser Index: Every issue.
Editorial Index: Annual. Subject. January.
Indexed or Abstracted Online: AMI; ABI/Inform; Trade & Industry Index; Predicasts.
Special Issues:
National Computer Conference Preview. $5. May.
DC 50—the 50 largest companies doing business in data communications. Started 1983. Published as a separate issue. $5. September.
Buyers Guide. Published as a separate issue. $25. November.
The Year in Review. $5. December.

0406. DATA MANAGEMENT.
505 Busse Hwy., Park Ridge, IL 60068.
Annual Subscription: $16. **Frequency:** Monthly.
Publisher: Data Processing Management Association.
Advertiser Index: Every issue.
Editorial Index: Annual. Subject/Title/Author. December.
Indexed Online: ABI/Inform; Trade & Industry Index.
Special Issues:
Profile of DPMA Executive Council. $3. January.
DPMA Distinguished Information Sciences Award/DPMA Annual Conference Proceedings. $3. December or January.

0407. DATA USER NEWS.
Superintendent of Documents, Government Printing Office, Washington, DC 20402.
Annual Subscription: $20. **Frequency:** Monthly.
Publisher: Bureau of the Census.
Editorial Index: Annual. Subject. December.

0408. DATAMATION.
875 Third Ave., New York, NY 10022.
Annual Subscription: $42. **Frequency:** Monthly.
Publisher: Technical Publishing Co.
Advertiser Index: Every issue.
Indexed Online: Trade & Industry Index.
Special Issues:
National Computer Conference (NCC) Preview. May.
Mainframe Survey. June.
Datamation 100. July.
Europe's Top 25 DP Companies. August.
DP Salary Survey. October.
Systems Software Survey. December.

0409. DEALERSCOPE.
115 Second Ave., Waltham, MA 02154.
Annual Subscription: Free to qualified persons. **Frequency:** Monthly.
Publisher: Bartex Publishing Group.
Special Issues:
Buyers Guide. $25 (to nonqualified). May/December.
Consumer Electronics Show. June.
Dealerscope 100. July.
Awards: Audio/Video Men of the Year. August.

0410. DECORATING RETAILER.
1050 North Lindbergh Blvd., St. Louis, MO 63132.

Annual Subscription: $27. **Frequency:** Monthly.
Publisher: National Decorating Products Association.
Advertiser Index: Every issue.
Special Issues:
   Cost of Doing Business Survey. $2.50. September.
   Directory of the Wallcoverings Industry. Started 1972.
      Published as a separate issue. $12. December.

0411. DECORATIVE PRODUCTS WORLD.
2911 Washington Ave., St. Louis, MO 63103.
Annual Subscription: $21. **Frequency:** Monthly.
Publisher: American Paint Journal Co.
Advertiser Index: Every issue.
Special Issues:
   American Occupational Medical Association—Annual
      Meeting Program/Abstracts Issues. $12. July.

0412. DEFENSE ELECTRONICS.
1170 E. Meadow Dr., Palo Alto, CA 94303.
Annual Subscription: $24. **Frequency:** Monthly.
Publisher: E. W. Communications.
Advertiser Index: Every issue.
Editorial Index: Annual. Subject. December or January.
Indexed Online: Trade & Industry Index.
Special Issues:
   Marketing Directory & Buyers Guide. Started 1979. $5.
      February or March.
   International Countermeasures Handbook. $5.
      September.
   Top 100 Defense Electronics Contractors. Started 1983.
      $5. September.
   Electronics Hardware Matrix of Airborne EW Systems.
      Started 1983. $5. October.

0413. DEFENSE MANAGEMENT JOURNAL.
U.S. Government Printing Office, Washington, DC 20402.
Annual Subscription: $11. **Frequency:** Quarterly.
Publisher: Department of Defense.
Editorial Index: Annual. Subject. December.

0414. DELI NEWS.
P.O. Box 66367, Mar Vista, CA 90066.
Annual Subscription: $15. **Frequency:** Monthly.
Publisher: Southern California Deli Council.
Special Issues:
   Directory of Delicatessen Products. Started 1966. $1.50.
      January.
   National Deli Seminar. $1.50. September.

0415. DENTAL LABORATORY REVIEW.
One East First St., Duluth, MN 55802.
Annual Subscription: $16. **Frequency:** Monthly.
Publisher: Harcourt Brace Jovanovich.
Advertiser Index: Every issue.
Special Issues:
   State of Industry Survey. $2. February.
   Salary Survey—growth of wages and benefits in industry.
      $2. Biennially. August or September.
   Buyers Guide. Started 1975. $7. October.

0416. DENTAL PRODUCTS REPORT.
4849 Golf Rd., Ste. 400, Skokie, IL 60077.
Annual Subscription: $33. **Frequency:** 11/yr.
Publisher: Irving-Cloud Publications.
Special Issues:
   Buyer's Guide—includes information on trends as well as top
      products. November.

0417. DESIGN ENGINEERING.
777 Bay St., Toronto, Ontario, Can. M5W 1A7.
Annual Subscription: $32/24. **Frequency:** Monthly.
Publisher: Maclean Hunter Ltd.
Advertiser Index
Editorial Index: Annual. Subject. December.
Special Issues:
   National Design Engineering Show and Conference. $6.
      March.
   Engineering Materials in Review. $6. April.
   Canadian CAD/CAM Exposition and Conference. $6.
      May.
   Bearing Technology Update. $6. June.
   Fluid Power and Controls Buyers Guide. Started 1963.
      $10. July.
   Canadian Design Engineering 2nd Annual Show-In-Print.
      $6. September.
   Mechanical Power Transmission Buyers' Guide. Started
      1965. $10. October.
   New Directions in Automation. $6. November.
   Fluid Couplings Report. $6. December.

0418. DESIGN NEWS.
221 Columbus Ave., Boston, MA 02116.
Annual Subscription: $40. **Frequency:** 24/yr.
Publisher: Cahners Publishing Co.
Advertiser Index: Every issue.
Special Issues:
   Power Transmission Directory/Design Engineering Show.
      $4. March.
   Aerospace. $4. April.
   Fluid Power Directory. $4. May.
   Fastening Directory/Design Product Showcase. $4. July.
   Energy Conservation. $4. August.
   Materials Directory/Automotive. $4. September.
   Home Appliances. $4. October.
   Electrical/Electronic Directory/Design Awards. $4.
      November.
   Significant New Components. $4. December.

0419. THE DESIGNER.
H D C Publications, 192 Lexington Ave., New York, NY 10016.
Frequency: Monthly.
Publisher: Same.
Advertiser Index: Every issue.
Special Issues:
   Designer File: Floorcovering. Started 1976. February or
      March.
   Designer File: Wallcovering. Started 1976. August.

0420. DESKTOP COMPUTING.
P.O. Box 917, Farmingdale, NY 11737.
Annual Subscription: $24.97. **Frequency:** Monthly.
Publisher: Wayne Green Inc.
Advertiser Index: Every issue.
Editorial Index: Annual. Subject. December.
Indexed Online: BRS.

0421. DIALYSIS & TRANSPLANTATION.
12849 Magnolia Blvd., North Hollywood, CA 91607.
Annual Subscription: $35. **Frequency:** Monthly.
Publisher: Creative Age Publications.
Advertiser Index: Every issue.
Editorial Index: Annual. Title. December.

0422. THE DIAPASON.
380 Northwest Highway, Des Plaines, IL 60016.
Annual Subscription: $10. **Frequency:** Monthly.
Publisher: American Institute of Organbuilders.
Editorial Index: Annual. Subject/Author. January.
Special Issues:
   American Musicological Society Convention. $2.
      November.

0423. DIE CASTING ENGINEER.
P.O. Box 3002, River Grove, IL 60171.
Annual Subscription: $18. **Frequency:** 6/yr.
Publisher: The Society of Die Casting Engineers.
Advertiser Index: Every issue.
Editorial Index: Biennial. Subject. Varies.
Special Issues:
   Die Casting Exposition & Congress. $3.50. September/
      October.

0424. DIESEL & GAS TURBINE WORLDWIDE.
13555 Bishop's Court, Brookfield, WI 53005.
Annual Subscription: $45. **Frequency:** 10/yr.
Publisher: Diesel & Gas Turbine Publications.
Advertiser Index: Every issue.

Special Issues:
Diesel & Gas Turbine Worldwide Catalog—reference book and buyers guide for diesel engines, natural gas engines, industrial gas turbines and accessories and transmission components. Published as a separate issue. $55. Not included in the subscription price. May.

0425. DIESEL PROGRESS NORTH AMERICAN.
13555 Bishop's Court, Brookfield, WI 53005.
Annual Subscription: $35. **Frequency:** Monthly.
Publisher: Diesel & Gas Turbine Publications.
Advertiser Index: Every issue.
Editorial Index: Subject/Title/Author. Available separately on request.
Indexed Online: Trade & Industry Index.
Special Issues:
Electrical Generating Systems Association Membership/Product Directory. $4. January.
Off-Highway OEM Yearbook. $4. March.
Association of Diesel Specialists Membership Directory. $4. April.
Annual Diesel Engine Roundup. Started 1979. $4. June.
Society of Automotive Engineers Show. $4. September.

0426. DIGITAL DESIGN.
1050 Commonwealth Ave., Boston, MA 02215.
Annual Subscription: Free (qualified engineers).
Frequency: Monthly.
Publisher: Morgan-Grampian Publishing.
Advertiser Index: Every issue.
Special Issues:
Computer Compatible Directory & Technology Review. Started 1981. Published as a separate issue. $4. October.
Salary Survey. Started 1983. $4. December.

0427. DIMENSIONS IN HEALTH SERVICE.
25 Imperial St., Toronto, Ontario, Can. M5P 1C1.
Annual Subscription: $29. **Frequency:** Monthly.
Publisher: Canadian Hospital Association.
Advertiser Index: Every issue.
Editorial Index: Annual. Subject/Author. December.
Special Issues:
Canadian Hospital Directory. Published as a separate issue. $37.50. Not included in the subscription price. September.
Annual Purchasing Issue. October.

0428. THE DISCOUNT MERCHANDISER.
2 Park Ave., New York, NY 10016.
Annual Subscription: $25. **Frequency:** Monthly.
Publisher: Schwartz Publications.
Advertiser Index: Every issue.
Indexed or Abstracted Online: ABI/Inform; Management Contents.
Special Issues:
Housewares (National Housewares Manufacturers Association). $3. January/July.
Toys/Sporting Goods (National Sporting Goods Association). $3. February.
Automotive Oil. $3. March.
Combination Stores. Started 1982. $3. April.
National Mass Retailing Institute Convention. $3. May.
True Look of the Discount Industry, Part 1: Marketing—includes $100 Million Club: Leading Discount Chains. Started 1961. $15. May.
True Look of the Discount Industry, Part 2: Merchandising. Started 1961. $15. June.
Hardware (National Hardware Show). $3. August.
Health and Beauty Aids. $3. September.
Automotive Parts. $3. November.
Presidents Round Table. Started 1970. $3. December.

0429. DISCOUNT STORE NEWS.
425 Park Ave., New York, NY 10022.
Annual Subscription: $20. **Frequency:** 26/yr.
Publisher: Lebhar-Friedman Inc.
Indexed Online: Trade & Industry Index.
Special Issues:
Consumer Electronics Show. $2. January/June.
National Sporting Goods Association Show. $2. January.
Spring Car Care. $2. February.
Toy Fair/Winter Hardware Show. $2. February.
Annual Product Movement Audit/Photo Marketing Association Show. $2. March.
MAGIC Show (men's apparel manufacturers, California). $2. March/October.
Off-Price Apparel Chain Census/Home Center Show. $2. March.
Housewares Show. $2. April/October.
Mass Retailing Institute Convention. $2. May.
Consumer Electronics Discount Chain Census. $2. June.
Mass Market Licensing Report/Discount Automotive Chain Census. $2. June.
Annual Statistical Analysis and Census of Discount Chains—the top chains, and department-by-department analysis. Started 1962. $20. July.
Discount Toy Chain Census/National Hardware Show. $2. August.
Catalog Showroom Census/Automotive Parts & Accessories Association Show/Consumer Electronics Magazine. $2. September.
Discount Sporting Goods Chain Census/SPARC Awards (supplier performance awards by retail categories—top manufacturers). $2. September.
AGMC (Association of General Merchandise Chains) Convention. $2. October.
Supplier Analysis Issue—top vendors by merchandise category. $2. November.
Full-Issue Profile of Leading Discount Chain—all merchandise categories, retail strategies, key executives. $2. December.

0430. DISTRIBUTION.
Chilton Way, Radnor, PA 19089.
Annual Subscription: $20. **Frequency:** Monthly.
Publisher: Chilton Company.
Advertiser Index: Every issue.
Editorial Index: Annual. Subject/Author. December.
Special Issues:
Intermodal Guide—names & addresses of key truck, air and steamship lines, railroads, ports, public warehouses. July.

0431. DIXIE CONTRACTOR.
P.O. Box 280, Decatur, GA 30031.
Annual Subscription: $15. **Frequency:** 26/yr.
Publisher: Dixie Contractor.
Advertiser Index: Every issue.
Special Issues:
Directory Issue—lists all construction machinery manufacturers in US; all construction machinery distributors in the Southeast. $10. March/September.

0432. DOGS IN CANADA.
43 Railside Rd., Don Mills, Ontario, Can. M3A 3L9.
Annual Subscription: $18. **Frequency:** Monthly.
Publisher: Apex Publishers & Publicity Ltd.
Special Issues:
Dogs Annual. $5. November.

0433. DOORS AND HARDWARE.
7711 Old Springhouse Rd., McLean, VA 22102.
Annual Subscription: $12.50. **Frequency:** Monthly.
Publisher: Door and Hardware Institute.
Advertiser Index: Every issue.
Editorial Index: Annual. Subject/Title/Author. January.
Special Issues:
Membership Directory. Published as a separate issue. January.
Convention Issue. May.
Buyers Guide. Published as a separate issue. Triennially. 1984 (Last).

0434. DRILLING CONTRACTOR.
3737 Westcenter, Houston, TX 77210.
Annual Subscription: $12. **Frequency:** Monthly.
Publisher: International Association of Drilling Contractors.
Advertiser Index: Every issue.
Special Issues:
 Offshore Annual Report. $2. May.
 International Association of Drilling Contractors Convention. $2. September.
 Production Operations. $2. October.
 Forecast. $2. November.
 Hotspots of Activity. $2. December.

0435. DRILLING, THE WELLSITE PUBLICATION.
P.O. Box 7000, Dallas, TX 75209.
Frequency: 13/yr.
Publisher: Associated Publishers Inc.
Advertiser Index
Special Issues:
 International Wellsite Report/Buyers Guide. February.
 Equipment and Services Issue. April.
 Drilling Technology. May.
 Offshore Technology Conference. May.
 Deep Hole Report. July.
 Annual Report to the Drilling Contractor—contract industry. Started 1940. September.
 Society of Petroleum Engineers Show. September.
 Annual Rotary Rig Census. Started 1953. October.
 LAGCOE Show (Lafayette Gulf Coast Oil Show) Review & Forecast. October.
 Review & Forecast. December.

0436. DRILLSITE.
1015 Centre St., North, Ste. 200, Calgary, Alberta, Can. T2E 2P8.
Annual Subscription: $12. **Frequency:** 6/yr.
Publisher: MacLean Hunter Ltd.
Advertiser Index: Every issue.
Special Issues:
 Drilling Muds and Mud Systems. February.
 Canada Society of Exploration Geophysicists Conference. April.
 Equipment Rentals and Leasing. June.
 Canadian Offshore Resources Exposition and Conference. August.
 Transportation. October.
 Downhole Services. December.

0437. DRUG & COSMETIC INDUSTRY.
757 Third Ave., New York, NY 10017.
Annual Subscription: $15. **Frequency:** Monthly.
Publisher: Harcourt Bruce Jovanovich.
Advertiser Index
Special Issues:
 Cosmetic, Toiletry & Fragrance Assoc. convention. $2. February.
 Chemical Specialities Manufactures Association Convention. $2. May.
 Packaging Exposition. $2. June.
 Drug and Cosmetic Catalog—manufactuers and distributors of raw materials, packaging and machinery components. Published as a separate issue. $15. October or August.
 Society of Cosmetic-Chemists Convention. $2. December.

0438. DRUG STORE NEWS.
425 Park Ave., New York, NY 10022.
Annual Subscription: $12. **Frequency:** 25/yr.
Publisher: Lebhar-Friedman Inc.
Indexed or Abstracted Online: AMI.
Special Issues:
 Top 100 Ethical Over-the-Counter Drugs. $2. March.
 Annual Report of the Chain Drug Industry. $10. April or May.
 Reference for Pharmacy Practice. Published as a separate issue. $2. April.
 Top 100 Pharmaceuticals. $2. April.
 Triple A Product Study. $2. July.
 Nielson Report on Drug Stores—marketing statistics. Started 1972. $2. September.
 Drug Wholesaler Annual Report. $2. October.
 Annual Consumer Study. $2. December.

0439. DRUG TOPICS.
680 Kinderkamack Rd., Oradell, NJ 07649.
Annual Subscription: $26. **Frequency:** Bimonthly.
Publisher: Medical Economics Company.
Special Issues:
 Prescription Survey. $2. April.
 Report on Consumer Spending. $2. July.
 Financial Planning Guide. $2. October.
 Business Outlook. $2. December.

0440. DUN'S BUSINESS MONTH.
875 Third Ave., New York, NY 10022.
Annual Subscription: $27. **Frequency:** Monthly.
Publisher: Technical Publishing.
Editorial Index: Semi-Annual. Subject. June.
Special Issues:
 Annual Report Section. May.
 Executive Jobs (typical compensation by region & industry). Started 1975. N. November.
 Industry Ratios; Retailing; Wholesaling; Manufacturing. November or later.
 Corporate Dividend Achievers/Five Best-Managed Companies/Good News (best business news of the year). Started 1979. December.

0441. EDN.
221 Columbus Ave., Boston, MA 02116.
Annual Subscription: $45. **Frequency:** 26/yr.
Publisher: Cahners Publishing Co.
Editorial Index: Annual. Subject. January (for previous November through October).
Special Issues:
 EDN Technical Article Database Index—subject index to technical articles in major electronics magazines and technical journals for previous 6 months. $12. January/August.
 Communication Technology. $4. March.
 Test & Measurement. $4. April.
 Computer Graphics. $4. May.
 Electro/Mini-Micro Shows (Eastern electronics shows). $4. May.
 National Computer Conference. $4. June.
 Product Showcase. $4. July (twice)/December (twice).
 Military Electronics. $4. August.
 Engineering Productivity. $4. September.
 WESCON Show (Western Electronics Show). $4. October.

0442. E•ITV.
51 Sugar Hollow Rd., Danbury, CT 06810.
Annual Subscription: $15. **Frequency:** Monthly.
Publisher: C. S. Tepfer Publishing.
Advertiser Index: Every issue.
Editorial Index: Annual. Subject/Title. January.
Special Issues:
 Audio in Television. Started 1973. $2. February.
 Directory of Production Houses. Started 1980. $2. May.
 Interactive Video; Video/Computer Interface. Started 1981. $2. June.
 Testing and Measuring the TV Signal. Started 1978. $2. September or October.
 Directory of Program Sources. Started 1976. $2. November or December.
 Equipment Directories. Started 1972. $2. 2/yr. Spring & Fall.

0443. EARNSHAW'S INFANTS, GIRLS AND BOYS WEAR REVIEW.
393 7th Ave., New York, NY 10001.
Annual Subscription: $12. **Frequency:** Monthly.
Publisher: Earnshaw Publications Inc.
Advertiser Index: Every issue.

Special Issues:
Buyers Guide to New York Market—children's wear apparel industry in New York City. Published as a separate issue. $2. March.
Directory—children's wear manufacturers and industry. $2. December.

0444. EBONY.
820 South Michigan Ave., Chicago, IL 60605.
Annual Subscription: $16.
Publisher: Johnson Publishing Co.
Special Issues:
Black America—in-depth treatment of a specific aspect of current life in Black America. $1.75. August.

0445. ECOLOGY.
Center for Environmental Studies, Arizona State University, Tempe, AZ 85287.
Annual Subscription: $60. **Frequency:** 6/yr.
Publisher: Ecological Society of America.
Editorial Index: Annual. Subject/Author. December.

0446. ECONOMETRICA.
5801 South Ellis Ave., Chicago, IL 60637.
Annual Subscription: $79. **Frequency:** 6/yr.
Publisher: Econometric Society/University of Chicago Press.
Editorial Index: Annual. Author. November.
Indexed Online: Management Contents.
Special Issues:
Annual Reports of the Econometric Society. January.
Fellows of the Econometric Society. May.
Program of North American Meetings of the Econometric Society. May/November.

0447. ECONOMIC REPORT.
Terminal Annex, P.O. Box 2097, Los Angeles, CA 90051.
Annual Subscription: Free. **Frequency:** 3/yr.
Publisher: Security Pacific National Bank.
Indexed Online: Predicasts.
Special Issues:
Long-Term U.S. Outlook Edition—5-year forecast. Includes GNP, interest rates, corporatae profits, specific industries. Free. Spring/Summer.
California Outlook Edition and U.S. Update. Free. Fall.
International Edition—includes world trade, commodity prices, industrial countries; developing world; developing country finance. Free. Winter.

0448. ECONOMIC REVIEW—FEDERAL RESERVE BANK OF ATLANTA.
P.O. Box 1731, Atlanta, GA 30301.
Annual Subscription: Free. **Frequency:** Monthly.
Publisher: Federal Reserve Bank of Atlanta.
Editorial Index: Annual. Subject. December.
Special Issues:
The Southeast in 1983—state-by-state outlook for the Sixth District (Florida, Georgia, Tennessee, Louisiana, Alabama, Mississippi), plus North and South Carolina. Free. One time only. February '83.
Interstate Banking—outlook. Free. One time only. May '83.
Displacing the Check—forecast to 1994 on check-writing and electronic funds transfer. Free. One time only. August '83.
Commercial Bank Surveillance. Free. One time only. November '83.

0449. ECONOMIC REVIEW—FEDERAL RESERVE BANK OF KANSAS CITY.
925 Grand, Research Division, Kansas City, MO 64198.
Annual Subscription: Free. **Frequency:** 10/yr.
Publisher: Federal Reserve Bank of Kansas City.
Editorial Index: Annual. Title. December.
Special Issues:
Outlook for the Economy/Outlook for Agriculture. Free. December.

0450. ECONOMIC WORLD.
60 East 42nd St., New York, NY 10165.
Annual Subscription: $50. **Frequency:** Monthly.
Publisher: Economic Salon, Ltd.
Advertiser Index
Indexed Online: Predicasts.
Special Issues:
Directory of Japanese Companies in the U.S. Published as a separate issue. $150. Not included in the subscription price. Triennially. 1982 (last).

0451. EDITOR & PUBLISHER.
575 Lexington Ave., New York, NY 10022.
Annual Subscription: $35. **Frequency:** Weekly.
Publisher: Ferdinand C. Teubner.
Indexed or Abstracted Online: Predicasts; Trade & Industry Index; AMI.
Special Issues:
Newspaper Advertising Executives. $1. January.
International Yearbook—directory of the newspaper industry. Lists U.S. and Canadian daily and Sunday newspapers with circulation, advertising rates and data, names of executives and department editors. Published as a separate issue. $50. Not included in the subscription price. March.
ANPA Pre- and Convention Issues—American Newspaper Publishers Association. $1. April.
Linage Issue. $1. May.
Newspaper Promotion Issue. $1. May.
ANPA/RI Production Management Conference Issues—Pre- and convention report. $1. June.
Syndicate Directory. $5. July.
Color Awards Issue. $1. September.
Southern Newspaper Publishers Association Convention Coverage. $1. September.
Food Editors Conference. $1. October.
Inland Daily Press Association Issue. $1. October.
Market Guide—provides market data on U.S. and Canadian newspaper markets. Statistics include: population, households, banking, automobile registrations, utilities, industries, retail, chain and discount stores. Published as a separate issue. $50. Not included in the subscription price. October.
Directory of Journalism Awards—awards for journalism, writing, photography, public service, cartooning and art. $3. December.
Newspaper Mergers and Acquisitions. $1. December.

0452. THE EDUCATION DIGEST.
P.O. Box 8623, Ann Arbor, MI 48107.
Annual Subscription: $15. **Frequency:** 9/yr.
Publisher: Prakken Publications, Inc.
Advertiser Index: Every issue.
Editorial Index: Annual. Subject/Author. May.
Indexed Online: Magazine Index.

0453. EDUCATIONAL DEALER.
19 Davis Dr., Belmont, CA 94002.
Annual Subscription: Free (controlled circulation). **Frequency:** Quarterly.
Publisher: Pitman Learning, Inc.
Advertiser Index: Every issue.
Special Issues:
Spring New Products. Started 1983. April.
Annual Buyers Guide & Directory of Suppliers. July.
Featured Product Preview—National School Supply & Equipment Association convention. Started 1982. October.

0454. EDUCATIONAL DIGEST.
777 Bay St., Toronto, Ontario, Can. M5W 1A7.
Annual Subscription: $42/22. **Frequency:** 6/yr.
Publisher: Maclean Hunter Ltd.
Advertiser Index: Every issue.
Special Issues:
AV Report. $11/6. January/February.
Teaching Aids Digest Supplements. $11/6. 3/yr. March/April/September/October/November/December.
Plant Maintenance. $11/6. May/June.

Educational Buyers Guide & Directory. $11/6. July/August.

0455. ELECTRIC COMFORT CONDITIONING NEWS.
2132 Fordem Ave., Madison, WI 53704.
Annual Subscription: $20. **Frequency:** Monthly.
Publisher: EIP Inc.
Special Issues:
Electric Heating & Cooling Fact Book. March.

0456. ELECTRIC LIGHT & POWER.
1301 S. Grove Ave., Barrington, IL 60010.
Annual Subscription: $34. **Frequency:** Monthly.
Publisher: Technical Publishing Co.
Advertiser Index: Every issue.
Indexed Online: Trade & Industry Index.
Special Issues:
Electric Industry Man of the Year. Started 1976. $4. April.
Top 100 Electric Utilities—sales & financial performance. Started 1966. $4. June.
Top 50 Publicly Owned Electric Utilities. Started 1976. $4. July.
Top 100 Electric Utilities—operating performance. Started 1971. $4. August.
Electric Utility of the Year. Started 1969. $4. November.

0457. ELECTRIC POWER MONTHLY.
Superintendant of Documents, GPO, Washington, DC 20402.
Annual Subscription: $55. **Frequency:** Monthly.
Publisher: Energy Information Administration, National Energy Information Center.
Editorial Index: Annual. Subject/Title. Indexed in EIA Publications Directory.
Indexed or Abstracted Online: FEDEX.

0458. ELECTRICAL APPARATUS.
400 N. Michigan Ave., Chicago, IL 60611.
Annual Subscription: $20. **Frequency:** Monthly.
Publisher: Barks Publications, Inc.
Advertiser Index: Every issue.
Editorial Index: Annual. Subject. January.
Special Issues:
Electro Mechanical Bench Reference—manufacturers, distributors, special services, UL certified motor rebuilders, and training and educational sources of interest to the electrical aftermarket. Started 1974. Published as a separate issue. $5. January.

0459. ELECTRICAL BUSINESS.
443 Mt. Pleasant Rd., Toronto, Ontario, Can. M4S 2L8.
Annual Subscription: $40. **Frequency:** Monthly.
Publisher: Kerrwil Publications.
Advertiser Index: Every issue.
Special Issues:
Electrical Blue Book—buyers guide to Canada's electrical manufacturing, distribution industry. Started 1979. Published as a separate issue. $15. Not included in the subscription price. March.
CEDA Current Annual. Published as a separate issue. Not included in the subscription price. May.
Lighting Installations. $5. August.
Electrical Business Literature Review. $5. September.
Transformers & Switchgear. $5. October.
Electrical Heating. $5. November.
Site Location and Electrical Construction. $5. December.

0460. ELECTRICAL CONSTRUCTION AND MAINTENANCE.
1221 Ave. of the Americas, New York, NY 10020.
Annual Subscription: $15. **Frequency:** Monthly.
Publisher: McGraw-Hill Publications.
Advertiser Index: Every issue.
Editorial Index: Annual. Subject/Title/Author. February (available only separately for $2.50).
Indexed Online: Trade & Industry Index.
Special Issues:
Electrical Products Yearbook—new products with photos; product index; manufacturers literature. $10. September.

0461. ELECTRICAL CONSULTANT.
One River Rd., Cos Cob, CT 06807.
Annual Subscription: $12. **Frequency:** 6/yr.
Publisher: Cleworth Publishing Co., Inc.
Advertiser Index: Every issue.
Special Issues:
Standby-Emergency-Prime Power/Cogeneration and Automatic Switching. January.
UPS/Power Conditioning/Frequency Conversion/DC Systems and Monitoring. March.
Security-Life Safety/Communications and Energy Management Systems. May.
Power Factor Correction/Motors, Motor Controls and Switchgear. July.
Computer-Aided Design/Lighting and Electric Heating. September.
Circuit Protection/Substations and Distribution Systems. November.

0462. ELECTRICAL CONTRACTOR.
7315 Wisconsin Ave., Bethesda, MD 20814.
Annual Subscription: $12. **Frequency:** Monthly.
Publisher: National Electrical Contractors Association.
Advertiser Index: Every issue.
Special Issues:
Economic Forecast, Electrical Construction Industry. Started 1966. Annual. January.
Lighting. Started 1960. Annual. May.
NECA Convention/Exposition. Started 1943. Annual. October.
Product Literature Directory. Started 1970. Annual. December.

0463. THE ELECTRICAL DISTRIBUTOR.
111 Prospect St., Stamford, CT 06901.
Annual Subscription: $5. **Frequency:** Monthly.
Publisher: National Association of Electrical Distributors.
Advertiser Index: Every issue.
Special Issues:
Annual Electrical Industry Review & Forecast. January.
Convention Issue. June.
Mid Year Electrical Industry Business Review. September.
Supplier Promotion Directory. October.

0464. ELECTRICAL EQUIPMENT NEWS.
1450 Don Mills Rd., Don Mills, Ontario, Can. M3B 2X7.
Annual Subscription: $36.00/26.50. **Frequency:** 10/yr.
Publisher: Southam Communications Ltd.
Special Issues:
Product Review of Electra-Ex Montreal. $2.50. September.
Energy-Efficient Products Update. $2.50. October.
Lighting, Wire & Cable Update. $2.50. December.

0465. ELECTRICAL WHOLESALING.
P.O. Box 430, Hightstown, NJ 08520.
Annual Subscription: $10 (qualified)/30 (others).
Frequency: Monthly.
Publisher: McGraw-Hill Inc.
Advertiser Index: Every issue.
Editorial Index: Annual. Subject. December.
Special Issues:
Directory of Electrical Wholesaler Distributors—includes industry profile/statistics on percentages handling each product, sales breakdowns, etc. Published as a separate issue. Biennially (even years). February or March.
Industry Trends—includes 250 top electrical wholesalers. $5. Biennially (even years). April.
Market Planning Guidebook. Started 1979. $5. November.

0466. ELECTRICAL WORLD.
1221 Ave. of the Americas, New York, NY 10020.
Annual Subscription: $36. **Frequency:** Monthly.
Publisher: McGraw-Hill Publications, Co.
Advertiser Index: Every issue.
Editorial Index: Semi-Annual. Subject/Title. January/August (published separately. Available free by request).
Indexed or Abstracted Online: Predicasts; Magazine Index; Trade & Industry Index.
Special Issues:
   Generation Construction Survey—summary of all nuclear, fossil/steam, hydroelectric and combustion/turbine units planned or under construction. Started 1981. January.
   Annual Statistical Report—covers investor-owned systems, federal agencies, cooperatives and municipal, state, and public power district system for U.S. & major Canadian utilities; key areas: capital expenditures; transmission & distribution construction; generation capability; sales; financial, etc. Started 1905. $5. March/April.
   Maintenance Survey—U.S. & Canada—statistics on generation and transmission & distribution. Started 1983. $5. April or May.
   Edison Electric Institute Interview. $5. May.
   Buyer's Guide—companies supplying products and services to the electric utility industry. Started 1983. $5. June.
   Electric Utility Industry Technical Reference—classified guide to the year's technical papers. Started 1977. $5. June.
   Transmission & Distribution Construction Survey. Started 1966. $5. August.
   Electric Utility Industry Forecast. Started 1950. $5. September.
   Directory of Electric Utilities (U.S. & Canada). Published as a separate issue. $195. Not included in the subscription price. October.
   Steam Station Design Survey. Started 1967. $5. November.
   Annual Meeting Calendar. $5. December.

0467. ELECTRICITY CANADA.
777 Bay St., Toronto, Ontario, Can. M5W 1A7.
Annual Subscription: $29/25. **Frequency:** 11/yr.
Publisher: Maclean Hunter Limited.
Advertiser Index: Every issue.
Special Issues:
   Annual Electrical Buyers Guide—products, catalogs, distributors. $6. July/August.

0468. ELECTRI-ONICS.
17730 W. Peterson Rd., Libertyville, IL 60048.
Annual Subscription: $40. **Frequency:** Monthly.
Publisher: Lake Publishing Corporation.
Advertiser Index: Every issue.
Editorial Index: Annual. Subject. January.
Indexed or Abstracted Online: Compendex; CIN.
Special Issues:
   Printed Circuits Supplement. $5. February.
   Electri-Onics—buyers guide with commentary on terms and products used in manufacturing electrical/electronic products. Started 1974. Published as a separate issue. $25. June/July.
   Connections and Terminations Supplement. $5. October.
   Wire and Cable Supplement. $5. December.

0469. ELECTRONIC BUSINESS.
221 Columbus Ave., Boston, MA 02116.
Annual Subscription: $40. **Frequency:** 19/yr.
Publisher: Cahners Publishing Co.
Advertiser Index: Every issue.
Editorial Index: Annual. Subject. January.
Special Issues:
   Annual Forecast. $3. January.
   Top 100 Electronic Manufacturers; Update. $3. February/August.
   Top 10 Semiconductor Manufacturers. $3. March.
   Top 10 Interconnection Devices Manufacturers. $3. Annual. April.
   Plant Sites Special Report—Overseas; U.S. $3. May/November.
   Second Top 100 Manufacturers; Update. $3. May/November.
   Top Ten Semiconductor Production Equipment Manufacturers. $3. May.
   Top 100 Paid Executives. $3. June.
   Top 10 Manufacturers of Printers. $3. June.
   Top 20 Electronics Distributors/Midyear Outlook. $3. July.
   Top 10 Printed Circuit Manufacturers/Top 10 Printed Circuit Production Materials Manufacturers/Top 10 Printed Circuit Production Equipment Manufacturers. $3. September.
   Top 10 Super Minicomputer Manufacturers. $3. September.
   Top 10 Terminals Manufacturers. $3. September.
   Top 10 Automatic Test Equipment Manufacturers. $3. October.
   Top 10 Capacitors Manufacturers. $3. November.
   Top 10 Semiconductor Memories Manufacturers/Military Electronics. $3. December.

0470. ELECTRONIC COMPONENT NEWS.
Chilton Way, Radnor, PA 19089.
Annual Subscription: $35. **Frequency:** Monthly.
Publisher: Chilton Co.
Advertiser Index: Every issue.
Special Issues:
   Telecommunications Circuits/SOUTHCON Show. $3. January.
   Semiconductor Memories. $3. February.
   Connectors for Flat Cables. $3. March.
   Oscilloscopes and Logic Analyzers. $3. April.
   Microprocessors and Peripheral Chips. $3. May.
   Computer Graphic Circuits. $3. June.
   Microcomputers and Microcomputer Boards for the O.E.M./National Computer Conference. $3. July.
   Meters and Multimeters. $3. August.
   Modems and Multiplexers/MIDCON Show. $3. September.
   Software Development Systems/NORTHCON Show. $3. October.
   Disc Drives/WESCON Show and Mini/Micro West Show. $3. November.
   Displays. $3. December.

0471. ELECTRONIC DESIGN.
50 Essex St., Rochelle Park, NJ 07662.
Annual Subscription: $45. **Frequency:** 26/yr.
Publisher: Hayden Publishing Co. Inc.
Advertiser Index: Every issue.
Special Issues:
   Top 10 Electronic Design Firms. $5. January.
   Career Extra—job recruitment & newspaper. Published as a separate issue. May/November.
   Electro Show Preview. May.
   National Computer Conference Preview. June.
   Gold Book—master directory and catalog; product index; manufacturers (including foreign) and sales offices; distributors; trade names. Published as a separate issue. $55. Not included in the subscription price. July.
   WESCON (Western Electronics Convention) Show Preview/Career Survey. October.
   Designers & Reference. December.

0472. ELECTRONICS.
P.O. Box 430, Hightstown, NJ 08520.
Annual Subscription: $19. **Frequency:** 26/yr.
Publisher: McGraw-Hill Inc.
Advertiser Index: Every issue.
Indexed or Abstracted Online: NEXIS; Trade & Industry Index.
Special Issues:
   Electronics Buyers Guide. Published as a separate issue. $35. January.
   World Market Forecast. Published as a separate issue. $6. January.
   World Semiconductor Report. $6. June.

Technology Update. $6. October.
Executive Outlook. $6. December.

0473. ELECTRONICS & COMMUNICATIONS.
1450 Don Mills Rd., Don Mills, Ontario, Can. M3B 2X7.
Annual Subscription: $23. **Frequency:** 6/yr.
Publisher: Southam Communications Ltd.
Special Issues:
Electronic Procurement Index for Canada (EPIC). $25. June.

0474. ELECTRO-OPTICS.
270 St. Paul, Denver, CO 80206.
Annual Subscription: $35/year. **Frequency:** Monthly.
Publisher: Cahners Publishing Co.
Advertiser Index: Every issue.
Special Issues:
Vendor Selection Guide (Buyers Guide Issue). Started 1971. $10. November.

0475. EMERGENCY MEDICAL SERVICES.
12849 Magnolia Blvd., North Hollywood, CA 91607.
Annual Subscription: $12. **Frequency:** Monthly.
Publisher: Creative Age Publications.
Advertiser Index: Every issue.
Editorial Index: Annual. Title. December.
Special Issues:
Emergency Medical Services Annual Buyers Guide. Started 1977. Published as a separate issue. $10. October.

0476. EMPLOYEE BENEFIT PLAN REVIEW.
222 West Adams St., Chicago, IL 60606.
Annual Subscription: $20. **Frequency:** Monthly.
Publisher: Charles D. Spencer & Associates.
Advertiser Index: Every issue.
Editorial Index: Semi-Annual. Subject. January/July.
Indexed or Abstracted Online: ABI/Inform; Management Contents; Insurance Abstracts.
Special Issues:
Health Care Plan Sales Statistics. Started 1960. $2. April.
Pension Statistical Issue. Started 1960. $2. May.

0477. EMPLOYEE SERVICES MANAGEMENT.
20 N. Wacker Dr., Chicago, IL 60606.
Annual Subscription: $12. **Frequency:** 10/yr.
Publisher: National Employee Services and Recreation Association.
Advertiser Index: Every issue.
Editorial Index: Annual. Subject. December/January.
Special Issues:
Fitness and Health. $1.50. February.
NESRA Conference Preview. $1.50. March.
Employee Services. $1.50. April.
Administration. $1.50. May/June.
New Directions. $1.50. July.
Conference Review. $1.50. August.
Employee Travel. $1.50. September.
Sports Programs. $1.50. October.
Programming Techniques. $1.50. November.
Buyers Guide/Forecasts. $1.50. December/January.

0478. EMPLOYMENT AND EARNINGS.
U.S. Government Printing Office, Washington, DC 20402.
Annual Subscription: $39. **Frequency:** Monthly.
Publisher: U.S. Department of Labor.
Special Issues:
Benchmark Issue—Establishment Data, Revised Seasonally Establishment Data. $7.50.
Annual Averages Household Data/Preliminary Establishment Data. $6. January.
Quarterly Averages, Household Data. $6. January/April/July/October.
Revised Seasonally Adjusted Household Data. $6. January/February.
Annual Averages Detailed Industry, Establishment Data. $6. March.
Annual Averages States and Areas—Establishment Data/Area Definitions/Annual Averages, Local Area Unemployment Statistics. $6. May.
Women Employment—Detailed Industry, Establishment Data. $6. Monthly.

0479. EN ROUTE.
2973 Weston Road, Weston, Ontario, Can. M9N 3R3.
Annual Subscription: $24/yr. **Frequency:** Monthly.
Publisher: Southam Printing Ltd. (Airmedia Division).
Special Issues:
Demographics. $1. May.
Corporate Fitness Programs. $1. July.
Franchising. $1. September.
100 Favorite Canadian Restaurants. $1. October.
Consumer Guide to Home Entertainment Systems. $1. December.

0480. ENERGY PROGRESS.
345 East 47th St., New York, NY 10017.
Annual Subscription: $20. **Frequency:** Quarterly.
Publisher: American Institute of Chemical Engineers.
Editorial Index: Annual. Subject/Title/Author. December.

0481. ENERGY SYSTEMS PRODUCT NEWS.
250 West 34 St., New York, NY 10119.
Annual Subscription: $12. **Frequency:** 6/yr.
Publisher: Business Communications Inc.
Advertiser Index: Every issue.
Special Issues:
Buyers Guide and Catalog File. $10. July.

0482. ENERGY USER NEWS.
7 East 12th St., New York, NY 10003.
Annual Subscription: $45. **Frequency:** Weekly.
Publisher: Fairchild Publications.
Indexed Online: Trade & Industry Index.
Special Issues:
HVAC: Technology Report. $2. January.
Steam Traps: Technology Report. $2. January.
Annual EMS (Energy Management Systems) Technology Report. $2. February.
Annual Oil Forecast: Supply/Demand. $2. February.
Lighting Controls: Technology Report. $2. February.
Motors: Technology Report. $2. March.
National Plant Engineering & Maintenance Show. $2. March.
Industrial Energy Conservation Technology Conference. Started 1979. $2. April.
Multi-Fuel Boilers: Technology Report. $2. April.
Annual Electricity Forecast: Supply//Demand. $2. May.
Directory of Energy Consultants. Started 1978. $10. May.
Roof & Wall Insulation: Technology Report. $2. May.
Lighting: Technology Report. $2. June/September.
Annual EMS Service & Maintenance Feature. $2. July.
EMS Power Line Carrier: Technology Report. $2. July.
Annual Gas Forecast: Supply/Demand. $2. August.
Facility Management Systems: Technology Report. $2. August.
Variable Speed Drives: Technology Report. $2. August.
Annual Coal Forecast: Supply/Demand. $2. September.
Heat Recovery: Technology Report. $2. October.
Meters & Monitors: Technology Report. $2. October.
Combustion Controls & Analyzers: Technology Report. $2. November.
Annual Review & Forecast Issue/Energy & Technology Buyers Guide—includes year's product guides. $10. December.
Heat Pumps: Technology Report. $2. December.
Heat Scanners: Technology Report. $2. December.

0483. ENGINEERING & CONTRACT RECORD.
1450 Don Mills Rd., Don Mills, Ontario, Can. M3B 2X7.
Annual Subscription: $36.00/26.50. **Frequency:** Monthly.
Publisher: Southam Communications Ltd.
Advertiser Index: Every issue.

Special Issues:
   Canada's Top 200 Contractors. $2.50. June.
   Literature Review. $2.50. November.

0484. ENGINEERING DIGEST.
111 Peter St., Ste. 411, Toronto, Ontario, Can. M5V 2W2.
Annual Subscription: $24. **Frequency:** 10/yr.
Publisher: Canadian Engineering Publications Ltd.
Advertiser Index: Every issue.
Editorial Index: Annual. Title. January.

0485. ENGINEERING EDUCATION.
11 Dupont Circle, Ste. 200, Washington, DC 20036.
Annual Subscription: $26/$30 (foreign). **Frequency:** 8/yr.
Publisher: American Soceity for Engineering Education.
Advertiser Index: Every issue.
Editorial Index: Annual. Subject/Title/Author. May.
Special Issues:
   Effective Teaching. Started 1969. $2.75. February.
   Engineering College Research and Graduate Study—annual directory. Started 1967. $14. March.
   ASEE Profile—(review & directory of ASEE activities & members). Started 1968. $7.50. October.

0486. ENGINEERING & MINING JOURNAL.
1221 Ave. of the Americas, New York, NY 10020.
Annual Subscription: $20. **Frequency:** Monthly.
Publisher: McGraw-Hill Publishing Co.
Advertiser Index: Every issue.
Editorial Index: Annual. Subject/Author. Available separately in Spring for $2.
Indexed or Abstracted Online: Predicasts; Trade & Industry Index; Compendex.
Special Issues:
   Annual Project Survey—new mine and processing construction. $3. January.
   Annual Mineral Commodities Survey—production statistics. $3. March.
   International Directory of Mining—mines/plants; consultants; statistics. Started 1968. Published as a separate issue. $60. Not included in the subscription price. August.
   American Mining Congress Equipment Exposition (metal mining). $3. Every 4 yrs. September.
   Buyers Guide. $3. September.
   Annual Mining Nation Profile. $3. Annual. November.

0487. ENGINEERING NEWS-RECORD.
1221 Ave. of the Americas, New York, NY 10020.
Annual Subscription: $33. **Frequency:** Weekly.
Publisher: McGraw-Hill, Inc.
Advertiser Index: Every issue.
Editorial Index: Semi-Annual. Subject. July/January.
Indexed or Abstracted Online: Management Contents; NEXIS.
Special Issues:
   Annual Report and Forecast. $2. January.
   "Construction Man of the Year". $2. February.
   Quarterly Cost Reports. $2. March/June/September/December.
   Top 400 Contractors. $2. April.
   Top 500 Design Firms. $2. May.
   Executive Compensation. $2. July.
   Top International Contractors. $2. July.
   Top International Design Firms. $2. July.
   Top Specialty Contractors. $2. August.
   Preliminary Forecast. $2. October.
   Water Pollution Report. $2. October.
   Buildings Report. $2. November.
   Directory of Contractors. Published as a separate issue. $28.95. Not included in the subscription price. Biennially. 1983 (Last).
   Directory of Design Firms. Published as a separate issue. $28.95. Not included in the subscription price. Biennially. 1984 (Last).

0488. ENGINEERING TIMES.
1450 Don Mills Rd., Don Mills, Ontario, Can. M3B 2X7.
Annual Subscription: $49/39. **Frequency:** Monthly.
Publisher: Southam Communications Ltd.
Special Issues:
   Engineering Products News—new products. $2. March/June/September/December.
   Engineers Data Portfolio. $2. March/June/September/December.

0489. ENGINEER'S DIGEST.
2500 Office Center, Willow Grove, PA 19090.
Annual Subscription: Free (qualified persons). **Frequency:** Monthly.
Publisher: Walker-Davis Publications.
Advertiser Index: Every issue.
Editorial Index: Every issue. Subject. Monthly.
Special Issues:
   National Plant Engineering & Maintenance Show. March.

0490. ENTREE.
7 East 12 St., New York, NY 10003.
Annual Subscription: $20. **Frequency:** 11/yr.
Publisher: Fairchild Publications.
Special Issues:
   Annual Buyers Guide and Annual Survey. Started 1980. August.

0491. ENVIRONMENTAL PROGRESS.
345 East 47th St., New York, NY 10017.
Annual Subscription: $20. **Frequency:** Quarterly.
Publisher: American Institute of Chemical Engineers.
Editorial Index: Annual. Subject/Title/Author. November.

0492. ENVIRONMENTAL SCIENCE & TECHNOLOGY.
1155 16th Street, NW, Washington, DC 20036.
Annual Subscription: $20 (members)/25 (nonmembers)/110 (libraries). **Frequency:** Monthly.
Publisher: American Chemical Society.
Advertiser Index: Every issue.
Editorial Index: Annual. Subject/Author. December.

0493. EVALUATION ENGINEERING.
1282 Old Skokie Rd., Highland Park, IL 60035.
Annual Subscription: $43. **Frequency:** 8/yr.
Publisher: Nelson Associates.
Advertiser Index: Every issue.
Special Issues:
   Automatic Test Equipment Annual Reference/Directory. $6. April.
   Test Equipment/Services. $6. July/August.
   ESD/EOS Reference/Directory. $6. October.
   Electronic Test Labs/Services. $6. November/December.

0494. EXECUTIVE.
2973 Weston Rd., Weston, Ontario, Can. M9N 3R3.
Annual Subscription: $39.50/30.00. **Frequency:** Monthly.
Publisher: Southam Printing (Airmedia Division).
Special Issues:
   Forecast. $2.50. January.
   Industrial Locations. $2.50. May.
   Corporate Fitness Programs. $2.50. July.
   Franchising. $2.50. September.
   Business Poll. $2.50. November.

0495. THE EXECUTIVE COMBINATION.
3740 Campus Dr., Newport Beach, CA 92660.
Annual Subscription: $12. **Frequency:** Monthly.
Publisher: Executive Publications, Inc.
Special Issues:
   California's largest companies. $2. June.
   California's most profitable companies. $2. July.
   California's fastest growing companies. $2. September.
   Economic Outlook. $2. October.

0496. EXECUTIVE GOLFER.
2171 Campus Dr., Irving, CA 92715.
Annual Subscription: $5.25. **Frequency:** 6/yr.
Publisher: Pazdur Publishing Inc.
Special Issues:
Private Country Club Guest Policy Directory—lists leading U.S. private golf and country clubs with data on guest policies (including reciprocal), green fees, names of head pros, yardage, ratings. Started 1976. Published as a separate issue. $15. March.
Golf Resort Guide—best golf resorts for corporate meetings. Free. November/December.

0497. EXECUTIVE RECRUITER NEWS.
Templeton Rd., Fitzwilliam, NH 03447.
Annual Subscription: $54. **Frequency:** Monthly.
Publisher: Kennedy & Kennedy, Inc.

0498. FDA CONSUMER.
U.S. Government Printing Office, Washington, DC 20403.
Annual Subscription: $19. **Frequency:** 10/yr.
Publisher: Department of Health & Human Services.
Editorial Index: Annual. Subject. December/January.

0499. FAMILY CIRCLE.
488 Madison Ave., New York, NY 10022.
Annual Subscription: $.75 single issue. **Frequency:** 17/yr.
Publisher: Family Circle, Inc.
Special Issues:
Family Circle Great Ideas How to Be Pretty and Trim. Started 1977. Published as a separate issue. $2.25. Not included in the subscription price. April.
Family Circle Great Ideas Fashions & Crafts. Started 1974. Published as a separate issue. $2.25. Not included in the subscription price. July.
Family Circle Great Ideas 210 Kitchen Ideas. Started 1977. Published as a separate issue. $1.95. Not included in the subscription price. August.
Family Circle Great Ideas Christmas Helps—gift and food ideas. Started 1962. Published as a separate issue. $2.25. Not included in the subscription price. October.
Family Circle Great Ideas Decorating Made Easy—decorating and remodeling. Started 1977. Published as a separate issue. $2.25. Not included in the subscription price. October.

0500. FAMILY MOTOR COACHING.
8291 Clough Pike, Cincinnati, OH 45244.
Annual Subscription: $15. **Frequency:** Monthly.
Publisher: Family Motor Coach Association.
Advertiser Index: Every issue.
Special Issues:
Member Directory Issue. $8.95. January.

0501. FARM BUILDING NEWS.
260 Regency Court, Waukesha, WI 53186.
Annual Subscription: $8.95. **Frequency:** 8/yr.
Publisher: American Farm Building Services.
Advertiser Index: Every issue.
Special Issues:
Farm Builders Buyers Guide—product and company listings; association addresses, etc. Started 1978. $3. October.

0502. FARM EQUIPMENT QUARTERLY.
P.O. Box 1060, Exeter, Ontario, Can. N0M 1S0.
Annual Subscription: $30/20. **Frequency:** Quarterly.
Publisher: Agricultural Information Services Ltd.
Special Issues:
Farm Equipment Directory. Published as a separate issue. $5. October.

0503. FARM & POWER EQUIPMENT.
9701 Gravois Ave., St. Louis, MO 63123.
Annual Subscription: $11. **Frequency:** Monthly.
Publisher: ADmore Publishing.
Advertiser Index: Every issue.
Special Issues:
Directory of Manufacturers, Trade Names, Products. $10. January.
Fertilizers & Application Equipment. $1. February.
Energy Update. $1. March.
Cost of Doing Business/Dealer Survey. $1. May.
Trailers & Trucks. $1. July.
Service Shop. $1. August.
National Farm & Power Equipment Dealers Association Convention Issue. $1. September.
Lawn & Garden Equipment. $1. November.
Industrial Equipment Review. $1. December.

0504. FARM STORE MERCHANDISING.
2501 Wayzata Blvd., Minneapolis, MN 55440.
Annual Subscription: $15. **Frequency:** Monthly.
Publisher: Miller Publishing Co.
Advertiser Index: Every issue.
Special Issues:
Ag Chemicals. $1. February.
Feed & Grain Handling. $1. May.
Farm Store Trade Show Issue. $1. July.
Custom Application. $1. August.
Animal Health. $1. October.
Fertilizer Outlook. $1. November.
Buyers Guide Annual Product Directory. $1. December.

0505. FARM SUPPLIER.
Sandstone Bldg., Mt. Morris, IL 61054.
Annual Subscription: $15. **Frequency:** Monthly.
Publisher: Watt Publishing Co.
Advertiser Index: Every issue.
Special Issues:
Farm Chemicals/Herbicides. $1. January.
Fertilizer Materials/Handling. $1. February.
Farm Chemicals/Insecticides. $1. March.
Livestock Insecticides. $1. April.
Feed and Grain Handling. $1. May.
Product Showcase. $1. June.
Custom Applicator Special. $1. August.
Animal Health Care. $1. September.
Hardware, Lawn and Garden. $1. October.
Application Equipment. $1. November.
Directory Issue. $1. December.

0506. FARMLINE.
Superintendent of Documents, GPO, Washington, DC 20402.
Annual Subscription: $16. **Frequency:** 11/yr.
Publisher: Economic Research Service.
Special Issues:
Crop Reporting Board Reports include: Agricultural Prices; Agricultural Price Summaries; Cattle; Celery; Cold Storage; Crop Production; Dairy Products; Egg Products; Eggs, Chickens and Turkeys; Grain Stocks; Hogs and Pigs; Livestock Slaughter; Milk Production; Non-Citrus Fruits; Potatoes and Sweet Potatoes; Poultry Slaughter; Rice Stocks; Vegetables.
Situation and Outlook Reports include: Agricultural Exports (Rice; Sugar and Sweetener; Tobacco; Vegetable; Wheat; World Agriculture); Cotton and Wool; Dairy; Fats and Oils; Feed; Fruit; Livestock and Poultry.
Calendar of Situation and Outlook Reports of the Economic Research Service; Crop and Livestock Reports of the Crop Reporting Board; and Supply/Demand Estimates of the World Agriculture Outlook Board. Lists release dates and ordering information. January/February and June.

0507. FASHION ACCESSORIES MAGAZINE.
22 South Smith St., Norwalk, CT 06850.
Annual Subscription: $24. **Frequency:** Monthly.
Publisher: Business Journals, Inc.
Advertiser Index: Every issue.
Special Issues:
Annual Umbrella Section. September.
Accessories Directory. Started 1970. Published as a separate issue. $10. Not included in the subscription price. December.
Annual Sunglass Section. December.

0508. FEDERAL HOME LOAN BANK BOARD JOURNAL.
U.S. Government Printing Office, Washington, DC 20402.
Annual Subscription: $39. **Frequency:** Monthly.
Publisher: Federal Home Loan Bank Board.
Editorial Index: Annual. Subject/Title/Author. December.
Indexed or Abstracted Online: ABI/Inform; Legal Resource Index; Trade & Industry Index; Management Contents.

0509. FEDERAL RESERVE BULLETIN.
Publishing Services, Mail Stop 138, Board of Governors of the Federal System, Washington, DC 20551.
Annual Subscription: $20. **Frequency:** Monthly.
Publisher: Board of Governors of the Federal Reserve System.
Editorial Index: Annual. Subject. December.
Special Issues:
 Annual Report of the Board of Governors of the Federal Reserve System. Published as a separate issue. Free. Not included in the subscription price. April.
 Guide to Statistical Releases—anticipated schedule of release dates. $2. June/December.
 Annual Statistical Digest—final corrected statistics for previous year. Published as a separate issue. $7.50 (price varies each year). Not included in the subscription price. December.

0510. FEDERATION OF AMERICAN HOSPITALS REVIEW.
1405 North Pierce, Ste. 311, Little Rock, AR 72207.
Annual Subscription: $15. **Frequency:** 6/yr.
Publisher: Federation of American Hospitals.
Advertiser Index: Every issue.
Special Issues:
 Directory of Investor-Owned and Managed Hospitals. Started 1973. Published as a separate issue. $25. Not included in the subscription price. October.

0511. FEED & FARM SUPPLY DEALER.
1077 St. James St., P.O. Box 6900, Winnipeg, Manitoba, Can. R3C 3B1.
Annual Subscription: $15/13. **Frequency:** 6/yr.
Publisher: Sanford Evans Communications Ltd.
Special Issues:
 Directory of Farm Machinery & Equipment. $5. February.
 Feed, Agchemicals & Supplies Directory Annuaire. $5. December.

0512. FEED INDUSTRY.
7535 Office Ridge Circle, Eden Prairie, MN 55344.
Annual Subscription: $12.50. **Frequency:** Quarterly.
Publisher: Communications Marketing Inc.
Advertiser Index: Every issue.
Special Issues:
 Red Book—reference book and buyers guide; state and federal government regulations on feed ingredients; compliance officers; nutritional information. $12.50. Spring.

0513. FEEDLOT MANAGEMENT.
2501 Wayzata Blvd., Minneapolis, MN 55440.
Annual Subscription: $15. **Frequency:** Monthly.
Publisher: Miller Publishing Co.
Advertiser Index: Every issue.
Special Issues:
 Cattle Feeder's Planner—reference issue. $10. September.

0514. FEEDSTUFFS.
Box 1289, Minneapolis, MN 55440.
Annual Subscription: $37.50. **Frequency:** Weekly.
Publisher: Miller Publishing Co.
Advertiser Index: Every issue.
Editorial Index: Quarterly. Subject/Title/Author. April/July/October/January.
Indexed Online: Predicasts; Trade & Industry Index.
Special Issues:
 Feedstuffs Reference Issue—buyers guide and marketing, technical information relating to feed and animal production. Started 1969. Published as a separate issue. $10. July.

0515. FENCE INDUSTRY.
6285 Barfield Rd., Atlanta, GA 30328.
Annual Subscription: $24. **Frequency:** Monthly.
Publisher: Communications Channels Inc.
Advertiser Index: Every issue.
Editorial Index: Annual. Subject/Title/Author. January.
Special Issues:
 Forecast. $2.50. January.
 Security/Access Control. $2.50. February.
 Recreational Fencing—pools, tennis courts, playgrounds, etc. $2.50. March.
 International Fence Industry Association Convention Report. $2.50. April.
 Farm & Ranch Fencing. $2.50. May.
 Specialty/Ornamental Fencing. $2.50. June.
 Annual Fence Dealer Market Survey—statistics on dollar volume by type of fence product; by type of customer; gross dollar volume by population; capital investments; number and salaries of employees; price fluctuations; etc. Started 1971. Published as a separate issue. $50. Not included in the subscription price. July.
 Highlights of Fence Dealer Market Survey. $2.50. July.
 Highway & Road Fencing Systems and Barriers. $2.50. August.
 Dealer Survey, Year-to-Date. $2.50. September.
 Tools & Equipment. $2.50. October.
 Security Fencing. $2.50. November.
 Fence Industry Directory. Started 1960. Published as a separate issue. $10. December.

0516. FIBER OPTICS AND COMMUNICATIONS NEWSLETTER.
138 Brighton Ave., Boston, MA 02134.
Annual Subscription: $215. **Frequency:** Monthly.
Publisher: Information Gatekeepers, Inc.
Special Issues:
 International Fiber Optics and Communications Handbook and Buyers Guide. Published as a separate issue. $50. Not included in the subscription price. July.

0517. FIBER PRODUCER.
1760 Peachtree Rd., NW, Atlanta, GA 30357.
Annual Subscription: $30. **Frequency:** 6/yr.
Publisher: W. R. C. Smith Publishing Co.
Advertiser Index: Every issue.
Special Issues:
 Buyers Guide. Started 1973. $10. December.

0518. FIBEROPTICS REPORT.
119 Russell St., P.O. Box 1111, Littleton, MA 01460.
Annual Subscription: $140. **Frequency:** 22/yr.
Publisher: Advanced Technology Publications.
Special Issues:
 Annual Economic Review and Outlook. $45. January.

0519. FIELD & STREAM.
P.O. Box 2822, Boulder, CO 80322.
Annual Subscription: $11.94. **Frequency:** Monthly.
Publisher: CBS Publications.
Special Issues:
 Fishing Annual. Started 1976. Published as a separate issue. $2.25. Not included in the subscription price. February.
 Bass Fishing Annual. Started 1977. Published as a separate issue. $2.25. Not included in the subscription price. March.
 Recreational Vehicles. $1.75. March.
 Camping. $1.75. May.
 Hunting Annual. Started 1975. Published as a separate issue. $2.25. Not included in the subscription price. August.
 Deer Hunting Annual. Started 1978. Published as a separate issue. $2.25. Not included in the subscription price. September.

0520. 50 PLUS.
99 Garden St., Marion, OH 43302.
Annual Subscription: $15. **Frequency:** Monthly.
Publisher: Retirement Living Magazine Co.

Special Issues:
   Health. $1.50.   January.
   Cruise Travel. $1.50.   April/October.
   Annual Round-up of Over-50 Athletes. $1.50.   December.

0521. FILM COMMENT.
140 West 65 St., New York, NY 10019.
Annual Subscription: $12.   **Frequency:** 6/yr.
Publisher: Film Society of Lincoln Center.
Editorial Index: Annual. Subject/Title/Author. January/February.
Special Issues:
   Report on Film Industry/Critics' 10 Favorites. $2.   January/February.
   Year in Review/Oscar Predictions. $2.   March/April.

0522. THE FILM JOURNAL.
1600 Broadway, Suite 605, New York, NY 10019.
Annual Subscription: $25.   **Frequency:** 20/yr.
Publisher: Pubsun Corp.
Advertiser Index: Every issue.
Special Issues:
   Anniversary Issue—with blue sheets.   Started 1966. $2.   January.
   Showest Convention Issue. $2.   February.
   Adult Film Issue.   Started 1979. $2.   March.
   Show-A-Rama Convention.   Started 1966. $2.   April.
   Erotica Film Awards.   Started 1979. $2.   June.
   Distribution Guide—buyers guide.   Started 1956. $2.   August.
   Equipment, Concession & Services Buyers Guide.   Started 1979. $2.   September.
   National Association of Theater Owners Convention.   Started 1965. $2.   November.

0523. FILM QUARTERLY.
University of California Press, Berkeley, CA 94720.
Annual Subscription: $10.   **Frequency:** Quarterly.
Publisher: University of California Press.
Editorial Index: Annual. June.
Special Issues:
   Annual Film Book Review Round-up.   Started 1978. $2.50.   June.

0524. FINANCIAL ANALYSTS JOURNAL.
1633 Broadway, 14th Floor, New York, NY 10019.
Annual Subscription: $36.   **Frequency:** 6/yr.
Publisher: Financial Analysts Federation.
Editorial Index: Subject/Author. Cumulative indexes by subject and author; 1942-66, $3.00; 1967-72, $3.00; annual 1972, 1973, 1974, 1975, $2.00 each. Cumulative index for 1975-82 planned for early 1984 (price to be established).

0525. FINANCIAL EXECUTIVE.
10 Madison Ave., P.O. Box 1938, Morristown, NJ 07960.
Annual Subscription: $33.   **Frequency:** Monthly.
Publisher: Financial Executives Institute.
Editorial Index: Annual. Subject/Author. December.
Indexed Online: ABI/Inform; Management Contents.

0526. THE FINANCIAL POST.
P.O. Box 9100, Postal Station A, Toronto, Ontario, Can. M5W 1V5.
Annual Subscription: $39.50/29.50.   **Frequency:** Weekly.
Publisher: Maclean Hunter Ltd.
Editorial Index: Each issue.
Special Issues:
   Oil and Gas. $1.   April.
   Financial Post 500.   Started 1966.   Published as a separate issue. $3.50.   June.
   Conferences and Conventions.   Started 1969.   Published as a separate issue. $3.50.   August.
   Survey of Industrials.   Started 1926.   Published as a separate issue. $36.   Not included in the subscription price.   September.
   Survey of Mines and Energy Resources.   Started 1925.   Published as a separate issue. $48.   Not included in the subscription price.   September.
   Canadian Markets.   Started 1924.   Published as a separate issue. $75.   Not included in the subscription price.   November.
   Directory of Directors.   Started 1931.   Published as a separate issue. $59.   Not included in the subscription price.   November.

0527. FINANCIAL TIMES OF CANADA.
920 Yonge St., Suite 500, Toronto, Ontario, Can. M4W 3L5.
Annual Subscription: $52/17.   **Frequency:** Weekly.
Publisher: Same.
Special Issues:
   Investment Opportunities—annual guide. $1.   January.
   Atlantic Canada. $1.   February.
   Business Equipment. $1.   March.
   Mining. $1.   April.
   Annual Reports. $1.   May/October.
   Stockbroker Services. $1.   May.
   Business Travel/Oil & Gas. $1.   June.
   Guide to Government. $1.   July or August.
   Industrial Locations—listings by province, cities and towns of industrial sites, incentives, transportation, manpower resources, site selection, etc. $1.   August.
   Financial Institutions. $1.   September.
   New West. $1.   October.
   Forecast. $1.   November.
   High Tech. $1.   December.

0528. FINANCIAL WORLD.
P.O. Box 10750, Des Moines, IA 50340.
Annual Subscription: $41.95.   **Frequency:** Biweekly.
Publisher: Financial World Partners.
Indexed or Abstracted Online: Trade & Industry Index; ABI/Inform; Management Contents; Magazine Index.
Special Issues:
   Economy Forecast Issue.   Started 1960. $2.   January.
   Chief Executive of the Year.   Started 1973. $2.   March.
   Annual Report Award Issue.   Started 1943. $2.   November.
   Best Brokerage Firm Issue.   Started 1977. $2.   December.

0529. FINGERTIP FACTS & FIGURES.
1619 Massachusetts Ave., NW, Washington, DC 20036.
Annual Subscription: $15.   **Frequency:** Monthly.
Publisher: National Forest Products Association.
Special Issues:
   Quarterly Supplement—quarterly data for current year and 2 prior years plus annual data for past 8-10 years on lumber production, consumption, orders, stocks, shipments, and foreign trade by products and region.   February/May/August/November.

0530. FIRE COMMAND.
Batterymarch Park, Quincy, MA 02269.
Annual Subscription: $13.   **Frequency:** Monthly.
Publisher: National Fire Protection Association.
Advertiser Index: Every issue.
Editorial Index: Annual. Author. December.
Special Issues:
   Fire Fighter Injuries—statistics/National Fire Protection Association meeting & Fire Safety Exhibit. $1.   May.
   Fire Fighter Fatalities—statistics/International Association of Fire Chiefs Convention and Show. $1.   September.

0531. FIRE ENGINEERING.
875 Third Ave., New York, NY 10022.
Annual Subscription: $14.95.   **Frequency:** Monthly.
Publisher: Technical Publishing.
Advertiser Index: Every issue.
Editorial Index: Annual. Subject. December.
Special Issues:
   Product Review Literature. $3.   April.
   Fire Equipment Buyers Guide. $4.   June.
   International Association of Fire Chiefs Conference Issue. $3.   September.
   Emergency Medical Services Buyers Guide. $4.   October.

0532. FIRE JOURNAL.
Batterymarch Park, Quincy, MA 02269.
Annual Subscription: $17. **Frequency:** 6/yr.
Publisher: National Fire Protection Association.
Advertiser Index: Every issue.
Editorial Index: Annual. Subject/Author. November.
Special Issues:
U.S. Fire Loss Statistics for Previous Year (property)—by type of fire, etc. $3. September.
Fire Protection Reference Directory—includes buyers guide for fire protection industry. Published as a separate issue. $12.50 (free to members). Not included in the subscription price. December.

0533. THE FISHERMEN'S NEWS.
Fishermen's Terminal, C-3 Bldg., Room 110, Seattle, WA 98119.
Annual Subscription: $6. **Frequency:** 22/yr.
Publisher: Fishermen's News Inc.
Advertiser Index: Every issue.
Special Issues:
Pacific Fisheries Review—summary of prior year's fishing season and forecast for coming year. Includes a New Vessels Section describing vessels built for the Pacific Coast industry during the preceding year. Started 1974. Published as a separate issue. $2. February.

0534. FISHERY BULLETIN.
Superintendent of Documents, GPO, Washington, DC 20402.
Annual Subscription: $21. **Frequency:** Quarterly.
Publisher: National Marine Fisheries Service.
Editorial Index: Annual. Subject/Title/Author. October.

0535. FISHING GAZETTE.
P.O. Box 907, Rockland, ME 04841.
Annual Subscription: $20. **Frequency:** Monthly.
Publisher: Fishing Gazette Publishing Corp.
Advertiser Index: Every issue.
Special Issues:
International Shrimp Issue. $5. June.
Annual Directory & Reference Issue. $5. July.
Seafood Brands Issue. $5. August.

0536. FISHING TACKLE TRADE NEWS.
P.O. Box 70, Wilmette, IL 60091.
Annual Subscription: $25. **Frequency:** 10/yr.
Publisher: Fishing Tackle Trade News.
Advertiser Index: Every issue.
Special Issues:
National Sporting Goods Association Trade Show Preview/Muskie Tackle Market/Lures Product Review. $2.50. January.
Fly Tackle Market. $2.50. February.
Inland Striper Market; National Fishing Week Coverage. $2.50. March.
Small Ticket Items/Pan Fishing. $2.50. April.
Saltwater Tackle Market. $2.50. May.
Great Lakes Tackle Market. $2.50. June.
American Fishing Tackle Manufacturers Association Show/Market Analysis/Statistical Reports/Trends & New Products. $2.50. July/August.
Marine Trades Show/Merchandising Trends for New Year. $2.50. September.
Catalog of Catalogs—2-volume set of manufacturers' catalogs of fishing tackle. Started 1981. Published as a separate issue. $20. October.
Ice Fishing Market Preview/Reels Product Review. $2.50. October.
Walleye Market/Rods Product Review. $2.50. November/December.

0537. FLEET OWNER.
1221 Ave. of the Americas, New York, NY 10021.
Annual Subscription: $25. **Frequency:** Monthly.
Publisher: McGraw-Hill Inc.
Advertiser Index: Every issue.
Special Issues:
Maintenance Shop Issue/Buyers Guide. $2.50. March.
Fleet Owner Awards Issue. $2.50. May.
Specifications and Buyers Directory. $2.50. October.

0538. FLOOR COVERING NEWS.
777 Bay St., Toronto, Ontario, Can. M5W 1A7.
Annual Subscription: $26/22. **Frequency:** 10/yr.
Publisher: MacLean Hunter Ltd.
Special Issues:
Canadian Carpet Chart—directory. $5/4. May.
Canadian Resilient Chart—directory. $5/4. June.
Contract Chart—directory. $5/4. July/August.

0539. FLOOR COVERING WEEKLY.
FDR Station, P.O. Box 6052, New York, NY 10150.
Annual Subscription: $20. **Frequency:** Weekly.
Publisher: Hearst Business Communications.
Advertiser Index: Special issues.
Special Issues:
Floor Coverings International—product & export information. Started 1980. Published as a separate issue. $1. April/October.
Specifiers' Guide to Contract Floor Covering. Started 1977. Published as a separate issue. $15. May.
Summer Market Guides. $1. June/July.
Local Product Source Directory—manufacturers and distributors. Started 1976. Published as a separate issue. $12.50. November.

0540. FLOORING.
120 West Second St., Duluth, MN 55802.
Annual Subscription: $12. **Frequency:** Monthly.
Publisher: Harcourt Brace Jovanovich.
Advertiser Index: Every issue.
Special Issues:
Flooring Directory and Buying Guide. Started 1945. $6. October.

0541. FLORIDA BUILDER.
3300 Henderson Blvd., Ste. 105, Tampa, FL 33609.
Annual Subscription: $10. **Frequency:** Monthly.
Publisher: Peninsula Publishing Co.
Special Issues:
Products Directory. Started 1948. $1.25. February.
Cement/Concrete. Started 1980. $1.25. June.
Wood. Started 1961. $1.25. September.

0542. FLORIDA TREND.
P.O. Box 611, St. Petersburg, FL 33731.
Annual Subscription: $18. **Frequency:** Monthly.
Publisher: Florida Trend, Inc.
Special Issues:
Florida Real Estate/Construction. Started 1981. $2. January.
Annual Economic Yearbook of Florida. Started 1965. $3. April.
Directory of Florida Public Companies. Started 1970. $2. July.
Golden Spoon Restaurant Awards. Started 1967. $2. August.
Florida Financial Review. Started 1975. $2. October.

0543. FLORISTS' REVIEW.
310 S. Michigan Ave., Chicago, IL 60604.
Annual Subscription: $21. **Frequency:** Weekly.
Publisher: Florists' Publishing Co.
Advertiser Index: Every issue.
Editorial Index: Semi-Annual. Subject/Title. June/December.
Special Issues:
Valentine's Day Issue/Energy Conservation. $1. January.
New Varieties/Garden Supplies/Wholesale Florist's Issue. $1. February.
Easter/New Technology. $1. March.
Mother's Day. $1. April.
Greenhouses/Brides. $1. May.
Ohio Short Course/Society of American Florists Convention Issue. $1. June.
Giftware/Interior Plantscaping. $1. July.

FTD Convention/Growers' Trade Show. $1.   August.
Autumn/BPI Convention. $1.   September.
Mass Marketing/Christmas Issue. $1.   October.
New Varieties. $1.   November.
Special Foliage/Wholesale Florist and Florist Suppliers America Trade Fair/The Year in Review. $1.   December.

0544. FLOTATION SLEEP INDUSTRY.
P.O. Box 19531, Irvine, CA 92713.
Annual Subscription: $17.50.   **Frequency:** Monthly.
Publisher: Hester Communications Inc.
Advertiser Index: Every issue.
Special Issues:
Flotation Sleep Industry Buyers Guide (Supplier Source Directory).   Started 1976.   Published as a separate issue. $15.   December.

0545. FLYING.
P.O. Box 2772, Boulder, CO 80302.
Annual Subscription: $17.98.   **Frequency:** Monthly.
Publisher: Ziff-Davis Publishing.
Advertiser Index: Every issue.
Editorial Index: Annually. Subject. February.
Special Issues:
Buyers Guide—directory of aircraft and avionics.   Started 1965.   Published as a separate issue. $2.95.   Not included in the subscription price.   January or February.

0546. FLYING MODELS MAGAZINE.
P.O. Box 700, Newton, NJ 07860.
Annual Subscription: $16.   **Frequency:** Monthly.
Publisher: Carstens Publications Inc.
Advertiser Index: Every issue.
Editorial Index: Annual. Subject/Title/Author. January.
Special Issues:
Buyers Guide.   Monthly.

0547. FOCUS ON THE BAKING INDUSTRY.
106 Lakeshore Rd. East, Ste. 209, Port Credit, Ontario, Can. L5G 1E3.
Annual Subscription: $10.   **Frequency:** 6/yr.
Publisher: Naef Publishing Ltd.
Advertiser Index: Every issue.
Editorial Index: Annual. Subject/Title/Author. February.
Special Issues:
Buyers Guide Directory. $5.   February.
American Society of Bakery Engineers Report. $2.   April.
Bakery Council Canada. $2.   June.
Doughnut Month Preview. $2.   August.
Bakery Showcase Issue. $2.   Biennially (even yrs).   October, December.

0548. FOOD & DRUG PACKAGING.
1 East First St., Duluth, MN 55802.
Annual Subscription: $36.   **Frequency:** Monthly.
Publisher: Harcourt Brace Jovanovich.
Advertiser Index: Every issue.
Special Issues:
International Exposition for Food Processors Show. $4.   January.
Interpack Show. $4.   April.
Cosmo/Expo Show. $4.   May.
Packaging Machinery Manufacturers Institute Show. $4.   October.
Package of the Year Awards. $4.   December.

0549. FOOD ENGINEERING.
P.O. Box 2036, Radnor, PA 19089.
Annual Subscription: $36.   **Frequency:** Monthly.
Publisher: Chilton Company.
Advertiser Index: Every issue.
Editorial Index: Annual. Subject/Title/Author. Available separately by request.
Indexed or Abstracted Online: Foods Ad Libra; Agricola.
Special Issues:
Ingredients Report.   May.
Directory of U.S. Food Plants—every location with more than 20 employees, including headquarters and R & D locations.   Started 1976.   Published as a separate issue. $395.   Not included in the subscription price.   July.
New Processing & Packaging Concepts.   July.
Food Engineering Master.   Published as a separate issue. $55.   Not included in the subscription price.   August.
State of the Food Industry Report.   August.
New Food Plants.   September.
New Food Product Introductions.   October.
Food Industry Capital Expenditures.   November.
Food Industry Salary Review.   December.

0550. FOOD ENGINEERING INTERNATIONAL.
Chilton Way, Radnor, PA 19089.
Annual Subscription: $45.   **Frequency:** 10/yr.
Publisher: Chilton Company.
Advertiser Index: Every issue.
Special Issues:
PakEx/BrewEx Show Report.   January/February.
Process Equipment Report.   May.
Heating & Cooking Technologies.   July/August.
Plant Sanitation/Pollution Control Report.   October.
New Food Products Survey.   December.

0551. FOOD IN CANADA.
777 Bay St., Toronto, Ontario, Can. M5W 1A7.
Annual Subscription: $30/24.   **Frequency:** 10/yr.
Publisher: Maclean Hunter Ltd.
Special Issues:
Encyclopedia of Food Chemicals. $12.   April.
Statistical Review & Forecast. $16.   July.
Buyers Guide. $17.   October.

0552. FOOD PROCESSING.
301 East Erie St., Chicago, IL 60611.
Annual Subscription: $24.   **Frequency:** Monthly.
Publisher: Putman Publishing Co.
Advertiser Index: Every issue.
Special Issues:
Foods of Tomorrow—research on new products and ingredients. $2.   January/April/July/October.
New Food Plants—construction and engineering trends. $2.   June.
Food Processing World Wide Guide & Directory to Ingredients, Equipment & Supplies.   Started 1978.   Published as a separate issue. $25.   July.
Top 100 Food Companies.   2.   December.

0553. FOOD PRODUCTION/MANAGEMENT.
2619 Maryland Ave., Baltimore, MD 21218.
Annual Subscription: $20.   **Frequency:** Monthly.
Publisher: The Canning Trade, Inc.
Advertiser Index: Every issue.
Special Issues:
Convention Program Issue: National Food Processors Association & Food Processing Machinery & Suppliers Association International Exposition for Food Processors. $3.   January.
Agricultural Issue. $3.   February.
Convention Reports on NFPA & FPM&SA. $3.   March.
Directory of the Canning, Freezing, Preserving Industries.   Published as a separate issue. $70.   Not included in the subscription price.   Biennially (even years).   April.
Institute of Food Technologists Program. $3.   May.
Containers. $3.   June.
Almanac of the Canning, Freezing, Preserving Industries—standards and specifications, statistics, government regulations.   Published as a separate issue. $29.50.   Not included in the subscription price.   July.
Advertisers Buyers Guide—by manufacturers and product type. $3.   August.
National Frozen Food Association Convention Program. $3.   October.
Fall Convention Programs and Reports. $3.   November.

0554. FOOD SERVICE & HOSPITALITY.
980 Yonge St., Ste. 400, Toronto, Ontario, Can. M4W 2H8.
Annual Subscription: $24.   **Frequency:** Monthly.
Publisher: Mitch Kostuch.
Advertiser Index: Every issue.
Special Issues:
   Franchise Issue. $10.   February.
   Buyer's Guide.   Started 1981. $10.   June.
   Top 100.   Started 1972. $10.   September.

0555. FOODSERVICE EQUIPMENT SPECIALIST.
270 St. Paul St., Denver, CO 80206.
Annual Subscription: $25.   **Frequency:** Monthly.
Publisher: Cahners Publishing Co.
Advertiser Index: Every issue.
Special Issues:
   Buyers Guide.   Started Pre-1970.   Published as a separate issue. $25.   January.
   Forecast.   Started 1983.   January.
   National Restaurant Association Show Issues.   Started Pre-1970.   April or May.
   Giants—largest equipment dealers and distributors. Started 1976.   June.
   Dealer of the Year.   Started 1982.   July.
   National Association of Food Equipment & Manufacturers Show Issues.   Started 1973.   2/yr.   August or September and November.
   New York Hotel/Motel Show Issue.   Started Pre-1970. October.

0556. FOODSERVICE PRODUCT NEWS.
342 Madison Ave., New York, NY 10173.
Annual Subscription: Free.   **Frequency:** 10/yr.
Publisher: Young/Conway Publications, Inc.
Advertiser Index: Every issue.
Special Issues:
   Product Review.   January.

0557. FOOTWEAR NEWS.
P.O. Box 1402, Riverton, NJ 08077.
Annual Subscription: $39.   **Frequency:** Weekly.
Publisher: Fairchild Publications.
Special Issues:
   Financial Review. $1.15.   July.
   Directory.   Started 1975.   Published as a separate issue. $17.95.   Biennially (even years).   December.
   Financial Forecast. $1.15.   December.

0558. FORBES.
60 Fifth Ave., New York, NY 10011.
Annual Subscription: $36.   **Frequency:** Biweekly.
Publisher: Forbes Inc.
Editorial Index: Semi-Annual.   Subject.   June/December.
Indexed or Abstracted Online: Information Bank; Predicasts; CIN; ABI/Inform; Management Contents; Trade & Industry Index; Magazine Index.
Special Issues:
   Annual Report on American Industry. $3.   January.
   Banking Survey: 100 largest bank holding companies; 50 largest trust operations; 25 largest savings & loan associations. $3.   April.
   Annual Reports. $3.   May.
   Largest Employers: jobs and productivity. $3.   May.
   Top 500 U.S. Companies (Sales, Profits, Assets, Market Value). $3.   May.
   Who Gets the Most Pay: Forbes 500 Lists. $3.   June.
   Spolight on International Business: 125 largest foreign investments in the U.S.; 125 largest in U.S. multinationals; 125 largest.   July.
   Mutual Fund Ratings. $3.   August.
   Forbes 400: Richest People in the U.S.   Started 1982. Published as a separate issue.   September.
   Up and Comers (companies with high growth rates). October.
   Earnings Forecast for the Forbes 500.   November.

0559. FOREIGN AFFAIRS.
58 East 68 St., New York, NY 10021.
Annual Subscription: $22.   **Frequency:** Quarterly.
Publisher: Council on Foreign Relations.
Advertiser Index: Every issue.
Indexed or Abstracted Online: Information Bank; Magazine Index; Management Contents.
Special Issues:
   America and the World.   Published as a separate issue. February.

0560. FOREIGN SERVICE JOURNAL.
2101 E. St. NW, Washington, DC 20037.
Annual Subscription: $10.
Editorial Index: Annual.   Subject/Title/Author.   March.

0561. FOREST FARMER.
P.O. Box 95385, Atlanta, GA 30347.
Annual Subscription: $25.   **Frequency:** 10/yr.
Publisher: Forest Farmers Association.
Special Issues:
   Forest Farmer Manual.   Published as a separate issue. $15.   Biennially.   March.

0562. FOREST INDUSTRIES.
500 Howard St., San Francisco, CA 94105.
Annual Subscription: $30.   **Frequency:** Monthly.
Publisher: Miller Freeman Publications.
Advertiser Index: Every issue.
Indexed Online: Trade & Industry Index.
Special Issues:
   Annual Review. $3.   January.
   Directory of the Forest Products Industry—includes wood harvesting; primary and secondary forest products producers; wholesalers; industry statistics; forest area maps; grade stamps; agencies and organizations; buyers' guide. Indexed by type of operation, lumber specialties. Published as a separate issue. $80.   Not included in the subscription price.   January.
   Annual Panel Review—statistics on wood-based paneling in North America. $3.   April.
   Annual Lumber Review—statistics on the lumber industry in the U.S. and Canada. $3.   July.
   Pulpwood Annual. $3.   August.
   Electronics and Computer Technology. $3.   September.
   Buyers Guide and Suppliers Showcase—review of new woods equipment and mill equipment recently introduced in the North American forest products industry; classified directory of products and services; supplier index; directory of government agencies, research facilities, and industry associations.   Started 1982. $3.50.   December.

0563. FOREST PRODUCTS JOURNAL.
2801 Marshall Ct., Madison, WI 53705.
Annual Subscription: $60.   **Frequency:** Monthly.
Publisher: Forest Products Research Society.
Advertiser Index: October.
Editorial Index: Annual.   Subject/Title/Author.   December.
Special Issues:
   Yearbook Issue. $5.   October.

0564. FORM MAGAZINE.
433 E. Monroe Ave., Alexandria, VA 22301.
Annual Subscription: $18.   **Frequency:** Monthly.
Publisher: National Business Forms Association.
Advertiser Index: Every issue.
Editorial Index: Annual.   Subject.   January.
Special Issues:
   Convention Issue.   Started 1969. $1.50.   September.

0565. FORTUNE MAGAZINE.
1271 Ave. of the Americas, New York, NY 10020.
Annual Subscription: $36.   **Frequency:** 26/yr.
Publisher: Time Inc.
Indexed or Abstracted Online: ABI/Inform; Magazine Index; Management Contents; Trade & Industry Index; Predicasts; Information Bank; CIN.

Special Issues:
Survey of Corporate Reputations.   Started 1983. $3.
    January.
Top 50 Deals of the Year. $3.   January.
18 Month Economic Forecast. $3.   January/July.
Inventory Survey. $3.   February/May/August/
    November.
Fortune 500: Largest U.S. Industrial Corporations. $3.
    April or May.
Hall of Fame for U.S. Industrial Corporations.   Started 1975.
    $3.   April.
Home Builders Survey. $3.   April/October.
Executive Mood Survey. $3.   May/November.
Service 500 (includes 100 largest diversified service; 100
    largest commercial U.S. banks; 100 largest diversified
    financial companies; 50 largest life insurance companies; 50
    largest retailing companies; 50 largest transportation
    companies; and 50 largest utilities). $3.   June.
50 Largest Industrial Corporations in the World. $3.
    August.
50 Leading U.S. Industrial Exporters, Ranked by Total
    Exports. $3.   August.
International 500: Largest Industrial Corporations Outside the
    U.S. $3.   August.
100 Largest Commercial Banks Outside the U.S. $3.
    August.
Business Coups and Catastrophies. $3.   December.
Products of the Year. $3.   December.

0566. FOUNDATION NEWS.
1828 L St., NW, Washington, DC 20036.
Annual Subscription: $24.   **Frequency:** 6/yr.
Publisher: Council on Foundations, Inc.
Editorial Index: Annual. Subject/Author. November/
December.

0567. FOUNDRY MANAGEMENT & TECHNOLOGY.
1111 Chester Ave., Cleveland, OH 44114.
Annual Subscription: $35.   **Frequency:** Monthly.
Publisher: Penton/IPC.
Advertiser Index: Every issue.
Editorial Index: Annual. Title/Author. Available separately in
December by request (free).
Special Issues:
Business Outlook Survey Issue.   Started 1892. $4.
    January.
American Foundrymen's Society Congress Preview; Report.
    (Note: AFP Exposition in conjunction with AFP Congress
    held triennially, starting April 1984.).   Started 1932. $4.
    April and June.
Where-To-Buy Directory of Manufacturers.   Started 1981.
    $4.   September.
Metalcasting in Review/Foundry Catalog File (Note: Catalog
    file was separate biennial release through December
    1981.).   Started 1892. $4.   December.

0568. FRETS.
Box 2120, Cupertino, CA 95015.
Annual Subscription: $16.95.   **Frequency:** Monthly.
Publisher: GPI Publications.
Advertiser Index: Every issue.
Editorial Index: Irregular. Title/Author.
Special Issues:
Reader's Poll Ballot—best artist in various acoustic string
    categories. $1.75.   September.
Reader's Poll Winners. $1.75.   December.

0569. FROZEN FOOD AGE.
230 Park Ave., New York, NY 10017.
Annual Subscription: $16.   **Frequency:** Monthly.
Publisher: Frozen Food Age Publishing Corp.
Special Issues:
Seafoods. $2.   January.
Concentrates—citrus review & forecast. $2.   February.
Food Marketing Institute and National Restaurant Association
    Conventions. $2.   May.
Frozen Vegetable Pack. $2.   June.
Annual Kings (New Jersey) Super Markets Survey
    Association. $2.   August or September.
National Frozen Food Association Convention. $2.
    October or November.
National Food Brokers Association Convention. $2.
    December.

0570. FUEL OIL NEWS.
P.O. Box 360, Whitehouse, NJ 08888.
Annual Subscription: $11.   **Frequency:** Monthly.
Publisher: Publex Corp.
Advertiser Index: Every issue.
Special Issues:
Directory of Oil Handling Equipment. $1.   February.
Directory of Solar Suppliers. $1.   March.
Directory of EDP Suppliers. $1.   April.
Fuel Merchants Association of New Jersey Convention. $1.
    May.
National Association of Oil Heating Service Managers
    Convention. $1.   June.
Mid-Year Statistical Report. $1.   July.
Directory of Solid & Multi-Fuel Equipment. $1.   August.
Pennsylvania Petroleum Association Convention. $1.
    Biennially (even years).   September.
Directory of State Associations. $1.   October.
Futures Trading. $1.   November.
Source Book/Suppliers Directory/Statistics.   Started 1978.
    $5.   December.

0571. FUELOIL/OIL HEAT AND SOLAR SYSTEMS.
200 Commerce Rd., Cedar Grove, NJ 07009.
Annual Subscription: $14.   **Frequency:** Monthly.
Publisher: Industry Publications Inc.
Advertiser Index: Annually.
Editorial Index: Annual. Subject. December.
Indexed Online: Trade & Industry Index.
Special Issues:
Directory Issue.   Started 1924. $2.   Biennially.
    February.
Show Issue—Fuel Merchants Association of New Jersey
    Trade Show.   Started 1957. $2.   May.
Service Management Study—analysis of oilburner service
    management from heating oil dealer's standpoint, including
    operating costs, wages, profit and loss, productivity.
    Started 1941. $2.   June.
Show Issue—National Association of Oil Heat Service
    Managers Trade Show.   Started 1954. $2.   June.
Solar Issue.   Started 1971. $2.   August.
Fueloil Dealer Management Analysis—analysis of heating oil
    market from retail dealer's standpoint, including operating
    costs, margins and profits, wages, performance data, truck
    sizes, output comparisons.   Started 1932. $2.
    September.

0572. FUND RAISING MANAGEMENT.
224 7th St., Garden City, NY 11530.
Annual Subscription: $30.   **Frequency:** Monthly.
Publisher: Hoke Communications Inc.
Editorial Index: Annual. Title. January.
Indexed or Abstracted Online: ABI/Inform; Management
Contents.

0573. FUR AGE WEEKLY.
127 West 30 St., New York, NY 10001.
Annual Subscription: $31.   **Frequency:** Weekly.
Publisher: Same.
Special Issues:
Canadian Fur Fair Issue.   Started 1980. $.55.   April.
U.S. Fur Expo.   Started 1983. $.55.   May.
Wholesale Fur Source Directory: New York, Toronto and
    Montreal (with advertisers index).   Started 1933.
    Published as a separate issue. $10.   June.
Tri-City Fur Source Building-by-Building Directory: New York,
    Toronto and Montreal (with advertisers index).   Started
    1978.   Published as a separate issue. $15.   October.

0574. FURNITURE DESIGN AND MANUFACTURING.
1020 South Wabash Ave., Chicago, IL 60605.
Annual Subscription: $25. **Frequency:** Monthly.
Publisher: Delta Communications.
Advertiser Index: Every issue.
Special Issues:
  Supply Source Directory. $10.   June.
  International Woodworking Machinery & Furniture Supply Fair. $2.50.   Biennially (even years).   September.
  Woodworking Machinery & Furniture Supply Fair. $2.50.   Biennially (odd years).   September.

0575. FURNITURE MANUFACTURING MANAGEMENT.
P.O. Box 38629, Germantown, TN 38138.
Annual Subscription: $20. **Frequency:** 11/yr.
Publisher: Association Publications, Inc.
Advertiser Index: Every issue.
Special Issues:
  Directory and Buyers Guide.   Started 1964. $20.   May.

0576. FURNITURE PRODUCTION.
804 Church St., Nashville, TN 37203.
Annual Subscription: $15. **Frequency:** Monthly.
Publisher: Production Publishing Co.
Special Issues:
  International Woodworking Machinery and Furniture Supply Fair. $1.50.   Biennially (even years).   September.
  Blue Book (Directory of Supply Sources).   December.

0577. FURNITURE WORLD.
127 East 31st St., New York, NY 10016.
Annual Subscription: $8. **Frequency:** Monthly.
Publisher: Towse Publishing.
Advertiser Index: Every issue.
Special Issues:
  Market Buying Guide.   Published as a separate issue. $2.   April/October.
  The History of Furniture Styles—includes design awards: top 100 manufacturer's designs with greatest consumer acceptance.   Published as a separate issue. $2.   May.

0578. FUTURE SURVEY.
4916 St. Elmo Ave., Bethesda, MD 20814.
Annual Subscription: $45 (indiv.)/65 (libraries). **Frequency:** Monthly.
Publisher: World Future Society.
Editorial Index: Annual. Subject/Author. December.
Special Issues:
  Future Survey Annual—over 1,000 abstracts published in magazine during year, reorganized by subjects, with cumulative subject and author indexes, commentary, charts, etc.   Started 1979.   Published as a separate issue.   December.

0579. GARDEN SUPPLY RETAILER.
P.O. Box 67, Minneapolis, MN 55440.
Annual Subscription: $15. **Frequency:** Annual.
Publisher: Miller Publishing Co.
Advertiser Index: Every issue.
Special Issues:
  National Hardware Show. $1.   August.
  Garden Industry of America Show. $1.   September.
  Green Book—buyers guide to the home/lawn & garden and power equipment industry.   Started 1976.   Published as a separate issue. $10.   Not included in the subscription price.   November.

0580. GAS DIGEST.
Box 35819, Houston, TX 77235.
Annual Subscription: $17.50. **Frequency:** Monthly.
Publisher: TriPlek Publications.
Special Issues:
  Midwest Gas News.   Published as a separate issue.   March.
  Southern Gas Association Convention News.   Published as a separate issue.   April.
  Texas Gas Association Convention News.   Published as a separate issue.   June.

0581. GAS INDUSTRIES.
P.O. Box 558, Park Ridge, IL 60068.
Annual Subscription: $15. **Frequency:** Monthly.
Publisher: Gas Industries E&A News Inc.
Advertiser Index: Every issue.
Editorial Index: Annual. Subject. February.
Special Issues:
  Construction Equipment.   January.
  Corrosion Control.   March.
  Distribution Conference Issue.   April.
  Transmission Conference Issue.   May.
  Annual Metering and Instrumentation Issue.   August.
  American Gas Association Annual Meeting.   October.
  Annual Product Roundup.   December.

0582. THE GENEALOGICAL HELPER.
P.O. Box 368, Logan, UT 84321.
Annual Subscription: $15.50. **Frequency:** 6/yr.
Publisher: George B. Everton, Jr.
Advertiser Index: Every issue.
Editorial Index: Every issue. Subject. January/March/May/July/September/November.
Special Issues:
  Genealogist Exchange: 'Bureau of Missing Ancestors'—lists surnames of persons sought by researchers. $4.   6/yr.   January/March/May/July/September/November.
  Family Associations and their leaders. $4.   May.
  Directory of Genealogical Societies, Libraries and Professionals. $4.   July.
  Directory of Genealogists. $4.   September.

0583. GENIE-CONSTRUCTION.
310 Victoria Ave., Ste. 201, Westmount, Quebec H3Z 2M9.
Annual Subscription: $26.50. **Frequency:** Monthly.
Publisher: Southam Communications Ltd.
Advertiser Index: Every issue.

0584. GEOPHYSICS.
P.O. Box 3098, Tulsa, OK 74101.
Annual Subscription: $40. **Frequency:** Monthly.
Publisher: Society of Exploration Geophysicists.
Advertiser Index: Every issue.
Editorial Index: Annual. Subject/Title/Author. December (cumulative subject, title, author, index published separately).
Special Issues:
  Society of Exploration Geophysicists Yearbook (Roster Issue of Leading Edge).   Published as a separate issue. $20.   May.

0585. GERMAN AMERICAN TRADE NEWS.
666 Fifth Ave., New York, NY 10103.
Annual Subscription: $9. **Frequency:** Bimonthly.
Publisher: German American Chamber of Commerce.
Special Issues:
  American Subsidiaries of German Firms—includes number of employees, percentage owned by parent companies, products and services, geographical U.S. listing.   Published as a separate issue. $55.   Not included in the subscription price.   March.
  Buyers Guide to Imported German Products—lists representatives, agents, and/or subsidiaries of German companies in the U.S.   Published as a separate issue. $25.   Not included in the subscription price.   November.

0586. GEYER'S DEALER TOPICS.
51 Madison Ave., New York, NY 10010.
Annual Subscription: $16. **Frequency:** Monthly.
Publisher: Geyer-McAllister Publications.
Advertiser Index: Every issue.
Special Issues:
  Geyer's Who Makes It Directory-office product manufacturers.   Published as a separate issue. $3.50.   April.
  NOMDA Convention Issue—National Office Machine Dealers Association. $3.50.   July.
  NOPA Convention—National Office Products Association. $3.50.   September.

0587. GIFTS & DECORATIVE ACCESSORIES.
51 Madison Ave., New York, NY 10010.
Annual Subscription: $24. **Frequency:** Monthly.
Publisher: Geyer-McAllister Publications.
Advertiser Index: Every issue.
Editorial Index: Annual. Subject. January.
Indexed Online: Trade & Industry Index.
Special Issues:
  Chicago Midwest Market Review. January/July.
  Northeast Highlights. Published as a separate issue. $4. February/July.
  Gourmet Merchandising. Published as a separate issue. $4. March.
  Bridal Merchandising. April/September.
  National Stationery Highlights. Published as a separate issue. $4. April.
  Atlanta Highlights. Published as a separate issue. $4. May/November.
  N.Y. Tabletop & Accessories Show Highlights. Published as a separate issue. $4. May/October.
  Awards Issues. July/August.
  Miami Highlights. Published as a separate issue. $4. July.
  Dallas Highlights. Published as a separate issue. $4. August/December.
  Buyers Directory—gifts, china and glass, lamps and house accessories, greeting cards and special stationery. Published as a separate issue. September.
  Immediate Delivery Merchandise. November.
  Atlantic City Highlights. Published as a separate issue. $4. December.
  Collectibles Issue. December.
  Trends & Forecast Issue. December.
  Western Highlights. Published as a separate issue. $4. December/June.

0588. GIFTS & TABLEWARES.
1450 Don Mills Rd., Don Mills, Ontario, Can. M3B 2X7.
Annual Subscription: $24/18. **Frequency:** 6/yr.
Publisher: Southam Communications Ltd.
Advertiser Index: Every issue.
Special Issues:
  Toronto Spring Gift Show. $2. January/February.
  Montreal Spring Gift Show. $2. March/April.
  Montreal Fall Gift Show. $2. July/August.
  Toronto Fall Gift Show. $2. September/October.

0589. GIFTWARE BUSINESS.
1515 Broadway, New York, NY 10036.
Annual Subscription: $10. **Frequency:** Monthly.
Publisher: Gralla Publications.
Advertiser Index: Every issue.
Special Issues:
  Directory of Suppliers. September.

0590. THE GLASS INDUSTRY.
110 East 42nd St., New York, NY 10017.
Annual Subscription: $25. **Frequency:** Monthly.
Publisher: Ashlee Publishing Co.
Advertiser Index: Every issue.
Special Issues:
  The Glass Industry Directory Issue. Started 1965. Published as a separate issue. $12. October.

0591. GOLF COURSE MANAGEMENT.
1617 St. Andrews Dr., Lawrence, KS 66044.
Annual Subscription: $24. **Frequency:** Monthly.
Publisher: Golf Course Superintendents Association of America.
Advertiser Index: Every issue.
Editorial Index: Annual. Subject. December or January.

0592. GOLF DIGEST.
P.O. Box 10177, Des Moines, IA 50340.
Annual Subscription: $17.95. **Frequency:** Monthly.
Publisher: Golf Digest/Tennis Inc.
Advertiser Index: Every issue.
Special Issues:
  Most Improved Golfers—instruction for amateurs and pros. $1.75. January.
  Golf Record Book/Amateur Rankings/Places to Play—courses in U.S., Canada, Mexico, Caribbean. $2.25. February.
  Hole-in-One Roundup/Records. $2.25. March.
  Junior Golf Camps. $1.75. April.
  U. S. Open Preview. $1.75. June.
  Women Golfers Week Package. $1.75. August.
  World Series of Golf. $1.75. September.
  Places to Meet—meeting and convention guide. $1.75. October.
  America's 100 Greatest Courses. $1.75. Biennially. November (odd yrs).
  Golf Equipment. $1.75. Annual. December.

0593. GOLF MAGAZINE.
380 Madison Ave., New York, NY 10017.
Annual Subscription: $11.94. **Frequency:** Monthly.
Publisher: Times Mirror Magazines.
Advertiser Index: Every issue.
Indexed Online: Magazine Index.
Special Issues:
  PGA Tournament. $1.25. January.
  Yearbook—review of the year, statistics, annual tour schedules, ladies PGA/Golf South. $1.95. February.
  Equipment Buying Guide. $1.25. March.
  Masters Tournaments/Golfwear Guide. $1.25. April.
  Camps and Schools. $1.25. May.
  U.S. Open. $1.25. June.
  British Open/Golf Shoes. $1.25. July.
  PGA Championship. $1.25. August.
  50 Greatest Courses in the World. $1.25. September.
  Meeting Facilities. $1.25. October.
  College Golfers of the Year. $1.25. November.
  All-America Team/Florida Golf Guide. $1.25. December.

0594. GOVERNMENT PRODUCT NEWS.
1111 Chester Ave., Cleveland, OH 44114.
Annual Subscription: $24. **Frequency:** Monthly.
Publisher: Penton/IPC Publications.
Advertiser Index: Every issue.
Indexed Online: Trade & Industry Index.
Special Issues:
  Government Specifier's Reference File. $2.50. January.
  Section on Plant Maintenance. $2.50. March.
  Office Equipment Buyers Guide. $2.50. April.
  Budget Planning Aids. $2.50. Biennially. June/July.
  Section on Public Works. $2.50. September.
  Section on Parks and Recreation. $2.50. October.
  Grounds Maintenance Buyers Guide. $2.50. November.
  Product Preview. $2.50. December.
  Section on Material Handling. $2.50. Irregular.

0595. GRADUATING ENGINEER.
1221 Ave. of the Americas, New York, NY 10020.
Annual Subscription: $16. **Frequency:** Quarterly.
Publisher: McGraw-Hill Publishing Co.
Advertiser Index: Every issue.
Special Issues:
  Women Engineers. Published as a separate issue. $5. Not included in the subscription price. February.
  Computer Careers. Published as a separate issue. $5. Not included in the subscription price. October.
  Minority Engineers. Published as a separate issue. $5. Not included in the subscription price. October.

0596. GRAIN AGE.
7535 Office Ridge Circle, Eden Prairie, MN 55344.
Annual Subscription: $15. **Frequency:** Monthly.
Publisher: Communications Marketing, Inc.
Advertiser Index: Every issue.
Special Issues:
  Grain Elevator and Processing Society Conference Issue. $1.25. February.
  National Grain & Feed Association Convention Issue. $1.25. March.

Association of Operative Millers Convention Issue. $1.25. April.
Dust Control & Conditioning. $1.25. May.
Construction, Expansion, Maintenance. $1.25. June.
Hedging & the Futures Market. $1.25. August.
Transportation. $1.25. September.
Annual Operators Manual. Started 1974. $1.25. October.
World Food Picture. $1.25. December.

0597. GRAIN JOURNAL.
1600 East Lincoln, Decatur, IL 62521.
Annual Subscription: $15. **Frequency:** 10/yr.
Publisher: Country Journal Publishing.
Advertiser Index: Every issue.
Special Issues:
Special Reference Issue for Grain Storage Industry. October/November.
Outlook. December.

0598. GRAIN STORAGE & HANDLING.
4800 Main St., Kansas City, MO 64112.
Annual Subscription: Free to qualified persons. **Frequency:** Bimonthly.
Publisher: Sosland Publishing Co.
Advertiser Index: Every issue.
Special Issues:
Grain Elevator and Processing Society Show Issue. Started 1980. Published as a separate issue. 0. March.

0599. GRANTS MAGAZINE.
233 Spring St., New York, NY 10013.
Annual Subscription: $27. **Frequency:** Quarterly.
Publisher: Plenum Publishing Co.
Editorial Index: Annual. Title. December.

0600. GRAPHIC ARTS MONTHLY.
875 Third Ave., New York, NY 10022.
Annual Subscription: $40. **Frequency:** 13/yr.
Publisher: Technical Publishing Co.
Advertiser Index: Every issue.
Indexed Online: Trade & Industry Index.
Special Issues:
Buyers Guide—by manufacturers and distributors, product, brand names. Includes financial, operating ratio and industry market information. Started 1978. $30. June.

0601. GRAPHIC ARTS PRODUCT NEWS.
300 West Adams St., Chicago, IL 60606.
Annual Subscription: Free (qualified persons). **Frequency:** 6/yr.
Publisher: Maclean Hunter Publishing Corp.
Advertiser Index: Every issue.
Special Issues:
Quick Printing Equipment Update. October/November.
Best of Year—product review. December/January.

0602. GREETINGS MAGAZINE.
309 Fifth Ave., New York, NY 10016.
Annual Subscription: $10. **Frequency:** Monthly.
Publisher: Mackay Publications.
Advertiser Index: Every issue.
Special Issues:
Buyers Guide Directory. Started 1964. Published as a separate issue. $7. June.

0603. GROCERS' SPOTLIGHT.
22725 Mack Ave., St. Clair Shores, MI 48080.
Annual Subscription: $15. **Frequency:** 15/yr.
Publisher: Shamie Publishing Co.
Special Issues:
Market Studies: Mega West (Western Edition). $30/50 (combined). August.
Market Studies: Mega 2 (Midwest Edition). $35/50 (combined). August.
Annual Legislative Update. Started 1980. $2. November.
National Food Brokers Association Convention. $2. December.

0604. GROCERY DISTRIBUTION MAGAZINE.
307 North Michigan Ave., Chicago, IL 60601.
Annual Subscription: $20. **Frequency:** 6/yr.
Publisher: Same.
Special Issues:
Directory of Equipment/Fixtures/Services. Started 1975. $5. November/December.

0605. GROUND WATER AGE.
135 Addison, Elmhurst, IL 60126.
Annual Subscription: $20. **Frequency:** Monthly.
Publisher: Scott Periodicals.
Advertiser Index: Every issue.
Editorial Index: Biennial. Subject. Irregular.
Special Issues:
NWWA Convention Daily. Started 1971. Published as a separate issue. $4. Not included in the subscription price. September.
National Water Well Association Convention Preview. Started 1972. $4. September.

0606. GROUNDS MAINTENANCE.
P.O. Box 12901, Overland Park, KS 66212.
Annual Subscription: $24. **Frequency:** Monthly.
Publisher: John Wickersham.
Advertiser Index: Every issue.
Editorial Index: Annual. Subject. December.
Special Issues:
Golf Course Manual—seed, sod, and plants; irrigation; chemicals and fertilizers; accessories and materials. Started 1975. Published as a separate issue. $2. November.
Grounds Care Manual. $2. December.

0607. GUITAR PLAYER.
Box 2100, Cupertino, CA 95015.
Frequency: Monthly.
Publisher: GPI Publications.
Advertiser Index: Every issue.
Editorial Index: Title/Author. Irregular.
Special Issues:
Reader's Poll Ballot—best artist in various categories (classical, jazz, rock, etc.). $2.50. September.
Reader's Poll Winners. $2.50. December.

0608. HANDLING & SHIPPING MANAGEMENT.
Penton Plaza, Cleveland, OH 44114.
Annual Subscription: $30. **Frequency:** Monthly.
Publisher: Penton/IPC.
Advertiser Index: Every issue.
Editorial Index: Annual. Subject. December.
Special Issues:
Outlook Issue. $2.50. January.
International Distribution Outlook. February.
Export/Import. July.
Ports Directory. September.
Report on National Council of Physical Distribution Management. December.

0609. HANDLOADER MAGAZINE.
P.O. Box 3030, Prescott, AZ 86302.
Annual Subscription: $13. **Frequency:** 6/yr.
Publisher: Wolfe Publishing Co., Inc.
Advertiser Index: Every issue.
Editorial Index: Annual and Biennial. Subject/Title/Author. November/December.

0610. HARBOUR & SHIPPING.
C310 - 355 Burrard St., Vancouver, British Columbia, Can. V6G 2A9.
Annual Subscription: $28/20. **Frequency:** Monthly.
Publisher: Progress Publishing Co. Ltd.
Advertiser Index: Every issue.
Special Issues:
Annual Shipbuilding Edition. $3. March.
Annual Shipping Directory. $3. May.
Annual Marine Engine Review. Started 1928. $3. July.
Annual B.C. Ports Issue. $3. October.

0611. HARDWARE AGE.
Chilton Way, Radnor, PA 19089.
Annual Subscription: $7. **Frequency:** Monthly.
Publisher: Chilton Co.
Advertiser Index: Every issue.
Indexed Online: Trade & Industry Index.
Special Issues:
Directory of Hardlines Distributors. Published as a separate issue. $135. Not included in the subscription price. Biennially.
National Hardware Convention Preview. $1.50. October.
Buyer's Guide—Who Makes It, products & manufacturers. $10. December.

0612. HARDWARE MERCHANDISER.
7300 North Cicero, Lincolnwood, IL 60646.
Annual Subscription: $20. **Frequency:** Monthly.
Publisher: Irving-Cloud Publishing Co.
Advertiser Index: Every issue.
Editorial Index: Annual. Subject. December.
Special Issues:
Winter Hardware Show. January.
National Homecenter Show. February.
Southern Hardware Convention. April.
National Hardware Show. August.
Merchandiser of the Year/National Hardware Convention. October.

0613. HARDWARE MERCHANDISING.
777 Bay St., Toronto, Ontario, Can. M5W 1A7.
Annual Subscription: $44/20. **Frequency:** 10/yr.
Publisher: Maclean Hunter Limited.
Advertiser Index: Every issue.
Special Issues:
Canadian Hardware Show. $4. January.
Top 100—guide to retail/wholesale buying influences. Started 1982. Published as a separate issue. $20. Biennially. July.
Western Hardware-Housewares Home Improvement Show. $4. September.
Canadian Home Improvement Show. $4. October.

0614. HARDWARE RETAILING.
770 North School Rd., Indianapolis, IN 46224.
Annual Subscription: $4. **Frequency:** Monthly.
Publisher: National Retail Hardware Association.
Advertiser Index: Every issue.
Editorial Index: Annual. Subject. December.
Special Issues:
Product Knowledge Handbook. Started 1967. Published as a separate issue. $5. Biennially. May (even yrs).
Hardware Show Issue. Started 1949. $1. August.
Price Study Issue. $1. October.
Advertising Workbook. $1. December.

0615. HARPER'S.
P.O. Box 2622, Boulder, CO 80322.
Annual Subscription: $18. **Frequency:** Monthly.
Publisher: Harper's Magazine Foundation.
Editorial Index: Semi-Annual. Subject/Title/Author. Published separately; available free by request.
Indexed Online: Magazine Index.

0616. HARVARD BUSINESS REVIEW.
Soldiers Field, Boston, MA 02163.
Annual Subscription: $30. **Frequency:** 6/yr.
Publisher: Graduate School of Business Administration.
Advertiser Index: Every issue.
Editorial Index: Annual. Subject/Author. November/December; cumulative index 1971-83 in January/February issue.
Indexed or Abstracted Online: HBR; AMI; Information Bank; Magazine Index; Trade & Industry Index; ABI/Inform; Insurance Abstracts; Predicasts.

0617. HARVARD LAW REVIEW.
Gannett House, Cambridge, MA 02138.
Annual Subscription: $32. **Frequency:** 8/yr.
Publisher: Harvard Law Review Association.
Editorial Index: Annual. Subject/Title/Author. June.
Abstracted Online: ABI/Inform; Management Contents; Legal Resource Index.
Special Issues:
The Supreme Court: Review of Previous Term. $7.50. November.

0618. HEALTH.
P.O. Box 3700, Bergenfield, NJ 07621.
Annual Subscription: $18. **Frequency:** 10/yr.
Publisher: Family Media, Inc.
Indexed Online: Magazine Index.
Special Issues:
All-Breakthroughs Issue—This year's giant leaps in health and medicine. Started 1980. $1.50. March.

0619. HEALTH CARE.
1450 Don Mills Rd., Don Mills, Ontario, Can. M3B 2X7.
Annual Subscription: $22. **Frequency:** 8/yr.
Publisher: Southam Communications Ltd.
Advertiser Index: Every issue.
Special Issues:
Directory/Health Care Buyer's Guide. Started 1960. May.

0620. HEALTH CARE FINANCING REVIEW.
U.S. Government Printing Office, Washington, DC 20402.
Annual Subscription: $15. **Frequency:** Quarterly.
Publisher: Health Care Financing Administration.
Indexed or Abstracted Online: Medlars; Health Planning & Administration; Medline.
Special Issues:
Trends—historical data that highlight economic development in the health care sector. Started 1983 (fall). September/December/March/June.
Annual Supplement—single theme issue on subject of critical concern to health care financing. Started 1984. Published as a separate issue. Varies.

0621. HEALTH CARE SYSTEMS.
1515 Broadway, New York, NY 10036.
Annual Subscription: $36 (U.S.)/65 (foreign). **Frequency:** Monthly.
Publisher: Gralla Publications, Inc.
Advertiser Index: Every issue.
Special Issues:
Directory of Health Care Suppliers/Hospital Design-Construction-Furnishing Issue. $4. January.
Annual Operating Room Survey. Started 1982. $4. March.
Infection Control. $4. May.
Annual Decubitus Round Table. Started 1980. $4. June.
Who's Who in Hospital Management and Contract Services. $4. August.
Annual Medicare Records Survey. Started 1982. $4. October.
Hospital Software Guide. Started 1983. $4. November/December.

0622. HEALTH EDUCATION.
AAHPERD Publications, P.O. Box 704, Waldorf, MD 20601.
Annual Subscription: $42. **Frequency:** Bimonthly.
Publisher: American Alliance for Health, Physical Education, Recreation, & Dance.
Advertiser Index: Every issue.
Editorial Index: Annual. Title/Author. November/December.
Special Issues:
AAHPERD Directory of Institutions—institutions offering graduate and undergraduate programs. Published as a separate issue. $6. Biennially (even years). September/October.

0623. HEALTH FOODS BUSINESS.
567 Morris Ave., Elizabeth, NJ 07208.

Annual Subscription: $25. **Frequency:** Monthly.
Publisher: Howmark Publishing Co.
Advertiser Index: Every issue.
Special Issues:
　State of the Industry (annual review).　$2.50.　January.
　Annual Survey Issue (statistics).　Started 1976.　$5.　March.
　Wholesaler Directory (regional guide).　$5.　May.
　Pre-Show Issue.　$2.50.　June.
　Show Issue (National Natural Foods Association Convention).　$2.50.　July.
　Purchasing Guide (directory of suppliers).　Started 1974.　$25.　November.

0624. HEALTH INDUSTRY TODAY.
2009 Morris Ave., Union, NJ 07083.
Annual Subscription: $8.50.　**Frequency:** Monthly.
Publisher: Cassak Publications.
Advertiser Index: Every issue.
Editorial Index: Semi-Annual. Subject. Varies.
Indexed or Abstracted Online: Predicasts.
Special Issues:
　Industry Forecast Issue.　Not included in the subscription price.　January.
　Health Industry Buyers Guide—hospitals and physicians supply; laboratory supply; oxygen therapy supply; home healthcare; X-ray supply; orthopedic appliance; international section; trade and brand names; product classification index and advertisers index.　Started 1940.　Published as a separate issue.　$20.　Not included in the subscription price.　September.

0625. HEALTH INSURANCE UNDERWRITER.
145 North Ave., Hartland, WI 53029.
Annual Subscription: $7.　**Frequency:** 11/yr.
Publisher: National Association of Health Underwriters.
Special Issues:
　National Association of Health Underwriters Convention Issue.　July/August.

0626. HEALTHCARE FINANCIAL MANAGEMENT.
1900 Spring Rd., Oak Brook, IL 60521.
Annual Subscription: $40.　**Frequency:** Monthly.
Publisher: Healthcare Financial Management Association.
Advertiser Index: Every issue.
Editorial Index: Quarterly. Subject/Author. March/June/September/December (full index in December issue).
Indexed or Abstracted Online: ABI/Inform; Management Contents; Trade & Industry Index.
Special Issues:
　HFMA National Institute Theme Announcement.　$4.　February.
　Tax Exempt Hospital Revenue Bonds Survey.　Started 1979.　$4.　April/October.
　Computers in Health Care/New Officers and Directors.　$4.　June.
　HFMA National Institute.　$4.　June.
　HFMA Annual Report.　$4.　September.

0627. HEARING INSTRUMENTS.
1 East 1st St., Duluth, MN 55805.
Annual Subscription: $16/20.　**Frequency:** Monthly.
Publisher: Harcourt Brace Jovanovich Publications, Inc.
Advertiser Index: Every issue.
Special Issues:
　Forecast Issue.　January.
　Product Reviews.　5/yr.　February/April/June/September/October.
　Directory of Hearing Health Care Products.　Started 1949.　May.
　Survey of Hearing Aid Dispensers.　Started 1939.　May.
　Special Instruments Buying Guide.　Started 1973.　August.

0628. THE HEARING JOURNAL.
West Bare Hill Rd., Box L, Harvard, MA 01451.
Annual Subscription: $16.　**Frequency:** Monthly.
Publisher: The Laux Company.
Advertiser Index: Every issue.
Editorial Index: Annual. Subject/Title/Author. February.
Special Issues:
　Annual Directory of Hearing Aid Manufacturers and Suppliers.　$4.　November or December.

0629. HEATING/COMBUSTION EQUIPMENT NEWS.
One Penn Plaza, New York, NY 10001.
Annual Subscription: $12.　**Frequency:** 6/yr.
Publisher: Business Communications Inc.
Advertiser Index: Every issue.
Special Issues:
　Buyers Guide—equipment, services and engineering information for process heat and combustion operations in the primary and secondary metalworking and metalforming, diecasting, heat treating, glass, ceramics, cement and petrochemical industries.　$10.　October.

0630. HEATING/PIPING/AIR CONDITIONING.
1111 Chester Ave., Cleveland, OH 44114.
Annual Subscription: $30.　**Frequency:** Monthly.
Publisher: Penton/IPC.
Advertiser Index: Every issue.
Editorial Index: Annual. Subject/Title/Author. June.
Indexed Online: Compendex; ISMEC.
Special Issues:
　HPAC Info-Dex: Mechanical Systems Information Index—manufacturers directory with all products classified including trade names; trade associations; code-making authorities; technical books and manuals.　Started 1934.　$15.　June.

0631. HEATING, PLUMBING, AIR CONDITIONING.
1450 Don Mills Rd., Don Mills, Ontario, Can. M3B 2X7.
Annual Subscription: $39.50/30.00.　**Frequency:** Monthly.
Publisher: Southam Communications Ltd.
Advertiser Index: Every issue.
Special Issues:
　Bath & Kitchen Marketer Supplement—for retailers and contractors selling bathroom & kitchen fixtures, cabinets, accessories, renovations.　Started 1979.　Published as a separate issue.　$2.　February/May/July/October.
　Buyers' Guide.　$12.　August.
　Trade Show Issues.　Published as a separate issue.　$2.　Alternate years: May/March or September.

0632. HEAVY CONSTRUCTION NEWS.
777 Bay St., Toronto, Ontario, Can. M5W 1A7.
Annual Subscription: $54/26.　**Frequency:** 24/yr.
Publisher: Maclean Hunter Ltd.
Advertiser Index: Every issue.
Special Issues:
　Construction Forecast.　January.
　Construction Equipment Outlook.　February.
　Concrete Construction Outlook/Roadbuilding Outlook.　March.
　Steel Construction Outlook.　April.
　Mid-Year Construction Equipment Review.　June.
　Roads & Transportation Construction Update.　September.
　Roadbuilding Review.　November.
　Contractor's Handbook.　December.

0633. HEAVY DUTY TRUCKING.
P.O. Box W, Newport Beach, CA 92660.
Annual Subscription: $30.　**Frequency:** Monthly.
Publisher: HIC Corporation.
Advertiser Index: Every issue.
Special Issues:
　Parts & Service Buyers Guide.　Started 1979.　January.
　Truck Show Issue.　Started 1968.　March.
　Trailer Issue.　Started 1977.　April.
　Maintenance.　Started 1973.　May.
　Winterizing Issue.　Started 1971.　September.
　American Trucking Association Issue.　Started 1970.　October.
　Calendar of Events (following year).　Started 1980.　December.
　Safety Issue.　Started 1978.　Varies.

0634. HIGHWAY & HEAVY CONSTRUCTION.
875 Third Ave., New York, NY 10022.
Annual Subscription: $30. **Frequency:** Monthly.
Publisher: Technical Publishing Co.
Advertiser Index: Every issue.
Special Issues:
CONEXPO Preview (Construction Equipment Exposition and Road Show). $3. Every 6 yrs (last 1981). January.
Forecast. $3. January.
Contractor Marketing. $3. March.
Infrastructures. $3. May.
Airports. $3. July.
Bridge Replacements. $3. September.
Trucks & Construction. $3. November.

0635. HISTORY OF POLITICAL ECONOMY.
6698 College Station, Durham, NC 27708.
Annual Subscription: $32 (institutional)/24 (individual).
Frequency: Quarterly.
Publisher: Duke University Press.
Editorial Index: Annual. Author. December.

0636. HOBBY MERCHANDISER.
490 Rte. 9, Rd. 3, P.O. Box 420, Englishtown, NJ 07726.
Annual Subscription: $12. **Frequency:** Monthly.
Publisher: Hobby Publications Inc.
Special Issues:
Hobby Industry Association Trade Show. $1. January.
Hobby Publications Annual Directory. Published as a separate issue. $15. June.
Fall and Christmas Merchandising—buyers guide, ornaments, books, arts. $1. August.

0637. HOG FARM MANAGEMENT.
2501 Wayzata Blvd., Minneapolis, MN 55440.
Annual Subscription: $15. **Frequency:** Monthly.
Publisher: Miller Publishing Co.
Advertiser Index: Every issue.
Editorial Index: Annual. Subject. December.
Special Issues:
American Pork Congress Preview Issue. $1. March.
Pork Producer's Planner—reference issue. $10. December.

0638. HOISERY & UNDERWEAR.
757 Third Ave., New York, NY 10017.
Annual Subscription: $16. **Frequency:** Monthly.
Publisher: Harcourt Brace Jovanovich.
Advertiser Index: Every issue.
Special Issues:
Directory of Fashion Names in Legwear. Started 1982. $2. February.
Resource Guide to Private Label Manufacturers. Started 1984. $2. August.
Buyers Guide to Support & Control Top Pantyhose. Started 1976. $2. September.

0639. HOME & AUTO.
757 Third Ave., New York, NY 10017.
Annual Subscription: $15. **Frequency:** Biweekly.
Publisher: Harcourt Brace Jovanovich Publishers.
Advertiser Index: Every issue.
Editorial Index: Annual. Subject. January.
Indexed Online: Trade & Industry Index.
Special Issues:
Home & Auto Show Dailies—Automotive Parts & Accessories Association. Started 1969. Published as a separate issue. March/August.
Home & Auto Buyers Guide. Started 1936. $6. July.

0640. HOME GOODS RETAILING.
777 Bay St., Toronto, Ontario, Can. M5W 1A7.
Annual Subscription: $46/22. **Frequency:** Monthly.
Publisher: Maclean Hunter Ltd.
Special Issues:
Toronto Furniture Market. $6. January.
Calgary Furniture Market. $6. May.
Montreal Furniture Market. $6. June.
VCR Guide. $6. November.

0641. HORIZONS.
Office of Public Affairs, Agency for International Development, Washington, DC 20523.
Annual Subscription: Free. **Frequency:** Monthly.
Publisher: Agency for International Development.
Editorial Index: Subject. January.

0642. THE HORN BOOK MAGAZINE.
31 St. James Ave., Boston, MA 02116.
Annual Subscription: $25. **Frequency:** 6/yr.
Publisher: The Horn Book Inc.
Advertiser Index: Every issue.
Editorial Index: Annual. Subject/Title/Author. December.
Abstracted Online: Magazine Index.
Special Issues:
Newbery-Caldecott Awards. $4.50. April.
Newbery-Caldecott Award Speeches. $4.50. August.
Boston Globe-Horn Book Awards. $4.50. October.

0643. HORSE & RIDER.
41919 Moreno, P.O. Box 555, Temecula, CA 92390.
Annual Subscription: $12. **Frequency:** Monthly.
Publisher: Horse & Rider Magazine.
Special Issues:
All-Western Yearbook—for Western-oriented horse owner, breeder and trainer. Articles on training pleasure horses, improving riding skills, veterinary advice, feeding and nutrition, grooming, etc. Also feature articles on movie cowboy and rodeo personalities; saddles, bits and spurs; equine schools; horse shows; famous horses; hoof care and shoeing. Published as a separate issue. $3. Not included in the subscription price. May.

0644. HORTICULTURE, THE MAGAZINE OF AMERICAN GARDENING.
3300 Walnut St., Boulder, CO 80323.
Annual Subscription: $18. **Frequency:** Monthly.
Publisher: Horticulture Associates.
Editorial Index: Annual. Subject/Title/Author. January.
Indexed Online: Magazine Index.

0645. HOSPITAL FORUM.
830 Market St., San Francisco, CA 94102.
Annual Subscription: $20. **Frequency:** 6/yr.
Publisher: Association of Western Hospitals.
Advertiser Index: Every issue.
Editorial Index: Annual. Subject/Author. November/December.
Special Issues:
Association of Western Hospitals Convention. $3.50. May/June.
Hospital Architecture and Building—13 Western states. $3.50. July/August.

0646. HOSPITAL GIFT SHOP MANAGEMENT.
12849 Magnolia Blvd., North Hollywood, CA 91607.
Annual Subscription: $35. **Frequency:** Monthly.
Publisher: Creative Age Publications.
Advertiser Index: Every issue.
Editorial Index: Annual. Title. December.

0647. HOSPITAL PRACTICE.
575 Lexington Ave., New York, NY 10022.
Annual Subscription: $25. **Frequency:** Monthly.
Publisher: HP Publishing Company.
Editorial Index: Annual. Subject/Author. December.
Indexed Online: BRS/Pre-Med.

0648. HOSPITAL PROGRESS.
4455 Woodson Rd., St. Louis, MO 63134.
Annual Subscription: $25. **Frequency:** Monthly.
Publisher: Catholic Health Association of the U.S.
Advertiser Index: Every issue.
Editorial Index: Annual. Subject/Author. December.
Special Issues:
Convention Report: Catholic Health Association. $3. July.

0649. HOSPITAL TOPICS.
3807 Bond Place, Sarasota, FL 33582.
Annual Subscription: $30. **Frequency:** 6/yr.
Publisher: Hospital Topics, Inc.
Editorial Index: Annual. Author. July/August.
Indexed Online: Medline.
Special Issues:
   Hospital Topics Central Service: Programs and Management; Technology; Infection Control. Started 1975. Published as a separate issue. $30. Not included in the subscription price. Triennially. June (last issue 1981).

0650. HOSPITALS.
211 East Chicago Ave., Suite 700, Chicago, IL 60611.
Annual Subscription: $35. **Frequency:** 24/yr.
Publisher: American Hospital Publishing.
Advertiser Index: Every issue.
Editorial Index: Annual. Subject/Author. December.
Indexed Online: Trade & Industry Index.
Special Issues:
   Annual Convention Factbook. Started 1982. Published as a separate issue. $3. July.

0651. HOTEL & MOTEL MANAGEMENT.
One East First St., Duluth, MN 55802.
Annual Subscription: $16. **Frequency:** Monthly.
Publisher: Harcourt Brace Jovanovich.
Advertiser Index: Every issue.
Indexed Online: Trade & Industry Index.
Special Issues:
   Guest Security and Fire Safety. January.
   Energy. February.
   Food & Beverage. May.
   Interior Design. June.
   Product Guide. Started 1981. July.
   Buyer's Guide Directory. Published as a separate issue. $7. December.
   Technology Guide. December.

0652. HOUSE BEAUTIFUL.
Box 10083, Des Moines, IA 50385.
Annual Subscription: $13.97. **Frequency:** Monthly.
Publisher: Hearst Magazines.
Indexed or Abstracted Online: Magazine Index.
Special Issues:
   Building Manual. Started 1935. Published as a separate issue. $2.50. Not included in the subscription price. February/July.
   Home Decorating. Started 1962. Published as a separate issue. $2.50. Not included in the subscription price. March/June/September/November.
   Home Remodeling. Started 1964. Published as a separate issue. $2.50. Not included in the subscription price. March/May/August/October.
   Kitchens/Baths. Started 1980. Published as a separate issue. $2.50. Not included in the subscription price. April/September.
   Houses & Plans. Started 1957. Published as a separate issue. $2.50. Not included in the subscription price. December.

0653. HOUSEWARES.
1 East First St., Duluth, MN 55802.
Annual Subscription: $16. **Frequency:** 21/yr.
Publisher: Harcourt Brace Jovanovich.
Advertiser Index: Every issue.
Special Issues:
   Housewares Show Stopper Editions—Chicago Housewares Shows coverage, including new product literature; sales and merchandising trends; calendar; manufacturers seeking representatives; and representatives open for new lines. Published as a separate issue. $1.50. Not included in the subscription price. January/July.
   Directory. $1.50. May.

0654. HYDRAULICS & PNEUMATICS.
1111 Chester Ave., Cleveland, OH 44114.
Annual Subscription: $35. **Frequency:** Monthly.
Publisher: Penton/IPC.
Advertiser Index: Every issue.
Editorial Index: Annual. Subject/Title/Author. January.
Indexed or Abstracted Online: Trade & Industry Index.
Special Issues:
   Designers Guide to Fluid Power Products. Started 1956. $10. January.
   Fluid Power Handbook & Directory. Published as a separate issue. $30. Not included in the subscription price. Biennially. January (odd years).
   Design Engineering Show. $6. March.
   Technical Literature File. $6. July.
   Fluid Power Show & Conference. $6. November.

0655. HYDROCARBON PROCESSING.
P.O. Box 2608, Houston, TX 77001.
Annual Subscription: $10. **Frequency:** Monthly.
Publisher: Gulf Publishing Co.
Advertiser Index: Every issue.
Editorial Index: Annual. Subject/Author. December (not published in 1982).
Indexed Online: CA Search; Compendex; CIN.
Special Issues:
   Maintenance Report—maintenance in oil refining and petrochemicals. $2. January.
   HPI Construction Boxscore—worldwide listing of new construction in oil refining, petrochemicals, and gas processing. Published as a separate issue. $2. Not included in the subscription price. 3/yr. February/June/October.
   Gas Processing Report. $2. April.
   American Petroleum Institute Report. Started Y. $2. May.
   Hydrocarbon Processing Catalog—pre-filed manufacturers' catalogs of equipment, materials and services for processing crude oil, natural gas and petrochemicals. Published as a separate issue. $40. Not included in the subscription price. June.
   Refining Developments. $2. Biennially (odd years). September.
   Refining Handbook. $2. Biennially (even years). September.
   Environmental Processes. $2. October.
   Petrochemical Developments. $2. Biennially (even years). November.
   Petrochemicals Hanbook. $2. Biennially (odd years). November.

0656. IBM SYSTEMS JOURNAL.
C/o IBM Corporation, Armonk, NY 10504.
Annual Subscription: $15. **Frequency:** Quarterly.
Publisher: IBM Corporation.
Editorial Index: Annual. Subject/Author. Cumulative index (1975-81) available annually.
Abstracted Online: CA Search; Compendex; ABI/Inform; Scisearch.

0657. ICAO BULLETIN (published in three editions: English, Spanish, and French.).
1000 Sherbrooke St. West, Montreal, Quebec, Can. H3A 2R2.
Annual Subscription: $15 (surface)/20 (air). **Frequency:** Monthly.
Publisher: International Civil Aviation Organization.
Editorial Index: Annual. Subject. February.
Special Issues:
   Annual Report on International Civil Aviation. Started 1947. July.
   Special Report: ICAO Assembly. Started 1950. Triennally. November (1983).

0658. ICP SOFTWARE BUSINESS REVIEW.
9000 Keystone Crossing, P.O. Box 40946, Indianapolis, IN 46240.
Annual Subscription: Controlled. **Frequency:** 6/yr.

Publisher: International Computer Programs, Inc.
Advertiser Index: Every issue.
Special Issues:
ICP Million Dollar Awards—best-selling software of year. Started 1972. April/May.
ICP 200—Top U.S. software product and service companies (ranking by revenue). Started 1979. June/July.

0659. ITE JOURNAL.
525 School St. SW, Washington, DC
Annual Subscription: $20. **Frequency:** Monthly.
Publisher: Institute of Transportation Engineers.
Advertiser Index: Every issue.
Editorial Index: Annual. Subject/Title/Author. December.
Special Issues:
Awards Issue. $2. September.

0660. IMPACT.
400 East 51 St., New York, NY 10022.
Annual Subscription: $112. **Frequency:** 24/yr.
Publisher: M. Shanken Communications, Inc.
Editorial Index: Annual. Subject. December.
Special Issues:
Impact American Beer Market Review and Forecast—same data as Wine Review. Published as a separate issue. $150. Not included in the subscription price.
Impact American Distilled Spirits Market Review and Forecast—same data as Wine Review. Published as a separate issue. $150. Not included in the subscription price.
Impact American Wine Market Review and Forecast—brand sales data; advertising expenditures by brand and company; analysis of the year's marketing achievements and failures; market trends; market shares; projections to 1990. Published as a separate issue. $150. Not included in the subscription price.

0661. IMPLEMENT AND TRACTOR.
P.O. Box 72901, Overland Park, KS 66212.
Annual Subscription: $10. **Frequency:** Monthly.
Publisher: Intertech Publishing Corp.
Special Issues:
Engineering Concepts Issue. $2. January.
Product File—directory and buying guide for farm, industrial and shop equipment and supplies; parts and components with listings of manufacturers under appropriate categories. Also covers farm and industrial equipment wholesalers, jobbers, agents; importers and export agencies; brand names; mailing addresses of manufacturers. Published as a separate issue. $5. January.
Red Book—comparative specifications, operating data, sales and service information on most popular types of powered agricultural and industrial equipment. Published as a separate issue. $5. March.
Shows and Conventions. $2. August.
Equipment Distribution. $2. October.
Market Statistics Issue. $2. November.

0662. IMPORT CAR.
11 South Forge St., Akron, OH 44304.
Annual Subscription: $20. **Frequency:** Monthly.
Publisher: Babcox Automotive Publications.
Advertiser Index: October.
Special Issues:
Auto International Show/Specialty Equipment Manufacturing Association Show. January/October.
Best Import Cars of the year. February.
Auto Racing. May.
U. S. Market Report. August.
Auto Mechanical Show Report. December.

0663. IMPRESSIONS.
15400 Knoll Trail Dr., Dallas, TX 75248.
Annual Subscription: $18. **Frequency:** Monthly.
Publisher: Gralla Publications.
Advertiser Index: Every issue.
Editorial Index: Annual. Subject. December.
Special Issues:
Directory of Imprinted Sportswear Industry Suppliers. Started 1983. June.

0664. INC. MAGAZINE.
38 Commercial Wharf, Boston, MA 02110.
Annual Subscription: $21. **Frequency:** Monthly.
Publisher: Inc. Publishing Corp.
Indexed or Abstracted Online: NEXIS; ABI/Inform; Magazine Index; Trade & Industry Index; Management Contents.
Special Issues:
Inc 100—the 100 fastest growing publicly held companies in the country. Started 1979. $2.50. May.
Executive Compensation Survey. Started 1979. $2.50. September.
Report on the States—ranks 50 states for small business climate. Started 1981. $2.50. October.
Inc 500—the 500 fastest growing privately held companies in the country. Started 1981. $2.50. December.

0665. INCENTIVE MARKETING INCORPORATING INCENTIVE TRAVEL.
633 Third Ave., New York, NY 10017.
Annual Subscription: $32. **Frequency:** Monthly.
Publisher: Bill Communications Inc.
Advertiser Index: Every issue.
Special Issues:
Incentive Travel Directory of Suppliers. Started 1981. Published as a separate issue. $3. January.
Incentive Merchanise Directory of Suppliers. Started 1950. Published as a separate issue. $3. February.
FACTS—survey and statistics on incentive industry. Started 1967. Published as a separate issue. $15. December.

0666. INCOME OPPORTUNITIES.
380 Lexington Ave., New York, NY 10017.
Annual Subscription: $12. **Frequency:** Monthly.
Publisher: Davis Publications Inc.
Special Issues:
Sales and Small Business Directory—listing of approximately 200 business opportunities in mail order, franchises, retailing and direct selling. Published as a separate issue. $1.75. March/October.

0667. INDEPENDENT RESTAURANTS.
2132 Fordem Ave., Madison, WI 53704.
Annual Subscription: $24. **Frequency:** Monthly.
Publisher: EIP, Inc.
Indexed or Abstracted Online: AMI; Trade & Industry Index.
Special Issues:
Directory of Foodservice Equipment, Supplies and Services. $2. May.
Fact Book of Electric Foodservice Equipment—buyers guide to manufacturers, by product category. Published as a separate issue. $2. Not included in the subscription price. September.

0668. INDEX MEDICUS.
Superintendent of Documents, GPO, Washington, DC 20402.
Annual Subscription: $195. **Frequency:** Monthly.
Publisher: National Institutes of Health.
Editorial Index: Monthly. Subject/Author. Every issue; Cumulated Index Medicus Annual available separately; price varies.
Indexed or Abstracted Online: Medline.
Special Issues:
Medical Subject Headings. Published as a separate issue. $15. January.
Bibliography of Medical Reviews. $18. Monthly. Monthly.

0669. INDUSTRIAL AND LABOR RELATIONS REVIEW.
Cornell University, Ithaca, NY 14853.
Annual Subscription: $14 (indiv.)/18 (institution).
 Frequency: Quarterly.
Publisher: New York State School of Industrial and Labor

Relations.
Editorial Index: Annual. Title/Author. July.
Indexed or Abstracted Online: ABI/Inform; Management Contents; Social Scisearch; Trade & Industry Index.

0670. **INDUSTRIAL CHEMICAL NEWS.**
633 Third Ave., New York, NY 10017.
Annual Subscription: $24. **Frequency:** Monthly.
Publisher: Bill Communications.
Advertiser Index: Every issue.
Editorial Index: Annual. Subject/Author. December.
Special Issues:
  Computers in Chemistry.   Started 1983. $2.   April.
  Biotechnology.   Started 1982. $2.   May.
  Specialties Chemicals.   Started 1983. $2.   June.
  Salary Survey.   Started 1980. $2.   October.
  Forecast Issue.   Started 1982. $2.   December.

0671. **INDUSTRIAL DESIGN.**
330 West 42nd St., New York, NY 10036.
Annual Subscription: $36. **Frequency:** Bimonthly.
Publisher: Design Publications Inc.
Advertiser Index: Every issue.
Special Issues:
  Annual Design Review 1983.   Started 1954. $10. Annual.   September/October.
  30th Anniversary Issue.   Started 1983. $8.   One time only.   November/December.

0672. **INDUSTRIAL DEVELOPMENT/SITE SELECTION HANDBOOK.**
1954 Airport Rd., NE, Atlanta, GA 30341.
Annual Subscription: $39. **Frequency:** 6/yr.
Publisher: Conway Publications, Inc.
Editorial Index: Subject/Title/Author. One cumulative index through 1979.
Indexed Online: Management Contents; Trade & Industry Index.
Special Issues:
  The 50 Legislative Climates for Industry. $7.   January/February.
  Site Selection Handbook: Geo-Corporate Index—directory of corporate real estate executives in leading U.S. manufacturing firms.   Started 1977.   Published as a separate issue. $15.   February.
  Site Selection Handbook: Geo-Economic Index—over 7,000 development agencies, public & private, U.S. and global.   Started 1977.   Published as a separate issue. $15.   May.
  Site Selection Handbook: Geo-Political Index—political officials involved in economic development, U.S. and global.   Started 1977.   Published as a separate issue. $15.   September.
  Environmental Planning Award. $7.   November/December.
  Site Selection Handbook: Geo-Sites Index—a directory of prepared office and industrial parks, including contact names, acreage and square footage, absorption rate, costs.   Started 1977.   Published as a separate issue. $15.   November.

0673. **INDUSTRIAL DISTRIBUTION.**
875 Third Ave., New York, NY 10022.
Annual Subscription: $50. **Frequency:** Monthly.
Publisher: Technical Publishing Co.
Advertiser Index: Every issue.
Editorial Index: Semi-Annual. Subject. December/June.
Indexed Online: Management Contents.
Special Issues:
  Triple Industrial Supply Convention: American Supply & Machinery Manufacturers Association; National Industrial Distributors Association; Southern Industrial Distributors Association. $6.   May.
  Survey of Distributor Operations.   Started 1946. $6.   July.
  Power Transmission Distributors Association Convention. $6.   October.
  Computer Update.   Started 1980. $6.   November.
  Directory of Industrial Distributors—lists 14,000 headquarters and branch units of industrial distributors in United States, Canada, Puerto Rico.   Published as a separate issue. $275.   Not included in the subscription price.   Every four years.   Varies (next issue 1985).

0674. **INDUSTRIAL ENGINEERING.**
25 Technology Park, Norcross, GA 30092.
Annual Subscription: $35. **Frequency:** Monthly.
Publisher: Institute of Industrial Engineers.
Advertiser Index: Every issue.
Editorial Index: Annual. Subject/Author. December.
Indexed or Abstracted Online: Management Contents.
Special Issues:
  IIE Fall Conference Report/Productivity Projects in Service & Support Industries.   Started 1980. $4.   January.
  Facilities Planning & Design; CAD.   Started 1980. $4.   March.
  Material Handling/Survey of Industrial Engineers' Use of Computers.   Started 1978. $4.   April.
  Productivity Engineering Show-in-Print/Corporate Managers Roundtable/Productivity Projects in Manufacturing.   Started 1978. $4.   May.
  Warehousing and Distribution/Salary Survey.   Started 1980. $4.   June.
  IIE Annual Conference and Productivity Engineering.   Started 1980. $4.   July.
  The Automated Factory, including Robots, Bar Coding, CAD/CAM, Other New Technologies.   Started 1980. $4.   September.
  Manufacturing Information Systems.   Started 1983. $4.   October.
  Cellular Manufacturing Systems.   Started 1980. $4.   November.
  Office Systems.   Started 1980. $4.   December.

0675. **INDUSTRIAL EQUIPMENT NEWS.**
One Penn Plaza, New York, NY 10001.
Annual Subscription: $36. **Frequency:** Monthly.
Publisher: Thomas Publishing Co.
Advertiser Index: Every issue.
Indexed Online: Trade & Industry Index.
Special Issues:
  OEM/Materials & Components Show. $3.   February.
  Plant Operation & Maintenance Show. $3.   March.
  Material Handling. $3.   April.
  Electrical Equipment & Supplies. $3.   May.
  Computerized Manufacturing Show. $3.   June.
  Packaging & Shipping. $3.   July.
  Power Transmission. $3.   August.
  Machine Tool Show. $3.   September.
  Electronics Show. $3.   October.
  Chemical Process Equipment Show. $3.   November.

0676. **INDUSTRIAL FABRIC PRODUCTS REVIEW.**
345 Cedar Bldg., Suite 450, St. Paul, MN 55101.
Annual Subscription: $24. **Frequency:** Monthly.
Publisher: Industrial Fabrics Association International.
Advertiser Index: Every issue.
Editorial Index: Annual. Title. December.
Special Issues:
  Buyers Guide and Directory—supply sources, testing labs, trade names, textile schools, company listings.   Published as a separate issue. $20.   February.
  New Products. $5.   March.
  Industrial Issue. $5.   June.
  Convention (IFAI Show) Issue. $5.   October.
  Government Products. $5.   November.
  Equipment/Findings. $5.   December.

0677. **INDUSTRIAL FINISHING.**
Hitchcock Bldg., Wheaton, IL 60187.
Annual Subscription: $40. **Frequency:** Monthly.
Publisher: Hitchcock Publishing Co.
Editorial Index: Annual. Subject. January.
Indexed Online: Trade & Industry Index.

Special Issues:
   Painting and Plating (Paint Con) Trade Show Issue.   Started 1982.   March.
   Directory.   Started 1984.   September.
   New Product and Literature Review.   Started 1981.   September.
   Paint Industries Show.   Started 1982.   Biennially (even years).   October.

0678. INDUSTRIAL HEATING.
1000 Killarney Dr., Pittsburgh, PA 15234.
Annual Subscription: Free.   **Frequency:** Monthly.
Publisher: National Industrial Publishing Co.
Advertiser Index: Every issue.
Editorial Index: Annual. Subject. January.
Special Issues:
   Annual Review & Forecast. $3.50.   February.
   Heat Treating. $3.50.   August.
   Iron and Steel Production. $3.50.   September.
   International Update. $3.50.   October.

0679. INDUSTRIAL HYGIENE NEWS.
8650 Babcock Blvd., Pittsburgh, PA 15237.
Annual Subscription: Free (if qualified).   **Frequency:** 6/yr.
Publisher: Rimbach Publishing Co.
Advertiser Index: Every issue.
Special Issues:
   Analytical Instruments/Directory of Analytical Laboratories. January.
   Health Surveillance Systems/Medical Screening Instruments/Plant Engineering Show/American Occupational Health Conference.   March.
   Catalog & Buyers Guide—arranged by product and manufacturer.   Started 1983.   Published as a separate issue.   April.
   American Industrial Hygiene Conference/Chem Pro Show/ Air Pollution Control Association Conference.   May.
   Dosimeters.   July.
   Noise Measuring Instruments/Hearing Conservation/Eye, Face, Body Protection.   September.
   Annual Catalog Review.   December.

0680. INDUSTRIAL MACHINERY NEWS.
P.O. Box 5002, Southfield, MI 48086.
Annual Subscription: $40.   **Frequency:** Monthly.
Publisher: Hearst Business Media Corp.
Advertiser Index: Every issue.
Special Issues:
   Serial Number Reference Book for Metalworking Machinery. Published as a separate issue. $34.95 (HC)/24.95 (PB). Not included in the subscription price.   Every 5 yrs.
   International Machine Tool Show Edition.   Started 1971. September.
   Metalworking Buyers Guide—lists metalworking machinery, equipment, products, tooling, accessories, supplies and services.   Started 1982.   Published as a separate issue. $25.   Not included in the subscription price.   December.

0681. INDUSTRIAL MAINTENANCE & PLANT OPERATION.
Chilton Co., Radnor, PA 19089.
Annual Subscription: $48.   **Frequency:** Monthly.
Publisher: Thomas R. Stillman.
Advertiser Index: Every issue.
Special Issues:
   National Plant Engineering & Maintenance Show.   Started 1949. $4.   March.

0682. INDUSTRIAL MINERALS.
Metal Bulletin Inc., 708 Third Ave., New York, NY 10017.
Annual Subscription: $132.   **Frequency:** Monthly.
Publisher: Metal Bulletin Ltd.
Advertiser Index: Every issue.
Editorial Index: Semi-Annual. Subject/Title. January/July.
Indexed or Abstracted Online: CIM.
Special Issues:
   Industrial Minerals Directory—non-metallics used in ceramics/refractories/abrasives/glass/chemicals/ construction/ paint/paper/plastics industries. Lists international companies mining non-metallic minerals. Includes address, executive staff, companies, mine and plant locations, mining and processing techniques, current production and annual capacity, minerals produced, sales agents, etc. Second section is buyers guide (by mineral) showing suppliers in most countries of the world.   Started 1977.   Published as a separate issue. $67.80.   Not included in the subscription price.   Every 5 yrs.

0683. INDUSTRIAL PRODUCT IDEAS.
777 Bay St., Toronto, Ontario, Can. M5W 1A7.
Annual Subscription: $24/13.   **Frequency:** 6/yr.
Publisher: Maclean Hunter Ltd.
Advertiser Index: Every issue.
Special Issues:
   Plant Management Show Guide.   Started 1975. $4. Biennially.   April.
   Production Show Guide (alternate years w/Plant Management Show Guide).   Started 1975. $4. Biennially.   April.
   Energy Conservation Issue.   Started 1980. $4.   June.
   Material Handling Show Guide.   Started 1975. $4. September.
   Maintenance and Safety.   Started 1981. $4.   October.
   High Technology.   Started 1982. $4.   November.

0684. INDUSTRIAL SAFETY & HYGIENE NEWS.
201 King of Prussia Rd., Radnor, PA 19089.
Annual Subscription: $30.   **Frequency:** Monthly.
Publisher: Chilton Company.
Special Issues:
   Noise Protection.   Started 1980. $2.75.   January.
   Industrial Hygiene Instrumentation.   Started 1980. $2.75. February.
   Fire/Security.   Started 1982. $2.75.   March.
   Industrial Hygiene Engineering Controls/American Industrial Hygiene Conference. $2.75.   May.
   Emergency Aid. $2.75.   June.
   Personal Protective Equipment Directory. $2.75.   July.
   National Safety Congress. $2.75.   October.
   Services Directory. $2.75.   November.

0685. INDUSTRY WEEK.
Penton Plaza, 1111 Chester Ave., Cleveland, OH 44114.
Annual Subscription: $30.   **Frequency:** 26/yr.
Publisher: Penton/IPC.
Advertiser Index: Every issue.
Editorial Index: Semi-Annual. Subject. August/February.
Indexed or Abstracted Online: Trade & Industry Index; Management Contents; Magazine Index.
Special Issues:
   Economists' Business Outlook. $1.50.   September.
   Annual Excellence in Management Award.   Started 1977. $1.50.   October.
   Chief Executive Officer's Annual Forecast.   Started 1972. $1.50.   November.

0686. INFORMATION MANAGEMENT.
101 Crossways Pk. West, Woodbury, NY 11797.
Annual Subscription: $12.   **Frequency:** Monthly.
Publisher: PTN Publishing Corp.
Indexed Online: Management Contents.
Special Issues:
   Micrographics and Image Management. $2.   April.

0687. INFOSYSTEMS.
Hitchcock Bldg., Wheaton, IL 60188.
Annual Subscription: $55.   **Frequency:** Monthly.
Publisher: Hitchcock Publishing Co.
Advertiser Index: Every issue.
Indexed or Abstracted Online: ABI/Inform; Predicasts; Trade & Industry Index.
Special Issues:
   New Product Review. $5.   January.
   Software Review (new or newly enhanced).   Started 1977. $5.   February/July.

Microcomputer Software Review. Started 1983. $5. March/August.
Micrographics Salary Survey. Started 1978. $5. April.
Micrographics Usage Survey. Started 1971. $5. April.
Data Processing Salary Survey. Started 1959. $5. June.

0688. INSIDE RADIO.
1930 East Marlton Pike, Ste. C-13, Cherry Hill, NJ 08003.
Annual Subscription: $150. **Frequency:** Weekly.
Publisher: Inside Radio, Inc.
Special Issues:
Directory—includes listings of group owners; representatives; syndicators; trade associations; consultants; trade press; brokers; hardware/software; FCC; satellite systems, etc. Published as a separate issue. Spring/Fall.

0689. INSTITUTIONAL DISTRIBUTION.
633 Third Ave., New York, NY 10017.
Annual Subscription: $40. **Frequency:** Monthly.
Publisher: Bill Communications.
Advertiser Index: Every issue.
Indexed or Abstracted Online: Trade & Industry Index.
Special Issues:
Food, Equipment Product Savvy—collections of "Product Savvy" article published in previous issues. Started 1981. Published as a separate issue. $4. May/September.
Distributor Shows. $4. October.
Top 50. $4. December.

0690. INSTITUTIONAL INVESTOR.
488 Madison Ave., New York, NY 10022.
Annual Subscription: $110. **Frequency:** Monthly.
Publisher: Institutional Investor Inc.
Advertiser Index: Every issue.
Editorial Index: Annual. Subject/Title/Author.
Indexed or Abstracted Online: Management Contents.
Special Issues:
International Edition. $125/yr.
Pensions Directory (US). Started 1972. Published as a separate issue. $25. January.
Mergers & Acquisitions. Started 1981. $14. February.
Country Credit Ratings. Started 1979. $14. 2/yr. March/September.
Foreign Banks in London. Started 1978. $14. March.
Underwriting Sweepstakes (US). Started 1972. $14. March.
Ranking America's Biggest Brokers/Investment Bankers. Started 1981. $14. April.
Global Banking Directory—World's Top 100 Banks. Started 1981. Published as a separate issue. $50. May.
Public Finance Directory. Started 1981. $14. June.
CFO Directory (Chief Corporate Financial Officers). Started 1982. Published as a separate issue. $25. July.
Global Banking Ranking. Started 1978. $14. July.
Institutional Investor Directory. Started 1982. Published as a separate issue. $150. July.
Insurance Broker Directory. Started 1983. $14. August.
Top 300 Money Managers. Started 1975. $14. August.
Art Market. Started 1981. $14. September.
Best Annual Reports. Started 1972. $14. September.
Best Hotels. Started 1977. $14. September.
Foreign Banks in U.S. (US). Started 1976. $14. September.
All American Research Team. Started 1972. $14. October.
Risk Manager Directory. Started 1980. Published as a separate issue. $25. November.

0691. INSTRUCTOR.
1 East First Street, Duluth, MN 55802.
Annual Subscription: $18. **Frequency:** 9/yr.
Publisher: Harcourt Brace Jovanovich.
Advertiser Index: Every issue.

Special Issues:
Children's Trade and Library Books. $2.50. May/November.
Encyclopedias. $2.50. May.
Instructor's Computer Directory for Schools. Started 1982. Published as a separate issue. $19.95. Not included in the subscription price. August.

0692. THE INSTRUMENTALIST.
1418 Lake St., Evanston, IL 60201.
Annual Subscription: $15.50. **Frequency:** Monthly.
Publisher: James T. Rohner.
Advertiser Index: Every issue.
Editorial Index: Annual. Title. July.
Special Issues:
Directory of Summer Camps & Workshops. $2. March or April.
Buyers Guide (Music Industry Cos.). $2. July.
Directory of Music Organizations. $2. September.
Directory of Music Schools. $2. December.

0693. I & C S (Instruments & Control Systems).
Chilton Way, Radnor, PA 19089.
Annual Subscription: $40. **Frequency:** Monthly.
Publisher: Chilton Co.
Advertiser Index: Every issue.
Special Issues:
Programmable Controls (PC). $4. January.
Flow Monitoring. $4. February.
Motor Controls. $4. March.
Pressure Monitoring. $4. April.
Temperature Monitoring. $4. June.
ISA (Instrument Society of America) Show. $4. September.
Buyers Guide. Published as a separate issue. $4. October.
WESCON Show/Level Monitoring. $4. October.
Control Relays. $4. November.

0694. INSURANCE ADVOCATE.
45 John St., New York, NY 10038.
Annual Subscription: $20. **Frequency:** Weekly.
Publisher: Roberts Publishing Corp.
Special Issues:
Review of Year's Events. $2. January.
Industrial Inflation Survey of Replacement Costs. $2. July.
Inland Marine Statistical Issue—premiums and losses in inland marine insurance, countrywide for U.S. insurance companies and groups. Started 1943. $2. July.
Ocean Marine Statistical Issue—premiums and losses for ocean marine business, countrywide and for N.Y. State. Started 1943. $2. August.

0695. INSURANCE FIELD.
4325 Old Shepherdsville Rd., P.O. Box 18630,
Annual Subscription: Free. **Frequency:** Annual.
Publisher: Insurance Field Co.
Advertiser Index: Every issue.
Special Issues:
Life Insurers Conference. Started 1951. $2. June.
American Association of Managing General Agents. Started 1971. $2. July.
Independent Insurance Agents of America/National Association of Life Underwriters. Started 1957. $2. October.
National Association of Professional Surplus Lines Offices. Started 1980. $2. December.

0696. INSURANCE JOURNAL.
P.O. Box 42030, Los Angeles, CA 90042.
Annual Subscription: $20. **Frequency:** 26/yr.
Publisher: Insurance Journal Inc.
Special Issues:
Life Insurance. $1. February.
Computer & Word Processing. $1. March.
Professional Insurance Agents Association Convention. $1. May.

Statistical Review. $6. May.
Special Marketing Directory. $6. July.
California Workers' Compensation. $1. August.
National Association of Professional Surplus Lines Offices Convention. $1. September.
Independent Insurance Agents of America. $1. October.
National Association of Independent Insurers Convention. $1. October.

0697. INSURANCE SALES MAGAZINE.
P.O. Box 564, Indianapolis, IN 46206.
Annual Subscription: $8. **Frequency:** Monthly.
Publisher: Rough Notes Company, Inc.
Advertiser Index: Every issue.
Editorial Index: Annual. Subject. January.
Special Issues:
All Star Honor Roll—outstanding life insurance salespersons. Started 1922. $1. April.
Brokerage and Impaired Risk. Started 1979. $1. October.

0698. INTECH.
P.O. Box 12227, 67 Alexander Dr., Research Triangle Park, NC 27709.
Annual Subscription: $14 (free to members). **Frequency:** Monthly.
Publisher: Instrument Society of America.
Advertiser Index: Every issue.
Editorial Index: Annual. Subject/Title/Author. December.
Special Issues:
ISA Spring show. $2.50. March.
ISA Directory of Instrumentation—U.S. and Canada, for control and instrumentation engineers. Specifications; manufacturer's catalogs; sales offices and representatives; trade name index. Started 1979. Published as a separate issue. $115. Not included in the subscription price. July.
ISA Fall Show. $2.50. September.

0699. INTERFACES.
290 Westminister Street, Providence, RI 02903.
Annual Subscription: $22. **Frequency:** 6/yr.
Publisher: The Institute of Management Science.
Indexed or Abstracted Online: ABI/Inform; Management Contents.
Special Issues:
Special Practice Issue—prize winning papers on the practice of management science. December.

0700. INTERIOR DESIGN.
850 Third Ave., New York, NY 10022.
Annual Subscription: $34.95. **Frequency:** Monthly.
Publisher: Whitney Communications.
Advertiser Index: Every issue.
Editorial Index: Annual. Subject. December (in the buyers guide).
Indexed or Abstracted Online: Trade & Industry Index.
Special Issues:
Interior Design Buyers Guide—keyword index; product index; source index; regional directory to sources, showrooms and representatives; editorial index to articles published during the year. Started 1971. Published as a separate issue. $10. December.

0701. INTERIOR TEXTILES.
370 Lexington Ave., New York, NY 10017.
Annual Subscription: $12. **Frequency:** 6/yr.
Publisher: Columbia Communications.
Advertiser Index: Every issue.
Indexed or Abstracted Online: Trade & Industry Index.
Special Issues:
Annual Industry Directory. Started 1925. $5. August/September.

0702. INTERIORS.
1515 Broadway, New York, NY 10036.
Annual Subscription: $23. **Frequency:** Monthly.
Publisher: Billboard Publications, Inc.
Advertiser Index: Every issue.
Special Issues:
Annual Interiors Awards—12 categories, including executive office, financial & hospitality design/A-Z Directory of Interior Awards Sources/Designer of the Year. Started 1980. $3.50. January.
Lighting Equipment Directory. Started 1982. $3.50. April.
Interiors Initiative. Started 1973. $3.50. May.
Directory of Fabric and Wallcoverings. Started 1983. $3.50. July.
A.I.A. (American Institute of Architects) Product Display Competition Winners/Annual Seating Directory. $3.50. August.
Corporate Client Giants. $3.50. November.
Contract Floor Covering Directory. Started 1982. $3.50. December.

0703. INTERLINE REPORTER.
2 West 46 St., New York, NY 10036.
Annual Subscription: $5. **Frequency:** Monthly.
Publisher: Interline Inc.
Special Issues:
Sales Conference—for travel personnel. $1. September.

0704. INTERNATIONAL AEROSPACE ABSTRACTS.
555 West 57th St., New York, NY 10019.
Annual Subscription: $650. **Frequency:** Semimonthly.
Publisher: American Institute of Astronautics and Aeronautics.
Editorial Index: Annual. Subject/Author. January.

0705. THE INTERNATIONAL EXECUTIVE.
P.O. Box 861, White River Junction, VT 05001.
Annual Subscription: $30. **Frequency:** 3/yr.
Publisher: Foundation for the Advancement of International Business Administration.

0706. INTERNATIONAL INSURANCE MONITOR.
150 West 28th St., New York, NY 10001.
Annual Subscription: $22.50. **Frequency:** 8/yr.
Publisher: International Media Inc.
Editorial Index: Subject/Title. Cumulative index (1976-1980) available separately.
Abstracted Online: Insurance Abstracts.
Special Issues:
Europe and the Common Market. $3. January/February.
United Kingdom. $3. March.
International Reinsurance. $3. April/May.
Middle East Market. $3. June/July/August.
International Union of Marine Insurance and Monte Carlo Rendezvous. $3. September.
Western Hemisphere. $3. October.
Far East, Japan, Australasia. $3. November.
Corporate Risk Management. $3. December.

0707. INTERNATIONAL LABORATORY.
808 Kings Highway, P.O. Box 827, Fairfield, CT 06430.
Annual Subscription: $63. **Frequency:** 9/yr.
Publisher: International Scientific Communications Inc.
Advertiser Index: Every issue.
Special Issues:
American Laboratory and International Laboratory Buyers Guide. Published as a separate issue. January.
Chemical—Clinical Analysis. $7. January/February.
Laboratory Automation. $7. March.
Analytical Techniques. $7. April.
Spectroscopy. $7. May.
Chromatography. $7. June.
Chemical Analysis. $7. July/August.
Environmental Analysis. $7. September.
Microscopy. $7. October.
Separation Techniques. $7. November/December.

0708. INTERNATIONAL TAX JOURNAL.
14 Plaza Rd., Greenvale, NY 11548.
Annual Subscription: $90. **Frequency:** Bimonthly.

Publisher: Panel Publishers.
Editorial Index: Annual. Subject/Author. August.
Indexed or Abstracted Online: ABI/Inform; Management Contents; Trade & Industry Index.

0709. INTERNATIONAL TRADE FORUM.
ITC, Palais des Nations, 1211 Geneva 10, , Switzerland
Annual Subscription: $12. **Frequency:** Quarterly.
Publisher: International Trade Centre.
Editorial Index: Annual. Subject. January/March.
Indexed or Abstracted Online: Management Contents; Trade & Industry Index.

0710. INTIMATE FASHION NEWS.
95 Madison Ave., New York, NY 10016.
Annual Subscription: $10. **Frequency:** 24/yr.
Publisher: Mackay Publishing Corp.
Special Issues:
Market Merchandisers (Summer; Warmwear/Transitional; Fall & Winter; Holiday; Spring/Summer). $.50. 5/yr. January/March/May/August/November.
Post-Mastectomy & Maternity Fashions. $.50. February/July.
Annual Suppliers Section. $.50. March.
Large-Size Issue. $.50. April.
Designer/Licensing. $.50. June.
Directory. Published as a separate issue. $2.50. October.
Machinery/Equipment/Supplies. $.50. December.
Fibers and Fabrics. $.50. Twice in September.

0711. INVENTION MANAGEMENT.
85 Irving St., P.O. Box 436, Arlington, MA 02174.
Annual Subscription: $96. **Frequency:** Monthly.
Publisher: Richard A. Onanian.
Editorial Index: Annual. Title. December.

0712. INVESTMENT DEALERS' DIGEST.
150 Broadway, New York, NY 10038.
Annual Subscription: $195. **Frequency:** Weekly.
Publisher: Dealers Digest Inc.
Advertiser Index: Supplements only.
Special Issues:
Mutual Fund Directory. Started 1938. Published as a separate issue. $50. Not included in the subscription price. January/November.
Corporate Financing Directory. Started 1943. Published as a separate issue. $125. Not included in the subscription price. February/October.
Corporate Syndicate Personnel Directory (investment bankers and their syndicate personnel). Published as a separate issue. $25. Not included in the subscription price. March/September.

0713. IRON AGE.
Chilton Way, Radnor, PA 19089.
Annual Subscription: $55. **Frequency:** 36/yr.
Publisher: Chilton Co.
Advertiser Index: Every issue.
Editorial Index: Semi-Annual. Subject/Author. January/July.
Indexed Online: Trade & Industry Index; ABI/Inform; Predicasts.
Special Issues:
Forecasts & Statistical Summaries. $2.50. January.
Design Engineering Show. $2.50. March.
Welding Show. $2.50. March.
Steel Industry Outlook. $2.50. May.
Steel/Non-Ferrous Industry Financial Analysis. $2.50. May.
Steel Service Center Institute Meeting. $2.50. May.
International Machine Tool Show. $2.50. August.

0714. IRON & STEEL ENGINEER.
3 Gateway Center, Ste. 2350, Pittsburgh, PA 15222.
Annual Subscription: $28. **Frequency:** Monthly.
Publisher: Association of Iron and Steel Engineers.
Special Issues:
Directory Iron and Steel Plants—U.S., Canadian, and selected foreign steel producers and suppliers. Started 1916. Published as a separate issue. $30. Not included in the subscription price. February.
Association of Iron and Steel Engineers Spring Conference Issue. $4. March.
AISE Annual Convention/Iron and Steel Exposition. $4. September.

0715. IRON & STEELMAKER.
410 Commonwealth, Warrendale, PA 15086.
Annual Subscription: $30. **Frequency:** Monthly.
Publisher: Iron & Steel Society of American Institute of Mining, Metallurgical and Petroleum Engineers.
Editorial Index: December. Author. December.
Special Issues:
Annual Review & Membership Directory. Started 1982. Published as a separate issue. July.

0716. ITALIAN AMERICAN BUSINESS.
Via Agnello, 12, 20121 Milan, , Italy
Annual Subscription: $30. **Frequency:** Monthly.
Publisher: American Chamber of Commerce in Italy.
Advertiser Index: Every issue.
Special Issues:
Directory. Started 1964. Published as a separate issue. $50. Not included in the subscription price. February.

0717. JEWELER/GEM BUSINESS.
5870 Hunters Lane, El Sobrante, CA 94803.
Annual Subscription: $12.50. **Frequency:** 6/yr.
Publisher: Gemstone Publications.
Advertiser Index: Every issue.
Special Issues:
Tucson Show. $2.50. January/February.
Pearls. $2.50. March/April.
Watches. $2.50. May/June.
African Jewelry. $2.50. July/August.
Buyers Guide. $2.50. November/December.

0718. JEWELERS' CIRCULAR-KEYSTONE.
Chilton Way, Radnor, PA 19089.
Annual Subscription: $24. **Frequency:** Monthly.
Publisher: Chilton Co.
Advertiser Index: Every issue.
Editorial Index: Annual. Subject. January.
Indexed or Abstracted Online: Trade & Industry Index.
Special Issues:
Retail Jewelers of America Show Issues. $4. January/February/July/August.
Brand Name and Trademark Guide—guide to symbols stamped on jewelry store products. Published as a separate issue. $14.95. Not included in the subscription price. Every 4 years. May (next issue 1984).
Jewelers' Almanac—statistics on jewelry industry, including independents vs. chains, etc. Started 1975. Published as a separate issue. $5. June.
Jewelers' Directory—buying guide for retailers, wholesalers, manufacturers. List suppliers cross-indexed under 1000 categories of merchandise and service. Published as a separate issue. $9. June.
Tabletops Issue—china, giftware, crystal, collectibles. $4. December.
Report on Jewelry Store Sales by SMSA. Started 1967. Published as a separate issue. $10. Not included in the subscription price. Every 5 years. Varies (last issue 1977).
Sterling Flatware Pattern Index—loose-leaf reference book listing and illustrating patterns of U.S. companies since 1832. Periodic revision update sheets. Published as a separate issue. $49.95. Not included in the subscription price. Irregular. Varies (last update 1977).

0719. JEWELRY MAKING, GEMS AND MINERALS.
P.O. Box 687, Mentone, CA 92359.
Annual Subscription: $9.50. **Frequency:** Monthly.

Publisher: Gemac Corp.
Advertiser Index: Every issue.
Editorial Index: Annual. Subject. September.
Special Issues:
Tucson Trade Show Guide. $1.50. January.
Directory Issue (for consumers). Started 1978. $1.50. September.

0720. JOBBER NEWS.
109 Vanderhoof Ave., Ste. 101, Toronto, Ontario, Can. M4G 2J2.
Annual Subscription: $15/12. **Frequency:** 13/yr.
Publisher: Wadham Publications Ltd.
Special Issues:
Marketplace Report on Autobody Business. $2.50. August.
Business Management. $2.50. September.
Jobber Annual Marketing Guide. Started 1976. Published as a separate issue. $2.50. October.
Marketplace Report on Western Canada. $2.50. December.

0721. JOBBER TOPICS.
7300 North Cicero Ave., Lincolnwood, IL 60646.
Annual Subscription: $20. **Frequency:** Monthly.
Publisher: Irving Cloud Publishing Co.
Advertiser Index: Every issue.
Special Issues:
Pacific Automotive Show. $2.50. January.
Big "I" Show—International Automotive Service Industries. $2.50. February.
Automotive Engine Rebuilders Association Show. $2.50. June.
Jobber Topics' Annual Directories & Marketing Issue. Started 1933. $15. July.
Automotive Warehouse Distributors Association Convention/Automotive Parts and Accessories Show/Specialty Equipment Manufacturers Association Show/Auto Internacionale. $2.50. October.

0722. THE JOURNAL.
One Penn Plaza, New York, NY 10001.
Annual Subscription: $60. **Frequency:** Bimonthly.
Publisher: National Commercial Finance Conference.
Editorial Index: Annual. Subject. December.
Special Issues:
Convention Preview and Report of The National Commercial Finance Conference. June/August.
Report on Legislative and Judicial Developments. December.

0723. JOURNAL AMERICAN WATER WORKS ASSOCIATION.
6666 West Quincy Ave., Denver, CO 80235.
Annual Subscription: $20 (members)/40 (nonmembers).
Frequency: Monthly.
Publisher: American Water Works Association.
Advertiser Index: Every issue.
Editorial Index: Annual. Subject/Title/Author. December.
Indexed or Abstracted Online: Waternet; Biosis; CA Search; Compendex; Aqualine.
Special Issues:
American Water Works Association Conference. $2. April.
Buyers Guide. Started 1975. Published as a separate issue. $2. November.

0724. JOURNAL OF ACCOUNTANCY.
1211 Ave. of the Americas, New York, NY 10036.
Annual Subscription: $20. **Frequency:** Monthly.
Publisher: American Institute of Certified Public Accountants.
Advertiser Index: Every issue.
Editorial Index: Semi-Annual. Subject/Author. June/December.
Indexed or Abstracted Online: Legal Resource Index; Trade & Industry Index; Management Contents; ABI/Inform; Insurance Abstracts.

0725. JOURNAL OF ACCOUNTING, AUDITING AND FINANCE.
210 South St., Boston, MA 02111.
Annual Subscription: $48.
Publisher: Warren, Gorham & Lamont.
Editorial Index: Biennial. Subject/Author. Fall.
Indexed or Abstracted Online: Management Contents; ABI/Inform; Predicasts; Insurance Abstracts.

0726. JOURNAL OF ADVERTISING RESEARCH.
3 East 54th St., New York, NY 10022.
Annual Subscription: $50. **Frequency:** 6/yr.
Publisher: Advertising Research Foundation.
Advertiser Index: Every issue.
Editorial Index: Annual. Author. December.
Indexed or Abstracted Online: ABI/Inform; Management Contents; AMI.
Special Issues:
Annual Report and Yearbook: Advertising Research Foundation. Started 1980. Published as a separate issue. $35. Not included in the subscription price. February/March.

0727. JOURNAL OF AIRCRAFT.
1633 Broadway, New York, NY 10019.
Annual Subscription: $165. **Frequency:** Monthly.
Publisher: American Institute of Astronautics and Aeronautics.
Editorial Index: Annual. Subject/Author. December.
Indexed or Abstracted Online: Recon (limited access—NASA contractors only).

0728. JOURNAL OF APPLIED PHYSICS.
335 East 45 St., New York, NY 10017.
Annual Subscription: $300. **Frequency:** Monthly.
Publisher: American Institute of Physics.
Special Issues:
Magnetism and Magnetic Materials Conference. Published as a separate issue. $50. July.

0729. JOURNAL OF BROADCASTING.
1771 N Street NW, Washington, DC 20036.
Annual Subscription: $17.50. **Frequency:** Quarterly.
Publisher: Broadcast Education Association.
Editorial Index: Annual. Subject/Title/Author. Fall issue. Twenty-five year cumulative index issued in 1982, available at $5.

0730. JOURNAL OF CHROMATOGRAPHIC SCIENCE.
P.O. Box 48312, Niles, IL 60648.
Annual Subscription: $80. **Frequency:** Monthly.
Publisher: Preston Publications Inc.
Advertiser Index: Every issue.
Editorial Index: Annual. Subject/Author. December.
Indexed or Abstracted Online
Special Issues:
International Chromatography Guide—listing of products and supplier. $15. February.
Pittsburgh Conference—papers. Started 1983. $15. March.
User's Needs—articles on equipment and instruments. Started 1982. $15. September.

0731. JOURNAL OF CLIMATE AND APPLIED METEOROLOGY.
45 Beacon St., Boston, MA 02108.
Annual Subscription: $120. **Frequency:** Monthly.
Publisher: American Meteorological Society.
Editorial Index: Annual. Subject/Author. December (Available separately for $15).
Abstracted Online: MGA.

0732. JOURNAL OF COATINGS TECHNOLOGY.
1315 Walnut St., Ste. 832, Philadelphia, PA 19107.
Annual Subscription: $20. **Frequency:** Monthly.
Publisher: Federation of Societies for Coatings Technology.
Advertiser Index: Every issue.
Editorial Index: Annual. Subject/Title/Author. December.
Abstracted Online: CA Search.
Special Issues:
Convention Issue. $3. Varies.

0733. JOURNAL OF COMMERCE (CANADA).
2000 West 12 Ave., Vancouver, British Columbia, Can. V6J 2G2.
Annual Subscription: $234/195. **Frequency:** Semiweekly.
Publisher: Southam Communications Ltd.
Special Issues:
Annual Forecast/Waterproofing. January.
Roadbuilding/Housebuilding/Concrete. February.
Industrial Parks (Western Canada) Supplement. Published as a separate issue. March.
Scaffolding and Lifting Devices/Construction Bonding/Municipal Water Treatment. March.
Pipeline Construction/Paints, Coatings & Wall Coverings/Roofing. April.
Municipal Buyers (Western Canada) Supplement. Published as a separate issue. May.
Valves & Meters/Architecture & Interiors/Brick & Masonry/Steel. May.
Sewage & Water/Equipment Showcase. June.
Engineering Fabrics/Insulation. July.
Road Surfacing & Maintenance/Solid Waste/Pre-Cast Concrete. August.
Parks & Landscaping/Heaters/Roads & Transportation Construction. September.
Industrial & Commercial Development Locations/Flooring. October.
Ports & Marine Construction/Safety, Fire Protection & Security Systems/Storage Tanks. November.
Leaders (Western Canada) Supplement. Published as a separate issue. December.
Standby Power/Windows & Doors/Earthmoving & Hauling. December.

0734. JOURNAL OF COMMERCIAL BANK LENDING.
1616 Philadelphia National Bank Building, Philadelphia, PA 19107.
Annual Subscription: $21.50. **Frequency:** Monthly.
Publisher: Robert Morris Associates.
Editorial Index: Annual. Subject/Title. August.
Indexed or Abstracted Online: Management Contents; ABI/Inform; CIS.

0735. JOURNAL OF COMMUNICATION.
P.O. Box 13358, Philadelphia, PA 19101.
Annual Subscription: $20. **Frequency:** Quarterly.
Publisher: Annenberg School of Communications.
Editorial Index: Annual. Title/Author. Fall.
Indexed Online: ERIC; AMI; Social Scisearch.

0736. JOURNAL OF CONSUMER RESEARCH.
250 South Wacker Dr., Chicago, IL 60606.
Annual Subscription: $25 (members of sponsoring organizations)/$50 (nonmembers). **Frequency:** Quarterly.
Publisher: The Journal of Consumer Research.
Editorial Index: Annual. Author. March.
Indexed or Abstracted Online: Management Contents; Social Scisearch; AMI.

0737. JOURNAL OF ECONOMIC LITERATURE.
1313 21st Ave. South, Ste. 809, Nashville, TN 37212.
Annual Subscription: $100. **Frequency:** Quarterly.
Publisher: American Economic Association.
Editorial Index: Annual. Title/Author. December.
Indexed or Abstracted Online: Predicasts; ABI/Inform; Management Contents.
Special Issues:
Annotated Listing of New Books. March/June/September/December.
Contents of Current Periodicals (includes a subject/author and selected abstracts). March/June/September/December.

0738. JOURNAL OF EDUCATION FOR LIBRARIANSHIP.
471 Park Lane, State College, PA 16801.
Annual Subscription: $20. **Frequency:** 5/yr.
Publisher: Association for Library Information Science Education.
Editorial Index: Subject/Title/Author. Fifteen-year Cumulative Index, 1960/75 ($10); and five-year Cumulative Index, 1975/80 ($5), available separately.
Abstracted Online: Social Scisearch.
Special Issues:
Directory Issue—lists all accredited library schools plus 30 graduate library programs that are members of ALISE. $5. Winter.

0739. JOURNAL OF ELECTRONIC MATERIALS.
420 Commonwealth Dr., Warrendale, PA 15086.
Annual Subscription: $100. **Frequency:** 6/yr.
Publisher: The Metallurgical Society of AIME.
Editorial Index: Subject/Author. November.
Indexed or Abstracted Online: CA Search.

0740. JOURNAL OF ENERGY.
1633 Broadway, New York, NY 10019.
Annual Subscription: $85. **Frequency:** Bimonthly.
Publisher: American Institute of Astronautics and Aeronautics.
Editorial Index: Annual. Subject/Author. December.
Indexed or Abstracted Online: Recon (limited access—NASA contractors only).

0741. JOURNAL OF FINANCE.
100 Trinity Place, New York, NY 10006.
Annual Subscription: $35. **Frequency:** 5/yr.
Publisher: American Finance Association.
Editorial Index: Annual. Title/Author. December.
Indexed or Abstracted Online: ABI/Inform; Management Contents.
Special Issues:
American Finance Association Annual Meeting Report. $7. May.

0742. JOURNAL OF FINANCIAL AND QUANTITATIVE ANALYSIS.
127 Mackenzie Hall, University of Washington, DJ-10, Seattle, WA 98195.
Annual Subscription: $20 (Indiv.)/$30 (Institutions), plus $5 for outside U.S. **Frequency:** 5/year.
Publisher: Western Finance Association.
Editorial Index: Annual. Author. December.
Indexed or Abstracted Online: Management Contents.

0743. JOURNAL OF GUIDANCE, CONTROL AND DYNAMICS.
1633 Broadway, New York, NY 10019.
Annual Subscription: $85. **Frequency:** Bimonthly.
Publisher: American Institute of Astronautics and Aeronautics.
Editorial Index: Annual. Subject/Author. December.
Indexed or Abstracted Online: Recon (limited access—NASA contractors only).

0744. JOURNAL OF HEALTH & SOCIAL BEHAVIOR.
1722 N Street, NW, Washington, DC 20036.
Annual Subscription: $21. **Frequency:** Quarterly.
Publisher: American Sociological Association.
Editorial Index: Annual. Author. December.

0745. JOURNAL OF HOME ECONOMICS.
2010 Massachusetts Ave., NW, Washington, DC 20036.
Annual Subscription: $16. **Frequency:** Quarterly.
Publisher: American Home Economics Association.
Advertiser Index: Every issue.
Editorial Index: Quarterly. Title/Author. Winter.
Special Issues:
American Home Economics Association Meeting. $4. Spring.

0746. JOURNAL OF HOUSING.
2600 Virginia Ave., NW, Washington, DC 20037.
Annual Subscription: $24. **Frequency:** 6/yr.
Publisher: National Association of Housing and Redevelopment Officials.
Editorial Index: Annual. Subject/Title/Author. Published separately in February; available for $3.00.

0747. JOURNAL OF INSURANCE.
110 William St., New York, NY 10038.
Annual Subscription: $9. **Frequency:** 6/yr.
Publisher: Insurance Information Institute.
Editorial Index: Annual. Subject/Title/Author. January.
Indexed or Abstracted Online: ABI/Inform; Management Contents.
Special Issues:
Insurance Facts (yearbook of statistics on the property/casualty insurance industry). Published as a separate issue. $6. Not included in the subscription price. Winter.

0748. JOURNAL OF LEARNING DISABILITIES.
11 East Adams #1209, Chicago, IL 60603.
Annual Subscription: $32. **Frequency:** 10/yr.
Publisher: Professional Press Inc.
Advertiser Index: Every issue.
Editorial Index: Subject/Author. December.
Special Issues:
Computers in School: educational software program reviews. $3.50. 10/yr. Every issue.

0749. JOURNAL OF MARKETING.
250 South Wacker Dr., Chicago, IL 60606.
Annual Subscription: $30/individuals; $50/institutions; $15/AMA members. **Frequency:** Quarterly.
Publisher: American Marketing Association.
Advertiser Index: Every issue.
Editorial Index: Annual. Subject/Author. Summer.
Indexed or Abstracted Online: Management Contents; AMI.

0750. JOURNAL OF MARKETING RESEARCH.
250 South Wacker Dr., Chicago, IL 60606.
Annual Subscription: $36 (individuals)/54 (institutions)/18 (AMA members). **Frequency:** Quarterly.
Publisher: American Marketing Association.
Advertiser Index: Every issue.
Editorial Index: Subject/Title/Author. November.

0751. JOURNAL OF METALS.
420 Commonwealth Dr., Warrendale, PA 15086.
Annual Subscription: $80. **Frequency:** Monthly.
Publisher: The Metallurgical Society of AIME.
Advertiser Index: As needed.
Editorial Index: Annual. Subject/Author.
Indexed or Abstracted Online: CA Search.
Special Issues:
New Products and Processes Buyers Guide. Started 1983. $7. February.
Annual Review of Extractive Metallurgy. $7. April.
Membership Directory (distributed only to members of Metallurgical Society). Published as a separate issue. June.

0752. THE JOURNAL OF NURSING ADMINISTRATION.
11 Lakeside Park, Wakefield, MA 01880.
Annual Subscription: $29.95. **Frequency:** 11/yr.
Publisher: Concept Development Inc.
Editorial Index: Annual. Title/Author. December.
Special Issues:
Consultant Directory. Started 1978. $10. 2/yr. February & July/August.

0753. JOURNAL OF OCCUPATIONAL MEDICINE.
2340 South Arlington Hts. Rd., Arlington Hts., IL 60005.
Annual Subscription: $30. **Frequency:** Monthly.
Publisher: American Occupational Medical Association.
Advertiser Index: Every issue.
Editorial Index: Annual. Subject/Author. December.
Indexed or Abstracted Online: CA Search; Medline; Scisearch; Trade & Industry Index.
Special Issues:
American Occupational Medical Association—Annual Meeting Program/Abstracts Issues. Started 1977. $3.50. February and April.

0754. JOURNAL OF PHYSICAL EDUCATION, RECREATION AND DANCE.
P.O. Box 704, Waldorf, MD 20601.
Annual Subscription: $42. **Frequency:** 9/yr.
Publisher: American Alliance for Health, Physical Education, Recreation, & Dance.
Advertiser Index: Every issue.
Editorial Index: Annual. Subject/Author. November/December.
Special Issues:
Buyers Guide. $4. January.
Show Issue—AAHPERD Convention. $4. March.

0755. JOURNAL OF PHYSICAL OCEANOGRAPHY.
45 Beacon St., Boston, MA 02108.
Annual Subscription: $120. **Frequency:** Monthly.
Publisher: American Meterological Society.
Editorial Index: Annual. Subject/Author. December (Cumulative Index, 1971/80, available for $10).
Abstracted Online: MGA.

0756. JOURNAL OF PROPERTY MANAGEMENT.
430 North Michigan Ave., Chicago, IL 60611.
Annual Subscription: $18. **Frequency:** 6/yr.
Publisher: Institute of Real Estate Management.
Advertiser Index: Every issue.
Indexed or Abstracted Online: Management Contents; Trade & Industry Index; ABI/Inform.
Special Issues:
Economic Outlook, Parts 1 & 2. $3.50. January/February & March/April.

0757. JOURNAL OF REAL ESTATE TAXATION.
210 South St., Boston, MA 02111.
Annual Subscription: $54. **Frequency:** Quarterly.
Publisher: Warren, Gorham and Lamont.
Editorial Index: Annual. Title/Author. Summer.
Indexed or Abstracted Online: ABI/Inform; Management Contents.

0758. JOURNAL OF RETAILING.
P.O. Box 465, Hanover, PA 17331.
Annual Subscription: $18. **Frequency:** Quarterly.
Publisher: New York University Institute of Retail Management.
Editorial Index: Biennial (even years). Author. Spring.
Indexed or Abstracted Online: Management Contents; AMI.

0759. JOURNAL OF SMALL BUSINESS MANAGEMENT.
West Virginia University, Morgantown, WV 26506.
Annual Subscription: $15. **Frequency:** Quarterly.
Publisher: Bureau of Business Research.
Editorial Index: Annual. Subject/Title/Author. October.
Indexed Online: Management Contents; Magazine Index.

0760. JOURNAL OF SPACECRAFT & ROCKETS.
1633 Broadway, New York, NY 10019.
Annual Subscription: $85. **Frequency:** Bimonthly.
Publisher: American Institute of Astronautics and Aeronautics.
Editorial Index: Annual. Subject/Author. December.
Indexed or Abstracted Online: Recon (limited access—NASA contractors only).

0761. JOURNAL OF SYSTEMS MANAGEMENT.
24587 Bagley Rd., Cleveland, OH 44017.
Annual Subscription: $17.50. **Frequency:** Monthly.
Publisher: Association for Systems Management.
Editorial Index: Annual. Subject. December.
Abstracted Online: Management Contents; Trade & Industry Index.

0762. JOURNAL OF TAXATION.
210 South St., Boston, MA 02111.
Annual Subscription: $84. **Frequency:** Monthly.
Publisher: Warren, Gorham & Lamont, Inc.
Editorial Index: Semi-Annual. Subject. June/December.
Special Issues:
Annual Survey of Income Tax Returns Processed by Computer Service Bureaus. Started 1966. October.

0763. **JOURNAL OF THE ACOUSTICAL SOCIETY OF AMERICA.**
335 East 45 St., New York, NY 10017.
Annual Subscription: $165. **Frequency:** Monthly.
Publisher: American Institute of Physics.
Advertiser Index: Every issue.
Editorial Index: Five-year cumulative indexes from 1938; last issued 1974-78. Subject/Title/Author.
Indexed or Abstracted Online: SPIN.

0764. **JOURNAL OF THE AIR POLLUTION CONTROL ASSOCIATION.**
P.O. Box 2861, Pittsburgh, PA 15230.
Annual Subscription: $95/45 (nonprofit Libraries & Institutions). **Frequency:** Monthly.
Publisher: Air Pollution Contron Association.
Advertiser Index: Every issue.
Editorial Index: Annual. Subject/Author. December.
Special Issues:
Product Guide. $3. March.
Governmental APC Agency Directory. Started 1983. $7.50. April.
Annual Meeting Preview. $7.50. May.
Consultant Guide. $7.50. December.

0765. **JOURNAL OF THE AMERICAN CONCRETE INSTITUTE.**
P.O. Box 19150, Detroit, MI 48219.
Annual Subscription: $60. **Frequency:** 6/yr.
Publisher: American Concrete Institute.
Editorial Index: Annual. Subject/Title/Author. March/April.
Special Issues:
American Concrete Institute Convention. $6. October.

0766. **JOURNAL OF THE AMERICAN DIETETIC ASSOCIATION.**
430 North Michigan Ave., Chicago, IL 60611.
Annual Subscription: $27.50. **Frequency:** Monthly.
Publisher: American Dietetic Association.
Advertiser Index: Every issue.
Editorial Index: Semi-Annual. Subject/Author. June/December.

0767. **JOURNAL OF THE AMERICAN GERIATRICS SOCIETY.**
P.O. Box 465, Hanover, PA 17331.
Annual Subscription: $44 (individual)/55 (institutions).
Frequency: Monthly.
Publisher: W. B. Saunders Co.
Advertiser Index: Every issue.
Editorial Index: Annual. Subject/Author. January.
Indexed Online: Medline.

0768. **THE JOURNAL OF THE AMERICAN MEDICAL ASSOCIATION.**
535 North Dearborn St., Chicago, IL 60610.
Annual Subscription: $52. **Frequency:** 4/month.
Publisher: American Medical Association.
Advertiser Index: Every issue.
Editorial Index: Semi-Annual. Subject/Author. June/December.
Indexed or Abstracted Online: Index Medicus; Medline.
Special Issues:
Continuing Education Courses for Physicians. January/July.
Official Call: AMA Annual Meeting. April.
Olympic Issue. Started 1984. July.
Medical Education in the US. September.
Contempo (developments in medicine). October.
Official Call: AMA Interim Meeting. October.

0769. **JOURNAL OF THE AMERICAN OIL CHEMISTS SOCIETY.**
508 South Sixth St., Champaign, IL 61820.
Annual Subscription: $50. **Frequency:** Weekly.
Publisher: American Oil Chemists Society.
Advertiser Index: Every issue.
Editorial Index: Annual. Subject/Author. December.
Abstracted Online: CIN.
Special Issues:
American Oil Chemists Society Conference Proceedings. $12 (members)/16 (nonmembers). February.
American Oil Chemists Society Membership Directory. Published as a separate issue. Free (to members only). Not included in the subscription price. Biennially (odd yrs). August.

0770. **JOURNAL OF THE AMERICAN PLANNING ASSOCIATION.**
1776 Massachusetts Ave., NW, Washington, DC 20036.
Annual Subscription: $30. **Frequency:** Quarterly.
Publisher: American Planning Association.
Editorial Index: Annual. Title/Author. Fall.
Indexed or Abstracted Online: ABI/Inform; Management Contents.
Special Issues:
Periodical Literature in Urban Studies & Planning—contents pages of journals. Winter, Spring, Summer, Fall.

0771. **JOURNAL OF THE AMERICAN SOCIETY FOR INFORMATION SCIENCE.**
605 Third Ave., New York, NY 10158.
Annual Subscription: $75. **Frequency:** 6/yr.
Publisher: American Society for Information Science.
Editorial Index: Annual. Subject/Author. November/December.

0772. **JOURNAL OF THE AMERICAN STATISTICAL ASSOCIATION.**
806 15th St., NW, Washington, DC 20005.
Annual Subscription: $55. **Frequency:** Quarterly.
Publisher: American Statistical Association.
Editorial Index: Annual. Author. December.

0773. **JOURNAL OF THE AMERICAN VETERINARY MEDICAL ASSOCIATION.**
930 North Meacham Rd., Schaumburg, IL 60196.
Annual Subscription: $50. **Frequency:** 24/yr.
Publisher: American Veterinary Medical Association.
Advertiser Index: Every issue.
Editorial Index: Semi-Annual. Subject/Title/Author. June 15/December 15.
Special Issues:
Small Animals. $3. January/March.
Equine Animals. $3. February.
Companion Animals. $3. April/June/August/November.
AVMA Convention Reports. $3. May/August.
All-Species. $3. July.
Large Animals. $3. September/October.
Membership Directory. Published as a separate issue. $30. December.
Wild Life/Laboratory Animals. $3. December.

0774. **JOURNAL OF THE ASSOCIATION FOR COMPUTING MACHINERY.**
11 West 42nd St., New York, NY 10036.
Annual Subscription: $60. **Frequency:** Quarterly.
Publisher: Association for Computing Machinery.
Editorial Index: Annual. Subject/Author. October.

0775. **JOURNAL OF THE ATMOSPHERIC SCIENCES.**
45 Beacon St., Boston, MA 02108.
Annual Subscription: $120. **Frequency:** Monthly.
Publisher: American Meteoroligical Society.
Editorial Index: Annual. Subject/Author. December.
Abstracted Online: MGA.

0776. **JOURNAL OF THE PRESTRESSED CONCRETE INSTITUTE.**
201 North Wells, Ste. 1410, Chicago, IL 60606.
Annual Subscription: $19. **Frequency:** 6/yr.
Publisher: Prestressed Concrete Institute.
Advertiser Index: Every issue.
Editorial Index: Annual. Subject/Author. November/December.
Special Issues:
Prestressed Concrete Institute Convention Issue. Started 1973. $4.50. July/August.
PCI Journal 25-Year Index 1956-1981. Started 1982. Published as a separate issue. $30. One time only.

0777. JOURNAL WATER POLLUTION CONTROL FEDERATION.
2626 Pennsylvania Ave., NW, Washington, DC
Annual Subscription: $95. **Frequency:** Monthly.
Publisher: Water Pollution Control Federation.
Advertiser Index: Every issue.
Editorial Index: Annual. Subject/Title/Author. December.
Special Issues:
Yearbook. $11. March.
Literature Review Issue. Started 1968. $24. June.
Annual Conference Issue—Water Pollution Control Federation. Started 1928. $11. September.

0778. JOURNALISM EDUCATION.
University of South Carolina, Columbia, SC 29208.
Annual Subscription: $15 (free to members). **Frequency:** Quarterly.
Publisher: Association for Education in Journalism and Mass Communications.
Special Issues:
Association for Education in Journalism and Mass Communications Convention Report—includes reports of annual meetings of Association of Schools of Journalism and Mass Communications, and American Society of Journalism School Administrators. $5. January.
Journalism Directory—includes Association for Education in Journalism and Mass Communications membership roster, and list of graduate and undergraduate programs in journalism, and faculties. Published as a separate issue. $15 (free to members). Not included in the subscription price. February.

0779. JOURNALISM QUARTERLY.
University of South Carolina, Columbia, SC 29208.
Annual Subscription: $20. **Frequency:** Quarterly.
Publisher: Association for Education in Journalism and Mass Communications.
Editorial Index: Annual. Subject/Author. Spring issue; separate cumulative indexes by subject, author, and book reviews by authors: 1924-63, 1964-73, available at $5 each.

0780. JUVENILE MERCHANDISING.
370 Lexington Ave., New York, NY 10017.
Annual Subscription: $12/yr. **Frequency:** Monthly.
Publisher: Columbia Communications.
Advertiser Index: Every issue.
Special Issues:
Directory. $2. November/December.

0781. KEYBOARD.
Box 2110, Cupertino, CA 95015.
Annual Subscription: $18.95. **Frequency:** Monthly.
Publisher: GPI Publications.
Advertiser Index: Every issue.
Editorial Index: Irregular. Title/Author.
Special Issues:
Reader's Poll Ballot—best artist in various keyboard categories (acoustic and electric). $2. September.
Reader's Poll Winners. $2. December.

0782. KITCHEN & BATH BUSINESS.
1515 Broadway, New York, NY 10036.
Annual Subscription: $18. **Frequency:** Monthly.
Publisher: Gralla Publications.
Advertiser Index: Every issue.
Editorial Index: Annual. Subject. February.
Special Issues:
Annual Directory & Product Guide. $5. February.
Annual Who's Who in Kitchen Cabinets/Cabinet Industry Market Profile. $5. July.
Distributor Directory & Independent Representative Guide. Started 1983. $5. August.
Annual Cabinet Industry Report. $5. December.

0783. KNITTING TIMES/APPAREL WORLD.
386 Park Ave. South, New York, NY 10016.
Annual Subscription: $30. **Frequency:** Weekly.
Publisher: National Knitwear & Sportswear Association.
Advertiser Index: Every issue.
Special Issues:
Knitting Yarn Fair Directory. Started 1979. Published as a separate issue. August.
Buyer's Guide & Knitwear/Apparel Directory. Started 1930. Published as a separate issue. $15. September.
Trimmings, Accessories & Supplies Exposition Directory. Started 1980. October.
Yearbook. Started 1930. Published as a separate issue. $15. November.

0784. LAB ANIMAL.
475 Park Ave. South, New York, NY 10016.
Annual Subscription: $11.75. **Frequency:** 8/yr.
Advertiser Index: Every issue.
Editorial Index: Annual. Subject/Title/Author. November/December.
Special Issues:
Buyers Guide—suppliers/manufacturers of products and services for laboratory animal scientists. $1.75. October.

0785. LABORATORY EQUIPMENT.
P.O. Box 1952, Dover, NJ 07801.
Annual Subscription: $12. **Frequency:** Monthly.
Publisher: Gordon Publications.
Advertiser Index: Every issue.
Special Issues:
Budget Planning. $1. January/July.
Pittsburgh Conference on Analytical Chemistry & Applied Spectroscopy. $1. February.
Liquid Chromatography. $1. March.
Computerization. $1. April.
Pittsburgh Wrap-up/Electronic Equipment Market. $1. May.
Microscopic/Optic/Photographic. $1. June.
Specialty Chemicals. $1. July.
Gas Chromatography. $1. August.
Basic Laboratory Equipment. $1. September.
Spectroscopy. $1. October.
Vacuum Market Business Package. $1. November.
Filtration Equipment. $1. December.

0786. LABORATORY MANAGEMENT.
475 Park Ave. South, New York, NY 10016.
Annual Subscription: $22. **Frequency:** Monthly.
Publisher: Media Horizons.
Advertiser Index
Editorial Index: Annual. Subject/Author. January.
Special Issues:
Gold Book—directory of manufacturers and products. $2. December.

0787. LABORATORY PRODUCT NEWS.
1450 Don Mills Rd., Don Mills, Ontario, Can. M3B 2X7.
Annual Subscription: $26.50/20. **Frequency:** Bimonthly.
Publisher: Southam Communications Ltd.
Advertiser Index: Every issue.
Special Issues:
Laboratory Buyers' Guide—instruments, apparatus, materials and supplies. Products keyed to manufacturers and Canadian distributors. Started 1970. Published as a separate issue. AnnuallY. November.

0788. LAND AND WATER.
P.O. Box 1376, Fort Dodge, IA 50501.
Annual Subscription: $12. **Frequency:** 8/yr.
Publisher: Land and Water Inc.
Advertiser Index: Every issue.
Editorial Index: Annual. Subject. September.

0789. LANDSCAPE ARCHITECTURE MAGAZINE.
1190 East Broadway, Louisville, KY 40204.
Annual Subscription: $24. **Frequency:** 6/yr.
Publisher: American Society of Landscape Architects.
Advertiser Index: Every issue.
Editorial Index: Annual. Subject/Author. January/February.

Special Issues:
American Society of Landscape Architects Awards. $4. September.

0790. THE LANDSCAPE CONTRACTOR.
4 A East Wilson St., Batavia, IL 60510.
Annual Subscription: $12. **Frequency:** Monthly.
Publisher: Better Business Communicators.
Advertiser Index: Every issue.
Special Issues:
Mid-Am Trade Show. January.
Illinois Landscape and Contractors Association Trade Show. July.

0791. LAPIDARY JOURNAL.
P.O. Box 80937, San Diego, CA 92138.
Annual Subscription: $12. **Frequency:** Monthly.
Publisher: Lapidary Journal Inc.
Advertiser Index: Every issue.
Editorial Index: Annual. Subject/Author. March.
Indexed or Abstracted Online: Magazine Index.
Special Issues:
Rockhound Buyers Guide—articles on lapidary; rockhound dealer list; geographical index of dealers; where-to-find-it product index; gem and mineral clubs and bulletins. $3. Annual. April.

0792. LASER FOCUS WITH FIBEROPTIC TECHNOLOGY.
119 Russell St., P.O. Box 1111, Littleton, MA 01460.
Annual Subscription: $42. **Frequency:** Monthly.
Publisher: Advanced Technology Publications.
Advertiser Index: Every issue.
Editorial Index: Annual. Subject. December.
Special Issues:
Buyers Guide. Started 1965. Published as a separate issue. $30. Not included in the subscription price. January.

0793. LASER REPORT.
119 Russell St., P.O. Box 1111, Littleton, MA 01460.
Annual Subscription: $140. **Frequency:** 22/yr.
Publisher: Advanced Technology Publications.
Special Issues:
Annual Economic Review and Outlook. $45. January.

0794. LAW AND ORDER.
P.O. Box 1150, Skokie, IL 60077.
Annual Subscription: $12. **Frequency:** Monthly.
Publisher: Hendon, Inc.
Advertiser Index: Every issue.
Special Issues:
Buyers Guide and Dealers Directory. Started 1956. $4. January.

0795. LAW ENFORCEMENT COMMUNICATIONS.
475 Park Ave. South, New York, NY 10016.
Annual Subscription: $10. **Frequency:** 4/yr.
Publisher: United Business Publications.
Advertiser Index: Every issue.
Special Issues:
June Specification & Purchasing Guide. Started 1976. $5. June.

0796. LAWN CARE INDUSTRY.
7500 Old Oak Blvd., Cleveland, OH 44130.
Annual Subscription: $16. **Frequency:** Monthly.
Publisher: Harcourt Brace Jovanovich Inc.
Advertiser Index: Every issue.
Special Issues:
State of the Industry. Started 1977. Published as a separate issue. $2. June.
Professional Lawn Care Show Extras. Started N. Published as a separate issue. Not included in the subscription price. November (2 issues).
Supplier Marketplace—directory. Started 1982. $2. December.

0797. THE LEATHER MANUFACTURER.
Box 198, Cambridge, MA 02140.
Annual Subscription: $16. **Frequency:** Monthly.
Publisher: Shoe Trades Publishing Co.
Advertiser Index: Every issue.
Special Issues:
Outlook Issue. $1.50. January.
Preview of Spring Leather Shows. $1.50. February.
Report on Tanners' Council and Hide Skin and Leather Association Spring Conventions. $1.50. March.
Milwaukee Symposium Report. $1.50. May.
American Leather Chemists Asociation. $1.50. July.
Preview of Fall Leather Shows. $1.50. September.
Semaine du Cuir Report. $1.50. October.
Tanners' Council of America Leather Garment Show Preview. $1.50. October.
Report on Tanners' Council & Hide Skin & Leather Association Conventions. $1.50. December.

0798. LEATHER & SHOES.
1800 Oakton St., Des Plaines, IL 60018.
Annual Subscription: $16. **Frequency:** Monthly.
Publisher: Rumpf Publishing Co.
Advertiser Index: Every issue.
Editorial Index: Annual. Subject/Title/Author. December.
Indexed Online: Predicasts.
Special Issues:
Forum—industry leaders forecast. $1.50. January.
Leather Buyer's Guide—(U.S. & Canadian tanners, includes brand name index). Started 1962. Published as a separate issue. $5. February.
National Shoe Fair Preview. $1.50. February/August.
American Leather Chemists Association Convention Preview. $1.50. June.
Chain Shoe Stores Directory. Started 1964. $1.50. July.
New Products Review. $1.50. August.
Manufacturers Catalogs Currently Available. $1.50. December.

0799. L'EPICIER.
1001 Maisonneuve Blvd. West, Montreal, Quebec, Can. H3A 3E1.
Annual Subscription: $44/18. **Frequency:** 10/year.
Publisher: Maclean Hunter Ltd.
Advertiser Index: Every issue.
Special Issues:
Grocery Buying Guide (in French)—covers food distribution in Quebec. $12. August.

0800. LIBRARY JOURNAL.
P.O. Box 1427, Riverton, NJ 08077.
Annual Subscription: $55. **Frequency:** 20/yr.
Publisher: R. R. Bowker Co.
Advertiser Index: Every issue.
Indexed Online: Magazine Index; Trade & Industry Index.
Special Issues:
Year in Review. $3.50. January.
Fund Raising in Libraries. $3.50. February.
Spring Announcements. $4.95. February.
Books to be Published. $3.50. March/November.
First Novelists—authors' interviews. $3.50. March/ October.
Sci/Tech/Business/Popular Medical Books. $3.50. March/November.
Best Reference Books. $3.50. April.
Buyers Guide. $3.50. April.
Association Publishing. $3.50. May.
American Library Association Conference Preview & Round-up. $3.50. June/August.
Information Technology. $3.50. June.
Special Libraries Association Conference Report. $3.50. August.
Fall Announcements. $4.95. September.
Paperbacks. $3.50. September.
Religious/Inspirational Books. $3.50. October.
Small Presses. $3.50. November.

Architectural/Design/Maintenance—review of new library construction, etc. $3.50. December.
Placement Salaries—survey of starting salaries for new graduates of library schools. $3.50. Varies (summer).
Price Indexes—study of cost of American periodicals and serial services. $3.50. Varies (summer).

0801. LIBRARY QUARTERLY.
5801 Ellis Ave., Chicago, IL 60636.
Annual Subscription: $30 (institution)/20 (individual).
Frequency: Quarterly.
Publisher: University of Chicago Press.
Editorial Index: Annual. Author. October.

0802. LIBRARY TRENDS.
University of Illinois Press, Journals Dept., P.O. Box 5081, Station A, Champaign, IL 61820.
Annual Subscription: $20. **Frequency:** Quarterly.
Publisher: Grad School of Library & Information Science Publications Office.
Editorial Index: Annual. Subject. April.

0803. LIFE.
541 North Fairbanks Court, Chicago, IL 60611.
Annual Subscription: $24. **Frequency:** Monthly.
Publisher: Time Inc.
Indexed Online: Magazine Index.
Special Issues:
Year in Pictures. Started 1980. $3. January.
Special Olympics Issue. Started 1984. Published as a separate issue. $3. One time special issue. June.

0804. LIFE ASSOCIATION NEWS.
1922 F St. NW, Washington, DC 20006.
Annual Subscription: $3 (free to members). **Frequency:** Monthly.
Publisher: National Association of Life Underwriters.
Advertiser Index: Every issue.
Editorial Index: Annual. Subject/Author. January.
Indexed or Abstracted Online: Insurance Abstracts.
Special Issues:
Association for Advanced Life Underwriting Conference. May.
Life Agency Management Program, at General Agents and Managers Conference. May or June.
Million Dollar Round Table. August.
National Association of Life Underwriters Convention. November.
American Society of Chartered Life Underwriters Meeting Forum. December.
Life Insurance Marketing and Reseach Association Meeting. December or January.

0805. LIFE & HEALTH NATIONAL UNDERWRITER.
420 East 4th St., Cincinnati, OH 45202.
Annual Subscription: $30. **Frequency:** Weekly.
Publisher: National Underwriter Co.
Indexed or Abstracted Online: ABI/Inform Management Contents; Insurance Abtracts.
Special Issues:
Convention Planning (includes calendar). $1.50. January or February.
Financial Review. $1.50. January or February.
Pension Review. Started 1983. $1.50. January or February.
Review and Forecast. $1.50. January or December.
Information Industry. $1.50. February.
Agency Management Review. $1.50. March or April.
Association for Advanced Underwriting Conference. $1.50. March.
Employee Benefits/Group Insurance Review. $1.50. April.
In-Force Leaders Ranking (over 800 companies). $1.50. May.
Life Insurance Conference. $1.50. May.
Risk & Insurance Management Society Conference. $1.50. May.
Health Insurance Review (includes rankings of health "experience" of companies). $1.50. June.
Life Premium Income Rankings (almost 300 companies). $1.50. June.
National Association of Insurance Commissioners Report. $1.50. June.
Full Financial Services Report. $1.50. July.
Million Dollar Roundtable Report. $1.50. July.
National Association of Health Underwriters Conference. $1.50. July.
Insurance Marketing Review. $1.50. August.
National Association of Life Companies Conference. $1.50. August.
Home Office Management Review. $1.50. September.
Life Office Management Association Conference. $1.50. September.
National Association of Life Underwriters Special. $1.50. September.
Chartered Life Underwriters Conference. $1.50. October.
International Association for Financial Planning Conference. $1.50. October.
American Council of Life Insurance Conference. $1.50. November.
FYI (For Your Information) annual review. $1.50. November.
Life Insurance Marketing Research Association Conference. $1.50. November.

0806. LIQUOR STORE MAGAZINE.
352 Park Ave. South, New York, NY 10010.
Annual Subscription: $20. **Frequency:** 9/yr.
Publisher: Jobson Publishing Corp.
Advertiser Index: Every issue.
Special Issues:
Package Power supplement—newspaper advertising mats with line art available to stores selling liquor, wine, beer. April/October.

0807. LOCKSMITH LEDGER.
1800 Oakton, Des Plaines, IL 60018.
Annual Subscription: $24. **Frequency:** Monthly.
Publisher: Nickerson & Collins Co.
Special Issues:
Security Register—buyers guide with brand name listings, plus directory of regional and national security-related trade associations. Started 1969. Published as a separate issue. $5. January.
Associated Locksmiths of America Convention. $3. August.

0808. LODGING.
888 Seventh Ave., New York, NY 10019.
Annual Subscription: $30. **Frequency:** Monthly.
Publisher: American Hotel & Motel Association.
Advertiser Index: Every issue.
Editorial Index: Irregular. Subject/Title. Cumulative index (1976-1980) available separately.
Special Issues:
American Hotel & Motel Association Convention Issue. $4. March.
Buyers Guide for Hotels/Motels. $10. April.
International Hotel, Motel & Restaurant Show Issue. $4. September.
American Hotel & Motel Association Resources Issue—services available to members. November.

0809. LODGING & FOOD-SERVICE EAST.
131 Clarendon St., Boston, MA 02116.
Annual Subscription: $17. **Frequency:** 7/yr.
Publisher: HSI, Inc.
Special Issues:
Suppliers Showcase/Product Guide—for hotels, restaurants and institutions (nursing homes, colleges, etc.). February.
Northeast Foodservice and Lodging Exposition. April.
Annual Beverage Issue. June.
Annual Food Service Sectors Review. August/September.
International Hotel/Motel & Restaurant Show. October.

Eastern Distributors & Brokers Survey.   December.

0810. LODGING HOSPITALITY.
P.O. Box 95759, Cleveland, OH 44101.
Annual Subscription: $30. **Frequency:** Monthly.
Publisher: Penton/IPC, Inc.
Advertiser Index: Every issue.
Indexed or Abstracted Online: Trade & Industry Index.
Special Issues:
Products Data Guide—annual buyers guide.   Started 1974. $3.   March.
Lodging's 300—profile of the 300 top performing lodging properties in U.S.   Started 1975. $3.   August.
Designer Circle Awards—hotel interior design competition.   Started 1982. $3.   November.

0811. LOGGING & SAWMILLING JOURNAL.
777 Bay St., Toronto, Ontario, Can. M5W 1A7.
Annual Subscription: $48/25. **Frequency:** Monthly.
Publisher: Maclean Hunter Ltd.
Advertiser Index: Every issue.
Special Issues:
Directory/Desk Calendar. $15.   November.

0812. LOS ANGELES MAGAZINE.
1888 Century Park East, #920, Los Angeles, CA 90067.
Annual Subscription: $19. **Frequency:** Monthly.
Publisher: Same.
Indexed Online: Magazine Index.
Special Issues:
Health & Beauty Guide. $2.25.   January.
Home & Condo/Interiors Guide. $2.25.   2/yr.   February/July.
Weekends. $2.25.   May.
Restaurant Guide.   Started 1976.   Published as a separate issue. $3.95.   August.
Sun Circuit. $2.25.   October.
Christmas Gift Guide. $2.25.   2/yr.   November/December.

0813. LUBRICATION ENGINEERING.
838 Busse Hwy., Park Ridge, IL 60068.
Annual Subscription: $35. **Frequency:** Monthly.
Publisher: American Society of Lubrication Engineers.
Advertiser Index: Every issue.
Editorial Index: Annual. Subject/Title/Author. January.
Special Issues:
ASLE Annual Meeting. $5.   April.

0814. LUGGAGE & LEATHERGOODS NEWS.
501 Oakdale Rd., Downsville, Ontario, Can. M3N 1W7.
Annual Subscription: $10/7. **Frequency:** 9/yr.
Publisher: Page Communications.
Special Issues:
Directory Issue.   November.

0815. THE LUMBER CO-OPERATOR.
339 East Ave., Rochester, NY 14604.
Annual Subscription: $15. **Frequency:** Monthly.
Publisher: Northeastern Retail Lumbermens Association.
Advertiser Index: Every issue.
Special Issues:
Convention Issue—NRLA.   Started 1950. $1.50.   December.

0816. MLO/MEDICAL LABORATORY OBSERVER.
P.O. Box 543, Oradell, NJ 07649.
Annual Subscription: $44. **Frequency:** Monthly.
Publisher: Medical Economics Co., Inc.
Advertiser Index: Every issue.
Editorial Index: Annual. Subject/Author. December.
Special Issues:
Clinical Laboratory Reference—annual directory of diagnostic products & services.   Started 1974.   Published as a separate issue. $17.50.   June.

0817. THE MACARONI JOURNAL.
P.O. Box 1008, Palatine, IL 60067.
Annual Subscription: $14. **Frequency:** Monthly.
Publisher: National Pasta Association.
Advertiser Index: Every issue.
Special Issues:
Anniversary Issue/Buyers Guide/World Round-up.   Started 1919. $2.50.   April.

0818. MACHINE AND TOOL BLUE BOOK.
Hitchcock Bldg., Wheaton, IL 60187.
Annual Subscription: $50. **Frequency:** Monthly.
Publisher: Hitchcock Publishing Co.
Advertiser Index: Every issue.
Editorial Index: Annual. Subject. February.
Special Issues:
Machine & Tool Directory and Buyers Guide.   Started 1952.   Published as a separate issue. $30.   Not included in the subscription price.   February.

0819. MACHINE DESIGN.
Penton Plaza, 1111 Chester Ave., Cleveland, OH 44114.
Annual Subscription: $50. **Frequency:** 28/yr.
Publisher: Penton/IPC.
Advertiser Index: Every issue.
Indexed Online: Trade & Industry Index.
Special Issues:
Materials Reference Issue. $6.   April.
Electrical and Electronics Reference Issue. $6.   May.
Mechanical Drives Reference Issue. $6.   June.
Fluid Power Reference Issue. $6.   September.
Fastening and Joining Reference Issue. $6.   November.

0820. MAGAZINE AGE.
6931 Van Nuys Blvd., Van Nuys, CA 91405.
Annual Subscription: $36. **Frequency:** Monthly.
Publisher: Freed Crown Lee Publishing, Inc.
Advertiser Index: Every issue.
Special Issues:
Top 100 Consumer Magazines. $2.50.   January.
Top 100 Business Magazines/Travel Magazines/Consumer Computer Magazines. $2.50.   February.
Business Computer Magazines/Consumer Apparel Magazines. $2.50.   March.
Consumer Food Magazines/Television-Cable Guide Magazines. $2.50.   April.
Doctors, Dentists, Nurses Magazines/Consumer Automotive Magazines. $2.50.   May.
100 Largest Consumer Ad Gainers. $2.50.   June.
Consumer Toiletries and Cosmetics Magazines. $2.50.   July.
Buyers Guide to Magazines (ad pages, revenue, editorial categories, ad categories, circulation, contact research, with three-year trends, for largest consumer and trade magazines).   Started 1981.   Published as a separate issue. $10.   August.
Liquor Advertising/Consumer Science and Technology Magazines. $2.50.   August.
Cigarette Advertising. $2.50.   September.
Business-to-Business Advertising/Consumer Electronics Advertising/Home Service Magazines. $2.50.   October.
Corporate Advertising/College & Youth Market. $2.50.   November.
Advertising to Professionals/The Affluent Market. $2.50.   December.

0821. THE MAGAZINE ANTIQUES.
551 Fifth Ave., New York, NY 10176.
Annual Subscription: $38. **Frequency:** Monthly.
Publisher: Straight Enterprises, Inc.
Advertiser Index: Every issue.
Editorial Index: Annual. Subject/Title/Author.
Indexed Online: Magazine Index.
Special Issues:
American Furniture.   Started 1970's. $4.   May.
American Paintings.   Started 1970's. $4.   November.

0822. MAINTENANCE SUPPLIES.
101 West 31 St., New York, NY 10001.
Annual Subscription: $20. **Frequency:** Monthly.
Publisher: MacNair-Dorland Co.
Advertiser Index: Every issue.
Special Issues:
  Show and Sell. $2. April.
  Maintenance Chemicals—markets and marketing. $2. June.
  International Sanitary Supply Association Exhibition. $2. September.
  Buyers Guide. $2. November.

0823. MANAGEMENT ACCOUNTING.
919 Third Ave., New York, NY 10022.
Annual Subscription: $42. **Frequency:** Monthly.
Publisher: National Association of Accountants.
Advertiser Index: Every issue.
Editorial Index: Annual. Subject. June.
Indexed or Abstracted Online: Management Contents; ABI/Inform.
Special Issues:
  Profile of National Association of Accountants' New President. Published as a separate issue. $4. July.
  Annual Report of the National Association of Accountants. Published as a separate issue. $4. October.

0824. MANAGEMENT OF WORLD WASTES.
6285 Barfield Rd., Atlanta, GA 30328.
Annual Subscription: $23. **Frequency:** Monthly.
Publisher: Communications Channels Inc.
Advertiser Index: Every issue.
Editorial Index: Annual. Subject/Title/Author. January.
Special Issues:
  Waste Industry Buyers Guide. $3. February.
  Sanitation Industry Yearbook. Started 1963. Published as a separate issue. $3. December.

0825. MANAGEMENT WORLD.
2360 Maryland Rd., Willow Grove, PA 19090.
Annual Subscription: $18. **Frequency:** Monthly.
Publisher: Administrative Management Society.
Advertiser Index: Every issue.
Editorial Index: Annual. Title. December.
Indexed Online: Management Contents.
Special Issues:
  Guide to Telecommunications. Started 1981. $3.50. March.
  Guide to Word Processing. Started 1981. $3.50. April.
  Guide to Small Business Computers. Started 1981. $3.50. July.
  Guide to Copiers. Started 1981. $3.50. September.
  Guide to Dictation. Started 1981. $3.50. November.

0826. MANAGERIAL PLANNING.
P.O. Box 70, Oxford, OH 45056.
Annual Subscription: $30. **Frequency:** Bimonthly.
Publisher: Planning Executives Institute.
Editorial Index: Annual. Subject. September/October.
Indexed or Abstracted Online: ABI/Inform; Management Contents.

0827. MANUFACTURED HOUSING BUSINESS.
29901 Agoura Rd., Agoura, CA 91301.
Annual Subscription: $12. **Frequency:** Monthly.
Publisher: T.L. Enterprises, Inc.
Advertiser Index: Every issue.
Special Issues:
  Directory and Buyers Guide—lists manufacturers, product categories and brand names; suppliers and products; distributors and wholesalers; manufacturer's representatives; associations and special services. Started 1957. $1.50. January.
  Directory of Mobile & Modular Housing Manufacturers & Distributors: Pocket Edition. Published as a separate issue. $5. Not included in the subscription price. February.

0828. THE MANUFACTURING CONFECTIONER.
175 Rock Rd., Glen Rock, NJ 07452.
Annual Subscription: $15. **Frequency:** Monthly.
Publisher: M C Publishing.
Advertiser Index: Every issue.
Editorial Index: Annual. Subject/Author. December.
Special Issues:
  Equipment & Supplies Directory. $5. July.

0829. MANUFACTURING ENGINEERING.
P.O. Box 930, Dearborn, MI 48121.
Annual Subscription: $26. **Frequency:** Monthly.
Publisher: Society of Manufacturing Engineers.
Advertiser Index: Every issue.
Editorial Index
Special Issues:
  Cutting Tools. January.
  Automatic Forming. February.
  WESTEC Show. March.
  Society of Manufacturing Engineers Annual Show. April.
  Nontraditional Machining. May.
  Grinding. June.
  Workholding. July.
  Machine Controls/Nontraditional Machines. August.
  Flexible Manufacturing Systems. September.
  AUTOFACT 5 Show—Automatic Manufacturing/Robotics. October.
  Testing & Inspection. November.
  The Machine Tool Industry—an overview. December.

0830. MARINE FISHERIES REVIEW.
Superintendent of Documents, GPO, Washington, DC 20402.
Annual Subscription: $8.75. **Frequency:** Quarterly.
Publisher: National Marine Fisheries Service.
Editorial Index: Annual. Subject/Title/Author. October/December.

0831. MARKETING.
777 Bay St., Toronto, Ontario, Can. M5W 1A7.
Annual Subscription: $42/32. **Frequency:** Weekly.
Publisher: MacLean Hunter Ltd.
Advertiser Index: March.
Special Issues:
  Canadian Premiums & Incentives Supplements (Annual Source Directory in May; Annual Show Guide in August). $3/.85. February/May/August/November.
  Creativity (Annual Awards Issue in March) Supplements. $3/.85. March/June/September/December.
  Direct Marketing Report & Guide. $3/.85. July.
  Forecast Issue. $3/.85. July.
  Guide to Canadian Business Publications. $3/.85. October.
  Annual Advertising Agencies Report. $3/.85. November.
  Daily Newspaper Report. $3/.85. November.

0832. MARKETING AND MEDIA DECISIONS.
1140 Ave. of the Americas, New York, NY 10036.
Annual Subscription: $40. **Frequency:** Monthly.
Publisher: Decisions Publications.
Advertiser Index: Every issue.
Editorial Index: Annual. Subject. February.
Indexed or Abstracted Online: AMI; Trade & Industry Index.
Special Issues:
  Business to Business Advertising. Started 1984. Published as a separate issue. $3. April.
  15 Marketing Successes of Year. Started 1982. Published as a separate issue. $3. May or June.
  National Ad Expenditures in Newspapers. Started 1978. $3. June.
  Top 200 Advertised Brands. Started 1971. $3. July.
  Media Cost Forecast. Started 1971. $3. September or October.
  Media Costs. Started 1982. Published as a separate issue. $3. September or October.

0833. MARKETING COMMUNICATIONS.
475 Park Ave. South, New York, NY 10016.
Annual Subscription: $15. **Frequency:** Monthly.
Publisher: United Business Publications.
Advertiser Index: Every issue.
Indexed or Abstracted Online: AMI (Mead Data Central).
Special Issues:
  The Retailing 1,000—nation's top retailers by title. Started 1979. $5. February.
  Directory of Special Agencies—primarily sales promotion. Started 1981. $1.50. April.
  The Big Spenders—the top 225 brands, their marketing teams and agencies by name, title & address. Started 1978. $5. June.
  Directory of Point-of-Purchase Producers & Suppliers. Started 1977. $1.50. July.
  Directory of Corporate-Sponsored Sporting Events. $1.50. November.

0834. MARKETING NEWS.
250 South Wacker Dr., Ste. 200, Chicago, IL 60606.
Annual Subscription: $24/36 (libraries & institutions). **Frequency:** Biweekly.
Publisher: American Marketing Association.
Abstracted Online: ABI/Inform; Predicasts; AMI.
Special Issues:
  Marketing Research. Started 1975. $1.75. 3/yr. January/May/September.
  Marketing Managers. Started 1983. $1.75. March.
  Marketing Education. Started 1975. $1.75. August.
  Technology for Marketing & Marketing Research. Started 1979. $1.75. November.

0835. MARKING INDUSTRY.
2640 N. Halsted Street, Chicago, IL 60614.
Annual Subscription: $12. **Frequency:** Monthly.
Publisher: Marking Devices Publishing Co.
Advertiser Index: March (buyers' guide).
Special Issues:
  Marking Products and Equipment—buyers guide, with advertiser index, product index, trade name index. Published as a separate issue. $10. March.

0836. MART MAGAZINE.
Berkshire Common, Pittsfield, MA 01201.
Annual Subscription: $30. **Frequency:** Monthly.
Publisher: Morgan-Grampian Publishing Co.
Advertiser Index: Every issue.
Special Issues:
  Review and Outlook/Consumer Electronics Show. Started 1967. $3. January/June or July.
  Air Conditioning. Started 1976. $3. February.
  Microware Ovens/Floor Care Products. Started 1978. $3. March.
  Annual Survey—Consumer Attitudes on Computer Hardware and Software. Started 1980. $3. April.
  National Housewares Manufactures Association Show. Started 1970. $3. April/October.
  Telephones. Started 1982. $3. May/November.
  Consumer Survey on Personal Computers. Started 1984. $3. June.
  Home & Auto Radios. $3. July.
  National Hardware Show/Electronic Furniture. August.
  Video Hardware & Software, with Consumer Survey. Started 1978. $3. September.
  Video Disk Hardware and Software. $3. December.

0837. MASS MARKET RETAILERS.
One Park Ave., New York, NY 10016.
Annual Subscription: $10. **Frequency:** 24/yr.
Publisher: Racher Press Inc.
Special Issues:
  Retailer of the Year. Started 1984. January.
  Annual Report of the Mass Retailing Industries. Started 1983. May or October.
  Health and Beauty Aids Study. Started 1983. July or September.
  Over-the-Counter Drug Study. Started 1984. August.
  Sales Survey. Started 1984. October.
  Company Profile (Full Issue Study). Started 1983. December.

0838. MASS TRANSIT.
337 National Press Bldg., Washington, DC 20045.
Annual Subscription: $25/45 (international). **Frequency:** Monthly.
Publisher: Mass Transit Magazine.
Advertiser Index: Every issue.
Indexed Online: Trade & Industry Index.
Special Issues:
  Suppliers Guide. Started 1979. Annual. February.
  Guide to Consultants. Started 1977. Annual. August.
  Guide to Subways. Started 1981. Biennially. November.
  Bus Guide. Started 1980. Annual. December.

0839. MATERIAL HANDLING ENGINEERING.
1111 Chester Ave., Cleveland, OH 44114.
Annual Subscription: $30. **Frequency:** Monthly.
Publisher: Penton/IPC.
Advertiser Index: Every issue.
Editorial Index: Annual. Subject. December.
Special Issues:
  Handbook & Directory. Started 1954. Published as a separate issue. $25. December.

0840. MATERIALS ENGINEERING.
Penton Plaza, Cleveland, OH 44114.
Annual Subscription: $30. **Frequency:** Monthly.
Publisher: Penton/IPC.
Advertiser Index: Every issue.
Abstracted Online
Special Issues:
  Top 20 Awards Issue. $3. November.
  Materials Selector—Product information with separated data sections on: comparisons of materials; irons and steels; non-ferrous metals, plastics; rubber and elastomers; ceramics, glass, carbon and mica; fibers, felts, wood and paper; finishes and coatings; composite materials; parts and forms; joining and fastening; equipment and services. Started 1957. Published as a separate issue. $17.50. December.

0841. MATERIALS MANAGEMENT & DISTRIBUTION.
777 Bay St., Toronto, Ontario, Can. M5W 1A7.
Annual Subscription: $32/23. **Frequency:** Monthly.
Publisher: Maclean Hunter Ltd.
Advertiser Index: Every issue.
Special Issues:
  Materials Handling Handbook and Buyers Guide. Started 1956. Published as a separate issue. $12. June.
  Transportation & Distribution Journal—desk diary for traffic distribution. Started 1980. Published as a separate issue. $10. November.

0842. MATERIALS PERFORMANCE.
1440 S. Creek, Houston, TX 77084.
Annual Subscription: $50. **Frequency:** Monthly.
Publisher: National Association of Corrosion Engineers.
Advertiser Index: Every issue.
Editorial Index: Annual. Subject/Author. December.
Special Issues:
  Corrosion Engineering Buyers Guide. $10. July.

0843. MEAT INDUSTRY.
P.O. Box 72, Mill Valley, CA 94942.
Annual Subscription: $32. **Frequency:** Monthly.
Publisher: Oman Publishing, Inc.
Advertiser Index: Every issue.
Editorial Index: Annual. Subject/Title. December.
Special Issues:
  January-Western States Convention Preview. Started 1955. $3. January.
  Sausage Issue. Started 1960. $3. June.
  Top 100 Packers Issue. Started 1978. $3. July.

American Meat Institute Convention Preview. Started 1955. $3. September or October.

0844. MEAT PLANT.
9701 Gravois Ave., St. Louis, MO 63123.
Annual Subscription: $12. **Frequency:** Monthly.
Publisher: ADmore Publishing.
Advertiser Index: Every issue.
Special Issues:
Financial Management. $1. January.
Cured & Smoked Meats. $1. March.
Sausage Issue/Buyers Guide. $1. April.
Fresh Meats Issue. $1. May.
Review of State Association Conventions. $1. June.
Review of American Association of Meat Processors Convention. $1. August.
American Meat Institute Convention. $1. September.
Fall Buyers Guide. $1. October.
Sanitation & Safety Issue. $1. November.
Packaging Issue. $1. December.

0845. MEAT PROCESSING.
241 Frontage Rd., Ste. 32, Hinsdale, IL 60521.
Annual Subscription: $25. **Frequency:** Monthly.
Publisher: Davies Publishing Co.
Advertiser Index: Every issue.
Special Issues:
Top 100 Packers. $2. July.
American Meat Institute Show. Started 1962. $2. September.
Future Trends. Started 1980. $2. November.
Directory/Buyers Guide. Started 1962. $2. December.

0846. MECHANICAL ENGINEERING.
345 East 47th St., New York, NY 10017.
Annual Subscription: $28. **Frequency:** Monthly.
Publisher: American Society of Mechanical Engineers.
Advertiser Index: Every issue.
Editorial Index: Annual. Subject/Title/Author. December.
Indexed or Abstracted Online: Compendex.
Special Issues:
Transportation Trends. January.
Non-destructive Evaluation. February.
Design Engineering/Vibration & Sound. March.
Codes & Standards Centennial. April.
Gas Turbines. May.
Pressure Vessels & Piping. June.
Failure Analysis. July.
Computer-Aided Engineering. August.
Medical Devices & Sporting Equipment. September.
Flexible Manufacturing. October.
Industrial Safety & Risk Assessment. November.
Industrial Energy Conservation. December.

0847. MEDIA INDUSTRY NEWSLETTER.
18 East 53rd Street, New York, NY 10022.
Annual Subscription: $112. **Frequency:** Weekly.
Publisher: M.I.N. Publishing Co.
Abstracted Online: AMI.
Special Issues:
5-Year Summary of Advertising Pages and Revenues. $2.50. January.

0848. MEDICAL ECONOMICS.
P.O. Box 55, Oradell, NJ 07649.
Annual Subscription: $54. **Frequency:** Biweekly.
Publisher: Medical Economics Co.
Advertiser Index: Every issue.
Editorial Index: Semi-Annual. Subject. January/July.

0849. MEDICAL ELECTRONICS & EQUIPMENT NEWS.
532 Busse Hwy., Park Ridge, IL 60068.
Annual Subscription: $25. **Frequency:** 6/yr.
Publisher: Reilly Publishing.
Advertiser Index: Every issue.
Special Issues:
Product Comparison Chart: Patient Monitors. January/February.
Product Comparison Chart: Diagnostic Ultrasound. March/April.
Product Comparison Chart: Cardiac Pacemakers. May/June.
Product Comparison Chart: Infusion Pumps. July/August.
Product Comparison Chart: Neonatal Monitors. September/October.
Product Comparison Chart: Digital Radiography. November/December.

0850. MEDICAL GROUP MANAGEMENT.
4101 East Louisiana Ave., Denver, CO 80222.
Annual Subscription: $29. **Frequency:** 6/yr.
Publisher: Medical Group Management Association.
Advertiser Index: Every issue.
Editorial Index: Annual. Subject/Author. January/February.
Indexed Online: Medlars.

0851. MEDICAL GROUP NEWS.
P.O. Box 36, Glencoe, IL 60022.
Annual Subscription: $18. **Frequency:** 6/yr.
Publisher: Same.
Special Issues:
Computer & Diagnostics in Clinics. Started 1970. $1.50. 2/yr. January/February & July/August.
Clinic Construction & Renovation. Started 1972. $1.50. September/October.

0852. MEDICAL INSTRUMENTATION.
1901 North Fort Myer Dr., Ste. 602, Arlington, VA 22209.
Annual Subscription: $60. **Frequency:** 6/yr.
Publisher: Association for the Advancement of Medical Instrumentation.
Advertiser Index: Every issue.
Editorial Index: Annual. Subject/Title/Author. November/December.
Indexed or Abstracted Online: Medline; Compendex.
Special Issues:
AAMI Annual Meeting Issue. Started 1973. $12.50. January/February or March/April.

0853. MEDICAL MARKETING & MEDIA.
31 Bailey Ave., Ridgefield, CT 06877.
Annual Subscription: $35. **Frequency:** Monthly.
Publisher: CPS Communications, Inc.
Advertiser Index: Every issue.
Editorial Index: Annual. Subject. December.
Abstracted Online: AMI.

0854. MEDICAL MEETINGS.
West Bare Hill Rd., P.O. Box L, Harvard, MA 01451.
Annual Subscription: $24. **Frequency:** Bimonthly & 2 directories.
Publisher: The Laux Co., Inc.
Advertiser Index: Every issue.
Special Issues:
Facilities Guide. Started 1978. Published as a separate issue. $15. April.
Directory of Medical Associations and Meetings. Started 1977. Published as a separate issue. $15. October.

0855. MEDICAL POST.
77 Bay St., Toronto, Ontario, Can. M5W 1A7.
Annual Subscription: $43/27. **Frequency:** 26/yr.
Publisher: MacLean Hunter Ltd.
Editorial Index: Annual. Subject. February.
Special Issues:
Report on Royal College of Surgeons Annual Convention. $4.50. October.
Report on Canadian Medical Association Annual Convention. $4.50. November.

0856. MEDICAL PRODUCTS SALES.
550 Frontage Rd., Northfield, IL 60093.
Annual Subscription: $22. **Frequency:** Monthly.
Publisher: McKnight Medical Communications.
Advertiser Index: Every issue.
Special Issues:
Health Industry Distributors Association Show. August.

0857. MEETING & CONVENTIONS.
One Park Ave., New York, NY 10016.
Annual Subscription: $30. **Frequency:** Monthly.
Publisher: Ziff-Davis Publishing Co.
Advertiser Index: Every issue.
Special Issues:
    International Directory of Facilities, Destinations, Services. Started 1969. $3. March.
    Incentive Travel From A to Z. Started 1978. $3. July.
    Meeting Market Report. Started 1972. $3. Biennially (even years). December.

0858. MEETING NEWS.
1515 Broadway, New York, NY 10036.
Annual Subscription: $36. **Frequency:** Monthly.
Publisher: Gralla Publications.
Advertiser Index: Every issue.
Special Issues:
    Directory of Sites, Suppliers, Services. Started 1978. $4. January.
    Incentive Travel Planning Guide. $4. February/April/August/October.
    Inside Resorts. $4. March/May/September/November.
    Dollars & Census Survey. $4. November.

0859. MEETINGS & INCENTIVE TRAVEL.
1450 Don Mills Rd., Don Mills, Ontario, Can. M3B 2X7.
Annual Subscription: $20.00/16.50. **Frequency:** 6/yr.
Publisher: Southam Communications Ltd.
Special Issues:
    Annual Directory/Product Round-Up and Literature Review. $2. July/August.
    Incentive Travel Report/Cruising/Fitness. $2. September/October.
    Audio-Visual Report/Canadian Resorts. $2. November/December.

0860. MEN'S WEAR OF CANADA.
501 Oakdale Rd., Downsview, Ontario, Can. M37 1W7.
Annual Subscription: $50/37. **Frequency:** 5/yr.
Publisher: Page Communications.
Special Issues:
    Sources. $5. January.
    Fall. $5. March.
    Winter. $5. June.
    Spring. $5. September.
    Sources Calendar. $5. December.

0861. MERCHANDISING.
1515 Broadway, New York, NY 10036.
Annual Subscription: $33. **Frequency:** Monthly.
Publisher: Gralla Publications.
Advertiser Index: Every issue.
Indexed or Abstracted Online: Trade & Industry Index; Management Contents.
Special Issues:
    Annual Statistical & Marketing Report—shipments of consumer electronics (including computers), major appliances, housewares for previous year. Started 1922. $15. March.
    Annual Consumer Survey—charts purchasing plans for the coming year. Started 1972. $4. July.
    Annual Directory—list of suppliers of consumer electronics, major appliances, housewares. Started 1980. $4. November.

0862. MERGERS & ACQUISITIONS.
229 South 18th St., Philadelphia, PA 19103.
Annual Subscription: $95. **Frequency:** Quarterly.
Publisher: The Hay Group.
Editorial Index: Annual. Title. March.
Indexed or Abstracted Online: ABI/Inform; Predicasts; PAIS; Legal Resource Index; Management Contents.
Special Issues:
    Mergers & Acquisitions Almanac & Index. Started 1982. Published as a separate issue. $40. March.

0863. METAL CENTER NEWS.
7 East 12th St., New York, NY 10003.
Annual Subscription: $35. **Frequency:** Monthly.
Publisher: Fairchild Publications.
Advertiser Index: Every issue.
Special Issues:
    Metal Distribution Annual. Started 1976. Published as a separate issue. $10. January.
    Non ferrous Issue/Copper & Brass Servicenter Association. $5. April.
    Steel Service Center Institute Convention Issues. $3. May/June.
    Service Center Salesmen. Started Y. $5. September.
    Service Center Equipment. $5. October.
    Aluminum Issue/National Association of Aluminum Distributors Convention. $5. November.
    Profile of a Service Center. $5. December.

0864. METAL FINISHING.
1 University Plaza, Hackensack, NJ 07601.
Annual Subscription: $28. **Frequency:** Monthly.
Publisher: Metals and Plastics Publications Inc.
Advertiser Index: Every issue.
Editorial Index: Annual. Title. December.
Special Issues:
    Metal Finishing Guidebook Directory. Published as a separate issue. January.

0865. METAL PROGRESS.
Metals Park, OH 44073.
Annual Subscription: $36. **Frequency:** 15/yr.
Publisher: American Society for Metals.
Advertiser Index: Every issue.
Editorial Index: Semi-Annual. Subject. January/July.
Indexed Online: Compendex.
Special Issues:
    Technology Forecast. $3.50. January.
    Society of Automotive Engineers Show Preview. $3.50. February.
    Testing & Inspection Buyers Guide and Directory. Published as a separate issue. $15. February.
    Highlights of Surtech & Surface Coating Exposition. $3.50. May.
    Materials & Processing Databook. Published as a separate issue. $15. June.
    Preview of American Society for Metals Congress. $3.50. September.
    Heat Treating Buyers Guide and Directory. Published as a separate issue. $15. November.

0866. METAL STAMPING.
27027 Chardon Rd., Richmond Hts., OH 44143.
Annual Subscription: $25. **Frequency:** Monthly.
Publisher: American Metal Stamping Association.
Special Issues:
    Sources for Stamping—membership directory of AMSA, and buyers guide. Published as a separate issue. $35. Not included in the subscription price. January.

0867. METALWORKING DIGEST.
Box 1952, Dover, NJ 07801.
Annual Subscription: $9. **Frequency:** 9/yr.
Publisher: Gordon Publications.
Advertiser Index: Every issue.
Special Issues:
    Machine Tools. January/February/July/August.
    Cutting Tools. March/September.
    Machine Controls. April or May.
    Pressroom Equipment/Robot 8 Show. May.
    Tooling & Accessories. June.
    International Machine Tool Show. July/August.
    Measurement & Inspection Equipment. October or March.
    Metal Cleaning, Coating & Finishing Equipment. November/December or October.

0868. **METEOROLOGICAL AND GEOASTROPHYSICAL ABSTRACTS.**
45 Beacon St., Boston, MA 02108.
Annual Subscription: $450. **Frequency:** Monthly.
Publisher: American Meteorological Society.
Editorial Index: Monthly. Subject/Author. Monthly. Indexes available separately: Annual Indexes, 1976-83, $150; Cumulative Index, 1950-1959, $200; Cumulative Index, 1970-1975, $300.
Abstracted Online: MGA.

0869. **METROPOLITAN (A.K.A. METRO).**
2500 Artesia Blvd., Redwood Beach, CA 90278.
Annual Subscription: $12. **Frequency:** 7/yr.
Publisher: Bobit Publishing Co.
Advertiser Index: Every issue.
Editorial Index: Annual. Subject. January/February.
Special Issues:
Annual Fact Book—statistics, and a directory of personnel in transit supply industry. Started 1969-70. $10. September.

0870. **METROPOLITAN LIFE STATISTICAL BULLETIN.**
1 Madison Ave., New York, NY 10010.
Frequency: Quarterly.
Publisher: Metropolitan Life Foundation.
Editorial Index: Annual. Subject. October/December.
Indexed Online: Management Contents.
Special Issues:
Statistics on longevity, mortality, cost containment, disability, health, population, accidents, etc. Irregular. Irregular.

0871. **METROPOLITAN TORONTO BUSINESS JOURNAL.**
3 First Canadian Pl., P.O. Box 60, Toronto, Ontario, Can. M5X 1C1.
Annual Subscription: $20/18. **Frequency:** 10/yr.
Publisher: Board of Trade of Metropolitan Toronto.
Special Issues:
Metro's Top Employers—top 500 in metropolitan Toronto. $1.75. June.

0872. **MICROCOMPUTING.**
P.O. Box 997, Farmingdale, NY 11737.
Annual Subscription: $24.97. **Frequency:** Monthly.
Publisher: Wayne Green Inc.
Advertiser Index: Every issue.
Editorial Index: Annual. Subject. December.

0873. **MICROWAVE JOURNAL.**
610 Washington St., Dedham, MA 02026.
Annual Subscription: $36. **Frequency:** Monthly.
Publisher: Horizon House-Microwave.
Advertiser Index: Every issue.
Editorial Index: Annual. Subject/Title/Author. December.
Indexed Online: Predicasts.

0874. **MICROWAVE SYSTEMS NEWS.**
1170 East Meadow Dr., Palo Alto, CA 94303.
Annual Subscription: $30 (free to qualified readers).
Frequency: Monthly.
Publisher: EW Communications Inc.
Advertiser Index: Every issue.
Special Issues:
Microwave System Designer's Handbook. Started 1983. Published as a separate issue. $4. November.

0875. **MICROWAVES & RF.**
50 Essex St., Rochelle Park, NJ 07662.
Annual Subscription: $30. **Frequency:** Monthly.
Publisher: Hayden Publishing Co.
Advertiser Index: Every issue.
Editorial Index: Annual. Subject. December.
Special Issues:
Test & Measurement Techniques. $3. January.
Semiconductor Applications. $3. February.
Communications. $3. March.
Radar Technology. $3. April.
RF & Microwave Technology Review/International Microwave Symposium. $3. May.
Communications. $3. August.
Military Electronics. $3. September.
Microwaves & RF Product Data Directory—manufacturers, data sheets, and applications information. Started 1973. Published as a separate issue. $23. October.
Solid State Design. $3. October.
Signal-Processing Technology. $3. November.

0876. **MID-WEST CONTRACTOR.**
P.O. Box 766, Kansas City, MO 64141.
Annual Subscription: $30. **Frequency:** 24/yr.
Publisher: Construction Digest Inc.
Advertiser Index: Every issue.
Special Issues:
Buyers Guide and Directory. $3. March.

0877. **MIDWEST PURCHASING.**
1127 Euclid Ave., Ste. 970, Cleveland, OH 44115.
Annual Subscription: $30. **Frequency:** Monthly.
Publisher: Purchasing Management Association of Cleveland, Inc.
Special Issues:
Roster: National Association of Purchasing Management. $25. April.
Buyers Guide. $3. July.
Metals Guide. $3. September.

0878. **THE MILITARY ENGINEER.**
607 Prince St., P.O. Box 180, Alexandria, VA 22313.
Annual Subscription: $24. **Frequency:** 7/yr.
Publisher: The Society of American Military Engineers.
Editorial Index: Annual. Subject/Title/Author. December.
Special Issues:
Red Book—reports on engineering programs by 5 Chiefs of Engineers: Air Force, Army, Navy, Coast Guard, National Oceanic and Atmospheric Administration. $4. January/February.
White Book—Technology Transfer. Started 1982. $4. April.
Gold Book—Directory of Sustaining Members. $4. May/June.

0879. **MILITARY MARKET MAGAZINE.**
475 School St. SW, Washington, DC 20024.
Annual Subscription: $20. **Frequency:** Monthly.
Publisher: Army Times Publishing Company.
Advertiser Index: Every issue.
Special Issues:
Buyers Guide—manufacturers selling to military resale systems. $5. January.
Almanac & Directory—statistics on retail sales of commissary and exchange systems, military population etc.; plus subject listing of products available for resale. $5. July.

0880. **MILLIMETER MAGAZINE.**
826 Broadway, New York, NY 10003.
Annual Subscription: $25. **Frequency:** Monthly.
Publisher: Millimeter Magazine Inc.
Advertiser Index: Every issue.
Special Issues:
Annual Animation Issue. Started 1975. $3.25. February.
Commercial Production Directory/TV Commercial Directors. Started 1978. Published as a separate issue. $35. Not included in the subscription price. Fall.

0881. **MILLING & BAKING NEWS.**
4800 Main St., Kansas City, MO 64112.
Annual Subscription: $52. **Frequency:** Weekly.
Publisher: Sosland Publishing Co.
Advertiser Index: Every issue.
Editorial Index: Annual. Subject. December.
Indexed or Abstracted Online: Predicasts.
Special Issues:
Market Analysis: White Bread. $2. January.
Baking Directory/Buyers Guide. Published as a separate issue. $20. March.
Market Analysis: Sweet Goods. $2. March.

Association of Operative Millers, Annual Meeting. $2. May or June.
Market Analysis: Variety Breads. $2. May/June.
Market Analysis: Cookies and Crackers. $2. July.
Grain Directory/Buyers Guide. Published as a separate issue. $20. September.
Market Analysis: Doughnuts. $2. September.
Market Analysis: Specialty Baked Goods. $2. November.
Milling Directory/Buyers Guide. Published as a separate issue. $20. November.

0882. MINES MAGAZINE.
Colorado School of Mines, Chauvenet Hall, P.O. Box 1410, Golden, CO 80402.
Annual Subscription: $15. **Frequency:** M (10/yr).
Publisher: Colorado School of Mines.
Advertiser Index: Every issue.
Editorial Index: Annual. Subject/Title/Author. December.
Special Issues:
Coal Mining. February.
Chemistry. March.
Environmental Issues. April.
Management. May.
Alternative Energy Sources. June.
Basic Engineering. September.
Research. October.
Construction. November.
Undersea Mining. December.

0883. MINI-MICRO SYSTEMS.
221 Columbus Ave., Boston, MA 02116.
Annual Subscription: $45. **Frequency:** Monthly.
Publisher: Cahners Publishing Co.
Advertiser Index: Every issue.
Indexed Online: Trade & Industry Index.
Special Issues:
Peripherals Digest—selection guide to computer peripheral products. Started 1982. Published as a separate issue. $4. April/November.
Technology Overview. $4. December.

0884. MINING CONGRESS JOURNAL.
1920 N Street, NW, Washington, DC 20036.
Annual Subscription: $20. **Frequency:** Monthly.
Publisher: American Mining Congress.
Advertiser Index: Every issue.
Editorial Index: Annual. Subject/Author. December.
Special Issues:
Review of the Year: Environment, Public Lands; Surface Mining; Safety and Health. $2. February.
American Mining Congress Convention Preview. $2. April.
Product Literature Guide. $2. June.
American Mining Congress International Mining Show Report. $2. December.

0885. MINING ENGINEERING.
Caller No. D., Littleton, CO 80127.
Frequency: Monthly.
Publisher: Society of Mining Engineers (American Institute of Mining, Metallurgical and Petroleum Engineers).
Advertiser Index: Every issue.
Editorial Index: Annual. Subject/Title/Author. December.
Indexed or Abstracted Online: CA Search; Compendex.
Special Issues:
Annual Review. Started 1949. $5. May.
SME Membership Directory. Started 1959. $100. July.
SME Fall Meeting Pre-Show Report. Started 1969. $3.50. 3 out of 4 years. September or October.

0886. MINING/PROCESSING EQUIPMENT.
13 Emery Ave., Randolph, NJ 07869.
Annual Subscription: $10. **Frequency:** Monthly.
Publisher: Gordon Publications.
Special Issues:
Drilling & Blasting Equipment. $2. February.
Coal Mining Equipment. $2. March/September.
Underground Mining. $2. May or July.
Bulk Material Handling. $2. June or April.
American Mining Congress International Coal Show Review. $2. Every 4 yrs. July (1984).
Mine Maintenance. $2. August or October.
Surface Mining. $2. September.
Grushing, Grinding, Screening Equipment. $2. October.
Pumps and Compressors. $2. November or September.
Product Equipment Review/Power and Power Distribution. $2. December.

0887. MOBILE/MANUFACTURED HOME MERCHANDISER.
203 North Wabash, Ste. 1819, Chicago, IL 60601.
Annual Subscription: $24. **Frequency:** Monthly.
Publisher: RLD Group, Inc.
Advertiser Index: Every issue.
Indexed Online: Trade & Industry Index.
Special Issues:
Supply Mart & Buyers Guide. Started 1968. $2. September.
Manufactured Housing Producers Guide. Started 1972. $2. November.

0888. MODERN AFRICA.
386 Park Ave. South, New York, NY 10016.
Annual Subscription: $40. **Frequency:** 6/yr.
Publisher: Johnston International Publishing Corp.
Advertiser Index: Every issue.
Special Issues:
Electrical Energy Systems in Africa. Started 1979. January/February.
Telecommunications in Africa. Started 1979. May/June.
Water Resources in Africa. Started 1979. May/June.
Construction in Africa. Started 1978. July/August.
Patterns of Progress—annual statistical round-up of economic performance by country. Started 1978. July/August.
Agriculture in Africa. Started 1978. September/October.
Business Equipment in Africa. Started 1981. November/December.

0889. MODERN ASIA.
386 Park Ave. South, New York, NY 10016.
Frequency: 11/yr.
Publisher: Johnston Int. Pub. Corp.
Advertiser Index: Every issue.
Special Issues:
Executive Aircraft. Started 1980. March.
Water Resources Technology. Started 1975. April.
Telecommunications. Started 1978. May.
Construction. Started 1975. June.
Patterns of Progress—annual regional economic review. Started 1975. July.
Agriculture. Started 1972. September.
Information Processing. Started 1981. October.

0890. MODERN BREWERY AGE (Brewers Edition—February/April/June/August/October/December; Wholesaler's Edition—January/March/May/July/September/November. Subscription to either includes weekly "Modern Brewery Age Tabloid.").
22 South Smith St., Norwalk, CT 06855.
Annual Subscription: $40. **Frequency:** 6/yr.
Publisher: Business Publications, Inc.
Advertiser Index: Every issue.
Special Issues:
Annual Statistical and Year End Roundup. Started 1960. $3. February/March.
Convention Issue: National Beer Wholesalers & Master Brewers Association. $3. August/September.
Transportation Issue. Started 1979. $3. November.
Blue Book—annual directory; lists all brewers & beer wholesalers, importers, statistics, legal regulations, etc. Started 1968. Published as a separate issue. $70. Not included in the subscription price. Spring.

0891. MODERN BULK TRANSPORTER.
1602 Harold St., Houston, TX 77006.
Annual Subscription: $15. **Frequency:** Monthly.
Publisher: Tunnell Publications Inc.
Advertiser Index: Every issue.
Special Issues:
Tank Cleaning Directory. Started 1980. $2. March.
Gross Revenue Report. Started 1965. $2. May.
Fuel Oil/Propane. $2. September.
Tank Truck Buyers Guide. Started 1978. $2. October.
Truck Buying Specifications. $2. November.

0892. MODERN CASTING.
Golf & Wolf Rds., Des Plaines, IL 60016.
Annual Subscription: $25. **Frequency:** Monthly.
Publisher: American Foundrymen's Society.
Advertiser Index: Every issue.
Editorial Index: Annual. Subject/Title/Author. January; available separately (free).
Indexed Online: Compendex.
Special Issues:
Forecast for the Foundry Industry. $3. January.
American Foundrymen's Society Casting Congress and CASTEXPO Preview, Review. Started 1938. $3. 2/yr. April/June.
Directory of Metalcasting and Foundry Consultants. Published as a separate issue. Free. Biennially. July.
Buyers Guide—for equipment manufacturers and suppliers for foundry industry. Started 1963. $15. November.
Census of World Casting Production. $3. December or January.

0893. MODERN DAIRY.
702 Weston Rd., Ste. 101, Toronto, Ontario, Can. M6N 3R2.
Annual Subscription: $23/14. **Frequency:** 6/yr.
Publisher: Maccan Publishing Co. Ltd.
Advertiser Index: Every issue.
Special Issues:
Buyers Guide. Started 1964. $5. March/April.

0894. MODERN GROCER.
370 Lexington Ave., New York, NY 10017.
Annual Subscription: $10. **Frequency:** Weekly.
Publisher: Grocers Publishing Co., Inc.
Special Issues:
Annual Market Report. Started 1945. $10. May.
Annual Directory and Buyers Guide. Started 1978. Published as a separate issue. $45. Not included in the subscription price. September.

0895. MODERN HEALTHCARE.
740 North Rush St., Chicago, IL 60611.
Annual Subscription: $35. **Frequency:** Monthly.
Publisher: Crain Communications, Inc.
Advertiser Index: Every issue.
Editorial Index: Quarterly. Subject/Title/Author. Quarterly.
Indexed Online: Management Contents.
Special Issues:
Economic Outlook/Environmental Assessment. Started 1974. $3. January.
Design & Construction Survey—includes a ranking of largest projects and client lists of completed and awarded projects—U.S. & Foreign. Started 1974. $3. February.
American College of Hospital Administrators' Young Administrator of the Year Award. $3. March.
Risk Management/Insurance. Started 1978. $3. April.
Multi-Unit Providers Survey—ranking and analysis of centrally managed multihospital systems; U.S. acute care hospitals; sponsoring multihospital systems; psychiatric hospitals; alternative services; nursing homes; home health care; health maintenance organizations; dialysis services; government hospitals. Started 1977. $3. May.
Financing Health Care. Started 1979. $3. June.
American Hospital Association Convention Preview. Started 1979. $3. July or August.
Contract Management & Shared Services Survey. Started 1977. $3. July or August.
Equipment Planning. Started 1977. $3. October.
The Cole Survey of Top Management Conpensation in Hospitals. Started 1969. $3. November or December.

0896. MODERN JEWELER.
7950 College Blvd., Shawnee Mission, KS 66201.
Annual Subscription: $12. **Frequency:** Monthly.
Publisher: Vance Publishing Corp.
Advertiser Index: Every issue.
Editorial Index: Annual. Title. January.
Special Issues:
The Modern Extra—Special report on jewelry trade shows. Started 1983. Published as a separate issue. 2/yr. March/September.

0897. MODERN MACHINE SHOP.
6600 Clough Pike, Cincinnati, OH 45244.
Annual Subscription: $24. **Frequency:** Monthly.
Publisher: Gardner Publications, Inc.
Advertiser Index: Every issue.
Editorial Index: Annual. Subject. December.
Indexed Online: Trade & Industry Index.
Special Issues:
NC/CAM Guidebook—directory of numerical control machines; control systems; computer-aided manufacturing systems; software services. Started 1970. Published as a separate issue. $5. January.

0898. MODERN MATERIALS HANDLING.
270 St. Paul St., Denver, CO 80206.
Annual Subscription: $45. **Frequency:** 18/yr.
Publisher: Cahners Publishing Co.
Advertiser Index: Every issue.
Indexed or Abstracted Online: ABI/Inform; Trade & Industry Index; Management Contents.
Special Issues:
Casebook/Directory—reference issue featuring actual case histories, manufacturers listings, company address, phone numbers. Published as a separate issue. $5. October.

0899. MODERN OFFICE PROCEDURES.
1111 Chester Ave., Cleveland, OH 44114.
Annual Subscription: $24/yr. **Frequency:** Penton/IPC Inc.
Advertiser Index: Every issue.
Editorial Index: Annual. Subject. January.
Indexed Online: Trade & Industry Index; Magazine Index; Management Contents; ABI/Inform.
Special Issues:
Buyers Reference—buyers guide to office equipment. Started 1972. $2.50. January.
Office Automation Update. Started 1981. $2.50. February.
Personal Computers. Started 1981. $2.50. May.
Furniture Trends. Started 1981. $2.50. June.
Personal Computer Users Profile. Started 1983. $2.50. 5/yr. June/July/October/November/December.
Furniture Industry Report. $2.50. September.
Telephone Systems Update. Started 1981. $2.50. October.
Reprographics. Started 1976. $2.50. November.
Electronic Office Design Awards. Started 1983. $2.50. December.

0900. MODERN PAINT & COATINGS.
6255 Barfield Rd., Atlanta, GA 30328.
Annual Subscription: $24. **Frequency:** Monthly.
Publisher: Communications Channels Inc.
Advertiser Index: Every issue.
Editorial Index: Annual. Subject/Title/Author. January.
Special Issues:
Annual Review & Forecast. $2.50. January.
Symposium & Paint Show Issue. $2.50. February.
Production Issue. $2.50. May.
Paint Red Book—directory of the paint and coatings industry. Started 1968. Published as a separate issue. $29.50. Not included in the subscription price. June.

Convention & Show Issue—Federation of Societies for Paint Technology. $2.50.   October.
Paint Show & Convention Wrap-Up. $2.50.   December.

0901. MODERN PLASTICS.
P.O. Box 602, Hightstown, NJ 08520.
Annual Subscription: $26.   **Frequency:** Monthly.
Publisher: McGraw-Hill Publications Co.
Advertiser Index: Every issue.
Editorial Index: Annual. Subject/Author. Varies.
Indexed or Abstracted Online: CIN; Trade & Industry Index.
Special Issues:
Materials & Markets Review—plastics performance for previous year; annual sales of individual resins; market growth.   Started 1960. $4.50.   January.
Machinery—special report on new processing developments; volume and dollar statistics on machinery sales.   Started 1960. $4.50.   April.
Show-in-Print—new products and equipment.   Started 1980. $4.50.   June.
U.S. National Plastics Exposition. $4.50.   Triennially. June.
Chemicals & Additives—special report reviews new materials; industry developments; new applications; sales statistics for previous year.   Started 1965. $4.50. September.
Modern Plastics Encyclopedia—950+ page hardcover; reference handbook for information on plastics materials and their formulations and properties, processing techniques, machinery and related equipment. Four sections: 1) textbook; 2) design guide; 3) engineering databank; 4) suppliers directory, with trade and brand names.   Started 1936.   Published as a separate issue. $34.95 (library edition).   October.

0902. MODERN PURCHASING.
Box 9100, Postal Stn. A, Toronto, Ontario, Can. M5W 1V5.
Annual Subscription: $44/21.   **Frequency:** 10/yr.
Publisher: Maclean Hunter Ltd.
Advertiser Index: Every issue.
Editorial Index: Annual. Subject. March.
Special Issues:
Office Products. $8/4.   April.
Packaging. $8/4.   April/July-August/November.
Value Analysis. $8/4.   May/September.
Transportation. $8/4.   3/yr.   June/October/December.
Materials Handling. $8/4.   September.
Materials Management. $8/4.   3/yr.   January-February/June/November.

0903. MODERN RAILROADS.
2020 West Oakton St., Park Ridge, IL 60068.
Annual Subscription: $40.   **Frequency:** Monthly.
Publisher: Enright/Reilly Publishing Co.
Advertiser Index: Every issue.
Special Issues:
Capital Spending Analysis/Man-of-the-Year Award.   Started 1964. $5.   January.
New Technology. $5.   February.
American Railway Engineering Association Show State of the Industry. $5.   March.
Signaling and Communications Show. $5.   March.
Multi-Modal Systems Report. $5.   April/November.
Amtrack Issue/Rail Transit Directory—city by city.   Started 1972. $5.   May.
Golden Freight Car Award—to RR with best freight marketing program. $5.   September.
Track and Roadway Show. $5.   October.
State of the Industry. $5.   December.

0904. MODERN VETERINARY PRACTICE.
P.O. Drawer KK, Santa Barbara, CA 93102.
Annual Subscription: $28.   **Frequency:** Monthly.
Publisher: American Veterinary Publications.
Advertiser Index: Every issue.
Editorial Index: Annual. Subject/Author. December.

0905. MONDAY REPORT ON RETAILERS.
777 Bay St., Toronto, Ontario, Can. M5W 1A7.
Annual Subscription: $249.   **Frequency:** Weekly.
Publisher: Maclean Hunter Ltd.
Editorial Index: Semi-Annual. Subject. January/July.
Special Issues:
Directory of Restaurant & Fast Food Chains in Canada.   Started 1980.   Published as a separate issue. $85.   Not included in the subscription price.   February.
Canadian Directory of Shopping Centres.   Started 1975.   Published as a separate issue. $175.   Not included in the subscription price.   July.
Directory of Retail Chains in Canada.   Started 1976.   Published as a separate issue. $159.   Not included in the subscription price.   October.

0906. MONEY.
P.O. Box 2519, Boulder, CO 80322.
Annual Subscription: $25.95.   **Frequency:** Monthly.
Publisher: Time Inc.
Editorial Index: Annual. Subject. January.
Indexed or Abstracted Online: ABI/Inform; Magazine Index; Trade & Industry Index; Management Contents.
Special Issues:
Best Investments for Coming Year. $2.95.   January.
How To Cut Your Taxes. $2.95.   February.
New York Stock Exchange Top Stocks of Previous Year. $2.95.   February.
American Stock Exchange and OTC Top Stocks of Previous Year.   Started 1982. $2.95.   March.
Top Mutual Funds.   Started 1983. $2.95.   April.
Focus on Cars. $2.95.   August.

0907. MONTHLY CATALOG OF UNITED STATES GOVERNMENT PUBLICATIONS.
Superintendent of Documents, U.S. Government Printing Office, Washington, DC 20402.
Annual Subscription: $125.   **Frequency:** Monthly.
Publisher: U.S. Government Printing Office.
Editorial Index: Monthly. Subject/Title/Author. Editorial Index in each issue, subject/author/title ($9.50 single copy); Cumulative Annual Index in December, subject/author/title, published separately, $27.
Special Issues:
Directory of United States Govenment Periodicals and Subscription Publications: Price List No. 36.   Published as a separate issue.   Free on request.   Not included in the subscription price.   Spring/Summer/Fall/Winter.

0908. MONTHLY WEATHER REVIEW.
45 Beacon St., Boston, MA 02108.
Annual Subscription: $120.   **Frequency:** Monthly.
Publisher: American Meteorological Society.
Editorial Index: Annual. Subject/Author. December.
Abstracted Online: MGA.

0909. MORTGAGE BANKING.
1125 15th St. NW, Washington, DC 20005.
Annual Subscription: $27.   **Frequency:** Monthly.
Publisher: Mortgage Bankers Association of America.
Advertiser Index: Every issue.
Editorial Index: Annual. Subject/Title/Author. January.
Indexed or Abstracted Online: Trade & Industry Index; Management Contents; ABI/Inform.
Special Issues:
Financial Institutions Buyers Guide.   Started 1983.   Published as a separate issue. $2.50.   April.
Mortgage Bankers Association of America Convention. $2.50.   October.

0910. THE MOTHER EARTH NEWS.
P.O. Box 70, Hendersonville, NC 28791.
Frequency: 6/yr.
Publisher: The Mother Earth News, Inc.
Editorial Index: Subject/Title/Author. Vols. 1-60 available separately for $20; updates issued irregularly.

0911. MOTOR.
555 W. 57 St., New York, NY 10019.
Annual Subscription: $12. **Frequency:** Monthly.
Publisher: The Hearst Corporation.
Special Issues:
  Motor Handbook—a reference guide for repairs and servicing; includes specifications for almost every make, year, and model of cars, light-trucks, etc. Published as a separate issue. $5. March or April.

0912. MOTOR/AGE.
Chilton Way, Radnor, PA 19089.
Annual Subscription: $12/yr. **Frequency:** Monthly.
Publisher: Chilton Co., Inc.
Advertiser Index: Every issue.
Indexed Online: Trade & Industry Index.
Special Issues:
  Tool & Equipment Buyers Guide. Started 1970. $2.50. March.
  Who's Who—directory of Big "I" Show (International Automotive Service Industries). Published as a separate issue. $2.50. March.
  Dealer Services. Started 1977. $2.50. June.
  Technical Reference. Started 1979. $2.50. September.

0913. MOTOR IN CANADA.
1077 St. James St., Box 6900, Winnipeg, Manitoba, Can. R3C 3B1.
Annual Subscription: $18. **Frequency:** Monthly.
Publisher: Sanford Evans Communications Ltd.
Advertiser Index: Every issue.
Special Issues:
  Directory Issue. $2.50. February.
  Manitoba. $2.50. April.
  British Columbia. $2.50. June.
  Saskatchewan. $2.50. August.
  Alberta. $2.50. November.
  Manufacturers & Rebuilders Directory. $2.50. December.

0914. MOTORCYCLE PRODUCT NEWS.
P.O. Box 2338, Van Nuys, CA 91405.
Annual Subscription: $18. **Frequency:** Monthly.
Publisher: Freed Crown Lee Publishing, Inc.
Advertiser Index: Every issue.
Special Issues:
  Motorcycle Product News Trade Directory—buyers guide for motorcycle trade; products & services available from manufacturers and distributors & service centers. Started 1974. Published as a separate issue. $12. January.

0915. MOUNTAIN STATES BANKER.
912 Baltimore, Ste. 900, Kansas City, MO 64105.
Annual Subscription: $15. **Frequency:** Monthly.
Publisher: Mountain States Publishing Co.
Special Issues:
  Convention Reports: Colorado Bankers Association; New Mexico Bankers Association; Utah Bankers Association; Wyoming Bankers Association. Started 1982. $3. June or July.
  American Bankers Association Convention Report. $3. October or November.

0916. MULTI-HOUSING NEWS.
1515 Broadway, New York, NY 10036.
Annual Subscription: $30. **Frequency:** Monthly.
Publisher: Gralla Publications.
Advertiser Index: Every issue.
Editorial Index: Annual. Title. December.
Special Issues:
  Semi-Annual Housing Statistics. Started 1980. $3. January/July.
  Finance Directory. Started 1972. $3. February.
  Product and Services Directory. Started 1969. $3. July.
  Marketing Services Directory. Started 1982. $3. September.

0917. MUSEUM NEWS.
1055 Thomas Jefferson St., Rm. 428, Washington, DC 20007.
Annual Subscription: $20. **Frequency:** 6/yr.
Publisher: American Association of Museums.
Advertiser Index: Every issue.
Editorial Index: Annual. Subject/Author. August.
Special Issues:
  Annual Meeting: American Association of Museums. June.

0918. MUSIC TRADES MAGAZINES.
P.O. Box 432, Englewood, NJ 07631.
Annual Subscription: $10. **Frequency:** Monthly.
Publisher: Music Trades Corp.
Advertiser Index: Every issue.
Special Issues:
  Purchasers Guide to the Music Industries—directory of musical instrument manufacturers and wholesalers, trade associations, music publishers, etc. Started 1897. Published as a separate issue. $3. December.

0919. NC SHOP OWNER.
1221 Ave. of the Americas, New York, NY 10020.
Annual Subscription: $10. **Frequency:** Monthly.
Publisher: McGraw-Hill, Inc.
Advertiser Index: Every issue.
Special Issues:
  Shop-Owner's Buying Guide. $3. March.
  Tooling Round-up. $3. September.

0920. NFAIS NEWSLETTER.
112 South 16th St., Ste. 1130, Philadelphia, PA 19102.
Annual Subscription: $45. **Frequency:** Bimonthly.
Publisher: National Federation of Abstracting and Information Services.
Special Issues:
  Member Service Statistics Issue—statistics from 1958 to date on documents covered by NFAIS. Started 1974. $10. February.
  Miles Conrad Memorial Lecture Issue. Started 1975. $10. April.

0921. NOMDA SPOKESMAN.
810 Lively Blvd., P.O. Box 707, Wood Dale, IL 60191.
Annual Subscription: Free to members. **Frequency:** Monthly.
Publisher: National Office Machine Dealers Association.
Advertiser Index: Every issue.
Special Issues:
  Forecast. January.
  National Office Machine Dealers Association Convention. Published as a separate issue. June/July.
  Who's Who Directory. Published as a separate issue. September.

0922. NOPA SPECIAL REPORT.
301 N. Fairfax St., Alexandria, VA 22314.
Annual Subscription: $30. **Frequency:** Bimonthly.
Publisher: National Office Products Association.
Special Issues:
  NOPA Membership Directory and Buyers Guide. Published as a separate issue. $55/$12 (members). Not included in the subscription price. January.
  NOPA Convention Guide. $5.50. September.

0923. NRA NEWS.
311 First St., NW, Washington, DC 20001.
Annual Subscription: $125. **Frequency:** 11/yr.
Publisher: National Restaurant Association.
Editorial Index: Annual. Subject. February.
Special Issues:
  Quarterly Crest Report (Consumer Behavior). February/May/August/November.
  Annual Report on Size and Scope of Industry. June/July.
  Forecast. December.

0924. THE NATION.
P.O. Box 1953, Marion, OH 43305.

Annual Subscription: $35. **Frequency:** Weekly.
Publisher: The Nation.
Editorial Index: Semi-Annual. Subject/Title/Author. February/August.

0925. NATIONAL CIVIC REVIEW.
47 East 68th St., New York, NY 10021.
Annual Subscription: $25 (members)/10 (libraries only).
Frequency: 11/yr.
Publisher: National Municipal League.
Editorial Index: Annual. Subject/Author. February.

0926. NATIONAL DEFENSE.
1700 North Moore St., Ste. 900, Arlington, VA 22209.
Annual Subscription: $25. **Frequency:** 10/yr.
Publisher: American Defense Preparedness Association.
Advertiser Index: Every issue.
Editorial Index: Annual. Subject/Title/Author. March.
Special Issues:
Partners in Prepardness—defense industry capabilities of corporate members of ADPA. Started 1977. $4. May/June.
Directory Issue—includes Directory of ADPA Members (individual and corporate); procurement and R & D officials of all branches of the military; "think tanks"; and "honor roll" of corporate members. Started 1981. $4. October.

0927. NATIONAL DEVELOPMENT (published in two English editions, *National Development/ASIA* and *National Development/Middle East/Africa*, and one Spanish edition, *Dessarollo Nacional*.).
P.O. Box 5017, Westport, CT 06881.
Annual Subscription: $60. **Frequency:** 9/yr.
Publisher: Intercontinental Publications.
Advertiser Index: Every issue.
Special Issues:
International Road Federation Supplement. $10. January/February.
International Water Directory—manufactures of water equipment and supplies. $10. March.
International Power Directory. $10. June/July.
International Communications Directory. $10. September.

0928. NATIONAL FISHERMAN.
21 Elm St., Camden, ME 04843.
Annual Subscription: $18. **Frequency:** Monthly.
Publisher: Journal Publications Inc.
Advertiser Index: Every issue.
Editorial Index: Subject. May (in yearbook issue).
Indexed Online: Trade & Industry Index.
Special Issues:
Southern Fisheries. $1.95. February.
In-shore Fisheries. $1.95. April.
Yearbook—review plus theme article. Published as a separate issue. $4. May.
Fishing Gear. $1.95. August.
West Coast Supplement—mailed to West Coast subscribers. Monthly. Monthly.
Seafood Business Report. $1.95. Varies.

0929. NATIONAL GEOGRAPHIC.
17th and M Sts., NW, Washington, DC 20036.
Annual Subscription: $15. **Frequency:** Monthly.
Publisher: National Geographic Society.
Editorial Index: Semi-Annual. Subject/Title/Author. February or March/August or September.
Special Issues:
Cumulative Editorial Indexes Vol. I-1888-1946; Vol. II-1947-76 (out-of-print); Supplement-1977-82 (soft cover, $1.00). All include map index. Revised Vol. II-1947-1983 scheduled for publication mid-1984.
Map supplements. $1.90. Varies.

0930. NATIONAL GLASS BUDGET.
P.O. Box 7138, Pittsburgh, PA 15213.
Annual Subscription: $18. **Frequency:** 24/yr.
Publisher: LJV Incorporated.
Abstracted Online: CA Search.
Special Issues:
Raw Materials for GlassMaking. Started 1983. March.
Glass Factory Directory. Started 1912. Published as a separate issue. $10. Not included in the subscription price. April.
Glass Plant Engineering. Started 1983. May.
Glass Manufacturing Machinery. Started 1983. September.

0931. NATIONAL HOG FARMER.
1999 Shepard Rd., St. Paul, MN 55116.
Annual Subscription: Controlled circulation. **Frequency:** Monthly.
Publisher: Webb Co.
Special Issues:
American Pork Congress Issue. $1. February.
Pork Producer Buying Guide. Started 1975. Published as a separate issue. $1. November.

0932. NATIONAL MALL MONITOR.
2280 US 19 N, Ste. 264, Clearwater, FL 33515.
Annual Subscription: $45. **Frequency:** 6/yr.
Publisher: National Mall Monitor, Inc.
Advertiser Index: Every issue.
Editorial Index: Annual. Subject. November/December.
Special Issues:
Top 50 Shopping Center Managers/Top 10 Management Companies/Southeast Land Use. January/February.
Retail Tenant Directory—lists 3400 shopping mall retailers in 42 categories, including off-price and factory outlet. Includes sales volume & total square footage. Arranged geographically & alphabetically. Started 1977. Published as a separate issue. $125 (both volumes). Not included in the subscription price. 2/yr. March/September.
Top 50 Open Center Developers/Centers of Excellence/Southwest Land Use. March/April.
Renovations/Far West Land Use. May/June.
Top Retailers/Midwest Land Use. July/August.
Marketing/Demographics/Shopping Center Management Buyers Guide, Urban Edition. September/October.
Products & Services/Parking Systems & Services. November/December.

0933. NATIONAL PARKS.
1701 18th Street, NW, Washington, DC 20009.
Annual Subscription: $15. **Frequency:** Bimonthly.
Publisher: National Parks & Conservation Association.
Editorial Index: Annual. Subject/Author. November/December.
Special Issues:
Annual Report/Alaska Special Issue. Started 1981. $3. April.

0934. NATIONAL PETROLEUM NEWS.
950 Lee St., Des Plaines, IL 60016.
Annual Subscription: $36.50. **Frequency:** Monthly.
Publisher: Hunter Publishing Co.
Advertiser Index: Every issue.
Editorial Index: Semi-Annual. Subject. June/December.
Special Issues:
NPN Factbook Issue (compilation of oil marketing facts). Published as a separate issue. $35. June.

0935. NATIONAL REAL ESTATE INVESTOR.
6255 Barfield Rd., Atlanta, GA 30328.
Annual Subscription: $41. **Frequency:** Monthly.
Publisher: Communication Channels, Inc.
Advertiser Index: Every issue.
Special Issues:
Forecast Issue—conditions in leasing, financing, construction and investment trends. $3.75. February.
Directory Issue—includes annual salary survey. Started 1959. Published as a separate issue. $20. June.

Annual Review Issue—round-up real estate investment conditions in major cities. $3.75. November.

0936. NATIONAL SAFETY NEWS.
444 North Michigan Ave., Chicago, IL 60611.
Annual Subscription: $19 (members)/24 (nonmembers).
Frequency: Monthly.
Publisher: National Safety Council.
Advertiser Index: Every issue.
Editorial Index: Annual. Subject/Title/Author. December.
Special Issues:
  Equipment Buyer's Guide—safety equipment manufacturers & products listed. $2.35 members/$3.40 non-members. March.
  Fire Protection & Security Issue. $2.35 members/3.40 nonmembers. June.
  Safety Literature Supplement. Started 1970. $2.35 members/3.40 nonmembers. July.
  National Safety Council Congress Issue (show guide). Started 1978. $2.35 members/3.40 nonmembers. October.
  Literature/Catalog Issue—safety equipment. $2.35 members/3.40 nonmembers. December.

0937. NATIONAL UNDERWRITER PROPERTY AND CASUALTY.
420 East 4th St., Cincinnati, OH 45202.
Annual Subscription: $30. **Frequency:** Weekly.
Publisher: National Underwriter Co.
Indexed or Abstracted Online: ABI/Inform; Insurance Abstracts; Management Contents.
Special Issues:
  Convention Calendar and Planning Issue. $1.50. January/February.
  Domestic Market Report: California & Farwest; Midwest; East; South (one per issue). Started 1983. $1.50. January/April/August/December.
  Financial & Investment Review. Started 1982. $1.50. January or March.
  Review and Forecast. $1.50. January/December.
  Information Industry Report. $1.50. February.
  International Market Report: London & Europe; Pacific/Asia; North America; Third World (one per issue). $1.50. February/June/September/November.
  Captive Insurance Review. $1.50. March.
  Risk and Insurance Management Society Conference. $1.50. April or May.
  Risk Management Review. $1.50. April.
  Auto Insurance Review. $1.50. May.
  Property-Casualty Premium Ranking Tables. $1.50. May or June.
  International Brokerage Report. $1.50. June or July.
  National Association of Insurance Commissioners Conference. $1.50. June.
  National Association of Insurance Brokers Conference. $1.50. July.
  Insurance Marketing Review. $1.50. August.
  Loss Control and Safety Review. $1.50. August.
  Reinsurance Review. $1.50. August.
  Independent Insurance Agents of America Conference. $1.50. September or October.
  International Union of Marine Insurance Conference. $1.50. September or October.
  Marine Insurance Review. $1.50. September.
  Monte Carlo Rendezvous Conference. $1.50. September.
  National Association of Mutual Insurance Companies Conference. $1.50. September or October.
  Society of CPCU (Chartered Property and Casualty Underwriters) Conference. $1.50. September or October.
  Excess & Surplus Lines Review. $1.50. November.
  FYI (For Your Information) Annual Review. $1.50. November.
  National Association of Independent Insurers Conference. $1.50. November.
  Hemispheric Insurance Conference Report. $1.50. December.

0938. NATIONAL UTILITY CONTRACTOR.
1235 Jeff Davis, Ste. 606, Arlington, VA 22202.
Annual Subscription: $15. **Frequency:** Monthly.
Publisher: National Utility Contractors Association.
Special Issues:
  National Utility Contractor Association Convention Issue. $1.50. January.
  Buyers Guide—for utility construction industry. $1.50. October.
  Contractors' Library—product literature review. $1.50. December.

0939. NATION'S BUSINESS.
1615 H Street NW, Washington, DC 20062.
Annual Subscription: $22. **Frequency:** Monthly.
Publisher: Chamber of Commerce of the United States.
Special Issues:
  Economic Forecast. $2.25. January.
  Annual Report of the Chamber of Commerce of the United States. $2.25. May.

0940. NATION'S CITIES WEEKLY.
1301 Pennsylvania Ave., NW, Washington, DC 20004.
Annual Subscription: $80. **Frequency:** Weekly.
Publisher: National League of Cities.
Special Issues:
  Congressional Cities Conference. February.
  Congress of Cities Conference. November.

0941. NATION'S RESTAURANT NEWS.
425 Park Ave., New York, NY 10022.
Annual Subscription: $18. **Frequency:** 26/yr.
Publisher: Lebhar-Friedman.
Special Issues:
  Forecast & Trends. $1. January.
  2nd Tier Chains—just behind the top 100. $1. March.
  National Restaurant Association Show/Fine Dining Hall of Fame Awards (Top 10 Restaurants). Started 1980. $1. May.
  Top 100 Chains (Part 1: Annual Report; Part 2: Menu and Operational Analysis). $1. August.
  Top 25 Volume Restaurants. $1. September.
  MUFSO (Multi-Unit Food Service Operators) Conference. $1. October.
  Company Profile. $1. December.
  Bar Management Supplement. $1. Varies.
  Metropolitan Area Market Study. $1. Several times a year. Varies.

0942. NATURAL HISTORY.
P.O. Box 4300, Bergenfield, NJ 07621.
Annual Subscription: $15. **Frequency:** Monthly.
Publisher: American Museum of Natural History.
Editorial Index: Annual. Subject/Author. Available separately in March or April by request.
Indexed Online: Magazine Index.

0943. NEW ENGLAND ADVERTISING WEEK.
100 Boylston St., Boston, MA 02116.
Annual Subscription: $20. **Frequency:** Weekly.
Publisher: Same.
Special Issues:
  Annual Client-Agency Issue. Started 1965. $5. March.
  Complete Guide to New England Markets and Media. Started 1972. $15. December.

0944. NEW ENGLAND ECONOMIC INDICATORS.
600 Atlantic Ave., Boston, MA 02106.
Annual Subscription: Free. **Frequency:** Monthly.
Publisher: Federal Reserve Bank of Boston.
Editorial Index: Annual. Subject/Title. December.

0945. NEW ENGLAND ECONOMIC REVIEW.
600 Atlantic Ave., Boston, MA 02106.
Annual Subscription: Free. **Frequency:** 6/yr.
Publisher: Federal Reserve Bank of Boston.
Editorial Index: Annual. Subject/Title/Author. December.

0946. NEW ENGLAND REAL ESTATE JOURNAL.
P.O. Box 55, Accord, MA 02018.
Annual Subscription: $30. **Frequency:** Weekly.
Publisher: Same.
Special Issues:
 Connecticut Real Estate Journal—bound-in supplement published 4th week of each month. Monthly.
 Massachusetts Real Estate Journal—bound-in supplement published 1st week of each month. Monthly.
 Hartford County, Connecticut. Started 1982. Published as a separate issue. March.
 Shopping Center Report. Started 1970. $2.50. March.
 Economic Development Edition. Started 1966. Published as a separate issue. $2.50. April or May.
 Fairfield County, Connecticut. Started 1982. Published as a separate issue. April.
 Route I-495, Massachusetts. Started 1982. Published as a separate issue. May.
 Commercial & Office Space Edition. Started 1968. $2.50. July.
 Banking & Finance Report. Started 1981. $2.50. October.
 End of Year Review. Started 1965. $2.50. December.

0947. NEW EQUIPMENT DIGEST.
Penton Plaza, Cleveland, OH 44114.
Annual Subscription: $30. **Frequency:** Monthly.
Publisher: Penton/IPC Inc.
Advertiser Index: Every issue.
Editorial Index: Monthly. Subject.
Special Issues:
 Design. $3. February.
 Plant Operation & Maintenance. $3. March.
 Material Handling. $3. April.

0948. NEW JERSEY BUSINESS.
50 Park Place, Newark, NJ 07102.
Annual Subscription: $12. **Frequency:** Monthly.
Publisher: New Jersey Business and Industry Association.
Special Issues:
 New Jersey Business and Industry Association's Outlook Conference. $1. February.
 Industrial-Office Parks. Started 1959. $1. April.
 New Jersey Top 100 Employers. Started 1973. $1. May.
 New Jersey Business & Industry Association's Golf Day (largest amateur golf outing in nation). Started 1971. $1. September.

0949. NEW YORK MAGAZINE.
Box 2979, Boulder, CO 80322.
Annual Subscription: $32. **Frequency:** 50/yr.
Publisher: News Group Publications Inc.
Special Issues:
 Women's Fashion. $1.50. March/September.
 Interior Design. $1.50. April.
 Spring Travel. $1.50. April.
 Summer Entertaining. $1.50. May.
 Summer Pleasures/Double Issue. $3. July.
 Men's Fashion. $1.50. September.
 Fall Preview. $1.50. October.
 Holiday Entertaining. 1.50. November.
 Island Travel. $1.50. November.
 Christmas Gifts. $1.50. December.

0950. THE NEW YORK TIMES BOOK REVIEW.
229 West 43rd St., New York, NY 10036.
Annual Subscription: $22. **Frequency:** Weekly.
Publisher: The New Yok Times.
Editorial Index: A (and biweekly). Author.
Indexed or Abstracted Online: Information Bank.
Special Issues:
 Spring Preview. January.
 Religion. April.
 Spring Children's Books. April.
 Summer Reading. June.
 University Presses. June.
 Fall Preview. September.
 Business/Finance/Economy. October.
 Fall Children's Books. November.
 Christmas Books. December.

0951. NON-FOODS MERCHANDISING.
P.O. Box 1226, Darien, CT 06820.
Annual Subscription: $20. **Frequency:** Monthly.
Publisher: Charleson Publishing.
Special Issues:
 Housewares Focus (for supermarkets). January/July.
 GM (general merchandise) Focus (for supermarkets). April/October.
 HBA (health & beauty aids) Focus (for supermarkets). September.
 Food Brokers and Non Foods (for supermarkets). December.

0952. NONWOVENS INDUSTRY.
26 Lake St., P.O. Box 555, Ramsey, NJ 07446.
Annual Subscription: $26. **Frequency:** Monthly.
Publisher: Rodman Publishing Co.
Advertiser Index: Every issue.
Editorial Index: Annual. Subject/Title/Author. January.
Special Issues:
 Diaper Update. Started 1970. $3. January.
 Technical Association of the Pulp and Paper Industry Seminar. Started 1973. $3. April.
 Fabric Manufacturers Directory. Started 1971. June.
 Machinery Directory. Started 1971. $3. July.
 Fibers/Chemicals/Films Directory. Started 1979. $3. November.
 Year-End Wrap-Up/Forecast Issue. Started 1973. $3. December.

0953. THE NORTHERN MINER.
7 Labott Ave., Toronto, Ontario, Can. M5A 3P2.
Annual Subscription: $40. **Frequency:** Weekly.
Publisher: Northern Miner Press Ltd.
Special Issues:
 Hemlo Update—gold exploration. January.
 Metals—international markets. February.
 Exploration. March.
 Technology & Equipment. April.
 Drilling: Mining, Oil & Gas. May.
 Canadian Mines Handbook. Published as a separate issue. $25 hardcover/$22 paperback. Not included in the subscription price. June.
 Junior Mining. June.
 New Mining Projects. July.
 Underground and Open Pit Mining. August.
 International Mining. September.
 Gold and Silver. October.
 Annual Number—forecast. November.
 Capital Projects. December.

0954. NORTHWEST FARM EQUIPMENT JOURNAL.
P.O. Box 16-367, St. Paul, MN 55116.
Annual Subscription: $5. **Frequency:** 6/yr.
Publisher: Northwest Farm Equipment Journal.
Advertiser Index: December/August/April.
Special Issues:
 Buyers Manual Marketing Directory. $10. April.

0955. NUCLEAR NEWS.
555 North Kensington Ave., LaGrange Park, IL 60525.
Annual Subscription: $130. **Frequency:** Monthly.
Publisher: American Nuclear Society.
Advertiser Index: Every issue.
Editorial Index: Annual. Subject/Author. January.
Indexed Online: Compendex.
Special Issues:
 Buyer's Guide—lists nuclear power oriented products and services with companies identified. Alphabetical listing by nation; worldwide listing of nuclear power plants including locations, unit size, on line data and percentage of completion. Started 1969. Published as a separate issue. $57. March.

ANS Annual Meeting. Started 1974. Published as a separate issue. $13. April.
ANS Winter Meeting. Started 1973. Published as a separate issue. $13. September.

0956. THE NURSE PRACTITIONER: THE AMERICAN JOURNAL OF PRIMARY HEALTH CARE.
109 West Mercer, Seattle, WA 98119.
Annual Subscription: $23. **Frequency:** 10/yr.
Publisher: Vernon Publications Inc.
Editorial Index: Annual. Author. November/December.
Indexed or Abstracted Online: Index Medicus.

0957. NURSING HOMES.
4000 Albemarle St., Washington, DC 20016.
Annual Subscription: $25. **Frequency:** 24/yr.
Publisher: Heldref Publications.
Advertiser Index: Every issue.
Editorial Index: Annual. Title/Author. December.

0958. NURSING OUTLOOK.
555 West 57th St., New York, NY 10019.
Annual Subscription: $20. **Frequency:** 6/yr.
Publisher: American Journal of Nursing Co.
Editorial Index: Annual. Subject/Author. November/December.
Indexed Online: Medline.

0959. NUTRITIONAL SUPPORT SERVICES.
12849 Magnolia Blvd., North Hollywood, CA 91607.
Annual Subscription: $35 a year. **Frequency:** Monthly.
Publisher: Creative Age Publications.
Advertiser Index: Every issue.
Editorial Index: Annual. Title. December.

0960. OCEAN INDUSTRY.
P.O. Box 2608, Houston, TX 77001.
Annual Subscription: $15. **Frequency:** Monthly.
Publisher: Gulf Publishing Co.
Advertiser Index: Every issue.
Special Issues:
North Sea Report. February.
Offshore Technology Conference Preview plus International Report. Annualy. April.
Digest of Industry Technical Papers. Started 1983. May.
Subsea Operations. July.
Offshore Europe Conference plus Mid East & Mediterrean Report. August.
Directory of Marine Drilling Rigs. September.
Industry Facts & Forecasts. Started 1979. October.
New Technical Ideas & Equipment. December.

0961. THE OFFICE.
P.O. Box 1231, Stamford, CT 06904.
Annual Subscription: $30. **Frequency:** Monthly.
Publisher: Office Publications, Inc.
Advertiser Index: Every issue.
Editorial Index: Semi-Annual. Subject/Title. June/December.
Special Issues:
Annual Forum Issue/Buying Plans Survey. $4. January.
Buyers Guide: Desktop and Programmable Calculators. $4. February.
Buyers Guide: Micrographic Readers and Reader-Printers. $4. March.
Buyers Guide: Electronic Typewriters. $4. May.
Buyers Guide: Copying Equipment. $4. July.
Buyers Guide: Business (Mini) Computers. $4. October.
Buyers Guide: Word Processors/Dictating Machines. $4. November.
Buyers Guide: Moveable Partitions. $4. December.

0962. OFFICE ADMINISTRATION AND AUTOMATION.
51 Madison Ave., New York, NY 10010.
Annual Subscription: $19. **Frequency:** Monthly.
Publisher: Geyer-McAllister Publications, Inc.
Advertiser Index: Every issue.
Editorial Index: Annual. Subject. December.
Special Issues:
Automated Office Awards. $3.50. January.
"Offices of the year" awards. Started 1950. $3.50. May.
Telephone Systems. $3.50. August.
Comprehensive Software Update. $3.50. September or October.
Stand-Alone Word/Info Processing Systems. $3.50. November or October.
Copiers Review and Specifications and OAA Industry Source Guide (Directory). $3.50. December.

0963. OFFICE EQUIPMENT & METHODS.
777 Bay St., Toronto, Ontario, Can. M5W 1A7.
Annual Subscription: $60/22. **Frequency:** 10/yr.
Publisher: Maclean Hunter Ltd.
Advertiser Index: Every issue.
Editorial Index: Annual. Subject. December.
Special Issues:
Copy/Duplication Report. March.
Temporary Help Report. April.
Small Business Systems Report. May.
Office Environment Report. June.
In-Plant Printing Report. July/August.
Word Processing Report. September.
Records Management Report. October.
Integrated Office Report. November.
Buyers' Guide and Directory. $15. December.

0964. OFFICE PRODUCTS DEALER.
Hitchcock Building, Wheaton, IL 60187.
Annual Subscription: $35. **Frequency:** Monthly.
Publisher: Hitchcock Publishing Company.
Advertiser Index: Every issue.
Editorial Index: Annual. Subject/Title/Author. February.
Special Issues:
NEOCON Showcase—special section on National Exposition of Contract Interior Furnishings. Started 1981. May.
NOMDA Showcase—special section on National Office Machine Dealers Association annual convention & exhibition. June.
NOPA Showcase—special section on National Office Products Association annual convention & exhibition. September.
COMDEX Showcase—special selection on trade show and conference for computer dealers. Started 1982. November.
Annual Directory & Dealer Buying Guide. Started 1983. December.

0965. OFFSHORE.
P.O. Box 1260, Tulsa, OK 74101.
Annual Subscription: Free (Controlled). **Frequency:** 14/yr.
Publisher: Pennwell Publishing Co.
Advertiser Index: Every issue.
Editorial Index: Annual. Subject/Title. January.
Indexed Online: NEXIS.
Special Issues:
Southeast Asia/Rig Construction. January.
Marine Transportation Boat Census. March.
Offshore Technology Conference (OTC). May.
Deepwater Drilling. June.
Worldwide Exploration and Drilling. Published as a separate issue. June.
North Sea. September.
Offshore Buyer's Guide. Published as a separate issue. October.
Marine Construction. November.
Offshore Forecast. December.

0966. THE OIL DAILY.
850 Third Ave., New York, NY 10022.
Annual Subscription: $297. **Frequency:** Daily (business days).
Publisher: Whitney Communications Co.
Indexed or Abstracted Online: Information Bank; Trade & Industry Index.
Special Issues:
Gas Processors Association Meeting. $1.50. March.

National Petroleum Refiners Association Meeting. $1.50. March.
Society of Independent Gasoline Marketers of America Meeting. $1.50. April.
Offshore Technology Conference. $1.50. May.
Annual Giants Issue. $1.50. July.
Annual Midyear Economics Issue. $1.50. August.
World Petroleum Congress. $1.50. Annual. August/September.
Annual Winter Fuel Outlook. $1.50. September.
International Association of Drilling Contractors Meeting. $1.50. September.
Petroleum Equipment Institute Meeting. $1.50. September.
World Energy Conference. $1.50. September.
American Gas Association Meeting. $1.50. October.
American Institute of Chemical Engineers Meeting. $1.50. October.
American Petroleum Institute. $1.50. November.
Independent Petroleum Association of America Meeting. $1.50. November.
Annual International Energy Issue. $1.50. December.

0967. OIL & GAS JOURNAL.
P.O. Box 1260, Tulsa, OK 74101.
Annual Subscription: $31. **Frequency:** Weekly.
Publisher: PennWell Publishing Co.
Advertiser Index: Every issue.
Editorial Index: Annual. Subject/Author. February.
Abstracted Online: NEXIS; CIN; Trade & Industry Index.
Special Issues:
Pipeline Construction Survey/Forecast/Review. January.
Capital Spending Survey. February.
Annual Refining/Petrochemical/Production Numbers. March or April.
Worldwide Construction Report. April/October.
Offshore Report/API (American Petroleum Institute) Refining Report. May.
Exploration/Development USA. Started 1982. June.
Annual Gas Processing Number. July.
Midyear Forecast/Review. July.
Annual Pipeline Number. August.
Annual Drilling Issue. September.
Ethylene Report. September.
Annual Geophysical Report. October.
Independent Operations. October.
NPRA Index Issue. October.
Annual API Issue. November.
Pipeline Economics. November.
Worldwide Report. December.
Middle East Report. Irregular.

0968. OIL & GAS (OGD'S) DIGEST.
915 Antoine at Katy Fwy., Houston, TX 77024.
Annual Subscription: $39. **Frequency:** Monthly.
Publisher: OGD Publishing Co.
Advertiser Index: Every issue.
Special Issues:
Offshore Technology Conference (OTC) Report. April.
Forecast. December.

0969. OIL, GAS & PETROCHEM EQUIPMENT.
1421 South Sheridan, P.O. Box 1260, Tulsa, OK 74101.
Annual Subscription: $20. **Frequency:** Monthly.
Publisher: PennWell Publishing Co.
Advertiser Index: December.
Special Issues:
Energy Conservation Equipment & Services. $2. February.
Refining/Petrochem/Gas Processing Equipment & Services. $2. March.
Safety/OSHA Equipment & Services. $2. April.
Offshore Equipment & Services. $2. May.
Maintenance Equipment & Services. $2. June.
Filtration & Separation Equipment & Services. $2. July.
Heating & Cooling Equipment & Services. $2. August.
Drilling & Production Equipment & Services. $2. September.
Instrumentation & Controls for the Petroleum Industry. $2. October.
Pipeline Equipment & Services. $2. November.
Pumps & Accessories for the Petroleum Industry. $2. December.

0970. OIL PATCH.
P.O. Box 53574, Lafayette, LA 70505.
Annual Subscription: $20. **Frequency:** Monthly.
Publisher: Uppercase Publications Inc.
Advertiser Index: Every issue.
Special Issues:
Annual Equipment Guide/Forecast. $3. December.

0971. OILWEEK.
1015 Centre St. N., Ste. 200, Calgary, Ontario, Can. T2E 2P8.
Annual Subscription: $27. **Frequency:** Weekly.
Publisher: MacLean Hunter Ltd.
Advertiser Index: Every issue.
Editorial Index: Annual. Subject/Title. January or February.
Special Issues:
Natural Gas Report—lists all Canadian gas processing plants: location, capacities & cost. January.
Service and Supply Industry Report. January.
Annual Review and Forecast—complete statistical report on all sectors of industry. February.
Computer, Communications and Data Processing Report in Petroleum Industry. February.
Energy Equipment News. Published as a separate issue. February, April, September and November.
Service Industry Training Programs Report. February.
Atlantic Canada. March.
Oil Sands and Mining Report—includes coal, metals and minerals mining exploration activities of petroleum companies. March.
Canada Overseas Directory. Published as a separate issue. April.
Canada Society of Exploration Geophysicists Conference. April.
First Quarter Review and Forecast. April.
Pipeline Contractors Association of Canada Convention. April.
Canadian Chemical Conference. May.
Offshore Report. May.
Refinery Report and Petrochemical Processing Conference—annual survey of Canada's refining and petrochemical industries, including plant capacities, locations, planned expansions and additions, and marketing and demand projections. May.
Energy Report; includes nuclear, geothermal, coal gasification. June.
First Canadian Offshore Buyer's Guide—alpha listings of suppliers; Canadian branch offices/reps of foreign countries; breakdown by province; alpha product listings. Published as a separate issue. June.
Mid-Year Pipeline Report. July.
Mid-Year Review and Forecast. July.
Canadian Offshore Resources Exposition and Conference. August.
LNG Project Report. August.
New Products and Services. August.
Heavy Oil Report. September.
Petrochemical Report. September.
Petroleum Careers. September.
Geophysical Report. October.
Third Quarter Review and Forecast. October.
Annual Pipeline Forecast—includes foldout pipeline map, construction data, contract information. November.
Annual Report and Financial Issue. Started 1976. November.
Petroleum Marketing Report—statistics. November.
Annual Drilling and Service Rig Issue—includes drilling mud chart. December.
Year in Review. December.

0972. OPERATIONS RESEARCH.
428 East Preston St., Baltimore, MD 21202.
Annual Subscription: $90. **Frequency:** 6/yr.
Publisher: Operations Research Society of America.
Editorial Index: Annual. Subject/Author. November/December.

0973. OPPORTUNITY MAGAZINE.
6 North Michigan Ave., Ste. 1405, Chicago, IL 60602.
Annual Subscription: $12. **Frequency:** Monthly.
Publisher: Opportunity Press, Inc.
Advertiser Index: September & February.
Special Issues:
Product Guide & Directory Issue. Started 1960. $1.50. February.
Sales Training Issue. Started 1979. $1.50. June.
Marketing Issue. Started 1979. $1.50. September.

0974. OUTDOOR CANADA.
953A Eglinton Ave., East, Toronto, Ontario, Can. M4G 4B5.
Annual Subscription: $9.77. **Frequency:** 8/yr.
Publisher: Ron Kaighin.
Special Issues:
Outdoor Canada Fishing Annual. Started 1981. $2. April.

0975. OUTDOOR LIFE.
380 Madison Ave., New York, NY 10017.
Annual Subscription: $13.94. **Frequency:** Monthly.
Publisher: Times-Mirror Magazines, Inc.
Indexed Online: Magazine Index.
Special Issues:
Outdoor Life's Midwest Fishing Guide. Started 1977. Published as a separate issue. $2.50. Not included in the subscription price. February.
Outdoor Life's Southern Fishing Guide. Started 1978. Published as a separate issue. $2.50. Not included in the subscription price. February.
Outdoor Life's Deer and Big Game Annual—with state-by-state forecasts. Started 1982. Published as a separate issue. $2.50. Not included in the subscription price. August.

0976. OWNER OPERATOR.
P.O. Box 2030, Radnor, PA 19089.
Annual Subscription: $9. **Frequency:** 6/yr.
Publisher: Chilton Publications.
Advertiser Index: Every issue.
Special Issues:
Cost per Mile Analysis Update/Directory: Who's Who in Washington; Trucking Special Events; Income Tax Calendar. $2. January/February.
Buyers Guide—trucks and accessories. $2. March/April.
Annual Size, Weight, Reciprocity Guide—rules of the road for the 48 states. $2. May/June.
Truck and Major Component Guide—new trucks, axles, transmissions, engines, fifth wheels/Christmas Sweepstakes. $2. November/December.

0977. PMLA.
62 Fifth Avenue, New York, NY 10011.
Annual Subscription: $60 (institutions). **Frequency:** 6/yr.
Publisher: Modern Language Association.
Editorial Index: Annual. Author. October.
Indexed Online: MLA Bibliography.
Special Issues:
MLA International Bibliography—with author/subject index. Published as a separate issue. $500. Not included in the subscription price. January.
Directory. $35. September.
Convention Program. $20. November.

0978. PPI-PULP & PAPER INTERNATIONAL.
500 Howard St., San Francisco, CA 94105.
Annual Subscription: $45. **Frequency:** Monthly.
Publisher: Miller Freeman Publications.
Advertiser Index: Every issue.
Special Issues:
PPI International Pulp & Paper Directory. Started 1975. Published as a separate issue. $77. Not included in the subscription price. Biennially. June.
Annual Review—includes production and trade figures for all major paper—producing countries; also details on all market pulp suppliers and their products. Started 1959. Published as a separate issue. $20. July.

0979. PSA JOURNAL.
2005 Walnut St., Philadelphia, PA 19103.
Annual Subscription: $25. **Frequency:** Monthly.
Publisher: Photographic Society of America.
Advertiser Index: Every issue.
Editorial Index: Annual. Title. December.
Indexed Online: Magazine Index.
Special Issues:
Calendar Exhibitions. $2.50.
PSA Membership Directory. Started 1940. $2.50. Biennially (even years).
Techniques Supplement. $2.50.
Who's Who in Exhibition Photography. May.

0980. PACIFIC BANKER & BUSINESS.
109 West Mercer St., Seattle, WA 98119.
Annual Subscription: $15. **Frequency:** Monthly.
Publisher: Vernon Publications.
Advertiser Index: Every issue.
Editorial Index: Annual. Subject/Title. December.
Special Issues:
Blue Chart Issues—analysis of bank and savings and loan performance in Alaska, Arizona, California, Hawaii, Idaho, Montana, Nevada, Oregon, Utah and Washington. $2. March/April/September/October.

0981. PACIFIC BUILDER & ENGINEER.
109 Mercer St., C19081, Seattle, WA 98119.
Annual Subscription: $14. **Frequency:** 24/yr.
Publisher: Vernon Publications.
Special Issues:
Forecast. $5. January.
CONEXPD (Construction Equipment Exposition & Road Show). $5. Every 6 yrs. February.
Buyer's Guide & Directory. $10. March.
Sewer & Water. $5. May.
Trucks. $5. November.

0982. PACIFIC TRAVEL NEWS.
274 Brannan St., San Francisco, CA 94107.
Annual Subscription: Free. **Frequency:** Monthly.
Publisher: Pacific Area Travel Association.
Advertiser Index: Every issue.
Editorial Index: Annual. Subject. January.
Special Issues:
Pacific Area Travel Association Preview & Review. April/May/June.
Pacific Hotel Directory & Travel Guide—hotel rates, transportation services, 32 countries in area. Published as a separate issue. $15. June/December.
American Society of Travel Agents Convention. September.
Orient. December.

0983. PACIFIC YACHTING.
202-1132 Hamilton St., Vancouver, British Columbia, Can.
Annual Subscription: $18.
Publisher: MacLean Hunter Ltd.
Advertiser Index: Every issue.
Special Issues:
Services Directory. Started 1981. Published as a separate issue. $2.25. October.

0984. PACKAGE ENGINEERING.
270 St. Paul St., Denver, CO 80206.
Annual Subscription: $35. **Frequency:** Cahners Publishing Co.
Advertiser Index: Every issue.
Editorial Index: Annual. Subject/Title. January.

Special Issues:
Packaging Encyclopedia—industry information, with educational articles. Published as a separate issue. $4. March.
Buyers Guide—machinery, container, material and supply sources. $4. October.

0985. PACKAGE PRINTING.
401 North Broad St., Philadelphia, PA 19108.
Annual Subscription: $16. **Frequency:** Monthly.
Publisher: North American Publishing Co.
Advertiser Index: Every issue.
Special Issues:
1983-84 Buyer's Guide & Directory. Started 1980. $10. December.

0986. THE PACKER.
P.O. Box 2939, Shawnee Mission, KS 66202.
Annual Subscription: $37.50. **Frequency:** Weekly.
Publisher: Agricultural Division of Vance Publishing Corp.
Special Issues:
North American Export (bound-in supplement). $1. March/June/August/December.
Produce Packaging and Materials Handling Digest. $1. April.
Supermarket Floral Guide—retailers buyers directory. $1. June.
Produce Availability and Merchandising Guide—source of supply directory. Started 1970. $1. July.
Focus (Review & Outlook). Started 1978. $1. December.
Produce & Floral Retailing (bound-in supplement). $1. Monthly.

0987. PAINTING & WALLCOVERING CONTRACTOR.
7223 Lee Highway, Falls Church, VA 22046.
Annual Subscription: $8. **Frequency:** Monthly.
Publisher: Painting & Decorating Contractors of America.
Advertiser Index: December.
Editorial Index: Annual. Subject/Author. December.
Special Issues:
Painting & Decorating Contractors of America Yearbook (listing all PDCA members). $1.50. July.

0988. PAPER, FILM & FOIL CONVERTER.
300 West Adams St., Chicago, IL 60606.
Annual Subscription: $32. **Frequency:** Monthly.
Publisher: Maclean Hunter Publishing Co.
Advertiser Index: Every issue.
Editorial Index: Annual. Subject. January.
Special Issues:
Vacuum Metallizing Packaging and Award Winners. Started 1980. $4. March.
Flexible Packaging & Folding Cartons and Award Winners. Started 1960. $4. April.
Trade Show-in-Print. Started 1975. $4. May.
Buyers Guide & Directory. Started 1956. $7. June.
Converting Machinery & Materials Show. $4. Biennially. October.
Packaging Machinery Manufacturers Institute Show. $4. Biennially. October.

0989. PAPER, PAPERBOARD AND WOOD PULP MONTHLY STATISTICAL SUMMARY.
260 Madison Ave., New York, NY 10016.
Annual Subscription: $220. **Frequency:** Monthly.
Publisher: American Paper Institute.
Special Issues:
Statistics of Paper, Paperboard and Wood Pulp—annual summary. Published as a separate issue. $175. Not included in the subscription price. September.

0990. PAPER SALES.
One East 1st St., Duluth, MN 55802.
Annual Subscription: $10. **Frequency:** Monthly.
Publisher: Harcourt, Brace Jovanovich Inc.
Advertiser Index

Special Issues:
Paper Yearbook. Started 1943. Published as a separate issue. $50. Not included in the subscription price. June.
National Paper Trade Association Convention/Exhibitions. October.

0991. PAPER TRADE JOURNAL.
133 East 58th St., New York, NY 10022.
Annual Subscription: $19. **Frequency:** 24/yr.
Publisher: Vance Publishing Corp.
Advertiser Index: Every issue.
Editorial Index: Annual. Subject/Title. January.
Abstracted Online: CIN.
Special Issues:
American Paper Institute Paper Week Issue. $2. March.
Technical Association of the Pulp & Paper Industry (TAPPI) Meeting. $2. March.
Papermaker's Conference Issue. $2. April.
Top 50 Paper Companies. Started 1975. $2. June.
Chemical Survey of Pulp & Paper Industry. Started 1976. $2. August.
Focus on Economics for Pulp/Paper. Started 1977. $2. December.
Papermaker of Year. Started 1976. $2. December.

0992. PAPERBOARD PACKAGING.
120 West 2nd St., Duluth, MN 55802.
Annual Subscription: $11. **Frequency:** Monthly.
Publisher: Harcourt, Brace, Jovanovich, Inc.
Advertiser Index: Every issue.
Editorial Index: Annual. Subject. December.
Special Issues:
Buyers Forecast. $3. January.
Statistics. $3. August or September.
Official Container Directory—buyers guide with boxplant listings. Published as a separate issue. $45 (for 2 issues). Not included in the subscription price. Spring/Fall.

0993. PARK MAINTENANCE.
P.O. Box 1936, Appleton, WI 54913.
Annual Subscription: $9. **Frequency:** Monthly.
Publisher: Madison Publishing Division.
Advertiser Index: Every issue.
Editorial Index: Annual. Subject. December.
Special Issues:
Swimming Pool Issue with Buyers Guide. March.
Turf Research Issue. July.
Buyers Guide. October.

0994. PARKING.
2000 K Street, NW, Ste. 350, Washington, DC 20006.
Annual Subscription: $20. **Frequency:** Quarterly.
Publisher: National Parking Association.
Special Issues:
National Parking Association Convention—owners and operators of off-street parking facilities. $5. April.

0995. PARKS & RECREATION.
3101 Park Center Dr., Alexandria, VA 22302.
Annual Subscription: $8/15 (nonmembers). **Frequency:** Monthly.
Publisher: National Recreation and Park Association.
Advertiser Index: Every issue.
Editorial Index: Annual. Subject/Title/Author. January.
Special Issues:
Buyers Guide—companies supplying products and services to private and governmental park and recreation agencies. January.
Trends—new developments in programming and products in the park and recreation field. May.
NRPA Congress Issue. September.

0996. PASSENGER TRANSPORT.
1225 Connecticut Ave., Washington, DC 20036.
Annual Subscription: $36/yr. **Frequency:** Weekly.

Publisher: American Public Transportation Association.
Editorial Index: Semi-Annual. Subject/Title. January/July (available separately on request; free to subscribers).

0997. PATIENT CARE.
16 Thorndal Cir., Darien, CT 06820.
Annual Subscription: $42. **Frequency:** 22/yr.
Publisher: Patient Care Communications, Inc.
Editorial Index: S; Cumulative. Subject. June/December, Cumulative index every 5 years by subject. Last index (1978-82) in December 1982.

0998. PENSION WORLD.
6255 Barfield Rd., Atlanta, GA 30328.
Annual Subscription: $37. **Frequency:** Monthly.
Publisher: Communication Channels, Inc.
Advertiser Index: Every issue.
Editorial Index: Annual. Subject/Title/Author. January.
Special Issues:
 ERISA Compliance Calendar. Started 1977. $3.50. January.
 Common Stock Analysis of Bank Pooled Pension Funds. Started 1972. $3.50. May.
 Directory of Insurance Co. Employee Benefits Services. Started 1980. $3.50. July.
 State Retirement Systems Survey. Started 1974. $3.50. August.
 Real Estate Portfolio Manager Directory. Started 1978. $3.50. September.
 Directory of Professional Benefits Administration Firms. $3.50. October or November.
 Directory of Master and Directed Trust Services. Started 1976. $3.50. December.

0999. PENSIONS & INVESTMENT AGE.
740 Rush St., Chicago, IL 60611.
Annual Subscription: $60. **Frequency:** 26/yr.
Publisher: Crain Communications.
Special Issues:
 Top 1000 Pension Funds Ranked by Total Assets—includes profiles of top 200 funds; special rankings for top 25 corporate funds; top 25 public funds; top 10 union funds. $3. January.
 Corporate Finance Directory. Started 1984. $2.50. February or March.
 Microcomputer Products & Services for Treasury Management. Started 1984. $2.50. February or March.
 P.I.P.E.R. (Pensions and Investments Performance Evaluation Report) Index—survey of 200 pooled equity and fixed income accounts of banks and insurance companies. $2.50. March/May/August/November.
 Directory of Investment Advisers—(rankings and profiles of over 600 banks, insurance companies and investment counselors; includes top 25 realty advisers; top 25 foreign advisers; top 25 master trustees; indexes by advisers, type & geographic location. $3.50. April.
 Annual Report Finder—Free corporate reports. $2.50. May.
 Directory of International Investment Advisers—profiles of 90 companies; ranking of top 20 advisers. $2.50. May.
 Master Trust/Custodian Banks Directory—ranking & profile of top U.S. & Canadian firms. $2.50. June.
 Cash Management Market Directory—includes profiles of largest cash management banks and consultants; associations and calendar of events. Started 1983. $2.50. July.
 Survey of Pension Fund Statistics and Corporate Financial Statistics as Reported in Annual Reports of Fortune 100 Companies. Started 1983. $2.50. July.
 Directory of Canadian Investment Advisers—profiles of over 50 firms; ranking of top 10. $2.50. August.
 Directory of Investment Management Consultants. $2.50. August.
 Survey of Cash Management Banks—cash managers of the 2000 largest U.S. non-financial corporations. Started 1981. $2.50. August.

 Directory of Real Estate Advisers—profiles of over 100 firms; rankings of top 10 equity, mortgage and foreign funds advisers. $2.50. Annual. September.
 Institutional Brokerage Research Survey—poll of chief investment officers at 500 largest investment institutions on the quality of Wall Street Research. $2.50. Annual. September.
 Microcomputer Products & Services for Investment Managers. Started 1983. $2.50. Annual. October.
 Review and Outlook. $2.50. December.

1000. PERSONNEL ADMINISTRATOR.
30 Park Dr., Berea, OH 44017.
Annual Subscription: $30. **Frequency:** Monthly.
Publisher: American Society for Personnel Administration.
Advertiser Index: Every issue.
Editorial Index: Annual. Subject/Author. December.
Indexed or Abstracted Online: Management Contents; Trade & Industry Index; Predicasts.
Special Issues:
 American Society For Personnel Administration Conference Issue. $4. June.

1001. PERSONNEL JOURNAL.
P.O. Box 2440, Costa Mesa, CA 92626.
Annual Subscription: $34. **Frequency:** Monthly.
Publisher: A. C. Croft, Inc.
Advertiser Index: Every issue.
Editorial Index: Annual. Subject/Author. December.
Indexed Online: Predicasts; Management Contents.

1002. PEST CONTROL TECHNOLOGY.
4012 Bridge Ave., Cleveland, OH 44113.
Annual Subscription: $18. **Frequency:** 13/yr.
Publisher: GLE Inc.
Advertiser Index: Every issue.
Editorial Index: Annual. Title/Author. April.
Special Issues:
 Buyer's Guide and Pesticide Label Book. Started 1982. Published as a separate issue. $1.50. April.

1003. PET AGE.
207 South Wabash, Chicago, IL 60659.
Annual Subscription: $25. **Frequency:** Monthly.
Publisher: H. H. Backer Associates.
Advertiser Index: Every issue.
Special Issues:
 Pet Industry Spring Market Trade Show. $2.50. March.
 The Directory—trade associations in the pet industry. $45. September.
 Pet Industry Christmas Market Trade Show. $2.50. October.

1004. THE PET DEALER.
567 Morris Ave., Elizabeth, NJ 07208.
Annual Subscription: $14. **Frequency:** Monthly.
Publisher: Howmark Publishing Corp.
Advertiser Index: Every issue.
Special Issues:
 Industry Outlook. Started 1979. $3.50. January.
 Annual Purchasing Guide. Started 1972. $28. April.
 Annual Store Management Section. Started 1977. $3.50. June.
 Survey of Pet Shops/Stores. Started 1977. $5. December.

1005. PETFOOD INDUSTRY.
Sandstone Bldg., Mount Morris, IL 61054.
Annual Subscription: $8. **Frequency:** 6/yr.
Publisher: Watt Publishing Co.
Advertiser Index: Every issue.
Special issues:
 Directory of Private Label Manufacturers. $5. January/February.
 Yearbook/Buyers Guide. $5. May/June.
 Pet Food Institute Convention. September/October.

1006. PETROLEUM ENGINEER INTERNATIONAL.
P.O. Box 1589, Dallas, TX 75221.
Annual Subscription: $16. **Frequency:** 15/yr.
Publisher: Energy Publications.
Editorial Index: Annual. Subject/Title/Author. March.
Special Issues:
  Rig Locator. $3.   February.
  Deep Well Report/Land Rig Locator/Ocean Technology Report. $3.   March.
  Downhole Tools and Technology. $3.   April.
  Offshore Report. $3.   May.
  Energy Operations and Equipment Forecast. $3.   July.
  Drilling Technology Report/Land Rig Locator. $3.   September.
  European Offshore Report/Offshore Rig Locator. $3.   October.
  Offshore Operations Report. $3.   November.

1007. PETROLEUM EQUIPMENT.
P.O. Box 360, Whitehouse, NJ 08888.
Annual Subscription: $15. **Frequency:** 6/yr.
Publisher: Publex Corp.
Special Issues:
  Petroleum Equipment Institute Show Issue.   Started 1979. $3.   October.

1008. PETS/SUPPLIES/MARKETING.
One East First Street, Duluth, MN 55802.
Annual Subscription: $16. **Frequency:** Monthly.
Publisher: Harcourt Brace Jovanovich Inc.
Advertiser Index: Every issue.
Editorial Index: Annual. Subject/Title/Author. November.
Indexed Online: Trade & Industry Index.
Special Issues:
  Annual Industry Statistical Report. $2.   June.
  Annual Directory and Buying Guide—listings of product manufacturers/importers and livestock suppliers; pet supply wholesalers and their coverage by states. $45.   December.

1009. PHI DELTA KAPPAN.
P.O. Box 789, Bloomington, IN 47402.
Annual Subscription: $20. **Frequency:** M 10/yr.
Publisher: Phi Delta Kappa.
Editorial Index: Annual. Author. June.
Indexed Online: Magazine Index; ERIC.
Special Issues:
  Annual Gallup Poll of Public Attitudes Toward the Public Schools.   Started 1969. $2.50.   September.

1010. PHILANTHROPY MONTHLY.
P.O. Box 989, New Milford, CT 06776.
Annual Subscription: $72. **Frequency:** 11/yr.
Publisher: Non-Profit Report, Inc.
Editorial Index: Annual. Subject/Title/Author. January.
Special Issues:
  Survey of State Laws Regulating Charitable Solicitations. Published as a separate issue. $96.   Not included in the subscription price.   Annually w/supplements.   January.
  United Way Survey of Funds.   February or March.
  Philanthropy Monthly's Policy Conference Preview.   Started 1977.   September or October.
  Distinguished Service to Philanthropy Award.   Started Y.   December.
  Legal Alert for Charitable Giving—review of state and federal decisions.   Published as a separate issue. $96 (for all). Not included in the subscription price.   Winter/Spring/Summer/Fall.

1011. PHOTO MARKETING.
3000 Picture Place, Jackson, MI 49201.
Annual Subscription: $10. **Frequency:** Monthly.
Publisher: Photo Marketing Association.
Advertiser Index: Every issue.
Editorial Index: Annual. Subject/Title. December (available separately on request).
Special Issues:
  Photo Marketing Association Convention Issue.   Started 1924. $2.   2/yr.   Varies Spring & Fall.

1012. PHOTOGRAMMETRIC ENGINEERING AND REMOTE SENSING.
210 Little Falls St., Falls Church, VA 22046.
Annual Subscription: $35. **Frequency:** Monthly.
Publisher: American Society of Photogrammetry.
Advertiser Index: Every issue.
Editorial Index: Annual. Subject/Author. December and cumulative 1934-1979.
Special Issues:
  Complete Index to Photogrammetric Engineering and Remote Sensing, vols. I-XLV, 1934-1979.   Published as a separate issue. $15.
  Directory.   Started 1960. $10.   March.
  Yearbook—annual convention, awards, committee reports. Started 1960. $5.   July.

1013. PHOTOGRAPHIC TRADE NEWS.
101 Crossways Park West, Woodbury, NY 11797.
Annual Subscription: $6. **Frequency:** Twice a month.
Publisher: PTN Publishing Corp.
Special Issues:
  Forecast/Retailer of the Year. $2.   January.
  PTN Master Buying Guide and Directory.   Published as a separate issue. $10.   Not included in the subscription price.   January.
  State of the Industry Issue.   Started 1975. $2.   September.

1014. PHOTOMETHODS.
P.O. Box 5860, Cherry Hill, NJ 08034.
Annual Subscription: $15. **Frequency:** Monthly.
Publisher: Ziff-Davis Publishing Co.
Advertiser Index: Every issue.
Special Issues:
  Audiovisual Issue.   Started 1980. $1.50.   March.
  Focus: Directory Issue.   Started 1979.   December.

1015. PHOTOVIDEO.
777 Bay St., Toronto, Ontario, Can. M5W 1A7.
Annual Subscription: $19/16. **Frequency:** 8/yr.
Publisher: Maclean Hunter Ltd.
Advertiser Index: Every issue.
Special Issues:
  Buyers Guide—for photo/video trade.   Started 1970. $12.   April.

1016. THE PHYSICIAN AND SPORTSMEDICINE.
4530 W. 77th St., Edina, MN 55435.
Annual Subscription: $34. **Frequency:** Monthly.
Publisher: McGraw-Hill.
Advertiser Index: Every issue.
Editorial Index: Annual. Subject/Author. December.
Indexed Online
Special Issues:
  American College of Sports Medicine Show.   Started 1982. $4.   May.

1017. PHYSICS IN CANADA.
151 Slater St., Ste. 805, Ottawa, Ontario, Can. K1P 5H3.
Annual Subscription: $10. **Frequency:** 6/yr.
Publisher: Canadian Association of Physicists.
Special Issues:
  Congress Issue—abstracts of papers presented at C.A.P. annual convention.   May.

1018. PHYSICS TODAY.
335 East 45 St., New York, NY 10017.
Annual Subscription: $45. **Frequency:** Monthly.
Publisher: American Institute of Physics.
Advertiser Index: Every issue.
Editorial Index: Subject/Author. December.

1019. PIMA MAGAZINE.
2400 East Oakton St., Arlington Heights, IL 60005.
Annual Subscription: $24. **Frequency:** Monthly.
Publisher: Paper Industry Management Association.
Advertiser Index: Every issue.
Indexed Online: Predicasts.
Special Issues:
Pulp and paper mill catalog—includes Engineering Handbook section; buyers guide; statistics. Started 1923. Published as a separate issue. $3. January.
Membership Directory. Started 1944. Published as a separate issue. July.
Paper Industry Management Association Conference Issue—includes "Man of Year" award. $3. August.

1020. PIPE LINE INDUSTRY.
P.O. Box 2608, Houston, TX 77001.
Annual Subscription: $12. **Frequency:** Monthly.
Publisher: Gulf Publishing Company.
Advertiser Index: Every issue.
Editorial Index: Annual. Subject/Title/Author. Available separately on request.
Special Issues:
Construction Report & Forecast. $2. January.
Pipeline Catalog—product and service catalogs of industry suppliers. Indexed by manufacturers and product. Started 1955. Published as a separate issue. $20. Not included in the subscription price. October.

1021. PIPELINE.
Box 22267, Houston, TX 77027.
Annual Subscription: $5. **Frequency:** 7/yr.
Publisher: Oildom Publishing.
Advertiser Index: Every issue.
Special Issues:
Review and Forecast. Started Y. $3. January.
Telecommunications & Control. Started Y. $3. March.
Corrosion Control. Started Y. $3. April.
Alaska-Canada-Arctic Pipelines. Started Y. $3. June.
International Pipelines. Started Y. $3. August.
Annual Directory of Pipe Lines. Started Y. $30 (purchased separately). October.
Slurry Pipeline Issue. Started Y. $3. December.

1022. PIPELINE & GAS JOURNAL.
Box 1589, Dallas, TX 75221.
Annual Subscription: $12. **Frequency:** 14/yr.
Publisher: Energy Publications Div., Harcourt Brace Jovanovich.
Advertiser Index: Every issue.
Editorial Index: Annual. Title/Author. February.
Indexed Online: Trade & Industry Index.
Special Issues:
Construction Forecast. $2. January.
Corrosion and Pipe Protection. $2. February.
Maintenance & Operations Report. $2. March.
Offshore Pipeline Construction. $2. April.
Pipeline and Gas Distribution Buyers' Guide and Handbook. $7. April.
Gas Pipelines/Gas Distribution. $2. May.
Liquid and Slurry Pipelines. $2. June.
125th Anniversary Issue (1984)/New Product Review. $2. July.
P&GJ 500—top companies. $2. August.
Construction Innovations. $2. September.
International Pipeline Construction Forecast/American Gas Association Convention. $2. October.
Peakshaving/Underground Storage/LNG. $2. November.
Gas Distribution Report and Forecast. $2. December.

1023. PIPELINE & UNDERGROUND UTILITIES CONSTRUCTION.
3314 Mercer St., P.O. Box 22267, Houston, TX 77027.
Annual Subscription: $12. **Frequency:** Monthly.
Publisher: Oildom Publishing Co.
Advertiser Index: Every issue.
Special Issues:
Review & Forecast; Pipe Line Contractors Convention. $5. January.
Distribution Contractors Convention. $5. February.
Canadian Pipe Line Issue. $5. April.
Pipeline and Underground Utilities Construction Directory. $5. June.
Pipe Line Buyers Guide Issue. $5. August.
International Pipe Line Issue. $5. September.
ARCTIC Pipe Line Issue. $5. October.
Utility Pipe Line Issue. $5. November.

1024. PIT & QUARRY.
205 West Wacker Dr., Chicago, IL 60606.
Annual Subscription: $12. **Frequency:** Monthly.
Advertiser Index: Every issue.
Editorial Index: Annual. Subject. December.
Indexed Online: Trade & Industry Index.
Special Issues:
Outlook/Review. $2. January.
Lime and Agricultural Limestone. $1.50. May.
Cement Reports—new technology and plants, including international. $2. July.
Buyers Guide. $1.50. August.
Maintenance. $1.50. October.

1025. PLAN AND PRINT.
10116 Franklin Ave., Franklin Park, IL 60131.
Annual Subscription: $15. **Frequency:** Monthly.
Publisher: International Reprographic Association.
Advertiser Index: Irregular.
Editorial Index: Annual. Subject/Title. Available on request (bound volumes).
Special Issues:
American Institute for Design & Drafting—Convention. March.
International Reprographic Association Convention. April.
Product Directory. August.
Management. December.

1026. PLANNING.
1313 East 60th St., Chicago, IL 60637.
Annual Subscription: $29. **Frequency:** Monthly.
Publisher: American Planning Association.
Editorial Index: Annual. Subject. December.
Special Issues:
American Planning Association Conference Issue—topic is planning in city that hosts the conference. $3.50. February or March.

1027. PLANT ENGINEERING.
1301 South Grove Ave., Barrington, IL 60010.
Annual Subscription: $50. **Frequency:** 26/yr.
Publisher: Technical Publishing Co.
Advertiser Index: Every issue.
Indexed Online: Compendex; CA Search.
Special Issues:
Directory & Specification Catalog—a specifying catalog, product directory, and technical reference manual with indexes to products, manufacturers, and suppliers. Started 1966. Published as a separate issue. $35. March.
National Plant Engineering & Maintenance Show Preview. Started 1951. $3. March.
National Material Handling Show and Seminar Workshop Preview. Started 1968. $3. Biennially. April.
The Best of Plant Engineering—articles awarded the highest ratings by readers during the previous year are republished. Started 1977. $3. December.

1028. PLANT MANAGEMENT & ENGINEERING.
777 Bay St., Toronto, Ontario, Can. M5W 1A7.
Annual Subscription: $50/23. **Frequency:** Monthly.
Publisher: Maclean Hunter Ltd.
Advertiser Index: Every issue.
Special Issues:
Security Systems. Started 1980. $5. January.
Compressed Air. Started 1980. $5. February.

Plant Maintenance.   Started 1980. $5.   March.
Power Transmission.   Started 1980. $5.   May.
Health and Safety.   Started 1980. $5.   June.
HVAC Heating Ventillating and Air Conditioning.   Started 1980. $5.   July.
Plant Layout Design and Construction.   Started 1980. $5.   August.
Materials Handling.   Started 1980. $5.   September.
Energy Management.   Started 1980. $5.   October.
Pumps, Valves, Piped Systems.   Started 1980. $5.   November.
Process Equipment & Controls.   Started 1980. $5.   December.

1029. **PLANT/OPERATIONS PROGRESS.**
345 East 47th St., New York, NY 10017.
Annual Subscription: $20.   **Frequency:** Quarterly.
Publisher: American Institute of Chemical Engineers.
Editorial Index: Annual. Subject/Title/Author. October.

1030. **PLANT SERVICES.**
301 East Erie, Chicago, IL 60611.
Annual Subscription: $24.   **Frequency:** Monthly.
Publisher: Putman Publishing Company.
Advertiser Index: Every issue.
Special Issues:
Plant Engineering & Maintenance Show. $5.   March.
Heating, Ventilation & Air Conditioning. $5.   May.
Electrical Systems. $5.   June.
Fluid Handling. $5.   September.
Plant Utilities. $5.   October.
Power Transmission. $5.   December.

1031. **PLASTICS BUSINESS.**
443 Mt. Pleasant Rd., Toronto, Ontario, Can. M4S 2L8.
Annual Subscription: $35/25.   **Frequency:** 7/yr.
Publisher: Kerrwil Publications Ltd.
Advertiser Index: Every issue.
Special Issues:
Plast-Ex Show Issue & Directory. $5.   April/May.
New Products & Equipment. $5.   June/July.
Export Directory. $5.   August/September.
Plastics Design in Electrical/Electronic Products. $5.   October/November.
Industry Trends. $5.   December.

1032. **PLASTICS COMPOUNDING.**
1129 East 17th Ave., Denver, CO 80218.
Annual Subscription: $21.   **Frequency:** 6/yr.
Publisher: Industry Media, Inc.
Advertiser Index: Every issue.
Editorial Index: Annual. Subject/Author. November/December.
Special Issues:
Plastics Compounding Redbook—buyers guide for resin producers formulators and compounders.   Started 1981.   Published as a separate issue. $20.   October.

1033. **PLASTICS DESIGN FORUM.**
1129 East 17th Ave., Denver, CO 80218.
Annual Subscription: $18.   **Frequency:** 6/yr.
Publisher: Industry Media, Inc.
Advertiser Index: Every issue.
Editorial Index: Annual. Subject. November/December.
Special Issues:
Focus Issue.   Started 1981.   Published as a separate issue. $3.50.   Varies.

1034. **PLASTICS DESIGN & PROCESSING.**
17730 West Peterson Rd., Libertyville, IL 60060.
Annual Subscription: Free (qualified persons).   **Frequency:** 6/yr.
Publisher: Lake Publishing Corp.
Advertiser Index: Every issue.
Editorial Index: Annual. Title. December/January.
Special Issues:
Plastics Desk Manual—plastics materials, processes, and equipment.   Started 1980.   Published as a separate issue.   September/October.

1035. **PLASTICS ENGINEERING.**
#14 Fairfield Dr., Brookfield Center, CT 06805.
Annual Subscription: $24.   **Frequency:** Monthly.
Publisher: Society of Plastics Engineers.
Advertiser Index: Every issue.
Editorial Index: Annual. Subject/Author. December.
Special Issues:
ANTEC—abstracts of papers to be presented at Annual Technical Conference in May. $3.   March.
Additives. $3.   June.
Society of Plastic Engineers Directory (Sections & Divisions). $3.   October.
Society of Plastics Engineers Member Roster. $20.   December.

1036. **PLASTICS MACHINERY & EQUIPMENT.**
1129 East 17th Ave., Denver, CO 80218.
Annual Subscription: $30.   **Frequency:** Industry Media, Inc.
Advertiser Index: Every issue.
Editorial Index: Annual. Subject. December.
Special Issues:
Source Book for Extruders.   Started 1982.   Published as a separate issue. $20.   March.
Source Book for Injection Molders.   Started 1981.   Published as a separate issue. $20.   November.

1037. **PLASTICS TECHNOLOGY.**
633 Third Avenue, New York, NY 10017.
Annual Subscription: $30.   **Frequency:** Monthly.
Publisher: Bill Communications.
Advertiser Index: Every issue.
Editorial Index: Annual. Subject. December.
Abstracted Online: CIN.
Special Issues:
Manufacturing Outlook.   Started 1976. $3.   January.
Extrusion Survey. $3.   February.
Injection Molding Survey. $3.   April.
Compounding Ingredients. $3.   May.
Plastics Manufacturing Handbook & Buyers Guide.   Started 1967.   Published as a separate issue. $40.   June.
Government Regulation.   Published as a separate issue. $3.   July.
Auxiliary Equipment. $3.   October.

1038. **PLASTICS WORLD.**
P.O. Box 5391, Denver, CO 80217.
Annual Subscription: $40.   **Frequency:** Monthly.
Publisher: Cahners Publications.
Advertiser Index: Every issue.
Editorial Index: Annual. Subject/Title. March (Directory Issue).
Abstracted Online: Predicasts; Trade & Industry Index; CIN.
Special Issues:
Top 500 Plastics Processing Plants/50 Outstanding Materials of Year. $4.   January.
50 Outstanding Equipment Developments of Year. $4.   February.
Plastics World Directory—listing of plastic resins and additives by producer; processors by state; machinery suppliers, mold & die makers; trade names.   Started 1979.   Published as a separate issue. $25.   March.
Better Way Design Awards. $4.   May.
Building Construction Materials and Methods Review. $4.   July.
National Plastics Exposition. $4.   Triennially.   August (last issue 1982).

1039. **PLATING AND SURFACE FINISHING.**
1201 Louisiana Ave., Winter Park, FL 32789.
Annual Subscription: $30 (nonmembers).   **Frequency:** Monthly.
Publisher: American Electroplaters' Society.
Advertiser Index: Every issue.

Editorial Index: Annual. Subject/Author. December.
Indexed or Abstracted Online: CA Search; Compendex; Technical Data Digest; Bulletin Analytique.
Special Issues:
SUR/FIN: Annual Technical Conference and Exhibit of Surface Finishing. Started 1950. May.

1040. PLAY METER.
P.O. Box 24970, New Orleans, LA 70184.
Annual Subscription: $50. **Frequency:** 24/yr.
Publisher: Skybird Publishing Co. Inc.
Editorial Index: Annual. Subject. December.
Special Issues:
Directory—names & addresses of manufacturers, distributors, importers, and support companies for coin-operated amusement machine industry. $15. March.
Arcades. $4. May/June.
Buyers Guide. $4. October.
State of the Industry. $4. November.
Amusement & Music Operators Association Conference. $4. December/January.
Year in Review. $4. December.

1041. PLAYBOY.
919 North Michigan Ave., Chicago, IL 60611.
Annual Subscription: $22. **Frequency:** Monthly.
Publisher: Playboy Enterprises, Inc.
Editorial Index: Annual. Subject/Title/Author. Annual indexes, 1979-83, available separately for $5.95 each. Cumulative indexes 1974-78, $12; 1969-73, $12; 1953-68, $50.
Indexed Online: Magazine Index.
Special Issues:
Playmate Review. $3.50. January.
The Year in Sex (pictorial). $3.50. February.
Annual Music Survey. $3.50. April.
The Year in Movies. $3.50. May.
Pro Football Preview. $3.50. August.
Pigskin Preview. $3.50. September.
Annual Music Poll (Ballot)/Sex in Cinema. $3.50. November.
College Basketball Preview/Sex Stars of Year/Christmas Gift Guide. $3.50. December.

1042. PLAYS, THE DRAMA MAGAZINE FOR YOUNG PEOPLE.
8 Arlington St., Boston, MA 02116.
Annual Subscription: $15. **Frequency:** 8/yr.
Publisher: Plays, Inc.
Editorial Index: Annual. Subject/Title/Author. May.

1043. PLAYTHINGS.
51 Madison Ave., New York, NY 10010.
Annual Subscription: $16. **Frequency:** Monthly.
Publisher: Geyer-McAllister.
Advertiser Index: Every issue.
Indexed Online: Trade & Industry Index.
Special Issues:
January Hobby Show Issue. $3.50. January.
Toy Fair Issue. $8. February.
Regional Show Highlights. $3.50. March.
Playthings Directory. Started 1925. Published as a separate issue. $16. May.

1044. PLYWOOD & PANEL WORLD.
P.O. Box 2268, Montgomery, AL 36197.
Annual Subscription: $24. **Frequency:** Monthly.
Publisher: Hatton-Brown Publishers Inc.
Advertiser Index: Every issue.
Special Issues:
Annual Worldwide Directory & Buyer's Guide. Started 1979. $5. January.

1045. POLLUTION ENGINEERING.
1935 Shermer Rd., Northbrook, IL 60062.
Annual Subscription: $15. **Frequency:** Monthly.
Publisher: Pudvan Publishing.
Advertiser Index: Every issue.
Editorial Index: Annual. Subject/Title. December.
Abstracted Online: Pollution Abstracts.
Special Issues:
The Case for Computerization—special editorial supplement. Started 1984. $2. January.
Consultants/Services Telephone Directory. Started 1976. $10. May.
Environmental Products Telephone Directory. Started 1975. $10. October.
Specifiers Guide to Chemical Manufacturers. Started 1984. $5. November.
Annual EPA Report & Forecast. $2. December.

1046. POLLUTION EQUIPMENT NEWS.
8650 Babcock Blvd., Pittsburgh, PA 15237.
Annual Subscription: Free (qualified persons). **Frequency:** 6/yr.
Publisher: Rimbach Publishing Co.
Advertiser Index: Every issue.
Special Issues:
Water Quality Instrumentation. February.
Analytical Instrumentation/Groundwater Pollution Monitoring/Chem Pro Show/American Industrial Hygiene Conference/Powder & Bulk Solid Show. April.
Air Quality Instrumentation/Air Pollution Control Association/Hazardous Materials Management Conference. June.
Water Conditioning Equipment. August.
Air Pollution Abatement Products/Hazardous Wastes Management. October.
Catalog and Buyers Guide—by product, manufacturer, and catalog insert section. Started 1977. Published as a separate issue. November.
Valves, Pumps, pH Instruments/Annual Catalog Review. December.

1047. POOL INDUSTRY CANADA.
1450 Don Mills Rd., Don Mills, Ontario, Can. M3B 2X7.
Annual Subscription: $15/11. **Frequency:** Quarterly.
Publisher: Southam Communications Ltd.
Advertiser Index: Every issue.
Special Issues:
Directory Issue. $2. January.

1048. POOL & SPA NEWS.
3923 West 6th St., Los Angeles, CA 90020.
Annual Subscription: $9.50. **Frequency:** 25/yr.
Publisher: Leisure Publications.
Advertiser Index: Every issue.
Editorial Index: Annual. Subject. December.
Special Issues:
Directory—manufacturers & distributors in swimming pool & spa industry. Started 1969. Published as a separate issue. $14.75. January.
National Swimming Pool Institute Convention. $2.50. November.
Forecast. $2.50. December.

1049. POPULAR MECHANICS.
P.O. Box 10064, Des Moines, IA 50350.
Annual Subscription: $11.97. **Frequency:** Monthly.
Publisher: The Hearst Corporation.
Editorial Index: Annual. Subject. January.
Indexed Online: Magazine Index.
Special Issues:
Home Ideas Guide. Started 1972. $1.25. April.
Car Care Guide. Started 1973. $1.25. May/October.
Outdoor Living Guide. Started 1981. $1.25. June.
Home Energy Guide. Started 1977. $1.25. September.

1050. POPULAR PHOTOGRAPHY.
P.O. Box 2775, Boulder, CO 80302.
Annual Subscription: $13.97. **Frequency:** Monthly.
Publisher: Ziff-Davis Publishing Co.
Advertiser Index: Every issue.
Editorial Index: Annual. Subject/Author.
Indexed Online: Magazine Index.
Special Issues:
Photography Annual. Published as a separate issue. $3.50. June.

Photography Buyers Guide. Published as a separate issue. $3.50. Varies.

1051. POPULAR SCIENCE.
Boulder, CO 80302.
Annual Subscription: $13.94/yr. **Frequency:** Monthly.
Publisher: Times Mirror Magazines, Inc.
Advertiser Index: Irregular.
Editorial Index: Annual. Subject/Author. March (5-yr and 10-yr cumulative indexes from 1972 $5 and $10).
Indexed or Abstracted Online: Magazine Index; CompuServ.
Special Issues:
Cars, imported—buyers guide. Started 1980. February.
Outdoor Power Equipment. Started 1980. March.
Outdoor Recreation Equipment—camping, bicycles, mopeds, RVs. Started 1970. March.
Home Improvement Ideas—hardware products. Started 1978. 3/yr. May/September/October.
Home Heating Products. Started 1972. October.
Consumer Electronics. Started 1977. November.

1052. POULTRY DIGEST.
Sandstone Building, Mt. Morris, IL 61054.
Annual Subscription: $15. **Frequency:** Monthly.
Publisher: Watt Publishing Co.
Advertiser Index: Every issue.
Editorial Index: Annual. Subject. December.
Special Issues:
Who's Who in the Egg and Poultry Industries. Started 1929. Published as a separate issue. $45. Not included in the subscription price. June.

1053. POULTRY & EGG MARKETING.
P.O. Box 1338, Gainesville, GA 30503.
Annual Subscription: $12. **Frequency:** Monthly.
Publisher: Poultry & Egg News.
Advertiser Index: Every issue.
Special Issues:
Southeastern International Convention Issues. Started 1962. $2. January/February.
National Independent Poultry and Food Distributors Association Man-of-The-Year Award. $2. Annual. March.
Pacific Egg and Poultry Association Convention. $2. March.
Retail Merchandising of Eggs and Poultry. $2. April.
Poultry Distributor Directory. Started 1973. $2. Annual. May.
New Products. Started 1982. $2. June/December.
Egg Market Trends & Outlook. $2. July.
Processor-Further Processor Directory. Started 1981. $2. Annual. August.
Brand Name Marketing. $2. October.
Egg Marketing Directory. Started 1974. $2. Annual. November.

1054. THE POULTRY TIMES.
P.O. Box 1338, Gainesville, GA 30503.
Annual Subscription: $7. **Frequency:** Weekly.
Publisher: Gannett Co., Inc.
Advertiser Index: January.
Special Issues:
International Poultry Convention. Started 1956. $.50. 3/yr. January (two issues)/February.
New Products Marketing Showcase. Started 1975. $.50. April/October.
Outlook. December.

1055. POULTRY TRIBUNE.
Sandstone Building, Mt. Morris, IL 61054.
Annual Subscription: $15. **Frequency:** Monthly.
Publisher: Watt Publishing Co.
Advertiser Index: Every issue.
Special Issues:
Export-Import Opportunities. $1.50. September.

1056. POWER ENGINEERING.
1301 South Grove Avenue, Barrington, IL 60010.
Annual Subscription: $34. **Frequency:** Monthly.
Publisher: Technical Publishing Co.
Advertiser Index: Every issue.
Editorial Index: Annual. Subject/Title/Author. Published separately; free on request; January.
Special Issues:
New Generating Capacity: When, Where, and by Whom—summary of utility plans for all new generating capacity. Includes listing of ten leading utilities in committed new capacity, and listing of major consulting engineers and constructors with summary of their jobs. Started 1972. $4. April.
New Generating Plants. Complete listing of all new capacity planned by electric utilities, with major suppliers and consultants identified. Started 1969. Published as a separate issue. $4. Not included in the subscription price. April.

1057. POWER MAGAZINE.
P.O. Box 521, Hightstown, NJ 08520.
Annual Subscription: $13. **Frequency:** Monthly.
Publisher: McGraw-Hill Publishing Co.
Advertiser Index: Every issue.
Editorial Index: Subject. Available separately on request.
Indexed Online: Trade & Industry Index.
Special Issues:
Electric Utility Generation Planbook—workbook for engineers and consultants designing electric utility generating plants. Started 1973. Published as a separate issue. $10. Not included in the subscription price. April.
International Power Systems (published jointly with **Electrical World**). Started 1983. Published as a separate issue. $15. Not included in the subscription price. June.
Industrial Plant Energy Systems Guidebook—workbook for engineers designing and operating industrial plant energy systems. Started 1972. Published as a separate issue. $10. Not included in the subscription price. September or October.
Buyers Guide. Started 1982. $2. November.

1058. POWER TRANSMISSION DESIGN.
1111 Chester Ave., Cleveland, OH 44114.
Frequency: Monthly.
Publisher: Penton/IPC.
Advertiser Index: Every issue.
Editorial Index: Every 3 yrs. Subject. Irregular.
Indexed or Abstracted Online: Compendex, INSPEC.
Special Issues:
Power Transmission Handbook—engineering data; manufacturers' catalog; component directory; trade names; where-to-buy. Published as a separate issue. $25. Biennially (even years). January.
Product Specification Guide. Started 1961. $3. January.
Controls for Power Transmission Systems. Started 1974. $3. February.
Design Engineering Show Review. $3. March or April.
Distributor Special. Started 1979. $3. June.
Annual Prize Literature Awards. Started 1978. $3. December.

1059. PRACTICAL ACCOUNTANT.
964 Third Ave., New York, NY 10155.
Annual Subscription: $42. **Frequency:** Monthly.
Publisher: Institute for Continuing Professional Development, Inc.
Editorial Index: Annual. Subject/Author. January.
Indexed or Abstracted Online: ABI/Inform; Management Contents.
Special Issues:
Accountants Buying Guide—includes computer systems; applications software; word processors; accounting systems, forms & supplies; publishers; reference tables, etc. Started 1983. Published as a separate issue. $3.50. May.

1060. PRECIOUS GEM INVESTOR.
5870 Hunters Lane, El Sobrante, CA 94803.
Annual Subscription: $30. **Frequency:** 6/yr.
Publisher: United Lapidary Wholesalers.
Advertiser Index: Every issue.
Special Issues:
Gemstone Price Index. Started 1982. $5. Monthly. Monthly.

1061. PREMIUM/INCENTIVE BUSINESS.
1501 Broadway, New York, NY 10036.
Annual Subscription: $33. **Frequency:** Monthly.
Publisher: Gralla Publications.
Advertiser Index: Every issue.
Editorial Index: Annual. Subject. December.
Special Issues:
Directory of Premium Suppliers & Services. February.
Premium Incentive Show Planner. April.
Industry Report. July.
Business Gift Buying Guide. August.

1062. PRESSTIME.
Dulles International Airport, Box 17407, Washington, DC 20041.
Annual Subscription: $100 (nonmembers). **Frequency:** Monthly.
Publisher: American Newspaper Publishers Association Research Institute.
Editorial Index: Semi-Annual. Subject. January/July.

1063. PREVENTION MAGAZINE.
33 East Minor St., Emmaus, PA 18049.
Annual Subscription: $12.97. **Frequency:** Monthly.
Publisher: Rodale Press Inc.
Editorial Index: Annual. Subject. March.
Indexed Online: Magazine Index; Newsearch.

1064. PRICE WATERHOUSE REVIEW.
1251 Ave. of the Americas, New York, NY 10020.
Annual Subscription: Free (limited quantities). **Frequency:** Quarterly.
Publisher: Price Waterhouse & Co.
Editorial Index: Cumulative. Subject/Title/Author. 25-year cumulative index, 1955-80, available separately.

1065. PRINTING IMPRESSIONS.
401 North Broad St., Philadelphia, PA 19108.
Annual Subscription: $35. **Frequency:** Monthly.
Publisher: North American Publishing Co.
Advertiser Index: Every issue.
Special Issues:
Sheet-Fed Presses. $5. January.
Web Presses. $5. April.
Business Forms Presses. $5. May.
Graphic Arts Marketplace—directory of graphic arts equipment and suppliers. $40. July.
Phototypesetting Equipment. $5. August.

1066. PROCESSED PREPARED FOODS.
5725 East River Rd., O'Hare Plaza, Chicago, IL 60631.
Annual Subscription: $45. **Frequency:** Monthly.
Publisher: Gorman Publishing.
Advertiser Index
Indexed or Abstracted Online: Trade & Industry Index; Predicasts.
Special Issues:
National Food Processors Association Pre-Show. $5.50. January.
Capital Spending Update. $5.50. February.
New Products Contest-Retail. Started 1977. $5.50. May.
50 Largest Prepared Food Companies/Warehouse Directory. $5.50. July.
Ingredient Innovations. $5.50. August.
Research & Development Review/American Meat Institute Preview/Processor of the Year Award. $5.50. September.
New Products Contest-Food Service. $5.50. October.
Prepared Foods Trends and Statistics. $5.50. November.
Buyer's Guide. $19. December.

1067. PRODUCT MARKETING AND COSMETIC & FRAGRANCE RETAILING.
124 East 40 St., New York, NY 10016.
Annual Subscription: $35. **Frequency:** Monthly.
Publisher: U.S. Business Press.
Advertiser Index: Every issue.
Editorial Index: Annual. Subject/Title. December.
Indexed or Abstracted Online: AMI; Trade & Industry Index.
Special Issues:
Annual Advertising Expenditure Study/Consumer Expenditure Study. Started 1979. $25. August.
Department Store Retailer Profiles. $3. October.
Fragrance Forecasts. $3. November.

1068. PRODUCTS FINISHING.
6600 Clough Pike, Cincinnati, OH 45244.
Annual Subscription: $18. **Frequency:** Monthly.
Publisher: Gardner Publications, Inc.
Advertiser Index: Every issue.
Editorial Index: Annual. Subject. December.
Special Issues:
Products Finishing Directory—manufacturers and suppliers in metal and plastics finishing industry. Published as a separate issue. $6. October.

1069. PROFESSIONAL BUILDER.
270 St. Paul St., Denver, CO 80206.
Annual Subscription: $30. **Frequency:** Monthly.
Publisher: Cahners Publishing Co.
Advertiser Index: Every issue.
Indexed Online: Trade & Industry Index.
Special Issues:
Giants In Housing—financial/personal profile on America's builders with annual sales volume of $15 million and up; plus profile on building industry. Started 1969. $10. July.

1070. PROFESSIONAL FURNITURE MERCHANT.
9600 West Sample Rd., Coral Springs, FL 33065.
Annual Subscription: $20. **Frequency:** Monthly.
Publisher: Vista Publications.
Advertiser Index: Every issue.
Editorial Index: Annual. Subject/Title/Author. February.
Special Issues:
Winter Markets Issue. Started 1968. $4. January.
Annual Resource Directory. Started 1968. $8. February.
Spring Market Issue. Started 1968. $4. April.
Summer Markets Issue. Started 1968. $4. July.
Fall Market Issue. Started 1968. $4. October.

1071. THE PROFESSIONAL PHOTOGRAPHER.
1090 Executive Way, Des Plaines, IL 60018.
Annual Subscription: $22.10. **Frequency:** Monthly.
Publisher: PPA Publications & Events, Inc.
Advertiser Index: Every issue.
Editorial Index: Annual. Subject/Title/Author. December.
Special Issues:
Portrait Photography. $3.25. Not included in the subscription price. February.
Video Production & Marketing. $3.25. Not included in the subscription price. March.
Wedding Photography. $3.25. Not included in the subscription price. April.
Directory of Professional Photography—Photographers, Buyers, Suppliers, Studios. Started 1940. Published as a separate issue. $25. Not included in the subscription price. June.
Professional Photographers of America Convention. $3.25. Not included in the subscription price. June.
Commercial Photography. $3.25. Not included in the subscription price. August.
Industrial Photography. $3.25. Not included in the subscription price. November.

1072. PROFESSIONAL PILOT.
West Bldg., Washington National Airport, Washington, DC 20001.
Annual Subscription: $24. **Frequency:** Monthly.
Publisher: Queensmith Communications.
Advertiser Index: Every issue.
Special Issues:
  Helicopter Association of America Convention.   January.
  Fixed Base Operator Profile & Contest Ballot.   February.
  International Operations.   March.
  Salary Survey/Hanover Air Show Preview.   April.
  Regional Profiles (commuter lines).   May.
  FBO Directory and Contest Awards.   June.
  Turbo Props and Public Service Helicopters.   July.
  National Business Aircraft Association Convention.   September.
  Top 10 Regionals.   October.
  Jets of the 80's.   November.
  Recognition and Awards.   December.

1073. PROFESSIONAL SAFETY.
850 Busse Hwy., Park Ridge, IL 60068.
Annual Subscription: $25. **Frequency:** Monthly.
Publisher: American Society of Safety Engineers.
Advertiser Index: Every issue.
Editorial Index: Annual. Subject/Title/Author. January.

1074. PROFESSIONAL SANITATION MANAGEMENT.
1019 Highland Ave., Largo, FL 33540.
Annual Subscription: $30. **Frequency:** 6/yr.
Publisher: Environmental Management Association.
Advertiser Index: Every issue.
Editorial Index: Annual. Title/Author. December.
Special Issues:
  Sanitation Floor Care.   Started 1969.   February/March.
  Grounds Maintenance.   Started 1969.   April/May.
  Who's Who in Sanitation Management.   Started 1969. June/July.
  EMA National Conference Issue.   Started 1969.   August/September.
  Pest Management.   Started 1969.   October/November.
  Maintenance Cleaners & Chemicals.   Started 1969. December/January.

1075. PROGRESSIVE ARCHITECTURE.
P.O. Box 95759, Cleveland, OH 44101.
Annual Subscription: $25 (professionals)/36 (nonprofessionals). **Frequency:** Monthly.
Publisher: Reinhold Publishing.
Advertiser Index: Every issue.
Editorial Index: Annual. Subject. December.
Special Issues:
  Awards Issue.   Started 1954. $7.   January.
  Energy-Conscious Design Issue.   Started 1979. $7. April.
  Interior Design.   Started 1977. $7.   September.
  Preservation and Re-use.   Started 1972. $7. November.

1076. PROGRESSIVE GROCER.
P.O. Box 10246, Stamford, CT 06902.
Annual Subscription: $35. **Frequency:** Monthly.
Publisher: Maclean Hunter Media/Progressive Grocer.
Advertiser Index: Every issue.
Editorial Index: Annual. Subject. January.
Indexed Online: Foods Ad Libra; Trade & Industry Index; AMI.
Special Issues:
  Outstanding Independent Supermarkets. $3.50.   March.
  Annual Report of the Grocery Industry.   Started 1934. $25.   April.
  Product Usage Guide—annual product sales. $3.50. July.
  Marketing Guidebook—facts, figures, key personnel; market shares; company information; volume figures; demographics.   Published as a separate issue. $195. Not included in the subscription price.   October.
  Retail Equipment. $3.50.   December.

1077. PUBLIC ADMINISTRATION REVIEW.
1120 G St., NW, Ste. 500, Washington, DC 20005.
Annual Subscription: $40. **Frequency:** 6/yr.
Publisher: American Society for Public Administration.
Editorial Index: Annual. Subject/Title/Author. December.
Indexed or Abstracted Online: Trade & Industry Index; ABI/Inform; Management Contents.

1078. PUBLIC OPINION QUARTERLY.
52 Vanderbilt Ave., New York, NY 10017.
Annual Subscription: $28. **Frequency:** Quarterly.
Publisher: Elsevier Science Publishing Co.
Editorial Index: Annual. Subject/Author. Winter.
Indexed or Abstracted Online: AMI; PAIS.

1079. PUBLIC POWER.
2301 M St., NW, Washington, DC 20037.
Annual Subscription: $25. **Frequency:** 6/yr.
Publisher: American Public Power Association.
Advertiser Index: Every issue.
Editorial Index: Annual. Subject/Author. November/December.
Special Issues:
  Directory of local publicly owned electric utilities.   Started 1962.   Published as a separate issue. $20.   January/February.

1080. PUBLIC RELATIONS JOURNAL.
845 Third Ave., New York, NY 10022.
Annual Subscription: $28. **Frequency:** 13/yr.
Publisher: Public Relations Society of America.
Editorial Index: Annual. Subject. January.
Special Issues:
  The Year Ahead/Public Relations Society of America Conference Roundup. $3.   January.
  Directory Issue—membership roster.   Published as a separate issue. $35.   Not included in the subscription price.   September.

1081. PUBLIC RELATIONS REVIEW.
7100 Baltimore Blvd., Ste. 500, College Park, MD 20740.
Annual Subscription: $25 (individual)/33 (institution). **Frequency:** Quarterly.
Publisher: Communication Research Association, Inc.
Editorial Index: Annual. Subject/Title/Author. December.
Indexed Online: AMI; Management Contents.
Special Issues:
  Annual Bibliography of Public Relations—over 200 books, periodicals, abstracts, etc. Includes titles of dissertations and theses.   Started 1973. $7.   Winter.

1082. PUBLIC ROADS.
U.S. Government Printing Office, Washington, DC 20402.
Annual Subscription: $10. **Frequency:** Quarterly.
Publisher: U.S. Department of Transportation.
Editorial Index: Annual. Title/Author. June.

1083. PUBLIC UTILITIES FORTNIGHTLY.
1700 North Moore St., Ste. 2100, Arlington, VA 22209.
Annual Subscription: $72. **Frequency:** 26/yr.
Publisher: Public Utilities Reports, Inc.
Advertiser Index: Every issue.
Editorial Index: Semi-Annual. Subject. January/July.
Indexed Online: Trade & Industry Index; Legal Resource Index; Management Contents.
Special Issues:
  Utility Finance. $3.50.   February.
  Power. $3.50.   April.
  Electric. $3.50.   June.
  Telecommunications. $3.50.   September.
  Gas. $3.50.   October.

1084. PUBLIC WORKS MAGAZINE.
200 South Broad St., Ridgewood, NJ 07451.
Annual Subscription: $30. **Frequency:** Monthly.
Publisher: Public Works Journal Corporation.
Advertiser Index: Every issue.

Editorial Index: Annual. Subject/Author. January (published separately; included with subscription).
Indexed Online: Trade & Industry Index.
Special Issues:
Highway and Transportation. Published as a separate issue. January.
Roadside Maintenance/Erosion Control. Published as a separate issue. March.
Public Works Manual—catalog file on products, services and firms active in public works, including street and highway, water works, environmental waste control. Covers all phases of design, construction, operation and maintenance. Started 1937. Published as a separate issue. $10. April.
American Water Works Association Convention. Published as a separate issue. June.
County/Regional. Published as a separate issue. July.
Winter Preparedness. $2.50. August.
American Public Works Association Convention/Institute of Traffic Engineers Convention. Published as a separate issue. September.
Water Pollution Control Federation Convention. Published as a separate issue. October.

1085. PUBLISHERS WEEKLY.
205 East 42 St., New York, NY 10017.
Annual Subscription: $68. **Frequency:** Weekly.
Publisher: R. R. Bowker Co.
Advertiser Index: Spring Announcements, Fall Announcements.
Editorial Index: Semi-Annual. Subject. Usually February and August, available separately on request (free). An author index to book review of forthcoming books appears in second issue of each month.
Indexed Online: Trade & Industry Index.
Special Issues:
Bowker Memorial Lecture. $2. January.
Spring Announcements—with index to advertised books. $4.95. February.
Spring Children's Books/Bologna Book Fair. $4.95. February.
Annual Summary—U.S. book industry statistics, titles, prices, sales trends; year in review, fiction and non-fiction bestsellers (hard and paper). $2. March.
Spring Religious Books. $2. March.
Business Books. $2. April.
Paperback Summer Announcements. $2. April.
Sci-Tech Books. $2. April.
Summer Announcements. $2. April.
Association of American Publishers Meeting. $2. May.
National Association of College Stores Convention. $2. May.
National Book Awards. $2. May.
ABA Convention Issue. $4.95. June.
AAP Annual Statistics—Industry sales by book categories. $2. July.
AAUP Convention. $2. July.
ABA Convention Round-Up. $2. July.
American Association of University Presses Book Show. $2. July.
Fall Children's Books. $4.95. July.
Christian Booksellers Association Convention. $2. August.
Christmas Books Issue. $2. August.
Fall Announcements. $4.95. August.
International (Frankfurt) Book Fair Issue—includes statistics on international book trade. $4.95. September.
Religious Books. $2. September.
Spring Previews. $4.95. September.
Frankfurt Book Fair Round-Up. $2. November.
Books in Education. $2. December.
Scientific, Business, Professional & Technical Books Preview. $2. December.

1086. PULP & PAPER.
500 Howard St., San Francisco, CA 94105.
Annual Subscription: $35. **Frequency:** Monthly.
Publisher: Miller Freeman Publications.
Advertiser Index: Every issue.
Editorial Index: Annual. Subject/Author. December.
Indexed Online: Trade & Industry Index.
Special Issues:
Outlook/Survey of Capital Spending Plans by U.S. and Canadian Companies. $3.50. January.
Coating Annual/Register of Adhesives & Binders. $3.50. May.
Worldwide Roundup—country-by-country data. $3.50. August.
Annual Engineering Review. $3.50. September.
Annual Chemicals Review—usage, supplies, pricing. $3.50. October.
Post's Pulp & Paper Directory—includes U.S. & Canadian mills and converting plants; industry executives; producers; sales organizations; capacity and production statistics; associations, schools & information sources; mill maps for each state and province; buyers guide. Started 1975. Published as a separate issue. $65. Not included in the subscription price. October.
Buyers Guide—includes guidelines to product selection and application; directory of equipment and supplies; directory of chemicals; directory of technical and consulting services; directory of market pulp grades; trade names; manufacturers and suppliers. Started 1975. Published as a separate issue. $20. November.

1087. PULP & PAPER CANADA.
310 Victoria Ave., Ste. 201, Westmount, Quebec, Can. H3Z 2M9.
Annual Subscription: $28. **Frequency:** Monthly.
Publisher: Southam Communications Ltd.
Advertiser Index: Every issue.
Editorial Index: Annual. Title/Author. December.
Special Issues:
Convention Issue—Canadian Pulp and Paper Association (CPPA) Technical Section. Published as a separate issue. $3 (Can.)/5 (foreign). Annual. March.
Pulp and Paper Canada Annual and Directory. Published as a separate issue. $42 (Can.)/62 (foreign). Not included in the subscription price. November.

1088. PULP & PAPER JOURNAL.
777 Bay St., Toronto, Ontario, Can. M5W 1A7.
Annual Subscription: $48/25. **Frequency:** 9/yr.
Publisher: Maclean Hunter Ltd.
Advertiser Index: Every issue.
Editorial Index: Annual. Subject/Title/Author. November.
Special Issues:
Annual Forecast & Spending Plans. Started 1948. $15. May.
Directory/Desk Calendar. Started 1969. Published as a separate issue. $12. November.

1089. PURCHASING MAGAZINE.
270 St. Paul St., Denver, CO 80206.
Annual Subscription: $30. **Frequency:** 24/yr.
Publisher: Cahners Publishing Co.
Advertiser Index: Every issue.
Indexed or Abstracted Online: Management Contents; Trade & Industry Index.
Special Issues:
Report to Chief Executive Officer. $2. January.
Chemical Report. $2. February.
Valve Analysis—case studies and idea notebook for buyers. $2. March.
Metals Report. $2. May.
Design Report—changing technology's affect on design teams & source selection. $2. June.
Top Industrial Salesmen Awards. $2. August.
Industrial Distribution Report. $2. September.
Plant Maintenance Report. $2. November.
Salary Survey: Comprehensive study of compensation in the purchasing profession/Economic Forecast. $2. December.

1090. PURCHASING WORLD.
P.O. Box 1030, Barrington, IL 60010.
Annual Subscription: $46. **Frequency:** Monthly.
Publisher: Technical Publishing Co.
Indexed Online: ABI/Inform; Management Contents.
Special Issues:
Economic Forecast—includes specific industries. $4. January/July.
Business Systems Data File—office equipment, furniture, computers, copiers, electronic typewriters and facsimile equipment. Started 1982. $4. April/October.
Purchasing Salaries At Top 500 Industrial Firms. $4. September.
Purchasing Salaries At Second 500 Industrial and Smaller Firms. $4. October.

1091. QUALIFIED REMODELER.
8 South Michigan Ave., Chicago, IL 60603.
Annual Subscription: $30. **Frequency:** 10/yr.
Publisher: Qualified Remodeler, Inc.
Advertiser Index: Every issue.
Special Issues:
Energy. Started 1979. $2. May.
Custom Remodeling—Case Histories & Products. Started 1977. $2. August.
"The Leaders"—Remodeling Profile Series. Started 1979. $2. September.
5-Yr Remodeling Forecast. Started 1979. Published as a separate issue. $2. October.
Remodeling Design Awards. Started 1977. $2. October.
Annual New Products Guide. Started 1977. $5. November.

1092. QUALITY.
Hitchcock Building, Wheaton, IL 60189.
Annual Subscription: $45. **Frequency:** Monthly.
Publisher: Hitchcock Publishing Co.
Advertiser Index: Every issue.
Editorial Index: Annual. Title.
Special Issues:
Test & Measurement Equipment Buyers Guide. $4. July.

1093. QUARTERLY JOURNAL—COMPTROLLER OF THE CURRENCY.
Communications Division, Washington, DC 20219.
Annual Subscription: $50/yr. **Frequency:** Quarterly.
Publisher: Comptroller of the Currency.
Special Issues:
Comptroller's Report of Operations. Started 1982.
Enforcement Actions. Started 1982.

1094. QUARTERLY REVIEW.
33 Liberty Street, New York, NY 10045.
Annual Subscription: Free. **Frequency:** Quarterly.
Publisher: Federal Reserve Bank of New York.
Special Issues:
Annual Report of the Federal Reserve Bank of New York. Published as a separate issue. April.
Monetary Policy and Open Market Operations Review. Spring.
Treasury and Federal Reserve Foreign Exchange Operations Review. Spring.

1095. QUICK FROZEN FOODS.
7500 Old Oak Blvd., Middleburg Hgts., OH 44130.
Annual Subscription: $13. **Frequency:** Monthly.
Advertiser Index: Every issue.
Special Issues:
National Food Brokers Association Convention Report/Ethnic Foods Survey. $2. January.
Orange Juice Concentrates Report/Seafood Survey. $2. February.
Processors and Distributors Construction & Equipment Buying Plans. $2. March.
Directory of Frozen Food Processors. Published as a separate issue. $55. Not included in the subscription price. June.
Retailers Building/Buying Survey. $2. June.
Warehouse/Transportation Survey. $2. June.
Pizza Survey. $2. July.
Ingredients Issue. $2. September.
Frozen Food Almanac—statistics. $2. October or November.
Frozen Foods State of the Industry. $2. November or December.
National Frozen Food Convention Issue. $2. November.

1096. THE QUILL.
840 N. Lake Shore Dr., Suite 801W, Chicago, IL 60611.
Annual Subscription: $12. **Frequency:** 11/yr.
Publisher: Society of Professional Journalists—Sigma Delta Chi.
Special Issues:
Awards: Listing of Society's SDX Distinguished Service Awards and Other National Journalism Awards. Started 1960s. $1.25. June.

1097. QUILL & QUIRE.
56 The Esplanade, Ste. 213, Toronto, Ontario, Can. M5E 1A7.
Annual Subscription: $35. **Frequency:** Monthly.
Publisher: Key Publishers Co., Ltd.
Advertiser Index: Every issue.
Special Issues:
Backlist. January.
Canadian Publishers Directory. Started 1935. Published as a separate issue. $9.50. May/November.
Fall Announcement. September.
Education. October.
Book Manufacturing. November.
Book Collectors. December.

1098. RNM IMAGES.
1800 Oakton St., Des Plaines, IL 60018.
Annual Subscription: $30. **Frequency:** Monthly.
Publisher: Nickerson & Collins Co.
Advertiser Index: Every issue.
Special Issues:
Buyers Guide Directory—products and services in radiology and nuclear medicine. Started 1980. January.

1099. RPM WEEKLY.
6 BrentCliffe Rd., Toronto, Ontario, Can. M4G 3Y2.
Annual Subscription: $95 (first class); $75 (second class).
Frequency: Weekly.
Publisher: RPM Music Publications Ltd.
Advertiser Index: Every issue.
Editorial Index: Subject.
Special Issues:
Big Country Music Special Edition—Highlighting Big Country Awards. $1. September.
Canadian Music Industry Directory—(record companies, radio stations, etc.). Published as a separate issue. $15. Irregular.

1100. RQ.
50 East Huron St., Chicago, IL 60611.
Annual Subscription: $20. **Frequency:** Quarterly.
Publisher: Reference and Adult Services Division, American Library Association.
Advertiser Index: Every issue.
Editorial Index: Annual. Subject/Title/Author. Summer.
Indexed or Abstracted Online: LISA; ERIC; Magazine Index; Social Scisearch.

1101. RSC - REFRIGERATION SERVICE AND CONTRACTING.
1800 Oakton St., Des Plaines, IL 60018.
Annual Subscription: $16. **Frequency:** Monthly.
Publisher: Nickerson & Collins Co.
Advertiser Index: Every issue.
Editorial Index: Annual. Title. December.
Special Issues:
ASHRAE Show Issue. January.
Test Instruments. April.
Commercial/Industrial Retrofit. July.
Energy Management/Controls. September.

RSES Conference Report.   December.

1102. RSI - ROOFING, SIDING, INSULATION.
1 East First St., Duluth, MN
Annual Subscription: $16.   **Frequency:** Monthly.
Publisher: Harcourt, Brace, Jovanovich.
Advertiser Index: Every issue.
Special Issues:
Handbook of Single-Ply Roofing Systems.   Started 1982. Published as a separate issue. $11.95.   Not included in the subscription price.   January.
Directory and Buying Guide. $6.   April.

1103. RVBUSINESS.
29901 Agoura Rd., Agoura, CA 91301.
Annual Subscription: $12.   **Frequency:** Monthly.
Publisher: T. L. Enterprises, Inc.
Advertiser Index: Every issue.
Special Issues:
Pocket Directory of Recreational Vehicle Manufacturers and Distributors.   Published as a separate issue. $5.   Not included in the subscription price.   February.
Directory and Buyers Guide—lists recreational vehicle manufacturers; product categories and brand names; suppliers; supplier products; distributors and wholesalers; manufacturer's representatives; associations and special services.   Started 1972.   Published as a separate issue. $9.   December.

1104. RAILROAD MODEL CRAFTSMAN.
P.O. Box 700, Newton, NJ 07860.
Annual Subscription: $18.   **Frequency:** Monthly.
Publisher: Carstens Publications Inc.
Advertiser Index: Every issue.
Editorial Index: Annual. Subject/Title/Author. June.
Special Issues:
Planning Aids Showcase for FBO resale items (FBO—Fixed-base operations, ie., airport businesses offering flight training, aircraft sales, etc.).   Monthly.

1105. RAILWAY TRACK & STRUCTURES.
508 Birch St., Bristol, CT 06010.
Annual Subscription: $5.   **Frequency:** Monthly.
Publisher: Simmons-Boardman Pub. Corp.
Advertiser Index: Every issue.
Editorial Index: Annual. Subject/Title/Author. January.
Special Issues:
Preview of Year Ahead. $2.   January.
Vegetation Control—herbicides. $2.   February.
American Railway Engineering Association Convention. $2. March.
Grade Crossing Safety. $2.   May.
Track Subgrade Stabilizaion. $2.   June.
Track Contractor's Directory. $2.   July.
Railroad Tie Issue. $2.   August.
Convention Reports: American Railway Bridge & Building Association; Roadmasters & Maintenance-of-Way Association. $2.   October.

1106. THE REAL ESTATE APPRAISER AND ANALYST.
645 North Michigan Ave., Chicago, IL 60611.
Annual Subscription: $25.   **Frequency:** Quarterly.
Publisher: Society of Real Estate Appraisers.
Editorial Index: Annual. Subject/Author. December.
Indexed or Abstracted Online: Management Contents; Trade & Industry Index; ABI/Inform.

1107. REAL ESTATE FORUM.
30 East 42 St., New York, NY 10017.
Annual Subscription: $50.   **Frequency:** Monthly.
Publisher: Real Estate Forum Inc.
Advertiser Index: Every issue.
Special Issues:
Annual Review. $4.25.   January.
Corporate/Consulting—services & success stories. $4.25. March or April.
Shopping Centers—mall development, financing, etc. $4.25.   May.
International—foreign investment in U.S.; major overseas projects; Canadian real estate review. $4.25.   June.
Mid-Year Office Review—city-by-city analysis. $4.25. July.
Multi-Family Housing—apartment development and redevelopment trends; condo & co-op conversions. $4.25.   August.
Industrial-key sections of U.S. $4.25.   September.
Real Estate Financing/Mortgage Market. $4.25. October.
National Association of Realtors Convention/Suburban Office Report. $4.25.   November.

1108. REAL ESTATE NEWS.
720 South Dearborn St., Chicago, IL 60605.
Annual Subscription: $18.   **Frequency:** Weekly.
Publisher: James P. Sirois.
Advertiser Index: Annual.
Special Issues:
Annual "Forecast & Review".   Started 1945. $1. February.
Chicago Real Estate Board Annual Outing. $1.   July.

1109. REAL ESTATE REVIEW.
210 South St., Boston, MA 02111.
Annual Subscription: $44.   **Frequency:** Quarterly.
Publisher: Warren, Gorham & Lamont.
Editorial Index: Biennial. Subject/Title/Author. Winter.

1110. REALTY.
80-34 Jamaica Ave., Woodhaven, NY 11421.
Annual Subscription: $12.   **Frequency:** Biweekly.
Publisher: Leader Observer, Inc.
Special Issues:
Energy.   Started 1979. $1.50.   June.
Conversion, Maintenance & Modernization.   Started 1979. $1.50.   October.
Anniversary Issue.   Started 1950. $3.   December.

1111. REALTY AND BUILDING.
12 East Grand Ave., Chicago, IL 60611.
Annual Subscription: $20.   **Frequency:** Weekly.
Publisher: Realty and Building, Inc.
Advertiser Index: February and October.
Special Issues:
Annual Review/Outlook.   Started 1888. $.50. February.
The REHAB Market.   Started 1980. $.50.   April.
Office/Industrial/Commerical Market.   Started 1975. $.50.   June.
Chicago Real Estate Board Installation Issue.   Started 1945. $.50.   October.

1112. RECREATION CANADA.
333 River Rd., Ottawa, Ontario, Can. K1L 8B9.
Annual Subscription: $32 (U.S.)/$27 (Can.).   **Frequency:** 5/yr.
Publisher: Canadian Parks/Recreation Association.
Advertiser Index: Every issue.
Special Issues:
Leisure and the Elderly.   February.
Leisure Environments.   April.
Politics in Recreation.   July.
Marketing Recreation Services.   September.
Festivals.   December.

1113. REEVES JOURNAL, PLUMBING-HEATING-COOLING.
7335 Topanga Canyon Blvd., Canoga Park, CA 91303.
Annual Subscription: $20.   **Frequency:** 11/yr.
Publisher: Western Trade Publishing Co.
Advertiser Index: Every issue.
Special Issues:
Solar Special. $2.   April.
N.A.P.H.C.C. (National Association of Plumbing, Heating, Cooling Contractors) Convention. $2.   June.
Bath and Kitchen Products Directory. $2.   August.

1114. REFRIGERATED TRANSPORTER.
1602 Harold St., Houston, TX 77006.
Annual Subscription: $15. **Frequency:** Monthly.
Publisher: Tunnell Publications Inc.
Advertiser Index: Every issue.
Special Issues:
  (Truck) Power Guide. Started 1975. $2. October.
  Body, Trailer & Equipment Guide. Started 1976. $2. November.
  LTL Guide (Less-than-Trailer Load). Started 1972. $2. December.

1115. RENTAL EQUIPMENT REGISTER.
2048 Cotner Ave., Los Angeles, CA 90025.
Annual Subscription: $25. **Frequency:** Monthly.
Publisher: Miramar Publishing Co.
Advertiser Index: Every issue.
Editorial Index: Subject. Cumulative index, 1958-1982, $25.
Special Issues:
  American Rental Association Convention. Semiannual. January/February.
  Lawn and Garden Equipment Rentals. March.
  Product Directory and Buyers Guide. June.
  Contractor/Industrial Equipment Rentals. August.
  California Rental Association Convention. Semiannual. September/November.

1116. RENTAL PRODUCT NEWS.
1233 Janesville Ave., Ft. Atkinson, WI 53538.
Annual Subscription: $25. **Frequency:** 10/yr.
Publisher: Johnson Hill Press.
Advertiser Index: Every issue.
Special Issues:
  Rental Product News Showcase—annual product catalog/buyer's guide. Started 1979. $20. October.

1117. RESEARCH & DEVELOPMENT.
1301 South Grove Ave., Barrington, IL 60010.
Annual Subscription: $36. **Frequency:** Monthly.
Publisher: Technical Publishing Co.
Advertiser Index: Every issue.
Editorial Index: Annual. Subject/Author. December.
Indexed or Abstracted Online: Compendex; Information Bank.
Special Issues:
  R & D Funding and Expenditures. $4. January.
  R & D Telephone Directory—for buyers and specifiers of instrumentation, equipment, supplies, components, chemicals and materials. Product and company name listings. Published as a separate issue. $9. February.
  R & D Salary Survey. $4. March.
  New Research Laboratory Review. $4. May.
  Scientist of the Year—award in applied science. $4. October.

1118. RESEARCH QUARTERLY FOR EXERCISE AND SPORT.
P.O. Box 704, Waldorf, MD 20601.
Annual Subscription: $40. **Frequency:** Quarterly.
Publisher: American Alliance for Health, Physical Education, Recreation, & Dance.
Editorial Index: Annual. Subject/Title/Author. December; ten-year cumulative indexes covering 1930-1970.
Special Issues:
  AAHPERD Centennial Issue. $4. One time only. March 1985.

1119. RESORT MANAGEMENT.
4501 Mission Bay Dr., San Diego, CA 92109.
Annual Subscription: $15. **Frequency:** Monthly.
Publisher: Western Speciality Publications.
Special Issues:
  Annual Directory of 100 Leading Newspapers in Resort and Hotel Advertising—listings of rates, circulation, personnel, dates of special sections. Started 1957. $1.50. February.
  Resort Hotel Advertising Linage and Revenue for Top 25 U.S. Newspapers—and comparison w/previous year. Six-month and year-end (12-month) reports. Started 1957. $1.50. October/April.
  Annual Directory of Leading Consumer Magazines in Resort and Hotel Advertising—rates, circulation, personnel, special editions. Started 1957. $1.50. November.
  Resort and Hotel Advertising Linage and Revenue for All Consumer Magazines—and comparison w/previous year. Six-month and year-end (12-month) reports. Started 1957. $1.50. November/March.

1120. RESOURCES IN EDUCATION (RIE).
Government Printing Office, Washington, DC 20402.
Annual Subscription: $70. **Frequency:** Monthly.
Publisher: Educational Resources Information Center.
Editorial Index: Every issue. Subject/Author. Each issue has an index to abstracts, by Subject, Author, Institution, and Publication Type. A semiannual index is available separately. $21 for January-June and July-December; $12 for single issue.
Indexed or Abstracted Online: ERIC.

1121. RESPIRATORY CARE.
Box 35886, Dallas, TX 75235.
Annual Subscription: $30. **Frequency:** Monthly.
Publisher: American Association for Respiratory Therapy.
Advertiser Index: Every issue.
Editorial Index: Annual. Subject/Author. December.
Indexed or Abstracted Online: CA Search; Medline.
Special Issues:
  American Association for Respiratory Therapy Meeting. $3. October.

1122. RESTAURANT BUSINESS.
633 Third Ave., New York, NY 10017.
Annual Subscription: $40/mo. **Frequency:** 15/yr.
Publisher: Restaurant Business, Inc.
Advertiser Index: Every issue.
Indexed or Abstracted Online: Trade & Industry Index; Predicasts.
Special Issues:
  Turnaround Strategy—profiles of company strategies for profits. $5. January.
  Franchising in the Economy (summary of U.S. Department of Commerce Analysis). $10. March.
  Restaurant Business Leadership Awards. Started 1983. $5. May.
  Restaurant Growth Index—includes top 100 restaurant markets. Started 1968. $10. September.
  International Issue. $5. November.
  Presidents' Forecast. $5. December.

1123. RESTAURANT HOSPITALITY.
1111 Chester Ave., Cleveland, OH 44114.
Annual Subscription: $40. **Frequency:** Monthly.
Publisher: Penton/IPC, Inc.
Advertiser Index: Every issue.
Indexed Online: Trade & Industry Index.
Special Issues:
  Product Reference File (food service product listings). Started 1970. $4. January.
  Kitchen Design Awards. Started 1984. $4. February.
  Restaurant Hospitality 500 (500 top grossing restaurants-U.S.). Started 1976. $10. June.
  Composite Performance Index (chain profitability index). Started 1982. $4. July.
  Top 100 Chains. Started 1983. $4. August.
  State of the Industry Report. Started 1978. $4. September.
  Top of the Table Awards—most beautiful tables in American restaurants. Started 1965. $4. November.

1124. RESTAURANTS & INSTITUTIONS.
1350 East Touhy Ave., Des Plaines, IL 60018.
Annual Subscription: $50.
Publisher: Cahners Publishing Co.

Advertiser Index: Every issue.
Indexed Online: Trade & Industry Index.
Special Issues:
  Annual Report.   Started 1976. $4.   January or March.
  Culinary Olympics Cookbook. $4.   Biennially.   January.
  Job$ Survey: Food Service Salaries. $4.   January or March.
  Buyer's Guide—products & services for the food service industry. $20.   February.
  Menu Census—regional food preferences. $4.   March or June.
  Ivy Awards (restaurants inducted into the Society of Ivy). $4.   May.
  National Restaurant Association Convention Preview. $4.   May.
  Annual 400: Part 1: financial analysis of America's largest food services/lodging organizations.   Started 1966. $20.   July or August.
  Food Buying Trends. $4.   July or September.
  400 Part II: menu & marketing strategies. $20.   July or August.
  Next 100 Growth Chains. $4.   August or November.
  Tastes of America—consumer survey of eating-out habits & preferences.   Started 1981.   October.

1125. RETAIL CONTROL.
100 West 31st St., New York, NY 10001.
Annual Subscription: $20.   **Frequency:** 10/yr.
Publisher: National Retail Merchants Association.
Editorial Index: Annual. Subject/Author. December.

1126. REVIEW OF ECONOMICS AND STATISTICS.
35 New Street, Worcester, MA 01605.
Annual Subscription: $63.   **Frequency:** Quarterly.
Publisher: Department of Economics; Harvard University.
Editorial Index: Annual. Title/Author. November.
Indexed or Abstracted Online: Trade & Industry Index; Magazine Index; ABI/Inform; Management Contents.

1127. THE REVIEW OF SCIENTIFIC INSTRUMENTS.
335 East 45th St., New York, NY 10017.
Annual Subscription: $165.   **Frequency:** Monthly.
Publisher: American Institute of Physics.
Advertiser Index: Every issue.
Editorial Index: Every 5 yrs. Varies (last issued 1978).
Indexed or Abstracted Online: SPIN.

1128. REVIEW OF TAXATION OF INDIVIDUALS.
210 South St., Boston, MA 02111.
Annual Subscription: $58.   **Frequency:** Quarterly.
Publisher: Warren, Gorham & Lamont.
Editorial Index: Annual. Title/Author. Fall.

1129. REVIEW OF THE GRAPHIC ARTS.
7599 Kenwood Rd., Cincinnati, OH 45236.
Annual Subscription: $4.   **Frequency:** 9/yr.
Publisher: International Association of Printing House Craftsmen.
Editorial Index: Biennially (odd years). Subject. January.
Special Issues:
  Copy Preparation and Pre Press Update.   Started 1980.   March.
  Convention Preview.   Started 1960.   July.
  Plates and Press Update.   Started 1980.   September.
  Club Directory.   Started 1974.   October.
  Bindery, Finishing and Paper Update.   Started 1980.   November.

1130. REVIEW—FEDERAL RESERVE BANK OF ST. LOUIS.
Research Dept., P.O. Box 442, St. Louis, MO 63166.
Annual Subscription: Free.   **Frequency:** 10/yr.
Publisher: Federal Reserve Bank of St. Louis.
Editorial Index: Annual. Title/Author. December.
Special Issues:
  Agricultural Outlook.   February.
  Review of Federal Open Market Committee.   April or June/July.

1131. RIFLE.
P.O. Box 3030, Prescott, AZ 86302.
Annual Subscription: $13.   **Frequency:** 6/yr.
Publisher: Wolfe Publishing Co.
Advertiser Index: Every issue.
Editorial Index: A and biennial. Subject/Title/Author. November/December.

1132. RISK MANAGEMENT.
205 East 42nd St., New York, NY 10017.
Annual Subscription: $36.   **Frequency:** Monthly.
Publisher: Risk and Insurance Management Society, Inc.
Advertiser Index: Every issue.
Editorial Index: Annual. Subject. January.
Indexed or Abstracted Online: ABI/Inform; Management Contents.
Special Issues:
  Risk and Insurance Management Society Conference. $3.   June.

1133. RN MAGAZINE.
680 Kinderkamack Rd., Oradell, NJ 07649.
Annual Subscription: $19.   **Frequency:** Monthly.
Publisher: Medical Economics Co.
Advertiser Index: Every issue.
Editorial Index: Annual. Subject/Author. December.
Indexed Online: Trade & Industry Index.

1134. ROAD & TRACK.
1255 Portland Place, P.O. Box 5333, Boulder, CO 80321.
Annual Subscription: $17.94.   **Frequency:** Monthly.
Publisher: CBS Publications.
Advertiser Index: Every issue.
Editorial Index: Annual. Subject. December.
Indexed Online: Magazine Index.
Special Issues:
  Guide to Sports & GT Cars.   Started 1972.   Published as a separate issue. $2.95.   Not included in the subscription price.   January.
  Road Test Annual & Buyer's Guide.   Started 1968.   Published as a separate issue. $2.95.   Not included in the subscription price.   February.

1135. ROBOTICS TODAY.
P.O. Box 930, Dearborn, MI 48121.
Annual Subscription: $36.   **Frequency:** 6/yr.
Publisher: Society of Manufacturing Engineers.
Advertiser Index: Every issue.
Special Issues:
  Robots Show.   February.
  Sensor-based Robots.   June.
  Robotic Arc Welding.   August.
  Standardization in Robots.   October.
  Robotic Assembly.   December.

1136. ROCK & GEM.
17337 Ventura Blvd., Encino, CA 91316.
Annual Subscription: $12.   **Frequency:** Monthly.
Publisher: Miller Magazines, Inc.
Advertiser Index: Every issue.
Editorial Index: Annual. Subject. January.
Special Issues:
  Rockhound and Lapidary Handbook.   Started 1973. $1.75.   April.

1137. ROCK PRODUCTS.
300 West Adams St., Chicago, IL 60606.
Annual Subscription: $35.   **Frequency:** Monthly.
Publisher: Maclean Hunter Publishing Corp.
Advertiser Index: Every issue.
Editorial Index: Annual. Subject/Title/Author. December.
Special Issues:
  Buyers Guide. $5.   January.
  Cement Demographics. $3.   5/yr.   February/June/August/October/December.
  Rock & Concrete World — international supplement. $3.   February/May/August/November.
  International Cement. $5.   April.

Aggregates. $3. September or November.
Forecast. $3. December.

1138. ROLLING STONE.
P.O. Box 2983, Boulder, CO 80322.
Annual Subscription: $15.95. **Frequency:** 24/yr.
Publisher: Straight Arrow Publishers, Inc.
Editorial Index: Cumulative (1967-79). Subject.
Indexed Online: Magazine Index.
Special Issues:
Beatles Twentieth Anniversary. Started 1984. $1.75. One time only. February.
College Issues. $1.75. March/September.
Readers & Critics Music Poll. $1.75. March.
Top 100 Albums of Year. $2.50. December/January.

1139. ROTOR & WING INTERNATIONAL.
740 Rush St., Chicago, IL 60611.
Annual Subscription: $20. **Frequency:** Monthly.
Publisher: PJS Publications.
Advertiser Index: Every issue.
Special Issues:
Helicopter Association of America Convention. $2. January.
Annual International Buyers Guide. Published as a separate issue. $5. June.

1140. ROUGH NOTES.
1200 North Meridian, Indianapolis, IN 46204.
Annual Subscription: $8. **Frequency:** Monthly.
Publisher: The Rough Notes Co.
Advertiser Index: Every issue.
Indexed or Abstracted Online: Insurance Abstracts.
Special Issues:
Computers and Management Concepts. $1. January.
Excess, Surplus and Specialty Markets. $1. March.
Personal Lines. $1. May.
Collecting the Premium. $1. August.
Industrial and Corporate Accounts. $1. September.
The Insurance Market Place—reference guide to excess & surplus facilities, non-standard specialty lines and Lloyds of London representatives, aviation, marine and international coverages. Started 1962. Published as a separate issue. Free. September.
Service After A Loss; Claims Procedures. $1. October.
Life Insurance in the P/C Agency. $1. November.
Increasing Next Years' Business. $1. December.

1141. RUBBER & PLASTICS NEWS.
Command Building, Ste. 10, 34 North Hawkins Ave., Akron, OH 44313.
Annual Subscription: $28. **Frequency:** 26/yr.
Publisher: Crain Communications.
Editorial Index: Quarterly. Subject/Title. January/April/July/October.
Special Issues:
Urethanes. $1.25. April/October.
American Chemical Society, Rubber Division Meeting FAX Book (technical papers). $1.25. May/October.
Rubbicana—Buyers Guide of companies that supply materials, equipment & services to rubber product manufacturers in U.S. & Canada. Also: complete directory of U.S. & Canadian rubber manufacturers. $1.25. December.

1142. RUBBER WORLD.
1867 West Market St., Akron, OH 44313.
Annual Subscription: $19. **Frequency:** Monthly.
Publisher: Lippincott & Peto, Inc.
Advertiser Index: Every issue.
Editorial Index: Annual. Subject. February.
Indexed or Abstracted Online: CIN; Trade & Industry Index.
Special Issues:
Technical Service/Forecast. $3. January.
Blue Book—materials, compounding ingredients and machinery for rubber. Published as a separate issue. $50. Not included in the subscription price. February.
Custom Mixing. $3. February.
Machinery & Equipment. $3. July.
Chemicals & Materials. $3. October.
Wire & Cable. $3. November.

1143. RUDDER.
318 Sixth St., Annapolis, MD 21403.
Annual Subscription: $15.94. **Frequency:** Monthly.
Publisher: Petersen Publishing Co.
Advertiser Index: Every issue.
Special Issues:
Boat Show. $1.75. January.
Mid-Atlantic & Northeast Chartering. $1.75. March.
Fitting Out. $1.75. April.
Caribbean Chartering. $1.75. September.
Boat Show Preview. $1.75. October.

1144. RUNNER'S WORLD.
P.O. Box 366, Mountain View, CA 94042.
Annual Subscription: $14.95. **Frequency:** Monthly.
Publisher: Runners World Magazine Co.
Advertiser Index: Every issue.
Indexed Online: Magazine Index.
Special Issues:
Runners World Annual. Started 1980. Published as a separate issue. $2.95. January.
Runners World Shoe Issue. Started 1977. $2.50. October.

1145. RUNNING & FITNESS.
2420 K St. N.W., Washington, DC 20037.
Annual Subscription: $20. **Frequency:** Bimonthly.
Publisher: American Running & Fitness Association.
Special Issues:
Survey of Sports-Oriented Podiatrists. January/February.
Fitness Resorts, Running Camps, and Race Vacations. March/April.
Survey of Sportsmedicine Clinics. July/August.
Survey of Sports-Oriented Orthopedists. November/December.

1146. RURAL AND URBAN ROADS.
380 Northwest Hwy., Des Plaines, IL 60016.
Annual Subscription: $17.50. **Frequency:** Monthly.
Publisher: Scranton-Gillette Communications, Inc.
Advertiser Index: Every issue.
Special Issues:
Public Roads Maintenance & Paving. $2. January.
Roadsides & Environment. $2. February.
Asphalt Road Recycling, Rehabilitation. $2. March.
Bridge Maintenance. $2. April or May.
Snow & Ice Control. $2. June.
Concrete Pavement Recyling & Rehabilitation. $2. July.
Traffic Control & Safety. $2. August.
Sources of Public Funding. $2. September.

1147. RURAL ELECTRIFICATION.
1800 Massachusetts Ave., NW, Washington, DC 20036.
Annual Subscription: $16. **Frequency:** Monthly.
Publisher: National Rural Electric Cooperative Association.
Advertiser Index: Every issue.
Editorial Index: Annual. Subject. January, February or March.
Special Issues:
Annual Meeting Report Issue. Started 1946. $5. February, March or April.
Directory of Rural Electric Cooperatives. Started 1977. $5. July.
Alternate Enery Sources. Started 1980. $5. December.

1148. SMPTE JOURNAL.
862 Scarsdale Ave., Scarsdale, NY 10583.
Annual Subscription: $55. **Frequency:** Monthly.
Publisher: Society of Motion Picture & Television Engineers.
Editorial Index: Annual. Subject/Author. December.
Special Issues:
Technical Conference Programs and Equipment Exhibits Listings. $6. January/September.

Progress Report—advances in motion picture and TV technology; U.S. and foreign. $6. April.

1149. SALES AND MARKETING MANAGEMENT IN CANADA.
416 Moore Ave., Ste. 303, Toronto, Ontario, Can. M4G 1C9.
Annual Subscription: $25/15. **Frequency:** Monthly.
Publisher: Ingmar Communications Ltd.
Advertiser Index: Every issue.
Special Issues:
Industrial Advertising/Merchandising. $3. January.
Report on Quebec/Co-op Advertising. $3. February.
Trade Shows, Exhibits, Meetings, Conventions/Public Relations. $3. March.
Direct Mail Marketing/Sales Training. $3. April.
Report on Western Canada/Packaging & Graphic Design. $3. May.
Broadcast Advertising/Marketing Research & Product Development. $3. June.
Annual Buyers Guide. $15. July.
Incentives & Motivation/Magazine Advertising. $3. August.
A/V Video Presentations/Official A/V Show Guide. $3. September.
Annual Business Publication Directory/Advertising Agencies. $3. October.
Newspaper Advertising/Sales Forecasting. $3. November.
Sales Promotion/Hi-Tech Marketing. $3. December.

1150. SALES & MARKETING MANAGEMENT.
633 Third Ave., New York, NY 10017.
Annual Subscription: $38. **Frequency:** Monthly.
Publisher: Bill Communications.
Advertiser Index: Every issue.
Editorial Index: Annual. Subject. April.
Indexed or Abstracted Online: ABI/Inform; Magazine Index; Trade & Industry Index; Management Contents.
Special Issues:
Awards Issue: Product Marketing Awards; Business Executive Dining Awards (Top 100 Restaurants for Business Dining in U.S. and Canada). Started 1976. $5. January.
Survey of Selling Costs—statistical information on a broad range of selling expenses. Started 1973. Published as a separate issue. $30. February.
Survey of Industrial Purchasing Power—industrial data for approximately 2800 counties; also lists industries by S.I.C. code. Started 1974. Published as a separate issue. $30. April.
Survey of Buying Power—statistical data on population, households, income and retail sales for metro areas, counties and cities in the U.S. and Canada. Started 1928. Published as a separate issue. $60. July.
Survey of Executive Compensation. $5. August.
Fleet Cars. $5. October.
Survey of Buying Power Part II—5-year projections, TV and newspaper markets. Started 1973. Published as a separate issue. $30. October.

1151. SAM ADVANCED MANAGEMENT JOURNAL.
135 West 50th St., New York, NY 10020.
Annual Subscription: $19.
Publisher: Society for Advancement of Management.
Editorial Index: Annual. Title. Fall.

1152. SANITARY MAINTENANCE.
P.O. Box 694, Milwaukee, WI 53201.
Annual Subscription: $20. **Frequency:** Monthly.
Publisher: Trade Press Publication Co.
Advertiser Index: Every issue.
Editorial Index: Annual. Subject/Title. December.
Special Issues:
Annual Buyers Guide. Started 1956. $7.50. January.
Floor Maintenance Issue. Started 1956. $3. May.
What's New Issue (review of new products). Started 1978. $2. August.
International Sanitary Supply Association Convention Issue. $2. December.
The Sanitary Supply Market Survey. Started 1981. Published as a separate issue. Free. Irregular.

1153. SASKATCHAWAN MOTORIST.
200 Albert St., North, Regina, Sas., Can. S4R 5E2.
Frequency: Quarterly.
Publisher: Provincial Publications Ltd.
Special Issues:
Vacation Planning. March/April.
Camping & Travel Canada. May/June.
Exotic Destinations. September/October.
Winter Driving & Winter Vacations. November/December.

1154. SAVINGS BANK JOURNAL.
200 Park Ave., New York, NY 10166.
Annual Subscription: $25. **Frequency:** Monthly.
Publisher: National Association of Mutual Savings Banks.
Advertiser Index: Every issue.
Editorial Index: Annual. Title. December.
Indexed or Abstracted Online: ABI/Inform; Management Contents.
Special Issues:
Annual Outlook. $3. January.
Bank Operations Conference Preview. $3. January or February.
New Bank Building Review. $3. 3/yr. February/June/September.
100 Largest Savings Banks—by deposit size. $3. March/September.
Operations Conference Report. $3. March or April.
Industry Policy Conference Report. $3. April.
Thrift Marketers' Convention Report. $3. April or May.
NAMSB Annual Conference/Reference Issue—lists association officers and committees. $3. June.
Balance Sheet Trends/Savings Bank Association of New York Annual Meeting/Vermont Bankers Association Convention. $3. August.
State Savings Bank Association Conventions: New York, Maine, New Hampshire. $3. October.
State Savings Bank Association Conventions: Massachusetts, Connecticut. $3. November.
Mortgage Bankers Association Convention Report/Robert Morris Associates Annual Conference. $3. December.

1155. SAVINGS INSTITUTIONS.
111 East Wacker Dr., Chicago, IL 60601.
Annual Subscription: $24. **Frequency:** Monthly.
Publisher: U.S. League of Savings Institutions.
Advertiser Index: Every issue.
Editorial Index: Annual. Subject. December.
Indexed or Abstracted Online: Management Contents; ABI/Inform; Trade & Industry Index.
Special Issues:
100 Largest Savings Associations. Started Pre-1963. $2. February.
Savings and Loan Source Book—data on the savings institution business; federal agencies; personal income and housing demographics; mortgage lending; savings and loan operations; Federal Home Loan Banks by district. Published as a separate issue. Free. Not included in the subscription price. July.

1156. SCHOOL BUS FLEET.
2500 Artesia Blvd., Redondo Beach, CA 90278.
Annual Subscription: $12. **Frequency:** 6/yr.
Publisher: Bobit Publishing Co.
Advertiser Index: Every issue.
Editorial Index: Annual. Subject. December/January.
Special Issues:
Annual Fact Book—A directory of key personnel in the student transportation field, including suppliers, officials and association officers. Started 1973-74. $5. January/February.

1157. SCHOOL BUSINESS AFFAIRS.
720 Garden St., Park Ridge, IL 60068.
Annual Subscription: $25. **Frequency:** Monthly.

Publisher: Association of School Officials of U.S. and Canada.
Advertiser Index: Every issue.
Editorial Index: Annual. Subject.
Special Issues:
   Facilities Planning & Operations. $1.50.   January.
   Alternate Sources of Revenue. $1.50.   February.
   Membership Directory/Buyers Guide. $30.   March.
   Pupil Transportation. $1.50.   April.
   Data Processing. $1.50.   May.
   Insurance and Risk Management. $1.50.   June.
   Energy Management. $1.50.   July.
   Back-to-School Product Preview. $1.50.   August.
   ABSO Annual Meeting Program and Report. $1.50.
      September/November.
   Accounting & Financial Reporting. $1.50.   October.
   School Food Service. $1.50.   November.
   The Best of "SBA". $1.50.   December.

1158. SCHOOL LIBRARY JOURNAL.
205 East 42 St., New York, NY 10017.
Annual Subscription: $47.   **Frequency:** 10/yr.
Publisher: R. R. Bowker Co.
Advertiser Index: Every issue.
Editorial Index: Title/Author. December.
Special Issues:
   School Certification Requirements Update. $4.   January.
   Paperbacks for Young Adults. $4.   February.
   Spring Books/ALA Mid-Winter Conference Report. $4.
      March.
   Best Books for Spring/Buyers Guide to A/V Materials. $4.
      May.
   ALA Conference Round-up. $4.   August.
   SLJ Annual Books Review Policy Statement/Paperback
      Giveaways—free material to write away for. $4.
      September.
   Fall/Winter Juvenile Books to Come. $4.   October.
   Year-End Round Up/Best Books of the Year. $4.
      December.

1159. SCHOOL PRODUCT NEWS.
1111 Chester Ave., Cleveland, OH 44114.
Annual Subscription: $24.   **Frequency:** Monthly.
Publisher: Penton/IPC.
Advertiser Index: Every issue.
Special Issues:
   Buyers Guide.   Started 1971. $2.50.   January.
   Census of School Expenses.   Started 1977. $2.50.
      March.
   Annual Administrator Calendar—calendar and roster of
      education associations and conventions.   Started 1973.
      $2.50.   August.
   Architectural Emphasis.   Started 1980. $2.50.
      December.

1160. SCHOOL SHOP.
P.O. Box 8623, Ann Arbor, MI 48107.
Annual Subscription: $12.   **Frequency:** Monthly.
Publisher: Prakken Publications, Inc.
Advertiser Index: Every issue.
Editorial Index: Annual. Subject/Title/Author. May.
Special Issues:
   Directory of Suppliers. $2.50.   April.
   Directory of State and Federal Officials in Industrial
      Vocational Education. $1.50.   September.
   Shop Teachers Service—free and low-cost teaching aids.
      $1.50.   October.
   Instructional Media Directory—print and non-print. $1.50.
      December.

1161. SCIENCE.
1515 Massachusetts Ave., NW, Washington, DC 20005.
Annual Subscription: $53 (members)/$90 (nonmembers).
Frequency: Weekly.
Publisher: American Association for the Advancement of
   Science.
Editorial Index: Quarterly. Author. March/June/September/
   December.

Special Issues:
   Biotechnology. $2.50.   February.
   Gordon Research Conference. $2.50.   March/October.
   AAAS Pre-Convention Issue. $2.50.   April.
   Book Issue—reviews of scientific books. $2.50.   May.
   Guide to Scientific Instruments—lists 2000 instrument
      categories and 2000 company names and addresses under
      the appropriate product category.   Started 1962.
      Published as a separate issue. $10.   September.
   Instruments—new instruments, techniques, methods.
      $2.50.   October.

1162. SCIENCE NEWS.
231 West Center St., Marion, OH 43302.
Annual Subscription: $27.50.   **Frequency:** Weekly.
Publisher: Science Service, Inc.
Editorial Index: Semi-Annual. Subject/Author. June/
   December.
Indexed Online: Magazine Index.

1163. SCIENTIFIC AMERICAN.
415 Madison Ave., New York, NY 10017.
Annual Subscription: $24.   **Frequency:** Monthly.
Publisher: Scientific American, Inc.
Editorial Index: Annual. Title/Author. December; separate
   cumulative index by author and key word, May 1948-June
   1978: $45.
Indexed Online: Magazine Index.

1164. SCOPE CAMPING NEWS.
P.O. Box 30, Hyde Park, Ontario, Can. N0M I2O.
Annual Subscription: $6.   **Frequency:** 6/yr.
Publisher: Merton Publications Ltd.
Special Issues:
   Canadian Campground Guide.   Published as a separate
      issue. $3.   Not included in the subscription price.
      March.

1165. SEA FRONTIERS.
3979 Rickenbacker Cwy., Virginia Key, Miami, FL 33149.
Annual Subscription: $15.   **Frequency:** Bimonthly.
Publisher: International Oceanographic Foundation.
Editorial Index: Annual. Subject. December.
Indexed Online: Magazine Index.

1166. SEA PORTS & THE SHIPPING WORLD.
4634 St. Catherine St. West, Montreal, Quebec, Can.
H3Z 2W6.
Annual Subscription: $20.   **Frequency:** Monthly.
Publisher: Gallery Publications Limited.
Special Issues:
   Spring Issue—featuring companies, clubs and associations
      connected with the Canadian shipping/marine industry.
      Published as a separate issue. $10.   May.
   Annual—featuring personalities connected with the Canadian
      shipping/marine industry.   Published as a separate issue.
      $10.   December.

1167. SEA TECHNOLOGY.
1117 North 19th St., Arlington, VA 22209.
Annual Subscription: $20.   **Frequency:** Monthly.
Publisher: Compass Publications, Inc.
Advertiser Index: Every issue.
Editorial Index: Annual. Subject/Author. December.
Special Issues:
   Annual Review/Forecast.   Started 1964. $1.75.
      January.
   Navigation & Positioning.   Started 1964. $1.75.   March.
   Offshore Technology.   Started 1964. $1.75.   April.
   Buyers Guide/Directory—for those concerned with design
      engineering and application of equipment and services in
      the marine environment. Products and services; ocean
      research and survey vessels; educational institutions;
      federal government.   Published as a separate issue.
      $1.75.   September.
   Geophysical Survey.   Started 1964. $1.75.   September.
   Undersea Defense.   Started 1964. $1.75.   November.
   Commercial Diving.   Started 1964. $1.75.   December.

1168. SEA TRADE.
11/12 Bury Street, London, , England EC3 5AT.
Annual Subscription: $105. **Frequency:** Monthly.
Publisher: Sea Trade Publications, Ltd.
Editorial Index: Annual. Subject. January (as a separate supplement).
Special Issues:
  Annual Review: Shipping and Shipbuilding. July or August.
  Arab Shipping—statistics, articles and directories for Algeria, Bahrain, Egypt, Iraq, Jordan, Kuwait, Lebanon, Libya, Mauritania, Morocco, Oman, Qatar, Saudi Arabia, Somalia, Sudan, Syria, Tunisia, Yemen. Includes ship and company indexes. Started 1978. Published as a separate issue. Varies.
  Far East Shipping—articles, directories and statistics for China, Hong Kong, Indonesia, Japan, Malaysia, North & South Korea, Philippines, Singapore, Taiwan, Thailand and Vietnam. Started 1981. Published as a separate issue. Varies.
  Latin America Shipping—statistics, articles & directories for Argentina, Bolivia, Brazil, Chile, Colombia, Costa Rica, Cuba, Dominican Republic, Ecuador, El Salvador, Guatemala, Honduras, Mexico, Nicaragua, Panama, Paraguay, Peru, Uruguay, Venezuela. Started 1979. Published as a separate issue. Varies.
  Sea Trade U.S. Yearbook—includes statistics, and review articles on shipbuilding, shipping, parts etc.; directories of companies, associations etc.; index of ships. Started 1979. Published as a separate issue. Varies.

1169. SEATTLE BUSINESS.
215 Columbia St., Seattle, WA 78104.
Annual Subscription: $15. **Frequency:** Monthly.
Publisher: Seattle Chamber of Commerce.
Special Issues:
  Seattle/King County Office Leasing Guide. $1.50. January.
  Economic Review. $1.50. April.
  Industrial Parks Guide. $1.50. August.

1170. THE SECRETARY.
2440 Pershing Rd. #G10, Kansas City, MO 64108.
Annual Subscription: $12. **Frequency:** 9/yr.
Publisher: Professional Secretaries International.
Editorial Index: Annual. Subject. November/December.

1171. SECURITY MANAGEMENT.
1600 North Ft. Myer Dr., Ste. 1200, Arlington, VA 22209.
Annual Subscription: $27. **Frequency:** Monthly.
Publisher: American Society for Industrial Security.
Advertiser Index: Every issue.
Editorial Index: Annual. Subject. December.
Indexed or Abstracted Online: ABI/Inform; Management Contents.

1172. SECURITY WORLD.
P.O. Box 5510, Denver, CO 80206.
Annual Subscription: $35. **Frequency:** Monthly.
Publisher: Cahners Publishing Co.
Advertiser Index: Every issue.
Editorial Index: Annual. Subject/Title/Author. December.
Special Issues:
  Risk Control: Insurance & Security/Conference Issue. $4. January.
  Fire & Arson/Safes & Vaults. $4. February.
  Employee Crime Prevention Education. $4. March.
  Industrial Espionage/Access Control. $4. April.
  Establishing a Security Department/Security Hardware/Conference. $4. May.
  Retail Security/Anti-Shoplifting Devices. $4. June.
  Transportation Security/Lighting. $4. July.
  Security Budgets & Salaries/Accounting Security/Conference. $4. August.
  Computer Security/Fire Extinguishing Systems. $4. September.
  How to Select a Guard Company/Mobile Communications. $4. October.
  Firearms Issues; Ballistic Materials. $4. November.
  "The Source"—Buyers Guide. Started 1960. $20. December.

1173. SEED WORLD.
380 Northwest Highway, Des Plaines, IL 60016.
Annual Subscription: $10. **Frequency:** Monthly.
Publisher: Scranton Gillette Communications.
Advertiser Index: Every issue.
Special Issues:
  Garden Seed. January.
  Seed Trade Buyers Guide & Directory—seed and closely allied companies; state seed laws; statistics of the seed industry; etc. Started 1917. Published as a separate issue. $10. January.
  Equipment. February.
  Grass Seed. April.
  International Convention. May.
  Convention Report: American & Canadian Seed Association. August.
  Flower Seed. September.
  Farm Seed. October.
  Corn, Sorghum & Soybean. November.

1174. SEEDSMEN'S DIGEST.
10714 Manchester Rd., St. Louis, MO 63122.
Annual Subscription: $15. **Frequency:** Monthly.
Publisher: The Webb Co.
Advertiser Index: Every issue.
Editorial Index: Subject. December.
Special Issues:
  State Conventions. $2. January/July.
  All-America Selections—award winning flowers and vegetables. $2. March.
  Equipment and Seed Conditioning. $2. April.
  International Seed Trade/American Seed Trade Association Convention. $2. June.
  Grasses. $2. August.
  Flowers. $2. September.
  Corn. $2. October.
  Sorghum. $2. November.
  Southern Seedmen's Association Convention. $2. December.

1175. SELLING DIRECT.
6255 Barfield Rd., Atlanta, GA 30338.
Annual Subscription: $10. **Frequency:** Monthly.
Publisher: Communication Channels, Inc.
Special Issues:
  Direct Selling Directory—of products, services and advertisers. Started 1955. $1.50. February.

1176. SERVICE REPORTER DISTRIBUTOR.
1098 South Milwaukee Ave., P.O. Box 745, Wheeling, IL 60090.
Annual Subscription: $10. **Frequency:** Monthly.
Publisher: Technical Reporting Corp.
Advertiser Index: Every issue.
Special Issues:
  International Buyers Guide—air conditioning, heating, refrigerating, ventilating equipment. Started 1979. $10. December.

1177. SEW BUSINESS.
P.O. Box 1331, Fort Lee, NJ 07024.
Annual Subscription: $15. **Frequency:** Monthly.
Publisher: Wilsir Publications.
Advertiser Index: Every issue.
Special Issues:
  Art Needlework Supplement. Started 1960. $2. 5/yr. January/February/May/August/November.
  Quilt Quarterly. Started 1980. $2. March/June/September/December.
  Annual National Directory and Buyers Guide. Started 1960. $7.50. July.

1178. SHOE SERVICE.
154 West Hubbard St., Chicago, IL 60610.
Annual Subscription: $9. **Frequency:** Monthly.

Publisher: Shoe Service Institute of America.
Advertiser Index: Every issue.
Editorial Index: Annual. Subject/Title. December.
Special Issues:
Shoe Service Institute of America Convention Issues. $1.25. June/December.

1179. **SHOOTING INDUSTRY.**
591 Camino de la Reina, San Diego, CA 92108.
Annual Subscription: $12.50. **Frequency:** Monthly.
Publisher: Publishers' Development Corp.
Advertiser Index: Every issue.
Special Issues:
Buyers Guide & Directory—manufacturers & wholesalers of firearms and accessories. May.
National Shooting Sports Foundation Show. Started 1979. December.

1180. **SHOPPING CENTER WORLD.**
6255 Barfield Rd., Atlanta, GA 30328.
Annual Subscription: $37. **Frequency:** Monthly.
Publisher: Communication Channels, Inc.
Advertiser Index: Every issue.
Special Issues:
Census of the Shopping Center Industry. $3.50. Biennially. January.
International Council of Shopping Centers Annual Convention. $3.50. May.
Product/Service Directory. $3.50. August.
Finance Directory. $3.50. October.

1181. **SHOPPING CENTRE CANADA.**
777 Bay St., Toronto, Ontario, Can. M5W 1A7.
Annual Subscription: $36/27. **Frequency:** Quarterly.
Publisher: Maclean Hunter Publications.
Advertiser Index: Every issue.
Special Issues:
Sources-directory of suppliers to the Canadian shopping center industry. Started 1980. $20. September.

1182. **SIERRA.**
530 Bush Street, San Francisco, CA 94108.
Annual Subscription: $8. **Frequency:** 6/yr.
Publisher: Sierra Club.
Editorial Index: Annual. Title/Author. November/December.
Indexed Online: Magazine Index.
Special Issues:
Outing Issue—complete list of Sierra Club outings. $1.50. January.

1183. **SIGNAL.**
5641 Burke Centre Parkway, Burke, VA 22015.
Annual Subscription: $23.25. **Frequency:** Monthly.
Publisher: Armed Forces Communications and Electronics Association.
Advertiser Index: Every issue.
Editorial Index: Annual. Title/Author. October.
Special Issues:
Capabilities Issue (Group membership listing). January.
Convention Issue (AFCEA International). August.

1184. **SKI.**
P.O. Box 2795, Boulder, CO 80302.
Annual Subscription: $11.94. **Frequency:** 8/yr.
Publisher: Times Mirror Magazines.
Special Issues:
Olympics Issue. $1.75. Every 4 yrs. February.
Aspen Winter National. $1.75. Annual. March.
Guide to Summer Ski Camps. $1.75. April.
Annual Buyers Guide. Started 1982. $1.75. September.

1185. **SKI AREA MANAGEMENT.**
P.O. Drawer D, North Salem, NY 10560.
Annual Subscription: $15. **Frequency:** Bimonthly.
Publisher: Beardsley Publishing Corp.
Advertiser Index: Every issue.
Special Issues:
Annual Survey of New Lift Construction. Started 1963. $2.50. January.
National Ski Areas Association Convention & Trade Show. Started 1963. $2.50. May.
Ski Area Supplier & Product Directory. Started 1963. $2.50. November.

1186. **SKI BUSINESS.**
975 Post Road, Darien, CT 06820.
Annual Subscription: $15. **Frequency:** 11/yr.
Publisher: Nick Hock Associates Inc.
Special Issues:
Ski Buying Shows Preview Issue. Started 1982. March.
Ski Market Research Issue. Started 1980. June/July.

1187. **SKIING.**
P.O. Box 2777, Boulder, CO 80302.
Annual Subscription: $11. **Frequency:** 7/yr.
Publisher: Ziff-Davis Publishing Co.
Indexed or Abstracted Online: Magazine Index.
Special Issues:
Buying Guide. $1.75. September.
Vacation Guide. $1.75. October.

1188. **SKILLINGS' MINING REVIEW.**
202 West Superior St., Ste. 700, Duluth, MN 55802.
Annual Subscription: $17. **Frequency:** Weekly.
Publisher: David N. Skillings, Jr.
Advertiser Index: Every issue.
Editorial Index: Annual. Title. December.
Special Issues:
Minnesota AIME (American Institute of Mining Engineers)/Mining Symposium Program. Started 1972. $2. January.
Compilation of Company Iron Ore Shipments. $1. July.
Minnesota Iron Ore Operations. $2. August.
American Mining Congress International Mining Show. $1. September.

1189. **SKIN DIVER.**
8490 Sunset Blvd., Los Angeles, CA 90069.
Annual Subscription: $11.94. **Frequency:** Monthly.
Publisher: Petersen Publishing Co.
Editorial Index: Annual. Subject/Title. December.
Indexed or Abstracted Online: Magazine Index.
Special Issues:
Australia Travel Guide. $1.75. July.
Bahamas Travel Guide. $1.75. August.

1190. **SKYLINES.**
1221 Massachusetts Ave., NW, Washington, DC 20005.
Annual Subscription: $5. **Frequency:** Monthly.
Publisher: Building Owners and Managers Association International.
Special Issues:
Occupancy Survey. January/August, varies.

1191. **SMALL SYSTEMS WORLD.**
950 Lee St., Des Plaines, IL 60016.
Annual Subscription: $30. **Frequency:** Monthly.
Publisher: Hunter Publishing Co.
Advertiser Index: Every issue.
Editorial Index: Annual. Subject/Author. December.
Indexed Online: ABI/Inform.
Special Issues:
Small Business Systems. January.
National Computer Conference Preview. May.
Survey of Small-System Manufacturing Software. Started 1978. August.

1192. **SMALL WORLD.**
393 7th Ave., New York, NY 10001.
Annual Subscription: $7. **Frequency:** Monthly.
Publisher: Earnshaw Publications.
Advertiser Index: Every issue.
Special Issues:
Juvenile Products Show Issue. $2. October.
Directory. $10. December.

1193. SMITHSONIAN MAGAZINE.
900 Jefferson Drive, SW, Washington, DC 20560.
Annual Subscription: $17. **Frequency:** Monthly.
Publisher: Smithsonian Institution.
Editorial Index: Annual. Subject/Title/Author. May.
Indexed Online: Magazine Index.

1194. SNACK FOOD.
1 East First St., Duluth, MN 55802.
Annual Subscription: $16. **Frequency:** Monthly.
Publisher: Harcourt, Brace, Jovanovich.
Advertiser Index: Every issue.
Editorial Index: Annual. Subject. December.
Special Issues:
Packaging. Started 1972. $2. May/November.
State of the Snack Food Industry Report. Started 1968. $2. June.
Buying Guide. Started 1960. $5. August.
New Plant/Expansions. Started 1982. $2. September.
Flavors & Ingredients. $2. October.

1195. SNIPS.
407 Mannheim Rd., Bellwood, IL 60104.
Annual Subscription: $9. **Frequency:** Monthly.
Publisher: Snips Magazine, Inc.
Advertiser Index: Every issue.
Special Issues:
Seasonal Market Reports—heating/air conditioning market. Started 1930. $2. 3/yr. January/March/September.
New Products. Started 1982. $2. August.
International Heating, Air Conditioning and Refrigeration Preshow Issue. Started 1930. $2. December.

1196. SNOWMOBILE CANADA.
3414 Park Ave., Ste. 221, Montreal, Quebec, Can. H2X 2H5.
Annual Subscription: $7. **Frequency:** 4/yr.
Publisher: CRV Publications Canada Ltd.
Advertiser Index: Every issue.
Special Issues:
Snowmobile Canada Buyers Guide. Started 1971. $2. October.

1197. SNOWMOBILE SPORTS.
1255 Yonge St., Ste. 105, Toronto, Ontario, Can. M4T 1W6.
Annual Subscription: $2.50. **Frequency:** 2/yr.
Publisher: Leisure Publications.
Special Issues:
Snowmobile Sports Annual. October.
Snowarama Show. December/January.

1198. SOAP/COSMETICS/CHEMICAL SPECIALTIES.
101 West 31st St., New York, NY 10001.
Annual Subscription: $20. **Frequency:** Monthly.
Publisher: MacNair-Dorland Company.
Advertiser Index: Every issue.
Editorial Index: Annual. Title. April.
Indexed or Abstracted Online: CIN; Trade & Industry Index.
Special Issues:
Soap and Detergent Association Meeting. $3.50. January.
Cosmetics, Toiletry & Fragrance Association Meeting. $3.50. February.
Markets & Marketing Techniques. $3.50. March.
Blue Book Buyer's Guide. Published as a separate issue. April.
Technical and Regulatory. $3.50. August.
Chemical Specialties Manufacturers Association Meeting. $3.50. December.

1199. SOCIAL PSYCHOLOGY QUARTERLY.
1722 N. St., NW, Washington, DC 20036.
Annual Subscription: $21. **Frequency:** Quarterly.
Publisher: American Sociological Association.
Editorial Index: Annual. Author. December.

1200. SOCIAL SECURITY BULLETIN.
Superintendent of Documents, U.S. Government Printing Office, Washington, DC 20402.
Annual Subscription: $29. **Frequency:** Monthly.
Publisher: Social Security Administration.
Editorial Index: A (Cumulative author, title, subj. index, 1938-79). Title/Author. December.
Special Issues:
Annual Statistical Supplement. Started 1949. Published as a separate issue. $7. October.

1201. SOCIOLOGY OF EDUCATION.
1722 N Street, NW, Washington, DC 20036.
Annual Subscription: $21. **Frequency:** Quarterly.
Publisher: American Sociological Association.
Editorial Index: Annual. Author. October.

1202. SOFTALK.
P.O. Box 60, North Hollywood, CA 91603.
Annual Subscription: $24. **Frequency:** Monthly.
Publisher: Softalk Publishing, Inc.
Advertiser Index
Special Issues:
Top Software Programs of Year. Started 1980. $3. April.
Holiday Gift Guide. Started 1980. $3. December.

1203. SOLAR AGE.
Church Hill Rd., Harrisville, NH 03450.
Annual Subscription: $24. **Frequency:** Monthly.
Publisher: SolarVision, Inc.
Editorial Index: Annual. Subject. December.
Indexed or Abstracted Online: Trade & Industry Index.
Special Issues:
Solar Products Specification Guide. Published as a separate issue. $125. Not included in the subscription price. 3/yr. February/June/November.

1204. SOLAR ENGINEERING & CONTRACTING.
P.O. Box 3600, Troy, MI 48099.
Annual Subscription: $24. **Frequency:** Monthly.
Publisher: Business News Publishing Co.
Advertiser Index: Every issue.
Editorial Index: Annual. Subject. November.
Special Issues:
Master Catalog—directory of manufacturers of solar equipment; product listing; laboratories. Started 1982. Published as a separate issue. $15. July.

1205. SOLID STATE TECHNOLOGY.
14 Vanderventer Ave., Port Washington, NY 11050.
Annual Subscription: $30. **Frequency:** Monthly.
Publisher: Technical Publishing Co.
Advertiser Index: Every issue.
Editorial Index: Annual. Subject/Title/Author. December or January.
Special Issues:
Solid State Processing and Production Buyers Guide and Directory. Published as a separate issue. $50. Not included in the subscription price. February.

1206. SOLUTIONS.
8823 North Industrial Rd., Peoria, IL 61525.
Annual Subscription: $25. **Frequency:** 7/yr.
Publisher: Fluid Fertilizer Industry.
Editorial Index: Annual. Subject/Title/Author. Cumulative index 1956-79, $25; with annual updates, $5; available separately. Cumulative index 1956-84, $25, available early 1985.
Special Issues:
Fluid Fertilizer Industry Convention Preview. November/December.

1207. SOUND AND VIBRATION.
P.O. Box 40416, Bay Village, OH 44140.
Annual Subscription: $10. **Frequency:** Monthly.
Publisher: Acoustical Publications, Inc.
Advertiser Index: Every issue.
Special Issues:
Instrumentation Buyers Guide. $1. March.

Materials and Systems for Noise and Vibration Control Buyers Guide. $1. July.
Dynamic Measurement Instrumentation Buyers Guide. $1. November.

1208. SOUND CANADA.
7240 Woodbine Ave., Markham, Ontario, Can. L3R 1A4.
Annual Subscription: $11.99. **Frequency:** Monthly.
Publisher: Chimo Media Ltd.
Advertiser Index: Every issue.
Special Issues:
Cassette Buying Guide. $1.50. January.
Audio Test Reports. $1.50. March.
Car Stereo Standards. $1.50. May.
Audio Preview. $3.95. August.
Cartridge-Turntable Buying Guide. $1.50. September.
Speaker Buying Guide. $1.50. November.

1209. SOUND & COMMUNICATIONS.
156 East 37th St., New York, NY 10016.
Annual Subscription: $15. **Frequency:** Monthly.
Publisher: Sound Publishing Company.
Advertiser Index: Every issue.
Special Issues:
Blue Book Directory—buyers guide. Started 1960. $8.50. August.
Annual Economic Review. Started 1977. $2. December.

1210. THE SOUTHERN BANKER.
6195 Crooked Creek Rd., Norcross, GA 30092.
Annual Subscription: $18. **Frequency:** Monthly.
Publisher: McFadden Business Publications.
Advertiser Index: Every issue.
Special Issues:
Buyers Guide. $3. April.
Southern Bankers Directory. Started 1937. Published as a separate issue. $37.50. Not included in the subscription price. April/October.
Bank Directors. $3. August.
American Bankers Association Convention. $3. September.

1211. SOUTHERN FUNERAL DIRECTOR.
Box 7368, Atlanta, GA 30357.
Annual Subscription: $20. **Frequency:** Monthly.
Publisher: John W. Yopp Publications.
Advertiser Index: Every issue.
Special Issues:
Regulations—compilation of state board rules regulating the industry in all 50 states.

1212. SOUTHERN PULP & PAPER.
75 Third St., NW, Atlanta, GA 30308.
Annual Subscription: $18. **Frequency:** Monthly.
Publisher: Ernest H. Abernathy Publishing Co.
Advertiser Index: Every issue.
Special Issues:
Mill & Personnel Directory—directory of mills in the 17 Southern states: production; equipment; products; key personnel; photographs. $10. October.

1213. SOUVENIRS AND NOVELTIES.
401 North Broad St., Philadelphia, PA 19108.
Annual Subscription: $12. **Frequency:** 7/yr.
Publisher: Kane Communications, Inc.
Advertiser Index: Every issue.
Special Issues:
New York Stationery Show and Buyers Guide. Published as a separate issue. $5. April/May.
Buyers Guide. $5. August.
Suppliers (Advertisers) Guide. $5. September.
Smoky Mountain Gatlinburg Gift Show. Started 1968. $5. October/November.

1214. SPA AND SAUNA TRADE JOURNAL.
P.O. Box 19531, Irvine, CA 92713.
Annual Subscription: $17.50. **Frequency:** Monthly.
Publisher: Hester Communications Inc.
Advertiser Index: Every issue.
Special Issues:
Spa and Sauna Buyers Guide—supplier directory for hot water products. Started 1976. Published as a separate issue. $15. December.

1215. SPECIAL LIBRARIES.
235 Park Ave. South, New York, NY 10003.
Annual Subscription: $36 (nonmembers). **Frequency:** Monthly.
Publisher: Special Libraries Association.
Advertiser Index: Every issue.
Editorial Index: Annual. Subject/Title/Author. October.
Indexed or Abstracted Online: Elcom; Inspec; LISA; PAIS; Trade & Industry Index.
Special Issues:
SLA Conference Report. Started 1910. Published as a separate issue. $1. August.
Who's Who in Special Libraries—member listing, association history, officers, bylaws, award winners. Started 1930. Published as a separate issue. $15.50. Not included in the subscription price. December.

1216. SPECIALTY ADVERTISING BUSINESS.
1404 Walnut Hill Lane, Irving, TX 75062.
Annual Subscription: $21. **Frequency:** Monthly.
Publisher: Specialty Advertising Association International.
Advertiser Index: Every issue.
Special Issues:
Vinyl and Leather Items. Started 1982. January.
Writing Instruments. Started 1981. March.
Watchables—buttons, badges, insignias, emblems, and appliques. Started 1982. April.
Calendars. Started 1981. May.
Balloons, Inflatables and Electronics. Started 1984. June.
Sports Accessories and Food Gifts. Started 1984. July.
Automotive Accessories, Key Tags. Started 1983. September.
Glassware. Started 1982. October.
Wearables (Imprinted Sportswear). Started 1982. November.

1217. SPECIALTY & CUSTOM DEALER.
11 South Forge St., Akron, OH 44304.
Annual Subscription: $20. **Frequency:** Monthly.
Publisher: Babcox Automotive Publications.
Advertiser Index: Every issue.
Special Issues:
Buyers Directory. Started 1981. January.
Complete Year's Racing Schedules. April.
Pacific Wholesalers Association Membership Directory and Map. Started 1974. June.
Indianapolis 500. July.
Specialty Cars. November.
Specialty Equipment Manufacturers Association Show Review. December.

1218. SPECIFYING ENGINEER.
270 St. Paul St., Denver, CO 80206.
Annual Subscription: $35. **Frequency:** Monthly.
Publisher: Cahners Publishing Co.
Advertiser Index: Every issue.
Editorial Index: Annual. Subject. January.
Special Issues:
Specifier's Guide to Mechanical/Electrical Products. Published as a separate issue. $4. September.

1219. SPINNING WHEEL: THE MAGAZINE OF ANTIQUES & EARLY CRAFTS.
1981 Moreland Pkwy., Bldg. 4A, Annapolis, MD
Annual Subscription: $15. **Frequency:** 6/yr.
Publisher: Pegasus Ltd.
Advertiser Index: Every issue.
Editorial Index: Annual. Subject. January/February.

1220. THE SPORTING GOODS DEALER.
1212 North Lindbergh, St. Louis, MO 63132.
Annual Subscription: $30. **Frequency:** Monthly.
Publisher: Same.
Advertiser Index: Every issue.
Special Issues:
  Leadership Awards—in marketing. $3. January.
  Best Promotions of the Year. $3. February.
  The Sporting Goods Directory—lists manufacturers for over 200 sporting goods product categories; wholesalers; import/export; independent manufacturers representatives; sports census. Started 1910. Published as a separate issue. $20. Not included in the subscription price. May.
  Youth Market Profile. $3. July.
  Annual Hunting Survey/Operating Costs Survey. $3. August.
  AFTMA (Fishing Tackle) Show Review. $3. September.
  Post Olympics Report. $3. Olympic years. October.
  SGMA (Sporting Goods) Show Review. $3. November.
  Calendar of Industry Events/SHOT (Hunting) Show/Over 50 Market. $3. December.

1221. THE SPORTING NEWS.
1212 North Lindbergh St., P.O. Box 56, St. Louis, MO 63166.
Annual Subscription: $39.95. **Frequency:** Weekly.
Publisher: The Sporting News Publishing Co.
Indexed Online: Magazine Index.
Special Issues:
  American Basketball Association All-Star Game. $1.50. January.
  Collegiate Football Bowls. $1.50. January.
  National Football League Super Bowl. $1.50. January.
  The Sporting News Man of the Year. $1.50. January.
  Olympic Update. $1.50. 3/yr. February/May/October.
  United States Football League Preview. $1.50. February.
  Baseball Spring Training. $1.50. March.
  College Basketball All-America. $1.50. March.
  Official Baseball Record Book. Published as a separate issue. $9.95. March.
  Sporting News Baseball Yearbook. Started 1982. Published as a separate issue. $2.95. Not included in the subscription price. March.
  Master's Golf Tournament. $1.50. April.
  NFL Draft Preview. $1.50. April.
  National Hockey League Playoffs. $1.50. April.
  Official Baseball Guide. Published as a separate issue. $9.95. April.
  Opening of Baseball Season. $1.50. April.
  Indianapolis 500. $1.50. May.
  Kentucky Derby. $1.50. May.
  Official Baseball Dope Book. Published as a separate issue. $9.95. May.
  Official Baseball Register. Published as a separate issue. $9.95. May.
  U.S. Open Golf Tournament. $1.50. June.
  All-Star Baseball Game. $1.50. July.
  British Open Golf Tournament. $1.50. July.
  National Football Guide. Published as a separate issue. $9.95. July.
  Sporting News College Football Yearbook. Started 1982. Published as a separate issue. $2.95. Not included in the subscription price. July.
  Sporting News Pro Football Yearbook. Started 1982. Published as a separate issue. $2.95. Not included in the subscription price. July.
  Wimbledon Tennis Tournament. $1.50. July.
  Football Register. Published as a separate issue. $9.95. August.
  Professional Golf Association Preview. $1.50. August.
  Collegiate Football Preview. $1.50. September.
  Pro-Football Review. $1.50. September.
  U.S. Open Tennis. $1.50. September.
  Official National Basketball Association Guide. Published as a separate issue. $9.95. October.
  Opening of Hockey Season. $1.50. October.
  Pro-Basketball Preview. $1.50. October.
  Sporting News Pro/College Basketball Yearbook. Started 1982. Published as a separate issue. $2.95. Not included in the subscription price. October.
  World Series Issue. $1.50. October.
  Christmas Gifts Issue. $1.50. November.
  College Basketball Preview. $1.50. November.
  College Basketball Season Opening. $1.50. December.
  College Football All-America. $1.50. December.
  Hockey Guide. Published as a separate issue. $9.95. December.
  Hockey Register. Published as a separate issue. $9.95. December.
  Major-Minor League Convention. $1.50. December.
  Official World Series Records Book. Published as a separate issue. $9.95. December.

1222. SPORTS AFIELD.
P.O. Box 10069, Des Moines, IA 50350.
Annual Subscription: $15. **Frequency:** Monthly.
Publisher: The Hearst Corp.
Special Issues:
  Fishing Annual. Started 1977. Published as a separate issue. $1.95. January.
  Bass. Started 1977. Published as a separate issue. $1.95. March.
  Fishing Secrets. Started 1977. Published as a separate issue. $1.95. March.
  Hunting Annual. Started 1977. Published as a separate issue. $1.95. August.
  Hunting Hotspots. Started 1977. Published as a separate issue. $1.95. August.
  Deer. Started 1977. Published as a separate issue. $1.95. September.

1223. SPORTS ILLUSTRATED.
541 North Fairbanks Court, Chicago, IL 60611.
Annual Subscription: $48. **Frequency:** Weekly.
Publisher: Time Inc.
Indexed Online: Magazine Index.
Special Issues:
  Super Bowl Insert. Started 1972. $1.75. January.
  Winter Olympic Preview. Started 1984. Every four years. February.
  Year In Sports Special. Started 1977. Published as a separate issue. $2.50. February.
  Indy 500 Insert. Started 1972. $1.75. May.
  Summer Olympic Preview. Started 1984. Published as a separate issue. Every four years. July.
  Pro/College Football Special. Started 1982. Published as a separate issue. $2.50. September.
  U.S. Open Tennis Insert. Started 1972. $1.75. September.
  World Series Insert. Started 1972. $1.75. October.

1224. SPORTS MERCHANDISER.
1760 Peachtree Rd., NW, Atlanta, GA 30357.
Annual Subscription: $40. **Frequency:** Monthly.
Publisher: W.R.C. Smith Publishing Company.
Advertiser Index: Every issue.
Special Issues:
  National Sporting Goods Association Shows. $4. January/October.
  Annual Tennis Survey. $4. February.
  Annual Retail Sales Survey. $4. April.
  American Fishing Tackle Manufacturers Association Show. $4. July.
  Sporting Goods Manufacturers Association Show. $4. September.
  Annual Footwear Survey. $4. October.
  Annual Softgoods Survey. $4. November.
  SHOT (Hunting) Show. $4. December.

1225. SPORTS RETAILER.
1699 Wall St., Mt. Prospect, IL 60056.
Annual Subscription: $30. **Frequency:** Monthly.
Publisher: National Sporting Goods Association.
Advertiser Index: Every issue.

Special Issues:
  Industry Outlooks/National Sporting Goods Association Convention and Show. $2.50. January.
  Skiing/Ski Council of America Snow Show/Ski Industries America Trade Show. $2.50. March.
  Sporting Goods Market—Annual Research Report on the State of the Industry. Published as a separate issue. $85. Not included in the subscription price. March.
  Fishing Tackle/American Fishing Tackle Manufacturers Association Show. $2.50. July.
  SPOGA and ISPO Trade Shows—International Sporting Goods Expositions. $2.50. July.
  Buying Guide. Published as a separate issue. $20. Not included in the subscription price. August.
  Sporting Goods Manufacturers Association Convention. $2.50. September.
  NSGA Fall Market. $2.50. October.
  Cost of Doing Business Survey. $2.50. November.
  800/Connection Directory. $2.50. December.

1226. SPORTS TRADE CANADA.
380 Wellington St. W., Toronto, Ontario, Can. M5V 1E3.
Annual Subscription: $37.50/18.00. **Frequency:** Bimonthly.
Publisher: Page Publications Limited.
Advertiser Index: Every issue.
Special Issues:
  Buying Guide. Started 1973. $10. June.

1227. SPORTSTYLE.
1 Sportstyle Center Dr., P.O. Box 921, Farmingdale, NY 11737.
Annual Subscription: $23.94. **Frequency:** 21/yr.
Publisher: Fairchild Publications.
Special Issues:
  SportStats—statistics on active sportswear industry. $1. June or April.
  Year-End Review. December.

1228. SQUARE DANCING.
462 North Robertson Blvd., Los Angeles, CA 90048.
Annual Subscription: $10. **Frequency:** Monthly.
Publisher: American Square Dance Society.
Advertiser Index: Every issue.
Special Issues:
  1982-83 Directory of Square Dancing—listing of contacts, organizations, publications, etc., in U.S. and Canada and 41 countries. $1.25. August.

1229. STATE GOVERNMENT NEWS.
P.O. Box 11910, Lexington, KY 40578.
Annual Subscription: $15. **Frequency:** Monthly.
Publisher: Council of State Governments.
Editorial Index: Annual. Subject. April.
Special Issues:
  Survey of Major Legislative Issues. Started 1976. January or February.
  Year-end Review of State Laws. Started 1974. January or February.
  Governors' Messages. Started 1972. March.
  Annual Report. Started 1980. Published as a separate issue. November.

1230. STEREO REVIEW.
P.O. Box 2771, Boulder, CO 80302.
Annual Subscription: $9.98. **Frequency:** Monthly.
Publisher: Ziff-Davis Publishing Co.
Advertiser Index: Every issue.
Editorial Index: Annual. Subject. December.
Indexed Online: Magazine Index.
Special Issues:
  Record of the Year Awards. Started 1960's. $1.50. February.
  Tape Issue. Started 1960's. $1.50. March.
  Loudspeakers Issue. Started 1960's. $1.50. August.

1231. STORES.
100 West 31 St., New York, NY 10001.
Annual Subscription: $9. **Frequency:** Monthly.
Publisher: National Retail Merchants Association.
Indexed or Abstracted Online: AMI; Trade & Industry Index.
Special Issues:
  National Retail Merchants Association Convention. $2. February.
  Top 100 Department Stores. $2. July.
  Top 100 Specialty Chains. $2. August.
  MOR: NRMA's Merchandising and Operating Results of Department and Specialty Stores. $2. October.
  FOR: NRMA's Financial and Operating Results. $2. November.

1232. SUCCESSFUL MEETINGS.
633 Third Ave., New York, NY 10017.
Annual Subscription: $37.50. **Frequency:** Monthly.
Publisher: Meetings Inc.
Advertiser Index: Every issue.
Editorial Index: Annual. Subject. January.
Indexed Online: ABI/Inform; Management Contents.
Special Issues:
  Facilities Guide (Hotels, Convention Bureaus, Auditoriums). Started 1958. Published as a separate issue. $20. April.
  Sites Guide (Meeting Sites). Started 1976. Published as a separate issue. $20. November.

1233. SUGAR Y AZUCAR.
2050 Center Ave., Fort Lee, NJ 07024.
Annual Subscription: $24. **Frequency:** Monthly.
Publisher: RUSPAM Communications Inc.
Advertiser Index: Every issue.
Editorial Index: Annual. Subject/Title/Author. February.
Special Issues:
  Yearbook. Started 1932. $35. Not included in the subscription price. February.

1234. SUPER SERVICE STATION.
7300 North Cicero Ave., Lincolnwood, IL 60646.
Annual Subscription: $20. **Frequency:** Monthly.
Publisher: Irving-Cloud Publishing Co.
Advertiser Index: Every issue.
Special Issues:
  Buyers Showcase Annual. Started 1980. $2.50. March.
  Spring Car Care. Started 1955. $2.50. April.
  Winter Car Care. Started 1955. $2.50. September.
  New Car Service & Technical Features. Started 1960. $2.50. October.

1235. SUPERMARKET BUSINESS.
25 West 43rd St., New York, NY 10036.
Annual Subscription: $32. **Frequency:** Monthly.
Publisher: Fieldmark Media, Inc.
Advertiser Index: Every issue.
Editorial Index: Annual. Subject. December.
Indexed or Abstracted Online: Trade & Industry Index; Predicasts.
Special Issues:
  Hair Care. April.
  Baked Foods Merchandiser. $3.50. August.
  Consumer Expenditures Study—sales by type of product through retail outlets. Started 1948. $15. September.
  Top 50 publicly owned food chains. $3.50. October.
  Store Planners Equipment Directory. $3.50. November.
  Instore Business. Irregular.

1236. SUPERMARKET NEWS.
7 East 12th St., New York, NY 10003.
Annual Subscription: $30. **Frequency:** Weekly.
Publisher: Fairchild Publications.
Indexed or Abstracted Online: Trade & Industry Index; Predicasts.
Special Issues:
  Dynamic Independents—profiles of successful independent food retailers. $1. March.
  FMI Section—Critical Issues. $1. May.
  Market Profiles—articles and market shares for 25 major U.S. cities for retail food sales. July or August or September.

Building Traffic—promotion, merchandising, advertising. $1. October.
Departmental Merchandising. $1. November.
General Merchandise. $1. Usually January.

1237. SUPPLY HOUSE TIMES.
7574 Lincoln Ave., Skokie, IL 60077.
Annual Subscription: $36. **Frequency:** Monthly.
Publisher: Horton Publishing Co.
Advertiser Index: Every issue.
Special Issues:
Purchasing & Inventory Control. Started 1975. January.
Wholesale Distributors Association. Started 1972. February.
Southern Wholesalers Association. Started 1972. April.
Salesmanship. Started 1974. June.
Manufacturers Representative Issue. Started 1974. August.
American Supply Association. Started 1970. November.
Wholesaler of the Year. Started 1964. December.

1238. SURVEY OF CURRENT BUSINESS.
Government Printing Office, Washington, DC 20402.
Annual Subscription: $30. **Frequency:** Monthly.
Publisher: U.S. Department of Commerce, Bureau of Economic Analysis.
Editorial Index: Annual. December.
Indexed or Abstracted Online: Management Contents; Trade and Industry Index; ABI/Inform.
Special Issues:
Plant and Equipment Expenditures, BEA Survey. $4.75. 5/yr. January/March/June/September/December.
Plant and Equipment Expenditures, Planned. $4.75. January.
State Personal Income Review. $4.75. 5/yr. January/April/July/August/October.
Federal Fiscal Programs Analysis. $4.75. February or March.
Inventories and Sales, Manufacturing and Trade. $4.75. February/May/August/November.
Pollution Abatement, Expenditures in Constant and Current Dollars. $4.75. February or March.
Capital Expenditures by Majority-Owned Foreign Affiliates of U.S. Companies—review, and planned. $4.75. March/September.
Corporate Profits. $4.75. 8/yr. March/April/May/June/August/September/November/December.
U.S. International Transactions. $4.75. March/June/September/December.
County and Metropolitan Area Personal Income. $4.75. April.
County & Metropolitan Area Personal Income Review. $4.75. April.
Gross National Product by Industry. $4.75. April/July.
International Travel and Passenger Fares. $4.75. May or June.
Foreign Direct Investment in the U.S. $4.75. June or August.
Pollution Abatement, Capital Expenditures by Business. $4.75. June.
Federal Sector. $4.75. 3/yr. July/August/November.
Fixed Nonresidential Business and Residential Capital in the U.S. $4.75. August.
International Investment Position of the U.S. $4.75. August.
U.S. Direct Investment Abroad. $4.75. August.
Capital Consumption and Profits of Nonfinancial Corporations. $4.75. September.
Motor Vehicles, Current Model Year Survey. $4.75. October.
State and Local Government Fiscal Position Review. $4.75. December, January or February.
Business Statistics. Published as a separate issue. Not included in the subscription price. Biennially (odd yrs) Varies.

1239. SURVEY OF WALL ST. RESEARCH.
P.O. Box 689, Rye, NY 10580.
Annual Subscription: $59. **Frequency:** 6/yr.
Publisher: Nelson Publications.
Editorial Index: Each issue. Subject.
Special Issues:
National Directory of Wall St. Research—industry research by Wall St. security analysts, by industry. Started 1975. Published as a separate issue. $159. Not included in the subscription price. February.
Insider Transactions: Who's Buying Who—S.E.C. 13-D filings (owners with more than 5% of stock in a public company). $10. 6/yr. Each issue.

1240. SWIMMING POOL AGE & SPA MERCHANDISER.
6255 Barfield Rd., Atlanta, GA 30328.
Annual Subscription: $15. **Frequency:** Monthly.
Publisher: Communications Channels, Inc.
Advertiser Index: Every issue.
Special Issues:
Swimming Pool Institute Convention. Started 1949. $3. October.
Data and Reference Annual—directory of suppliers, manufacturers' representatives, wholesale distributors of pools (public and residential) with catalog file. Started 1933. Published as a separate issue. $15. Spring.
Industry Market Report. Started 1970. $3. Fall.

1241. SWIMMING WORLD—JUNIOR SWIMMER.
P.O. Box 45497, Los Angeles, CA 90045.
Annual Subscription: $16. **Frequency:** Monthly.
Publisher: Swimming World.
Advertiser Index: Every issue.
Editorial Index: Annual. Subject. December.
Special Issues:
Men's NCAA Water Polo Championships. $1.75. January.
U.S.S. International Meet Results. $1.75. February.
European Meets Results. $1.75. March.
Major Collegiate Dual Meets & Conference Championships. $1.75. April.
Major Collegiate Championships for Men and Women. $1.75. May.
California State Jr. College Championships/U.S. National Swimming Championships/U.S. Jr. Olympics Championships. $1.75. June.
Special Olympics Preview Issue/U.S. Olympics Trials. $1.75. Olympic years. July.
Major International Olympic Trials Meets. $1.75. Olympic years. August.
Special Olympics Issue. $1.75. Olympic years. September.
U.S. National Championships/Jr. National Championships. $1.75. October.
Swimming World Annual—photos, statistics. $1.75. December.

1242. SYMPHONY MAGAZINE.
633 E Street, NW, Washington, DC 20004.
Annual Subscription: $25. **Frequency:** Bimonthly.
Publisher: American Symphony Orchestra League.
Advertiser Index: Every issue.
Editorial Index: Annual. Subject/Author. February/March.

1243. TAPPI JOURNAL.
One Dunwoody Park, Atlanta, GA 30338.
Annual Subscription: $40. **Frequency:** Monthly.
Publisher: Technical Association of the Pulp and Paper Industry.
Advertiser Index: Every issue.
Editorial Index: Annual. Subject/Author. December.
Indexed or Abstracted Online: Paperchem; CIN.
Special Issues:
Exhibit Issue. Started 1965. $7.50. March.
Directory—TAPPI membership, committees, etc. Started 1982. Published as a separate issue. $75. April.
Salary Survey. $3.50. August.

1244. **TACK 'N TOGS MERCHANDISING.**
P.O. Box 67, Minneapolis, MN 55440.
Annual Subscription: $15. **Frequency:** Monthly.
Publisher: Robert M. Clarity.
Advertiser Index: Every issue.
Special Issues:
Tack'n Togs Book—buyers guide for marketers of horse and rider supplies. Published as a separate issue. $5. June.
Christmas Market. $1. August/October.
Fall Markets. $1. September.
Preview of Spring Clothing. $1. November.
Review & Forecast. $1. December.

1245. **TAX EXECUTIVE.**
1616 North Fort Myer Dr., Arlington, VA 22209.
Annual Subscription: $15. **Frequency:** Quarterly.
Publisher: Tax Executives Institute, Inc.
Editorial Index: Annual. Subject/Title/Author. October.
Indexed or Abstracted Online: Legal Resource Index; ABI/Inform; Management Contents.

1246. **TAX LAW REVIEW.**
210 South St., Boston, MA 02111.
Annual Subscription: $42. **Frequency:** Quarterly.
Publisher: Warren, Gorham & Lamont.
Editorial Index: Annual. Title/Author. Summer.
Indexed or Abstracted Online: ABI/Inform; Legal Resource Index; Management Contents; Insurance Abstracts.

1247. **TAX LAWYER.**
1155 East 60th St., Chicago, IL 60637.
Annual Subscription: $25. **Frequency:** Quarterly.
Publisher: American Bar Association, Section of Taxation.
Editorial Index: Annual. Subject/Title/Author. Summer.
Indexed or Abstracted Online: ABI/Inform; Insurance Abstracts; Management Contents; Legal Resource Index.
Special Issues:
Annual Report—important developments during the year; by laws & rules; convention program; committee reports. $6.50. Summer.
Review of Supreme Court Decisions in Taxation. $6.50. Winter.

1248. **TAXATION FOR ACCOUNTANTS.**
210 South St., Boston, MA 02111.
Annual Subscription: $48. **Frequency:** Monthly.
Publisher: Warren, Gorham and Lamont.
Editorial Index: Semi-Annual. Subject/Author. June/December.
Indexed or Abstracted Online: ABI/Inform; Insurance Abstracts; Management Contents.
Special Issues:
Survey of Tax Return Computer Service Bureaus. Started 1966. September.

1249. **TAXES.**
4025 West Peterson Ave., Chicago, IL 60646.
Annual Subscription: $60. **Frequency:** Monthly.
Publisher: Commerce Clearing House, Inc.
Editorial Index: Annual. Subject/Author. December.
Indexed Online: Trade & Industry Index.

1250. **TAXICAB MANAGEMENT.**
P.O. Box 2329, Asheville, NC 28802.
Annual Subscription: $12. **Frequency:** Monthly.
Publisher: International Taxicab Association, Inc.
Special Issues:
International Taxicab Association Convention. $1. October.

1251. **TEENS & BOYS MAGAZINE.**
210 Boylston St., Chestnut Hill, MA 02167.
Annual Subscription: $16. **Frequency:** Monthly.
Publisher: Larkin Publications.
Advertiser Index: March, October.
Special Issues:
Active Sportswear Annual. $2. January.
Boys & Young Men's Apparel Manufacturers Association Shows. $2. March/October.
Outerwear. $2. March.
Back-to-School. $2. 3/yr. May/June/July.
Teens & Boys Directory—listing of boyswear manufacturers in New York City. Includes showrooms, apparel trade associations, resident buying firms. Started 1940. Published as a separate issue. $3. June.
Holiday Merchandise. $2. August.

1252. **TELEPHONE ENGINEER & MANAGEMENT.**
124 South First St., Geneva, IL 60134.
Annual Subscription: $22. **Frequency:** 24/yr.
Publisher: Harcourt, Brace Jovanovich.
Advertiser Index: Every issue.
Editorial Index: Annual. Subject/Author. December.
Indexed or Abstracted Online: ABI/Inform; Trade & Industry Index.
Special Issues:
Annual Review & Forecast. Started 1962. $1.50. January.
Modern Telco Craftsman. $1.50. February/May/August/December.
Spring and Fall Construction Statistics. April/September.
Directory—includes directories of manufacturers and suppliers, U.S. & foreign telephone companies & associations; a buyer's guide. Started 1935. Published as a separate issue. $42. Not included in the subscription price. July.
Marketing. Started 1961. $1.50. July.
North American Telephone Association Convention Report. $1.50. November.
United States Independent Telephone Association Convention Report. $1.50. November.
Telecom Man of the Year. $1.50. December.

1253. **TELEPHONY.**
55 East Jackson, Chicago, IL 60604.
Annual Subscription: $26. **Frequency:** Weekly.
Publisher: Telephony Publishing Corp.
Advertiser Index: Every issue.
Editorial Index: Semi-Annual. Subject/Author. March/September.
Indexed Online: Trade & Industry Index; ABI/Inform.
Special Issues:
Review and Forecast. January.
Spring and Fall Construction. March/August.
Interface Convention Report. April.
Test Methods and Equipment. May.
Digital Technology. June.
International Communications Association Report. June.
Consumer Electronics Show Report. July.
International Conference on Communication Report. July.
Directory and Buyers Guide for the Telecommunications Industry—independent telephone cos.; interconnect companies; personnel of federal & state agencies, associations; industry statistics, etc. Published as a separate issue. $42. Not included in the subscription price. August.
Marketing Telecommunications Equipment & Services. August or September.
Mobile Telecommunications. August.
Telecommunications Power Systems & Equipment. October.
United States Independent Telephone Association Convention Report. November.
North American Telephone Association Convention Report. December.
International Issue. Monthly. Last issue each month.

1254. **TELEVISION DIGEST.**
1836 Jefferson Pl., NW, Washington, DC 20036.
Annual Subscription: $390. **Frequency:** Weekly.
Publisher: Television Digest, Inc.
Editorial Index: Semi-Annual. Subject. February/August.
Indexed or Abstracted Online: Newsnet.

Special Issues:
Cable & Sation Coverage Atlas—contour maps; zone maps; microwave system maps; earth station directory; top 100 cable system operators, etc. Published as a separate issue. $117. Not included in the subscription price.
Television & Cable Factbook: Vol I-Broadcast TV Stations; Vol II-Cable TV & Services. Lists every TV station in U.S., Canada and major foreign markets. All ownership and personnel; station coverage data maps; marketing demographics; cable subscriber counts & fees; corporate ownerships; franchise fees; advertising rates, etc. Published as a separate issue. $165 (2 volumes). Not included in the subscription price. Fall (Vol. I); Spring (Vol. II).

1255. TENNIS.
495 Westport Ave., P.O. Box 5350, Norwalk, CT 06856.
Annual Subscription: $11.95. **Frequency:** Monthly.
Publisher: Golf Digest/Tennis, Inc.
Indexed Online: Magazine Index.
Special Issues:
Directory of Tennis Camps. $1.75. January.
Tennis Annual—complete record book: men's and women's professional records; year's competition results; international championships; all-time records; photos; top 10 players; instruction portfolio. $2. February.
Fashion. $1.75. May/November.
U.S. Open. $1.75. September.
Indoor Tennis. $1.75. October.
Winter Resorts. $1.75. November.
Equipment. $1.75. December.

1256. TEXTILE CHEMIST AND COLORIST.
P.O. Box 12215, Research Triangle Park, NC 27709.
Annual Subscription: $30. **Frequency:** Monthly.
Publisher: American Association of Textile Chemists and Colorists.
Advertiser Index: Every issue.
Editorial Index: Each issue. Author.
Indexed or Abstracted Online: CA Search; World Textile Abstracts; Compendex.
Special Issues:
New Product Review. Started 1969. $3. January.
Buyers Guide—for dyeing and finishing products and services. Started 1969. $40. July.
American Association of Textile Chemists and Colorists Conference Report. Started 1969. $3. December.

1257. TEXTILE INDUSTRIES.
1760 Peachtree Rd., NW, Atlanta, GA 30357.
Annual Subscription: $50. **Frequency:** Monthly.
Publisher: W.R.C. Smith Publishing Co.
Advertiser Index: Every issue.
Editorial Index: Annual. Subject. January (available separately on request, for $1.50).
Indexed or Abstracted Online: Trade & Industry Index; Predicasts.
Special Issues:
Carpet Industry Forecast. $4. January or February.
Industry Trends. $4. January or February.
American Textile Manufacturers Institute Convention Report. $4. May or June.
International Buyers Guide. $4. June or July.

1258. TEXTILE RENTAL.
P.O. Box 1283, Hallandale, FL 33009.
Annual Subscription: $18. **Frequency:** Monthly.
Publisher: Textile Rental Services Association of America.
Advertiser Index: Every issue.
Editorial Index: Annual. Subject. January.
Special Issues:
Convention Issue. Started 1918. $1.50. May.
Trade Show. Started 1975. $1.50. Biennially. July.
Theme Issue-Marketing (topic this year). Started 1976. $1.50. September.
TRSA Annual Roster/Buyers Guide and Handbook. Published as a separate issue. December.

1259. TEXTILE WORLD.
P.O. Box 532, Hightstown, NJ 08520.
Annual Subscription: $33. **Frequency:** Monthly.
Publisher: McGraw-Hill Publications.
Advertiser Index: Every issue.
Indexed or Abstracted Online: Trade & Industry Index; CIN; Predicasts.
Special Issues:
Carpet Forecast. $5. May.
Buyers Guide. $10. July.
International Textile Manufacturers Association Convention Preview and Report. $5. September/December.

1260. THEATRE CRAFTS.
P.O. Box 630, Holmes, PA 19043.
Annual Subscription: $19.95. **Frequency:** 9/yr.
Publisher: Theatre Crafts Associates.
Advertiser Index: Every issue.
Special Issues:
Annual Directory of Manufacturers, Distributors and Suppliers of Products for the Performing Arts. $10. June/July.

1261. 33 METAL PRODUCING.
1221 Ave. of the Americas, New York, NY 10020.
Annual Subscription: $35.
Publisher: McGraw-Hill Publications Co.
Advertiser Index: Every issue.
Editorial Index: Annual. Subject/Title/Author. Available separately in February (free).
Indexed or Abstracted Online: Predicasts.
Special Issues:
Canadian Steel Industry Profile. $3. June.
World Steel Industry Data Handbook. Published as a separate issue. $95. Not included in the subscription price. November.
Economic Outlook. $3. December.

1262. TILE & DECORATIVE SURFACES.
17901 Ventura Blvd., Encino, CA 91316.
Annual Subscription: $25. **Frequency:** 10/yr.
Publisher: Jerry Fisher.
Advertiser Index: Every issue.
Special Issues:
Annual Directory and Buyer's Guide—tile contractors and distributors. Started 1960. $15. December.

1263. TIMBER HARVESTING.
P.O. Box 2268, Montgomery, AL 36197.
Annual Subscription: $8. **Frequency:** Monthly.
Publisher: Hatton-Brown Publishers, Inc.
Advertiser Index: Every issue.
Special Issues:
Woodlands Directory & Loggers Buying Guide. Started 1960. $5. January.

1264. TIMBER PROCESSING INDUSTRY.
P.O. Box 2268, Montgomery, AL 36197.
Annual Subscription: $24. **Frequency:** Annual.
Publisher: Hatton-Brown Publishers Inc.
Advertiser Index: Every issue.
Special Issues:
Lumbermen's Buying Guide. Started 1979. $5. August.

1265. TIME.
1271 Ave. of the Americas, New York, NY 10020.
Annual Subscription: $41. **Frequency:** Weekly.
Publisher: Time, Inc.
Special Issues:
Woman/Man of the Year. $1.50. January.

1266. TIRE REVIEW.
11 South Forge St., Akron, OH 44304.
Annual Subscription: $20. **Frequency:** Monthly.
Publisher: Babcox Automotive Publications.
Advertiser Index: Every issue.
Special Issues:
Purchasing Directory/National Tire Dealers & Retreaders Association Convention Issue. September.

1267. **TOBACCO INTERNATIONAL.**
551 Fifth Ave., New York, NY 10176.
Annual Subscription: $20. **Frequency:** 26/yr.
Publisher: Lockwood Trade Journal.
Advertiser Index: Every issue.
Special Issues:
Turkey/Bulgaria. $5. February.
Greece/Yugoslavia. $5. March.
Dixie Directory—leaf dealers, tobacco associations in Southern U.S. Published as a separate issue. $15. April.
Leaf Dealers. $5. May.
Africa. $5. June.
Import/Export. $15. July.
Latin America/Pakistan. $5. July.
Thailand. $5. August.
Japan/Tobacco Chemists/Philippines. $5. September.
Directory/Buyers Guide. Published as a separate issue. $15. October.
Korea. $5. October.
Italy/Cigars. $5. November.
India/Year-end. $5. December.
Tobacco Sciences Yearbook. Published as a separate issue. $15. Spring.

1268. **TODAY'S CATHOLIC TEACHER.**
2451 East River Rd., Dayton, OH 45439.
Annual Subscription: $11.95. **Frequency:** 8/yr.
Publisher: Peter Li, Inc.
Advertiser Index: Every issue.
Special Issues:
Textbook Survey—New & Revised. Started 1983. $2. January.
Summer School. Started 1975. $2. February.
National Catholic Educational Association Convention. Started 1970. $2. April.
Buyers Guide. Started 1981. $2. May.
Semester Opening (Back-To-School). Started 1966. $2. September.

1269. **TODAY'S TRANSPORT INTERNATIONAL** (published in Spanish as *Transporto Moderno*.).
P.O. Box 5017, Westport, CT 06881.
Annual Subscription: $35. **Frequency:** 6/yr.
Publisher: Intercontinental Publications.
Advertiser Index: Every issue.
Special Issues:
International Fleet Directory—manufacturers, suppliers, exporters. $10. February/March.
Annual Maintenance Issue. $10. August/September.

1270. **TOOLING & PRODUCTION.**
6521 Davis Industrial Parkway, Solon, OH 44139.
Annual Subscription: Controlled circulation. **Frequency:** Monthly.
Publisher: Huebner Publications, Inc.
Advertiser Index: Every issue.
Editorial Index: Annual. Subject. December or January.
Indexed Online: Trade & Industry Index.
Special Issues:
Numerical Controls. March.
Toolmaking. April.
Metal Stamping/Society of Manufacturing Engineers Tool Show. May.
Welding. June.
Grinding & Finishing. July.
Turning. August.
Metalforming. September.
Quality Assurance. October.
Factory Automation. November.
Materials. December.

1271. **TOP OF THE NEWS.**
50 East Huron St., Chicago, IL 60611.
Annual Subscription: $10 (individual)/20 (institution).
Frequency: Quarterly.
Publisher: Association for Library Services to Children and Young Adult Services, American Library Association.
Special Issues:
Caldecott Award Acceptance Speech/Newbery Award Acceptance Speech/Laura Ingalls Wilder Acceptance Speech. $5. Annual. Summer.

1272. **TOURIST ATTRACTIONS & PARKS.**
401 North Broad Street, Philadelphia, PA 19108.
Annual Subscription: $24. **Frequency:** Quarterly.
Publisher: Kane Communications, Inc.
Advertiser Index: Every issue.
Special Issues:
American Showman Carnival Routes & Fair Guide—by state. Published as a separate issue. $5. Spring.
Fair Date listings. Started 1981. $7.50. Spring.
International Association of Arena Managers (IAAM) Convention. Started 1981. $7.50. Summer.
International Association of Amusement Parks & Attractions Convention/International Amusement Fairs & Expositions Convention. Started 1972. $7.50. Fall.
American Showman Talent Guide. Published as a separate issue. $5. Winter.
Buyers Guide. Started 1973. $7.50. Winter.

1273. **TOY & HOBBY WORLD.**
P.O. Box 1226, Darien, CT 06820.
Annual Subscription: $30. **Frequency:** Monthly.
Publisher: U.S. Business Press, Inc.
Advertiser Index: Every issue.
Special Issues:
Electronics for Kids. Published as a separate issue. Bimonthly. January/March/May/July/September/November.
Licensing. Published as a separate issue. Bimonthly. January/March/May/July/September/November.
Toy Fair. February.
Trim-A-Tree Merchandising. Published as a separate issue. February.
Hobby Show. March.
Hobby Issue. July.
Directory of Toy Importers. December.

1274. **TOYS & GAMES.**
380 Wellington St. West, Toronto, Ontario, Can. M5V 1E3.
Annual Subscription: $18/15. **Frequency:** 6/yr.
Publisher: Page Publications Ltd.
Special Issues:
Toy Fair. $3. February.
Christmas Buying. $3. June.
Directory. $3. August.
Hobbies & Crafts. $3. October.
Games & Gaming/Year-End Forecast & Report/Calendar for New Year. $3. December.

1275. **TOYS, HOBBIES & CRAFTS.**
One East First St., Duluth, MN 55802.
Annual Subscription: $16. **Frequency:** Monthly.
Publisher: Harcourt Brace Jovanovich Inc.
Advertiser Index: Every issue.
Editorial Index: Annual. Subject.
Special Issues:
Selling Christmas Decorations. Started 1965. Published as a separate issue. $1.50. February/March.
Toy Trade News—tabloid presented five times during American Toy Fair. Published as a separate issue. $1.50. Not included in the subscription price. February.
Statistical Edition. $1.50. March.
Directory—buyers guide to toy industry. Started 1921. Published as a separate issue. $6. Not included in the subscription price. June.

1276. **TRACK & FIELD NEWS.**
P.O. Box 296, Los Altos, CA 94022.
Annual Subscription: $17.50. **Frequency:** Monthly.
Publisher: Track & Field News, Inc.
Special Issues:
Men's Annual Edition. Started 1964. $2. January.
Olympics Preview. Started 1952. $2. July.
Olympics. Started 1948. $2. August.

1277. TRAFFIC MANAGEMENT.
P.O. Box 17012, Denver, CO 80217.
Annual Subscription: $35. **Frequency:** Monthly.
Publisher: Cahners Publishing Co.
Advertiser Index: Every issue.
Indexed or Abstracted Online: ABI/Inform; Management Contents.
Special Issues:
Transportation/Distribution/Equipment Directory. Started 1982. Published as a separate issue. $35. Not included in the subscription price. March.
World Commerce Issue. Started 1963. $4. October.
Catalog of Physical Distribution Directories & Guides. Started 1972. $4. December.

1278. TRAFFIC SAFETY.
444 North Michigan Ave., Chicago, IL 60611.
Annual Subscription: $11.15 (members)/13.95 (nonmembers). **Frequency:** 6/yr.
Publisher: National Safety Council.
Editorial Index: Annual. Subject/Title/Author. November/December.
Special Issues:
Annual Traffic Statistics Story. Started 1957. May/June.
National Safety Congress and Exposition. Started 1912. September/October.
Traffic Accident Facts—statistical summary. Started 1962. November/December.

1279. TRAFFIC WORLD.
1435 G St., Ste. 815, Washington, DC 20005.
Annual Subscription: $108. **Frequency:** Weekly.
Publisher: The Traffic Service Corp.
Advertiser Index: Every issue.
Editorial Index: Semi-Annual. Subject/Title/Author. February/July.
Special Issues:
Perfect Shipping. Started 1948. $3.50. March.
Freight Vehicles & Equipment. Started 1958. $3.50. July.
Ports & Harbors. Started 1950. $3.50. September.
Air Freight Guide. Started 1962. $3.50. November.
Official Directory of Industrial and Commercial Traffic Executives—U.S. and Canadian firms with full or part-time traffic departments. Started 1935. Published as a separate issue. $50. Not included in the subscription price. November.

1280. TRAILER/BODY BUILDERS.
1602 Harold St., Houston, TX 77006.
Annual Subscription: $15. **Frequency:** Monthly.
Publisher: Tunnell Publications Inc.
Advertiser Index: Every issue.
Special Issues:
Truck Equipment Distributors Issue/National Truck Equipment Association Convention. Started 1970. $2. March.
Truck Trailer Manufacturers Association Convention. $2. June.
Buyers Guide. Started 1960. $10. July.
Truck Body & Equipment Association Convention. $2. December.

1281. TRAINING AND DEVELOPMENT JOURNAL.
600 Maryland Ave., SW, Ste. 305, Washington, DC 20024.
Annual Subscription: $40. **Frequency:** Monthly.
Publisher: American Society for Training & Development.
Advertiser Index: Every issue.
Editorial Index: Annual. Subject/Title/Author. December.
Indexed or Abstracted Online: ABI/Inform; Management Contents.
Special Issues:
Career Development. $5. February.
Organizational Development. $5. April.
American Society For Training and Development Annual Report. $5. May or June.
International Issue. $5. October.
Sales Training. $5. November.

1282. TRAINS.
1027 North Seventh St., Milwaukee, WI 53233.
Annual Subscription: $20. **Frequency:** Monthly.
Publisher: Kalmbach Publishing Co.
Advertiser Index: Every issue.
Editorial Index: Annual. Subject/Title/Author. January.
Indexed Online: Magazine Index.

1283. TRANSMISSION & DISTRIBUTION.
One River Rd., Cos Cob, CT 06807.
Annual Subscription: $22. **Frequency:** Monthly.
Publisher: Cleworth Publishing Co.
Advertiser Index: Every issue.
Special Issues:
T & D Specifiers and Buyers Guide—electrical power transmission and distribution products and services. By product, company, trade names. Started 1966. Published as a separate issue. $4. September.

1284. TRANSPORT TOPICS.
1616 P St. NW, Washington, DC 20036.
Annual Subscription: $30. **Frequency:** Weekly.
Publisher: American Trucking Associations.
Special Issues:
Management Outlook. Started 1940. $1. Not included in the subscription price. January.
Product Reviews. Started 1979. $1. Not included in the subscription price. 5/yr. February/May/July/August/November.
International Trucking Show. Started 1977. $1. Not included in the subscription price. March.
Fleet Maintenance. Started 1979. $1. Not included in the subscription price. April.
Financial Special. Started 1979. $1. Not included in the subscription price. June.
Equipment Review. Started 1940. $1. Not included in the subscription price. September.
ATA Convention. Started 1935. $1. Not included in the subscription price. October.
Year End Report. Started 1979. $1. Not included in the subscription price. December.

1285. TRAVEL AGENT.
2 West 46th St., New York, NY 10036.
Annual Subscription: $7. **Frequency:** 2/wk.
Publisher: American Traveler, Inc.
Special Issues:
Travel Industry Personnel Directory—air and shipline executives; domestic and foreign railroads; hotel representatives; tourist bureaus; travel trade associations; U.S. and Canada tour operators; car purchase and rental firms. Started 1930. Published as a separate issue. $12. Not included in the subscription price. January.
ASTA (American Society of Travel Agents) Convention Issue and Bluebook. September.

1286. TRAVEL & LEISURE.
1350 Ave. of the Americas, New York, NY 10019.
Annual Subscription: $15 (Amex cardmembers)/18 (non-cardmembers). **Frequency:** Monthly.
Publisher: American Express Publishing Corp.
Editorial Index: A; also 10-year cumulative. Subject/Author. July.

1287. TRAVEL PRINTOUT.
U.S. Travel Data Ctr., 1899 L St., NW, Washington, DC 20036.
Annual Subscription: $45. **Frequency:** Monthly.
Publisher: U.S. Travel Data Ctr.
Special Issues:
Travel Industry Outlook. Started 1976. January.
Summer Vacation Travel Outlook. Started 1981. June.
Economic Review of Travel in America. Started 1980. July.
National Travel Survey Quarterly Reports. Started 1979. 4/yr. Varies.

1288. TRAVEL WEEKLY.
One Park Ave., New York, NY 10016.
Annual Subscription: $20. **Frequency:** Semiweekly.
Publisher: Ziff-Davis Publishing Co.
Indexed Online: Trade & Industry Index.
Special Issues:
  Economic Survey. $1. January.
  World Travel Directory/Yearbook—lists wholesale tour operators in North Amercian market; cruise lines with North American offices or representatives; wholesalers for special interest tours; data on world destinations; names and addresses of worldwide retail travel agencies, etc. Started 1969. Published as a separate issue. $75. Not included in the subscription price. January.
  Spring/Summer Tour Directory. Started Y. $1. February.
  Telephone Directory of the Travel Industry. Started Y. $1. March.
  Travel Agency Guide to Business & Group Travel. $1. April/October.
  Fall/Winter Tour Directory. $1. July.
  Profit Guide. $1. August.
  ASTA (American Society of Travel Agents) Convention. $1. 4/yr. September (2) & October (2).

1289. TRUCK & OFF-HIGHWAY INDUSTRIES.
One Chilton Way, Radnor, PA 19089.
Annual Subscription: $30. **Frequency:** 6/yr.
Publisher: Chilton Co.
Advertiser Index: Every issue.
Special Issues:
  Off-Highway Vehicle Specifications Issue. Started 1980. $10. November/December.

1290. TRUSTEE.
211 East Chicago Ave., Ste. 700, Chicago, IL 60611.
Annual Subscription: $16. **Frequency:** Monthly.
Publisher: American Hospital Publishing, Inc.
Advertiser Index: Every issue.
Editorial Index: Annual. Subject/Author. December.
Indexed Online: Medline.
Special Issues:
  American Hospital Association Meeting Report. March.
  American Hospital Association Trustee Forum Meeting Report. August.

1291. TRUSTS & ESTATES.
6255 Barfield Rd., Atlanta, GA 30328.
Annual Subscription: $45. **Frequency:** Monthly.
Publisher: Communication Channels, Inc.
Advertiser Index: Every issue.
Editorial Index: Annual. Subject/Title/Author. January.
Indexed or Abstracted Online: Trade & Industry Index; ABI/Inform; Insurance Abstracts; Management Contents; Legal Resource Index.
Special Issues:
  Forecast/Investment Officer Survey. $3.75. January.
  Survey of Trust Operation Officers. Started 1983. $3.75. March.
  Bank Marketing Association Meeting. $3.75. November.
  Directory of Trust Institutions. Published as a separate issue. $19.50. December.

1292. TURBOMACHINERY INTERNATIONAL.
P.O. Box 5550, Norwalk, CT 06856.
Annual Subscription: $38. **Frequency:** 9/yr.
Publisher: Business Journals, Inc.
Advertiser Index: Every issue.
Special Issues:
  Gas Turbine Conference. Started 1959. $5. March or April.
  Turbomachinery International Handbook—catalog issue including equipment specifications, supplier directory and advertising. Started 1961. Published as a separate issue. $45. March.
  Maintenance & Aftermarket. Started 1983. $5. August.
  Turbomachinery Symposium. Started 1982. $5. October.

1293. TURKEY WORLD.
Sandstone Building, Mt. Morris, IL 61054.
Annual Subscription: $8. **Frequency:** 6/yr.
Publisher: Watt Publishing Co.
Advertiser Index: Every issue.
Special Issues:
  Breeder Issue. $1.50. September/October.
  National Turkey Federation Convention. $1.50. November/December.

1294. TYPEWORLD.
15 Oakridge Circle, Wilmington, MA 01887.
Annual Subscription: $20. **Frequency:** 17/yr.
Publisher: Blum Publications.
Special Issues:
  American Newspaper Publishers Association Convention. June.
  Directory—for word processing and typesetting systems. December.

1295. U.S. GLASS, METAL & GLAZING.
2701 Union Ave. Ext., Ste. 410, Memphis, TN 38112.
Annual Subscription: $12. **Frequency:** 6/yr.
Publisher: U.S. Glass Publications, Inc.
Advertiser Index: Every issue.
Special Issues:
  Outlook & Forecast Issue. Started 1973. $2. January/February.
  Glass Machinery & Equipment. Started 1982. $2. March/April.
  Convention Reports: Flat Glass Marketing Association, National Glass Dealers Association. Started 1966. $2. May/June.
  Sealants & Glazing Systems. Started 1967. $2. July/August.
  Mirrors, Stained & Decorative Glasses. Started 1978. $2. September/October.
  Buyers' Guide. Started 1968. $2. November/December.

1296. U.S. MEDICINE.
2033 M St., NW, Ste. 505, Washington, DC 20036.
Annual Subscription: $55. **Frequency:** Semimonthly.
Publisher: U.S. Medicine Inc.
Advertiser Index: Every issue.
Special Issues:
  Annual Issue—reports by the chiefs of the major federal medical services. Started 1966. Published as a separate issue. January.

1297. U.S. NEWS & WORLD REPORT.
P.O. Box 2629, Boulder, CO 80322.
Annual Subscription: $36. **Frequency:** Weekly.
Publisher: U.S. News & World Report, Inc.
Indexed or Abstracted Online: NEXIS; Newsearch; Information Bank.
Special Issues:
  Outlook (The Year Ahead). $1.95. December.

1298. UNITED STATES BANKER.
1 River Rd., Cos Cob, CT 06807.
Annual Subscription: $24. **Frequency:** Monthly.
Publisher: Cleworth Publishing Co.
Advertiser Index: Every issue.
Editorial Index: Semi-Annual. Subject. January/July.
Indexed or Abstracted Online: ABI/Inform; Management Contents.
Special Issues:
  Investment Outlook. Started 1979. $3. January.
  Secondary Mortgage Market Update. $3. February.
  Home Banking Review. $3. May.
  Housing Market. $3. July.
  Marketing and the Deregulated Environment. $3. September.
  Commercial Banking Review. Started 1960. $3. October.
  Thrift Institutions Review. Started 1960. $3. November.
  Asset-Based Financing. $3. December.

1299. UNITED STATES TOBACCO AND CANDY JOURNAL.
254 West 31st St., New York, NY 10001.
Annual Subscription: $24. **Frequency:** 24/yr.
Publisher: BMT Publications, Inc.
Editorial Index: Annual. Subject/Author. January or February.
Indexed Online: Trade & Industry Index.
Special Issues:
  Cigars. $1. January.
  National Candy Wholesalers Association Shows. $1. 2/yr. February & July.
  Supplier Directory: Who's Who in Tobacco/Confectionery Distribution—lists over 6000 distributers, alpha and by state. Started 1963. Published as a separate issue. $10. February.
  National Association of Tobacco Distributors Convention. $1. March.
  Sundries. $1. August.
  Supplier Directory—lists over 500 suppliers with product listings. Started 1963. Published as a separate issue. $10. October.
  Year-End Review. $1. December.

1300. UPHOLSTERING TODAY.
200 South Main St., P.O. Box 2411, High Point, NC 27261.
Annual Subscription: $15. **Frequency:** Monthly.
Publisher: Communications Today Ltd.
Advertiser Index: Every issue.
Editorial Index: Annual. Subject. April.
Special Issues:
  Spring Fabrics/Fibers/Nonwovens. March.
  Directory of Industry Resources. April.
  Sewing Machines, Needles and Thread. May.
  Furniture Equipment Supply Exposition/Sleeper and Recliner Mechanisms. June.
  Buttoning Equipment/Webbing, Springs and Suspension Systems. July.
  Foam and Cushioning Materials. August.
  L.A. Woodworking, Machinery & Furniture Supply Fair/Fall Fabrics/Fibers. September.
  Financial Services/Coated Fabrics. October.
  Packaging Equipment and Materials. November.
  Materials Handling Systems/Leather. December.

1301. UPHOLSTERY MANUFACTURING MANAGEMENT.
P.O. Box 38629, Germantown, TN 38138.
Annual Subscription: $10. **Frequency:** 6/yr.
Publisher: Associations Publications, Inc.
Advertiser Index
Special Issues:
  Directory of Supply Sources. Started 1983. $10. June.

1302. VARIETY.
154 W. 46 St., New York, NY 10036.
Annual Subscription: $65. **Frequency:** Weekly.
Publisher: Variety Inc.
Advertiser Index: Every issue.
Indexed or Abstracted Online: AMI; Trade & Industry Index.
Special Issues:
  Anniversary Edition—Includes top rental films of the year; all-time film grossers, gold records of the year—records selling one million or more copies and albums grossing one million plus. Started 1907. $2.50. January.
  National Association of Television & Program Executives Convention. $2.50. February.
  American Film Market. Started 1981. $2.50. March.
  International TV Annual. Started 1970. $2.50. April.
  International Film Annual—includes Cannes Film Festival. Started 1958. $2.50. May.
  Auditorium-Arena Annual. Started 1972. $2.50. July.
  Home Video Annual. $1.25. September.
  Radio-TV Preview and Review—season's new shows. Includes series titles listed alphabetically by network, time slots, suppliers, production staff head, cast regulars and semi-regulars and estimated production costs per segment. $1.25. September/October.
  International Film and Documentary Market, Milan (MIFED—Mercato Internazionale del Filme del Documentario). $1.25. October.
  Canadian Issue. $1.25. November.

1303. VENDING TIMES.
211 East 43 Street, New York, NY 10017.
Annual Subscription: $20. **Frequency:** Monthly.
Publisher: Vending Times, Inc.
Advertiser Index: Every issue.
Indexed Online: Trade & Industry Index.
Special Issues:
  Buyer's Guide—vending, coffee services, music and games. Started 1977. Published as a separate issue. $10. February.
  Census of the Industry. Started 1946. Published as a separate issue. $10. July.

1304. VENTURE.
35 West 45th St., New York, NY 10036.
Annual Subscription: $18. **Frequency:** Monthly.
Publisher: Venture Magazine, Inc.
Advertiser Index: Every issue.
Indexed Online: Management Contents.
Special Issues:
  New Issues Review and Forecast. $2. April.
  Venture 100—Largest companies still managed by their founders. $2. May.
  Venture Capital 100—survey of the nation's most active venture capitalists. Started 1982. $2. June.
  Venture Fast-Track 100—the largest businesses in the country started within the last decade and still run by their founders. Started 1982. $2. July.
  Entrepreneurial compensation—100 company founders and their remuneration. $2. September.
  Venture Capital Directory—names and addresses of venture capital companies. Started 1981. $2. December.

1305. VERTIFLITE.
217 North Washington St., Alexandria, VA 22314.
Annual Subscription: $25. **Frequency:** Bimonthly.
Publisher: American Helicopter Society.
Special Issues:
  Annual Membership Directory. Started 1976. Published as a separate issue. $5. January.

1306. VETERINARY ECONOMICS.
690 South 4th Street, P.O. Box 13265, Edwardsville, KS 66113.
Annual Subscription: $30. **Frequency:** Monthly.
Publisher: Veterinary Medicine Publishing Co.
Advertiser Index: Every issue.
Editorial Index: Annual. Subject/Title/Author. December.

1307. VETERINARY MEDICINE/SMALL ANIMAL CLINICIAN.
690 South 4th Street, P.O. Box 13265, Edwardsville, KS 66113.
Annual Subscription: $28. **Frequency:** Monthly.
Publisher: Veterinary Medicine Publishing Co.
Advertiser Index: Every issue.
Editorial Index: Annual. Subject/Title/Author. December.

1308. VIDEO SYSTEMS.
9221 Quivira Rd., Overland Park, KS 66212.
Annual Subscription: $25. **Frequency:** Monthly.
Publisher: Intertec Publishing.
Advertiser Index: Every issue.
Editorial Index: Annual. Subject. December.
Special Issues:
  Equipment Roundup: Character Generators. $3. February.
  National Association of Broadcasters Convention Preview; Review. Started 1979. $3. March/June.
  Video Index: Guide to Production Services. Started 1978. $5. May.
  Post-Production Facilities Review. $3. June.
  ENG (electronic new gathering) Camera Roundup. $3. September.
  Salary Survey—video production industry. $3. October.
  Video Index: Hardware Buyer's Guide. Started 1977. $10. November.

1309. VIDEODISK/VIDEOTEX.
520 Riverside Ave., Westport, CT 06880.
Annual Subscription: $52. **Frequency:** Quarterly.
Publisher: Meckler Publishing.
Editorial Index: Annual. Title/Author. Winter issue. Index divided into 3 sections: project title, producer/sponsor, and key project personnel.
Indexed or Abstracted Online: ABI/Inform; LISA; CompuMath.
Special Issues:
 Videodisc Projects Directory—individual current applications of videodisc and optical disc technology in education and industry. 4/yr. January/April/July/October.

1310. VIDEOGRAPHY.
P.O. Box 658, Holmes, PA 19043.
Annual Subscription: $15.75. **Frequency:** Monthly.
Publisher: Media Horizons.
Advertiser Index: Every issue.
Special Issues:
 Guide to Blank Tape. Started 1981. $2. January.
 Guide to Videocassette Recorders. Started 1977. $2. January.
 Guide to Mobile Production. Started 1979. $2. May or June.
 Guide to Video Software. Started 1977. $2. May or June.
 Guide to Videoconferencing. Started 1982. $2. May or June.
 Guide to Production Studios. Started 1977. $2. July or August.
 Guide to Postproduction Facilities. Started 1977. $2. August.
 Guide to 1-inch VTRs. Started 1980. $2. October.
 Annual Hardware Directory. Started 1978. $2. December.

1311. VISUAL MERCHANDISING & STORE DESIGN.
407 Gilbert Ave., Cincinnati, OH 45202.
Annual Subscription: $18. **Frequency:** Monthly.
Publisher: S.T. Publications.
Advertiser Index: Every issue.
Editorial Index: Annual. Subject. February.
Special Issues:
 National Retail Merchants Association Convention and Retailers Business & Equipment Exposition. $2. January.
 Buyers Guide—directory of goods and services in store design and retail display. Started 1982. $5. February.
 Lighting. Started 1980. $2. Biennially (odd years). March.
 California Visual Merchandising Market. $2. April.
 National Association of Display Industries Christmas Market. $2. June.
 Mannequins. Started 1977. $2. Biennially (odd years). August.
 Store Fixturing/Design. Started 1975. $2. October.
 National Association of Display Industries Spring Market. $2. December.

1312. VOC ED.
2020 North 14th St., Arlington, VA 22201.
Annual Subscription: $20. **Frequency:** Monthly.
Publisher: American Vocational Association.
Advertiser Index: Every issue.
Editorial Index: Annual. Subject/Author. February.
Special Issues:
 Buyers Guide. Started 1975. $2.50. January.
 Teaching Issue for Vocational Teachers. Started 1979. $2.50. August.
 American Vocational Association Convention. $2.50. December.

1313. VOGUE MAGAZINE.
350 Madison Ave., New York, NY 10017.
Annual Subscription: $24. **Frequency:** Monthly.
Publisher: Conde Nast Publishing.
Indexed Online: Magazine Index.
Special Issues:
 New York Collections. $2.50. February/September.
 Accessories. $2.50. March.
 Beauty/Health Special. $2.50. April/October.
 Summer Collections. $2.50. May.
 Fall Forecast. $2.50. July.
 Resort Collections. $2.50. November.

1314. THE VOLTA REVIEW.
3417 Volta Pl., NW, Washington, DC 20007.
Annual Subscription: $30/35 (Institutions). **Frequency:** 7/yr.
Publisher: A.G. Bell Association for the Deaf.
Editorial Index: Annual. Subject/Author. December.
Indexed or Abstracted Online: ERIC.
Special Issues:
 Monograph Issue. Started 1976. September.

1315. WWS/WORLD PORTS.
77 Moehring Dr., Blauvelt, NY 10913.
Annual Subscription: $25. **Frequency:** 7/yr.
Publisher: World Wide Shipping Guide, Inc.
Advertiser Index: Every issue.
Special Issues:
 Marketing/West Coast Ports. $4.75. February/March.
 South Atlantic Ports/Caribbean. $4.75. April/May.
 North Atlantic Ports/Containerization/Free Trade Zones. $4.75. June.
 Great Lakes Canadian Ports/Freight Forwarding/Custom Brokers. $4.75. July/August.
 American Association of Port Authorities Convention Report. $4.75. October/November.
 Foreign Ports. $4.75. October/November.
 Gulf Ports. $4.75. December/January.

1316. WALL STREET JOURNAL.
22 Cortlandt St., New York, NY 10007.
Annual Subscription: $94. **Frequency:** Daily.
Publisher: Dow Jones & Co.
Editorial Index: A; also monthly. Subject. Monthly, $300; annually, $280; combination, $500. Two sections: general news and corporate news. Monthy index contains daily Dow-Jones averages. Annual index contains averages for each month by day, and the editorial index to *Barron's Weekly*..
Indexed or Abstracted Online: Information Bank; AMI; Trade & Industry Index; Dow Jones News Retrieval; Predicasts.

1317. WALLCOVERINGS.
2 Sellect St., Stamford, CT 06902.
Annual Subscription: $12. **Frequency:** Monthly.
Publisher: Publishing Dynamics Inc.
Advertiser Index: Every issue.
Special Issues:
 Buyers Guide & Directory. September.

1318. WALLS & CEILINGS.
14006 Ventura Blvd., Sherman Oaks, CA 91423.
Annual Subscription: $10. **Frequency:** Monthly.
Publisher: R. F. Welch.
Advertiser Index: Every issue.
Editorial Index: Annual. Subject/Title. January.
Special Issues:
 Business Forecast. $1. February.
 Steel Framing. $1. August.
 New Products. $1. November.

1319. WARD'S AUTO WORLD.
28 West Adams St., Detroit, MI 48226.
Annual Subscription: $30. **Frequency:** Monthly.
Publisher: Ward's Communications Inc.
Indexed Online: Trade & Industry Index; Predicasts; AMI.
Special Issues:
 Dealer Survey—attitudes of automobile dealers to various industry issues/Midyear Marketing Outlook. Started 1978. $2.50. February.
 Emphasis of Engineering. $2.50. March.
 Import Evaluations. Started 1976. $2.50. May.

Automotive Yearbook—includes statistics, directories and buyers guide. Started 1938. Published as a separate issue. $95. Not included in the subscription price. June.
Supplier Survey and Outlook. $2.50. July.
Materials Issue. $2.50. September.
Rating The Year's New Models. $2.50. October.
Goofs & Goodies Survey of New Models. $2.50. November.
State of the Industry—interviews with top officers of 5 largest U.S. automobile manufacturers. Started 1971. $2.50. December.

1320. WAREHOUSE DISTRIBUTOR NEWS.
11 S. Forge St., Akron, OH 44304.
Annual Subscription: $25. **Frequency:** Monthly.
Publisher: Babcox Automotive Publications.
Advertiser Index: Every issue.
Special Issues:
Automotive Warehouse Distributors Association Convention. October.

1321. THE WASHINGTON MONTHLY.
2712 Ontario Rd., NW, Washington, DC 20009.
Annual Subscription: $24. **Frequency:** 11/yr.
Publisher: James Rice.
Special Issues:
Political Book Issue. Started 1971. $2. March.

1322. WASTE AGE.
1730 Rhode Island Ave. NW, Washington, DC 20036.
Annual Subscription: $22. **Frequency:** Monthly.
Publisher: National Solid Wastes Management & Association.
Advertiser Index
Special Issues:
Annual Review—report on national publicly held refuse companies. $3. August.

1323. WATCH & CLOCK REVIEW.
2403 Champa St., Denver, CO 80205.
Annual Subscription: $12. **Frequency:** Monthly.
Publisher: Golden Bell Press.
Advertiser Index: Every issue.
Special Issues:
Directory of Clock Manufacturers and Importers. $2. May.
Watch Resources Directory—finished watches. $2. November.

1324. WATER CONDITIONING AND PURIFICATION.
P.O. Box 42406, Tucson, AZ 85733.
Annual Subscription: $22. **Frequency:** Monthly.
Publisher: Publicom Inc.
Special Issues:
Annual Buyers Guide. Started 1959. $5. April.

1325. WATER & POLLUTION CONTROL.
1450 Don Mills Rd., Don Mills, Ontario, Can. M3B 2X7.
Annual Subscription: $24. **Frequency:** 6/yr.
Publisher: Southam Communications Ltd.
Advertiser Index: Every issue.
Editorial Index: Annual. Subject. May.
Special Issues:
Government Reference Manual—environmental who's who, gov't. legislation, gov't publications on environment. Started 1980. May.
Directory and Buyer's Guide—manufacturers & suppliers, equipment and products for water/sewage, industrial wastes, air pollution, noise abatement. Started 1965. $25. November.

1326. THE WATER SKIER.
P.O. Box 191, Winter Haven, FL 33882.
Annual Subscription: $4. **Frequency:** 7/yr.
Publisher: American Water Ski Association.
Advertiser Index: Every issue.
Editorial Index: Annual. Subject/Title. January.

1327. WATERWAYS JOURNAL.
319 North Fourth St., St. Louis, MO 63102.
Annual Subscription: $18. **Frequency:** Weekly.
Publisher: Waterways Journal Inc.
Advertiser Index: Every issue.
Special Issues:
Work Boat Show. $.50. January.
Water Resources Congress Meeting. $.50. March.
Inland Waterways Conference & Trade Show. $.50. August.
Gulf Intracoastal Canal Association Meeting. $.50. September.
Ohio Valley Improvement Association Meeting. $.50. October.
Annual Review and Directory. $.50. December.

1328. WEEDS TREES & TURF.
HBJ Publications, Duluth, MN 55802.
Annual Subscription: $15. **Frequency:** Monthly.
Publisher: Dick Gore.
Advertiser Index: Every issue.
Editorial Index: Annual. Title/Author. December.
Special Issues:
Golf Show Issue. January.
Weed Control Guide. March.
Insect Control Guide. May.
Buyers Guide. September.
Fertilizer Guide. November.

1329. WEIGHT WATCHERS MAGAZINE.
P.O. Box 2555, Boulder, CO 80321.
Annual Subscription: $11.97. **Frequency:** Monthly.
Publisher: American/Harlequin Inc.
Editorial Index: Monthly. Subject.
Special Issues:
Annual Reader Recipe Contest. Started 1968. $1.25. February/October.

1330. WELDING DESIGN & FABRICATION.
1111 Chester Ave., Cleveland, OH 44114.
Annual Subscription: $36. **Frequency:** Monthly.
Publisher: Penton/IPC.
Advertiser Index: Every issue.
Editorial Index: Annual. Subject/Title. December.
Special Issues:
Welder Safety & Health. $3. January.
Welding & Fabricating Data Book—buyers guide. Started 1958. Published as a separate issue. $25. Not included in the subscription price. Biennially (even years). January.
American Welding Society Welding Show. $3. March/April.
Nondestructive Testing. $3. September.

1331. WELDING JOURNAL.
550 LeJeune Rd. NW, Miami, FL 33126.
Annual Subscription: $36. **Frequency:** Monthly.
Publisher: American Welding Society/Welding Research Council.
Editorial Index: Subject/Author. December.

1332. WESTERN CANADA OUTDOORS.
P.O. Box 430, North Battleford, Saskatchewan, Can. S9A 3K2.
Annual Subscription: $6. **Frequency:** 6/yr.
Publisher: McIntosh Publishing Co.
Special Issues:
Annual Convention Issue. February.
Spring Issue. April.
Angling. June.
Hunting. August.
Big Game. October.
Winter Sports. December.

1333. WESTERN FISHERIES.
1132 Hamilton St., Ste. 202, Vancouver, British Columbia, Can. V6B 2S2.
Annual Subscription: $14. **Frequency:** Monthly.

Publisher: Maclean Hunter Ltd.
Advertiser Index: Every issue.
Special Issues:
  Gear Issue.   January.
  Annual Statistical Review.   June.
  New Boat Issue.   October.

1334. WESTERN HORSEMAN.
P.O. Box 27780, San Diego, CA 92127.
Annual Subscription: $12.   **Frequency:** Monthly.
Publisher: Western Horseman Inc.
Advertiser Index: Every issue.
Editorial Index: Annual. Title. December.
Abstracted Online
Special Issues:
  All-Breed Issue—major and lesser known breeds.   Started 1956. $1.50.   October.

1335. WESTERN MINER.
1201 Melville St., Vancouver, British Columbia, Can. V6E 2X9.
Annual Subscription: $25/15.   **Frequency:** Monthly.
Publisher: Western Miner Press Ltd.
Advertiser Index: Every issue.
Editorial Index: Subject/Title/Author. December.
Special Issues:
  Coal Miner Supplement. $3.   6/yr.   January/March/May/July/September/November.
  Coal Industry Review—producers and projects; overview of provinces.   Y.   March.
  Annual Spring Review—mineral, financial, policy reviews by federal and provincial governments in Canada.   Y.   April.

1336. WESTERN PAINT & DECORATING.
7335 Topanga Canyon Blvd., Canoga Park, CA 91303.
Annual Subscription: $12.   **Frequency:** 6/yr.
Publisher: Western Trade Publishing Co.
Advertiser Index: Every issue.
Special Issues:
  Annual Raw Materials and Equipment Source Directory. $2.   January/February.
  National Decorating Products Show/Federation of Societies for Coatings Technology Show. $2.   September/October.
  Annual Western Retail Dealers Source Directory (13 Western states). $2.   November/December.

1337. THE WHOLESALER.
135 Addison Ave., Elmhurst, IL 60126.
Annual Subscription: $20.   **Frequency:** Monthly.
Publisher: Scott Periodicals Corp.
Advertiser Index: Every issue.
Special Issues:
  Directory of Manufacturers Representatives—of plumbing, heating, air conditioning and piping. $30.   February.
  Profit & Market Survey—for distributors of plumbing, heating, air conditioning and piping.   Started 1959. $5.   April.
  Wholesaling 100 and HCR 50—list of 100 top plumbing, 50 top heating/cooling wholesalers.   Started 1971. $5.   July.
  Wholesaler Product Directory—classified guide to plumbing, heating, air conditioning, piping, and refrigeration products. Published as a separate issue. $5.   September.
  Air Conditioning and Refrigeration Wholesalers Convention/American Supply Association Convention. $5.   October.
  North American Heating & Wholesalers Convention. $5.   December.

1338. WILSON LIBRARY BULLETIN.
950 University Ave., Bronx, NY 10452.
Annual Subscription: $25.   **Frequency:** 10/yr.
Publisher: The H. W. Wilson Company.
Advertiser Index: Every issue.
Editorial Index: Annual. Subject/Author. September.
Indexed Online: Magazine Index.
Special Issues:
  International Librarianship. $3.   April.

1339. WINDOW ENERGY SYSTEMS.
345 Cedar Bldg., Ste. 450, St. Paul, MN 55101.
Annual Subscription: $24.   **Frequency:** Monthly.
Publisher: Industrial Fabrics Association International.
Advertiser Index: Every issue.
Special Issues:
  New Products Issue.   Started 1981.   January.
  Northeast Window Energy Show Program.   Started 1983.   February.
  Buyers Guide of Window Treatments.   Started 1981.   June.
  Annual Window Energy Show Program.   Started 1981.   August.

1340. WINES & VINES.
1800 Lincoln Ave., San Rafael, CA 94901.
Annual Subscription: $22.   **Frequency:** Monthly.
Publisher: Hiaring Company.
Advertiser Index: Every issue.
Special Issues:
  Brandy Issue. $2.50.   January.
  Vineyard Issue. $2.50.   February.
  Man-of-the Year Issue. $2.50.   March.
  Water Issue. $2.50.   April.
  Import/Export Issue. $2.50.   May.
  Enology Issue. $2.50.   June.
  Statistical Issue. $2.50.   July.
  Marketing Issue. $2.50.   September.
  Equipment and Supplies Issue. $2.50.   November.
  Champagne. $2.50.   December.
  Wine & Vines Annual Directory—listing of all wineries in U.S., Canada and Mexico; buyer's guide; industry roster; summary of state laws.   Published as a separate issue. $25.   December.

1341. WINGS.
1224-53 Ave. NE, Ste. 158, Calgary, Alberta, Can. T2E 7E2.
Annual Subscription: $18/15.   **Frequency:** 6/yr.
Publisher: Corvus Publishing Group Ltd.
Advertiser Index: Every issue.
Special Issues:
  General Aviation Buyers Guide.   February.
  Avionics Directory.   May.
  Air Shows.   August.
  Corporate Aviation in Canada.   September.
  NBAA Report.   November.

1342. WIRE JOURNAL INTERNATIONAL.
1570 Boston Post Road, Guilford, CT 06437.
Annual Subscription: $50.   **Frequency:** Monthly.
Publisher: Wire Association International.
Advertiser Index: Every issue.
Editorial Index: Annual. Subject. January.
Indexed Online: Compendex; CA Search.
Special Issues:
  Wire Dies & Equipment. $4.   January.
  Business Outlook. $4.   February.
  Measuring, Testing & Inspecting Equipment. $4.   March.
  Fabricating. $4.   April.
  Chemicals & Coatings. $4.   May.
  Wire Journal International Directory/Catalog.   Started 1965.   Published as a separate issue. $50.   May.
  Fine Wire. $4.   June.
  Wire Machinery Review. $4.   July.
  Fiber Optics. $4.   August.
  Plant Engineering. $4.   October.
  Fasteners. $4.   November.

1343. WOMAN'S DAY.
1515 Broadway, New York, NY 10036.
Annual Subscription: $11.85.   **Frequency:** 15/yr.
Publisher: CBS Publications.
Indexed Online: Magazine Index.
Special Issues:
  WD Diet & Exercise Guide.   Started 1977.   Published as a separate issue. $2.25.   Not included in the subscription price.   January.

WD 101 Needlework & Sweater Ideas.   Started 1969.
   Published as a separate issue. $2.25.   Not included in
   the subscription price.   February.
WD The Pleasures of Easy International Cooking.   Started
   1983.   Published as a separate issue. $2.25.   Not
   included in the subscription price.   March.
WD 101 Ways to Lose Weight and Stay Healthy.   Started
   1973.   Published as a separate issue. $2.25.   Not
   included in the subscription price.   April.
WD Remodeling Ideas.   Started 1975.   Published as a
   separate issue. $2.25.   Not included in the subscription
   price.   April/August.
WD Home Decorating.   Started 1972.   Published as a
   separate issue. $2.25.   Not included in the subscription
   price.   May/September.
WD Kitchen & Bath Guide.   Started 1971.   Published as a
   separate issue. $2.25.   Not included in the subscription
   price.   June/October.
WD Make Yourself Beautiful and Healthy.   Started 1981.
   Published as a separate issue. $2.25.   Not included in
   the subscription price.   June.
WD Simply Delicious Meals in Minutes.   Started 1977.
   Published as a separate issue. $2.25.   Not included in
   the subscription price.   July.
WD Granny Squares and Needlework Ideas.   Started 1973.
   Published as a separate issue. $2.25.   Not included in
   the subscription price.   August.
WD Great Holiday Baking Ideas.   Started 1977.   Published
   as a separate issue. $2.25.   Not included in the
   subscription price.   October.
WD Best Ideas for Christmas.   Started 1954.   Published as
   a separate issue. $2.25.   Not included in the subscription
   price.   November.
WD Dessert Lover's Cookbook.   Started 1980.   Published
   as a separate issue. $2.25.   Not included in the
   subscription price.   December.

1344. WOMEN IN BUSINESS.
9100 Ward Parkway, P.O. Box 8728, Kansas City, MO 64114.
Annual Subscription: $10.   **Frequency:** 6/yr.
Publisher: American Business Women's Association.
Special Issues:
   American Business Women's Association Convention. $2.
      November/December.

1345. WOOD & WOOD PRODUCTS.
P.O. Box 400, Prairie View, IL 60069.
Annual Subscription: $20.   **Frequency:** Monthly.
Publisher: Vance Publishing Co.
Advertiser Index
Indexed Online: Trade & Industry Index.
Special Issues:
   Outlook. $2.   January.
   Cabinet & Case Goods Product Review. $2.   February.
   High Technology. $2.   March.
   Reference Buying Guide.   Started 1963.   Published as a
      separate issue. $5.   March.
   Panel Products. $2.   April.
   Cabinets. $2.   May/November.
   Furniture Design—review of spring market. $2.   June.
   International Woodworking, Machinery & Furniture Supply
      Fair. $2.   June.
   Woodworking & Machinery Productivity Handbook. $2.
      August.
   Finishing. $2.   September.
   "How to" Issue. $2.   October.
   New Products Catalog. $2.   December.

1346. WOODALL'S CAMPGROUND MANAGEMENT.
500 Hyacinth Pl., Highland Park, IL 60035.
Annual Subscription: $10.   **Frequency:** Monthly.
Publisher: Woodall Publishing Co.
Advertiser Index: Every issue.
Special Issues:
   Buyers Guide.   March.
   National Campground Owners Association Convention
      Reports.   December.

1347. THE WORK BOAT.
P.O. Box 2400, Covington, LA 70434.
Annual Subscription: $20.   **Frequency:** Monthly.
Publisher: H.L. Peace Publications.
Advertiser Index: Every issue.
Editorial Index: Annual. Title/Author. February.
Special Issues:
   The Work Boat Show.   January.
   State of the Offshore Industry.   March.
   U.S. Inland Waterways.   April.
   Marine Diesel Engine Review.   June.
   Navigation & Communication.   August.
   America's Rivers.   October.
   Annual Construction Report.   December.

1348. WORKING WOMAN.
342 Madison Ave., New York, NY 10173.
Annual Subscription: $12.   **Frequency:** Monthly.
Publisher: HAL Publications, Inc.
Special Issues:
   WW Annual Salary Survey—business and professional
      women.   Started 1979. $2.   January.

1349. WORLD COAL.
500 Howard St., San Francisco, CA 94105.
Annual Subscription: $30.   **Frequency:** 6/yr.
Publisher: Miller Freeman Publications.
Advertiser Index: Every issue.
Editorial Index: Annual. Title/Author. November/December.
Special Issues:
   Annual Review & Buyers Guide—reviews of developments in
      major coal-producing nations; resource and production
      figures, import/export statistics; world trade developments;
      a report on trends in coal preparation; directory of coal
      exporters; buyers guide and manufacturers' directory.
      Started 1975. $6.   November/December.

1350. WORLD COFFEE & TEA.
P.O. Box 507, West Haven, CT 06516.
Annual Subscription: $24.   **Frequency:** Monthly.
Publisher: McKeana Publications.
Advertiser Index: Every issue.
Editorial Index: Annual. Subject. December.
Special Issues:
   Coffee & Tea Outlook/National Coffee Association
      Convention. $3.   January.
   Pacific Coast Coffee Association Convention. $3.   April.
   Office Coffee Service Red Book Directory Issue/National
      Coffee Service Association Convention. $3.   July.
   Green Coffee Issue/Green Coffee Association Convention.
      $3.   September.
   International Tea Issue/Tea Association Convention. $3.
      October.
   Plant and Plantation Equipment Issue. $3.   December.

1351. WORLD CONVENTION DATES.
79 Washington St., Hempstead, NY 11550.
Frequency: Monthly.
Publisher: Hendrickson Publishing Co.
Advertiser Index: Every issue.
Special Issues:
   U.S. Geographic Events Guide of Meetings, Conventions,
      Trade-Shows—by location and time, up to 20 years in
      future. Attendance, banquet, exhibit data.   Started 1916.
      Published as a separate issue. $30.   Spring.
   Canadian and International Events Guide.   Started 1980.
      Published as a separate issue. $10.   Summer.
   Generic Directory of Meetings, Conventions, Trade Shows,
      U.S. and international—by type of profession or industry, up
      to 20 years in future. Master alpha index by name;
      anticipated attendance, banquet and exhibit data.   Started
      1977.   Published as a separate issue. $30.   Fall.
   Event Planners Guide—hotels, convention, exposition and
      conference centers, convention and visitors bureaus, by city
      and state. Professional speakers, commercial and
      association speakers bureaus. Companies supplying
      services to conventions, by type of service.   Started 1979.
      Published as a separate issue. $30.   Winter.

Event Planners Guide—regional editions (N.E., S.E., Central, Plains & Western). $7.50.   Winter.

1352. WORLD DREDGING & MARINE CONSTRUCTION.
P.O. Box 17479, Irvine, CA 92713.
Annual Subscription: $10.   **Frequency:** Monthly.
Publisher: Wodcon Association.
Advertiser Index: Every issue.
Special Issues:
Worldwide Dredging and Marine Construction Forecast. $1.   January.
Directory of Dredge Fleets & Suppliers. $6.   March.
Electronic Advances in Dredging. $1.   May.
Dredge Mining. $1.   July.
Port & Harbor Construction. $1.   September.
Sand & Gravel Dredging. $1.   November.

1353. WORLD MINING.
500 Howard St., San Francisco, CA 94105.
Annual Subscription: $40.   **Frequency:** Monthly.
Publisher: Miller Freeman Publications.
Advertiser Index: Every issue.
Editorial Index: Annual. Subject/Title/Author. December.
Special Issues:
Yearbook—catalog of new product literature; technological surveys of developments in mineral exploration and mineral processing; mining trends and equipment; worldwide survey of production statistics by country; equipment and manufacturers directory.   Started 1948. $15.   August.

1354. WORLD OIL.
3301 Allen Parkway, Houston, TX 77019.
Annual Subscription: $12.   **Frequency:** 14/yr.
Publisher: Gulf Publishing Co.
Advertiser Index: Every issue.
Indexed or Abstracted Online: Trade & Industry Index; Predicasts; CIN.
Special Issues:
Outlook—statistics and forecast, U.S. & Abroad. $3.   February.
Offshore Technology Conference Preview. $3.   April.
Developments in Drilling & Completion Techniques.   Started 1980. $3.   May.
Guide To Drilling, Completion and Workover Fluids.   Started 1983. $3.   June.
Offshore Exploration & Production. $3.   July.
International Outlook.   Started 1946. $3.   August.
Drilling Progress Report.   October.
Production Progress Report.   November.

1355. WORLD PRESS REVIEW.
P.O. Box 915, Farmingdale, NY 11737.
Annual Subscription: $17.95.   **Frequency:** Monthly.
Publisher: The Stanley Foundation.
Indexed or Abstracted Online: Magazine Index.
Special Issues:
New Year Economic Outlook—survey of global opinion from foreign publications.   Started 1979.   Annully.   January.
International Editor of the Year Award.   Started 1975.   June.

1356. WORLD TENNIS.
1515 Broadway, New York, NY 10036.
Annual Subscription: $15.94.   **Frequency:** Monthly.
Publisher: CBS Consumer Publishing (for U.S. Tennis Association).
Advertiser Index: Every issue.
Indexed Online: Magazine Index.
Special Issues:
Tennis Camp Directory. $1.75.   January.
Top Tennis Resorts—by state/World Rankings. $1.75.   March.
French Open Preview. $1.75.   May.
Tennis Shoe Review. $1.75.   June.
Wimbledon Preview.   Started 1980. $1.75.   July.
Olympic Issue.   Every four yrs.   August.
U.S. Open Preview.   Started 1980. $1.75.   September.
Racket Annual—Equipment Evaluation.   Started 1982. $1.75.   December.

1357. WORLD WOOD.
500 Howard St., San Francisco, CA 94105.
Annual Subscription: $35.   **Frequency:** 6/yr.
Publisher: Miller Freeman Publications.
Advertiser Index: Every issue.
Special Issues:
World Wood Review—trade statistics and forest resource data on every major forested country of the world; overviews of developments in Africa, Asia, Europe, Latin America, Oceania, North America; annual production figures by country for major forest products categories.   Started 1975.   Published as a separate issue. $15.   August.

1358. WORLDWIDE PROJECTS.
P.O. Box 5017, Westport, CT 06881.
Annual Subscription: $70.   **Frequency:** 6/yr.
Publisher: Intercontinental Publications, Inc.
Advertiser Index: Every issue.
Special Issues:
Outlook Issue—international engineering construction opportunities/Supply Guide—for international products and services. $40.   October/November.

1359. THE WRITER.
8 Arlington St., Boston, MA 02116.
Annual Subscription: $15.   **Frequency:** Monthly.
Publisher: The Writer, Inc.
Editorial Index: Annual. Title/Author. December.
Indexed Online: Magazine Index.
Special Issues:
Articles Market: Sports, Recreation, Conservation, Outdoors. $1.50.   January.
Writer's Handbook—all markets, plus articles on how to write.   Published as a separate issue. $18.95.   Not included in the subscription price.   January.
Articles Market: Trade Journals and Business Magazines. $1.50.   February.
Poetry, Light Verse, Literary & Little Magazines Market. $1.50.   March.
Juvenile, Teen-Age, Young Adult Markets/City and Regional Publications Market. $1.50.   April.
Writers Conferences Calender/Popular Market (Men's and Adult Magazines, Detective & Mystery, Westerns, Science Fiction & Fantasy, Romance & Confession/Travel Articles). $1.50.   May.
Home, Garden & Women's Magazines/Fillers & Short Humor/Greeting Card Markets. $1.50.   June.
Book Publishers—adult fiction and nonfiction; juveniles. $1.50.   July.
General Magazine Articles. $1.50.   August.
Drama, Play Publishers. $1.50.   September.
Fiction for General Magazines/Syndicates. $1.50.   October.
Specialized Articles—health, education, agriculture, arts and the media, hobbies and collecting, popular and technical science, computing. $1.50.   November.
Religious and Denominational/Television Markets. $1.50.   December.

1360. WRITER'S DIGEST.
205 West Center St., Marion, OH 43305.
Annual Subscription: $18.   **Frequency:** Monthly.
Publisher: F & W Publishing.
Editorial Index: Annual. Subject. December.
Indexed Online: Magazine Index.
Special Issues:
Writer's Yearbook—annual reference tool for writers.   Started 1930.   Published as a separate issue. $2.95.   January.
Writer's Conference Directory and Education Guide. $1.50.   May.
Writer's Digest Writing Competition Winning Entries. $1.50.   October.

Guide to Reference Books and Books on Writing. $1.50. November.

1361. YACHT RACING/CRUISING.
401 North Broad St., Philadelphia, PA 19108.
Annual Subscription: $20. **Frequency:** 10/yr.
Publisher: North American Publishing Co.
Advertiser Index: Every issue.
Special Issues:
   Sailboard Catalog. Started 1981. $2. May.
   America's Cup. Published as a separate issue. $2. Every four years. September.

1362. YACHTING.
P.O. Box 2775, Boulder, CO 80302.
Annual Subscription: $18. **Frequency:** Monthly.
Publisher: Ziff-Davis Publishing Company.
Editorial Index: Annual. Subject/Author.
Special Issues:
   Boat Buyers Guide. Published as a separate issue. $3.95. Not included in the subscription price.
   Equipment Issue. $2.50. January.
   Spring Maintenance. $2. April.
   Chartering. $2. August.
   America's Cup. $2. Every 4 yrs. September.
   Boat Show Issue. $2. October.

Subject Index to Special Issues

A

Abrasive Engineering Society, conference; 0015
Abstracting services
   international business; 0705
Abstracts and indexes, statistics on; 0920
Accessories, fashion
   manufacturers directory; 0507
Accident statistics; 0870, 1278
Accounting
   See also Taxes
   automated data systems; 0234
   buyers guide; 1059
   doctoral programs survey; 0016
Acoustical Society of America; 0763
Acoustics
   instrument buying guides; 1207
   noise/vibration control buyers guide; 1207
Acquisitions
   See Mergers and acquisitions
Adcraft Club of Detroit; 0019
Adhesives
   directory of adhesives industry; 0020
Administrative Management Society; 0825
Advertising; 0019
   See also Advertising agencies; Advertising, farm; Marketing; Premiums and incentives; specific market
   annual HBA expenditures; 1067
   art direction; 0120
   awards; 0224, 0347
   bad ad awards; 0026
   broadcast; 1149
   budgets, business advertising survey; 0224
   business press; 0024
   business/professional; 0024, 0224
   business-to-business; 0820, 0832
   calendar; 0026
   Chicago market; 0024
   cigarette; 0820
   co-op; 0024
   co-op, in Quebec; 1149
   corporate; 0820
   corporate image; 0024
   creativity report; 0026
   design; 0026
   Detroit agency roster; 0019
   direct sales directory; 1175
   directories; 0026
   entertainment business; 0026
   5-year ad page revenues; 0847
   grocery trade market studies; 0603
   hardware industry workbook; 0614
   hotel and resort, ad linage and revenue; 1119
   independent services handbook; 0017
   industrial; 1149
   international markets; 0024
   liquor; 0820
   magazine; 0026, 1149
   magazine profiles; 0820
   marketing; 0026
   marketing to affluents; 0024
   marketing to women; 0024
   maturity market; 0024
   media buyers guide to magazines; 0820
   media costs/forecast; 0832
   media outlook; 0024
   New England market; 0018, 0943
   newspaper advertising executives; 0451
   newspaper advertising statistics; 0026, 0451, 0832, 1149
   outdoor; 0024
   page volume forecast; 0224
   radio; 0026
   readership studies; 0224
   regional markets; 0026
   research business review; 0024
   retail marketing; 0024
   salary survey; 0026
   specialty imprints; 1216
   suburban media; 0024
   television advertising rates; 1254
   television industry; 0026
   television marketing demographics; 1254
   test marketing; 0024
   to professionals; 0820
   top advertised brands; 0832
   top business advertisers; 0224
   top magazine ad gainers; 0820
   top magazines in hotel and resort advertising; 1119
   top newspapers in hotel and resort advertising 1119
   women and; 0026
   youth marketing; 0024
   100 leading advertisers; 0024
   100 top markets; 0024
   100 top media companies; 0024
Advertising agencies
   art directors; 0026
   best & worst clients; 0026
   Canadian; 0831, 1149
   for radio and TV; 0201
   for top brands; 0833
   international agency billing review; 0025
   new business report; 0017
   New England clients/agencies; 0018, 0943
   report; 0026
   special sales promotion; 0833
   top business advertisers; 0224
   top farm agencies; 0033
   top 100 broadcast billings; 0201
   U.S. agency income; 0024
Advertising, farm
   See also Agricultural marketing
   Canadian; 0033
   marketing research; 0033
   marketing services guide; 0033
   premiums and incentives; 0033
   top 150 print advertisers; 0033
   year-end forecast; 0033
Advertising Research Foundation
   annual report/yearbook; 0726
Aerosols; 0027
Aerospace
   See Aviation and aerospace
Aerospace Industries Association of America; 0028
Aerospace Medical Association; 0147
Africa
   economic performance statistics, by country; 0888
   industry profiles; 0888
   tobacco industry; 1267
Agency for International Development; 0641
Agribusiness
   in banking; 0051
   international consultants; 0034
   international outlook; 0034
   international show; 0034
Agricultural equipment
   buyers guide; 0037
   buyers manual; 0954
   cold storage; 0506
   costs; 0503
   dealer survey; 0503
   directory; 0503
   directory and buying guide; 0661
   directory, Canadian; 0502, 0511
   equipment review; 0503
   farm & ranch fencing; 0515
   farm show; 0037
   fertilizer; 0503
   harvesting; 0177
   irrigation; 0177
   lawn and garden; 0503
   machinery; 0036
   market statistics; 0661
   service shop management; 0503
   shows; 0661
   specifications; 0661
   trailers and trucks; 0503
Agricultural marketing
   See also Advertising, farm
   chemical and fertilizer; 0031
   irrigation; 0031
   packing and shipping; 0031
   pre-harvest; 0031
Agricultural supplies
   buyer's guide; 0504
   directory; 0505
   show; 0504
   showcase; 0505
Agriculture
   See also Agribusiness; Agricultural equipment; Agricultural marketing; Agricultural supplies; Agriculture, United States Department of; Poultry; Specific products
   alternate energy sources; 1147
   economic outlook; 0449, 1130
   exports; 0506
   farm manager survey; 0032
   farm show guide; 0033
   in Africa; 0888
   in Asia; 0889
   limestone; 1024
   prices; 0506
   rural electric cooperatives; 1147
   top 100 agricultural banks; 0032
   world agriculture; 0506
Agriculture, United States Department of
   crop and livestock reports; 0506
   situation and outlook reports; 0506
Agriculture, United States of
   agriculture outlook board; 0506
   world supply-demand estimates; 0506
Air cargo
   See Air transport industry
Air conditioning
   See also Refrigeration
   buyers guide; 1176
   buyers guide, Canadian; 0631
   consumer markets; 0836
   fact book; 0455
   industrial; 1030
   international show; 1195
   manufacturers directory; 0038, 0630
   seasonal market reports; 1195
   technology report; 0482
Air Conditioning and Refrigeration Wholesalers; 1337
Air Conditioning Contractors of America; 0379
Air Force Association, convention; 0039
Air freight
   See Air transport industry; Freight forwarding
Air Line Pilots Association International; 0041
Air Pollution Control Association; 0679, 0764
Air transport industry
   cargo directory; 0069
   cargo routing guide; 0344
   cargo statistics; 0042
   freight forwarding agents; 0069
   freight guide; 1279
   industry forecast; 0042
   international; 0148
   marketing statistics; 0042
Aircraft Owners and Pilots Association; 0007

commuter airline yearbook; 0350
  directory; 0430
  meeting; 0043
  yearbook; 0043
Airports
  airline ground support equipment directory; 0044
  aviation suppliers directory; 0044
  construction; 0634
Alaska
  construction; 0045, 0046
  electric power; 0046
  lumber; 0046
  mining; 0046
  national parks report; 0933
  native corporations; 0045
  petroleum; 0046
  pipelines; 1021
  transportation; 0046
Alexander Graham Bell Association for the Deaf; 1314
Alliance of Canadian Travel Associations; 0284
Aluminum
  distributors; 0863
  recycling; 0082
Amateur Hockey Association of the U.S.; 0067
American Academy of Facial and Plastic Reconstruction; 0117
American Academy of Optometry; 0076
American Accounting Association; 0016
American Alliance for Health, Physical Education, Recreation, and Dance; 0622, 0754, 1118
American Animal Hospital Association; 0400
American Arbitration Association; 0109
American Association for Respiratory Therapy; 1121
American Association for the Advancement of Science; 1161
American Association of Bovine Practitioners; 0400
American Association of Cereal Chemists; 0306
American Association of Community and Junior Colleges; 0349
American Association of Cost Engineers; 0385
American Association of Immunologists; 0180
American Association of Managing General Agents; 0695
American Association of Meat Processors; 0844
American Association of Museums; 0917
American Association of Petroleum Geologists; 0001
American Association of Physics Teachers; 0077
American Association of Port Authorities; 1315
American Association of Respiratory Therapy; 0002
American Association of Textile Chemists and Colorists; 0060, 1256
American Association of University Presses; 1085
American Bakers Association; 0152
American Bankers Association; 0915, 1210
  convention; 0003, 0051
  investments conference; 0189
American Bar Association; 0052, 1247
American Basketball Association; 1221
American Booksellers Association; 1085
American Business Women's Association; 1344
American Camping Association; 0239
American Ceramic Society; 0054, 0197, 0304
American Chamber of Commerce in Italy, directory; 0716
American Chemical Society; 0101, 0313, 0492
  Rubber Division; 1141
American College of Hospital Administrators, awards; 0895
American College of Sports Medicine; 1016
American Concrete Institute; 0765
American Council of Life Insurance; 0805
American Defense Preparedness Association; 0926
American Dietetic Association; 0766

American Economics Association; 0061
American Electroplaters' Society; 1039
American Federation of Information Processing Societies; 0102
American Finance Association; 0741
American Fishing Tackle Manufacturers Association; 0536, 1220, 1225
American Foundrymen's Society; 0567, 0892
American Gas Association; 0966, 1022
American Geriatrics Society; 0767
American Helicopter Society; 1305
American Home Economics Association; 0745
American Hospital Association; 0895, 1290
  convention factbook; 0650
American Hotel & Motel Association; 0808
  resources directory; 0808
American Industrial Health Conference; 0679, 1046
American Industrial Hygiene Association; 0070
American Industrial Hygiene Conference; 0684
American Institute for Design & Drafting; 1025
American Institute of Architects; 0114
  awards; 0702
American Institute of Astronautics and Aeronautics; 0128, 0704, 0727, 0740, 0743, 0760
  membership roster; 0004
American Institute of Biological Sciences; 0181
American Institute of Chemical Engineers; 0005, 0314, 0480, 0491, 0966, 1029
American Institute of Mining, Metallurgical and Petroleum Engineers; 0715, 0739, 0751, 0885, 1188
American Institute of Organbuilders; 0422
American Institute of Physics; 0077, 0728, 0763, 1018, 1127
American Institute of Plant Engineers; 0006
American Institute of Real Estate Appraisers membership directory; 0107
American Jewish Committee; 0342
American Leather Chemists Association; 0797
American Library Association; 0080, 0190, 0322, 0800, 1158
  Reference and Adult Services Division; 1100
American Management Association; 0351
American Marketing Association; 0749, 0750
American Meat Institute; 0843, 0844, 0845, 1066
American Medical Association; 0115, 0116, 0768
American Metal Stamping Association
  membership directory; 0866
American Meteorological Society; 0211, 0731, 0755, 0775, 0868, 0908
American Mining Congress; 0337, 0486, 0886, 1188
  convention and show; 0336, 0884
American Museum of Natural History; 0942
American Musicological Society; 0422
American Newspaper Publishers Association; 0451, 1294
  Research Institute; 1062
American Nuclear Society; 0955
American Occupational Medicine Association; 0753
American Occupational Therapy Association; 0075
American Oil Chemists Society; 0769
  membership directory; 0769
American Paper Institute; 0989, 0991
American Petroleum Institute; 0655, 0966, 0967
American Physiological Society; 0078
American Planning Association; 0770, 1026
American Pork Congress; 0637
American Public Power Association; 0189, 1079
American Public Transit Association; 0056
American Public Transportation Association; 0996
American Public Works Association; 0010, 0056, 0170
American Railway Bridge & Building Association; 1105

American Railway Engineering Association; 0903, 1105
American Rental Association; 1115
American Rose Society; 0090
American Seed Association; 1173
American Seed Trade Association; 1174
American Society for Cell Biology; 0180
American Society for Engineering Education; 0485
American Society for Head and Neck Surgery; 0117
American Society for Industrial Security; 1171
American Society For Information Science; 0771
American Society for Metals; 0865
American Society for Microbiology; 0180
American Society For Personnel Administration; 1000
American Society for Public Administration; 1077
American Society for Testing Materials; 0013
American Society for Training & Development; 1281
American Society of Agricultural Engineers; 0036
American Society of Association Executives; 0127
American Society of Bakery Engineers; 0152, 0547
American Society of Biological Chemists; 0180
American Society of Chartered Life Underwriters; 0334, 0804
American Society of Civil Engineers; 0330
American Society of Heating, Refrigerating and Air Conditioning Engineers; 0011, 0379, 1101
American Society of Journalism School Administrators; 0778
American Society of Landscape Architects; 0789
American Society of Lubrication Engineers; 0813
American Society of Mechanical Engineers; 0846
American Society of Safety Engineers; 1073
American Society of Sanitary Engineering; 0379
American Society of Travel Agents; 0012, 0285, 0982, 1285, 1288
American Sociological Association; 0095, 0744, 1201
American Square Dancing Society; 1228
American Statistical Association; 0772
American Stock Exchange
  top stocks; 0906
American studies; 0088
American Studies Association
  membership directory; 0088
American Subcontractors Association; 0379
American Supply Association; 0379, 1237, 1337
American Supply & Machinery Manufacturers Association; 0673
American Symphony Orchestra League; 1242
American Textile Machinery Association; 0060
  membership guide; 0098
American Textile Manufacturers Institute; 1257
American Trucking Association; 0633, 1284
American Veterinary Medical Association; 0400, 0773
American Vocational Association; 1312
American Water Ski Association; 1326
American Water Works Association; 0056, 0723, 1084
American Welding Society; 1330, 1331
Amusement industry
  See also Entertainment industry
  showman talent guide; 1272
Amusement parks and shows
  See also Auditoriums, arenas and stadiums
  buyers guide; 1272
  Carnival routes, circus and fair guide; 0099, 1272
  directory; 0099
  fair date listings; 1272
  rides and games, buyers guide; 0099
Amusements, coin-operated
  arcades; 1040

buyers guide; 1040
directory; 1040
industry survey; 1040
year in review; 1040
Amusements & Music Operators Association; 1040
Animal health care; 0504, 0505, 0773
Animation
production company directors; 0356
Antiques
annual; 0103
furniture, American; 0821
price guide; 0103
wholesale sources directory; 0104
Apiaries
See Beekeeping
Apparel
See also Knitware; Men's wear; Sportswear, active
horse and riders; 1244
needle trades show; 0186
off-price chains; 0429
Apparel, boys
active sportswear; 1251
directory; 1251
seasonal markets; 1251
Apparel, children's
directory; 0443
New York market buyers guide; 0443
Apparel, intimate
designer/licensing; 0710
directory; 0187, 0710
fabrics; 0710
large sizes; 0710
machinery/equipment/supplies; 0710
maternity & post-mastectomy; 0710
seasonal merchandising; 0710
suppliers; 0710
Appliances
See also Consumer electronics; Food service
calendar; 0105
directory; 0105, 0106
manufacturers profiles; 0106
microwave ovens; 0836
statistics; 0105
suppliers; 0105
trade show; 0106
Aquaculture
See Fish and fisheries
Arab banks, top 100; 0157
Arab shipping directory; 1168
Archaeological Institute of America; 0110
Archaeology
travel guides; 0110
Archery
bowhunting guide; 0112
directory; 0111
Architecture; 0733
American review; 0114
awards; 1075
best designed houses; 0113
Canadian yearbook; 0242
chain store design awards; 0307
costing yardsticks annual; 0242
energy conservation; 1075
Hospitals; 0621
interior design; 1075
preservation; 1075
World review; 0114
Arenas
See Amusement parks and shows; Auditoriums, arenas and stadiums
Argentina
banking; 0051
Armed Forces Communications and Electronics Association; 1183
Arson
See Fire protection
Art
advertising; 0120
American paintings; 0821
art market survey; 0690
books; 0048
instruction; 0048
journalism awards; 0451
national gallery guide; 0121
school directory; 0048
trade products; 0048
youth arts & crafts; 0124
Art directors; 0151
Artists; 0048
Artists' materials, directory and buyers guide; 0122, 0124
Arts
See also Performing arts
survey; 0324
Asbestos
company/product review; 0125
mining review; 0125
safety & health review; 0125
Asia, regional economic review; 0889
Asparagus, marketing; 0031
Assembly engineering
catalogue and reference handbook; 0126
high technology; 0126
productivity and costs; 0126
Associated Equipment Distributors; 0367
Associated General Contractors of America; 0371
Associated Locksmiths of America; 0807
Associated Public Safety Communications Officers; 0009
Association for Advanced Life Underwriting; 0804, 0805
Association for Computing Machinery; 0774
Association for Education in Journalism and Mass Communications; 0778, 0779
Association for Library and Information Science Education; 0738
Association for Library Services to Children, ALA; 1271
Association for Systems Management; 0761
Association for the Advancement of Medical Instrumentation; 0852
Association of American Nurserymen; 0083
Association of American Publishers; 1085
book sales statistics; 1085
Association of College & Research Libraries; 0322
Association of Diesel Specialists
membership directory; 0425
Association of General Merchandise Chains; 0429
Association of Iron and Steel Engineers; 0714
Association of Operating Room Nurses; 0008
Association of Operative Millers; 0881
Association of Professional Engineers of British Columbia, directory; 0149
Association of School Business Officials of U.S. and Canada; 1157
Association of Schools of Journalism and Mass Communications; 0778
Association of the U.S. Army; 0118
Association of Western Hospitals; 0645
Associations
awards; 0127
conferences; 0127
convention dates; 1351
management; 0127
management services directory; 0127
Astronomy
graduate programs; 0077
teaching and research staffs directory; 0077
Atlantic Providence Trucking Association; 0129
Attorneys
See Lawyers
Audio equipment
See also Sound recording
Canadian buying guides; 1208
home and auto, consumer markets; 0836
in television; 0442
loudspeakers; 1230
product review directory; 0130
Audio-visual communications
See also Video production industry
advertising presentations; 1149
biographical directory; 0132
Canadian industry source book; 0014
Canadian producers; 0200
corporate communications center guide; 0132
directory; 1160
equipment guide; 0132
producer directory; 0131
show; 0014, 0131, 1149
technology forecast; 0014
videotape production facilities guide; 0132
Audio-visual materials; 0190, 0397
motion picture lab services; 0132
school library buyers guide; 1158
slide lab services guide; 0132
Auditoriums, arenas and stadiums
annual listing; 1302
directory; 0099, 1232
Australia
banking; 0051
diver's travel guide; 1189
Austria
banking; 0051
Authors
See Writers
Auto Internacionale; 0721
Auto laundries, buyers guide; 0133
Automation
See also CAD/CAM; Robotics
construction statistics; 0137
factory; 0674, 1270
in banking; 0051
laboratory; 0079
Automobile dealerships
buyers guide; 0138
Automobile races
Indianapolis 500; 1221
Automobile rental firms, directory; 1285
Automobiles
See also Automobiles, imported; Automobiles, specialty; Automotive accessories; Automotive aftermarket; Automotive bodyshops; Automotive Industry
buyer's guide; 0292, 0906, 1134
consumer buyers guide; 0375, 1049
electric and non-petroleum, directory; 0023
fleet cars; 1150
imports evaluation; 1319
international show; 0721, 0912
new cars; 0119, 0141
new cars, Canadian; 0243
new model ratings; 1319
new models consumers surveys; 0310
road test annual; 1134
sports cars; 1134
Automobiles, imported
best annual; 0662
buyer's guide; 1051
market report; 0662
parts directory; 0144
racing; 0662
shows; 0662
Automobiles, specialty
buyers directory; 1217
racing schedule; 1217
shows; 1217
Automotive accessories
buyers guide; 0142
discount stores; 0429
show; 0134, 0142, 0298
Automotive aftermarket
auto service data book; 0243
auto trim products directory; 0135
brake buyers guide; 0195
buyers guide; 0142, 0639
chassis buyers guide; 0195
directory; 0134
engine rebuilders show; 0721
forecast, Canadian; 0243
marketing directory; 0721
oil; 0428
parts; 0428
parts and accessories show; 0721
products; 1051
rebuilders directory; 0144
rebuilders directory, Canada; 0913

rebuilders parts directory; 0144
repairs and servicing handbook/specifications; 0911
service industries show; 0721
service stations; 1234
shows; 0142, 0145, 0639
specialty equipment show; 0721
supplier and retailer profiles; 0142
tool & equipment buyers guide; 0195, 0243
warehouse distributors show; 0721, 1320
Automotive body shops
buyers guide; 0139
certification and training; 0188
directory; 0188
Automotive Engine Rebuilders Association; 0721
Automotive industry
See also Automobiles; Automotive aftermarket; Diesel engines
automotive electronics; 0140
automotive engineers show; 0425
battery manufacturers, buyers guide; 0720
Canadian autobody markets; 0720
Canadian directory; 0913
custom market; 0143
dealer attitude survey; 1319
dealer services; 0912
directory and catalog; 0140
engineering; 1319
European vehicles; 0140
forecast; 0143
import evaluations; 1319
imports; 0143
industry survey; 1319
Japan; 0143
jobber business management; 0720
jobber marketing guide, Canadian; 0720
marketing data; 0024, 0143
marketing forecast; 0143, 1319
materials; 0140, 1319
OEM suppliers; 0141
off-highway; 0140
passenger cars; 0140
SAE roster; 0140
service profits; 0143
showroom profits; 0143
shows; 0143
specifications & statistics; 0141
supplier survey; 1319
technical reference; 0912
tool/equipment buyers guide; 0912
western Canada; 0913
yearbook/buyers guide/statistics; 1319
year-end report; 0141
Automotive Parts & Accessories Association; 0142, 0429, 0639, 0721
Automotive Service Industries Convention; 0145
Automotive Warehouse Distributors Association; 0145, 0721, 1320
Autoramics
See Ceramic industry
Aviation and aerospace
See also Air transport industry; Airline industry; Airports; Aviation, business; Aviation, civil; Aviation, commercial; Avionics
aerospace abstracts; 0704
aerospace design; 0418
aerospace metals and machines; 0082
air show; 0148
aircraft directory; 0007
airplane maintenance; 0042
business flying; 0148
buyers guide; 0545
buyers guide, Canadian; 1341
computers; 0148
corporate, Canadian; 1341
forecast; 0148
helicopter air show; 0148
helicopter buyers' guide; 1139
helicopter convention; 1139
helicopters membership directory; 1305
international marketing directory; 0148
maintenance equipment review; 0146
review and forecast; 0028
shows; 1341
warfare, electronic; 0148

Aviation, business
awards; 1072
conventions; 1072
executive aircraft, Asia; 0889
FBO directory; 1072
helicopters; 1072
international; 1072
jet; 1072
regional commuter lines; 1072
salary survey; 1072
Aviation, civil
annual report; 0657
Aviation, commercial
buyers guide; 0244
corporate aircraft survey; 0216
directory, Canadian; 0244
purchasing handbook; 0216
review; 0241
salary survey; 0216
update; 0244
Avionics
buyers guide; 0244, 0545
directory; 0007
directory, Canadian; 1341
maintenance equipment review; 0146
Awards
books; 1085
business aircraft; 1072
children's books; 0190, 1271
electronic office design; 0899
food and drug packaging; 0548
food processing; 1066
food service; 1124
furniture design; 0577
hospital administrators; 0895
interior design; 0378, 0702
materials engineering; 0840
packaging; 0988
paper and pulp industry; 1019
papermaking; 0991
philanthropy service; 1010
restaurant; 1123
restaurant kitchen design; 1123
restaurant leadership; 1122
sporting goods; 1220
structural clay marketing; 0197
top manufacturers, discount stores; 0429
TV commercials; 0151
woman/man of the year; 1265

B

Babies; 0050
Bahamas
diver's travel guide; 1189
travel; 0284
Baking industry
bakers and distributors directory; 0152
Canadian buyers guide; 0547
directory and buyers guide; 0881
ingredients directory; 0153
packaging directory; 0153
processing systems directory; 0153
product market analysis reports; 0881
show; 0153, 0547
supermarket bakeries; 0152, 1235
suppliers buyers guide; 0152
Bank Administration Institute; 0154
Bank Marketing Association; 0155, 1291
Banking law
book review index; 0160
cases index; 0160
judicial decisions index; 0160
Banks and banking
See also Banking law; Banks, savings; Credit; Federal Reserve System; Finance; Mortgage banking; Trust institutions
ABA convention; 0003, 0051, 0156
agribusiness; 0051
agricultural credit; 0245
argicultural, top 100; 0032
ATM directory; 0154
automation; 0051
bank security; 0051

bank security directory; 0154
bankers' Washington guide; 0003
banking technology; 0051
Benelux; 0051
buyers guide; 0003, 1210
Canadian; 0249
cash management banks survey; 0999
cash management market directory; 0999
check processing equipment directory; 0154
check-writing forecast; 0448
coin/cash equipment directories; 0154
commercial; 0051
commercial bank surveillance; 0448
commercial banking review; 1298
community banking; 0003
convention; 1210
corporate financing directory; 0712
corporate syndicate personnel; 0712
correspondent banking; 0051
credit unions; 0051
deregulation; 1298
directors; 1210
electronic funds transfer; 0051, 0156
equipment directory; 0156
executive compensation; 0051
finance companies; 0051
finance industry survey; 0159
financial marketing services directory; 0155
financing; 1298
foreign banks in London; 0157, 0690
foreign banks in New York; 0157
foreign banks in the U.S.; 0690
holding companies; 0051
home banking; 1298
installment credit; 0051, 0389
insurance; 0051
international; 0051
international bankers; 0690
international data networks; 0051
interstate banking outlook; 0448
investment advisers directory; 0999
investment conference; 0189
IRA update; 0003
largest commercial banks (non-US); 0565
largest commercial banks (US); 0565
largest savings and loan associations; 0558
largest trust operations; 0558
marketing to the affluent; 0051
master and directed trust services directory; 0998
mortgage banking; 0051
mountain states conferences; 0915
oil-producing nations; 0051
outlook; 1298
overseas business, U.S. banks; 0069
Pacific states banking performance; 0980
pension funds performance evaluation; 0999
personnel & management; 0051
pooled pensions funds directory; 0998
premiums and incentives; 0155
professional education; 0051
real estate financing; 0051
savings & loan associations; 0051
secondary mortgage market; 1298
self-service banking; 0051
software review; 0156
southern bankers; 1210
statistical guide; 0051
telecommunications; 0051
thrift institutions; 1298
top banks; 0226
top holding companies; 0558
top investment banking firm; 0690
top profit performing; 0154
top 100 Arab banks; 0157
top 100 world banks; 0690
top 100s, 300s, 5000s; 0051
Top 500 world commercial banks; 0157
transaction cards; 0051
trust/custodian banks directory; 0999
trust management & operations; 0051
Banks, savings; 0051
balance sheet trends; 1154
marketing; 1154
mortgage banking; 1154
new buildings; 1154
operations conference; 1154

outlook; 1154
policy report; 1154
state associations; 1154
100 largest; 1154
Baseball
All-Star game; 1221
broadcasting; 0201
dope book; 1221
guide; 1221
record book; 1221
register; 1221
spring training; 1221
World Series; 1221
Basketball
ABA All-Star Game; 1221
annual preview; 1041
college; 1221
NBA guide; 1221
professional; 1221
Bathrooms
See Kitchens and bathrooms
Batteries; 0082
Battery manufacturers, automotive, buyers guide; 0162
Beans, marketing; 0031
Beatles; 0178, 1138
Beauty aids
See Cosmetics and fragrances; Health and beauty aids
Beauty care; 1313
Beauty culture; 0499
Beauty supplies
buying guide; 0066
convention; 0066
Bedding; 0164
See also Water beds
Beekeeping; 0053
Beer; 0173
See also Breweries
imported; 0165
market review and forecast; 0660
marketing; 0024
top 10 brands; 0174
Beverage industry
See also Beer; Beverages, alcoholic; Breweries; Liquor industry; Soft drinks
buyers guide; 0174
buyers guide, Canadian; 0246
buyers guide, Spanish; 0175
Canadian market leaders; 0171
conventions; 0173
directory; 0174
forecast; 0174
Hall of Fame; 0174
history; 0174
holiday packaging/merchandising; 0173
hotels; 0651
imports; 0171
international roundup; 0174
manual/statistics/buyers guide; 0172
market index; 0174
new products; 0171
NY/NJ beverage annual; 0173
restaurants/institutions; 0809
retailers industry report; 0173
top 10 companies; 0174
trucking; 0174
vending; 0049, 0287
wines, cordials, liqueurs exposition; 0173
women's issue; 0173
Beverages, alcoholic
See also Liquor industry; Wines
California industry directory; 0150
California legislation; 0150
sales by brand; 0226
Bibliographies
international business; 0705
Bicycles; 1051
buyers guide; 0176
dealer survey; 0176
Billiards; 0191
Biochemistry; 0101, 0180
Biology, cell; 0180
Biotechnology; 0670, 1161

Biscuit & Bakers Manufacturers Association; 0152
Blacks
Black Enterprise 100; 0182
career opportunities; 0182
corporate directors; 0217
United States; 0444
Board of Trade of Metropolitan Toronto; 0871
Boats and boating
America's Cup; 0184, 1362
boat show; 0183, 0184, 1143, 1362
buyers guide; 1362
Canadian buyers guide; 0247
Canadian services directory; 0983
chartering; 1362
maintenance/equipment; 1362
marine buyers guide; 0185
new boats; 1333
regional chartering; 1143
sailboat catalog; 1361
sailboat fitting-out; 1143
statistics and buyers guide; 0183
work boats; 1327
Bologna Book Fair; 1085
Bonds
See Investments; Municipal bonds; Securities trading
Book collectors; 1097
Book manufacturing; 1097
production techniques; 1129
Book publishing industry
See also Books
announcements by category; 1085
annual statistics; 1085
awards; 1085
book fairs; 1085
conventions; 1085
Books
See also Book publishing industry; Encyclopedias
awards; 0190, 0642, 1271
best reference; 0190, 0800
business; 0800, 0950, 1085
Canadian; 1097
children's; 0190, 0323, 0950, 1085, 1271
christian; 0325
Christmas; 0950
education; 1085
for school libraries; 1158
notable; 0190
nursing; 0074
outstanding academic; 0322
paperback; 0800, 1085
political; 1321
popular medical; 0800
popular reading; 0190
reference; 0080, 1360
religious; 0047, 0323, 0324, 0326, 0346, 0800, 0950, 1085
sales statistics; 1085
sci/tech; 0800, 1085, 1161
seasonal announcements; 0190, 0322, 0323, 0346, 0800, 0950, 1085
textbooks; 0339
university presses; 0950
vocational/technical; 0190
young adult; 0190
Booksellers
conference; 0323, 0325
Bottling; 0272
Bowker Memorial Lecture; 1085
Bowling
proprietors; 0191
tournaments and conventions; 0191
Bowling Proprietors Association of America, Inc.; 0192
Boy's and Young Men's Apparel Manufacturers Association; 1251
Brands
See also Marketing
top advertised; 0832
Brandy; 1340
Brass; 0082

Brazil
banking; 0051
Bread
See Baking industry
Breweries
See also Beer
brewing methods; 0196
buyers guide; 0196
conventions; 0890
directory; 0196, 0890
imports; 0196
plant equipment and maintenance; 0196
sales figures; 0196
statistics; 0890
statistics, Canada; 0246
wholesalers; 0890
Brick industry
autoclaymation; 0197
awards; 0197
convention; 0197
forecast; 0197
international markets; 0197
refractories; 0197
Brick Institute of America; 0197
Bridal merchandising; 0587
Brides; 0169
Bridges
construction and repair; 0170
construction equipment; 0366
maintenance; 1146
replacements; 0634
Broadcast Education Association; 0729
Broadcast engineering
Chinese edition; 0198
Broadcast engineers, salary survey; 0198
Broadcasting
See also Cable TV; Commercials, broadcast; Video production industry; Radio; Telecommunications; Television
advertising agencies; 0201
awards; 0201
baseball; 0201
broadcasting directory; 0688
Canadian buyers guide; 0199
Canadian radio stations; 1099
equipment manufacturers; 0201
farm; 0033
federal regulations; 0201
football; 0201
season's new shows; 1302
top markets; 1150
yearbook; 0201, 0201
Brokerage houses
See Investments; securities industry
Brushes, brooms, mops
buyers guide; 0203
Building
See also Building, home; Building, multi-housing; Construction; Home improvement; Manufactured housing; Remodeling
Alaska; 0045
brick & masonry; 0733
Canadian leaders; 0733
concrete; 0733
construction bonding; 0733
design award winners; 0204
directory/buyers guide; 0363
earth moving & hauling; 0733
equipment; 0733
forecast; 0363
forecast, western Canada; 0733
forecasts; 0113
historical data/statistics; 0368
industry profile; 1069
international directories; 0927
international opportunities; 1358
international supply guide; 1358
lifting devices; 0733
midwest contractors' buying guide; 0876
municipal buyers, Canada; 0733
new products; 0113, 0204
new technology; 0205
roofing/siding/insulation; 0733, 1102
scaffolding; 0733
steel; 0733

top builders; 1069
top design/construction giants; 0205
top owner-giants; 0205
truck and trailer equipment; 0363
unbuilt projects; 0204
waterproofing; 0733
windows & doors; 0733
Building, home
   See also Home improvement
   building manual; 0652
   convention; 0379
   home buyer survey; 0204
   plans; 0652
   survey; 0565
Building maintenance
   See also Sanitation industry
   buyers guide; 0331, 0822
   chemicals; 0822
   Exposition; 0822
   training; 0331
Building management
   buyers guide; 0208
   cleaning technology; 0208
   contract services; 0207
   energy loss control; 0207
   forecast; 0210
   grounds maintenance; 0208
   interiors; 0210
   remodeling; 0207, 0210
Building, multi-housing; 0916
Building Owners and Managers Association International; 0207, 1190
Building Services Contractors Association; 0208
Building supplies; 0209
Buildings, office
   occupancy survey; 1190
Bulgaria
   tobacco industry; 1267
Buses
   See Transportation
Business and industry
   See also Business, Canadian; Business, small; Corporations; Economics; International business; Venture capital
   annual news review; 0440
   Black leaders; 0182
   books; 0950
   CEO's forecast; 0685
   coups and catastrophies; 0565
   forecasts; 0226, 0565, 0685, 0939
   industry financial research; 1239
   industry ratios; 0440
   products of year; 0565
   statistics; 1238
Business, Canadian
   directory; 0021
   markets; 0526
   publications; 0831, 1149
   top 500; 0249, 0526
Business flying; 0148
Business forms
   customs forms; 0069
   directory of manufacturers & suppliers; 0220
   man of the year; 0220
   NBFA Convention; 0564
   trends and projections; 0220
Business opportunities directory; 0666
Business, small
   executive compensation; 0664
   source book; 0249
   state climate; 0664
   top companies; 0664
Business travel
   See Travel and tourism

C

Cable TV
   See also Television
   broadcast equipment buyers guide; 0198
   Canadian buyers guide; 0235
   Canadian stations; 0200
   Canadian Who's Who; 0235

construction forecast; 0237
contractors callbook; 0237
convention; 0236, 0237
convention reports, Canada; 0235
engineering demographics; 0198
equipment specifications; 0198
review & forecast; 0235
CAD/CAM; 0081, 0082, 0327, 0461, 0846
   computer numerical control census; 0268
   conference; 0417
   equipment show; 0675
   guidebook; 0897
   systems and software survey; 0253
Calculators, buyers guide; 0961
California
   alcoholic beverage laws; 0150
   economic outlook; 0447
   legislators biographies; 0150
   top companies; 0495
California Rental Association; 1115
Campers
   See Recreational Vehicles
Campground management, buyers guide; 1346
Camping; 0519
   Canadian campgrounds; 0238, 1153, 1164
   Sierra Club outings; 1182
Camping equipment; 1051
Camps
   children's; 0239
   music; 0692
Canada
   See also Specific listings
   camping; 1153
   convention events; 1351
   entertainment industry; 1302
   festivals; 1112
   fur industry; 0573
   government guide; 0527
   intimate apparel manufacturers; 0187
   investment advisers directory; 0999
   lumber statistics; 0562
   marketing; 1150
   paneling statistics; 0562
   pipelines; 1021
   ports; 1315
   power plant statistics; 0466
   pulp capital spending; 1086
   pulpwood mill maps; 1086
   real estate review; 1107
   steel industry profile; 1261
   top markets; 1150
   travel; 0283, 0284
   trust/custodian bank directory; 0999
   Utilities directory; 0466
   utilities maintenance survey; 0466
Canada Society of Exploration Geophysicists; 0436, 0971
Canadian Association of Physicists; 1017
Canadian Bankers Association; 0245
Canadian Cable Television Association; 0235
Canadian Chemical Conference; 0971
Canadian Electrical Distributors Association; 0459
Canadian Hospital Association; 0427
Canadian Industrial Traffic League; 0282
Canadian Information Processing Society; 0231
Canadian Institute of Chartered Accountants; 0234
Canadian Medical Association; 0855
Canadian Offshore Resources Exposition; 0273, 0436, 0971
Canadian Parks/Recreation Association; 1112
Canadian Pulp and Paper Association; 1087
Canadian Seed Association; 1173
Canadian Soft Drink Association; 0246
Canadian Welding Society; 0288
Candy and confectionery
   buyers brand survey; 0290
   buyer's guide; 0289
   candy bar survey; 0289
   chocolate survey; 0289
   conferences; 0289
   convention; 1299

directory; 0290, 0828, 1299
European report; 0289
packaging; 0289
review; 0290, 1299
vending machines; 0049
Cannes Film Festival; 1302
Canning
   See Food processing
Canoes and kayaks; 0291
Car wash
   See Auto laundries
Careers; 1281
   engineering; 0595
   for Blacks; 0182
   outlook for college graduates; 0310
   petroleum industry; 0971
   religion; 0047
Carnivals
   See Amusement parks and shows
Carpets
   See Floor coverings
Cars
   See Automobiles
Cartoons, awards; 0451
Catalog showrooms
   See also Discount trade
   annual consumer audit; 0299
   awards; 0298
   catalog publishers; 0299
   census; 0298, 0429
   market audit; 0299
   product selection; 0298
   rep guide; 0299
   seasonal promotion; 0298
   shows; 0298
   suppliers directory; 0298, 0299
   top firms; 0299
Catholic Health Association of the U.S.; 0648
Catholic Library Association; 0302
Catholic Press Association; 0301
Cats; 0303
Cattle, agricultural reports; 0506
CEDA
   See Canadian Electrical Distributors Association
Celery, crop reports; 0506
Cement
   See Concrete
Census statistics; 0058
Census, United States Bureau of; 0407
Ceramic hobby industry
   buyers guide; 0305
   youth crafts; 0124
Ceramic industry
   autoramics; 0304
   batching techniques; 0304
   Canadian directory; 0251
   Canadian membership roster; 0251
   container glass; 0304
   convention; 0304
   data book; 0304
   directory; 0054
   heat and combustion buyers guide; 0629
   industry giants; 0304
   international; 0304
   meeting; 0054
   membership roster; 0054
   raw materials handbook; 0304
   refractories; 0054
   review/forecast; 0304
Ceramic tile, directory and buyers guide; 1262
Cereal foods; 0306
Chain stores
   See also Discount trade
   annual census; 0307
   automotive, census; 0429
   capital expenditures; 0307
   chain drug industry annual report; 0438
   company profile; 0308, 0429, 0837
   construction forecast; 0307
   consumer electronics, census; 0429
   consumer study; 0308
   design awards; 0307
   industry report; 0837

off-price apparel, census; 0429
retailer of the year; 0837
sales survey; 0837
shows; 0307
sporting goods, census; 0429
top chains; 0308
top merchandising departments; 0308
top $100 million; 0307
toy, census; 0429
Chamber of Commerce of the United States; 0939
Champagne
   See Wine
Charitable organizations
   See Philanthropy
Chartered Life Underwriters; 0805
Cheese products
   See also Dairy products
consumer survey; 0402
convention; 0311
Chemical engineering
   See also Chemical process industry
industry directory; 0319
salary survey; 0313
show; 0314
Chemical industry
   See also Chemical process industry; Chemicals
awards; 0315
budgeting; 0313
buyers' guide; 0319
capital spending outlook; 0313
congressional outlook; 0313
construction directory; 0319
employment outlook; 0313
engineering and construction directory; 0319
equipment; 0315
facts & figures; 0313
financial reports; 0313
forecast; 0319
instruments; 0313
maintenance survey; 0319
outlook; 0318
plant capacity use survey; 0313
plants exposition; 0314
pollution control; 0315, 1045
R&D budget outlook; 0313
salary survey; 0313, 0318, 0319
show; 0315
top foreign; 0319
top 300; 0319
top 50 companies and products; 0313
world outlook; 0313
Chemical process industry
buyers guide; 0250, 0312
construction survey; 0312
Hydrocarbon processing; 0655
industry forecast; 0312
shows; 0312, 0317, 0675
Chemical specialties; 0670, 1198
Chemical Specialties Manufacturers Association; 0027, 0437, 1198
Chemicals
agricultural; 0261, 0328, 0504, 0511
analysis; 0079
beauty; 0316
building maintenance; 0822
buyers guide; 0250, 0316
coating; 0316
detergents; 0316
directory; 0318
forecast; 0670
in paper; 0991
insecticide buyer's guide; 1002
laboratory analysis; 0707
laboratory application review; 0101
laboratory buyers guide; 0101, 0180, 0785
oil chemists conference proceedings; 0769
petrochemicals; 0316
plastic industry statistics; 0901
pulp and paper industry; 1086
purchasing; 1089
rubber; 1142
salary survey; 0670
sanitation cleaners; 1074
shipping; 0316
tank trucks; 0891
Chemicals, food; 0551
Chemistry, analytical; 0013, 0785
Chicago advertising market; 0024
Chicago Real Estate Board; 1108, 1111
Children's wear; 0050
Chile
banking; 0051
China and glass; 0718, 0718
   See also Giftware; Tableware
buyers guide; 0587
directory; 0321, 0589
show; 0298
Christian Booksellers Association; 0323, 0325, 1085
Christian Century Foundation; 0324
Christianity; 0326
Christmas
books; 0950
books and music; 0325
cooking and entertaining ideas; 0169
crafts ideas; 0169
crafts merchandising; 0386
dance performances; 0404
decorations merchandising; 1275
food & gift ideas; 0499
gift guides; 0949, 1041, 1221, 1343
hobby merchandising; 0636
toy merchandising; 1273
Chromatography; 0079, 0180, 0730, 0785
Chromium; 0082
Churches
liturgy planning guide; 0332
Cigarettes
   See Tobacco industry
Circus
   See Amusement parks and shows
City planning; 1026
Civil engineering; 0330
Clay
   See Ceramic industry
Clio awards; 0151
Clocks
   See Watches and clocks
Clothing
   See Apparel
Club Managers Association of America; 0335
Coal and coal mining; 0882
   See also Mines and mining
buyers guide; 0336, 1349
Canadian exploration; 0971
Canadian gasification; 0971
Canadian industry review; 1335
company profile; 0336
convention; 0336, 0886
equipment; 0886
exporters directory; 1349
forecast; 0337, 0482
international review; 1349
laboratory application review; 0101
review and outlook; 0336
statistics; 1349
Coatings and finishes
   See Paints and coatings
Cobalt; 0082
Coffee
plantations; 1350
service; 0287, 1350
vending; 0049, 0287, 1303
Coin Laundry Association; 0057
Coin-operated machines
   See Laundry and dry cleaning; Vending machines
Collectibles; 0587, 0718
College stores; 0339
Colleges
   See Schools and universities
Colorado Bankers Association; 0915
Combination store
   See Discount trade
Commercials, broadcast
awards; 0151
directory; 0151
production directory; 0880
Commodity trading
   See Investments
Communications
   See also Audio-visual communications; Data communications; Telecommunications
international directory; 0927
public safety; 0009
Compensation
   See Executive compensation; Salary surveys
chemical industry survey; 0319
Computer graphics; 0228, 0354, 0356, 0441
Computer law; 0355
Computer software
accountant's buying guide; 1059
best-sellers; 0658, 1202
buyers guide; 0359, 0387, 0687
educational; 0387, 0397, 0691
for investment and treasury management; 0999
microcomputer review; 0687
office equipment; 0962
retail guide; 0178
small systems; 1191
systems survey; 0408
top companies; 0658
Computer-aided design
   See CAD/CAM
Computer-aided manufacturing
   See CAD/CAM
Computers
   See also CAD/CAM; Computer graphics; Computer software; Computers, personal; Data communications; Data processing
aerospace; 0148
and insurance; 0265
anti-theft security; 1172
benchmarks; 0228
business mini; 0961
Canadian census; 0231
Canadian shows; 0231, 0255
careers in; 0595
compatibles directory; 0426
computer games review; 0387
conference proceedings; 0102
consumer electronics show; 0374
dealer show; 0964
design; 0354
designers salary survey; 0426
directory/buyers guide; 0358
education; 0228
for medical diagnoses; 0851
gift guide; 1202
hardware review; 0359
in bioresearch; 0180
in chemistry; 0670
in mining; 0230
in petroleum industry; 0273, 0971
interfacing; 0228
mainframe survey; 0359, 0408
micro buyers guide; 0359
mini buyers guide; 0359, 0961
National Computer Conference; 0408
new chips; 0228
new product review; 0687
simulation; 0228
small business systems; 0825, 1191
storage; 0228
supermini buyers guide; 0359, 0469
terminals and peripherals buyers guide; 0359
top components manufacturers; 0469
video interface; 0442
Computers, personal; 0420, 0872
consumer survey; 0836, 0861
games; 0387
hardware and software buyers guide; 0387
marketing; 0024
merchandising report; 0861
mini-micro peripherals selection guide; 0883
supplier directory; 0861
users profile; 0899
Concrete
buyers guide; 0360, 0361
Canadian report; 0401

cement and demographics; 1137
cement reports; 0541, 1024
masonry; 0360
outlook; 0360
pipe; 0360
precast; 0360
ready-mixed; 0360
sourcebook; 0361
Confectionery
See Candy and confectionery
Conferences
See Conventions
Construction
See also Building; Concrete; Contractors; Highway construction; Pipelines; Window systems
agricultural; 0501
Alaska; 0046
awards; 0487
buyers guide; 0361, 0365, 0371, 0981
Canadian; 0206, 0401, 0483, 0583, 0632
chemical industry; 0319
convention; 0367
cost reports; 0487
directory; 0370, 0371, 0487
electrical tools; 0229
engineering; 0330
executive compensation; 0487
Florida; 0542
forecast; 0370, 0487, 0632, 0981
handbooks and manuals; 0369
in Africa; 0888
in Asia; 0889
international; 0487
legal aspects; 0369
literature review; 0483
marine; 0965, 0967
pipelines; 1023
product guide; 0369, 0541
public works; 0370
research & technology; 0046
seasonal aspects; 0370
statistics; 0368
trucks and trucking; 0370
utility contracting; 0370
walls & ceilings; 1318
wood; 0541
Construction equipment
Alaska; 0046
buyers guide; 0366
Canadian; 0632
conference; 0981
distribution directory; 0367
infrastructure; 0366
machinery manufacturers and distributors; 0431
show; 0634
specifications; 0364
top contractors equipment owners; 0366
top industrial equipment owners; 0366
Construction Specifications Institute; 0369
Consultants; 0229, 0373
Consumer electronics
annual report; 0105
awards, audio/video; 0409
buyers guide; 0374, 0409
computers; 0374
consumer surveys; 0836, 0861
discount stores; 0429
forecast; 0374
markets; 0024, 0836, 0861
outlook; 0836
product reviews; 1051
show; 0299, 0374, 0409, 0836, 1253
statistics; 0861
supplier directory; 0861
top companies; 0409
Consumer products
buyers guide; 0375
Consumer purchasing
buying power; 1150
forecast; 1150
Consumer surveys
See Specific listings
Containerization; 0069, 1315

Containers
See Packaging
Contractors
See also Construction
directory; 0371, 0487
top firms; 0487
Controls systems
See Instruments and controls
Convenience stores
chain store directory; 0381
convention; 0381
equipment guide; 0396
industry report; 0381, 0396
marketing trends; 0381
Conventions
Canadian; 0265, 0526
medical meeting facilities; 0854
planning directory; 1351
world dates; 1351
Cookbooks; 0169, 1124
Cookies and crackers
See Baking industry
Copper; 0082
Copper and Brass Servicenter Association; 0863
Copying equipment; 0961
Copyright newsletter; 0382
Corn; 0296, 1174
Corporate mergers
See Mergers and acquisitions
Corporate Officers
See Executives
Corporations
See also Business and industry; International business; Mergers and acquisitions
annual report awards; 0528
annual reports; 0440, 0558, 0999
balance sheet scoreboard; 0226
best-managed; 0440
Canadian directors; 0526
communications centers guide; 0132
corporate finance directory; 0712, 0999
corporate financial officers directory; 0690
corporate scoreboard; 0226
corporate-sponsored sports events; 0833
defense industry; 0926
dividend achievers; 0440
earnings forecast; 0226, 0558
executive compensation; 0226, 0558
fastest growing; 0558, 0664
5-year profits forecast; 0447
fixed business capital in U.S.; 1238
Florida; 0542
foreign; 0565
foreign corporate scoreboard; 0226
foreign investment in U.S.; 1238
industry ratios; 0440
inflation scoreboard; 0226
international; 0565
largest; 0565
largest employers; 0558
Minnesota; 0384
multinational: U.S. and foreign; 0558
nonfinancial; 1238
pension fund statistics; 0999
profits; 1238
R & D scoreboard; 0226
reputations survey; 0565
top California companies; 0495
top companies still run by founders; 1304
top deals; 0565
top service; 0565
top small companies; 0664
top 500 companies; 0558
Corrosion control; 0317
Corrosion engineering; 0842
Cosmetics and fragrances
See also Chemical specialties; Health and beauty aids
advertising expenditures; 1067
consumer expenditures; 1067
cosmetics directory; 0163
industry catalog; 0437
men's cosmetics directory; 0163
treatments directory; 0163
women's fragrance directory; 0163

Cosmetics, Toiletries and Fragrance Association; 0027, 0437, 1198
Cotton, crop reports; 0506
Council of State Governments; 1229
Council of State Housing Agencies; 0189
Council on Foreign Relations; 0559
Crafts and hobbies
See also Needlework
buyers guide; 0386, 0388, 0636, 1043, 1275
country; 0169
doll houses; 0386
holiday; 0169
seasonal merchandising; 0386, 0636
show; 0386, 0636, 1043, 1273, 1275
statistics; 1275
youth crafts; 0124
100 ideas; 0169
Credit
See also Banks and banking
consumer; 0389
consumer credit buyers guide; 0394
consumer credit managers directory; 0394
country credit ratings; 0690
manual of regulations; 0390
statistics; 0390
Credit Union National Association; 0392, 0393
Credit unions; 0391
Crop production reports; 0506
Currency; 1093
Custom house brokers; 0069

D

Dairy industry
buyers guide; 0403
buyers guide, Canadian; 0893
international; 0034
processor awards; 0403
show; 0403
Dairy products
See also Cheese products
agricultural reports; 0506
buyers guide; 0402
consumer surveys; 0402
government regulations; 0402
industry trends; 0402
ingredients and flavors; 0402
new products; 0402
packaging; 0402
Dallas-Fort Worth advertising market; 0024
Dance
See also Education; Square Dancing
awards; 0404
Christmas programs; 0404
college programs; 0404
directory of services, dancers; 0404
square dancing vacations; 0096
summer events; 0404
Data communications
See also Telecommunications
buyer's guide; 0405
design; 0354
top companies; 0405
year in review; 0405
Data processing
See also Computers; Information processing
awards; 0406
buyers guides; 0359
Datamation 100; 0408
design; 0354
directory, Canadian; 0255, 0357
for accountants; 0234
hardware roundup; 0359
in petroleum industry; 0971
managers' profiles; 0406
new product review; 0687
office equipment; 0359
salary survey; 0408, 0687
top companies; 0353
top 25 European DP companies; 0408
Data Processing Management Association; 0406
Dealer Bank Association; 0189
Defense industry; 0926, 1167

See also Electronics, military
Delicatessens; 0414
Demographics; 0479
  by state; 0058
  marketing to the affluent; 0051
  population statistics; 0870
  survey of buying power; 1150
Dental laboratories
  buyers guide; 0415
  industry review; 0415
  salary survey; 0415
Dental products
  buyers guide; 0416
Department stores
  See also Chain stores; Store design
  ratios; 1231
  retailer profile; 1067
  top companies; 1231
Design engineering
  See also Machine design; Materials engineering
  awards; 0418
  components; 0418
  directory; 0418, 0487
  electrical generating; 1057
  energy systems guidebook; 1057
  international; 0487
  plant planbook; 1057
  power transmission; 1058
  product showcase; 0418
  purchasing; 1089
  show; 0418, 0654, 0713
  show, Canadian; 0417
  top firms; 0487
Detergents
  See Soaps and detergents
Dialysis services; 0895
Diamonds
  See Jewelry
Diapers; 0952
Die casting
  See also Metalworking
Diesel engines
  See also Power plants
  international catalog/buyers guide; 0424
  review; 0425
  specialists directory; 0425
Direct mail
  See also Direct selling
Direct selling; 0024
  Canadian; 0831
  directory; 0973, 1175
  farm market; 0033
  marketing; 0973
  opportunities directory; 0666
  sales training; 0973
Disability statistics; 0870
Discount trade
  See also Catalog showrooms; Chain stores
  automotive; 0428, 0429
  combination stores; 0428
  company profile; 0429
  consumer electronics; 0429
  executives; 0428
  health and beauty aids; 0428
  industry statistics; 0429
  manufacturers' awards; 0429
  marketing statistics; 0428
  mass market licensing; 0429
  merchandising report; 0428
  off-price apparel; 0429
  product movement audit; 0429
  shows and conventions; 0429
  sporting goods; 0428, 0429
  top companies; 0428, 0429
  toys; 0428, 0429
Distilleries
  See Liquor industry
Distribution
  See also Materials handling; Transportation
  catalog of directories; 1277
  computer update; 0673
  convention; 0344, 0673
  directory; 0367, 0430, 0673, 1277
  international outlook; 0608

  outlook; 0608, 1089
  sales awards; 1089
  world commerce; 1277
Diving
  commercial; 1167
  travel guide; 1189
Documentary films
  See Motion pictures
Dogs
  See Pets
Doors; 0433
Doors and Hardware Institute; 0433
Doughnuts
  See Baking industry
Dredging; 1352
Drilling
  See also Drilling, offshore
  annual survey; 0967
  contract drilling report; 0435
  convention; 0434
  equipment; 0435, 0960, 0969, 1006
  forecast; 0434
  marine; 0960, 0965
  offshore; 1006
  offshore report; 0434
  production operations; 0434
  review and forecast; 0435
  rig locators; 1006
  rotary rig census; 0435
  technology; 0435, 1006
Drilling, offshore
  See also Petroleum industry
  downhole services, Canadian; 0436
  equipment and rigs; 0273, 0436, 0960, 0971
  equipment, Canadian; 0436
  muds and mud systems; 0436
Drug stores
  See also Drugs and pharmaceuticals
  consumer spending; 0439
  financial planning guide; 0439
  marketing statistics; 0438
  outlook; 0439
  prescription survey; 0439
Drugs and pharmaceuticals
  See also Drug stores
  advertising expenditures; 1067
  catalog; 0437
  chain drug industry; 0438, 0837
  consumer study; 0438, 1067
  conventions; 0437
  drug wholesalers; 0438
  packaging; 0437
  pharmacy reference guide; 0059, 0438
  prescription survey; 0439
  product study; 0438
  top over-the-counter; 0059, 0438
  top pharmaceuticals; 0438
Dry cleaning
  See Laundry and dry cleaning
Dyes
  buyer's guide, carpets; 0294

E

Earnings
  See Wages
Earth stations
  See Satellites and earth stations
Eastern States Veterinary Conference; 0400
Ecological Society of America; 0445
Econometric Society; 0446
Economic development
  agencies and officials directories; 0672
Economics
  See also Business and industry; Economy, U.S.
  bibliographies; 0737
  books; 0950
  forecast; 0528, 0685
  industrial nations survey; 0226
  Third World survey; 0226
Economy, U.S.
  outlook; 0449
  update and forecast; 0447

Education
  See also Education, Vocational; Schools and universities
  Accounting Doctoral Programs Survey; 0016
  arts & crafts; 0124
  audio visual; 0454, 1309
  banking; 0051
  books on; 1097
  Canadian buyers guide; 0454
  Catholic textbooks; 1268
  college dance programs; 0404
  computer directory; 0387, 0691
  construction cost report; 0092
  dance, buyer's guide; 0754
  dance, directory of institutions; 0622
  document abstracts; 1120
  early learning; 0050
  educator's buyers guide; 0092
  engineering; 0485
  for military and family; 0040, 0119
  Gallup poll opinion survey; 1009
  health, directory of institutions; 0622
  learning disabilities software; 0748
  maintenance cost report; 0092
  medical; 0768
  physical, buyer's guide; 0754
  physical, directory of institutions; 0622
  plant maintenance; 0454
  recreation, buyer's guide; 0754
  recreation, directory of institutions; 0622
  religious; 0047, 0324, 0326
  teaching aids; 0454
  videodisc applications; 1309
Education, vocational
  buyers guide; 1160, 1312
  government officials directory; 1160
  teacher training; 1312
Educational materials
  See also Audio-visual materials
  audio-visual aids; 0397, 0454, 1309
  buyers guide; 0453, 1159
  computers; 0397
  product review; 0453
  science; 0397
Educational Resources Information Center; 1120
Egg industry
  See also Poultry industry
  agricultural reports; 0506
  award; 1053
  directory; 1052
  export-import; 1055
Electric industry; 0465
  convention; 0463
  electromechanical bench reference; 0458
  review forecast; 0463
  site location, Canadian; 0459
  top wholesalers; 0465
Electric power industry
  See also Power plants; Utilities, electric
  Africa; 0888
  Alaska; 0046
  buyers guide; 1057, 1283
  directory; 0425
  government statistics; 0457
  international systems; 1057
  supply-demand forecast; 0482
  systems planbook; 1057
Electrical appliances
  See Consumer electronics
Electrical contractors; 0229, 0462
Electrical distributors; 0463
Electrical engineering; 1030
  circuit protection; 0461
  communications systems; 0461
  computer-aided design; 0461
  machine design; 0819
  motor controls; 0461
  substations; 0461
  switching; 0461
  systems; 0461
Electrical equipment; 0229, 0459, 0675, 1218
  Canadian; 0459, 0464, 0467
  insulation buyers guide; 0468
  plastics design; 1031
  yearbook; 0460

Electrical Generating Systems Association; 0425
Electronic funds transfer; 0051, 0156
Electronics
   See also Computers; Consumer electronics; Fiber optics; Microwaves; Optoelectronics; Printed circuits; Telecommunications
   automotive; 0140
   business forecast; 0469
   buyers guide; 0327, 0468, 0472
   Canadian; 0257, 0473
   careers; 0471
   components; 0470
   connectors and terminals; 0468
   design engineering directory; 0418, 0471
   designers' reference; 0471
   engineering productivity; 0441
   executive outlook; 0472
   microwave systems; 0874
   midyear outlook; 0469
   plant sites; 0469
   product showcases; 0441
   shows; 0327, 0441, 0470, 0471, 0675
   solid state buyers guide; 1205
   technical articles index; 0441
   technology update; 0472
   test and measurement; 0441
   test equipment directory; 0493
   testing laboratories; 0493
   top components manufacturers; 0469
   top contractors; 0412
   top design firms; 0471
   top distributors; 0469
   top manufacturers; 0469
   top paid executives; 0469
   wires and cables; 0468
   world market forecast; 0472
Electronics, military; 0327, 0441, 0469, 0875
   international counter measures handbook; 0412
   marketing directory & buyers guide; 0412
   matrix of airborne EW systems; 0412
   top defense contractors; 0412
   U.S. Air Force; 0039
   warefare, aviation; 0148
Electrophoresis; 0180
Electroplating; 1039
Employee benefits; 0223, 0805
   administration firms; 0998
   consultants directory; 0166
   Erisa calendar; 0998
   insurance company services; 0998
   statistics; 0476
Employee crime; 1172
Employers
   largest; 0558
   top Toronto; 0871
Employment
   advertising industry; 0024
   chemical industry; 0313
   statistics; 0478
   temporary help; 0963
Encyclopedias; 0691
Energy
   alternative energy sources; 0882
   Canadian; 0273, 0526, 0971
   construction equipment; 0366
   consultants directory; 0482
   engineering; 0330
   forecast; 0482
   home guide; 1049
   industrial; 0846
   international industry; 0966
   products update; 0464
Energy conservation
   architectural design; 1075
   chemical processing; 0315, 0317
   industrial; 0683
   insulation technology; 0482
   petroleum industry; 0969
   technology conference; 0482
Energy management systems; 0461, 0482
Engineering
   See also Specific field of engineering
   awards; 0253
   building; 0330
   codes and standards; 0846
   college research directory; 0485
   computer-aided; 0846
   control products; 0380
   design; 0846
   failure analysis; 0846
   international supply guide; 1358
   manufacturers' literature; 0373
   specifier's guide; 1218
Engineering, industrial
   CAD/CAM; 0674
   conference; 0674
   facilities planning; 0674
   factory automation; 0674
   manufacturing systems; 0674
   material handling; 0674
   office systems; 0674
   productivity projects; 0674
   warehousing and distribution; 0674
Engineers
   Canadian directory; 0149
   careers; 0595
   marine; 1347
   power plant consulting; 1056
   salary survey; 0674
   survey of computer use; 0674
Enology
   See Wine
Entertainment industry
   See also Amusement industry; Amusement parks and shows; Fairs and Festivals
   advertising report; 0026
   buyers guide; 0099
   directory of acts and attractions; 0099
   leisure facilities; 0099
   marketing; 0024
Environmental Management Association; 1074
Environmental protection
   See also Pollution control; Water pollution
   Canadian; 1325
   in hydrocarbon processing; 0655
   laboratory analysis; 0079, 0707
   planning award; 0672
   products directory; 1045
Environmental Protection Agency; 1045
Equitation
   See also Horse and riders
Estate planning
   See Trust institutions
Ethylene; 0967
Europe
   Eastern Bloc banking; 0051
   financial marketing review; 0051
   offshore report; 1006
   travel; 0283, 0284
European Economic Community
   banking; 0051
Executive compensation
   See also Salary surveys
   banking; 0051
   company founders; 1304
   electronics industry; 0469
   hospital administrators; 0895
   marketing and sales; 1150
   salary surveys; 0664
   survey; 0226
Executives
   business poll, Cananda; 0494
   chief executive of the year; 0528
   leadership awards; 0565
   mood survey; 0565
   survey of Black directors; 0217
Export/import
   See also International trade
   top exporters; 0565

F

Fabrics
   See Textile industry
Factory automation
   See Automation
Fairs and Festivals
   See also Amusement parks and shows
   directory; 0099
   western; 0099
Family Motor Coach Association; 0500
Far East
   ports; 0069
   shipping directory; 1168
Farm equipment
   See Agricultural equipment
Farms
   See Agriculture
Fashion industry
   forecast; 1313
   intimate apparel markets; 0187
   marketing data; 0024
   men's; 0949
   seasonal collections; 1313
   women's; 0949
Fast foods
   See also Restaurants; Snacks foods
   Canadian chains; 0905
   marketing data; 0024
   snack processing; 0153
Fastenings; 0418
Fats and oils, agricultural reports; 0506
Federal government
   See United States government listings
Federal Home Loan Banks; 1155
Federal Reserve Bank of Atlanta; 0448
Federal Reserve Bank of Boston; 0944, 0945
Federal Reserve Bank of Kansas City; 0449
Federal Reserve Bank of New York; 1094
Federal Reserve Bank of Philadelphia; 0225
Federal Reserve Bank of St. Louis; 1130
Federal Reserve System; 0509, 1094, 1130
Federation of American Hospitals; 0510
Federation of American Societies for Experimental Biology; 0180
Federation of Societies for Coating Technology; 0085, 0732, 1336
Federation of Societies for Paint Technology; 0900
Feed industry; 0505
   agricultural reports; 0506
   buyer's guide; 0512, 0514
   directory, Canadian; 0511
   handling; 0504
Fence industry; 0515
Fertilizers; 0031, 0504, 0505, 1024, 1206
   equipment; 0503
   guide; 1328
Fiber optics
   buyers guide; 0516
   economic review; 0518
   Laser industry buyers guide; 0792
   wire industry; 1342
Fibers
   See Textile industry
Film industry
   See Motion pictures
Film Society of Lincoln Center; 0521
Filmstrips, notable; 0190
Filters, laboratory; 0180
Filtration engineering; 0315, 0317, 0785
Finance
   See also Banks and banking; Credit
   commercial; 0722
   convention; 0722
   corporate financial officers directory; 0690
   industry survey; 0159
   largest companies; 0565
   Legislative and Judicial Developments; 0722
   public finance directory; 0690
Financial Analysts Federation; 0524
Financial Executives Institute; 0525
Fire protection; 1172
   buyer's guide; 0531, 0532, 0936
   convention; 0530, 0531
   emergency medical buyers guide; 0531
   fire fighter injuries; 0530
   industrial; 0684

property loss statistics; 0532
Firearms; 0062, 1172, 1179
Fish and fisheries
   annual statistics, Canadian; 1333
   aquaculture buyers guide; 0108
   regional fisheries; 0928
   seafood brands; 0535
   seafood business; 0928
   shrimp; 0535
Fishing
   See also Fishing tackle
   bass guide; 0519, 1222
   Canadian guide; 0974, 1332
   directory & reference; 0535
   guide; 0519, 1222
   midwest guide; 0975
   review and forecast; 0533
   southern guide; 0975
   yearbook; 0928
Fishing boats; 0533
Fishing tackle; 0928, 1333
   catalogs; 0536
   product reviews; 0536
   show; 0298, 0536, 1220, 1225
Fishing Tackle Manufacturers Association; 1224
Fitness and health
   See Health and fitness
Flat Glass Marketing Association; 1295
Flatware
   sterling flatware pattern index; 0718
Fleets
   See Trucks and trucking
Floor care products; 0836
Floor coverings
   buyers guide; 0411
   Canadian directory; 0538
   carpet chemicals; 0294
   carpet dyeing technology; 0060
   carpet industry forecast; 1257, 1259
   designers file; 0419
   export; 0539
   machinery and equipment; 0294
   source directory; 0539
   specifiers' guide; 0539
   summer market guides; 0539
   top manufacturers; 0294
Flooring; 0540, 0702
Florida
   advertising market; 0024
   construction; 0541, 0542
   economic yearbook; 0542
   financial review; 0542
   public companies directory; 0542
   real estate; 0542
   restaurant awards; 0542
Florida Irrigation Society; 0328
Florists; 0543
   Canadian buyers guide; 0258
Flotation sleep
   See Waterbeds
Flowers
   See also Gardens and gardening
   export; 0986
   packaging; 0986
   seedsmen awards; 1174
Fluid Fertilizer Industry; 1206
Food
   See also Baking industry; Food, institutional;
      Food processing industry; Frozen foods;
      Snack foods
   food editors conference; 0451
   ingredients; 0549
   new products; 0549, 0550
   pasta products; 0817
   specialty; 0490
Food brokers; 0262, 0951
Food, institutional; 0651
   distributor shows; 0689
   product savvy; 0689
   top 50 distributors; 0689
Food Marketing Institute; 0152, 0569
Food processing
   salary review; 0549

Food processing industry
   See also Frozen foods
   agriculture; 0553
   award; 1066
   buyers' guide; 0553, 1066
   Canadian buyers guide; 0551
   capital expenditures; 0549
   capital spending update; 1066
   cooking techniques; 0550
   directory; 0552, 0553
   engineering master; 0549
   equipment report; 0550
   food chemicals encyclopedia; 0551
   industry review; 0549
   ingredients; 0549, 1066
   new products; 0549, 0550, 1066
   packaging; 0553
   plants; 0549, 0552
   research and development; 0383, 0552, 1066
   sanitation & pollution control; 0550
   seafood business report; 0928
   show; 0548, 0550, 0553, 1066
   statistics; 0551, 0553, 1066
   top companies; 0552, 1066
   warehouse directory; 1066
Food Processing Machinery & Suppliers
   Association; 0553
Food service; 0554, 0941, 1123
   annual report; 1124
   awards; 1124
   beverages; 0809
   buyers guide; 0555, 0667, 1124
   buying trends; 1124
   convention; 0555
   dealer of the year; 0555
   eastern distributors; 0809
   equipment; 0667
   equipment dealers; 0555
   forecast; 0555
   hotels and motels; 0555
   new products contest; 1066
   product guide; 0556, 0809, 1123
   salary survey; 1124
   schools; 1157
   shows; 0809
   top organizations; 1124
   vending; 0287
Football; 1041, 1221
   broadcasting; 0201
   NFL Super Bowl; 1221
Footware
   See also Leather; Shoe industry
   Canadian; 0259
Footwear
   convention; 1178
   directory; 0557
   financial review; 0557
   new products; 0094
   running shoes; 1144
   shows; 0094
   sporting goods survey; 1224
   tennis shoes; 1356
Forest Farmer Association; 0561
Forest industries
   See also Lumber industry; Paper and pulp;
      Wood and wood products
   buyers guide; 0562
   Canadian; 0260
   capital expenditures; 0260
   directory; 0562
   electronics/computer technology; 0562
   farmer manual; 0561
   forest area maps; 0562
   loggers buying guide/woodlands directory; 1263
   lumbermen's buying guide; 1264
   mill automation; 0260
   pulpwood; 0562
   review; 0562
   statistics; 0529, 0562, 1357
   yearbook; 0563
Foundation for the Advancement of International
   Business Administration; 0705
Foundries; 0567
   See also Metalworking

Fragrances
   See Cosmetics and Fragrances
France
   banking; 0051
Franchising
   Canada; 0479, 0494
   opportunities directory; 0666
   restaurants; 1122
Frankfurt Book Fair; 1085
Freight forwarding; 0069
   See also Air transport industry; Ports
Frozen foods
   almanac/statistics; 0553, 1095
   citrus concentrates; 0569
   conventions; 0553, 0569, 1095
   equipment; 1095
   ethnic foods survey; 1095
   industry survey; 1095
   ingredients; 1095
   orange juice report; 1095
   pizza; 1095
   processors directory; 0553, 1095
   retailers building/buying; 1095
   seafood survey; 0569, 1095
   supermarket survey; 0569
   warehouse/transportation; 0569, 1095
Fruit growing
   See also Produce
Fruits, agricultural reports; 0506
Fruits, citrus; 0328
Fuel Merchants Association of New Jersey;
   0570, 0571
Fuel oil industry
   See also Petroleum industry
   conventions; 0570, 0571
   dealer management; 0571
   EDP suppliers directory; 0570
   equipment directory; 0570
   futures trading; 0570
   mid-year statistics; 0570
   service management; 0571
   state associations directory; 0570
   suppliers directory/statistics; 0570
   supply-demand forecast; 0482, 0966
Fund raising
   for associations; 0127
   in libraries; 0800
Funeral regulations; 1211
Fur industry; 0573
Furniture
   See also Woodworking
   buyer's guide; 0575, 0577
   casual; 0297
   contract furnishings show; 0378
   convention; 0576
   design awards; 0577
   design market review; 1345
   electronic; 0836
   equipment supply exposition; 1300
   historical style review; 0577
   industry calendar; 0297
   juvenile; 0050, 0780, 1192
   office furniture report; 0899
   resource directory; 1070
   seasonal markets; 1070
   seating directory; 0702
   show; 0266, 0574
   supply source directory; 0574, 0576
   upholstery directory; 1300
Futures trading
   See also Investments
   fuel oil; 0570
   grain industry; 0596
Futurism; 0578

G

Gallup marketing trends report; 0381
Games
   See Amusements, coin-operated; Toys
Garages
   See Parking, off-street

Gardens and gardening
   See also Flowers; Supplies
   ideas; 0169
   nurseries; 0083
   shows; 0579
   supplies; 0543
Gas, liquefied petroleum
   See also Pipelines
   buyer's guide; 1022
   Canadian plants; 0273, 0971
   construction; 0655
   distribution report; 1022
   equipment and services; 0969
   processing; 0655, 0967
   regional conventions; 0580
   supply-demand forecast; 0482
   top companies; 1022
Gas Processors Association; 0966
Gas turbines
   See Diesel engines; Turbomachinery
Gatlinburg Gift Show; 1213
Gems
   See also Jewelry; Jewelry making
   buyers guide; 0791
Genealogy; 0582
Geophysics; 0967
   See also Ocean science
   Canada; 0273, 0971
   yearbook; 0584
Germany
   banking; 0051
   corporations with U.S., subsidiaries; 0585
   U.S. imports, buyers guide; 0585
Gerontology; 1112
Gifts; 0375, 0812
Giftware
   awards; 0587
   buyers directory; 0587, 0589
   Canadian shows; 0588
   for florists; 0543
   forecast; 0587
   show; 0298, 0587
Glass
   See also Ceramic industry
   buyers guide (flat glass); 1295
   conventions; 1295
   materials, equipment, machinery; 0930, 1295
   mirrors; 1295
   sealants and glazing systems; 1295
Glass factories, directory; 0065, 0590, 0930
Glassware
   See China and glass
Glazing
   See Glass
Gold; 0082, 0953
   See also Jewelry
Golf; 0496, 0592, 0593, 0948, 1221
   See also Golf courses
   camps and schools; 0592, 0593
Golf Course Superintendents Association of America; 0591
Golf courses; 0592, 0593, 0606, 1328
Gordon Research Conference; 1161
Gourmet ware; 0587
Grain Elevator and Processing Society; 0596, 0598
Grain industry
   agricultural reports; 0296, 0506
   conferences; 0596
   directory and buyers guide; 0881
   futures; 0596
   maintenance; 0596
   operators' manual; 0596
   storage; 0597
   tranportation; 0596
   world food picture; 0596
Graphic arts
   See also Printing and typesetting
   advertising design; 0026, 1149
   advertising typography; 0120
   awards; 0347
   buyers guide; 0600
   directory; 1065
   market statistics; 0600
   product review; 0601
Grass
   See Lawns
Great Britain
   travel; 0283
Greece
   tobacco industry; 1267
   travel; 0283
Green Coffee Association; 1350
Greenhouses; 0097, 0258, 0543
Greeting cards; 0587, 0589, 0602
Grocery trade
   See also Chain stores; Convenience stores; Delicatessens; Supermarkets
   annual industry report; 1076
   Canadian; 0262, 0799
   convention; 0603
   directory; 0604, 0894
   equipment; 1076
   legislation; 0603
   market studies; 0024, 0603, 0894
   marketing guidebook/statistics; 1076
   product usage guide; 1076
   Quebec buying guide; 0799
   top supermarkets; 1076
Gross National Product
   by industry; 1238
   5-year forecast; 0447
Grounds maintenance; 1074
   See also Golf courses; Lawns
   government buying guide; 0594
   manual; 0606
Gulf Intracoastal Canal Association; 1327
Guns
   See Firearms
Gutenberg Festival; 0087

H

Hairdressers
   buying guide; 0066
Hanover Air Show; 1072
Harbors
   See Ports and harbor
Hardware
   advertising workbook; 0614
   buyers guide; 0433
   Canadian; 0613
   consumer product review; 1051
   convention; 0433, 0611
   discount stores; 0429
   hardlines directory; 0611
   merchandiser of the year; 0612
   price study; 0614
   product handbook; 0614
   show; 0298, 0579, 0612, 0614
Hazardous material; 0125
Hazardous materials; 1046
   See also Occupational safety
Health and beauty aids; 0428
   See also Cosmetics and fragrances; Drug stores; Drugs and pharmaceuticals
   chain industry report; 0438, 0837
   chemicals; 0316
   consumer study; 0438
   hair care products; 1235
   product study; 0438
   supermarket merchandising; 0951
Health and fitness; 1118, 1313
   beauty and health guide; 1343
   corporate fitness program; 0479, 0494
   diet and exercise guide; 1329, 1343
   marketing data; 0024
   over 50; 0520
Health care
   See also Hospitals; Medical equipment; Nurses and nursing
   Canadian; 0619, 0855
   clinic construction; 0851
   computers; 0626
   emergency medical services; 0475
   Federal medical services; 1296
   financing supplement; 0620
   giant leaps in health/medicine; 0618
   government regulations; 0002
   historical data; 0620
   home health care study; 0059, 0895
   insurance programs; 0476
   marketing data; 0024
   Medicare; 0620
   multi-unit providers rankings; 0895
   occupational medicine abstracts; 0753
   occupational therapy buyers guide; 0075
Health Care Financial Management Association; 0626
Health care products; 0428, 0624, 0856
Health education
   See Education
Health foods; 0623
Health Industry Distributors Association; 0856
Health maintenance organizations; 0895
Health surveillance systems; 0679
Hearing aids; 0627, 0628
Heating
   See also Fuel oil industry; Heating, industrial; Plumbing
   buyers guide; 1176
   Canadian buyers guide,; 0631
   consumer product review; 1051
   convention; 0379, 1337
   directory; 1337
   equipment technology reports; 0482
   fact book; 0455
   manufacturers directory; 0038, 0630
   manufacturers representatives; 1237, 1337
   profit and market survey; 1337
   seasonal market reports; 1195
   wholesalers; 1237, 1337
Heating, industrial; 1030
   international update; 0678
   review and forecast; 0678
Heating oil
   See Fuel oil industry
Helicopter Association of America; 1072, 1139
Helicopters
   See Aviation and aerospace
Hemispheric Insurance Conference; 0937
Herbicides
   See also Pesticides
   for highways; 0170
   guides; 1328
   railway track maintenance; 1105
Hide Skin and Leather Association; 0797
Highway construction
   See also Roads
   Alaska; 0046
   contractor marketing; 0634
   equipment; 0170, 0366
   fencing and barriers; 0515
   forecast; 0368, 0632, 0634
   Funding; 0170, 1146
   geotextiles; 0170
   herbicides for; 0170
   international; 0927
   maintenance and paving; 0170, 0634
   paving; 1146
   show; 0634
Hiking; 1182
Hispanic market; 0024
Hobbies
   See Crafts and hobbies
Hobby Industry Association; 0386, 0636
Hockey
   buyers guide; 0067
   NHL playoffs; 1221
   Olympics yearbook; 0067
   register; 1221
   summer camps; 0067
Hogs; 0506, 0931
   See also Meat industry
Holidays
   See Christmas; Crafts and Hobbies; Gifts
Home accessories
   See Giftware
Home centers; 0209, 0612
   See also Hardware; Home improvement

Home economics; 0745
Home furnishings; 0640
　See Interior design and decoration
Home Improvement; 1051
　See also Kitchens and bathrooms; Remodeling
　Canadian marketer; 0631
　Canadian retail-wholesale; 0613
　Canadian shows; 0613
　consumer guide; 1049
　country homes; 0169
　discount stores; 0429
　do-it-yourself; 0169
　remodeling plans; 0169, 0652, 1343
　trade shows; 0631
Hong Kong
　banking; 0051
Horse and riders; 0773
　breeds; 1334
　horse shows; 0643
　marketers buyers guide; 1244
　Western yearbook; 0643
Horse racing
　Kentucky Derby; 1221
Hosiery and underwear
　buyers guide; 0638
　private label manufacturers; 0638
Hospitality
　See Hotels and motels; Restaurants
Hospitals
　See also Health care; Nursing homes
　administration awards; 0895
　Canadian directory; 0427
　central service reference manual; 0649
　construction outlook; 0368
　convention; 0645, 0895
　decubitus review; 0621
　design, construction, furnishings; 0621
　economic outlook; 0895
　equipment; 0895
　executive compensation; 0895
　financing; 0895
　infection control; 0621
　insurance; 0895
　investor-owned directory; 0510
　managers & contract services; 0621, 0895
　medical records; 0621
　meetings; 1290, 1338
　multi-unit rankings; 0895
　new buildings; 0645
　operating room survey; 0621
　purchasing; 0427
　revenue bonds survey; 0626
　software guide; 0621
　suppliers directory; 0621
Hotels and motels
　See also Food service; Meetings and
　　conventions; Restaurants
　best hotels; 0690
　bibliography; 0383
　buyers guide; 0651, 0808
　Canadian buyers guide; 0554
　Canadian directory; 0263
　Canadian franchise; 0554
　construction outlook; 0368
　convention; 0808, 1232
　convention facilities; 1351
　directory; 1232
　educators' forum; 0383
　food and beverage; 0651
　interior design; 0651
　interior design awards; 0810
　magazine advertising; 1119
　newspaper advertising; 1119
　Pacific area directory; 0982
　product buyers guide; 0810
　product guide; 0809
　security and fire safety; 0651
　show; 0555, 0808, 0809
　technology guide; 0651
　top Canadian; 0554
　top growth chains; 1124
　top organizations; 1124
　top U.S.; 0810
House furnishings
　accessories, directory suppliers; 0297

Housewares
　Canadian; 0613
　consumer purchasing plans; 0861
　cookwear buyers guide; 0490
　directory; 0653, 0861
　discount stores; 0429
　floor care products; 0836
　show; 0653, 0836
　statistical and marketing report; 0861
　supermarket merchandising; 0951
Housing
　See also Buildings, home
　fixed residential capital in U.S.; 1238
Hunting
　Canada; 1332
　deer and big game guide; 0519, 0975
　guides; 1222
　hunters directory; 0068
　show; 1220, 1224
Hydraulics and pneumatics; 1030
　directory; 0418, 0654
　literature file; 0654
　product guide; 0417, 0654
　shows; 0654
Hydronics Institute; 0379

I

Ice cream
　See also Dairy products
　consumer survey; 0402
Illinois Landscape Contractors Association; 0790
Illustration awards; 0347
Immunology; 0180
Import/export trade
　airline and shipping directories; 0069
　attorneys; 0069
　banks; 0069
　custom brokers; 1315
　custom forms; 0069
　floor coverings; 0539
　foreign zones; 0069
　free trade zones; 1315
　German imports; 0585
　insurance; 0069
　Italian-American; 0716
　marketing; 0069
　materials handling; 0608
　ports; 0069
　tobacco; 1267
Incentive travel
　See Travel and tourism
Incentives
　See Premiums and incentives
Income, personal
　county/metropolitan area; 1238
　state; 1238
Independent Battery Manufacturers Association;
　0162
Independent Insurance Agents of America; 0695,
　0696, 0937
Independent Petroleum Association of America;
　0966
Indexes
　See Abstracts and indexes
India
　tobacco industry; 1267
Indianapolis 500
　See Automobile races
Industrial design
　annual review; 0671
Industrial espionage; 1172
Industrial Fabrics Association International; 0676
Industrial finishing; 0677
Industrial hazards
　See Hazardous materials; Occupational safety
Industrial hygiene; 0684
　show; 0679, 1046
Industrial locations
　See also Site selection
Industrial parks
　See also Site selection

　guide; 0071
　New Jersey; 0948
　site selection; 0071
　Western Canada; 0733
Industrial plants
　See also Plant engineering
　capacity use survey; 0313
Industrial wastes
　See Hazardous materials; Pollution control;
　　Sewage and waste disposal
Industry ratios
　See Business and industry
Inflation
　corporate adjusted earnings; 0226
Information industry; 0805, 0937
Information processing
　See also Computers; Data processing
　computer conference proceedings; 0102
　in Asia; 0889
Information science
　See Library/information science
Infrastructures; 0366, 0634
Ink, printing; 0072
Inland Daily Press Association; 0451
Inland Waterways Conference; 1327
Insecticides
　See Pesticides
Installment credit
　See Banking
Institute of Business Designers; 0378
Institute of Electrical and Electronics Engineers
　Computer Society; 0352
Institute of Food Technologists; 0553
Institute of Industrial Engineers; 0674
Institute of Management Science; 0699
Institute of Real Estate Management; 0756
Institute of Traffic Engineers; 1084
Institute of Transportation Engineers; 0659
Instrument Society of America; 0693
Instruments and controls
　See also Medical instruments
　analytical; 0679
　buyers guide; 0254, 0693, 1161
　chemical equipment; 0315
　chemical industry; 0313
　chemical processing; 0317
　directory; 0698
　electrical; 0229
　new products; 1161
　noise and vibration; 1207
　petroleum industry; 0273, 0969
　pollution monitoring; 1046
　products; 0380, 0693
　shows; 0693
Insurance
　See also Insurance companies; Insurance, life
　　and health; Insurance, property and casualty
　adjusting and claims; 0265
　agents/brokers; 0223
　asset allocation; 0167
　aviation; 0223
　banking; 0051
　brokers directory; 0690
　business lapse ratios; 0167
　California association conventions; 0696
　California marketing directory; 0696
　Canadian statistics; 0265
　commercial; 0286
　company changes; 0167
　computers; 0265, 0696
　convention guide; 0167
　dividend comparisons; 0167
　education; 0286
　employee benefits; 0223
　for associations; 0127
　for schools; 1157
　group insurance directory; 0166
　health care institutions; 0895
　international; 0223, 0706
　policy size; 0167
　reinsurance; 0265
　salespersons awards; 0697
　statistics; 0286, 0696, 0870
　stocks; 0167

surety; 0265
technology; 0167
Insurance Accounting and Systems Association; 0167, 0168
Insurance associations; 0695
Insurance companies
  employee benefits services directory; 0998
  investment advisers directory; 0999
  office management; 0265
  pension funds performance evaluation; 0999
  top companies; 0168
Insurance Information Institute; 0747
Insurance, life and health
  agency management; 0805
  annuities; 0167
  commissioners report; 0805
  conferences; 0695, 0805
  convention planning; 0805
  employee benefits/group insurance; 0805
  financial review; 0805
  full financial services; 0805
  health insurance company rankings; 0805
  health premiums; 0167
  home office management; 0805
  in property/casualty agency; 1140
  information round-up; 0805
  largest companies; 0565
  life premium income rankings; 0805
  marketing and research meeting; 0804
  marketing review; 0805
  million-dollar round table; 0804, 0805
  pension review; 0805
  statistics; 0870
  top companies; 0167
  top in-force leaders; 0805
  underwriters conferences; 0804
  underwriters convention; 0625
  universal; 0167
  whole life policies; 0167
Insurance, property and casualty
  accident premiums; 0167
  automobile; 0168, 0937
  captive insurance; 0937
  claims procedures; 1140
  conferences; 0937
  convention calendar; 0937
  corporate accounts; 1140
  corporate changes; 0168
  corporate risk management; 0706
  domestic regional market reports; 0937
  excess, surplus and specialty; 0168, 0937, 1140
  financial and investment review; 0937
  Fire loss statistics; 0532
  impaired risk; 0697
  information industry; 0937
  information round-up; 0937
  inland marine; 0168, 0694
  international brokerage; 0937
  international markets; 0937
  loss control/safety; 0937
  marine; 0069, 0223, 0265, 0694, 0937
  marketing; 0168, 0937
  medical malpractice; 0168
  new business; 1140
  personal lives; 1140
  premium distribution; 0168
  premium ranking tables; 0937
  reinsurance review; 0937
  replacement costs survey; 0694
  review and forecast; 0168, 0937
  review/forecast; 0694
  risk management; 0937, 1172
  statistics; 0747
  stock trends; 0168
Interest rates
  5-year forecast; 0447
Interior design; 0949
  contract furnishings show; 0378
  furniture design awards; 0577
  historical style review; 0577
Interior design and decoration; 0419, 0652, 1075
  See also Store design
  awards; 0378
  awards (industrial/office); 0702
  best interiors; 0113

Canadian markets; 0640
contract floor covering directory; 0702
country homes; 0169
decorative products buyers guide; 0411
decorative products show; 1336
designer of the year; 0702
directory/buyers guide; 0266, 0378, 0700, 0702
fabric and wallcoverings directory; 0702
furniture show; 0266
home decorating ideas; 0169, 0499, 1343
hotel awards; 0810
hotel industry; 0651
lighting directory; 0702
product finder; 0266
seating directory; 0702
textiles directory; 0701
top corporate clients; 0702
wallcoverings directory; 0410
who's who; 0378
window and wall ideas; 0169
Intermountain Veterinary Association; 0400
International Air Transport Association; 0042, 0043
International Amusement Fairs and Expositions; 1272
International Association for Financial Planning; 0805
International Association of Amusement Parks and Attractions; 0099, 1272
International Association of Arena Managers; 1272
International Association of Auditorium Managers; 0099
International Association of Drilling Contractors; 0434, 0966
International Association of Fire Chiefs; 0530, 0531
International Association of Printing House Craftsmen; 1129
International Automobile Service Industries; 0721, 0912
International Broadcast Commercials Association; 0151
International business; 0249
  Africa; 0888
  annual outlook; 1355
  Asia; 0889
  bibliographies; 0705
  foreign affiliates of U.S. companies, capital expenditures; 1238
  foreign investments in U.S.; 0558, 1238
  foreign investments in U.S. real estate; 1107
  free trade zones; 1315
  industrial nations survey; 0226
  Japanese companies in U.S.; 0450
  largest foreign companies; 0558
  largest multinationals in U.S.; 0558
  paper and pulp survey; 1086
  survey; 0447
  Third World outlook; 0226
  U.S. direct investment abroad; 1238
  U.S. international investment position; 1238
  U.S. international transactions; 1238
  U.S. overseas real estate projects; 1107
  U.S. subsidiaries of German firms; 0585
International Business Forms Industries; 0220
International Civil Aviation Organization; 0657
International Communications Association; 0348, 1253
International Council of Shopping Centers; 1180
International Fence Industry Association; 0515
International Oceanographic Foundation; 1165
International relations
  United States; 0559
International Reprographic Association; 1025
International Road Federation; 0927
International Sanitary Supply Association; 0822, 1152
International Society for Hybrid Microcircuits; 0327
International Taxicab Association; 1250
International Textile Machinery Association; 0060

International Textile Manufacturers Association; 1259
International trade
  See also Import/export trade
  economic report; 0447
  foreign trade zones; 0069
  forest products; 0529
  outlook; 0215
  trade fairs; 0215
  world commercial holidays; 0215
  world trade week; 0215, 0344
International Union of Marine Insurance; 0706, 0937
International Woodworking, Machinery & Furniture Supply Fair; 0576, 1345
Inventories and sales; 0565
  U.S. statistics; 1238
Investment firms
  See Investments; Securities industry
Investments; 0161
  See also Corporations; International business; Mortgage banking; Municipal bonds; Mutual funds; Pension funds; Securities industry; Securities trading; Trust institutions; Venture capital
  annual guide; 0527
  annual reports; 0527
  bankers conference; 0189
  Canadian industrial; 0526
  Canadian investment advisers directory; 0527, 0999
  commodities guide; 0345
  corporate earnings forecast; 0226
  corporate financing directory; 0712
  corporate syndicate personnel; 0712
  international investment advisers directory; 0999
  investment advisers directory; 0999
  largest foreign in U.S.; 0558
  management consultants directory; 0999
  new issues review, forecast; 1304
  opportunities; 0906
  real estate review; 0935
  review and outlook; 0999
  security analysts research; 0999, 1239
  software for investment managers; 0999
  software for treasury management; 0999
Iron and steel industry
  Canadian report; 0401, 1261
  capital equipment and financing; 0082
  construction outlook; 0632
  economic outlook; 1261
  financial analysis; 0713
  forecast/statistics; 0713
  international; 0082
  manufacturing; 0082
  market forecast; 0082
  ore shipments; 1188
  plants directory; 0714
  production; 0678
  service centers; 0863
  shows; 0713
  specialty steel; 0082
  stainless steel; 0082
  steel outlook; 0713
  world data handbook; 1261
Iron and Steel Society of AIME; 0715
Irrigation
  buyers guide; 0328
Italy
  banking; 0051
  tobacco industry; 1267
  U.S. business in; 0716

J

Japan
  banking; 0051
  Japanese companies in U.S.; 0450
  tobacco industry; 1267
Jewelers of America; 0299
Jewelry
  See also Jewelry making; Watches and clocks
  African; 0717

almanac/statistics; 0718
  brand name and trademark guide; 0718
  buyers guide; 0717
  Canadian directory; 0267
  Canadian shows; 0267
  casting; 0073
  diamonds; 0896
  directory; 0718
  electroplating; 0073
  gemstone price index; 1060
  lapidary handbook; 1136
  pearls; 0717, 0896
  show; 0073, 0298, 0896
  store sales by SMSA; 0718
Jewelry making
  buyers guide; 0791
  directory; 0719
  show; 0719
Jobbers
  See Automotive aftermarket
Journalism
  awards; 0301, 0451, 1096, 1355
  directory; 0301
  university programs and faculty; 0778
Juke boxes; 0295, 1040, 1303

K

Kentucky Derby
  See Horse racing
Kitchens and bathrooms
  See also Home improvement
  cabinet industry profile; 0782
  distribution directory; 0782
  product directory; 0782, 1113
  remodeling ideas; 0169, 0499, 0652, 1343
Knitwear; 0783
  apparel directory and buyers guide; 0783
  trimmings and accessories; 0783
  yarn directory; 0783
Korea
  tobacco industry; 1267

L

Labels, packaging; 0272
Laboratories
  directory of analytical laboratories; 0679
  directory of diagnostic products and services; 0816
  research laboratory profile; 1117
Laboratory animals; 0180, 0784
Laboratory equipment; 0180, 0624, 0785
  Canadian buyers guide; 0787
  directory; 0786
Laboratory techniques
  analytical techniques; 0707
  automation; 0079
  buyers guide; 0079, 0707
  Canadian reference guide; 0278
  chemical analysis; 0079, 0707
  chromatography; 0079, 0707
  environmental analysis; 0707
  microscopy; 0079, 0707
  reference guide; 0252
  separation; 0707
  spectroscopy; 0079
  thermal analysis; 0079
Lafayette Gulf Coast Oil Show; 0435
Landscape design
  awards; 0789
  contractors trade show; 0790
  nurseries; 0083
Lapidary
  See Jewelry
Laser industry
  See Fiber optics
Latin America
  shipping directory; 1168
  tobacco industry; 1267
Laundry and dry cleaning; 0338
  self-service; 0057

Law enforcement
  buyers guide; 0794, 0795
Lawns; 0505
  equipment buyers guide; 0503, 0579
  equipment rental; 1115
  golf course maintenance; 0606
  lawn mowers; 1051
  Lawncare industry; 0796
  seedsmen awards; 1174
  turf research; 0993
Lawyers
  directory; 0052
  marine and customs, directory; 0069
Lead; 0082
Leather
  See also Shoe industry
  buyer's guide; 0798
  Canadian directory; 0814
  industry outlook; 0797
  shows; 0298, 0797
  upholstery; 1300
Legal decisions
  banking; 0160
  supreme court review; 0617
Legislation
  state laws/issues; 1229
Librarians
  international librarianship; 1338
  professional literature; 0080
  salary survey; 0800
Libraries
  annual review; 0800
  buyers guide; 0800
  construction/design review; 0800
  fund raising; 0800
  information technology; 0800
Libraries, school
  audio-visual buyers guide; 1158
  certification requirements; 1158
  free materials; 1158
  recommended books; 1158
Library/information science
  graduate study programs; 0738
  schools; 0738
Licensing, mass market; 0429
Life Agency Management Program; 0804
Life Insurance Marketing Research Association; 0804, 0805
Lighting; 0462
  commercial; 0229
  equipment; 0482, 0702
  products update; 0464
  security; 1172
  store design; 1311
Linen rental; 1258
Lingerie
  See Apparel, intimate
Liquor industry
  See also Beverages, alcoholic; Wines
  bourbon; 0173
  Canadian distilleries; 0246
  liquor store advertising; 0806
  market review and forecast; 0660
  marketing; 0024
Livestock
  agricultural report; 0506
  cattle feeder's planner; 0513
  feed reference book; 0512
  management; 0177
  pork producer's planner; 0637
Locksmiths
  See Security systems
Logging
  See Forest industries; Lumber industry
Luggage
  Canadian directory; 0814
  show; 0298
Lumber industry
  See also Forest industries; Paper and pulp; Wood and wood products
  Alaska; 0046
  Canadian logging and sawmills directory; 0811
  retail lumbermen's convention; 0815

M

Machine design; 0819
  See also Design engineering
Machine tools; 0867
  See also Tools
  awards; 0081
  distributors; 0082
  European; 0082
  industry overview; 0829
  international show; 0081, 0082, 0713, 0867
  international tools; 0082
  Japanese; 0082
  show; 0081, 0082, 0136, 0675
  standings, international; 0081
  United States; 0082
Machinery
  See also Assembly engineering; Tools
  converting; 0988
  electrical discharge; 0082
  machine and tool directory; 0818
  NC/CAM guidebook; 0897
Magazines
  advertising buyers guide; 0820
  advertising data; 0024, 0026
  business magazine profiles; 0820
  consumer magazine profiles; 0820
  hotel and resort advertising; 1119
  top business; 0820
  top consumer; 0820
Magnetism, conference; 0728
Mail order
  opportunities directory; 0666
Management
  See also Office management
  association; 0127
  award; 0685
Management science; 0699
Manganese; 0082
Mannequins
  See Store design
Manufactured housing
  buyers guide; 0137, 0827, 0887
  pocket directory; 0827
  producers guide; 0887
  statistics; 0137
  top home producers; 0137
Manufacturers Agents National Association; 0029
Manufacturers representatives, directory; 0029
Manufacturing
  industry ratios; 0440
Manufacturing techniques
  See Engineering, industrial
Marine and maritime
  See also Boats and boating; Ports and harbors; Ships and shipbuilding
  attorneys; 0069
  boat census; 0965
  Canadian buyers directory; 0280
  Canadian organizations; 1166
  Canadian personalities; 1166
  construction report; 0733, 1347, 1352
  equipment review; 0610
  inland waterways conference; 1327
  insurance; 0265, 0694
  intracoastal conference; 1327
  marine engineers; 1347
  navigators and communications; 1347
  water resources congress; 1327
  waterways; 1327, 1347
  work boats; 1327
Marketing
  See also Advertising; Demographics; Direct mail; Direct selling; Marketing research; Merchandising
  aviation and aerospace directory; 0148
  awards; 1150
  bank marketing to the affluent; 0051
  Canadian awards; 0831
  Canadian markets; 0526, 0831, 1149, 1150
  consumer electronics dealers; 0409
  consumer purchasing; 1150
  corporate-sponsored sporting events; 0833

discount trade statistics; 0428
education; 0834
executive compensation; 1150
forecast; 1150
Gallup report; 0381
import-export; 0069
independent services handbook; 0017
industrial purchasing; 1150
managers; 0834
marketing agencies; 0833
newspaper markets statistics; 0451
point-of-purchase suppliers directory; 0833
product development; 1149
sales promotion agencies; 0833
selling costs survey; 1150
technology for; 0834
top brands by expenditures; 0833
top markets; 1150
top successes of year; 0832
top U.S. retailers; 0833
A/V presentations; 1149
Marketing research; 0024, 1149
    See also Marketing
    farm market; 0033
    technology for; 0834
Marking products, buyers guide; 0835
Mass Retailing Institute; 0429
Mass transit
    bus guide; 0838
    construction equipment; 0366
    consultants; 0838
    fact book/directory; 0869
    rail transit directory; 0903
    subway guide; 0838
    suppliers guide; 0838
Massachusetts
    real estate; 0946
Master Brewers Association; 0890
Materials engineering; 0840
Materials handling; 0317, 0902, 0947
    See also Distribution
    Canadian buyers guide; 0841
    Canadian show guide; 0683
    case histories/directory; 0898
    equipment; 0675
    for furniture; 1300
    government; 0594
    handbook/directory; 0839
    produce; 0986
    show; 1027
Measurement and inspection equipment; 0867
Meat industry
    buyers guide; 0844, 0845
    conventions; 0843, 0844
    cured and smoked; 0844
    forecast; 0845
    fresh; 0844
    packaging; 0844
    plant financial management; 0844
    pork congress; 0931
    pork producer buying guide; 0931
    sanitation and safety; 0844
    sausages; 0843
    top 100 packers; 0843, 0845
Mechanical Contractors Association of America; 0379
Mechanical engineering
    See Engineering
Media buying
    See also Advertising
    buyers' guide to magazines; 0820
Medical associations, meetings calendar; 0854
Medical equipment; 0179, 0846, 0849
Medical Group Management Association; 0850
Medical instruments; 0679
    See also Medical equipment
Medical Library Association; 0212
Medical media directory; 0179
Medical products
    See Health care products
Medical reviews bibliography; 0668
Medical services; 0531, 0816
Medical subject headings; 0668

Medicare
    See Health care
Medicine
    See also Health care; Hospitals
    developments in; 0768
    malpractice insurance; 0168
Medicine, aerospace
    directory; 0147
Medicine, nuclear
    buyers guide; 1098
Meetings and conventions
    AV Report; 0859
    Canadian directory; 0859
    convention hall directory; 0127
    golf resort guide; 0496
    guide; 0099
    international directory; 0857
    market report; 0857
    sites; 1232
    sites/suppliers/services directory; 0858
    survey; 0858
Men's wear
    Canadian seasonal markets; 0860
    show; 0429
Mercato Internazionale del Film e del Documentario; 1302
Merchandising
    See also Catalog showroom merchandising
    college stores; 0339
    consumer purchasing plans; 0861
    statistical and marketing report; 0861
    supermarkets; 0951
Mergers and acquisitions
    See also Corporations
    almanac and index; 0862
    newspaper; 0451
    top deals; 0565
Metal distribution
    See also Metals
    aluminum; 0863
    annual; 0863
    conventions; 0863
    copper and brass (non-ferrous); 0863
    equipment; 0863
    salesmen; 0863
    service center profile; 0863
    steel; 0863
Metallurgical Society of AIME; 0739, 0751
Metallurgy; 0101
    Canadian conference; 0230
Metals
    See also Metal distribution; Specific metals
    aerospace; 0082
    alloys; 0082
    Canadian mining and exploration; 0953, 0971
    contract shops; 0082
    economic outlook; 1261
    exchange trading; 0082
    heat treating buyers guide; 0865
    London exchange; 0082
    magnetic materials conference; 0728
    market mills; 0082
    materials databook; 0865
    metal casting; 0892
    metal finishing directory; 0864, 1068
    metal market; 0082
    pipe & tube; 0082
    precious; 0082
    purchasing; 0082, 0877, 1089
    scrap; 0082
    strategic; 0082
    surface coating exposition; 0865
    technology forecast; 0865
    testing and inspection buyers guide; 0865
Metalworking
    See also Assembly engineering; Foundries; Machinery; Metals; Tools
    buyers guide; 0081, 0680
    Canadian buyers guide; 0268
    die casting exposition; 0423
    equipment; 0867
    heat and combustion buyers guide; 0629
    machine tool show; 0680
    metal stamping directory; 0866
    numerical control buying guide; 0919

    serial number reference book; 0680
    tools; 1270
Meteorology; 0211
Metropolitan Life Foundation; 0870
Mexico
    travel; 0283
Microbiology
    See American Society for Microbiology
Microcomputers
    See Computers, personal
Micrographics; 0686
    salary survey; 0687
    usage survey; 0687
Microscopy
    See Laboratory techniques
Microwaves; 0875
    See also Electronics
Middle East
    Arab countries shipping directory; 1168
    petroleum; 0967
Midwest Gas Association; 0580
Military
    See also Military market
    Army Green Book; 0118
    defense procurement officials; 0926
    electronics; 0441
    engineering; 0878
    facilities construction outlook; 0368
    international balance; 0039
    R & D officials; 0926
Military market
    almanac/directory; 0879
    buyers guide; 0879
    educational opportunities; 0040, 0119
    retirement; 0040, 0119
    travel; 0040, 0119
Milk
    See also Dairy products
    agricultural reports; 0506
    consumer survey; 0402
Milling
    See also Baking industry
    directory and buyers guide; 0881
Millionaires
    richest people in U.S.; 0558
Mineral waters
    Canadian directory; 0246
Minerals, industrial; 0682
Mines and mining
    See also Coal and coal mining; Gold; Metals; Mining, Canadian
    Alaska; 0046
    annual review; 0884
    asbestos; 0125
    buyers guide; 0486
    capital projects; 0953
    construction outlook; 0368
    convention; 0884, 1188
    engineering review; 0885
    environmental issues; 0882
    equipment; 0886, 1353
    international; 0953
    international directory; 0486
    international statistics and yearbook; 1353
    iron ore shipments; 1188
    junior mining; 0953
    metals; 0953
    mineral commodities survey; 0486
    new projects; 0953
    open pit; 0953
    product review; 0884, 0886
    profile; 0486
    project survey; 0486
    research; 0882
    show; 0884, 0886
    undersea; 0882
Minicomputers
    See Computers, personal
Mining, Canadian; 0527
    buyers guide; 0269
    directory; 0230
    equipment & maintenance; 0230
    forecast; 0953
    gold mining; 0953

handbook; 0953
mine safety; 0230
mine survey; 0526, 1335
mines and mineral exploration; 0230, 0971
open pit; 0230
Minorities; 0595
Mobile homes
buyers guide; 0137
construction outlook; 0368
Mobile housing
See Manufactured housing
Model aircraft, buyers guide; 0546
Model railroads, buyers guide; 1104
Modern Language Association; 0977
Molybdenum; 0082
Monte Carlo Insurance Rendezvous; 0706, 0937
Mopeds; 0176, 1051
Mortality statistics; 0870
fire fighters; 0530
traffic accidents; 1278
Mortgage Bankers Association of America; 0909, 1154
Mortgage banking
See also Banks and banking; Investments
buyers guide; 0909
Mortgages; 0051, 1154
real estate financing; 1107
secondary mortgage market; 1298
Motels
See Hotels and motels
Motion pictures
adult films; 0522
animation; 0151, 0880
annual film reviews; 0194, 0521, 1041
art directors; 0151
awards predictions; 0521
buyers directory; 0194
convention; 0522
critics favorite; 0521
directory; 0151
distribution guide - buyers guide; 0522
engineers technical conference; 1148
equipment, concession & services buyers guide 0522
erotica film awards; 0522
film book reviews; 0523
film market U.S.; 1302
film processors, specifications; 0276
film/tape directors; 0151
industrial and training films; 0151
industrial film festival; 0151
international film and documentary market; 1302
international film annual; 1302
laboratory services guide; 0132
notable films; 0190
regional facilities; 0151
sex in cinema; 1041
shows; 0151, 0194
technology advances; 1148
top film grossers; 1302
Motor vehicles
See also Automobiles; Trucks and trucking
U.S. current model survey; 1238
Motorcycles
buyers guide; 0399
Canadian buyers guide; 0238
Motors
controls and switchgear; 0461
technology report; 0482
Multi-Housing Laundry Association; 0338
Multinational corporations; 0565
See also International business
Multi-Unit Food Service Operators; 0941
Municipal administration
See Public administration
Municipal Bond Analysts Association; 0189
Municipal Bonds
See also Investments
conferences; 0189
dealers directory; 0189
index to issues; 0189
Museums
national gallery guide; 0121

Music
See also Sound recordings
Canadian music industry; 1099
Christian; 0325
country music awards; 1099
country music bookings; 0099
guitarist poll winners; 0607
industry buyers guide; 0692
keyboard poll winners; 0781
organizations directory; 0692
schools directory; 0692
string players poll winners; 0568
summer camps and workshops directory; 0692
Music publishing
directory; 0295
Musical instruments
buyers' guide; 0918
Musicology
convention; 0422
Mutual Finance Officers Association; 0189
Mutual Funds; 0161
See also Investments
top performing; 0310, 0558, 0906

N

National Agricultural Marketing Association; 0033
National Association for the Advancement of Colored People; 0395
National Association of Accountants; 0823
National Association of Aluminum Distributors; 0863
National Association of Auto Trim Shops; 0135
National Association of Bedding Manufacturers; 0164
National Association of Broadcasters; 0151, 0198, 0201, 1308
National Association of Business Economists; 0219
National Association of College Stores; 0339, 1085
National Association of Convenience Stores; 0381
National Association of Corrosion Engineers; 0842
National Association of Counties; 0189
National Association of Credit Management; 0390
National Association of Display Industries; 1311
National Association of Electrical Distributors; 0463
National Association of Federally Licensed Firearms Dealers; 0062
National Association of Food Equipment Manufacturers; 0555
National Association of Health Underwriters; 0625, 0805
National Association of Home Builders; 0204, 0379
National Association of Housing and Redevelopment Officials; 0746
National Association of Independent Insurers; 0696, 0937
National Association of Insurance Brokers; 0937
National Association of Insurance Commissioners 0805, 0937
National Association of Life Companies; 0805
National Association of Life Underwriters; 0695, 0804
National Association of Mutual Insurance Companies; 0937
National Association of Mutual Savings Banks; 1154
National Association of Oil Heat Service Managers; 0570, 0571
National Association of Plumbing, Heating, Cooling Contractors; 0379, 1113
National Association of Printing Ink Manufacturers 0072

National Association of Professional Surplus Lines Offices; 0695, 0696
National Association of Purchasing Management; 0877
National Association of Realtors; 1107
National Association of State Treasurers; 0189
National Association of Television and Program Executives; 1302
National Association of Theatre Owners; 0522
National Association of Tobacco Distributors; 1299
National Audio-Visual Association; 0131, 0151
National Automatic Laundry and Cleaning Council 0338
National Automobile Dealers Association; 0143
National Basketball Association; 1221
National Beer Wholesalers; 0173, 0890
National Book Awards; 1085
National Business Aircraft Association; 1072, 1341
National Business Forms Association; 0220, 0564
National Cable Television Association; 0237
National Cable Television Institute; 0236
National Campground Owners Association; 1346
National Candy Wholesalers Association; 0290, 1299
National Catholic Educational Association; 1268
National Coffee Association; 1350
National Coffee Service Association; 1350
National Commercial Finance Conference; 0722
National Computer Conference; 0405, 0441, 0470, 0471, 1191
National Confectioners Association; 0289
National Consumer Credit Association; 0394
National Consumers Finance Association; 0389
National Council of Physical Distribution Management; 0608
National Decorating Products Association; 0410
National Electrical Contractors Association; 0229, 0462
National Employee Services and Recreation Association; 0477
National Exposition of Contract Interior Furnishings; 0964
National Farm and Power Equipment Dealers Association; 0503
National Federation of Abstracting and Information Services; 0920
National Fire Protection Association; 0530
National Food Brokers Association; 0569, 0603, 1095
National Food Processors Association; 0553, 1066
National Football League; 1221
National Forest Products Association; 0529
National Frozen Food Association; 0553, 0569, 1095
National Geographic Society; 0929
National Glass Dealers Association; 1295
National Grain and Feed Association; 0596
National Hardware Show; 0428, 0429, 0836
National Hockey League; 1221
National Housewares Manufacturers Association; 0299, 0428, 0836
National Independent Poultry and Food Distributors Association; 1053
National Industrial Distributors Association; 0673
National Institute of Ceramic Engineers; 0054
National Knitware & Sportswear Association; 0783
National League of Cities; 0189, 0940
National Liquor Stores Association; 0173
National Marine Fisheries Service; 0534, 0830
National Mass Retailing Institute; 0428
National Municipal League; 0925
National Natural Foods Association; 0623
National Oceanic and Atmospheric Administration 0878
National Office Machine Dealers Association; 0586, 0921, 0964

National Office Products Association; 0586, 0922, 0964
National Paint and Coatings Association; 0085
National Paper Trade Association; 0990
National Parking Association; 0994
National Parks and Conservation Association; 0933
National Pasta Association; 0817
National Petroleum Refiners Association; 0966
National Recreation and Park Association; 0056, 0995
National Restaurant Association; 0555, 0569, 0923, 0941, 1124
National Retail Merchants Association; 1125, 1231, 1311
National Rifle Association; 0089
National Rural Electric Cooperative Association; 1147
National Safety Congress; 0684, 1278
National Safety Council; 0936, 1278
National School Boards Association; 0091
National School Supply and Equipment Association; 0453
National Shooting Sports Foundation; 1179
National Ski Area Association; 1185
National Soft Drink Association; 0174
National Solid Wastes Management Association; 0056, 1322
National Sporting Goods Association; 0428, 0429, 0536, 1224, 1225
National Swimming Pool Institute; 1048, 1240
National Tire Dealers and Retreaders Association 1266
National Truck Equipment Association; 1280
National Turkey Federation; 1293
National Utility Contractors Association; 0938
National Water Well Association; 0605
Needlework
 buyers guide; 0386
 ideas; 0169, 0499, 1343
New England
 advertising markets; 0943
 real estate; 0946
New Jersey
 industrial parks; 0948
 top employers; 0948
New Jersey Business and Industry Association; 0948
New Jersey Licensed Beverage Association; 0173
New Jersey Liquor Stores; 0173
New Mexico Bankers Association; 0915
New York Academy of Medicine; 0213
New York State Beer Wholesalers; 0173
New York University Institute of Retail Management; 0758
Newberry and Caldecott Awards; 0190
Newbery and Caldecott Awards; 0642, 1271
Newfoundland
 travel; 0283
News outlook, annual; 1297
Newspapers
 ad expenditures; 0832
 advertising data; 0024, 0026
 advertising executives; 0451
 awards; 0451
 Canadian marketing report; 0831
 conventions; 0451
 food editors; 0451
 hotel and resort advertising; 1119
 linage; 0451
 mergers and acquisitions; 0451
 printing report; 0087
 promotion; 0451
 syndicate directory; 0451
 top markets; 1150
 yearbook; 0451
Nickel; 0082
Noise abatement
 See also Occupational safety
 Canadian buyers guide; 1325

Non-profit organizations
 See Philanthropy
North American Heating and Wholesalers; 1337
North American Telephone Association; 1252, 1253
North Sea
 offshore drilling; 0960
 oil exploration; 0965
Northeast Foodservice and Lodging Exposition; 0809
Northeastern Retail Lumbermen's Association; 0815
Nova Scotia, offshore forecasts; 0273
Novelties
 buyer's guide; 1213
 gift show; 1213
 sales guide; 1213
Nuclear power products
 See also Power plants
 buyer's guide; 0955
Nurseries (Horticulture)
 buyers guide; 0097
 container production; 0083
 convention; 0083
 energy conservation; 0083
 flower and garden; 0083
 foreign technology; 0083
 landscaping; 0083
 management; 0083
 trade show; 0083
Nurses and nursing
 administration consultant directory; 0752
 books; 0074
 directory of nursing organizations; 0074
 operating room nurses; 0008
Nursing homes
 See also Hospitals
 rankings; 0895
Nutrition
 See also Cereal foods; Health foods
 diet and exercise guide; 1343
 food processing encyclopedia; 0551
 low calorie recipes; 0169
 prenatal; 0050
Nuts
 See Fruit growing

O

Occupational medicine
 See Health Care
Occupational safety; 0683, 0846
 See also Fire safety
 asbestos safety; 0125
 catalog and buyers guide; 0679
 conference; 0679, 0684
 emergency medical aid; 0531, 0684
 equipment directory; 0684
 eye, face, body protection; 0679
 noise and hearing; 0679, 0684
 petroleum industry; 0969
 plant management; 1028
 welding; 1330
Ocean science
 buyers guide and directory; 1167
 geophysical survey; 1167
 navigation; 1167
 review and forecast; 1167
 undersea defense; 1167
Off-highway vehicles; 0140
 See also Agricultural Equipment; Construction Equipment
Office equipment; 0021, 0527, 0674
 See also Computers; Data processing
 automation; 0359
 buyers guide; 0586, 0899, 0922, 0961, 0964, 1090
 Canadian buyers guide; 0270, 0963
 Canadian dealers guide; 0271
 convention; 0586, 0921, 0964
 copiers; 0825, 0962
 dealers directory; 0921, 0964
 dictation machines; 0825, 0961

electronic office design awards; 0899
equipment reports; 0899
forecast; 0271, 0921
government equipment buying guide; 0594
in Africa; 0888
industry source guide; 0962
marking products; 0835
office automation; 0102, 0962
purchasing; 0902
show; 0298
software; 0962
typewriters; 0279
word processing; 0825, 0962
Offshore technology; 0434, 0967, 1006, 1167
 buyer's guide; 0965
 Canadian buyers guide; 0280
 conference; 0960, 0965, 0968, 1354
 equipment and services; 0960, 0969
 Europe; 0960
 exploration and production; 1354
 facts and forecasts; 0960, 0965, 0968
 marine drilling rigs directory; 0960
 North Sea; 0960, 0965
 pipeline construction; 1022
 Southeast Asia; 0965
 subsea technology; 0960
 technical papers digest; 0960
Offshore Technology Conference; 0435, 0966
Ohio Valley Improvement Association; 1327
Oil and gas exploration
 See also Offshore technology; Petroleum industry
 Canadian; 0526
 drilling; 0953
Oil rigs
 See Petroleum industry
Oil-producing nations
 and banking; 0051
Older Americans Month; 0030
Olympic games; 0768, 0803, 1184, 1220, 1223
 hockey; 0067
 swimming; 1241
 tennis; 1356
 track and field; 1276
 update; 1221
Operations Research Society of America; 0972
Optical discs
 See Video production industry
Optoelectronics
 See also Fiber optics
 buyers' guide; 0474
Orthopedists, sports; 1145
Otolaryngology; 0117, 0516
Outdoor living; 1049
 See also Camping

P

Pacific area
 travel; 0283, 0284
Pacific Automotive Show; 0145, 0721
Pacific Coast Coffee Association; 1350
Pacific Egg and Poultry Association; 1053
Pacific Rim
 banking; 0051
Packaging
 awards; 0988
 baking industry; 0153
 beverage industry; 0174
 boxmakers' buying guide; 0193
 buyers guide; 0984, 0988, 0992
 Canadian directory; 0272
 chemicals; 0317, 0319
 encyclopedia; 0984
 equipment; 0675
 food industry; 0549
 forecast; 0992
 furniture; 1300
 in sales promotion; 1149
 machinery directory; 0272
 package printing buyers guide; 0985
 purchasing; 0902
 show; 0272, 0988

statistics; 0992
Packaging, food and drug
   awards; 0548
   shows; 0548
Packaging Machinery Manufacturers Institute; 0548, 0988
Painting and Decorating Contractors of America; 0987
Paints and coatings; 0733
   buyer's guide; 0316, 0411
   chemical buyers directory; 0316
   conventions; 0085
   directory; 0900
   forecast; 0900
   industrial maintenance painting; 0086
   production; 0900
   raw materials directory; 1336
   regional dealers; 1336
   show; 0677, 0900
Pakistan
   tobacco industry; 1267
Paneling
   See Wood and wood products
Paper and pulp
   adhesives and binders; 1086
   buyers guide; 1019, 1086
   Canadian directory; 1087, 1088
   capital spending plans; 1086
   chemicals review; 0991, 1086
   coating; 1086
   convention; 0990, 0991
   directory; 1086
   economics focus; 0991
   engineering review; 1086
   exhibit; 1243
   forecast; 1088
   industry outlook; 1086
   international directory; 0978
   international survey; 1086
   mill and personnel directory; 1212
   mill maps; 1086
   papermaker award; 0991
   pulpwood annual review; 0562
   pulpwood buyers guide; 1086
   salary survey; 1243
   statistics; 0989, 1086
   top companies; 0991
   yearbook; 0990
Paper Industry Management Association; 1019
Parking, off-street; 0994
   parking lot maintenance; 0208
Parks and recreation; 0329, 0995
   government; 0594
   maintenance buyers guide; 0993
   programming trends; 0995
Partitions, moveable
   buyers guide; 0961
Pasta products; 0817
Patents and inventions; 0711
Pearls
   See Jewelry
Pennsylvania Petroleum Association; 0570
Pensions and pension funds
   administration firms directory; 0998
   bank pooled funds directory; 0998
   directory; 0690
   Erisa calendar; 0998
   insurance review; 0805
   investment services directory; 0166
   performance evaluation; 0999
   real estate vehicles for; 0166
   review and outlook; 0999
   state retirement systems survey; 0998
   statistics; 0476
   top corporate statistics; 0999
   top funds; 0166, 0999
Performing arts
   product buying guide; 1260
Perfumes
   See Cosmetics and Fragrances
Periodicals
   See also Magazines
   government periodicals directory; 0907
   subscription cost studies; 0800

Personnel administration
   conference; 1000
Pesticides
   buyer's guide and label book; 1002
   fruit; 0063
   guide; 1328
   laboratory review; 0101
   livestock; 0505
   pest management; 1074
Petfood; 1005
Petrochemicals; 0316, 0967
   See also Chemical process industry; Petroleum industry; Petroleum industry, Canadian
   Canadian; 0273, 0971
   catalog; 0655
   construction; 0655
   developments; 0655
   equipment and services; 0969
   handbook; 0655
   heat and combustion buyers guide; 0629
   maintenance; 0655
Petroleum Equipment Institute; 0966, 1007
Petroleum industry
   See also Offshore technology; Petrochemicals; Petroleum industry, Canadian; Pipelines
   Alaska; 0046
   capital spending survey; 0967
   conference; 0967
   construction; 0967
   conventions; 0435
   drilling; 0435, 0967, 1354
   equipment; 0046, 0435, 0969, 0970
   equipment forecast; 1006
   exploration yearbook; 0584
   factbook; 0934
   forecast/review; 0435, 0967, 1354
   geophysical; 0967
   giants; 0966
   international outlook; 1354
   maintenance; 0655
   Middle East; 0967
   midyear economic review; 0966
   offshore report; 0967, 1006, 1354
   petroleum geologists; 0001
   pipelines; 0967
   processing; 0655
   production report; 1354
   refining; 0655, 0967
   rig locators; 1006
   rotary rig census; 0435
   tank trucks; 0891
   wellsite report; 0435
   winter fuel outlook; 0966
Petroleum industry, Canadian
   Atlantic sites; 0273, 0971
   audit of industry performance; 0273
   capital spending; 0273
   careers in; 0971
   computers and data processing; 0273, 0971
   drilling and service rigs; 0971
   energy pricing report; 0273
   financial reporting; 0273, 0971
   government regulations; 0273
   heavy oil; 0273, 0971
   instruments and controls; 0273
   manpower reports; 0273
   marketing report; 0971
   offshore buyers guide; 0971
   offshore drilling equipment; 0436
   offshore drilling report; 0273, 0971
   offshore forecasts, Nova Scotia; 0273
   offshore resources exposition; 0273, 0971
   oil register, annual; 0273
   oil sands and mining; 0273, 0971
   overseas directory; 0971
   pipeline forecast, report; 0273, 0971
   refinery report; 0971
   reviews and forecasts; 0971
   service and supply industry; 0971
   well completions, statistics; 0273
Pets; 0773
   See also Petfood
   directory/buyers guide; 1004, 1008
   directory of trade associations; 1003
   dogs annual; 0432
   industry outlook; 1004

   industry statistics; 1008
   seasonal markets; 1003
   shop/store survey; 1004
   store management; 1004
Pharmacies
   See Drug stores; Drugs and pharmaceuticals
Phi Delta Kappa; 1009
Philanthropy; 1010
   state/federal decisions; 1010
Philippines
   tobacco industry; 1267
Phonograph records
   See Sound recording
Photo Marketing Association; 0299, 0429, 1011
Photogrammetry
   See Photography, aerial
Photographic Society of America; 0979
Photography
   See also Audio-visual communications; Motion pictures; Video production industry
   advertising; 0120
   annual; 1050
   awards; 0347
   buyers guide; 1013, 1050
   Canadian industry buyers guide; 1015
   discount stores; 0429
   exhibition calendar; 0979
   home video annual; 1302
   journalism awards; 0451
   laboratory equipment buyers guide; 0180
   membership directory; 0979
   photomarketing show; 0298
   professional directory; 1071
   retailer of the year; 1013
   techniques; 0979
   trade forecast; 1013
   video cameras; 1308
   year in pictures; 0803
Photography, aerial; 1012
Physical education
   See Education
Physicians
   continuing education for; 0768
Physics
   graduate programs; 0077
   teaching and research staffs directory; 0077
Pipeline Contractors Association of Canada; 0971
Pipelines; 0967
   Alaska; 1021
   Arctic; 1021, 1023
   buyer's guide; 1022, 1023
   Canadian; 0273, 0971, 1021, 1023
   construction; 0733, 1020, 1022
   construction directory; 1023
   construction forecasts; 1022
   corrosion; 1021
   directory; 1021
   equipment and services; 0969
   industry catalog; 1020
   international; 1021, 1023
   maintenance and operations; 1022
   new products; 1022
   peakshavings; 1022
   review and forecast; 1021
   slurry; 1021
   telecommunications; 1021
   top companies; 1022
   underground storage; 1022
   underground utilities; 1023
Piping; 0846
   chemical equipment; 0315
   manufacturers directory; 0630
Plant and equipment expenditures; 1238
Plant design and construction; 1028
Plant engineering; 0947, 1028
   See also Industrial plants
   best articles; 1027
   Canadian show guide; 0683
   conference; 0006
   directory and specification catalog; 1027
   maintenance; 0594, 1089
   show; 0482, 0675, 0681, 1027, 1030
Plant security; 1028

See also Security systems
Plastic surgery; 0117
Plastics
   See also Rubber; Society of Plastics Engineers
   additives; 0274, 0901, 1035
   Canadian directory and buying guide; 0274
   Canadian exports; 0274, 1031
   Canadian industry outlook; 0274
   compounders buyers guide; 1032
   construction methods; 1038
   design awards; 1038
   design focus; 1033
   desk manual; 0901, 1034
   directory/buyers guide; 1037, 1038
   encyclopedia; 0901
   equipment; 1037
   exposition; 1038
   extrusion; 1036, 1037
   finishing directory; 1068
   government regulation; 1037
   industry trends; 1031
   ingredients; 1037
   injection molding; 1036, 1037
   machinery sales statistics; 0901
   manufacturing outlook; 1037
   materials and markets review; 0901
   new products; 0901, 1031
   show; 1031
   top equipment; 1038
   top materials; 1038
   top processing plants; 1038
Platinum; 0082
Playgrounds
   See also Parks and recreation
   fencing; 0515
Plumbing
   See also Heating; Refrigeration
   Canadian buyers guide; 0631
   contractors convention; 0379
   convention; 1337
   directory; 1337
   manufacturers representatives directory; 1337
   profit and market survey; 1337
   top wholesalers; 1337
Plywood
   See Wood and wood products
Pneumatics
   See Hydraulics and pneumatics
Podiatrists, sports; 1145
Police
   See Law enforcement
Pollution control
   See also Environmental protection; Water pollution
   Canadian buyers guide; 1325
   catalog and buyers guide; 1046
   chemical equipment; 0315
   chemical manufacturers guide; 1045
   chemical processing; 0317
   computerization; 1045
   conference; 0679, 1046
   consultants/services directory; 0764, 1045
   environmental products directory; 1045
   food processing industry; 0550
   governmental agency directory; 0764
   laboratory application review; 0101
   product guide; 0764
   U.S. expenditures statistics; 1238
Pollution Control Federation; 0189
Pools
   See Swimming pools and spas
Pork
   See Meat industry
Ports
   Far East, directory; 0069
Ports and harbors; 1279
   Canadian; 0282, 0610, 1315
   Caribbean; 1315
   construction; 0733, 1352
   directory; 0430, 0608
   foreign; 1315
   free trade zones; 1315
   freight forwarding; 1315
   marketing; 1315
   port authorities convention; 1315

   regional U.S.; 1315
Potatoes and sweet potatoes; 0031, 0506
Poultry industry
   See also Egg industry
   agricultural reports; 0506
   award; 1053
   Canadian directory; 0240
   convention; 1053, 1054
   directory; 1052
   distributor directory; 1053
   export-import; 0202
   marketing; 0202, 1053
   new products; 1053, 1054
   outlook; 1053, 1054
   processor directory; 1053
   production; 0202
   top broiler companies; 0202
   trade show; 0202
   turkeys; 1293
Powder metal technology; 0082, 0293
Power and bulk solids; 1046
Power equipment, outdoor; 1051
   See also Agricultural equipment
Power plants
   See also Diesel engines; Electric power industry; Power transmission; Turbomachinery; Utilities; Utilities, electric
   Canadian nuclear energy report; 0971
   construction surveys; 0466
   consulting engineers; 1056
   electrical generating systems directory; 0425
   energy systems guidebook; 1057
   in Africa; 0888
   industry meetings calendar; 0466
   international systems; 1057
   new generating plants; 1056
   product buyers guide; 0481, 1057
   statistical report; 0466
   steam station design; 0466
   top proposed construction plans; 1056
Power Transmission; 1030
   buyers guide; 0417
   design engineering directory; 0418, 1058
   distributors; 0673, 1058
   equipment; 0675
   international directory; 0927
   literature awards; 1058
   product specifications; 1058
   show; 1058
   systems controls; 1058
Power Transmission Distributors Association; 0673
Premiums and incentives; 1149
   bank marketing; 0155
   business gift buying guide; 1061
   Canadian show guide; 0831
   Canadian source guide directory; 0831
   incentive industry statistics; 0665, 1061
   incentive travel guide; 0857, 0858
   incentive travel suppliers directory; 0665
   marketing; 0024
   suppliers and services directory; 0665, 1061
Pressure vessels; 0846
Prestressed Concrete Institute; 0776
Print Engineering
   conference; 0489
Printed circuits
   See also Electronics
   buyers guide; 0327
   new technologies; 0327
   top manufacturers; 0469
Printing and typesetting
   buyers guide; 0123, 0600
   Canadian buyers guide; 0276
   electronic printers; 1294
   for packaging; 0272
   forecast; 0087
   gravure update; 0087
   Gutenber Festival; 0087
   in-plant; 0963
   international buyers guide; 0123
   market statistics; 0600
   midyear report; 0087
   package printing buyers guide; 0985
   phototypesetting; 1065

   presses; 1065
   production techniques; 1129
   quick printing equipment; 0601
   top electronic printer manufacturers; 0469
   typesetting equipment specifications; 0276, 1294
Produce; 0986
   See also Vegetables
Productivity
   awards; 0268
   employees; 0558
   engineering; 0674
Professional Golf Association; 1221
Professional Insurance Agents Association; 0696
Professional Photographers of America; 1071
Professional Secretaries International; 1170
Propane gas
   See also Gas, liquefied petroleum
Public administration
   administration survey; 0056
   budget planning; 0594
   conferences and shows; 0056
   directory of public officals; 0056
   fiscal position review; 1238
   government specifiers reference file; 0594
   industry outlook; 0056
   leadership awards; 0056
   municipal index/equipment buyers guide; 0056
   office equipment buyers guide; 0594
   safety communications conference; 0009
   salary survey; 0056
Public relations
   annual forecast; 1080
   bibliography; 1081
Public Relations Society of America; 1080
Public Securities Association; 0189
Public service
   journalism awards; 0451
Public works
   See also Public administration
   Canadian buyers guide; 0329
   Canadian convention calendar; 0329
   construction; 0370
   county/regional; 1084
   grounds maintenance buyers guide; 0594
   leader awards; 0056
   maintenance and equipment; 1084
   manual/catalog file; 1084
   material handling; 0594
   parks and recreation; 0594
   plant maintenance; 0594
Public Works Association; 0010
Publishers and publishing
   See also Books; Magazines; Newspapers
   association publishing; 0127, 0800
   Canadian publishers directory; 1097
   small presses; 0800
   special issues in business publications; 0224
   university presses; 0950
Pulpwood
   See Forest industries; Paper and pulp
Pumps
   See also Valves and meters
   chemical equipment; 0315
   chemical processing; 0317
   pollution control; 1046
Purchasing; 0902
   See also Specific industry buyers guide
   buyers guide; 0877
   chemicals; 1089
   conference; 0877
   design teams; 1089
   economic forecast; 1089, 1090
   metals; 0877, 1089
   office equipment; 1090
   salary survey; 1089, 1090
   valves; 1089
Purchasing, industrial
   buying power survey; 1150
Purchasing Management Association of Cleveland; 0877

Q

Quarries
   See Stone products

R

R & D
   See Research and development
Radar technology; 0875
Radiators
   See Heating
Radio
   See also Broadcasting
   antennas and towers; 0348
   broadcast equipment buyers guide; 0198
   Canadian stations; 0200
   equipment review; 0348
   equipment specifications; 0198
   marketing data; 0024, 0026
   mobile telecommunications; 1253
   PBX; 0348
   two-way; 0348
Radiology
   buyers guide; 1098
Radios
   See Audio equipment
Railroads
   Amtrack; 0903
   capital spending analysis; 0903
   directory; 0430
   freight marketing award; 0903
   industry review; 0903
   man of the year; 0903
   multi-modal systems; 0903
   new technology; 0903
   rail transit directory; 0903
   shows; 0903
   track and structure maintenance; 1105
   U.S. and foreign directory; 1285
Real estate
   See also Industrial parks; Shopping centers; Site selection
   annual review; 1107, 1111
   bank housing market mortgage review; 1298
   banking and finance; 0946
   Canadian; 0248, 1107
   city-by-city office review; 1107
   commercial and office space market; 0071, 0946, 1107, 1111
   condominiums/co-ops; 1107
   Connecticut; 0946
   conventions; 1107
   conversion & modernization; 1110
   corporate/consulting; 1107
   corporate executives directory; 0672
   directory; 0935
   economic outlook; 0756
   energy; 1110
   financing; 0051, 1107
   Florida; 0542
   for pension funds; 0166
   forecast; 0935, 1108
   foreign investment guide; 0071
   industry spending plans; 0248
   international; 1107
   investment advisers directory; 0999
   Massachusetts; 0946
   multi-family housing; 1107
   New England; 0946
   portfolio manager directory; 0998
   rehab market; 1111
   review; 0935
   salary survey; 0935
   shopping centers; 0946, 1107
   suburban offices; 1107
   year-end review; 0946
Real estate management
   See Building management
Recipes
   Christmas; 0499, 1343
Recordings
   See Sound recordings
Records management; 0021

Recreation
   See also Education; Parks and recreation
   marketing; 1112
Recreational vehicles; 0143, 0500, 0519, 1051
   Canadian campgrounds; 1164
   Canadian guide; 0238
   directory/buyers guide; 1103
   pocket directory; 1103
Refineries, petroleum
   See Petroleum industry; Petroleum industry Canadian
Refrigeration
   See also Air conditioning
   buyers guide; 1176
   commercial, manufacturers directory; 0038
   convention; 0379, 1337
   directory; 1337
   energy management; 1101
   manufacturers representatives; 1337
   profit and market survey; 1337
   test instruments; 1101
   top wholesalers; 1337
Religion
   books; 0325, 0346, 0950
   Christian Bible schools; 0325
   Christian colleges; 0325
   Christian music; 0325
   Christian youth programs; 0325
   Easter missions; 0325
Remodeling
   See also Home improvement
   custom remodeling; 1091
   design awards; 1091
   5-year forecast; 1091
   new products; 1091
Rental services
   Canadian; 0277
   directory/buyers guide; 1115
   industrial equipment; 1115
   lawn and garden equipment; 1115
   product catalog; 1116
Reprographics; 0021, 0899
   See also Printing and typesetting
   management; 1025
   product directory; 1025
Research and development
   award; 1117
   buyers guide; 1117
   chemical industry; 0313
   conference; 1161
   corporate scoreboard; 0226
   funding; 1117
   laboratory profile; 1117
   salary survey; 1117
   U.S. research team directory; 0690
Resins
   See also Plastics
   marketing statistics; 0901
Resorts
   See also Travel and tourism
   magazine advertising; 1119
   newspaper advertising; 1119
   running and fitness; 1145
   tennis; 1255, 1356
Respiratory therapy; 0002, 1121
Restaurants
   See also Food service
   awards; 0542
   bar management; 0941
   bibliography; 0383
   business dining awards; 1150
   Canadian buyers guide; 0554
   Canadian directory; 0263, 0905
   Canadian favorites; 0479, 0554
   Canadian franchises; 0554
   chain performance index; 1123
   company profiles; 1122
   consumer behavior; 0923
   convention; 0941, 1124
   Florida; 0542
   food service products file; 1123
   forecast; 0923, 0941, 1122
   franchising; 1122
   growth index; 1122
   industry survey; 0923, 1123

   international; 1122
   Ivy awards; 1124
   kitchen design awards; 1123
   leadership awards; 1122
   Los Angeles guide; 0812
   menu census; 1124
   metropolitan area market studies; 0941
   profile; 0941
   second top chains; 0941
   show; 0808, 0941
   top chains; 0941, 1123
   top growth chains; 1124
   top of table awards; 1123
   top restaurants; 1123, 1124
   top volume; 0941
   top 100 markets; 1122
Retail Bakers of America; 0152
Retail Confectioners International; 0289
Retail Jewelers of America
   show; 0718
Retail trade
   See also Chain stores
   annual industry report; 0837
   Canadian chain store directory; 0905
   Canadian shopping center directory; 0905
   consumer purchases; 1150
   convention; 1231
   ratios; 1231
   top companies; 0565, 0833
   top markets; 1150
   top specialty chains; 1231
Retailing
   See also Marketing; Specific industries
   advertising report; 0026
   furniture directory; 1070
   furniture markets; 1070
   industry ratios; 0440
Retirement
   Erisa calendar; 0998
   for military; 0040, 0119
   maturity marketing data; 0024
   state systems survey; 0998
Retirement living; 0520
Rice, agricultural reports; 0506
Rifles
   See Firearms
Risk and Insurance Management Society; 0805, 0937, 1132
Roadmasters and Maintenance of Way Association; 1105
Roads
   See also Highway construction
   maintenance and paving; 0170, 1084, 1146
   public funding sources; 1146
   snow and ice control; 1146
   traffic control; 0170, 1146
Robert Morris Associates; 1154
Robotics; 0081, 0082, 0829, 1135
   show; 0867
Rock products
   See Stone products
Rockhound and lapidary guide; 0791, 1136
   See also Jewelry making
Rodeo personalities; 0643
Roofing
   See Building
Royal College of Surgeons; 0855
Rubber
   buyers guide; 1141
   chemicals; 1142
   equipment; 1142
   FAX book (technical papers); 1141
   industry forecast; 1142
   materials/ingredients directory; 1142
   urethanes; 1141
   wire and cable; 1142
Running
   See also Health and Fitness
   annual review; 1144
   shoes; 1144
   track and field; 1276

S

Safes and vaults; 1172
Safety and security
   See Security systems
Safety, industrial
   See Occupational safety
Salary surveys
   See also Executive compensation
   advertising; 0026
   broadcast engineers & managers; 0198
   business aircraft pilots; 1072
   business and professional women; 1348
   chemicals industry; 0670
   chemists; 0313
   computer designers; 0426
   contractors; 0487
   data processing; 0687
   dental laboratory industry; 0415
   engineers; 0313
   executive; 0440
   food processing industry; 0549
   food service; 1124
   industrial engineers; 0674
   librarians; 0800
   micrographics; 0687
   paper and pulp industry; 1243
   public administrators; 0056
   purchasing executives; 1090
   real estate; 0935
   research and development; 1117
   safety and security industry; 1172
   video production industry; 1308
Sales
   See also Marketing
   selling costs survey; 1150
Salesmanship
   product guide & directory; 0973
   training; 0973, 1281
Sanitation industry; 0981
   buyer's guide; 1152
   chemicals; 1074
   conference; 1074
   convention; 0379, 1152
   floor maintenance; 1152
   market survey; 1152
   new products; 1152
   Who's Who; 1074
Satellites and earth stations; 0348
   See also Telecommunications
Saunas
   buyers guide; 1214
Savings and loan associations; 0051
   top companies; 1155
Savings banks
   See Banks, savings
Savings Banks Association of Connecticut; 1154
Savings Banks Association of Maine; 1154
Savings Banks Association of Massachusetts; 1154
Savings Banks Association of New Hampshire; 1154
Savings Banks Association of New York; 1154
Sawmills
   See Lumber industry
Scandinavia
   banking; 0051
School administration
   See Schools and universities
School buses; 1156, 1157
Schools and universities
   See also Education
   administrator calendar; 1159
   advertising; 0026
   architecture; 1159
   art schools; 0048
   construction outlook; 0368
   equine; 0643
   expenses census; 1159
   graduate engineering and research directory; 0485
   journalism; 0778
   music; 0692
   parochial; 0300, 0325, 0326, 1268
   public opinion survey; 1009
   revenue sources; 1157
   school administration; 1157
   textile schools; 0676
   universities maintenance and construction costs; 0092
Science
   See Research and development; Specific science
Science fiction
   anthology; 0100
Sealants
   See Adhesives
Seaports
   See Ports and harbors
Seattle
   economic review; 1169
   industrial parks guide; 1169
   office leasing guide; 1169
Seattle Chamber of Commerce; 1169
Securities industry
   See also Mutual Funds; Securities trading; Security analysts
   best annual reports; 0690
   institutional investors directory; 0690
   mergers and acquisition survey; 0690
   risk managers survey; 0690
   top brokerage firms; 0528, 0690
   top 300 money managers; 0690
   underwriting sweepstakes; 0690
Securities trading
   industry research; 1239
   insider transactions filing; 1239
   insurance stocks; 0168
   top AMEX stocks; 0906
   top NYSE stocks; 0906
   top OTC stocks; 0906
Security analysts
   poll on Wall St. research; 0999
   research reports; 1239
Security systems; 0229, 0461, 0733, 1028
   banking; 0051
   buyers guide; 1172
   fencing; 0515
   locksmith/security directory; 0807
   office buildings; 0207, 0210
   salaries and budgets; 1172
   shoplifting; 1172
Seed and nurseries
   awards; 1174
   buyers guide/directory; 1173
   conventions; 1173, 1174
   equipment; 1173, 1174
   international trade; 1174
   seed varieties; 1173
Semiconductors
   See also Electronics
   top manufacturers; 0469
   world report; 0472
Sewage and waste disposal; 0329, 0733
   buyer's guide; 0824
   Canadian buyers guide; 1325
   construction outlook; 0368
   industry review; 1322
   yearbook; 0824
Sewing
   directory/buyers guide; 1177
   needlework; 1177
   quilts; 1177
Sewing machines; 1300
Sex stars; 1041
Sheet Metal and Air Conditioning Contractor National Association; 0379
Shipping
   See also Freight forwarding; Marine and maritime; Transportation
   chemicals; 0316
   directory; 0610
   freight steamship lines; 0069
Ships and shipbuilding
   annual review; 1168
   Arab/ship index; 1168
   Far East/ship index; 1168
   Latin America/ship index; 1168
   shipbuilding directory; 0610
   U.S. yearbook/ship index; 1168
Shoe industry
   See also Footware; Leather
   Canadian directory; 0259
   chain shoe stores directory; 0798
   industry leaders forecast; 0798
   leather buyers guide; 0798
   manufacturers catalogs; 0798
   new products; 0798
   shows; 0798
Shoe Service Institute of America; 1178
Shopping centers
   See also Retail trade
   Canadian directory; 0905
   census; 1180
   convention; 1180
   demographics; 0932
   directory; 1181
   finance directory; 1180
   management buyers guide; 0932
   marketing; 0932
   New England; 0946
   parking; 0932
   product/service directory; 1180
   real estate review; 1107
   regional U.S. land use; 0932
   renovations; 0932
   retail tenant directory; 0932
   top management and companies; 0932
   top open center developers; 0932
Shopping malls
   See Shopping centers
Shrimp
   See Fish and fisheries
Sierra Club; 1182
Sigma Delta Chi awards; 1096
Sigma Xi (Scientific Research Society); 0093
Silver; 0082
   See also Jewelry
Silverware
   See Tableware
Singapore
   banking; 0051
Site selection
   Canadian; 0249, 0494, 0527
   directories; 0672
   economic forecast; 0071
   electronics plant site; 0469
   finance directory; 0071
   reverse investment guide; 0071
Ski Council of America; 1225
Ski industry
   buying shows preview; 1186
   market research; 1186
   new lift construction; 1185
   ski area supplier/product directory; 1185
   trade show; 1225
Skiing; 1185
   buyer's guide; 1184, 1187
   ski camps guide; 1184
Slides
   See Audio-visual materials
Snack foods
   See also Fast foods
   buyers guide; 1194
   industry report; 1194
   plants and expansions; 1194
Snowmobiles
   Canadian buyers guide; 1196
   show; 1197
   sports annual; 1197
Soap and Detergent Association; 1198
Soaps and detergents
   buyers guide; 1198
   chemicals; 0316
   marketing; 1198
   meetings; 1198
   regulations; 1198
Social issues
   Blacks in U.S.; 0444
Social security
   statistical supplement; 1200

Society for Advancement of Management; 0022, 1151
Society of American Florists; 0543
Society of American Military Engineers; 0878
Society of Automotive Engineers; 0140, 0143, 0425, 0865
Society of Carbide & Tool Engineers; 0293
Society of Chartered Property and Casualty Underwriters; 0233, 0937
Society of Cosmetic Chemists; 0437
Society of Die Casting Engineers; 0423
Society of Exploration Geophysicists; 0584
Society of Independent Gasoline Marketers of America; 0966
Society of Ivy; 1124
Society of Manufacturing Engineers; 0082, 1135, 1270
   show; 0829
Society of Mining Engineers, AIMMPE; 0885
Society of Motion Picture and Television Engineers; 0151, 1148
Society of Petroleum Engineers; 0435
Society of Plastics Engineers; 1035
Society of Professional Journalists, Sigma Delta Chi; 1096
Society of Real Estate Appraisers; 1106
Soft drinks
   See also Beverage industry
   franchise company directory; 0174
   top 10 brands; 0174
Software
   See Computer software
Solar energy; 0571
   catalog/directory; 0038, 1204
   products specification guide; 1203
Solar heating; 1113
Sorghum; 1174
Sound
   See Acoustics
Sound and vibration; 0846
Sound equipment; 1208
   See Audio equipment; Sound recordings
Sound recordings
   annual music poll; 1041
   Beatles; 1138
   Canadian record companies; 1099
   country music source book; 0178
   gold records; 1302
   international buyers guide; 0178
   international directory; 0295
   international studio directory; 0178
   notables; 0190
   readers and critics poll; 1138
   record awards; 1230
   tapes; 1230
   top albums; 1138
Southeast, U.S.
   economic outlook; 0448
Southern Gas Association; 0580
Southern Industrial Distributors Association; 0673
Southern Newspaper Publishers Association; 0451
Southern Seedsmen's Association; 1174
Southern Wholesalers Association; 1237
Souvenirs
   See Novelties
Soybeans; 0296
Spas
   See Swimming pools and spas
Speakers bureaus; 0127, 1351
Special Libraries Association; 0800, 1215
Specialty Equipment Manufacturers Association; 0662, 0721, 1217
Spectroscopy; 0785
   See also Laboratory techniques
Sporting equipment
   engineering; 0846
Sporting goods; 0428
   best promotions; 1220
   business costs survey; 1225
   buying guide; 1225
   Canadian buying guide; 1226

   directory; 1220
   discount stores; 0429
   footwear survey; 1224
   industry events; 1220
   industry statistics; 1227
   market research report; 1225
   marketing awards; 1220
   operating costs survey; 1220
   outlook; 1225
   over 50 market; 1220
   retail sales survey; 1224
   seasonal market; 1225
   shows; 0298, 1220, 1225
   telephone directory; 1225
   tennis survey; 1224
   youth market profile; 1220
Sporting Goods Manufacturers Association; 1220, 1224, 1225
Sports
   See also Specific sport or event
   advertising report; 0026
   auto race; 1223
   baseball; 1223
   Canadian winter; 1332
   corporate-sponsored events, directory; 0833
   employee sports; 0477
   football; 1223
   gifts; 1221
   man of the year; 1221
   marketing; 0024
   over-50 athletes; 0520
   tennis; 1223
   track and field; 1276
   year in sports; 1223
Sports medicine clinics; 1145
Sports medicine, show; 1016
Sportswear, active; 1227
Square dancing
   directory; 1228
Stadiums
   See Auditoriums, arenas and stadiums
Standardization, scientific; 0013
State governments
   fiscal position review; 1238
   governor's messages; 1229
   review of legislation; 1229
Stationery; 1213
   buyers directory; 0587, 0589
Steamship lines
   See also Shipping; Travel and tourism
   directory; 0430
Steel
   See Iron and steel industry
Steel Service Center Institute; 0082, 0713, 0863
Stereophonic equipment; 0130
   See Audio equipment
Stock market
   See Investments; Securities industry; Securities trading
Stone products
   aggregates; 1137
   buyers guide; 1024, 1137
   cement and demographics; 1024, 1137
   industry outlook/review; 1024, 1137
   international market; 1137
   lime and agricultural limestone; 1024
   maintenance; 1024
Store design; 1311
   See also Interior design and decoration
Subways
   See Mass transit
Sugar
   yearbook; 1233
Sundries, merchandising; 1299
Sunglasses; 0507
Super Bowl
   See Football
Supermarkets
   See also Chain stores; Grocery trade
   baked foods; 1235
   consumer expenditures study; 1235
   equipment directory; 1235
   floral guide; 0986
   frozen foods survey; 0569

   general merchandise; 1236
   hair care products; 1235
   independents profile; 1236
   in-store bakeries; 0152
   instore business; 1235
   market profiles by city; 1236
   merchandising; 1236
   non-food merchandising; 0951
   produce packaging; 0986
   top independent; 1076
   top publicly owned chains; 1235
Supreme Court
   tax decisions; 1247
   term review; 0617
Surgical products
   See Health care products
Swimming
   annual statistics; 1241
   meets and championships; 1241
   Olympics; 1241
Swimming pools and spas
   buyers guide; 0993, 1214
   Canadian statistics; 0275
   convention; 1240
   directory; 1048, 1240
   directory, Canadian; 0275, 1047
   fencing; 0515
   hot tubs; 1214
   industry report; 1048, 1240
   show; 1048
Switzerland
   banking; 0051

T

Tableware; 0321
   See also China and glass; Giftware
Tanners, Council of America; 0797
Tantalum and Columbium; 0082
Tapes, audio; 1230
Taxes
   saving tips; 0906
   Supreme Court review; 1247
   tax return service bureaus; 1248
Tea; 1350
   plantations; 1350
Tea Association; 1350
Technical Association of the Pulp and Paper Industry (TAPPI); 0991, 1243
   nonwovens seminar; 0952
Telecommunications
   See also Communications; Telephone industry
   antennas and towers; 0348
   banking; 0051
   conferences; 0348
   directory/buyers guide; 1209, 1253
   economic review; 1209
   equipment reviews; 0348
   forecast; 0348
   in Africa; 0888
   in Asia; 0889
   marketing equipment/services; 1253
   microwave; 0348
   mobile; 1253
   office products guide; 0825
   power systems; 1253
   public utilities; 1083
   technology; 0441
Telecommunications Association; 0348
Telephone industry
   See also Telecommunications
   awards; 1252
   construction statistics; 1252, 1253
   consumer markets; 0836
   conventions; 1252, 1253
   digital technology; 1253
   directory/buyers guide; 1252, 1253
   international; 1253
   international conference; 1253
   marketing; 1252
   office systems; 0962
   review and forecast; 1252, 1253
   systems update; 0899
   test methods; 1253

Television
    See also Broadcasting; Motion pictures;
        Television, cable; Video production industry
    advertising; 0026, 0120
    animation; 0880
    broadcasting equipment buyers guide; 0198
    cable & station coverage atlas; 1254
    Canadian stations; 0200
    closed circuit equipment; 0348
    engineers technical conference; 1148
    equipment specifications; 0198
    industrial and educational, directories; 0442
    international annual; 1302
    photography; 1071
    production directory; 0151
    season's new shows; 1302
    shows; 0151
    syndication marketing; 0024
    technology advancement; 1148
    top markets; 1150
    TV and cable factbook; 1254
Television, cable
    See also Broadcasting
    atlas; 1254
    equipment review; 0348
    marketing; 0024
    yearbook; 0201
Tennis
    camps directory; 1255
    championship records; 1255
    equipment; 1255, 1356
    fashion; 1255
    French Open; 1356
    indoor; 1255
    Olympics; 1356
    shoes; 1356
    sporting goods survey; 1224
    top resorts; 1356
    top 10 players; 1255
    U.S. Open; 1221, 1255, 1356
    Wimbledon; 1221, 1356
    winter reports; 1255
    world rankings; 1356
Tennis courts
    fencing; 0515
Testing equipment
    See also Instruments and controls
    buyers guide; 1092
Texas Gas Association; 0580
Textile fibers
    buyers' guide; 0517
Textile finishing
    buyers guide; 1256
    coated; 1300
    conference; 1256
    new products; 1256
Textile industry
    See also Textile fibers; Textile finishing
    buyers guide; 1259
    Canadian industry manual; 0281
    carpet dyeing; 0060
    convention; 1257, 1259
    equipment/findings; 0676
    fabric directory; 0702
    financial survey; 0098
    flame retardants; 0060
    government products; 0676
    industrial fabric buyer's guide; 0676
    interior textiles directory; 0701
    international buyers guide; 1257
    new products; 0060, 0676
    nonwovens; 0952, 1300
    outlook; 0098
    process control buyers guide; 0060
    testing labs; 0676
    textile schools; 0676
    trends; 1257
    upholstery fabrics; 1300
    wet processing; 0060
Textile products, imprinted
    supplier directory; 0663
Textile Rental Services Association of America; 1258
Thailand
    tobacco industry; 1267

Theatre
    See Performing arts
Theatres
    See Motion pictures
Think tanks; 0926
Third World countries
    economic report; 0447
Tile
    See Ceramic tile
Tin; 0082
Tire industry
    convention; 1266
    purchasing directory; 1266
Tissue Culture Association; 0180
Titanium; 0082
Tobacco industry
    buyers guide; 1267
    cigars; 1267, 1299
    convention; 1299
    distributors directory; 1299
    Dixie directory; 1267
    foreign countries; 1267
    import/export; 1267
    leaf dealers; 1267
    marketing; 0024
    merchandising review; 1299
    show; 0298
    suppliers directory; 1299
    tobacco chemists; 1267
    tobacco sciences yearbook; 1267
    vending machines; 0049
Toiletries
    See Cosmetics and fragrances
Tools; 0293, 0818, 0919, 1270
    See also Machine tools; Metalworking
Toys
    See also Crafts and hobbies
    babies; 0050
    chain stores; 0429
    Christmas merchandising; 1273, 1274, 1275
    directory; 1043, 1274, 1275
    discount stores; 0428, 0429
    electronic; 0387, 1273
    fair; 1273, 1274
    forecast; 1274
    importers directory; 1273
    licensing; 1273
    show; 0298, 1043, 1275
    statistics; 1275
Track industry
    See also Railroads
    directory; 0430
Trade show industry
    best exhibit award; 0224
    buying trends survey; 0224
Traffic accidents; 1278
Traffic control; 0170
Traffic Management
    See also Transportation
    Canadian salary survey; 0282
    convention; 0344
    directory; 1277
    directory of traffic executives; 1279
Transportation; 0902
    See also Freight forwarding; Mass transit;
        Shipping; Trucks and trucking
    air freight guide; 1279
    Alaska; 0046
    Canadian directory; 0282
    convention; 0344
    directory; 1277
    distribution intermodal guide; 0430
    engineering; 0330, 0846
    freight vehicles; 1279
    largest companies; 0565
    perfect shipping; 1279
    ports and harbors; 1279
    security systems; 1172
Transportation engineers
    awards; 0659
Transportation, public
    See Mass transit
Travel and tourism
    See also Specific countries

    agents sales guide; 0284
    archaeological; 0110
    bluebook; 1285
    business and group travel; 0527, 1288
    Canadian auto travel; 1153
    Canadian incentive travel; 0859
    convention; 0285, 1285
    cruise guides; 0285
    diver's travel guide; 1189
    Easter missions; 0325
    economic forecast and review; 0285, 1287, 1288
    employee travel; 0477
    for associations; 0127
    for military market; 0040, 0119
    incentive travel; 0665, 0857, 0858
    island travel; 0284, 0949
    Los Angeles; 0812
    marketing; 0024
    over-50 cruises; 0520
    Pacific area; 0982
    personnel directory; 1285
    profit guide; 1288
    resorts guide; 0858
    sales conference; 0703
    seasonal tour directories; 1288
    ski vacation guide; 1187
    spring vacations; 0949
    telephone directory; 1288
    travel and passenger fares; 1238
    world directory; 1288
Truck Body and Equipment Association; 1280
Truck equipment; 1280
Truck Trailer Manufacturers Association; 1280
Trucks and trucking; 0981
    See also Diesel engines
    agricultural; 0503
    buyers guide; 0343, 0537, 0976
    calendar; 0633
    Canadian highway carriers guide; 0129, 0282
    component guide; 0976
    construction; 0365, 0370
    construction industry; 0363, 0634
    convention; 1284
    equipment buyers guide; 0214, 1280, 1284
    equipment distributors; 1280
    Federal agencies directory; 0976
    financial special; 1284
    fleet directory, international; 1269
    fleet maintenance; 1284
    fleet owner awards; 0537
    fleet reference annual; 0343
    international show; 1284
    maintenance; 0537, 0633, 1269
    management outlook; 1284
    mileage costs analysis; 0976
    off-highway; 0425, 1289
    parts and service buyers guide; 0633
    product reviews; 1284
    refrigerated; 1114
    revenue report; 0891
    rigging; 0401
    safety; 0633
    show; 0256, 0633
    state regulations directory; 0976
    survey; 0344
    sweepstakes; 0976
    tank cleaning directory; 0891
    tank truck buyer's guide; 0891
    top 100 carriers; 0343
    trailers; 0633
    truck and bus engineering; 0140
    year-end report; 1284
Trust institutions
    See also Banks and banking
    directory; 1291
    investment officer survey; 1291
    operation officers; 1291
    trust services; 0998
Trusts
    largest; 0558
Tungsten; 0082
Turbomachinery; 1292
    See also Power plants
Turkey
    banking; 0051

tobacco industry; 1267
Turkeys
  See Poultry industry
TV
  See Television
Typesetting
  See Printing and typesetting
Typewriters, buyers guide; 0961
Typography
  See Graphic arts; Printing and typesetting

U

Umbrellas; 0507
Underwater equipment; 0960
Underwear
  See Hosiery and underwear
Unemployment
  statistics; 0478
United Kingdom
  banking; 0051
United States Air Force
  Chief of Engineers report; 0878
  survey of United States commands; 0039
United States Army
  Chief of Engineers report; 0878
United States Coast Guard
  Chief of Engineers report; 0878
United States Football League; 1221
United States government agencies
  banker's guide to Washington; 0003
  for air pollution control; 0764
United States government fiscal programs
  analysis; 1238
United States government periodicals, directory; 0907
United States Independent Telephone Association 1252, 1253
United States League of Savings Institutions; 1155
United States National Plastics Exposition; 0901
United States Navy
  Chief of Engineers report; 0878
United States Tennis Association; 1356
United States Treasury
  foreign exchange operations; 1094
United Way, funds survey; 1010
Universities
  See Schools and universities
Urban planning; 0770
Urban redevelopment
  construction equipment; 0366
Utah Bankers Association; 0915
Utilities
  See also Power plants; Utilities, electric; Water sypply systems
  construction outlook; 0368, 0938
  contractors; 0370
  finance; 1083
  gas; 1083
  largest companies; 0565
  pipelines; 1023
  telecommunications; 1083
Utilities, electric; 1083
  See also Power plants
  awards; 0456
  buyer's guide; 0466
  directory; 0466, 1079
  generation construction survey; 0466
  industry forecast; 0466
  industry meetings calendar; 0466
  maintenance survey; 0466
  new generating plants; 1056
  proposed new plants; 1056
  rural electric cooperatives directory; 1147
  statistical report; 0466
  technical papers reference; 0466
  top companies; 0456
  top publicly-owned; 0456
  transmission and distribution construction survey; 0466

V

Vaccines
  antibodies buyers guide; 0180
Vacuum metallurgy; 0082
Valves and meters; 0733
  See also Pumps
  chemical equipment; 0315, 0317
  control valve selection guide; 0254
  pollution control; 1046
  purchasing; 1089
VCR
  See Videocassette recorders
Vegetables; 0097
  See also Produce
  agrichemical directory; 0328
  crop reports; 0506
  equipment directory for growers; 0328
  seedsmen awards; 1174
Vending machines
  beverage industry; 0174
  buyers guide; 1303
  Canadian; 0287
  industry census; 0049, 1303
  product directory; 0049
Venezuela
  banking; 0051
Ventilating equipment
  See also Air conditioning
  buyers guide; 1176
Venture capital
  See also Investments
  directory; 1304
  entrepreneurial compensation; 1304
  top company founders; 1304
  top venture capitalists; 1304
Vermont Bankers Association; 1154
Veterinary medicine; 0400
  See also Animal health care
Video production industry
  See also Audio-visual communications; Television
  Canadian equipment buyers guide; 1015
  equipment reviews; 1308
  hardware and software; 0836, 1308, 1310
  production facilities; 1310
  salary survey; 1308
  services guide; 1308
  video conferencing; 1310
  videodisc projects directory; 1309
  videotapes production facilities; 0132
Videocassette recorders; 1310
  buying guide; 0640
Vineyards; 0063
  See also Wines
Visual displays
  See Store design
Vocational Education
  See Education, vocational

W

Wages
  See also Employment; Salary surveys
  statistics; 0478
Wallcoverings
  buyer's guide; 0411, 1317
  designers file; 0419
  directory; 0410, 0702, 1317
Wallpaper
  See Wallcoverings
Warehouses; 0430, 0674
  See also Distribution
Waste disposal
  See Hazardous materials; Sewage and waste disposal
Watches and clocks
  clock manufacturers/imports directory; 1323
  Watch buyers guide; 0717
  Watch directory; 0718, 1323
Water beds, buyers guide; 0544

Water conditioning
  buyer's guide; 1324
Water pollution; 0487, 1046
  Canadian pollution control directory; 1325
  literature review; 0777
Water Pollution Control Federation; 0056, 0777, 1084
Water quality
  laboratory application review; 0101
Water resources
  in Africa; 0888
  in Asia; 0889
Water Resources Congress; 1327
Water supply systems
  buyers guide; 0723
  construction equipment; 0366
  construction outlook; 0368
  convention; 0605
  engineering; 0330
  international directory; 0927
  treatment; 0733
Waterways
  See also Marine and maritime
  inland; 1347
  offshore; 1347
  rivers; 1347
  show; 1347
Weed control
  See Herbicides
Welding
  buyers guide; 1330
  Canadian buyers guide; 0288
  robotic; 1135
  safety and health; 1330
  show; 0713, 1330
  testing; 1330
Welding Research Council; 1331
WESCON Show; 0693
Western Electronics Conventions; 0471
Western Finance Association; 0742
Wholesale Distributors Association; 1237
Wholesale Florist and Florist Suppliers of America 0543
Wholesaling
  industry ratios; 0440
Wilder, Laura Ingalls, award; 1271
Wildlife; 0773
Window displays
  See Store design
Window systems
  See also glass
  buyers guide; 1339
  new products; 1339
  sealants and glazing systems; 1295
  shows; 1339
Wine and Spirit Wholesalers of America; 0173
Wines
  See also Beverages, alcoholic; Liquor industry
  Canadian wineries; 0246
  directory; 1340
  import/export; 1340
  market review and forecast; 0660
  marketing data; 0024, 1340
  statistics; 1340
Wire Association International; 1342
Wire industry
  coatings; 1342
  directory/catalog; 1342
  equipment; 1342
  machinery; 1342
  outlook; 1342
  rubber; 1142
Women
  advertising markets; 0026
  employment; 0478
  engineering careers; 0595
Women, business and professional
  salary survey; 1348
Wood and wood products
  See also Forest industries; Lumber industry; Paper and pulp
  construction; 0541
  international statistics; 1357

worldwide directory and buyer's guide; 1044
Woodworking; 0576
  buying guide; 1345
  cabinets; 1345
  case goods; 1345
  industry outlook; 1345
  panel products; 1345
  product review; 1345
  productivity handbook; 1345
  show; 0574, 1300, 1345
Wool, agricultural reports; 0506
Word processors; 0962, 0963
  buyers guide; 0961
  directory; 1294
Workmen's compensation
  California; 0696
World Energy Conference; 0966
World Future Society; 0578
World Petroleum Congress; 0966
World trade
  See International trade
Writers
  awards; 1360
  conferences; 1359, 1360
  education guide; 1360
  first novelists; 0800
  handbook; 1359
  markets; 1359
  yearbook; 1360
Wyoming Bankers Association; 0915

Y

Yachts
  See Boats and Boating
Young Adult Services, American Libraries
  Association; 1271
Yugoslavia
  tobacco industry; 1267

Z

Zinc; 0082